The Collective Memory Reader

The
Collective Memory
Reader

Edited by

JEFFREY K. OLICK

VERED VINITZKY-SEROUSSI

DANIEL LEVY

OXFORD
UNIVERSITY PRESS

2011

OXFORD
UNIVERSITY PRESS

Oxford University Press, Inc., publishes works that further
Oxford University's objective of excellence
in research, scholarship, and education.

Oxford   New York
Auckland   Cape Town   Dar es Salaam   Hong Kong   Karachi
Kuala Lumpur   Madrid   Melbourne   Mexico City   Nairobi
New Delhi   Shanghai   Taipei   Toronto

With offices in
Argentina   Austria   Brazil   Chile   Czech Republic   France   Greece
Guatemala   Hungary   Italy   Japan   Poland   Portugal   Singapore
South Korea   Switzerland   Thailand   Turkey   Ukraine   Vietnam

Published by Oxford University Press, Inc.
198 Madison Avenue, New York, NY 10016

www.oup.com

Oxford is a registered trademark of Oxford University Press

Library of Congress Cataloging-in-Publication Data
The collective memory reader / edited by Jeffrey K. Olick,
Vered Vinitzky-Seroussi, and Daniel Levy.
   p.   cm.
Includes bibliographical references and index.
ISBN 978-0-19-533741-9; ISBN 978-0-19-533742-6 (pbk.)
1. Collective memory.
I. Olick, Jeffrey K., 1964– II. Vinitzky-Seroussi, Vered 1960–.
III. Levy, Daniel, 1962–
HM1033.C62   2011
302.01—dc22   2010014503

9 8 7 6
Printed in the United States of America

Contents

Preface and Acknowledgments

This volume has been a long time in the making, and arrives quite a bit behind schedule. We cannot lay all of this delay at the feet of the project's complexity: life is complicated too, and three lives in three different places are three times as complicated. But at least some of the delay was indeed due to the difficulties not only of searching through an enormous literature and editing a large number of challenging texts, but of tracing and obtaining the legal rights to reprint our excerpts of them. As difficult as this was, we are grateful to the many people—authors, in some cases their students or even children, publishers, editors, permissions departments, etc.—who made it less so. We received tremendous help in reaching our goal from many individuals responsible for protecting published texts; in most cases, individuals and institutions listened carefully to our requests and accommodated our challenges with impressive generosity. This book has indeed taken a village, but it was especially interesting how multitiered and global that village was. We enthusiastically thank all of the people at so many different presses, journals, and elsewhere who worked with us to overcome obstacles and make this unusual volume possible.

In the difficult and drawn-out process of searching for and obtaining rights, as well as in a wide variety of other tasks, we were lucky to have the help of two of the most creative and tenacious research assistants we could imagine—Jennifer Marie Silva and Tara Tober—who worked tirelessly and with impressive ingenuity over long years.

In the course of our work, we had more conversations with more people than we can possibly count about the idea and execution of the project. In the first place, two publishers sent our proposal to eight referees each; we learned a great deal from these sixteen responses and are grateful for the thought these anonymous individuals put into their reports, even if we could not possibly take up all of their suggestions, or allay all of their doubts. We also discussed details of the project with, and solicited suggestions from, a large number of individuals, including Ulrich Beck, Nachman Ben-Yehuda, Efrat Ben-Zeev, Maurice Bloch, Alon Confino, Astrid Erll, Gary Alan Fine, Bill Hirst, Andrew Hoskins, Siobhan Kattago, Olaf Kleist, Harold Marcuse, Allan

Megill, Oren Meyers, Dirk Moses, Klaus Neumann, Stephen Rutter, Howard Schuman, Barry Schwartz, Lyn Spillman, John Sutton, Natan Sznaider, John Torpey, Robin Wagner-Pacifici, Harald Welzer, and Eviatar Zerubavel. Where we heeded their advice and incorporated their suggestions, the result was substantially improved; where we could not, we appreciated the advice no less.

Jeffrey Olick is grateful to audiences at the Institute for Advanced Studies at Swinburne University in Melbourne, and to Klaus Neumann in particular, for listening to the outlines of the book and for helpful feedback he received there. Additionally, discussion following a lecture at Davidson College was a helpful test for the argument of the introduction. We are also grateful to Adam Brown, Yifat Gutman, and Amy Sodaro for their invitation to present the outlines of the volume and the argument of its introduction at the 2010 "Limits of Memory" conference they organized at The New School for Social Research, and to Vera Zolberg and Marianne Hirsch for their comments as respondents to our presentation.

All three of the editors benefited from the generosity of their home institutions—the University of Virginia, the Hebrew University of Jerusalem, and Stony Brook University—which provided research and travel support, as well as time off from regular duties, without which this project would not have been possible. The University of Virginia provided a partial financial subsidy for permission fees, as well as significant funds for research assistance. Vered Vinitzky-Seroussi thanks the Center for Cultural Sociology at Yale University for their generous hospitality during the year 2009–2010. Daniel Levy is grateful to the United University Professions for a small grant for research assistance.

Throughout, we have benefited from the heroic patience and unfailingly good advice of our editor, James Cook. James supported our ambitions for the book, which were driven by the desire to advance a field of study, rather than merely to sell copies for classroom use.

Finally, we want to acknowledge the important role of our families—our children Hannah, Benjamin, Netta, Ofri, and Ella and our spouses Bettina Winckler, Yair Seroussi, and Emily Miller. Without their encouragement and support, the work would not have been possible.

Original source information for all selections is listed below in order of appearance in this volume. The vast majority of texts were under copyright, and the editors and publisher gratefully acknowledge permission to reproduce previously published material. We have made every effort to trace copyrights to their proper holders, including U.S. and world holders for both original materials and translations. If we have inadvertently failed to do so properly, we apologize and request that copyright holders contact the publisher.

Edmund Burke. *Reflections on the Revolution in France.* London: John Sharpe, 1820 [49–54].

Alexis de Tocqueville. *Democracy in America, Volume 2.* Translated by Henry Reeve, Esq. Cambridge: Sever & Francis, 1863 [103–7, 119–21].

Friedrich Nietzsche. "On the Uses and Disadvantages of History for Life." Pp. 57–124 in *Untimely Meditations.* Translated by R. J. Hollingdale. Cambridge: Cambridge University Press, 1997 [60–83, 115, 120–21]. Reprinted with the permission of Cambridge University Press.

Ernest Renan. "What Is a Nation?" Pp. 8–22 in *Nation and Narration.* Edited by Homi K. Bhabha, translated by Martin Thom. London: Routledge, 1990 [11–12, 19–20]. Reproduced by permission of Taylor & Francis Books UK.

Sigmund Freud. *Totem and Taboo: Resemblances between the Psychic Lives of Savages and Neurotics.* Translated by Abraham Arden Brill. London: George Routledge & Sons, 1919 [262–64].

Sigmund Freud. *Moses and Monotheism.* Translated by Katherine Jones. New York: Vintage Books, 1967 [85–90, 169–71]. Copyright 1939 by Alfred A. Knopf, Inc., and renewed 1967 by Ernst L. Freud and Anna Freud. Used by permission of Alfred A. Knopf, a division of Random House, Inc.

Karl Marx. "The Eighteenth Brumaire of Louis Bonaparte." Pp. 594–617 in *The Marx-Engels Reader.* Edited by Robert C. Tucker. New York: W. W. Norton, 1978 [595–97]. Copyright © 1978, 1972 by W. W. Norton & Company, Inc. Used by permission of W. W. Norton & Company, Inc.

Karl Mannheim. "The Sociological Problem of Generations." Pp. 286–320 in *Essays on the Sociology of Knowledge.* Translated by Paul Kecskemeti. London: Routledge, 1952 [292–307]. Reproduced by permission of Taylor & Francis Books UK.

Walter Benjamin. "The Storyteller." Pp. 83–110 in *Illuminations.* New York: Schocken Books, 1969 [83–84, 86–91, 97–98]. Reprinted by permission of Houghton Mifflin Harcourt.

Walter Benjamin. "Theses on the Philosophy of History." Pp. 253–64 in *Illuminations.* New York: Schocken Books, 1969 [257–58]. Reprinted by permission of Houghton Mifflin Harcourt.

Ernst Gombrich. *Aby Warburg: An Intellectual Biography.* London: Phaidon Press, 1997 [239–43, 247–51, 254–59].

Theodor W. Adorno. "Valéry Proust Museum." Pp. 173–86 in *Prisms.* Translated by Samuel M. Weber. Cambridge: MIT Press, 1983 [175–76]. Reprinted with permission.

Theodor W. Adorno. "In Memory of Eichendorff." Pp. 58–79 in *Notes to Literature,* vol. 1. New York: Columbia University Press, 1991 [55–57]. Reprinted with permission of the publisher.

Lev Vygotsky. *Mind in Society.* Cambridge: Harvard University Press, 1978 [38–39, 50–51]. Copyright © 1978 by the President and Fellows of Harvard College. Reprinted by permission of the publisher.

Frederic Bartlett. *Remembering: A Study in Experimental and Social Psychology.* Cambridge: Cambridge University Press, 1995 [1932] [293–300]. Reprinted with the permission of Cambridge University Press.

Carl Becker. "Everyman His Own Historian." *American Historical Review* 37(2): 221–36. 1932 [230–36]. Reprinted by permission of the University of Chicago Press.

George Herbert Mead. "The Nature of the Past." Pp. 235–41 in *Essays in Honor of John Dewey.* New York: Henry Holt and Company, 1929 [235–40].

Charles Horton Cooley. *Social Process.* New York: Charles Scribner's Sons, 1918 [114–24].

Émile Durkheim. *The Elementary Forms of Religious Life*. Translated by Joseph Ward Swain. London: George Allen and Unwin, 1915 [420–23, 474–76].

Maurice Halbwachs. *The Collective Memory*. Translated by Francis J. Ditter Jr. and Vida Yazdi Ditter. New York: Harper & Row, 1980 [45–49, 80–87, 124–27]. Copyright 1950 by Presses Universitaires de France. English translation copyright © 1980 by Harper & Row, Publishers, Inc. Introduction copyright © 1980 by Mary Douglas. Reprinted by permission of HarperCollins Publishers.

Marc Bloch. "Mémoire collective, tradition et coutume: À propos d'un livre récent." *Revue de Synthèse Historique* 40: 73–83. 1925 [73–83]. Reprinted by permission of Fondation "pour la science—centre international de synthèse" Siège: Ècole normale supérieure 45, rue d'Ulm, F-75005 Paris.

Charles Blondel. "Revue critique: M. Halbwachs *Les cadres sociaux de la mémoire*." *Revue Philosophique* 101: 290–98. 1926 [290–98].

Roger Bastide. *The African Religions of Brazil: Toward a Sociology of the Interpenetration of Civilizations*. Translated by Helen Sabba. Baltimore: Johns Hopkins University Press, 1978 [240–59]. © 1978 The Johns Hopkins University Press. Reprinted with permission of The Johns Hopkins University Press.

W. Lloyd Warner. *The Living and the Dead: A Study of the Symbolic Life of Americans*. New Haven: Yale University Press, 1959 [278–79, 318–20, 474–76]. Reprinted with permission.

E. E. Evans-Pritchard. *The Nuer: A Description of the Modes of Livelihood and Political Institutions of a Nilotic People*. Oxford: Oxford University Press, 1940 [94–95, 102–8]. By permission of Oxford University Press, Inc.

Claude Lévi-Strauss. *The Savage Mind*. Chicago: University of Chicago Press, 1966 [233–44]. Reprinted by permission of George Weidenfeld and Nicolson, Ltd., an imprint of The Orion Publishing Group, London. Reprinted by permission of the University of Chicago Press.

Hans-Georg Gadamer. *Truth and Method*. New York: Continuum International, 1989 [262–67]. Reprinted with the permission of the publisher.

Edward Casey. *Remembering: A Phenomenological Study*. Bloomington: Indiana University Press, 1987 [247–57]. Reprinted by permission of Indiana University Press.

Peter Burke. "History as Social Memory." Pp. 97–113 in *Memory: History, Culture and the Mind*. Edited by Thomas Butler. Malden: Blackwell, 1989 [97–110]. Reproduced with the permission of Blackwell Publishing Ltd.

Allan Megill. "History, Memory, Identity." Pp. 41–62 in *Historical Knowledge, Historical Error: A Contemporary Guide to Practice*. Chicago: University of Chicago Press, 2007 [41–59]. Adapted and reprinted with permission from "Memory, History, Identity." *History of the Human Sciences* 11(3): 37–62. 1998.

Alon Confino. "Collective Memory and Cultural History: Problems of Method." *American Historical Review* 102(5): 1386–1403. 1997 [1393–97, 1402–3]. Reprinted by permission of the University of Chicago Press.

Yosef Haim Yerushalmi. *Zakhor: Jewish History and Jewish Memory*. Seattle: University of Washington Press, 1982 [6–21, 26, 86, 89–91, 93–95, 97, 99–101]. Reprinted by permission of the publisher.

Jan Assmann. *Moses the Egyptian: The Memory of Egypt in Western Monotheism*. Cambridge: Harvard University Press, 1997 [9–17]. Copyright © 1997 by the President and Fellows of Harvard College. Reprinted by permission of the publisher.

Jan Assmann. "Collective Memory and Cultural Identity." *New German Critique* 65: 125–33. 1995 [125–33]. Reprinted by permission of the author.

Peter Berger. *Invitation to Sociology: A Humanistic Approach*. New York: Doubleday, 1963 [54–65]. © 1963 by Peter L. Berger. Used by permission of Doubleday, a division of Random House, Inc.

Eviatar Zerubavel. "Social Memories: Steps towards a Sociology of the Past." *Qualitative Sociology* 19: 283–99. 1996 [284–90]. With kind permission from Springer Science and Business Media.

Jeffrey K. Olick. "Collective Memory: The Two Cultures." *Sociological Theory* 17(3): 338–48. 1999.

Robert Bellah, Richard Madsen, William M. Sullivan, Ann Swidler, and Steven M. Tipton. *Habits of the Heart: Individualism and Commitment in American Life*. Berkeley: University of California Press, 1985 [153–55]. © 1996 Regents of the University of California. Reprinted by permission of the University of California.

Anthony Smith. *The Ethnic Origins of Nations*. Malden: Blackwell, 1991 [174–79, 206–8]. Reproduced with permission of Blackwell Publishing Ltd.

Yael Zerubavel. *Recovered Roots: Collective Memory and the Making of Israeli National Tradition*. Chicago: University of Chicago Press, 1995 [6–12]. Reprinted by permission of the University of Chicago Press.

Barry Schwartz. *Abraham Lincoln and the Forge of American Memory*. Chicago: University of Chicago Press, 2000 [13–19, 298–303]. Reprinted by permission of the University of Chicago Press.

Michel Foucault. "Film in Popular Memory: An Interview with Michel Foucault." Translated by Martin Jordan. *Radical Philosophy* 11: 24–29. 1975 [24–29]. Reprinted with permission.

Popular Memory Group. "Popular Memory: Theory, Politics, Method." Pp. 43–53 in *Oral History Reader*. Edited by Robert Perks and Alistair Thomson. New York: Routledge, 1998 [43–53].

Raphael Samuel. *Theatres of Memory*. London: Verso, 1996 [242–47].

John Bodnar. *Remaking America: Public Memory, Commemoration and Patriotism in the Twentieth Century*. Princeton: Princeton University Press, 1993 [13–17]. © 1992 Princeton University Press. Reprinted by permission of Princeton University Press.

Roy Rosenzweig and David Thelen. *The Presence of the Past: Popular Uses of History in American Life*. New York: Columbia University Press, 1998 [115–17]. Reprinted with permission of the publisher.

Eric Hobsbawm. "Introduction: Inventing Traditions." Pp. 1–14 in *The Invention of Tradition*. Edited by Eric Hobsbawm and Terence Ranger. Cambridge: Cambridge University Press, 1983 [1–6]. Reprinted with the permission of Cambridge University Press.

Terence Ranger. "The Invention of Tradition Revisited: The Case of Colonial Africa." Pp. 62–111 in *Legitimacy and the State in Twentieth Century Africa*. Edited by Terence Ranger and Olufemi Vaughan. London: Macmillan, 1993 [75–82]. Reprinted with permission of Palgrave Macmillan.

Orlando Patterson. *Slavery and Social Death: A Comparative Study*. Cambridge: Harvard University Press, 2007 [5–10]. Copyright © 1982 by the President and Fellows of Harvard College. Reprinted by permission of the publisher.

Richard Sennett. "Disturbing Memories." Pp. 10–26 in *Memory*. Edited by Patricia Fara and Karalyn Patterson. Cambridge: Cambridge University Press, 1998 [11–25]. Reprinted with the permission of Cambridge University Press.

Michael Schudson. "The Past in the Present versus the Present in the Past." *Communication* 11: 105–13. 1989 [106–13]. Reprinted by permission of the publisher (Taylor & Francis, http://www.informaworld.com).

Gladys Lang and Kurt Lang. "Recognition and Renown: The Survival of Artistic Reputation." *American Journal of Sociology* 94(1): 79–109. 1988 [101–6].

Lori Ducharme and Gary Alan Fine. "The Construction of Nonpersonhood and Demonization: Commemorating the 'Traitorous' Reputation of Benedict Arnold." *Social Forces* 73(4): 1309–31. 1995 [1309–12, 1326–27]. Copyright © 1995 by the University of North Carolina Press. Used by permission of the publisher. www.uncpress.unc.edu

Wulf Kansteiner. "Finding Meaning in Memory: A Methodological Critique of Collective Memory Studies." *History and Theory* 41(2): 179–97. 2002. Reprinted with the permission of Ohio University Press, Athens, Ohio (www.ohioswallow.com).

Ron Eyerman. "The Past in the Present: Culture and the Transmission of Memory." *Acta Sociologica* 47(2): 159–169. 2004 [160–63].

Jeffrey Alexander. "Toward a Cultural Theory of Trauma." Pp. 1–30 in *Cultural Trauma and Collective Identity*. Edited by Jeffrey C. Alexander, Ron Eyerman, Bernhard Giesen, Neil J. Smelser, and Piotr Sztompka. Berkeley: University of California Press, 2004 [1–3, 8–13, 23–27].

André Leroi-Gourhan. *Gesture and Speech*. Cambridge: MIT Press, 1993 [258–65]. © 1993 Massachusetts Institute of Technology, by permission of The MIT Press.

Jack Goody. "Memory in Oral and Literate Traditions." Pp. 73–94 in *Memory*. Edited by Patricia Fara and Karalyn Patterson. Cambridge: Cambridge University Press, 1998 [73–77, 90–94].

Merlin Donald. *Origins of the Modern Mind: Three Stages in the Evolution of Culture and Cognition*. Cambridge: Harvard University Press, 1991 [308–23]. Copyright © 1991 by the President and Fellows of Harvard College. Reprinted by permission of the publisher.

Aleida Assmann. "Canon and Archive." Pp. 97–107 in *Cultural Memory Studies: An International and Interdisciplinary Handbook*. Berlin: Walter de Gruyter, 2008 [97–106].

Paul Connerton. *How Societies Remember*. Cambridge: Cambridge University Press, 1989 [70–76, 100–102]. Reprinted with the permission of Cambridge University Press.

Harald Welzer, Sabine Moller, Karoline Tschuggnall, Olaf Jensen, and Torsten Koch. "*Opa war kein Nazi:*" *Nationalsozialismus und Holocaust im Familiengedächtnis*. Frankfurt: Fischer, 2002 [202–4]. Translated by Daniel Levy and Jeffrey K. Olick. Reprinted by permission of the author.

Marianne Hirsch. "The Generation of Postmemory." *Poetics Today* 29(1): 103–28. 2008 [105–7].

John B. Thompson. "Tradition and Self in a Mediated World." Pp. 89–108 in *Detraditionalization: Critical Reflections on Authority and Identity*. Edited by Paul Heelas, Scott Lash, and Paul Morris. Malden: Blackwell, 1996 [95–99]. Reproduced with the permission of Blackwell Publishing Ltd.

George Lipsitz. *Time Passages: Collective Memory and American Popular Culture*. Minneapolis: University of Minnesota Press, 1990 [5–12]. Adapted and reprinted with permission from "This Ain't No Sideshow: Historians and Media Studies." *Critical Studies in Mass Communication* 5(2): 147–61. 1988. Reprinted by permission of the publisher (Taylor & Francis Ltd.).

Barbie Zelizer. "Why Memory's Work on Journalism Does Not Reflect Journalism's Work on Memory." *Memory Studies* 1(1): 79–87. 2008 [79–87].

Daniel Dayan and Elihu Katz. *Media Events: The Live Broadcasting of History*. Cambridge: Harvard University Press, 2006 [1–9, 211–13]. Copyright © 1992 by the President and Fellows of Harvard College. Reprinted by permission of the publisher.

Reinhart Koselleck. "War Memorials: Identity Formations of the Survivors." Pp. 285–326 in *The Practice of Conceptual History*. Translated by Todd Presner. Stanford: Stanford University Press, 2002 [287–93, 316–26]. Copyright © 2002 by the Board of Trustees of the Leland

Stanford Junior University. All rights reserved. Used with the permission of Stanford University Press, www.sup.org.

James E. Young. *At Memory's Edge: After-Images of the Holocaust in Contemporary Art and Architecture*. New Haven: Yale University Press, 2002 [90–96, 118–19]. Reprinted with permission.

Vered Vinitzky-Seroussi. "Commemorating a Difficult Past: Yitzhak Rabin's Memorials." *American Sociological Review* 67(1): 30–51. 2002.

M. Christine Boyer. *The City of Collective Memory: Its Historical Imagery and Architectural Entertainments*. Cambridge: MIT Press, 1994 [130–35]. © 1994 Massachusetts Institute of Technology, by permission of The MIT Press.

Danièle Hervieu-Léger. *Religion as a Chain of Memory*. Piscataway: Rutgers University Press, 2000 [123–30]. Copyright © 2000 by Polity Press. Reprinted by permission of Polity Press, Ltd., and Rutgers University Press.

Harald Weinrich. *Lethe: The Art and Critique of Forgetting*. Ithaca: Cornell University Press, 2004 [213–17]. Reprinted from Harald Weinrich, *Lethe: The Art and Critique of Forgetting*. Translated by Steven Rendall. English translation copyright © 2004 by Cornell University. Used by permission of the publisher, Cornell University Press.

Robin Wagner-Pacifici. "Memories in the Making: The Shapes of Things That Went." *Qualitative Sociology* 19(3): 301–22. 1996 [301–11, 319].

Edward Shils. *Tradition*. Chicago: University of Chicago Press, 1981 [326–30]. Reprinted with permission of Faber and Faber Ltd.

Ian Hacking. "Memory Sciences, Memory Politics." Pp. 67–88 in *Tense Past: Cultural Essays in Trauma and Memory*. Edited by Paul Antze and Michael Lambek. New York: Routledge, 1996 [70–82]. Adapted and reprinted with permission from "Memoro-Politics, Trauma and the Soul." *History of the Human Sciences* 7(2): 29–52. 1994.

Patrick Hutton. *History as an Art of Memory*. Burlington: University of Vermont Press, 1993 [xx–xxv]. © University Press of New England, Hanover, NH. Reprinted with permission.

Anthony Giddens. "Living in a Post-Traditional Society." Pp. 56–109 in *Reflexive Modernization: Politics, Tradition and Aesthetics in the Modern Social Order*. Edited by Ulrich Beck, Anthony Giddens, and Scott Lash. Stanford: Stanford University Press, 1994 [100–104]. Reprinted by permission of Polity Press Ltd. Copyright © 1994 by Ulrich Beck, Anthony Giddens, and Scott Lash. All rights reserved. Used with the permission of Stanford University Press, www.sup.org.

David Gross. *Lost Time: On Remembering and Forgetting in Late Modern Culture*. Amherst: University of Massachusetts Press, 2000 [140–52]. Copyright © 2000 by University of Massachusetts Press and published by the University of Massachusetts Press.

Jay Winter. *Remembering War: The Great War between Memory and History in the Twentieth Century*. New Haven: Yale University Press, 2006 [9–11, 278–82]. Reprinted with permission.

Andreas Huyssen. "Present Pasts: Media, Politics, Amnesia." *Public Culture* 12(1): 21–38. 2000 [21–22, 27–29, 31–38]. Copyright, 2000, Duke University Press. All rights reserved. Used by permission of the publisher.

Pierre Nora. "Reasons for the Current Upsurge in Memory." *Transit* 22: 1–8. 2002 [1, 4–8]. This article was first published in German in *Transit—Europäische Revue* no. 22/2002 and has been mediated by *Eurozine* (www.eurozine.com). © Transit © Pierre Nora.

Charles Maier. "A Surfeit of Memory? Reflections on History, Melancholy, and Denial." *History and Memory* 5: 137–51. 1992 [140–41, 147–50]. Reprinted by permission of Indiana University Press.

Fred Davis. *Yearning for Yesterday: A Sociology of Nostalgia.* New York: Free Press, 1979 [1–17, 101–16]. Reprinted with the permission of Philip Davis.

Svetlana Boym. "Nostalgia and Its Discontents." *Hedgehog Review* 9(2): 7–18. 2007 [7–18]. Reprinted by permission of University of Virginia Press.

Michel-Rolph Trouillot. "Abortive Rituals: Historical Apologies in the Global Era." *Interventions: International Journal of Postcolonial Studies* 2(2): 171–86. 2000 [173–85]. Reprinted by permission of the publisher (Taylor & Francis Ltd., http://www.informaworld.com).

Daniel Levy and Natan Sznaider. "Memory Unbound: The Holocaust and the Formation of Cosmopolitan Memory." *European Journal of Social Theory* 5(1): 87–106. 2002.

Mark Osiel. *Mass Atrocity, Collective Memory, and the Law.* New Brunswick: Transaction, 1997 [2–4, 6–9]. Reprinted by permission of the publisher.

Avishai Margalit. *The Ethics of Memory.* Cambridge: Harvard University Press, 2002 [6–11]. Copyright © 2002 by the President and Fellows of Harvard College. Reprinted by permission of the publisher.

Marc Augé. *Oblivion.* Minneapolis: University of Minnesota Press, 2004 [87–89]. Reprinted by permission of the publisher.

Paul Ricoeur. "Memory—Forgetting—History." Pp. 9–19 in *Meaning and Representation in History.* Edited by Jörn Rüsen. Oxford: Berghahn Books, 2006 [9–19].

The Collective Memory Reader

Introduction

Jeffrey K. Olick, Vered Vinitzky-Seroussi, and Daniel Levy

Memory, even conceived in its social dimensions, is hardly a new topic. "Zakhor!" (Remember!), commanded the Hebrew bible repeatedly, as for instance in Deuteronomy 32:7, when Moses instructed the assembly of Israel to "Remember the days of old / Consider the years of the many generations." Priests and politicians before and since have intuitively understood the cultic powers of the past to underwrite solidarity and motivate action. And poets, autobiographers, and philosophers alike have for millennia been parsing memory's complexities, pondering its mysteries, and extolling its import.

In the past thirty or so years, however, we seem to have entered a new phase in the contemplation of memory. Many commentators now refer to a "memory boom" that began sometime in the late 1970s and that has only begun to wind down since the turn of the millennium (though many see it as continuing undiminished).[1] The story goes something like this: following the decline of postwar modernist narratives of progressive improvement through an ever-expanding welfare state, nation-states turned to the past as a basis for shoring up their legitimacy. The decline of utopian visions supposedly redirected our gaze to collective pasts, which served as a repository of inspiration for repressed identities and unfulfilled claims. Without unifying collective aspirations, identity politics proliferated. And most often, these identities nursed a wound and harbored a grudge. The memory boom thus unleashed a culture of trauma and regret, and states are allegedly now judged on how well they atone for their past

---

1. While the present preoccupation with memory has its origins in the Western European context and associated debates about modernity, it has since permeated political-cultural debates in other context as well. See, for instance, Schwartz and Kim (2010); Stern (2010, 2006); Lee and Yang (2007); Makdisi and Silverstein (2006); Smith (2006); Judt (2005); Jelin (2003); Roudometof (2002); Wertsch (2002); Fujitani, White, and Yoneyama (2001); Fabian (1999); Roniger and Sznajder (1999); Verdery (1999); Duara (1997); Trouillot (1997); Tumarkin (1997); Mudimbe and Jewsiewicki (1993). This list is by no means exhaustive, or even extensive.

misdeeds rather than on how well they meet their fiscal obligations and inspire future projects. In the commercial sphere, these transformations in political legitimation were supposedly matched by a commodification of nostalgia, a popularization of history, and an interest in "memory," both individual and collective. Both of the latter—individual memory and collective memory—are seen to be at risk, the former by neurological decay and sensory overload, the latter by dying generations and official denial.

On the analytical side, the memory boom has supposedly also given rise to varieties of inquiry, including science, scholarship, memoir writing, curatorial work, oral history projects, and the like. While baby-boomers worry about the living death of Alzheimer's disease, neuroscientists search for its biological basis (Eichenbaum 2002; Pillemer 1998; Schachter 1997). While trauma victims seek to overcome their ongoing suffering from post-traumatic stress, psychologists develop frameworks for treatment (Leys 2000; Herman 1997; Caruth 1995). While past oppression has seemingly become the coin of identity, cultural theorists inquire into the origins of the politics of victimhood (Fassin and Rechtman 2009; Olick 2007; Bell 2006; Kaplan 2005; Edkins 2003; Antze and Lambek 1996). And while societies confront the legacies of their misdeeds, social and political scientists analyze the conditions for successful transition and salutary commemoration (Elster 2004; Vinitzky-Seroussi 2002; Teitel 2002; Minow 1999; McAdams 1997). All of these, and more, are constituents of what has come to be referred to as the new "memory studies," which has acquired its own journals, been elaborated in countless edited volumes, established research centers, received grants, and been the subject of university courses.[2]

At the same time, a powerful line of critique has argued that "memory studies" is merely part of a broader "memory industry" that has arisen in response to the "memory boom" and that as the boom inevitably goes bust, the industry it has generated will also disappear, or at least suffer a downturn (Rosenfeld 2009; Winter 2006; Berliner 2005; Klein 2000; Lowenthal 1998; Maier 1993). We agree that some of the scholarship as well as other products about memory that have arisen in response to the memory boom may indeed have been more trendy than durable. But, in the first place, it is not clear whether the production of a scholarly and cultural surplus is a sign of a field's decadence or of its fertility. In the second place, the transformations in attitudes toward the past of which the memory boom is a part have not been as superficial as the critique implies, in part because they are longer-term, more gradual, and more

2. Significant programs include, among many others, the Warwick Centre for Memory Studies, the Center for Interdisciplinary Memory Research in Essen, the Center for the Study of History and Memory at Indiana University, the research project titled "Social Memory and Historical Justice" at Swinburne Institute of Technology in Melbourne, the Collaborative Research Centre Memory Cultures at the University of Giessen, and the Luce Program in Individual and Collective Memory at Washington University in St. Louis. Major journals in the field, in addition to many special issues of more general journals, include *History and Memory* and *Memory Studies*. Edited volumes are too numerous to cite.

complex than they have often been characterized; the preoccupation with memory in all its different forms is a perennial one, though to be sure it is varied and changing.

In contrast to the critique of the "memory boom," then, our effort here begins from the premise that, far from declining in relevance, many of the analytical frameworks with which scholars have approached the issues highlighted under the rubric of memory studies represent the outlines of an increasingly important paradigm that unifies diverse interests across numerous disciplines, and consolidates long-standing perspectives within them, in perspicuous ways. Our contemporary interest in memory, we believe, is no mere fad, though it risks being mistaken for one if it is seen entirely from the present and if certain intellectual conditions for consolidating memory studies as a coherent field of inquiry are not met.

The Collective Memory Reader presents key texts—the selection of which we explain toward the end of this essay—that underwrite and express the long-standing, though surely intensifying, interest in memory. As the title indicates, however, our focus is on a particular kind of interest in memory, namely that which emphasizes its social or collective nature. Collective memory has been a key referent of memory studies since even before its consolidation in scholarly and public discourse in the 1920s and with increasing frequency since the 1980s. Before explaining the structure of this Reader and the principles that guided our selection and arrangement of materials, the present essay aims to specify where this interest in memory—and in collective memory in particular—came from and how it has developed, for again we see it as of much longer standing than any supposed contemporary memory boom, however important the concentration of interest in the last thirty years has been.

We emphasize first the transformations in our understanding of time that emerged with—or indeed constitute—modernity, for modernity's reconfiguration of the relations among past, present, and future has transformed the meaning and role of memory in essential ways. Next, in part prefiguring the organization of the readings that follow, we explore the history of thinking about and analyzing the social dimensions of memory leading up to the landmark work of the sociologist Maurice Halbwachs in 1925. While Halbwachs is often considered the founding father of contemporary memory studies, we demonstrate that his ideas did not emerge from a vacuum and that he was not the only scholar whose writings have contributed to, or should be seen as contributing to, contemporary memory studies; tracing out alternate sources of scholarly interest in memory, and the strange history of Halbwachs's canonization as a founding father, we argue, produces a richer and more coherent foundation for contemporary efforts. Finally, we examine transformations in the conditions of memory, and the ways in which we have studied it, in the contemporary period, the period that has supposedly given rise to the memory boom. Our goal in presenting these extensive discussions is twofold: first, we aim to correct what we see as a misleading narrative about the origins of contemporary memory studies; and second, we seek to highlight the ways in which the resources we provide in this Reader can help consolidate the future of this still-developing and, we argue, crucially important field of inquiry.

Memory and Modernity

Like everything else, memory has a history. *Memoria*, mother of the muses (including *Clio*, the muse of history), is the basic form of our relationship to the past, of our existence in time. But this relationship has clearly changed in profound ways over the course of history. Obviously, as many of the readings in the following pages show, many factors are at play in defining broad epochal differences. Contemporary historians of memory, for instance, have pointed to the importance of media technologies in shaping what it means to remember: being able to read and write fundamentally alters what we remember and how we remember it; societies that keep written records have a different relationship to the past than ones that do not. Walter Ong (1967, 2002), for instance, has shown that in the contemporary period, which is dominated by images and visual culture, rhetoric has regained the prominence it once enjoyed in manuscript culture. Drawing on Ong's insight, the historian Patrick Hutton (1993: 16) argues that "over the long run, the appreciation of memory as habit is displaced by one of memory as representation." Based on Ong's history of communications media, Hutton (1993: 16) thus links the changing modes of communication with different historical perspectives on memory: "orality with the reiteration of living memory; manuscript literacy with the recovery of lost wisdom; print literacy with the reconstruction of a distinct past; and media literacy with the deconstruction of the forms with which past images are composed." During this last stage of media literacy, moreover, memory has been marked by a high degree of self-reflexivity. This new kind of self-conscious memory thus simultaneously helps to explain the so-called memory boom and contributes to it.

Moreover, given what we now know about neural plasticity, it is clear that changes in the forms of memory are not merely sociocultural: a mind that was trained to remember telephone numbers is rather different from one that was not, or is not anymore; one that developed the capacity to perform long oral narratives is in important ways different from one that was trained to reproduce long written ones, and both of these are rather different from minds that can simply use Google to search for an inscribed original, or a snippet view of it. When we say that technologies of memory and the ways we use them have changed over time, therefore, we need to remember that the brain is also a technology of memory and that even its operations are historically malleable. Psychological study, even the most brain-oriented, is thus an essential part of the history of memory, not something that stands outside it.

Of course, neither brains nor technologies nor the interactions between them exhaust the outlines of the history of memory, or of history that explains changes in memory. At the most basic existential level, for instance, scholars commonly draw a distinction between the "cyclical" temporality of premodern societies and the "linear" temporality of modern ones (Eliade 1971), though there are good reasons to doubt the clarity with which such distinctions are often applied. Perhaps more convincingly, many have written of the history of the idea of progress, in which the horizon of expectation stretches farther beyond the space of experience after the birth of the modern age than it did before it. As Reinhart Koselleck (1985: 22) has put it, before the modern era, "the future of the end of the world is absorbed within time by the Church as a constituting element, and thus does not exist in a linear sense at the end point of time. . . . In contrast, the experience in a century of bloody struggles [the seventeenth] was, above all, that the religious wars did not herald final judgment. . . . This disclosed a new and unorthodox future." According to Koselleck (1985: 14), "There is thus a stark contrast between a world of prophecy, in which events are merely symbols of that which is already known . . . and one of prognosis, which produces time within which and out of which it weaves."

It is not difficult to extrapolate from such an account how the role of memory changes under such circumstances. From the Italian Renaissance through the age of Enlightenment, according to this kind of account, both the perception and reality of the rate of social change increased to an extent previously inconceivable. An acknowledgment of distance from the past is thus a hallmark of Western modernity, in which our sense of time—which treats past, present, and future as more clearly delineated than in previous epochs—yields a sense of difference from our ancestors. In other words, distance from the past only came to be understood and recognized as something that matters in the course of history. In the Renaissance, this sense of difference was new, and yet still different from our own. The present at that time was often seen as a matter of decline from a golden age of antiquity; by the seventeenth century, commentators were arguing vigorously in what was known as the "Querelles des anciens et des modernes" ("Quarrel between the Ancients and the Moderns") about the relative merits of the present and the past (DeJean 1997); it was only after this debate that belief in the superiority of the modern carried the day. But carry the day it did, with many positive consequences, and surely more negative ones than anticipated as well (Fritzsche 2004). What is most clear, though, is that the problem of our relation to the past arises in its present form only when we experience ourselves as having traveled far beyond it, as if to a foreign country (see especially Lowenthal 1985). And this has increasingly been the case over the last two or so centuries.

Beyond these transformations in temporality, moreover, related transformations in social structure altered the status of memory as well. The past is a foreign country not simply because it is long ago, but because it is often far away. In the age of mass immigration, for instance, distance from the past is quite literal, when residents of the "new world" define themselves in relation to the "old country" (Anderson 1991). But this sense of distance from the past is even more complex and of longer standing. One of the basic features of modernization adumbrated by sociologists is the increasing differentiation of society (Durkheim 1984 [1915]). Prior to the division of labor associated with the Industrial Revolution, the varieties of experience in localities and across short life spans were rather limited and uniform. And in such times and places, the foundations of cohesion were assumed rather than hypothetical: where experiences are largely identical among people both in a given time and place and across generations (a concept that itself depends on temporal differentiation and occurs only when there is marked social change; see Mannheim 1952 [1928], Schuman and Scott 1989), identity is manifest in the rhythms of everyday life and in the ritualism of cyclical communion. But where people from different milieus congregate together in polyglot urban settings, leaving behind both their earlier contexts and to some degree their earlier selves, where the labors of life are more highly differentiated than in rural households, where classes and guilds and interest groups form, the basis of agreement and the bonds of commonality are much less obvious, requiring vast new efforts and conceptual frameworks.

Before the age of the individual, then, the bonds of civility and foundations of solidarity were less *problematic* in the authentic sense of that term: how we belong together, and are constituted as groups, seemed more obvious and less in need of contemplation and special measures. The problem of *collective* memory thus arises in a particular time and a particular place (which is not to say there are not other versions of the problem elsewhere), namely where collective identity is no longer as obvious as it once was (Nora 1989; Megill 1998).

There have, of course, been other significant changes in the conditions for memory since the era of high modernity, but we reserve comment on those transformations—usually associated with "postmodernity"—for the moment; our purpose here is to draw out longer trajectories within which to situate the discontinuities assumed in diagnoses of the late twentieth-century memory boom.

The Long History of Memory Studies

Not only does memory have a history, so too does our analysis of it. As we saw, biblical texts enjoined groups to recall their common origins, in ways both similar to and different from the ways modern national leaders do. Classical philosophers like Plato and Aristotle provided enduring metaphors—like that of the mind as a wax tablet or of memorization as a sorting into bins (Coleman 2005; Carruthers 1990). Augustine of Hippo is not only credited with having invented the autobiography as a form of memory at the turn of the fifth century, but his spatial understanding of memory, based on the image of a staircase, also contributed to the remarkable techniques medieval and Renaissance orators developed for remembering long texts (Yates 1966); these techniques clearly rested on durable intuitions about how memorization works. And later, Enlightenment philosophers like John Locke found in memory the ultimate

source of the self, namely the awareness of self-sameness through time, pre-
saging our contemporary discourse of identity (Taylor 1992; Gergen 1991;
MacIntyre 1984; Erikson 1994; Mead 1934; James 1910). Contemporary
scholars who analyze memory can thus draw a lineage for their inquiries back
to these and other important insights.

Nevertheless, modern perspectives on memory and historicity are profoundly different from much of what came before (though differences are not
as absolute and exclusive as they are often portrayed). Part of the change in our
view of the past—and of history and memory as ways of framing it—might be
characterized as emanating from the triumph not only of the idea of progress
but also of the associated "logocentrism" of this Western modernity—the valuation of reason and rationality over other criteria. In terms of memory, this has
involved a shift from an emphasis on knowledge *from* the past about *how* to do
things to an emphasis on knowledge *about* the past *that* certain things happened (Hacking 1998); memory now seems to be not so much about preservation of folkways in ritual and repetition (see the discussion of Ong and Hutton
above), but about the acquisition of knowledge in learning and recitation, and
our analytical frameworks thus seek to parse these capacities.

In the late nineteenth century, avatars of logocentrism in the natural sciences—particularly Wilhelm Wundt (1897, 1910, 1912) and Hermann Ebbinghaus (1913), two of the founding fathers of experimental psychology—thus
began to study the cognitive substrata of remembering systematically with the
tools of modern science.[3] In the early twentieth century, writers like Richard
Semon (1921, 1923), whose work has proven generative for many later theorists
(though this is something of a well-kept secret; see Schacter 2001), sought to
understand cultural inheritance with the tools of evolutionary biology. Most
famously, Sigmund Freud approached the psychodynamics of memory as a
physician, though to be sure Freud had a deep, even overriding, appreciation
for the role of the irrational in psychic and cultural life. Psychoanalysis of various kinds, along with the anthropological study of mythologies, has thus undertaken the tasks of demystification, individual and social. Indeed, Ian
Hacking (1998: 209) has suggested that these new sciences of memory
"emerged as surrogate sciences of the soul, empirical sciences, positive sciences that would provide new kinds of knowledge in terms of which to cure,
help, and control the one aspect of human beings that had hitherto been resistant to positivist science." If previously we embraced memory as a source of
mystery and haunting, we thus now seek to solve those mysteries and exorcise
those demons with the tools of analysis.

Where we earlier derived meaning from worlds of myth, moreover, we now
establish truth through the study of history and have developed methodological
principles for doing so; indeed, the theory of history was one of the most

---

3. Efforts to clarify the neurological foundations of memory were conducted by Paul Broca as early as
(1861). For a comprehensive account of the history of memory research in psychology, see Danziger (2008).

important intellectual and political growth enterprises in the late nineteenth century. Perhaps the overwhelming result of logocentrism in historical thinking was the tradition of historicism, a manifestation of the Enlightenment's widespread belief that history was linear (or at least dialectical) and irreversible. The most famous such view is elaborated in Hegel's *Philosophy of History*, which offers a teleological account of history as "none other than the progress of the consciousness of freedom" (2007: 19).

Modern philosophies of history, however, can be understood in at least two distinct ways. On the one hand, a progressivist account allows the evaluation of different nations according to their relative advancement. For Hegel, the Prussian state was clearly the most advanced in history, the apotheosis of Reason. More generally, as Koselleck (1985) has formulated it, such views led to a perception of the "noncontemporaneity of the contemporaneous,"[4] namely the belief that some societies are more "advanced" than others existing at the same time; and such views, whether implicit or explicit, philosophical or political, allow a great deal, including the exploitation of those considered behind or inferior. On the other hand, historicism also gives rise to its seeming opposite, namely historical relativism—the belief that each particular culture has its own intrinsic principle, incommensurable and incomparable with any other according to any general scheme.[5]

Despite the strong apparent opposition between historicism and relativism, however, both led in the same direction: namely, to a new alliance between nation-states and a sense of the past. The connections between the rise of the nation-state and the status of history writing are well documented in the historiographical literature (Iggers 1968; Breisach 1995); the role of memory understood as broader than what professional historians produce has recently emerged as a topic for scholars of nationalism as well (e.g., Smith 1986).

To be sure, the triumph of logocentrism has never been absolute, and our contemporary set of interests in memory has as much to do with the reaction against it as with its triumph. Indeed, many scholars have characterized the late nineteenth century as experiencing a "crisis of memory" (Wolf 2002; Terdiman 1993). For the Enlightenment faith in progress brought with it a Romantic reaction, in which commitment to ever increasing prosperity was challenged by perceptions that modern rationality and order brought with them a soul-withering sterility. During a period in which science and administration

---

4. The term comes originally from the art historian Wilhelm Pinder's work on generations (1926), and is known through the sociologist Karl Mannheim's response to it (Mannheim 1952 [1928]). Koselleck (1985) interpellates the term for his purposes as a philosopher of history.

5. While Wundt, as already mentioned, is most often recognized as the founding father of experimental psychology and thus as an avatar of logocentrism, it is much less often noted that Wundt also espoused a form of cultural relativism as the founder of what he called *Völkerpsychologie* or cultural psychology, which attributed distinct psychological dispositions to unique cultural groups and called for the study of these cultural horizons of cognition. John D. Greenwood (2009) has thus argued that scholarly amnesia about Wundt's contributions is part and parcel of contemporary psychology's more general forgetting of the social.

were reaching a previously unimaginable apogee, writers like Henri Bergson, Marcel Proust, and Freud, among many others, as we will discuss in more detail below, thus inquired into the complex dimensions that lay beneath this modern veneer of rationality and control. The principal repository of these seething wellsprings: memory.

It is significant as well to acknowledge that logocentrism has proceeded in important regards via the distinction and development of the *individual* and individualism, and that it has led to the hegemony of individualistic approaches across many fields, including the modern experimental psychology deriving from Wundt and Ebbinghaus. Indeed, many logocentrists believed firmly that modern people are less constrained by social factors than their "primitive" predecessors, who they believed were utterly beholden to the group in a way moderns supposedly are not. Such a view sometimes led them to see collective solidarity—and the shared beliefs and practices that constitute it—as an outmoded form of social organization (Douglas 1986; Shils 1981). "Primitive" societies, in such a view, are societies of collective memory, while modern ones are societies of individual memory.

Nevertheless, within the same set of developments, the recognition that memory—modern as well as premodern—has social dimensions, or is even essentially social rather than individual, distributed rather than solipsistic, did indeed come to the fore in seemingly new ways as well. Perhaps this was because these theorists, or at least their politician counterparts, understood how important strong commitments can be ideologically when they are seen to be long-standing. As Mary Douglas (1986: 86) has written, history models itself on "naturalizing analogies," and such analogies brook no dissent because they make current arrangements appear inevitable.

Indeed, for many writers in the late nineteenth and early twentieth centuries, the problems of historical memory were seen to be a part of nature not just figuratively, but also literally. In the late eighteenth century, the French naturalist Jean-Baptiste Lamarck proposed a theory asserting that acquired traits become heritable: that if, because of environmental pressures, an organism develops a particular characteristic—for instance, builds up certain muscles at the expense of others because they are useful in obtaining food—such traits will be passed on to its offspring. One of the most important contributions of Charles Darwin's work decades later was to refute this proto-evolutionary theory through the elaboration of genetic, rather than acquired, inheritance and the principle of natural selection.

For many of those inspired by both Lamarck's problematic and Darwin's solution, however, genes were a sort of biological species-memory. On this basis, scholars like Ewald Hering (1905) and Samuel Butler (1880) asserted that cultural traits must be inscribed in the same way as physical ones. Perhaps the most durably important work in this tradition is that of Richard Semon, already mentioned above, who followed Hering and Butler in hypothesizing a social or cultural equivalent of genes. Semon, who had studied with the German evolutionist Ernst Haeckel, coined the term "engram"—now common in psychological discourse—to refer to hypothetical changes in the brain caused by the encoding of external stimuli: in other words, the physical traces of memory. This view contributed to later theories of memory as reconstruction rather than retrieval, since in this theory experiences were seen to be broken into constituent units for storage, which are then reassembled (in new combinations) later. On this basis, Semon (1921, 1923) developed a theory of "mnemes" (much later echoed by evolutionary psychologists like Richard Dawkins [1976]), coined to sound similar to "genes," and an approach to "mimetics," which like genetics was part of a theory of inheritance, though in this case of culture.

What is important here is that the study of cultural memory in the nineteenth century was conceived not as alien to the natural science of memory in biology, but as an extension of it. It was Semon's goal to identify what the mechanism of cultural inheritance might be, rather than hinting at some kind of mystical haunting by the past. To be sure, many writers of the time and later adopted a discreditable cultural Lamarckism, again the belief that acquired characteristics—in this case, memories—could be inherited without any concrete mechanism of coding or transmission.[6] Nevertheless, Semon's influence, though itself rather coded (Schacter 2001), was profound indeed.

While Freud dismissed Semon's theories, the question of inexplicit cultural aftereffects was a central one for him, particularly in his late books *Totem and Taboo* and *Moses and Monotheism*, in which Freud sought a cultural correlate for his ideas of the repressed memory and return of individual trauma. Indeed, Freud has also been charged with a sort of cultural Lamarckism, particularly in his claim that the Jewish people have been defined by the repressed memory of their murder of Moses (Yerushalmi 1993). In general, Freud drew much more on Wundt's neglected writings on cultural psychology than on Semon's, but his agenda was set by this general climate of interest in cultural heritability, influenced by the late nineteenth-century discourse on "organic memory" (Otis 1994).

In contrast to Freud, Carl Jung drew eagerly on Semon's ideas in developing his theory of the "collective unconscious" and its central source: "racial memory." Additionally, both Semon's ideas and Hering's were significant sources for the "iconological" theory of social memory articulated by the art historian Aby Warburg in the 1920s. And this line of thought has been a central theme in the development of contemporary theories of "cultural memory," as articulated most prominently by the Egyptologist Jan Assmann (2007).

---

6. A central idea here was that "ontogeny recapitulates phylogeny"—in other words, that the process of individual development reflects the entire history of the species (Gould 1977). For humans, this is the now common idea that the process of socialization is a matter of civilization, or the acquisition of all that the civilization has accomplished. After all, in the process of maturing, the child acquires a wide variety of social and cultural capacities—e.g., language and practical knowledge—that have taken ages to develop. Such acquisition was seen as a kind of deep cultural memory.

Memory and the Nation

Other than these often-forgotten debates in late nineteenth-century psychology, perhaps the key site in the story of thinking about social and cultural forms of memory is the rise of nationalism, and the understandings of history it depended on.

Whether to demonstrate the superiority of a particular nation in the scheme of human history, or to endow a sense of the nation's uniqueness and hence spiritual appeal as a special identity, nation-states in the late nineteenth century propagated interest in their pasts to an unprecedented extent. This is the famous "invention of tradition" thesis of Eric Hobsbawm and Terence Ranger (1983), who showed convincingly how European states in the decades before World War I sought to shore up the legitimacy they had been losing since the demise of absolutism and the introduction of democracy by generating a sense of historical endurance (often bogus) for their institutions and practices. Leaders had done this in earlier epochs too, of course, but in the late nineteenth century they did it with a new vigor and with new tools, including those of emerging mass literacy and coordinated administration (Weber 1976).

As Benedict Anderson (1991) showed in his famous book *Imagined Communities*, all nations are unities that are fundamentally imagined (which is different from saying they are imaginary). But imagining nations, Anderson argues in similar terms to Koselleck and Hutton quoted above, depended on the decline of earlier cultural models, including that of the written word as a privileged carrier of ontological truth and of cosmological time: "What has come to take the place of the medieval conception of simultaneity-along-time is, to borrow from [Walter] Benjamin, an idea of 'homogeneous, empty time,' in which simultaneity is, as it were, transverse, cross-time, marked not by prefiguring and fulfillment, but by temporal coincidence, and by clock and calendar" (Anderson 1991: 24). Because of transformations in the perception of time, therefore, the invention of tradition was both more possible and more effective in this period than it had previously been. At the same time, because of the advancements in record keeping and historical scholarship, it was also easier to debunk these inventions, though some historical myths have proven remarkably impervious to evidence. Again referring to Douglas's (1986) argument about naturalizing analogies, one often does not even think to question such assertions.

Whether from an Enlightenment philosophy heralding the superiority of Reason or a Romantic faith in the incommensurable uniqueness of cultures, then, nationalism was heavily invested in the past and produced new understandings of the relationship to it. As mentioned by Anderson and many others, for instance, nation-state builders often developed new calendars as an effective way to unify societies by standardizing temporal frames of reference (Landes 2000; Zerubavel 1989). In general, modern states solidify their power in part by manipulating assumptions about time and space, and they do so with both history and memory. According to Ana Maria Alonso (1988: 40), "Historical chronologies solder a multiplicity of personal, local, and regional historicities and transform them into a unitary national time." As Prasenjit Duara (1997: 4) puts it, again echoing Benjamin's characterization of the "empty, homogeneous time of the nation state," "National history secures for the contested and contingent nation the false unity of a self-same, national subject evolving through time." In the late nineteenth century, when nation-states were increasing their demands for allegiance and fiscal extraction from their populations, memory thus served as the handmaiden of nationalist zeal, history its high counsel (Olick 2003). Any threats to the sense of the shared past by dislocation, rampant growth, or the general unmooring of cultures from their origins produced a "memory crisis" and a redoubled search for its hidden recesses.

The parallels between the memory boom of the late nineteenth and late twentieth centuries are thus rather strong, and call into question the more dismissive assumptions that our current interest in memory is a dying contemporary fad of the last thirty years. To be sure, the memory boom of the late nineteenth century was tied up with the ascendancy of nationalism, while that of the late twentieth century is tied up with its decline (Nora 1989), and the nineteenth century was still the age of monuments, while ours, given the atrocious history of the last hundred years, is one of memorials (Mosse 1991). Nevertheless, it was in the context of the nineteenth-century boom that we began theorizing the political and social dimensions of memory (and other aspects of it as well) in ways recognizably linked to how we theorize them today. Moreover, late nineteenth-century critiques of the uses and misuses of history, particularly that of Friedrich Nietzsche (1997) (and a half-century later that of Herbert Butterfield [1965] and others who attacked "Whig history"), have clearly informed contemporary approaches to the relationship between history and memory and our widespread skepticism toward modernist narratives. This skepticism has obviously shaped—though not in any universally accepted way—contemporary scholarly work on memory.

Within this story of memory's rising apparent importance and our new modes of analyzing it, other factors like the rise of the press, the development of media like photography and film, and the digital revolution, obviously warrant attention, as they contributed to a media-theoretic perspective that has clearly advanced our understanding of memory. Also important were frameworks for characterizing the dehumanizing experiences of the First World War, in which, as Walter Benjamin (1969: 84) put it, "Never has experience been contradicted more thoroughly than strategic experience by tactical warfare, economic experience by inflation, bodily experience by mechanical warfare, moral experience by those in power." These cataclysms, according to Benjamin, left people not only without the conditions for telling stories in the heroic form of the epic or even the redemptive form of the novel, but with experiences that were in fact ultimately incommunicable. Indeed, many see in the First World War the beginning of the contemporary discourse of trauma, in which any linear relationship to experience and hence narratability is disrupted.[7] This discourse of trauma as a special kind of memory, developing since the late nineteenth century, through the First World War, and with particular vigor in the 1970s and 1980s, has been a major constituent of the contemporary memory boom; but it is clearly one with a long and complex history (Leys 2000; Caruth 1995).

War, moreover, has indeed changed memory in the contemporary age, though since there has always been war, such an explanation of the new memory boom obviously requires careful specification. Many of these themes, for instance, were already presaged in Paul Fussell's (1975) magisterial book, *The Great War and Modern Memory* (thus predating the alleged contemporary memory boom), which depicts how the experience of the war and its literary articulations were inscribed (Benjamin's thesis of incommunicability notwithstanding) into the memories of an entire generation.[8] Jay Winter (1995) has also written about how commemorations of World War I served to transform individual grief into public mourning. If World War I served as a catalyst for heroic memories, World War II and the atrocities associated with what came to be known as the Holocaust, by contrast, gave rise to more skeptical memories (e.g., Gillis 1994a; Young 1993; Maier 1988).

To be sure, the relationship between memory and war is not limited to these two epochal events, though, as we discuss later, both were the subject of recurrent anniversary commemorations at the end of the twentieth century, fueling the hunger for commemorative events more generally (Ashplant, Dawson, and Roper 2001). Public controversies around cultural and political dimensions of war commemoration have been a prominent feature of contemporary debates extending to other armed conflicts, e.g., the Vietnam War and the Enola Gay exhibit (see Lowenthal 1998; Zolberg 1998; Sturken 1997; Thelen 1995; Wagner-Pacifici and Schwartz 1991). The end of the Cold War along with the ethnic conflicts of the 1990s was yet another historical juncture that sustained interest in the memories of war and atrocities (Judt 2005).

The complexities of the foregoing account of memory's long history aside, two things are clear: since the late nineteenth century, memory seems to have become a top item on our intellectual and scientific, as well as public, agendas. And we have moved increasingly—though not nearly enough, as the texts in this volume imply—to seeing memory as a topic that extends far beyond the bounds of the individual mind. It is clear that "collective memory" has become

7. More accurately, the origins of the discourse of trauma are to be found in the context of the introduction of rail travel—which transformed perceptions of time and space—and of railway accidents—which produced invisible psychic traumas on a mass scale—in the late nineteenth century. See especially Schivelbusch (1987).

8. See also Klaus Theweleit's *Male Fantasies* (1987), which describes the war generation in Germany and the impact memories of the war had for their artistic sensibilities and, more important, for their political views, prefiguring the rise of Nazism. For a similar analysis applied to the United States after the Vietnam War, see also Sturken (1997).

one of the emblematic terms and concerns of our age, which we nevertheless define as longer than the last thirty years; the memory boom may be recent, but it was clearly a long time in the making. What is not yet clear is exactly what the term "collective memory" means, what issues it addresses, what inquiries it inspires, and whether the intellectual conditions presently exist or can be propagated for advancing, rather than merely recycling, the insights that have already been produced under its banner.

Maurice Halbwachs and the Concept of "Collective Memory"

What do we mean when we use the term "collective memory"? Memory, our common sense tells us, is a fundamentally individual phenomenon. What could be more individual than remembering, which we seem to do in the solitary world of our own heads as much as in conversation with others? Even when we reminisce, we often experience this as a process of offering up to the external world the images of the past locked away in the recesses of our own minds. We can remember by ourselves in the dark at night, as we drive alone along the highway, or as we half-listen to a conversation about something else. By the same token, lesions of the brain—caused perhaps by Alzheimer's disease or physical injury—are surely internal rather than social defects, preventing us as individuals from remembering. Memory—and by extension forgetting—thus seems not just fundamentally individual, but quintessentially so, as primal and lonely as pain. What can we possibly mean, then, when we refer to social or collective memory?

Contemporary use of the term "collective memory" traces itself largely to the sociologist Halbwachs, who published his landmark *Social Frameworks of Memory* (*Les cadres sociaux de la mémoire*) in 1925, though the term was by then in general use in a variety of contexts related and unrelated to sociology (common cognates in this regard were "public memory" and the already-discussed "racial memory," the use of which in fact predated Jung's). Halbwachs was not the only one to contribute to a social perspective on memory at the time and since. It is also true that many contemporary writers have taken little from him consciously except the term. But even when they are not apparently influenced by his arguments, many contemporary scholars at least acknowledge Halbwachs totemically. More important for many scholars, however, Halbwachs gave the term "collective memory" a theoretical weight previously unknown, and his ideas have indeed been generative for much of the more serious subsequent scholarship.

Halbwachs's interest in memory combined insights from two important figures in late nineteenth-century France, philosopher Henri Bergson and sociologist Émile Durkheim, both of whom were concerned—though in very different ways—with so-called advances of European "civilization." In the late nineteenth century, as we already discussed under the banner of logocentrism, powerful forces were pushing to overcome subjectivity, judgment, and variability in the name of science, organization, and control. Political and commercial elites, for instance, viewed the diversity of local times as a growing problem: like railroad tracks of different gauges, the diversity of times was an impediment to increasingly complex and widespread commerce and political power (Kern 1986). As a result, élites worked hard to standardize time in terms of homogeneous criteria. One good example was the establishment of time zones and Greenwich Mean Time.[9] Scientific advances—which discovered regularities behind apparent variations—lent support to these unifying and standardizing projects. The philosophical tradition, moreover, had long favored objectivist accounts, in which empirical variety is a mere illusion behind which lie perfect conceptual unities.

Like many other thinkers of the time, the philosopher Bergson was concerned by increasing rationalization and the unifying force of science. Along with writers like Proust and Freud, among many others, Bergson became preoccupied with memory because it seemed to him that precisely in an age in which historiography, biography, and other forms of record keeping were ordering history in an increasingly objective and complete manner, meaningful connections to our pasts, personal or shared, seemed to be waning. Thus influenced in part by Romantic perceptions that the logocentric conceptual universe was somehow sterile, Bergson rejected objectivist accounts, arguing that subjectivity is the only source of true philosophical knowledge (Terdiman 1993; Bergson 1988; Kern 1986). As a result, he undertook a radical philosophical analysis of the *experience* of time, highlighting memory as its central feature. Against accounts of memory as passive storage, he characterized remembering as active engagement. Against accounts of memory as the objective reproduction of the past, he characterized remembering as fluid and changing. Bergson thus posed the problem of memory in particularly potent ways for Halbwachs and other later theorists. His work on memory drew Halbwachs's attention to the difference between objective (often transcendental) and subjective apprehensions of the past: whereas new forms of record keeping measured time and recorded history in increasingly uniform and standardized ways, individual memory was still highly variable, sometimes recording short periods in intense detail and long periods in only the vaguest outline.[10] Following Bergson, this variability of memory was for Halbwachs the real point of interest.

Like Bergson, Durkheim considered transcendentalist accounts of time and space unjustified. Unlike Bergson, however, Durkheim located the variability of perceptual categories not in the vagaries of subjective experience, but in differences among forms of social organization. Where Bergson rejected objectivist and materialist accounts of time in favor of the variability of *individual*

---

9. Of course, the history of the standardization of time, which depended on the development and spread of mechanical clocks, predates these developments by centuries. See especially Landes (2000).

10. More recently, however, Zerubavel (2003) has demonstrated that this variable attention span characterizes social memory as well.

experience, Durkheim rejected such accounts by attending to the ways different *societies* produce different concepts of time: forms of time, like other basic categories, do not derive either from transcendental truths or from contingent interests, but are social facts, varying not according to subjective experience but according to the changing forms of social structure. Standardization and objectivism, according to Durkheim, were central ways modernizing societies were responding to increasing levels of differentiation and individuation. By connecting cognitive order (time perception) with social order (division of labor), Durkheim thus provided for Halbwachs a sociological framework for studying the variability of memory raised by Bergson.

In his landmark work on collective memory, Halbwachs thus drew from Bergson's problematization of time and memory, but addressed the issue through Durkheim's sociological lens.[11] Memory, for Halbwachs, is first of all a matter of how minds work together in society, how their operations are not simply mediated by social arrangements but are in fact structured by them: "It is in society that people normally acquire their memories. It is also in society that they recall, recognize, and localize their memories" (1992: 38). The forms memory takes thus vary according to social organization, and the groups to which any individual belongs are primary even in the most apparently individual remembering. Moreover, for Halbwachs, memory is framed in the present as much as in the past, variable rather than constant. Studying memory, as a result, is a matter not of reflecting philosophically on inherent properties of the subjective mind but of identifying its shifting social frames.

There are, nevertheless, a number of distinct aspects of collective remembering in Halbwachs, and different kinds of collective memory research since then have emphasized various of these aspects.[12] First, Halbwachs argued that it is impossible for individuals to remember in any coherent and persistent fashion outside of their group contexts; these are the necessary *social frameworks* of *individual* memory.[13] His favorite examples include the impossibility of being certain of any particular childhood memory: once we become adults, it is often impossible to say whether a memory of a childhood experience is more the result of stored features of the original moment or some kind of compilation out of stored fragments, other people's retellings, and intervening experiences.

11. It should be pointed out that Halbwachs's intellectual concerns were quite wide-ranging and that his interests in memory were part of his larger concern with what he called "social morphologies" (see Halbwachs 1960). Halbwachs's work on collective memory should not be isolated from his larger project, although this is not the place to provide a general intellectual portrait of Halbwachs. For a recent sketch highlighting Halbwachs's longer career, see especially Lepenies (2006). For a more comprehensive survey of Halbwachs's career and intellectual contributions, see Wetzel (2009).

12. For a more elaborated version of this argument, see Olick (1999a) and Olick and Robbins (1998). Moreover, this discussion is not meant to imply that all valuable work in contemporary memory studies is directly engaged with Halbwachs's original formulations.

13. See also Iwona Irwin-Zarecka (2007) for connections to Goffmanian frame theory.

The social frameworks in which we are called on to recall, moreover, are inevitably tied up with what and how we recall. Groups provide us the stimulus or opportunity to recall; they also shape the ways in which we do so, and often provide the materials. Following this argument, the very distinction between the individual and social components of remembering ceases to make absolute sense: "There is no point," Halbwachs (1992: 38) argued, "in seeking where . . . [memories] are preserved in my brain or in some nook of my mind to which I alone have access: for they are recalled by me externally, and the groups of which I am a part at any given time give me the means to reconstruct them." All individual remembering, that is, takes place with social materials, within social contexts, and in response to social cues. Even when we do it alone, we do so as social beings with reference to our social identities, and with languages and symbols that we may use in creative ways but certainly did not invent.

Halbwachs thus distinguished between "autobiographical memory" and "historical memory." The former concerns the events of one's own life that one remembers because they were experienced directly, though it also includes reference to events which one did not experience directly but around which one's memory is oriented. For instance, you are likely to remember what you were doing when an event designated historic by the group took place—such as the attacks of September 11, 2001—even if these events did not affect you directly in your individuality rather than in terms of the group of which you are a member. "Historical memory," in distinction, refers to residues of events by virtue of which groups claim a continuous identity through time. "Historical memory" of the U.S. Civil War, for instance, is part of what it means to be an American and is part of the collective narrative of the United States. But nobody still has "autobiographical memory" of the event.

This is the more authentically Durkheimian moment in Halbwachs's theory: Durkheim (1968 [1915]) developed a sociological approach to what he called "collective representations," symbols or meanings that are properties of the group whether or not any particular individual or even particular number of individuals share them. In this sense, very few people may be able to identify key figures or events of the Civil War, but those figures or events may nonetheless be important elements of American collective memory, and individuals may still be shaped by them (as an example, many more Americans are familiar with the first phrase of the Gettysburg Address—"Four score and seven years ago"—than could give a basic account of the issues Abraham Lincoln was raising in his most famous speech). Survey researchers may conclude that a particular image or event not remembered by very many people is no longer a part of the collective memory; but for a true Durkheimian, culture is not reducible to what is in people's heads. In an alternative tradition of work on "cultural memory" founded by Warburg (1999, 2008) and culminating more recently in the writings of Jan and Aleida Assmann (J. Assmann 2007; A. Assmann 1999), mentioned above, analysis of this latency is taken to be the most interesting part of memory studies.

Representations themselves, within the Durkheimian perspective, are not to be evaluated solely in terms of their origins, resonance, or distribution in any particular population. Collective memory, in this sense, has a life of its own, though this need not be as metaphysical as it sounds: work emphasizing the genuinely collective nature of social memory has demonstrated that there are long-term structures to what societies remember or commemorate that are stubbornly impervious to the efforts of individuals to escape them; powerful institutions, moreover, clearly support some histories more than others, provide narrative patterns and exemplars of how individuals can and should remember, and stimulate public memory in ways and for reasons that have little to do with the individual or aggregate neurological records. Many scholars of collective memory believe that without such a collectivist perspective, it is difficult to provide good explanations of why mythology, tradition, and heritage, among other long-term symbolic patterns, are as robust as they are.[14] A key task for contemporary work has been to understand the mechanisms of this robustness, which are often far from obvious.

Durkheimian approaches are often accused—and often rightly so—of being radically anti-individualist, conceptualizing society in disembodied terms, as an entity existing in and of itself, over and above the individuals who comprise it. Another important feature of Durkheimian sociology can be an unjustified assumption that these societies—constituted by "collective representations" which individuals may or may not share—are unitary. A Durkheimian approach to collective memory can thus lead us to attribute one collective memory or set of memories to entire, well-bounded societies.[15] Indeed, while not usually—though sometimes—articulated in terms of Durkheimian theory, many political discussions over the past two hundred years about cultural heritage have shared such assumptions: commemoration of certain historical events is essential, so the argument goes, to our sense of national unity; without substantial consensus on the past, social solidarity is in danger; there is either a "deep structure" or a stored-up legacy of shared culture that binds us together; without its pervasive influence, there is no "us" to bind. In more extreme versions, the "truth" of such accounts is seen as irrelevant in face of the need for them: any myth of belonging, it sometimes seems, even a patently absurd one, is better than none.

Halbwachs was in some ways more careful than his great mentor Durkheim, placing most of his emphasis on the multiple social frameworks of individual memories (Coser 1992). He characterized collective memory as plural, showing that shared memories can be effective markers of social differentiation. However, Halbwachs did lay the groundwork for a more radically collectivist, in addition to socially framed individualist, approach to memory. In some con-

14. To be sure, there are many critics who see this collectivism as a metaphysical Achilles' heel. See especially Kansteiner (2002) and Klein (2000), as well as our discussion below.

15. Like many such critiques, these are based on something of a straw-man version of Durkheim's positions.

trast to his idea that what individuals remember is determined by their group memberships but still takes place in their own minds, Halbwachs also focused on publicly available commemorative symbols, rituals, and technologies. As we just noted, some later theorists treat these symbols and representations as a vast cultural storehouse; this is a wise move, since the items in a cultural storehouse are real. Others, however, take an additional step and hypothesize a deep cultural structure, a set of rules, patterns, and resources that generates any particular representation (Lévi-Strauss 1983 [1964]; Douglas 1996; Elias 1996). In even more extreme versions, the structure of collective meanings is treated not as *conscience collective*, but as a "collective unconscious," which can indeed have mystical overtones (Jung 1968). One need not become a metaphysician, however, to believe there is an emergent dimension of collective remembering that is organized without direct reference to individuals.

Halbwachs, of course, is not the only important figure who comments on memory's social character, nor was he even the only important *early* thinker who developed such a perspective. In 1882, the French philosopher and political essayist Ernest Renan gave an important—and a century later quite famous—lecture in which he defined shared remembering as well as shared forgetting as constitutive elements of national identity. Somewhat earlier than Halbwachs, Warburg was developing his theory of artistic iconology, in which present images were seen as containing the accumulated residues of their long histories. At around the same time (and partly influenced by Halbwachs), the British experimental psychologist Frederick Bartlett (1995 [1932]) was redefining the purview of psychology to include elaborate attention to the social settings of remembering. In the same period, the sociologist Charles Horton Cooley (1918) was writing extensively on the social construction of reputations and fame, while his Chicago colleague George Herbert Mead (2000 [1932]) was elaborating a concept of shared memory as part of his "philosophy of the present."[16] The Russian literary philosopher Mikhail Bakhtin was developing his theory of genres as carriers of social memory (Morson and Emerson 1990), as his compatriots Lev Vygotsky, Ivan Pavlov, and Alexander Luria (Bakhurst 1990) were combining social insights with experimental methods in psychology. And these are just a few examples.

According to the mythology of the memory boom, such early work on social or collective memory, including that of Halbwachs, was nearly entirely forgotten, and was itself only recovered as a sort of invented tradition in the late 1970s and early 1980s as a slogan for the memory industry (though some of it, including many of the names just mentioned, as well as such figures as Semon, in fact has not yet been recovered, or has been recovered only partially in various corners). This account has some intuitive plausibility, though it tends to be overstated. After all, if the contemporary interest in memory is a unique result

16. In 1897, Cooley and Mead's Chicago colleague George Edgar Vincent had published a book (Vincent 1897) touting the Durkheimian perspective, in which he provided an extended discussion of Durkheim's ideas about collective memory—thus years before Halbwachs developed them.

of the transformations of the late twentieth century, what explains the earlier constellation of interest and the (often subterranean) continuities with it? Halbwachs, again, was not the first or the only one to use the term "collective memory," or cognates like "public memory" or "racial memory," and indeed the conceptual history of "collective memory" before Halbwachs remains an under-researched subject in intellectual history.[17] Moreover, the development and transmission of Halbwachs's ideas (to say nothing of the important ideas by the other seminal figures mentioned above) from the interwar years to the present are themselves rather complicated, not reducible to a simple forgetting followed by recovery; indeed, the memory of that development is confused by a variety of issues surrounding Halbwachs's life and work, as well as the complexities of twentieth-century history, to which we turn directly.

The Complex Inheritance of "Collective Memory"

Despite the way we conventionally tell stories of intellectual innovation, Halbwachs was far from a lone wolf. His development of the "collective memory" concept took place within a dialogue with close colleagues at the University of Strasbourg in the 1920s and early 1930s, including the psychiatrist Charles Blondel and the historians Marc Bloch and Lucien Febvre (Friedman 1996; Besnard 1983; Clark 1973). Halbwachs refined his arguments in response to critiques he received from these and other colleagues, and he developed his ideas substantially in the decades following publication of his first work on memory in 1925.

Indeed, the relations between Halbwachs and Bloch were quite important for both the formation of Halbwachs's ideas and their transmission to the present. In the first place, Bloch engaged with Halbwachs in private and in print, encouraging Halbwachs to refine his relationship to historiography; Halbwachs's second book on memory from 1941, *The Legendary Topography of the Holy Land*, was in part a response to Bloch's question as to whether Halbwachs's approach could account for historical inaccuracies in the collective memory.

In the second place, Bloch himself contributed to the transmission of Halbwachs's ideas, both directly and institutionally. Bloch not only wrote a prominent review of Halbwachs's 1925 book but also included a chapter on collective memory in his *Feudal Society* (Bloch 1961 [1939]) and extensively engaged with the concept, as well as with Durkheim's work on "collective representations." While "collective memory" was not explicitly a central theme in the work of Febvre, with whom Bloch founded the Annales school of historiography (the major twentieth-century school of historiography in France, and of key importance elsewhere as well), Halbwachs's work affected the development of that

17. For a rather different use of the term "collective memory," see Van Doren (1967).

tradition profoundly, and collective memory was always part of the basic lexicon of the *Annalistes* (Confino 1997). Both Bloch and Febvre took significant inspiration from the Durkheimian tradition represented close at hand by Halbwachs in underwriting what later came to be called "total history," an approach that emphasized large structures and long-term transformations (the "long *durée*") over events in the short term (the "conjuncture"). And their social-psychological emphasis on "ways of life" and "mentalities"—which gave rise to the vibrant "history of mentalities" of the 1960s and 1970s—was clearly related to Halbwachs's emphasis on a social-psychological topic like memory as well as by Durkheimian ideas about "collective psychology," their understanding of which was at least partly mediated by Halbwachs.

Indeed, part of the reemergence of the memory problematic in the 1980s was led by third-generation *Annalistes* such as Jacques LeGoff, who wrote an influential series of encyclopedia entries on history and memory (later collected in an eponymous book [LeGoff 1992]); in studies by Philip Ariès (1965) and Maurice Agulhon (1981) on funerary practices and the symbols of power, respectively; and then ultimately in Pierre Nora's grand encyclopedia on "lieux de memoire" of 1984–1992 (timed to engage with the problematics of the French Revolution bicentennial).[18]

It may seem that the reappearance of "collective memory" in the 1980s was unprepared and rather sudden, a result of such contemporary political concerns as that over French national identity in the age of mass immigration (Noiriel 1996) and at the moment of the bicentennial (Kaplan 1995). But clearly the term's relative invisibility in the 1950s through 1970s was more a matter of latency than nonexistence, and this latency was inscribed through Halbwachs's direct relations with Bloch and Febvre, whose works were better known and more consequential in those intervening years.

In sociology, the story is related, but somewhat distinct. In reference to the classical founders of sociology, Halbwachs himself was already a latecomer, a member of a second, post-charismatic generation, which is always easier to forget than the founders of a tradition. Moreover, the fate of the Durkheimian tradition in French sociology, to say nothing of sociology elsewhere, was shaky (Besnard 1983; Clark 1973; Marcel and Mucchielli 1999). Part of the problem was one of overreach: Durkheim and his followers were often quite imperialistic in their ambitions for their brand of sociology (Clark 1973), and the hopes for intellectual dominance were likely unrealizable under any circumstances.

18. As with most complex works—and as the theory of collective memory predicts—the reception of Nora's ideas has reduced a vast and profound effort to a few key ideas. Suffice it to say here that the reception of Nora is too often limited to a spatial understanding of his key distinction between worlds of memory (*milieux de mémoire*) and places of memory (*lieux de mémoire*), and his association of the former with premodernity and the later with contemporary society. However, Nora also focused on the history of memory itself and the attendant realignment of temporalities, which he referred to as a shift "from a history sought in continuity to a memory cast in the discontinuity of history." As such, his work bears some comparison to projects like Koselleck's (1985).

Both the psychologist Blondel and the historian Bloch, for instance, could not follow Halbwachs's implied assimilation of their disciplines.

By the same token, the political situation in France was clearly changing dramatically in the interwar years in such a way that was not hospitable to the politics of many members of the Durkheim circle. Several of Durkheim's pro-tégés had already been killed in the First World War (as had Durkheim's son, an event that is often said to have hastened Durkheim's own death). And many of those who survived were relatively left-leaning Jews in a time of increasing anti-Semitism and fascist agitation. Indeed, while not himself a Jew, Halbwachs died in 1945 in Buchenwald, having been arrested when he protested the mur-der of his Jewish in-laws (Coser 1992). Bloch was killed by the Nazis as well.

In the English-speaking world, the conditions for the reception of both Durkheim's and Halbwachs's work are also complex. Halbwachs's 1925 book received several favorable reviews in American sociology journals upon its publication, and Halbwachs was subsequently invited, though entirely for his reputation as a statistician (Topalov 1997), to spend a semester visiting the University of Chicago in 1930, where he gave a course on suicide as well as on French sociology. Halbwachs also subsequently published two papers, one each in the *American Journal of Sociology* and the *American Sociological Review*, explicating the Durkheimian concepts of "collective representations" and "col-lective psychology," and in this way surely played a significant role in establish-ing the canonical status of Durkheim for American sociologists (Halbwachs 1938, 1939). Nonetheless, Halbwachs had only limited opportunities during his visit to Chicago to call attention to his work specifically on memory.[19]

Throughout the 1930s and early 1940s, however, Halbwachs continued to develop his ideas about memory, both in his book *The Legendary Topography of the Holy Land* and in a series of essays that would later, posthumously, be col-lected in 1950 as *The Collective Memory* (which included extensive engagement with the psychologist Blondel). Alas, key passages were left out of that 1950 publication (due to misguided efforts by Halbwachs's sister to burnish his leg-acy) and were not restored until many years later by the work of Gerard Namer. When Halbwachs's collective memory essays were published in an English edition by Mary Douglas in 1980, the paperback carried a blurb from Herbert Blumer, the major legatee of Mead's symbolic interactionism in American sociology, whom Halbwachs had met during his stay in Chicago (Topalov 2008). Indeed, it was Chicago neo-Durkheimians like Edward Shils and Barry Schwartz who were most prominent in re-intensifying sociological interest in "collective memory" from the mid-1970s forward, though whatever lines of influence there might have been were highly indirect.

A translation of Halbwachs's book *The Causes of Suicide* was published in 1978 with an introduction by Anthony Giddens, who by that time was already

19. It is reported that at the time of Halbwachs's visit, Mead, then in the last year of his life, was reading Bergson, though we are not aware of any evidence one way or the other about Mead's awareness of Halbwa-chs (Topalov 2008).

enjoying a major international reputation. Strangely, however, when Douglas's English edition of *The Collective Memory* appeared two years later in 1980 (Douglas also by that time being quite well known), it received no notice at all, despite the blurb from Blumer.[20] Indeed, that edition quickly went out of print and has subsequently become something of a collector's item.

It was only twelve years later that the émigré American sociologist Lewis Coser, who had studied in Paris in the 1930s with members of the Durkheim circle, published a volume of selections from Halbwachs called *On Collective Memory*, a title rather easily confused with Halbwachs's own posthumous *The Collective Memory*.[21] Coser's edition included about half of the 1925 *Social Frameworks of Memory* as well as only the conclusion to *The Legendary Topography of the Holy Land*; it included nothing from *The Collective Memory*—there was obviously no point in reprinting what Douglas had already published. As a result of this much more accessible volume, made readily available in the University of Chicago Press's prestigious *Heritage of Sociology* series, much of the Halbwachs reception in anglophone literatures has thus centered on his earlier presentations.[22] At best, the developments within his thought—to say nothing of the discursive exchanges with Blondel and Bloch, whose residues were much more apparent in *The Collective Memory* and which were surely influential in the transit of Halbwachs's ideas in France—are caught up together into a relatively undifferentiated picture of Halbwachs's theories of memory despite their transformations over time. While we are able to provide excerpts of our first-ever translations of Bloch and Blondel's reviews of Halbwachs's 1925 book here, *The Collective Memory* from 1950 (from which we provide excerpts as well) has never been reissued in English since Douglas's 1980 version, neither simply as a reprint nor in a new edition that could take advantage of subsequent scholarship on Halbwachs (see note 20 above). This scholarship on Halbwachs is much better known in France and Germany, and its limited availability in English is quite regrettable.

Other Trajectories

Moreover, again in response to the emphasis on the supposed latency of "collective memory" between 1945 and the early 1980s, it is important to point out

---

20. Additionally, an important dissertation on Halbwachs's entire oeuvre by Suzanne Vromen (1975) was never published as a book, and there is still no full-length critical study on Halbwachs in English, though there are several in French and German, including, among others, Becker (2003, 2005); Egger (2003); Wetzel (2009); Namer (1987); and Marcel and Mucchielli (1999).

21. That title, however, was not Halbwachs's own; Halbwachs more likely favored some version of "The Individual Memory and the Collective Memory" (Douglas 1980).

22. In Germany, Halbwachs's (1925) book was translated and published in (1966), while *The Collective Memory* appeared in German only in (1991). However, the critical literature on Halbwachs in German has been much more extensive than it has been in English, including the translation of Halbwachs's collected works, and a large number of intellectual historical and conceptual studies of his thought, though this interest has been pursued mostly since the mid- to late (1990s).

that "collective memory" was never entirely absent elsewhere in those years (i.e., from the end of World War II until the supposed advent of the "memory boom" in the late 1970s and 1980s), nor was its relative hibernation due entirely to an inhospitable intellectual and political climate, though in some arenas the postwar years saw a resurgence of a modernist thinking that did not necessarily favor an interest in memory rather than scientific history and rationality (or engaged Marxism).

In French anthropology, for instance, Roger Bastide (1978) wrote important works engaging with the concept. So too did the Annales school archaeologist and historiographer Paul Veyne (1984). While the art historian Frances Yates (1966) did not employ the term "collective memory" in her famous study of Renaissance mnemotechnics, her book *The Art of Memory* is a landmark work for the history of memory in general, and of clear relevance to contemporary memory studies (Yates, perhaps not incidentally, worked for many years at the Warburg Institute at the University of London). Historian Bernard Lewis (1975) produced a volume on varieties of history—"remembered, recovered, and invented"—that presaged some of Hobsbawm and Ranger's (1983) more famous argument. Sociologists Georges Gurvitch (1963), Pitirim Sorokin (1970), Robert Faris (1967), Alfred Schutz (1964), Peter Berger (1963), Lloyd Warner (1959), Fred Davis (1979), and Franco Ferrarotti (1990), among others, all employed "collective memory" in various works during this period as well; while some of these works used "collective memory" merely incidentally, some were centered on it and are (or should be) important models for subsequent scholarship.

Additionally, systematic work on memory in disciplines besides sociology and history made significant progress in these years as well. While psychoanalysis and other kinds of psychotherapy did not see their most vigorous development of the trauma concept until after the Vietnam War, it is not clear that the development of the discourse of trauma—which of course had much older origins in the nineteenth century—was of a piece with the "memory boom" in other spheres, though there are obvious affinities of discourse (Farrell 1998). Nevertheless, the trajectories of the trauma discourse are at least somewhat autonomous—though to be sure only somewhat—from those of social scientific work on collective memory, despite the way in which "trauma" and "collective memory" are often tightly coupled in diagnoses of the "memory boom," which has tended to focus more on regrettable or horrible pasts than on proud ones. While not explicitly an engagement with the trauma concept, Philip Rieff's (1987) diagnosis of American culture as suffering the "triumph of the therapeutic," a diagnosis with some clear similarities to more recent discourse attributed to the transformations of the 1970s and 1980s, was first published in 1966, thus before any memory boom and subsequent reaction criticizing the contemporary triumph of victimhood.

In cognitive psychology, moreover, the experimental tradition founded by Ebbinghaus developed in important ways through the 1960s and 1970s as well, autonomously from the trajectories of historiography, sociology, and psychoanalysis. Perhaps most prominent here is the work of Endel Tulving (1985), whose models of the role of retrieval cues in recall at least hinted at exogenous factors in memory, as well as the later work of Ulric Neisser and colleagues (Neisser and Hyman 1982) on flashbulb memories (particularly powerful memories of significant events) and on "ecological" factors in recall. Nevertheless, as Greenwood (2009) points out, a clear concept of "the social," which underwrote American social psychology at the beginning of the twentieth century, has largely disappeared from the contemporary discipline (though see Coman et al. 2009 and Oishi, Kesebir, and Snyder 2009).

In this intermediate period as well, media theorists Ong (as already mentioned) and Eric Havelock (1988) also explored collective memory and its relation to writing and other forms of inscription, anticipating and laying a foundation for the later "cultural memory" work of Jan and Aleida Assmann (J. Assmann 2007; A. Assmann 1999). Additionally, while the anthropologist Jack Goody's (1986) work on similar themes to Ong and Havelock, namely his book *The Logic of Writing and the Organization of Society*, did not appear until 1986, this was a culmination of a great deal of work being produced by anthropologists from the 1950s through 1970s seeking to dismantle too-sharp distinctions between "primitive" and "complex" societies.

At the margins of traditional historiography, moreover, oral history, which was often, though not exclusively, motivated by a Marxist politics and which drew on "memory" in unprecedented (and to some extent unsurpassed) ways, had been developing steadily since the Second World War, and many important works appeared in the 1960s and 1970s (Perks and Thomson 1998). In many ways, it is important to note, historiography's skepticism toward "memory studies" is often tied up with its disdain of oral history, from which it often tries to maintain a distance. In the process, as we will argue below, historian critics of memory studies have often missed some of the novelty of memory studies because they associate it mostly with the project of oral history, which ascribes more importance to the "evidence" of individual memory than many "scientific" historians are comfortable doing, and perhaps rightly so given the very different aims of their enterprise. But "oral history" was always at least partly a political program as well as an epistemological one. Beyond oral history, the question of memory, heritage, and preservation also arose somewhat earlier and in different terms in Great Britain than the memory boom more generally is said to have arisen elsewhere, and key texts like those of Raphael Samuel (1996) and David Lowenthal (1985) were as much the results of ongoing debates as they were foundations for new ones (Wright 1985; Hewison 1987; Kaye 1991).

Beyond the "collective memory" tradition in so many ways founded by Halbwachs, other sources of social perspectives on memory had their own complex developmental trajectories as well. The ideas of Bakhtin, for instance, underwent a famously complex transit to their present influence, given the challenges of Soviet censorship (see especially Morson and Emerson 1990); there are similar complexities regarding the influence of the works of A. R. Luria

(1978), Vygotsky (1978), and others, whose legacies have required significant reconstructive efforts (Todes 2001); here too works like those of Yuri Lotman (2001) and the Tartu School of semiotics are worth mentioning, though their work has not been widely integrated into contemporary discussions (for an exception, see Wertsch 1988). In Western psychology, the limitations on Bartlett's ability to elaborate his social perspectives are well analyzed in Douglas's (1986) book *How Institutions Think*: Bartlett, Douglas argues, is an ironic demonstration of the powers of social frameworks to fail memory, a phenomenon Bartlett himself both discovered and suffered under. As we have already seen, Bartlett is only one such example; Wundt is another, given that he is largely known for founding experimental psychology, to the neglect of his work on cultural psychology.

Warburg's influence has been limited not only by the difficulties of his own biography—including mental illness—and his writing—which was aphoristic and telegraphic—but by the difficulties of establishing institutional legacies of a German Jew across the ruptures of the Holocaust. Nevertheless, Warburg did benefit from some extraordinary institutional and reputational entrepreneurship, not least through the work of the art historian and biographer E. H. Gombrich, who reconstructed Warburg's contributions to a theory of social memory out of the scant residue of Warburg's fragments (Gombrich 1986) (the contemporary Italian philosopher Giorgio Agamben [2000] has also drawn on Warburg's work). Warburg's influence, mediated by the Assmanns, has been important for the "cultural memory" tradition that has developed in European literary and media theory (for reviews, see Erll 2005 and Winthrop-Young 2005).

Other legacies for contemporary memory studies, moreover, are relatively unknown in the same way that the Annales school preserved implicit memory of Halbwachs. For instance, it is rarely mentioned that E. E. Evans-Pritchards's (1940) well-known work on the anthropology of time-awareness was influenced in part by his reading of Halbwachs. Beyond these trajectories, we have not even begun to assay work in other areas like the sociology of scientific reputations, a key topic in the work of Robert Merton (1973) that arguably can be assimilated to memory studies, though this has not widely happened (for exceptions see Olick and Robbins 1998; Fine 2001; Cubitt 2007). There are independent trajectories in art history (Saltzman 2006) and varieties of literary criticism as well (Sommer, Nünning, and Gymnich 2006; Nalbantian 2004; Singh, Skerrett, and Hogan 1994).

Our point, however, is this: given these facts, not too widely discussed in recent literature, some of the criticisms the "collective memory" concept faced upon its supposed reemergence in the 1980s and early 1990s appear at least somewhat overstated. Kerwin Klein (2000: 127), for instance, has claimed that "outside of experimental psychology and clinical psychoanalysis, few academics paid much attention to memory until the great swell of popular interest . . . that marked the seventies." Much hinges, apparently, on the meaning of "much attention." Noa Gedi and Yigal Elam (1996: 30), moreover, argued that collective memory was "an act of intrusion . . . forcing itself like a molten rock into an earlier formation . . . unavoidably obliterating fine distinctions." Read as intellectual history, this claim does not stand up to scrutiny: while "memory studies" may be a "new formation," "collective memory" and interest in it is not, and one might, moreover, question whether the fine distinctions it supposedly obliterated—such as among myth, tradition, and custom—were all that fine to begin with.

As conceptual critique, of course, the charge is more serious and warrants further examination. It is one that has been echoed elsewhere as well, even among distinguished contributors to memory studies, such as Alon Confino (1997: 1387), who wrote in the mid-1990s of a "sense that the term 'memory' is depreciated by surplus use, while memory studies lack a clear focus and have become predictable." This charge is connected to a similar-sounding one that is nonetheless distinct, namely that of the historian Charles Maier (1993), who famously asked around the same time whether we had in fact reached "a surfeit of memory." The important difference between these two points, however, is often conflated: one concerns memory scholarship, while the other concerns the visibility of memory in culture and politics. But memory studies is not to be dismissed along with the phenomena it studies; indeed, without the frameworks of "collective memory," we believe, it is impossible to determine how much memory there is and what kind it is, to explain its operation, and to evaluate whether there is indeed a "surfeit" or when, where, and why it might be seen as such. Before exploring these issues further, however, it is necessary to complete the story of the supposed rise of memory in the culture and politics of the second half of the twentieth century, and to explore its relation to the development of memory studies, remembering that the latter is not entirely reducible to the former.

Did the Holocaust Cause Memory Studies?

According to a much-quoted line by Pierre Nora, "Whoever says memory, says Shoah" (Mueller 2002: 14). More recently, Paul Connerton (2009: 1), whose 1989 book *How Societies Remember* is one of the seminal texts for contemporary memory studies, has claimed that the "frequent discussion of and the apparently high value ascribed to memory in recent years" is vitally connected to "the accumulated repercussions of the holocaustal [sic] events of the last century." Like other characterizations of the memory boom, this one requires scrutiny and does not necessarily bear up well under it (though such generalizations rarely do).[23] It is certainly true that the Holocaust has generated new and particularly intense forms of memory (Bartov 1996). When one speaks of the

23. For his part, Connerton looks beyond this conjunctural explanation and ascribes the memory boom to broader trends in modernity (his 2009 book is called *How Modernity Forgets*).

memory boom, one is indeed speaking in part—though far from exclusively—
of the vast terrains of Holocaust memory, and other terrains of memory
modeled on it.

Nazis as well as the Holocaust have been condensation symbols of evil over
many decades, though to be sure increasingly since the 1970s, with major
landmarks like the *Holocaust* TV miniseries (1979) and Steven Spielberg's
Schindler's List (1993); equally important for memory scholarship was Claude
Lanzmann's nine hour documentary from 1985, *Shoah*, which included reminiscences and testimony of witnesses and survivors. These aesthetic and intellectual confrontations have been matched by documentary and museological
ones as well, including the assembly of vast video and other testimonial archives
at many locations around the world, numerous museums and memorials, documentation collections, school curricula, and pilgrimage tourist sites. Indeed,
the proliferation of such sites, and those in other contexts modeled on them, is
a major part of what those who describe the memory industry are referring to.

However, it is not only the quantitative presence of Holocaust memory that
leads one to connect memory in general with the Holocaust in particular. The
Holocaust, after all, is not the first or only historical event to have generated
artistic and other responses. Rather, it is the specific content of these memories
and what they symbolize. In part due to the power of new media such as
photography and film, in part due to new political institutions like those developed to enforce universal human rights, in part because the victims were so
numerous, and in part because of the industrial method of the destruction, the
image of the Holocaust victim has not simply become first among images of
victims generally, but has supposedly placed the image of the victim at the core
of contemporary culture as a whole. The post-Holocaust landscape is one littered with victims, including not only the victims of the Holocaust but those
whose victimhood is often defined by the master image of the broken Auschwitz inmate, and unfortunately often compared to or measured against him
or her (Chaumont 2002).

For many Western scholars and artists, even given the horrors of trench
warfare in World War I the Holocaust marked the decisive turning point
because it was an event "at the limits," one that, according to the historian Saul
Friedländer, "tests our traditional conceptual and representational categories"
(1992: 4). Historians like Mosse (1991) and Winter (1995), as already mentioned, among others, have traced how the First World War led to new, more
introspective war memorials and to a general democratization of the cult of the
dead appropriate to the mass devastation. By the same token, these new forms
of consolation were made more public than ever before, and were often exploited to foment renewed nationalist sentiment, principally a desire for national
revenge. However, this no longer seemed possible or desirable after World War
II. The Holocaust, according to the philosopher Emmanuel Levinas (1988),
was simply impossible to describe as other than "useless suffering."

Just as modern science ushered in an era of progressive temporality, the
Holocaust is thus seen as having ushered in "traumatic temporality," the

hallmark of which is supposedly an inability to tell a linear narrative in which one thing comes after another; instead, as the survivor Jean Améry (1986 [1966]: 68–69) put it, "anyone who has been tortured remains tortured." The natural result of this, for Améry, is resentment, "which blocks the exit to the genuine human condition, the future" (69). Because "the time-sense of the person trapped in resentment is twisted around, disordered . . . the man of resentment cannot join in the unisonous peace chorus all around him, which cheerfully proposes: Not backward let us look but forward, to a better, common future!" (69). Neither the individual nor the society has the means to tell a redemptive narrative, Améry thus argued in 1966, and memory of the events and memory of other events after them are thus of a very different sort. Traumatic culture does not merely represent a pocket of dissent from modernist narratives; it undermines them at their core (sociologist Zygmunt Bauman [2000] has articulated a kindred thesis about the Holocaust and modernity).

Nevertheless, it is not entirely clear to what extent these developments are the results of the Holocaust itself and the transformations in perceptions it inevitably gave rise to, whether the effects of Holocaust consciousness were enabled by other, broader processes, or whether subsequent events retrospectively transformed the view of the Holocaust (and these three things can be true simultaneously). In the first place, according to sociologist Jeffrey Alexander (2004), for instance, memory of the Holocaust itself has since 1945 undergone a shift from a "progressive" narrative to a "trauma" narrative, or what he calls a "trauma drama." In the earlier frame, the Western Allies fought the good war against Nazi evil, triumphed, and were ushering in a new era of liberal prosperity and humanitarianism. By the 1960s, however, a new narrative regime was forming, one in which the events of the Holocaust—a term not previously in wide use—were seen as somehow universal and emblematic of the pathologies of modernity.[24] The Holocaust victim was no longer the exception to be marginalized with pity, but the exemplar with which each of us can identify. As Daniel Levy and Natan Sznaider (2005) have demonstrated, this dynamic is connected to wider processes of globalization, which they address in terms of a "cosmopolitanization" of memory cultures. This refers to practices that shift attention away from the territorialized nation-state and the ethnically bounded frameworks that are commonly associated with the notion of collective memory. In this view, moreover, the iconographic status of Holocaust memories is reflected in and contributes to the formation of a global memory imperative (Levy and Sznaider 2010; Olick 2007).

Moreover, the very distinction of the genocide of the European Jews as an event apart—the Holocaust—let alone the view of it as a trauma both individual and cultural emerged only after what trauma theorists might describe as a

---

24. It should be clear that Alexander is characterizing broader public culture. In their famous *Dialectic of Enlightenment* (2002 [1944]), for instance, Max Horkheimer and Theodor Adorno had already diagnosed what they saw as the barbaric core of modernity in the early 1940s, even before the Nazi exterminations had mobilized to their full extent.

period of latency. But unlike the "return of the repressed" in individual psychology, it is not clear what the mechanisms of such latency are for societies as
a whole (a debate, again, that goes back at least as far as Freud's *Moses and
Monotheism*), nor are all scholars in agreement about the evidence. American
historian Peter Novick (2000), for instance, has also traced the transformations of Holocaust discourse in the United States, arguing that memory of the
Holocaust was not a significant part of public discourse and American Jewish
consciousness until the 1970s and that it emerged as such for instrumental
reasons, namely to shore up Jewish identity in the American diaspora. Hasia
Diner (2009), by some contrast, has emphasized the presence of the past in
Jewish families and communities early on (see also Gerson and Wolf 2007). In
Germany as well, many scholars have spoken of a "silence" about the Nazi past
in the 1950s that was only broken by the New Left of the 1960s. While some
ways of talking about the past did change over time in Germany, however,
recent research has shown that it is inaccurate to speak of any sort of silence,
at least not a straightforward one (Moeller 2003; Olick 2005).

More convincing, perhaps, are explanations that emphasize the reactivation
or invigoration of Holocaust references in light of subsequent events. During
the U.S. civil rights movement of the 1960s, for instance, Martin Luther King
Jr. famously employed the Jewish Passover song "Let my people go" in his rhetoric (Walzer 1986), and many Jews saw parallels between their oppression by
the Nazis and the situation of American blacks in that period, and many other
oppressed groups subsequently adopted the redemptive narrative of civil rights
and the victim status of the Jews. The emancipatory claims of the civil rights
and subsequent movements thus profitably drew on, and in the process contributed to, memory of the Holocaust, as contemporary genocides are compared to it (and, given the origins of the term "genocide" in the wake of the
Holocaust, are defined by it).[25]

By the same token, the European transformations of 1989 also mobilized
Holocaust memory, if in different ways. In the first place, Cold War antipathies
had hindered exploration of Eastern European history and memory, and the
demise of the Soviet Union thus opened the door to new explorations (Lebow,
Kansteiner, and Fogu 2006). And in the second place, restitution claims that
had previously been impossible were now able to be pursued (Deak, Gross, and
Judt 2000; Diner and Wunberg 2007; Torpey 2006, 2003; Barkan 2000). The
emancipation from authoritarianism, moreover, invited comparison with
earlier such liberations (Courtois et al. 1999; Snyder 2009).

For many critics, however, the sum total of these developments has been
what Maier (1993), again, called a "surfeit of memory," which is intended as an
understatement, for the diagnosis is substantially more grim than a "surfeit."
According to Dominick LaCapra (1998: 8), "Recently the concern with the

---

25. Such "inter-textual" and "dialogical" qualities of memory are central topics in the theories of Olick
(1999, 2007).

problem of memory has become so widespread and intense that one is tempt-ed to take a suspicious view and refer to fixation." The literary critic Geoffrey Hartman (2002) refers to a Proustian *Schwärmerei* or unwholesome swarm-ing. Maier (1993: 140) argues that "we have in a sense become addicted to memory" and asks "whether an addiction to memory can become neurasthenic and disabling."

Despite the liberatory nature of many recent political developments, then, within the narrative of trauma culture the memory boom is often seen as a sort of pathology of the post-Holocaust era, resulting in a culture of complaint and a competition among victims. According to Maier (1993: 147), "Modern Amer-ican politics . . . has become a competition for enshrining grievances. Every group claims its share of public honor and public funds by pressing disabilities and injustices. National public life becomes the settlement of a collective mal-practice suit in which all citizens are patients and physicians simultaneously." As Schwartz (2009: 8) puts it (though he attributes the transformations to the social movements of the 1960s rather than to the Holocaust), "The moral and social leveling supporting the most congenial society in history . . . is precisely the kind of society in which great men and women and their achievements count for less, while the victimized, wounded, handicapped, and oppressed count for more than ever before."

Most important in this triumph of trauma and regret, then, is what it is seen to signal about our prospects. According to LaCapra (1998: 8), "In certain of its forms, the preoccupation with memory may indicate a failure of constructive will and divert attention from the needs of the present and the necessity of attempting to face the future." For Schwartz (2009: 17), "the discrediting of America's grand narratives is postmodernity's distinctive achievement. . . . As postmodernity disparages stories that Americans tell about themselves, the ori-enting past tense of the individual's life, the bond that once linked men and women to vital symbols of their cultural tradition, is weakened." Others, never-theless, highlight that these transformations were a long time in the making. As the literary critic Hartman (2002: 100) has put it, "We have known for a long time that there is great suffering in the world, suffering impossible to justify. . . . But we also know from the time of Job's so-called friends to that of Holocaust negationists, that suffering is explained or rationalized against all odds."

Although much can be said for the argument that the Holocaust was simply too much for common theodicies to rationalize its suffering, it is nevertheless not convincing to say that the events themselves overpowered theodicy, rather than that the conditions for theodicy had been moving toward a breaking point for a long time and that they were not truly as broken as such diagnoses claim (Neiman 2002). After all, although Hartman has been one of the most signifi-cant voices in articulating the ways in which the Holocaust caused a crisis of representation, his comments about the rationalization of suffering actually refer to a later period, at most to a failure of the triumphalist interpretation of the Holocaust to fulfill its promises: "Today we have entered a new period,"

Hartman says, referring to the 1990s. "Until recently, perhaps until news from Bosnia reached the screen, we clutched at the hope that had the indifferent masses in Germany or American known what was going on in the concentration camps, known with the same graphic detail communicated today by TV, surely the atrocities would not have continued" (2002: 100).

The rise of memory into what has been characterized as a boom thus clearly cannot be explained entirely by the "civilizational rupture" of the Holocaust, however important a moment it was, or by the emergence of "post-Nuremberg sensibilities," which is a description rather than explanation of the problem. The sources of the transformations, and their varieties, have simply been too diverse. Again, without wishing to advocate a technologically determinist view, it is relevant to recount some of the broader explanations in terms of media and social structure some theorists—including some whose interests in memory were indeed shaped by study of the Holocaust—have recently advanced. As Hartman (2002: 99) has argued, for instance,

> The substantial effects of film and telecommunications are having their impact. An 'information sickness,' caused by the speed and quantity of what impinges on us, and abetted by machines we have invented that generate endless arrays, threatens to overwhelm personal memory. The individual, we complain, cannot 'process' all this information, this incoming flak: public and personal experience are not being moved closer together but further apart.

In a similar vein, literary critic Andreas Huyssen (1994: 6) argues that "the evident crisis of the ideology of progress and modernization" signals "the fading of a whole tradition of teleological philosophies of history."

> The memory boom for Huyssen (1994: 7) "represents the attempt to slow down information processing, to resist the dissolution of time in the synchronicity of the archive, to recover a mode of contemplation outside the universe of simulation and fast-speed information and cable networks, to claims some anchoring space in a world of puzzling and often threatening homogeneity, non-synchronicity, and information overload."

In a marked departure from many of the critiques, however, Huyssen actually sees in these developments "a powerful stimulant for cultural and artistic creativity" (1994: 3).

The preceding account is thus in accord with that of Winter (2001: 53), who has emphasized that there are "distinctive sources of the contemporary obsession with memory" and that these "arise out of a multiplicity of social, cultural, medical, and economic trends and developments of an eclectic but intersecting nature." It is important to note, however, that these distinctive sources operate at different wavelengths: that is, some are conjunctural (e.g., the impact of 1989), some occur over decades (e.g., the "traditional conceptual and representational categories" Friedländer sees as tested by the Holocaust), some operate at the level of epochs (e.g., modernist teleologies of progress and philosophies of history), and some work at the level of eons (e.g., the technologies of memory ranging from oral narrative through writing, through electronic communication, storage, and retrieval). Additionally, there is much space for analysis of the ways in which these "eclectic" trends are or are not "intersecting:" Are such intersections coincidental (for instance, the bicentennial of the French Revolution and the collapse of the Soviet Union)? Are they co-produced but still theoretically independent (like the development of video recording and interest in oral history and others forms of testimonial preservation)? Or are they part of a tightly coupled political-cultural profile (Olick and Levy 1997; Olick 2007) (e.g., neoconservatism and the building of historical museums)? Identification of such a political-cultural profile is obviously no mere empiricist induction: it is part of a diagnosis which, in its more serious versions, draws on a sociohistorical theory that must include the kinds of considerations we have outlined in our history of memory in the foregoing pages and that inevitably places collective memory at its center.

Such distinctions as these between wavelength and kind of intersection, however, are not often addressed in diagnoses of the boom, which first concatenate these diverse sources into a single result and then often criticize the language of the result for being too general. Critics have thus charged that "ubiquitous" use of the term "memory" has led to a "dangerous overextension" (Fabian 1999) of it, such that the term suffers a "semantic overload" (Klein 2000) in which it "seems to be losing precise meaning in proportion to its growing rhetorical power" (Gillis 1994a: 3). As a result, they say, the "concept of memory may become indistinguishable from either identity or culture" (Fabian 1999: 51).[26]

To be sure, we do not disagree that use of the term "memory"—individual or collective—has been imprecise and occasionally profligate. But it is not clear to us what the source of this supposed overextension is and thus how seriously it is to be taken. In the first place, some overuse, for instance, is a matter of employment of the term in the memory boom itself: purveyors of exhibits, celebrations, artworks, and other such products often articulate their projects as addressing "memory," which is no more precise a label than most others used for promotional or broadly thematic purposes and of no greater concern for scholars.

In the second place, by the same token, some of the overextension comes from precisely those critics of "memory" wishing to identify a proliferation of various kinds of history-politics and other forms of historicity as a unitary phenomenon that they label a *memory* boom: after all, whatever rhetorical power memory has, it is often those of us trying to characterize a variety of products, processes, and practices as related who employ the umbrella term "memory" to cover phenomena that are not obviously articulated with that term (e.g., heritage tourism and nostalgia). The value of such an effort, of course, is to be assessed on the basis of what the concatenation adds—an

---

26. For a survey of these critiques, see Berliner (2005).

assessment that, again, requires a serious social-theoretic approach and imagination.

The third possible referent for such accusations is memory studies itself, including the varieties of serious research in various disciplines into mnemonic products and practices. And here surely the concern about conceptual precision is weightier. Before addressing this concern, however—a concern we believe requires institutional remedies, of which the present Reader is intended to be a part—we need to specify the unique contributions of memory studies.

What Is Memory Studies?

It is certainly true that memory studies is to some extent tied up with its moment, though like everything else we have addressed in the foregoing pages this relationship is complex too. First, scholarship on memory, individual or collective, has obviously contributed to the memory boom: witness, for instance, the wide use of the term "collective memory" beyond the provinces of academic sociology or the prestige accorded public debates by the reference to science and scholarship. Second, memory studies in the last thirty or so years has been motivated by some of the same interests as the memory boom, which has certainly reshaped the trajectories of research on memory, for example, the transformations in information technology, which pose new challenges to scholarship (especially in media studies, though also in other fields that pay more attention to media now than they did in the past), or the moral force of the Holocaust, which has drawn many scholars into memory studies. And third, memory studies has also sometimes been part of the memory boom itself. For surely the field would not have achieved the institutional status it has without the stirring up of interests by the politics of regret, the fear of memory loss, and the commodification of nostalgia, among other parts of the memory boom. Many of us have surely asserted such connections, particularly in our efforts to impress deans, obtain funding, and secure publication (including that of *The Collective Memory Reader!*).

None of this is either surprising or inappropriate. What is perhaps surprising is that it sometimes seems as if memory studies were being pronounced dead from the very moment of its supposed arrival. In contrast, our effort here is founded on the conviction that memory studies—and the terms "memory" and "collective memory"—adds unique and valuable perspective to our understanding in ways that would otherwise be missed. To be sure, part of this is because memory has such contemporary resonance and has assumed a peculiarly reflexive character in the contemporary era—that is, the coincidence of the memory boom and the potential consolidation of memory studies, with its widespread acceptance of social perspectives on remembering and on the intersections of wide varieties of mnemonic practices (Olick and Robbins 1998).

But part of it stems as well from the perennial nature of the questions "memory," individual or collective, raises. For memory, as Terdiman (1993: 9) puts it, "functions in every act of perception, in every act of intellection, in every act of language." From a phenomenological perspective every social act is permeated with memory. The philosopher Edward Casey (1987: xix) notes that "in the case of memory, we are always already in the thick of things. . . . Not only because remembering is at all times presupposed, but also because it is always at work: it is continually going on, often on several levels and in several ways at once. . . . Indeed, every fiber of our bodies, every cell of our brains, holds memories—as does everything physical outside bodies and brains, even those inanimate objects that bear the marks of their past histories upon them in mute profusion." As Philip Abrams (1982: 8) put it,

> Doing justice to the reality of history is not a matter of noting the way in which the past provides background to the present; it is a matter of treating what people do in the present as a struggle to create a future out of the past, of seeing that the past is not just the womb of the present but the only raw material out of which the present can be constructed.

Memory—relating past and present—is thus the central faculty of being in time, through which we define individual and collective selves: "I, entelechy," as James Joyce's Stephen Dedalus thought it, "form of forms, am I by memory." This insight remains as true, though in different ways, as it was a century ago when Joyce wrote it.

The new insight of memory studies is thus not merely that memory is omnipresent but that it is at once situated in social frameworks (e.g., family and nation), enabled by changing media technologies (e.g., the Internet and digital recording), confronted with cultural institutions (e.g., memorials and museums), and shaped by political circumstances (e.g., wars and catastrophes). Social frameworks and historical circumstances change over time and, with them, the aforementioned alignments of past, present, and future (e.g., the discourse of progress in modernity). Studying (and theorizing) memory allows us to shift our focus from time to temporalities, and thus to understand what categories people, groups, and cultures employ to make sense of their lives, their social, cultural, and political attachments, and the concomitant ideals that are validated—in short, the political, cultural, and social theories that command normative attention.

Whatever the waxing and waning of the public concern with "memory," then, memory studies clearly has a lot of work to do: as in economics, busts are as much its subject matter as booms. To be sure, as we have seen, the status of social memory studies as a field is not unproblematic or undisputed. Part of this certainly derives from the profligacy with which the terms "memory" and "collective memory" have been employed. But we question the extent to which that profligacy is the result of conceptual issues, how much it is the result of a conflationary critique that associates scholarship with the excesses of popular discourse, how much it is the result of rhetorical slippage and blurry boundaries between studies and boom, how much it is a response to widespread dilettantism (a common problem when scientific and lay terms coincide), and how much of it, instead, is due to the institutional conditions for memory studies as a field of scholarship.

In 1998, Olick and Robbins offered the following characterization of what they called "social memory studies:" "Scholars have viewed social memory narrowly as a subfield of the sociology of knowledge and broadly as 'the connective structure of societies.' They have seen it as involving particular sets of practices like commemoration and monument building and general forms like tradition, myth, or identity. They have approached it from sociology, history, literary criticism, anthropology, art history, and political science, among other disciplines. They have studied it in simple and complex societies,[27] from above and below, across the geographical spectrum. Social memory studies," that review announced, "is nevertheless, or perhaps as a result, a nonparadigmatic, transdisciplinary, centerless enterprise" (1998: 105–6).

Certainly, some of these qualities are inherent in the undertaking: the variety of practices, processes, and products memory studies touches on is vast indeed, and the range of methods—from the neuropsychological to the hermeneutic—reaches across the spectrum of academic inquiry. In part because of these qualities, however, which have kept potentially related inquiries within segregated disciplinary contexts, memory studies has not yet fully developed all of the institutional supports that underwrite the formation and operation of a coherent scholarly field. As already mentioned, it does now have several journals and book series, as well as a place within various disciplinary orthodoxies and their publication outlets, but these programs and centers operate independently and are often unaware of each other, and memory studies as of yet has no society or organization.

Even more important, we believe, are intellectual institutions. The 1998 assessment thus stated its goal as follows: "to (re-)construct out of the diversity of work addressing social memory a useful tradition, range of working definitions, and basis for future work in a field that ironically has little organized memory of its own" (1998: 106). In the last ten years, there has indeed been a good deal of progress, theoretical, conceptual, and empirical. Unfortunately, this progress has been hampered by continued lack of cross-disciplinary and cross-case reading, as well as by redundancy and lack of systematicity in the enterprise.

Finally, and most important, we believe, is the ironically lacking organized memory the 1998 review mentioned. As the sociologist Donald Levine (1995: 11) has argued, "Like all human communities, those organized to cultivate intellectual disciplines depend on some view of their past. Such views give their disciplines identity and direction, important for functioning effectively in the

27. The authors of that review were duly chastised for the outdated vocabulary of "simple and complex." There is nothing simple about premodern, non-Western societies.

present." In doing so, Levine not only contributes to memory studies—giving a clear demonstration of the value of the collective memory concept for understanding intellectual organization—but helps us understand part of the institutional conditions for the advancement of memory studies itself. For our assessment is that such a "life-story" for memory studies has failed to form robustly enough, partly because of the prominence of the memory boom narrative, and partly because memory studies requires a very capacious narrative indeed.

Within such disciplinary narratives, "classics" clearly assume a central place (Alexander 1987). This is one reason we have devoted so many of the foregoing pages to the seminal work of Halbwachs, though also including information about his complex reception along with reference to other classics, established and potential. For indeed, as already indicated, references to such iconic figures need to be more than totemic, lest, as Halbwachs himself might have put it, they risk becoming "dead memory," a past with which we no longer maintain an "organic" relationship. References to classics—acknowledged or forgotten—also make clear that the enterprise is much older and more persistently vibrant than typically described.

The time is thus ripe, we believe, for an effort to collect, present, organize, and evaluate past work and provide essential materials for future teaching and research on the questions raised under the rubric of collective memory. In the collection that follows, therefore, we aim to provide a foundational resource for research and teaching in the field, which includes not only a sense of history but also a body of exemplars, concepts, and tools for contemporary work.[28] While the field is too vast for comprehensive coverage, we intend our product to be an essential starting point for students and scholars, providing wide-ranging reference points in, and landmarks from, the extensive literature, and hence to be one version—surely to be challenged and revised—of a life-story for memory studies.

The Collective Memory Reader

The task has indeed been challenging. There are quite a few reasonable principles by which one could present such a complex, long-developing, and multidisciplinary field, and an extraordinary number of candidates for inclusion (we considered more than a thousand). One could well imagine an equally valuable Reader with only a small percentage of overlapping selections. It should be clear that we have left out many worthy candidates for inclusion. To include

---

28. We have greatly benefited from and highly recommend important assessments of the field such as Erll and Nünning (2008); Cubitt (2007); Irwin-Zarecka (2007); Jelin (2003); Misztal (2003); Wertsch (2002); Zelizer (1995); Hutton (1993); Coser (1992); Fentress and Wickham (1992); LeGoff (1992); Middleton and Edwards (1990); Connerton (1989); and Lowenthal (1985).

merely the ninety or so we have here has required great efforts of selection, exclusion, and condensation. How, then, have we proceeded?

In the first place, despite the foregoing discussion, the designation "memory studies" is still rather a broad one to constitute a coherent field. The full extent of what has been referred to as memory studies can include work across disciplines and even academic enterprises ranging from neuroscience to museology, and including the panoply of what critics mean when they employ the term "memory industry" pejoratively. And in this sense, the critics are correct: if all of these things are memory, or part of memory studies, what is not? It would, for instance, be misleading to imply that the interest of neuroscientists in the molecular and cellular bases of memory is principally due to the "memory boom" in late modern culture or is tightly associated with the interests of sociologists in commemoration and collective identity. The purpose of this volume, therefore, is somewhat more restricted than to assay the wide territories of all serious work on memory, which are likely too far-flung to constitute a field of study, though to be sure there are interesting questions to be asked about the epochal character of these diverse interests. Instead, we focus here on the kinds of "memory studies" that develop, employ, react to, and engage with the concept of "collective memory" and its cognates across the disciplines.

To be sure, as we have seen, the term "collective memory" is not a philosophically or operationally precise one, and its conceptual rather than signaling value may indeed have diminished over time as critiques and alternatives—e.g., cultural memory, communicative memory, social memory—have been articulated; moreover, much important relevant work employs none of these while yet advancing the discussion. There are thus many kinds of work on memory that we do not include within our purview, though we are aware of their potential relevance. Perhaps most important here are, toward one end of the spectrum, neurobiology of memory and cognitive psychology that does not directly address supra-individual influences (or addresses them only as determinants of individual outcomes), as well as psychoanalytic discourses about memory (though to be sure there are huge overlaps, and we include seminal texts from Freud that address *social* memory directly); and, toward the other end of the spectrum, areas like museum and preservation studies, which are certainly related but raise issues of professional practice that extend beyond our story here.

How, then, do we define our enterprise? Perhaps a better term than the more general "memory studies" and the more historical "collective memory studies" for the field we believe we are describing is "social memory studies," which we see as related to, but not identical with, the cognitive psychology of memory, oral history, museology, the literary analysis of memoir and autobiography, history and theory of the trauma concept, and the study of transitional justice or "transitology," among other enterprises. Unlike "collective memory studies," "social memory studies" does not raise confusions about its object of reference, recalling that for Halbwachs collective memory sometimes seems to include socially framed individual memory, and sometimes seems to refer only to the common memory of groups. And unlike other candidates, including "social studies of memory"—which sounds as if the social component is not in memory itself but only in the study of memory—"social memory studies" remains presuppositionally open to a variety of phenomena while pointing out that all remembering is in some sense social, whether it occurs in dreams or in pageants, in reminiscences or in textbooks.

Nevertheless, "collective memory" clearly still has its residual value as an emblem. And our goal here is to contribute to the consolidation of "collective memory," or "social memory studies," into a more coherent field than it has heretofore been by providing it with a more common set of references than it has so far acknowledged. This is, obviously, a more controversial and complex aim than it might at first appear. A principal source of this complexity, however, is the way in which social memory studies is crosscut by established disciplines. For the problematics of social memory are indeed rather different within its major disciplinary homes, which include first and foremost—but are not limited to—sociology, history, psychology, and anthropology.

Sociology

Within sociology—in which, as we have shown, the concept of "collective memory" was first formulated and has perhaps been elaborated theoretically to the greatest extent—the question of memory has been most clearly linked to issues of identity. It has rarely been pointed out, for instance, the extent to which Halbwachs's interest in group memory—family memory, religious memory, and class memory—was part of a Durkheimian effort to elaborate the mechanisms of social solidarity in a manner distinct from the Marxian emphasis on "consciousness," namely of the class variety. Halbwachs's work on memory followed on, and was part of, his long-standing interest in the living standards of the working class, but while he was on the Left politically, he was never tempted by Marxism in his scholarship. Is working-class identity to be understood wholly in terms of material circumstances—"class in itself"— and in terms of when and where it is transformed into political action—"class for itself"? Or are there other considerations? It is important in this regard to recall that Halbwachs was one of the most significant conduits for the introduction of Max Weber's writings into France (Lepenies 2006); Weber's critique of Marx, in which he argued for the consideration of status and party in addition to class, is surely relevant here as well, though Halbwachs's analysis remains wholly Durkheimian. Collective memory, divided into family memory, religious memory, and class memory, addresses many of the same questions Marx handled in terms of class consciousness but with a clearly different inflection.[29]

29. In an arguably similar manner, and at roughly the same time, Mannheim (1952 [1928]) sought to add "generation" to Weber's "class, status, and party" as axes of social organization.

On this and other bases, many sociologists have explored collective memory as a major source for, and carrier of, identities. From above, memory has thus been studied as an integrative force that overcomes individual and partisan interests and bequeaths to large collectivities a sense of purpose and obligation; as such, it allows for demands ranging from taxation to soldierly sacrifice. From below, memory has been studied as a force of opposition, endowing subgroups with a sense of distinctiveness, often deriving from a particularistic sense of continuity with previous generations, whether this leads to a special sense of pride, a special complaint, or often both.

At the same time, a great deal of the contemporary sociological literature on collective memory has been inspired by Halbwachs's and others' implication that memory is formed largely in the present rather than in the past and is thus to be seen from the perspective of contemporary interests. As such, sociological studies of collective memory emphasize processes of memory "entrepreneurship" as well as contestation about and through images of the past (this strategy of analysis is thus assimilable to Hobsbawm's [1983] "invention of tradition" perspective). We now take very much for granted "constructionist" approaches that emphasize the ways images of the past distort, are deployed for instrumental purposes, propagate myths, and so on. In the process, however, we should not forget the novelty and power of such perspectives, nor should we reduce them to a version of "lies my country told me." While such approaches can devolve into what Schwartz (2003: 11) has called "cynical muck-raking," they nevertheless provide important insights into the complex connections between knowledge and power, the disentangling of which is more profound than a simple unmasking.

Perhaps the most significant contribution of collective memory to sociology, however, has in our opinion been the way in which it has participated in a temporalization of sociological concepts and to a more processual theorization of modernity. Sociology, particularly American sociology, has long been a notoriously presentist enterprise, one that does better comparing present and past moments than it does identifying the paths from past to present and resisting the temptations of reification.[30] In one sense, then, Halbwachs may not be the best exemplar of temporalization: as J. Assmann (2006: 170) has written, emphasizing Halbwachs's interest in the present sources of memory, "Being a sociologist, Halbwachs had only limited interest in the past, in the 'vertical anchoring' of mankind." In our reading, this is a mischaracterization of Halbwachs's contribution, as well as of sociology overall. Nevertheless, Assmann's own contribution, which emphasizes that memory is not a timeless structure

---

30. As Abrams (1982: xvi) has put it, "It was not so much the relevance of history that sociologists failed to see as the relevance of time. Even when interest in the sociology of past societies was at its highest, and even among those who were themselves working on such historical questions, sociologists retained an impressive ability to ignore the fact that history happens in time. Accordingly, they also managed not to see either the possibility or the need to reconstitute the action and structure antinomy as a matter of process in time, to re-organize their investigations in terms of the dialectics of structuring."

but a fundamentally temporal process, is an example of the contribution attention to memory can make to a more genuinely historical approach in sociology. Moreover, sociological theorists of modernity such as Anthony Giddens (1991), who have paid greater attention than some of their predecessors and contemporary colleagues to such processual aspects, thus emphasize the complex reflexivity that is at the heart of late modernity.

Historiography

If collective memory has for sociologists been most closely associated with questions of identity and identity-politics, for historians the principal concern has been epistemological (Cubitt 2007; Ankersmit 2001; Hutton 1993). Here the divide has been between those who see history and memory as entirely distinct (usually with the implication that memory is inferior) and those who see them as continuous with each other. On the one side, for instance, R. G. Collingwood (1999 [1946]: 8) has argued vigorously for the distinction, because he believes that "history is a certain kind of organized and inferential knowledge, and memory is not organized, not inferential at all. If I say 'I remember writing a letter to So-and-so last week,'" Collingwood (1999: 8) continues, "that is a statement of memory, but it is not an historical statement. But if I can add 'and my memory is not deceiving me; because here is his reply,' then I am basing a statement about the past on evidence; I am talking history." By contrast, Hobsbawm (1997: 24–25) has argued that historians "compile and constitute the collective memory of the past," while Richard Hofstadter (1968: 3) has claimed that "memory is the thread of personal identity, history of public identity." In one of the most important synthetic and critical works early in the consolidation of memory studies, Hutton (1993) thus referred to history as "an art of memory." Others, for instance Yosef Yerushalmi (1996 [1982]: 101), have sought a compromise formula that preserves the distinction yet allows a relation: "historiography that does not aspire to be memorable is in peril of becoming a rampant growth." A century earlier, Nietzsche (1997) was critical of both "antiquarian history" (perhaps scientific, but sterile) and "monumental history" (memorable, but inevitably distorted). In the present, it sometimes seems as if the battle continues unashamedly between these two misconceived varieties (Funkenstein 1989).

In this context, it is also important to distinguish two threads that are often confused: namely, the evidentiary problem of relying on individual memory and the functional problem of the role of history as collective memory. Outside of the Annales tradition, as pointed out above, most historians' discussions of memory concern either oral history or the value of testimony and eyewitness accounts. But eyewitness accounts are notoriously unreliable. So while oral history has aimed at recuperating voices left out from traditional historiography, traditional historiography has been wary of such approaches, and perhaps rightly so. Of course, historians have also become increasingly less sanguine about the "objectivity" of documentary evidence and the generality of the view from above.

Nevertheless, this use of "memory" is rather distinct from the problematic of "collective memory," as well as from an assessment of the social function of history-writing. Indeed, while some of the most significant and profound writing about memory has been by historians, it is also true that the lion's share of skepticism about, and even disdain for, "memory" comes from historians as well. And this seems to be the reason. Often it seems as if the unreliability of individual memory is adduced as the reason to maintain the distinction between history and collective memory. But the poor epistemological status of memory—distorted and distorting—should have no bearing on history's interest in commemoration as an activity with a history (e.g., Kammen 1991). As Hutton (1993: 22) puts it, "To the historians' fascination with the commemorative practices of the past . . . we must juxtapose their reluctance to bear the taint of being identified with commemorative historical writing." Such juxtaposition has often led to conflation when historians have dismissed memory—individual or collective—wholesale or, again, as part of a passing fad whose disappearance is to be celebrated. But does the reliability of individual memory, or even the distortions of collective memory, say anything about the role history plays in society?

What, then, does a greater sensitivity to the advances of memory studies have to contribute to the historians' enterprise(s)? In the first place, as the Annales tradition demonstrates, it opens up vast new topics, namely commemoration, historical imagery, ritual, and the like, all of which have histories. Moreover, "the discrepancy between fact and memory," Alejandro Portelli (1991: 26) writes, "ultimately enhances the value of oral sources as historical documents because such discrepancies reveal how ordinary people caught up in historical events make sense of their experiences. This too is worthy of historical analysis."[31] A commemoration of a past event, moreover, is itself an event and thus worthy of historical analysis. Beyond this, memory as a practice of relating to the past, as well as the forms and symbol of group life, also clearly have histories and warrant rigorous investigation, for instance the kind of history of memory that media theorists in particular have offered, though not only this kind of history of technology.

To these contributions, Hutton and others have pointed out, one can also add a transformed view of historical processes that sees the two meanings of history—what happened and our study of what happened—as mutually constitutive. One version of this comes from the philosopher Hans-Georg Gadamer's (1975) reconstruction of philosophical hermeneutics, which encourages a "fusion of horizons" between past and present in an ongoing circle of interpretation. Another, related approach comes from J. Assmann's (1997: 9) articulation of "mnemohistory," which is "concerned not with the past as such, but only with the past as it is remembered," and is thus a sort of "reception theory applied to history." Mnemohistory, Assmann (1997: 9) argues, helps us understand

---

31. For a broader discussion, see Cubitt (2007: 87).

history as "the ongoing work of reconstructive imagination." Despite historiography's narrative and temporal commonsense, which is greater than sociology's, there is still room for greater temporalization of history's approach. And a greater appreciation of the complexities of memory can provide this.

Psychology

If sociology has principally seen social memory through the lens of identity, and history has seen it through the lens of reliability, the social memory problematics in both psychology and anthropology are rather more difficult to pinpoint (Hirst and Manier 2008). In regard to psychology, we have already referred to the overriding individualism of the field, whose method is controlled experimentation and whose focus is the individual mind (Danziger 2008; Greenwood 2009). Perhaps one of the most significant changes in some branches of psychology in recent years has been the move away from mind and toward the brain. Ironically, this may have meant a *greater* emphasis in some hands on "exogenous" factors, since neuroscience has discovered an even greater plasticity in the brain than might have been anticipated (we referred to this in the first pages of this introduction). By the same token, even the most physiological understandings of memory long ago abandoned straightforward ideas of memory as storage. Already at the turn of the twentieth century, we saw, Semon (1921, 1923) coined the term "engram," which refers to the basic units of memory. We now know that we do not perceive every aspect of a situation, that not every aspect of a situation we do perceive is converted into engrams, that a situation perceived as unitary is preserved in fragments (hence the value-added quality of the term "engrams"), and that the act of "remembering" often involves a new combination of stored engrams, noise, extrapolation, and features of the present. As such, remembering is a matter not of retrieval but of recombination and creation.

Nevertheless, in the view of some scholars who have become more interested in social memory, experimental psychology has been limited by its emphasis on recall. Other developments, already mentioned, thus include the turn toward ecological considerations and memory in "natural settings." Research has shown, for instance, that events socially defined as particularly significant yield different memory outcomes from those defined as mundane. While such interests have not often been directly connected to work on posttraumatic stress, moreover, the connections are obvious: traumatic events affect, and reside in, the brain in different ways than ordinary events; but at least some of the experience of trauma may be mediated by cultural categories (this is a central point of contention in the literature on trauma). Experimental psychology can also obviously bear on other contemporary issues like suggestibility, particularly in the debate over recovered versus false memory syndrome (Prager 2000).

Yet another important avenue toward social memory in psychology has been the development of ideas partly deriving from cognitive science: namely, the extension of the distributed cognition idea into a concept of distributed memory (Sutton 2006, 2003). The potential overlap between psychology and sociology here (particularly sociology that has developed methods for studying such operations, which include both network methods and traditional ethnography) is clear (Oishi, Kesebir, and Snyder 2009; Manier and Hirst 2008). What is even clearer is that there is at least as much to be gained by addressing, if not outright abandoning, the supposed barriers between individual and society that lie at the heart of psychology's disciplinary self-identity. This does not, as some fear, threaten psychology's scientific status (Coman et al. 2009). Psychology has thus seen the development of narrative (Bruner 1990), cultural (Shweder 1991; Cole 1996), and other approaches that have reached out—sometimes through the connections between memory and identity—to other social sciences, philosophy, and even literary criticism.

Anthropology

Beyond the media-theoretic considerations we outlined many pages ago (e.g., Goody and the orality-literacy question), the role of social memory studies in anthropology has been deeply tied up with some of anthropology's own disciplinary identity struggle. In particular, anthropology in the last fifty years has often been a struggle to overcome its definition as the study of premodern difference and to see itself as one that endeavors to dismantle the sharp dichotomies associated with "primitive" versus "complex" societies, between the "hot" and the "cold," and by extension between timeless societies of memory and custom and progressive societies of history and tradition. Anthropological interest in memory has thus been part of the effort to demonstrate the varieties of cultural organization, as well as the mixing of different temporalities in both preindustrial and industrial societies. As already mentioned, the work of Goody (1986) on orality and writing has been particularly key here. Recent anthropology's connections to history have also been complex and multidirectional, in face of earlier assumptions that anthropology was the study of societies that do not have history (see Wolf 1982). Premodern societies are not as ahistorical as previously assumed, and modern societies are rife with ahistorical forms of thought and representation (Sahlins 1987, 2004). Moreover, there are obvious synergies between anthropological work on myth and ritual and the "new cultural history," within which "collective memory" has been more prominent than in other corners of history, and which has benefited greatly from anthropological theory and methods (Ortner 1999; Hunt 1989; Chartier 1988).

A wide range of additional disciplines and fields have both contributed to, and benefited from, the consolidation of memory studies, including media studies (e.g., van Dijck 2007; Edy 2006; Hoskins 2004; Landsberg 2004; A. Assmann 1996; Thompson 1995; Zelizer 1992), urban studies (e.g., Jordan 2006; Crinson 2005; Ladd 1997; Hayden 1995; Boyer 1994;), geography (e.g., Foote and Azaryahu 2007; Jonker 1995; Boyarin 1994), gender studies (e.g., Hirsch and Smith 2002; Leydesdorff, Passerini, and Thompson 1996), cultural studies (e.g., Sturken 1997; Lipsitz 1990; Wallace 1996), literary criticism (e.g., Huyssen 2003; Wood 1999; Young 1993; Felman and Laub 1992), heritage and preservation studies (e.g., Koshar 2000; Kirshenblatt-Gimblett 1998; Handler and Gable 1997; Barthel 1996; Lowenthal 1996; Hewison 1987), museum studies (e.g., Crane 2000; Dubin 1999; Maleuvre 1999; Bennett 1995), archae-ology (e.g., Jones 2007; Kohl, Kozelsky, and Ben-Yehuda 2007; Alcock 2002; Ben-Yehuda 2002; Jones 2007), architecture (e.g., Bastéa 2004; Rosenfeld 2000; Young 2000), politics (e.g., Bell 2006; Booth 2006; Dienstag 1997; Schudson 1993; Rousso 1991), law (e.g., Wieviorka 2006; L. Douglas 2001; Osiel 1999; Teitel 2002), and certainly philosophy (e.g.,Whitehead 2008; Ricoeur 2004; Todorov 2003; Margalit 2002; Sutton 1998; MacIntyre 1984), each in at least somewhat distinctive ways and motivated by somewhat distinc-tive concerns. But to organize our selection and presentation of materials according to established disciplinary and field categories would be at cross purposes with our hope for memory studies: namely, that its transdisciplinary connections and relevances be promoted, without any suppression of impor-tant distinctions of concern and history. Instead, we have selected and orga-nized the materials that follow on the basis of our intention to fulfill both the narrative and conceptual requirements for memory studies' productive future, though to be sure some arbitrariness and bias is inevitable.

The five parts, then, are: Precursors and Classics; History, Memory, and Identity; Power, Politics and Contestation; Media and Modes of Transmission; and Memory, Justice, and the Contemporary Epoch. We introduce the (loosely) governing principles in short introductions to each part. Suffice it to say here that the allocation of a particular work to one or the other part, the order of the parts (with the exception of the first), and ultimately the content of each, could well have been (and at times was) different.

Criteria of Selection

What principle, then, has governed what we have done here? In the age of easy electronic access to previously published materials, the production of a Reader faces perhaps a greater bar of worthiness than in the past. Our overriding con-cern has thus been with the "value added" of any particular candidate for inclu-sion. This was always an imprecise calculus of difficulty of availability, fame, impact, and generativity.

First, it makes no sense to include the most obvious pieces that most people with the slightest interest in the field have at their fingertips or can include easily on a course syllabus without the access we provide, though to be sure some are so important that our narrative would make no sense without them (e.g., Hobsbawm). In such cases, and in others, "value added" is defined by the rigorous editing work we have done. Our goal has been to extract the key and durable ideas from complex texts, which are often interspersed with rich exam-ples and complex case narratives. We thus recognize that our editing has often involved a sort of editorial violence, in some cases perhaps too extreme. But every additional page from a given piece reduces the space remaining for others. And we have striven for more than simply a lightly-edited selection of our twenty or thirty favorite pieces; in the age of JSTOR, downloadable PDFs, and Google Books, a Reader, we believe, must provide more.

Second, the principle of value added may seem to be at odds with the standards of fame and impact, both rather nebulous concepts too. As we have demonstrated in the foregoing pages, impact is not always a straightforward process, nor is it always, or even usually, instantaneous and constant. So some of our choices have been recuperative. Additionally, sometimes a work is very well known in the sense of appearing frequently in references, but is actually rarely read because it is hard to obtain (a good example here is Bloch's 1925 review of Halbwachs, which was hard to find and in French).

Finally, generativity is no more precise a criterion. In the most mundane sense, this guided our editing within texts. Namely, we sought to carve out of often richly illustrative and complexly argued texts the central definition, concept, or novel idea that has been, or in our opinion should be, a stimulus to further thought. This is part of creating a life-story for the field. But it is also about laying the foundation for a more erudite future discourse and a more cumulative research enterprise. Mundanely, this has resulted in two rules, which we followed fairly rigorously throughout, with only a few exceptions: namely, no secondary commentary on the literature (including no introductory or overview texts, though there are by now many excellent ones [see note 28 above]) and no case studies or illustrations. Again, this is a trade-off in terms of time and space. As we argued to authors and publishers whose texts we have so vigorously edited, we intend our selections to lead readers to the original, more complete texts rather than to substitute for them.

We also recognize that such an aim as ours is not universally viewed as desirable. It might appear as if we are attempting to establish or represent a canon for memory studies. And canon-making can be a process of exclusion, selection, and ultimately as much destruction as construction. But it does not have to be if we refer instead to curricula and understand these as starting points rather than end points, as guides to and common ground for future discourse rather than as an effort to end such discourse. Within our grand posture is thus a rather more modest aim to invite debate, dissent, contestation, and continuous revision. But we believe such processes have to start somewhere. Too many studies in different fields announce the same conclusions as if they were new, remain within a small section of the literature without looking over the disciplinary hedges, or fail to speak in a language general enough to advance truly interdisciplinary dialogue, a value announced much more often than it is redeemed.

While inclusion in this volume does indeed imply an assertion of importance—"value added" to both the Reader and the reader—noninclusion should not be misinterpreted. Indeed, some of our personal favorites have not been included, for a variety of reasons. Again, some texts unfold their contributions principally through commentary on and engagement with the established literature (a worthy strategy that this Reader is meant to support); nevertheless, often this has made them difficult to excerpt in any coherent yet not overly long fashion. Other texts make their arguments by closely developing a case or subtly elaborating a description, which again made them difficult to excerpt. Beyond this, there were other outstanding and important texts with which we struggled but whose crucial fragments, for one reason or another, we could not coherently weave together (in many cases, this speaks very well of a text rather than poorly of it). As a result, this means that many wonderful works have not been included here.

Finally, we must acknowledge our own editorial biases. All three of us were trained as sociologists. Although we have read far and wide and strived for "balance" of some sort, this volume would surely look at least somewhat different had we been trained in different disciplines. By the same token, "collective memory," as we have shown, does have a special place in sociology, as sociology has a special place in memory studies, given both the historical origins of the concept and the definition of the subject matter. Just as well, any effort to "represent" different disciplines or areas proportionally would have entailed its own biases. Additionally, while our linguistic range includes English, German, Hebrew, and French, we have indeed been hampered by our relative ignorance of literature in other languages, just as the field itself is limited by the very poor conditions for the translation and exchange of ideas internationally. Again, by pointing out these biases we mean not simply to defend the choices we have made but to articulate that we look forward to the constructive reactions to this text and to the dialogue we hope will develop out of those reactions. We offer it as the continuation of a dialogue that is already ongoing but that we hope will now proceed somewhat more efficiently than it has to date.

REFERENCES

Abrams, Philip. *Historical Sociology.* Ithaca: Cornell University Press, 1982.

Agamben, Giorgio. *Potentialities: Collected Essays in Philosophy.* Trans. Daniel Heller-Rozen. Stanford: Stanford University Press, 2000.

Agulhon, Maurice. *Marianne into Battle: Republican Imagery and Symbolism in France, 1789–1880.* Trans. Janet Lloyd. Cambridge: Cambridge University Press, 1981.

Alcock, Susan E. *Archeologies of the Greek Past: Landscape, Monuments and Memories.* Cambridge: Cambridge University Press, 2002.

Alexander, Jeffrey C. "The Centrality of the Classics." In *Social Theory Today,* ed. Anthony Giddens and Jonathan H. Turner, 11–57. Stanford: Stanford University Press, 1987.

———. "Toward a Theory of Cultural Trauma." In *Cultural Trauma and Collective Identity,* ed. Jeffrey C. Alexander, Ron Eyerman, Bernhard Giesen, Neil J. Smelser, and Piotr Sztompka, 1–30. Berkeley: University of California Press, 2004.

Alexander, Jeffrey C., Ron Eyerman, Bernhard Giesen, Neil J. Smelser, and Piotr Sztompka, eds. *Cultural Trauma and Collective Identity.* Berkeley: University of California Press, 2004.

Alonso, Ana Maria. "The Effects of Truth: Re-Presentations of the Past and the Imagining of Community." *Journal of Historical Sociology* 1(1): 33–57, 1988.

Améry, Jean. *At the Mind's Limits: Contemplations by a Survivor on Auschwitz and Its Realities.* Trans. S. Rosenfeld and S. P. Rosenfeld. Bloomington: Indiana University Press, 1986 [1966].

Anderson, Benedict. *Imagined Communities: Reflections on the Origin and Spread of Nationalism.* 2nd ed. London: Verso, 1991.

Ankersmit, Frank R. *Historical Representation.* Stanford: Stanford University Press, 2001.

Antze, Paul, and Michael Lambek, eds. *Tense Past: Cultural Essays in Trauma and Memory.* London: Routledge, 1996.

Ariès, Philippe. *Centuries of Childhood: A Social History of Family Life.* Trans. Robert Baldick. New York: Vintage, 1965.

Ashplant, T. G., Graham Dawson, and Michael Roper, eds. *The Politics of War Memory and Commemoration.* London: Routledge, 2001.

Assmann, Aleida. "Text, Traces, Trash: The Changing Media of Cultural Memory." *Representations* 56: 123–34, 1996.

———. *Erinnerungsräume: Formen und Wandlungen des kulturellen Gedächtnisses.* Munich: C. H. Beck, 1999.

Assmann, Jan. *Moses the Egyptian: The Memory of Egypt in Western Monotheism.* Cambridge: Harvard University Press, 1997.

———. *Religion and Cultural Memory.* Trans. Rodney Livingstone. Stanford: Stanford University Press, 2006.

———. *Das kulturelle Gedächtnis.* Munich: C. H. Beck, 2007.

Bakhurst, David. "Social Memory in Soviet Thought." In *Collective Remembering,* ed. David Middleton and Derek Edwards, 203–26. Newbury Park: Sage, 1990.

Barkan, Elazar. *The Guilt of Nations: Restitution and Negotiating Historical Injustices.* New York: W. W. Norton, 2000.

Barthel, Diane. *Historic Preservation: Collective Memory and Historic Identity.* New Brunswick: Rutgers University Press, 1996.

Bartlett, Frederick. *Remembering: A Study in Experimental and Social Psychology.* Cambridge: Cambridge University Press, 1995 [1932].

Bartov, Omer. *Murder in Our Midst: The Holocaust, Industrial Killing, and Representation.* New York: Oxford University Press, 1996.

Bastéa, Eleni, ed. *Memory and Architecture.* Albuquerque: University of New Mexico Press, 2004.

Bastide, Roger. *The African Religions of Brazil: Toward a Sociology of the Interpenetration of Civilizations.* Trans. Helen Sebba. Baltimore: Johns Hopkins University Press, 1978.

Bauman, Zygmunt. *Modernity and the Holocaust.* Ithaca: Cornell University Press, 2000.

Becker, Annette. *Maurice Halbwachs: Un intellectuel en Guerres Mondiales, 1914–1945.* Paris: Agnès Viénot Éditions, 2003.

———. "Memory Gaps: Maurice Halbwachs, Memory and the Great War." *Journal of European Studies* 35(1): 102–13, 2005.

Bell, Duncan, ed. *Memory, Trauma and World Politics: Reflections on the Relationship between Past and Present.* London: Palgrave Macmillan, 2006.

Benjamin, Walter. *Illuminations: Essays and Reflections.* Ed. Hannah Arendt. Trans. Harry Zohn. New York: Harcourt, Brace, 1969.

Bennett, Tony. *The Birth of the Museum: History, Theory, Politics.* New York: Routledge, 1995.

Ben-Yehuda, Nachman. *Sacrificing Truth: Archeology and the Myth of Masada.* Amherst: Humanity Books, 2002.

Berger, Peter L. *Invitation to Sociology: A Humanistic Perspective.* New York: Anchor, 1963.

Bergson, Henri. *Matter and Memory*. Trans. N. M. Paul and W. S. Palmer. New York: Zone Books, 1988.

Berliner, David. "The Abuses of Memory: Reflections on the Memory Boom in Anthropology." *Anthropological Quarterly* 78(1): 197–211, 2005.

Besnard, Philippe, ed. *The Sociological Domain: The Durkheimians and the Founding of French Sociology*. Cambridge: Cambridge University Press, 1983.

Bloch, Marc. "Mémoire collective, tradition et coutume: À propos d'un livre récent." *Revue de Synthèse Historique* 40: 73–83, 1925.

———. *Feudal Society*. Trans. L. A. Manyon. 2 vols. New York: Routledge, 1961 [1939].

Booth, W. James. *Communities of Memory: On Witness, Identity, and Justice*. Ithaca: Cornell University Press, 2006.

Boyarin, Jonathan. *Remapping Memory: The Politics of TimeSpace*. Minneapolis: University of Minnesota Press, 1994.

Boyer, Christine M. *The City of Collective Memory*. Cambridge: MIT Press, 1994.

Breisach, Ernst. *Historiography: Ancient, Medieval, and Modern*. Chicago: University of Chicago Press, 1995.

Bruner, Jerome. *Acts of Meaning: Four Lectures on Mind and Culture*. Cambridge: Harvard University Press, 1990.

Butler, Samuel. *Unconscious Memory*. 4th ed. London: Ballantyne, Hanson and Co., 1880.

Butterfield, Herbert. *The Whig Interpretation of History*. New York: W. W. Norton, 1965.

Carruthers, Mary. *The Book of Memory: A Study of Memory in Medieval Culture*. Cambridge: Cambridge University Press, 1990.

Caruth, Cathy. *Trauma: Explorations in Memory*. Baltimore: Johns Hopkins University Press, 1995.

Casey, Edward S. *Remembering: A Phenomenological Study*. Bloomington: Indiana University Press, 1987.

Chartier, Roger. *Cultural History: Between Practices and Representations*. Trans. Lydia G. Cochrane. Cambridge: Polity Press, 1988.

Chaumont, Jean-Michel. *La concurrence des victimes: Génocide, identité, reconnaissance*. Paris: La Découverte, 2002.

Clark, Terry Nichols. *Prophets and Patrons: The French University and the Emergence of the Social Sciences*. Cambridge: Harvard University Press, 1973.

Cole, Michael. *Cultural Psychology: A Once and Future Discipline*. Cambridge: Harvard University Press, 1996.

Coleman, Janet. *Ancient and Medieval Memories: Studies in the Reconstruction of the Past*. Cambridge: Cambridge University Press, 2005.

Collingwood, Robin George. *The Idea of History*. Oxford: Clarendon, 1999 [1946].

Coman, Alin, Adam D. Brown, Jonathan Koppel, and William Hirst. "Collective Memory from a Psychological Perspective." *International Journal of Politics, Culture, and Society* 22(2): 125–41, 2009.

Confino, Alon. "Collective Memory and Cultural History: Problems of Method." *American Historical Review* 102(5): 1386–1403, 1997.

Connerton, Paul. *How Societies Remember*. Cambridge: Cambridge University Press, 1989.

———. *How Modernity Forgets*. Cambridge: Cambridge University Press, 2009.

Cooley, Charles Horton. *Social Process*. New York: Scribner's, 1918.

Coser, Lewis A. "Introduction: Maurice Halbwachs 1877–1945." In *On Collective Memory*, ed. Lewis A. Coser, 1–34. Chicago: University of Chicago Press, 1992.

Courtois, Stephane, Nicolas Werth, Jean-Louis Panne, Andrezej Paczkowski, Karel Bartosek, and Jean-Louis Margolin. *The Black Book of Communism*. Trans. Jonathan Murphy and Mark Kramer. Cambridge: Harvard University Press, 1999.

Craig, John E. "Sociology and Related Disciplines between the Wars: Maurice Halbwachs and the Imperialism of the Durkheimians." In *The Sociological Domain: The Durkheimians and the Founding of French Sociology*, ed. Philippe Besnard, 263–89. Cambridge: Cambridge University Press, 1983.

Crane, Susan. *Museums and Memory*. Stanford: Stanford University Press, 2000.

Crinson, Mark, ed. *Urban Memory: History and Amnesia in the Modern City*. London: Routledge, 2005.

Cubitt, Geoffrey. *History and Memory*. Manchester: Manchester University Press, 2007.

Danziger, Kurt. *Marking the Mind: A History of Memory*. Cambridge: Cambridge University Press, 2008.

Davis, Fred. *Yearning for Yesterday: Nostalgia, Art and Society*. New York: Free Press, 1979.

Dawkins, Richard. *The Selfish Gene*. New York: Oxford University Press, 1976.

Deak, Istvan, Jan T. Gross, and Tony Judt, eds. *The Politics of Retribution in Europe: World War II and Its Aftermath*. Princeton: Princeton University Press, 2000.

De-Brito, Alexandra, Carmen Enriquez, and Paloma Aguilar, eds. *The Politics of Memory: Transitional Justice in Democratizing Societies*. Oxford: Oxford University Press, 2001.

DeJean, Joan. *Ancients against Moderns: Culture Wars and the Making of a Fin de Siècle*. Chicago: University of Chicago Press, 1997.

Didur, Jill. *Unsettling Partition: Literature, Gender, Memory*. Toronto: University of Toronto Press, 2006.

Dienstag, Joshua F. *Dancing in Chains: Narrative and Memory in Political Theory*. Stanford: Stanford University Press, 1997.

Diner, Dan, and Gotthard Wunberg, eds. *Restitution and Memory: Material Restoration in Europe*. New York: Berghahn, 2007.

Diner, Hasia. *We Remember with Reverence and Love: American Jews and the Myth of Silence after the Holocaust, 1945–1962*. New York: New York University Press, 2009.

Douglas, Lawrence. *The Memory of Judgment: Making Law and History in the Trials of the Holocaust*. New Haven: Yale University Press, 2001.

Douglas, Mary. "Introduction: Maurice Halbwachs (1877–1945)." In *The Collective Memory*, ed. Mary Douglas, 1–21. New York: Harper Colophon, 1980.

———. *How Institutions Think*. Syracuse: Syracuse University Press, 1986.

———. *Purity and Danger: An Analysis of the Concepts of Pollution and Taboo*. London: Routledge and Kegan Paul, 1996.

Duara, Prasenjit. *Rescuing History from the Nation: Questioning Narratives of Modern China*. Chicago: University of Chicago Press, 1997.

Dubin, Steve. *Displays of Power: Memory and Amnesia in the American Museum*. New York: New York University Press, 1999.

Durkheim, Émile. *The Elementary Forms of the Religious Life*. Trans. J. W. Swain. London: Allen and Unwin, 1968 [1915].

———. *The Division of Labor in Society*. Trans. W. D. Halls. New York: Free Press. 1984 [1915].

Ebbinghaus, Hermann. *Memory: A Contribution to Experimental Psychology*. Trans. Henry A. Ruger. New York: Columbia University Press, 1913.

Edkins, Jenny. *Trauma and the Memory of Politics*. Cambridge: Cambridge University Press, 2003.

Edy, Jill A. *Troubled Past: News and the Collective Memory of Social Unrest*. Philadelphia: Temple University Press, 2006.

Egger, Stephen, ed. *Maurice Halbwachs: Aspekte des Werks*. Konstanz: UVK, 2003.

Eichenbaum, Howard. *The Cognitive Neuroscience of Memory*. New York: Oxford University Press, 2002.

Eliade, Mircea. *The Myth of the Eternal Return: Cosmos and History.* Trans. Willard R. Trask. Princeton: Princeton University Press, 1971.

Elias, Norbert. *The Germans.* Trans. Eric Dunning and Stephen Mennell. London: Polity Press, 1996.

Elster, Jon. *Closing the Books: Transitional Justice in Historical Perspective.* Cambridge: Cambridge University Press, 2004.

Erikson, Erik H. *Identity and the Life Cycle.* New York: W. W. Norton, 1994.

Erll, Astrid. *Kollektives Gedächtnis und Erinnerungskulturen: Eine Einführung.* Stuttgart: Metzler, 2005.

Erll, Astrid, and Ansgar Nünning. *Cultural Memory Studies: An International and Interdisciplinary Handbook.* Berlin: Walter de Gruyter, 2008.

Evans-Pritchard, E. E. *The Nuer: A Description of the Modes of Livelihood and Political Institutions of a Nilotic People.* Oxford: Oxford University Press, 1940.

Fabian, Johannes. "Remembering the Other: Knowledge and Recognition in the Exploration of Central Africa." *Critical Inquiry* 26: 49–69, 1999.

Faris, Robert E. L. *Chicago Sociology 1920–1932.* Chicago: University of Chicago Press, 1967.

Farrell, Kirby. *Post-Traumatic Culture: Injury and Interpretation in the Nineties.* Baltimore: Johns Hopkins University Press, 1998.

Fassin, Didier, and Richard Rechtman. *The Empire of Trauma: An Inquiry into the Condition of Victimhood.* Trans. Rachel Gomme. Princeton: Princeton University Press, 2009.

Felman, Shoshana, and Dori Laub. *Testimony: Crises of Witnessing in Literature, Psychoanalysis, and History.* London: Routledge, 1992.

Fentress, James J., and Chris Wickham. *Social Memory: New Perspectives on the Past.* Oxford: Blackwell, 1992.

Ferrarotti, Franco. *Time, Memory, and Society.* Westport: Greenwood Press, 1990.

Fine, Gary Alan. *Difficult Reputations: Collective Memories of the Evil, Inept, and Controversial.* Chicago: University of Chicago Press, 2001.

Foote, Kenneth E., and Maoz Azaryahu. "Towards a Geography of Memory: Geographical Dimensions of Public Memory and Commemoration." *Journal of Political and Military Sociology* 35(1): 125–44, 2007.

Forster, Kurt W. "Aby Warburg's History of Art: Collective Memory and the Social Mediation of Images." *Daedalus* 105(1): 169–76, 1976.

Freud, Sigmund. *Moses and Monotheism.* Trans. Katherine Jones. New York: Vintage Books, 1967.
———. *Totem and Taboo: Resemblances between the Psychic Lives of Savages and Neurotics.* Trans. Abraham Arden Brill. London: George Routledge & Sons, 1919.

Friedländer, Saul. Introduction to *Probing the Limits of Representation: Nazism and the Final Solution,* ed. Saul Friedländer, 1–21. Cambridge: Harvard University Press, 1992.

Friedman, Susan W. *Marc Bloch, Sociology, and Geography: Encountering Changing Disciplines.* Cambridge: Cambridge University Press, 1996.

Fritzsche, Peter. *Stranded in the Present: Modern Time and the Melancholy of History.* Cambridge: Harvard University Press, 2004.

Fujitani, Takashi, Geoffrey Miles White, and Lisa Yoneyama, eds. *Perilous Memories: The Asia Pacific War(s).* Durham: Duke University Press, 2001.

Funkenstein, Amos. "Collective Memory and Historical Consciousness." *History and Memory* 1: 5–26, 1989.

Fussell, Paul. *The Great War and Modern Memory.* New York: Oxford University Press, 1975.

Gadamer, Hans-Georg. *Truth and Method.* Trans. Joel Weinsheimer and Donald G. Marshall. New York: Continuum, 1975.

Gedi, Noa, and Yigal Elam. "Collective Memory—What Is It?" *History and Memory* 8(2): 30–50, 1996.

Gergen, Kenneth. *The Saturated Self: Dilemmas of Identity in Contemporary Life.* New York: Basic Books, 1991.

Gerson, Judith M., and Diane L. Wolf, eds. *Sociology Confronts the Holocaust: Memories and Identities in Jewish Diasporas.* Durham: Duke University Press, 2007.

Giddens, Anthony. *The Consequences of Modernity.* Stanford: Stanford University Press, 1991.

Gillis, John R. "Memory and Identity: The History of a Relationship." In *Commemorations*, ed. John R. Gillis, 3–24. Princeton: Princeton University Press, 1994a.

Gillis, John R., ed. *Commemorations: The Politics of National Identity.* Princeton: Princeton University Press, 1994b.

Gombrich, Ernst H. *Aby Warburg: An Intellectual Biography.* London: Phaidon, 1986.

Goody, Jack. *The Logic of Writing and the Organization of Society.* Cambridge: Cambridge University Press, 1986.

Gould, Steven Jay. *Ontogeny and Phylogeny.* Cambridge: Harvard University Press, 1977.

Greenwood, John D. *The Disappearance of the Social in American Social Psychology.* Cambridge: Cambridge University Press, 2009.

Gurvitch, Georges. *The Spectrum of Social Time.* Trans. Myrtle Korenbaum. New York: Springer, 1963.

Hacking, Ian. *Rewriting the Soul: Multiple Personality and the Sciences of Memory.* Princeton: Princeton University Press, 1998.

Halbwachs, Maurice. *Les cadres sociaux de la mémoire.* Paris: Librarie Félix Alcan, 1925.

———. "Individual Psychology and Collective Psychology." *American Sociological Review* 3(5): 615–23, 1938.

———. "Individual Consciousness and Collective Mind." *American Journal of Sociology* 44(6): 812–22, 1939.

———. *La topographie légendaire des Évangiles en Terre Sainte: Étude de mémoire.* Paris: Presses Universitaires de France, 1941.

———. *Population and Society: Introduction to Social Morphology.* Trans. Otis Dudley Duncan and Harold W. Pfautz. New York: Free Press, 1960.

———. *The Causes of Suicide.* Trans. Harold Goldblatt. London: London: Routledge and Kegan Paul, 1978 [1930].

———. *The Collective Memory.* Ed. Mary Douglas. Trans. Francis J. Ditter Jr. and Vida Yazdi Ditter. New York: Harper Colophon, 1980 [1950].

———. *On Collective Memory.* Ed. Lewis A. Coser. Chicago: University of Chicago Press, 1992.

Handler, Richard, and Eric Gable. *The New History in an Old Museum: Creating the Past at Colonial Williamsburg.* Durham: Duke University Press, 1997.

Hartman, Geoffrey. *The Longest Shadow: In the Aftermath of the Holocaust.* New York: Palgrave Macmillan, 2002.

Havelock, Eric A. *The Muse Learns to Write: Reflections on Orality and Literacy from Antiquity to the Present.* New Haven: Yale University Press, 1988.

Hayden, Dolores. *The Power of Place: Urban Landscape as Public History.* Cambridge: MIT Press, 1995.

Hegel, Georg W. F. *The Philosophy of History.* Trans. J. Sibree. New York: Cosimo, 2007.

Hering, Ewald. *On Memory and the Specific Energies of the Nervous System.* Chicago: Lakeside Press, 1905.

Herman, Judith Lewis. *Trauma and Recovery: The Aftermath of Violence—From Domestic Abuse to Political Terror.* New York: Basic Books, 1997.

Hewison, Robert. *The Heritage Industry*. London: Methuen, 1987.

Hirsch, Marianne, and Valerie Smith. "Feminism and Cultural Memory: An Introduction." *Signs* 28(1): 1–19, 2002.

Hirst, William, and David Manier. "Toward a Psychology of Collective Memory." *Memory* 16(3): 183–200, 2008.

Hobsbawm, Eric J. *On History*. New York: New Press, 1997.

Hobsbawm, Eric J., and Terence O. Ranger, eds. *The Invention of Tradition*. Cambridge: Cambridge University Press, 1983.

Hofstadter, Richard. *The Progressive Historians: Turner, Beard, Parrington*. New York: Alfred A. Knopf, 1968.

Horkheimer, Max, and Theodor W. Adorno. *Dialectic of Enlightenment*. Trans. Edmund Jephcott. Stanford: Stanford University Press, 2002 [1944].

Hoskins, Andrew. "Television and the Collapse of Memory." *Time and Society* 13(1): 109–27, 2004.

Hunt, Lynn, ed. *The New Cultural History*. Berkeley: University of California Press, 1989.

Hutton, Patrick H. *History as an Art of Memory*. Burlington: University of Vermont Press, 1993.

Huyssen, Andreas. *Twilight Memories: Marking Time in a Culture of Amnesia*. New York: Routledge, 1994.

———. *Present Pasts: Urban Palimpsests and the Politics of Memory*. Stanford: Stanford University Press, 2003.

Iggers, Georg. *The German Conception of History: The National Tradition of Historical Thought from Herder to the Present*. Middletown: Wesleyan University Press, 1968.

Irwin-Zarecka, Iwona. *Frames of Remembrance: The Dynamics of Collective Memory*. Piscataway: Transaction, 2007.

James, William. *Psychology: The Briefer Course*. New York: Henry Holt, 1910.

Jelin, Elizabeth. *State Repression and the Labors of Memory*. Trans. Judy Rein and Marcial Goody-Anatavia. Minneapolis: University of Minnesota Press, 2003.

Jones, Andrew. *Memory and Material Culture*. Cambridge: Cambridge University Press, 2007.

Jonker, Gerdien. *The Topography of Remembrance: The Dead, Tradition and Collective Memory in Mesopotamia*. Leiden: Brill, 1995.

Jordan, Jennifer. *Structures of Memory: Understanding Urban Change in Berlin and Beyond*. Stanford: Stanford University Press, 2006.

Joyce, James. *Ulysses*. New York: Modern Library, 1992 [1922].

Judt, Tony. *Postwar: A History of Europe since 1945*. New York: Penguin, 2005.

Jung, Carl Gustav. *The Archetypes and the Collective Unconscious (Collected Works of C. G. Jung, Vol. 9, Part 1)*. Trans. R. F. C. Hull. Princeton: Bollington, 1968.

Kammen, Michael. *Mystic Chords of Memory: The Transformation of Tradition in American Culture*. New York: Knopf, 1991.

Kansteiner, Wulf. "Finding Meaning in Memory: A Methodological Critique of Collective Memory Studies." *History and Theory* 41(2): 179–97, 2002.

Kaplan, E. Ann. *Trauma Culture: The Politics of Terror and Loss in Media and Literature*. New Brunswick: Rutgers University Press, 2005.

Kaplan, Steven Laurence. *Farewell, Revolution: Disputed Legacies: France, 1789/1989*. Ithaca: Cornell University Press, 1995.

Kaye, Harvey J. *The Powers of the Past: Reflections on the Crisis and the Promise of History*. Minneapolis: University of Minnesota Press, 1991.

Kern, Stephen. *The Culture of Time and Space*. Cambridge: Harvard University Press, 1986.

Kirshenblatt-Gimblett, Barbara. *Destination Culture: Tourism, Museums, and Heritage*. Berkeley: University of California Press, 1998.

Klein, Kerwin Lee. "On the Emergence of Memory in Historical Discourse." *Representations* 69: 127–50, 2000.

Kohl, Philip L., Mara Kozelsky, and Nachman Ben-Yehuda, eds. *Selective Remembrance: Archeology in the Construction, Commemoration and Consecration of National Pasts*. Chicago: University of Chicago Press, 2007.

Koselleck, Reinhart. *Futures Past: On the Semantics of Historical Time*. Trans. Keith Tribe. Cambridge: MIT Press, 1985.

Koshar, Rudy. *From Monuments to Traces: Artifacts of German Memory, 1870–1990*. Berkeley: University of California Press, 2000.

LaCapra, Dominick. *History and Memory after Auschwitz*. Ithaca: Cornell University Press, 1998.

Ladd, Brian. *The Ghosts of Berlin: Confronting German History in the Urban Landscape*. Chicago: University of Chicago Press, 1997.

Landes, David S. *Revolution in Time: Clocks and the Making of the Modern World*. Cambridge: Belknap Press, 2000.

Landsberg, Alison. *Prosthetic Memory: The Transformation of American Remembrance in the Age of Mass Culture*. New York: Columbia University Press, 2004.

Lebow, Richard Ned, Wulf Kansteiner, and Claudio Fogu, eds. *The Politics of Memory in Postwar Europe*. Durham: Duke University Press, 2006.

Lee, Ching Kwan, and Guobin Yang. *Re-envisioning the Chinese Revolution: The Politics and Poetics of Collective Memory in Reform China*. Stanford: Stanford University Press, 2007.

LeGoff, Jacques. *History and Memory*. Trans. Steven Rendall and Elizabeth Claman. New York: Columbia University Press, 1992.

Lepenies, Wolf. *The Seduction of Culture in German History*. Princeton: Princeton University Press, 2006.

Levinas, Emmanuel. "Useless Suffering." In *The Provocation of Levinas: Rethinking the Other*, ed. R. Bernasconi and D. Wood, 156–80. London: Routledge, 1988.

Levine, Donald. *Visions of the Sociological Tradition*. Chicago: University of Chicago Press, 1995.

Lévi-Strauss, Claude. *The Raw and the Cooked*. Chicago: University of Chicago Press, 1983 [1964].

Levy, Daniel, and Natan Sznaider. *Holocaust and Memory in the Global Age*. Trans. Assenka Oksilof. Philadelphia: Temple University Press, 2005.

———. *Human Rights and Memory*. University Park: Pennsylvania State University Press, 2010.

Lewis, Bernard. *History: Remembered, Recovered, Invented*. Princeton: Princeton University Press, 1975.

Leydesdorff, Selma, Luisa Passerini, and Paul Richard Thompson. *Gender and Memory*. New York: Oxford University Press, 1996.

Leys, Ruth. *Trauma: A Genealogy*. Chicago: University of Chicago Press, 2000.

Lipsitz, George. *Time Passages*. Minneapolis: University of Minnesota Press, 1990.

Lotman, Yuri. *Universe of the Mind: A Semiotic Theory of Culture*. Bloomington: Indiana University Press, 2001.

Lowenthal, David. *The Past Is a Foreign Country*. Cambridge: Cambridge University Press, 1985.

———. *Possessed by the Past: The Heritage Crusade and the Spoils of History*. Cambridge: Cambridge University Press, 1996.

————. *The Heritage Crusade and the Spoils of History.* Cambridge: Cambridge University Press, 1998.

Luria, A. R. *Cognitive Development: Its Cultural and Social Foundations.* Cambridge: Harvard University Press, 1978.

MacIntyre, Alasdair. *After Virtue: A Study in Moral Theory.* South Bend: University of Notre Dame Press, 1984.

Maier, Charles S. *The Unmasterable Past: History, Holocaust and German National Identity.* Cambridge: Harvard University Press, 1988.

————. "A Surfeit of Memory? Reflections on History, Melancholy and Denial." *History and Memory* 5(2): 136–52, 1993.

Makdisi, Ussama, and Paul A. Silverstein, eds. *Memory and Violence in the Middle East and North Africa.* Bloomington: Indiana University Press, 2006.

Maleuvre, Didier. *Museum Memories: History, Technology, Art.* Stanford: Stanford University Press, 1999.

Manier, David, and William Hirst. "A Cognitive Taxonomy of Collective Memories." In *Cultural Memory Studies: An International and Interdisciplinary Handbook,* ed. Astrid Erll and Ansgar Nünning, 253–62. Berlin: De Gruyter, 2008.

Mannheim, Karl. "The Sociological Problem of Generations." In *Essays on the Sociology of Knowledge,* ed. Paul Kecskemeti, 286–320. New York: Oxford University Press, 1952 [1928].

Marcel, Jean-Christophe, and Laurent Mucchielli. "Un fondement du lien social: La mémoire collective selon Maurice Halbwachs." *Technologies, Idéologies, Pratiques: Revue d'Anthropologie des Connaissances* 13(3): 63–88, 1999.

Margalit, Avishai. *The Ethics of Memory.* Cambridge: Harvard University Press, 2002.

McAdams, A. James. *Transitional Justice and the Rule of Law in New Democracies.* South Bend: University of Notre Dame Press, 1997.

Mead, George Herbert. *Mind, Self and Society.* Chicago: University of Chicago Press, 1934.

————. *The Philosophy of the Present.* Amherst: Prometheus, 2000 [1932].

Megill, Alan. "History, Memory and Identity." *History of the Human Sciences* 11(3): 37–62, 1998.

Merton, Robert K. *The Sociology of Science: Theoretical and Empirical Investigations.* Chicago: University of Chicago Press, 1973.

Middleton, David and Derek Edwards, eds. *Collective Remembering.* Newbury Park: Sage, 1990.

Minow, Martha. *Between Vengeance and Forgiveness: Facing History after Genocide and Mass Violence.* Boston: Beacon Press, 1999.

Misztal, Barbara A. *Theories of Social Remembering.* Berkshire: Open University Press, 2003.

Moeller, Robert G. *War Stories: The Search for a Usable Past in the Federal Republic of Germany.* Berkeley: University of California Press, 2003.

Morson, Gary, and Caryl Emerson. *Mikhail Bakhtin: Creation of a Prosaics.* Stanford: Stanford University Press, 1990.

Mosse, George L. *Fallen Soldiers: Reshaping the Memory of the World Wars.* New York: Oxford University Press, 1991.

Mucchielli, Laurent. *La découverte du social: Naissance de la sociologie en France (1870–1914).* Paris: La Découverte, 1998.

Mudimbe, V. Y., and B. Jewsiewicki, eds. *History Making in Africa: History and Theory,* Beiheft 32. Middletown: Wesleyan University Press, 1993.

Mueller, Jan-Werner, ed. *Memory and Power in Post-War Europe: Studies in the Presence of the Past.* Cambridge: Cambridge University Press, 2002.

Nalbantian, Suzanne. *Memory in Literature: From Rousseau to Neuroscience*. New York: Palgrave Macmillan, 2004.

Namer, Gerard. *Mémoire et société*. Paris: Meridiens Klincksieck, 1987.

Neiman, Susan. *Evil in Modern Thought: An Alternative History of Philosophy*. Princeton: Princeton University Press, 2002.

Neisser, Ulric, and Ira Hyman, eds. *Memory Observed: Remembering in Natural Contexts*. New York: Worth, 1982.

Nietzsche, Friedrich. *Untimely Meditations*. Trans. R. J. Hollingdale. Cambridge: Cambridge University Press, 1997.

Noiriel, Gérard. *The French Melting Pot: Immigration, Citizenship, and National Identity*. Trans. Geoffroy de Laforcade. Minneapolis: University of Minnesota Press, 1996.

Nora, Pierre. *Les lieux de mémoire*. 7 vols. Paris: Gallimard, 1984–1992.

———. "Between Memory and History: Les Lieux de Mémoire." Trans. Marc Roudebush. *Representations* 26: 7–24, 1989.

Novick, Peter. *The Holocaust in American Life*. New York: Mariner Books, 2000.

Oishi, Shigehiro, Selin Kesebir, and Benjamin H. Snyder. "Sociology: A Lost Connection in Social Psychology." *Personality and Social Psychology Review* 13(4): 334–53, 2009.

Olick, Jeffrey K. "Genre Memories and Memory Genres: A Dialogical Analysis of May 8, 1945 Commemorations in the Federal Republic of Germany." *American Sociological Review* 64(3): 381–402, 1999a.

———. "Collective Memory: The Two Cultures." *Sociological Theory* 17(3): 333–48, 1999b.

———. *In the House of the Hangman: The Agonies of German Defeat, 1943–1949*. Chicago: University of Chicago Press, 2005.

———. *The Politics of Regret: On Collective Memory and Historical Responsibility*. New York: Routledge, 2007.

Olick, Jeffrey K., ed. *States of Memory: Continuities, Conflicts, and Transformations in National Retrospection*. Durham: Duke University Press, 2003.

Olick, Jeffrey K., and Daniel Levy. "Collective Memory and Cultural Constraint: Holocaust Myth and Rationality in German Politics." *American Sociological Review* 62(6): 921–36, 1997.

Olick, Jeffrey K., and Joyce Robbins. "Social Memory Studies: From 'Collective Memory' to the Historical Sociology of Mnemonic Practices." *Annual Review of Sociology* 24(1): 105–40, 1998.

Ong, Walter J. *The Presence of the Word*. New Haven: Yale University Press, 1967.

———. *Orality and Literacy*. 2nd ed. London: Routledge, 2002.

Ortner, Sherry B. *The Fate of "Culture:" Geertz and Beyond*. Berkeley: University of California Press, 1999.

Osiel, Mark. *Mass Atrocity, Collective Memory, and the Law*. New Brunswick: Transaction, 1999.

Otis, Laura. *Organic Memory: History and the Body in the Late Nineteenth and Early Twentieth Centuries*. Lincoln: University of Nebraska Press, 1994.

Perks, Robert, and Alistair Thomson, eds. *The Oral History Reader*. London: Routledge, 1998.

Pillemer, David B. *Momentous Events, Vivid Memories*. Cambridge: Harvard University Press, 1998.

Pinder, Wilhelm. *Das Problem der Generationen in der Kunstgeschichte Europas*. Berlin: Frankfurter Verlagsanstalt, 1926.

Portelli, Alejandro. *The Death of Luigi Trastulli: Form and Meaning in Oral History*. Albany: State University of New York Press, 1991.

Prager, Jeffrey. *Presenting the Past: Psychoanalysis and the Sociology of Misremembering*. Cambridge: Harvard University Press, 2000.

Renan, Ernest. "What Is a Nation?" In *Nation and Narration*, ed. Homi K. Bhabha, trans. Martin Thom, 8–22. New York: Routledge, 1990.

Ricoeur, Paul. *Memory, History, Forgetting*. Trans. Kathleen Blamey and David Pallauer. Chicago: University of Chicago Press, 2004.

Rieff, Philip. *The Triumph of the Therapeutic: Uses of Faith after Freud*. Chicago: University of Chicago Press, 1987.

Roniger, Luis, and Mario Sznajder. *The Legacy of Human-Rights Violations in the Southern Cone*. Oxford: Oxford University Press, 1999.

Rosenfeld, Gavriel D. *Munich and Memory*. Berkeley: University of California Press, 2000.

———. "A Looming Crash or a Soft Landing? Forecasting the Future of the Memory 'Industry.'" *Journal of Modern History* 81(1): 122–58, 2009.

Roudometof, Victor. *Collective Memory, National Identity and Ethnic Conflict: Greece, Bulgaria, and the Macedonia Question*. Westport: Praeger, 2002.

Rousso, Henry. *The Vichy Syndrome: History and Memory in France since 1944*. Trans. Arthur Goldhammer. Cambridge: Harvard University Press, 1991.

Sahlins, Marshall D. *Islands of History*. Chicago: University of Chicago Press, 1987.

———. *Apologies to Thucydides: Understanding History as Culture and Vice Versa*. Chicago: University of Chicago Press, 2004.

Saltzman, Lisa. *Making Memory Matter: Strategies of Remembrance in Contemporary Art*. Chicago: University of Chicago Press, 2006.

Samuel, Raphael. *Theatres of Memory*. London: Verso, 1996.

Schacter, Daniel L. *Searching for Memory: The Brain, the Mind, and the Past*. New York: Basic Books, 1997.

———. *Forgotten Ideas, Neglected Pioneers: Richard Semon and the Story of Memory*. Philadelphia: Psychology Press, 2001.

———. *The Seven Sins of Memory*. New York: Mariner, 2002.

Schivelbusch, Wolfgang. *The Railway Journey: The Industrialization of Time and Space in the 19th Century*. Berkeley: University of California Press, 1987.

Schudson, Michael. *Watergate in American Memory*. New York: Basic Books, 1993.

Schuman, Howard, and Jacqueline Scott. "Generations and Collective Memories." *American Sociological Review* 54: 359–81, 1989.

Schutz, Alfred. "Making Music Together." In *Collected Papers II: Studies in Social Theory*, ed. Arvid Broderson, 159–78. The Hague: Martinus Nijhoff, 1964.

Schwartz, Barry. *Abraham Lincoln and the Forge of National Memory*. Chicago: University of Chicago Press, 2003.

———. *Abraham Lincoln in the Post-Heroic Era: History and Memory in Late Twentieth-Century America*. Chicago: University of Chicago Press, 2009.

Schwartz, Barry, and Mikyoung Kim, eds. *Northeast Asia's Difficult Past: Essays in Collective Memory*. Houndmills: Palgrave Macmillan, 2010.

Semon, Richard Wolfgang. *The Mneme*. Trans. Louis Simon. London: Allen & Unwin, 1921.

———. *Mnemic Psychology*. Trans. Bella Duffy and Vernon Lee. London: Allen & Unwin, 1923.

Shils, Edward. *Tradition*. Chicago: University of Chicago Press, 1981.

Shweder, Richard A. *Thinking through Cultures: Expeditions in Cultural Psychology*. Cambridge: Harvard University Press, 1991.

Singh, Amritjit, Joseph T. Skerrett, and Robert E. Hogan. *Memory, Narrative, and Identity: New Essays in Ethnic American Literatures*. Boston: Northeastern University Press, 1994.

Smith, Andrea L. *Colonial Memory and Postcolonial Europe*. Bloomington: Indiana University Press, 2006.

Smith, Anthony D. *The Ethnic Origins of Nations.* Oxford: Blackwell, 1986.

Snyder, Timothy. "Holocaust: The Ignored Reality." *New York Review of Books* 56 (July 16): 14–16, 2009.

Sommer, Roy, Ansgar Nünning, and Marion Gymnich. *Literature and Memory.* Tübingen: Francke A. Verlag, 2006.

Sorokin, Pitirim A. *Social and Cultural Dynamics.* Boston: Porter Sargent, 1970.

Stern, Steve J. *Remembering Pinochet's Chile: On the Eve of London 1998.* Durham: Duke University Press, 2006.

———. *Reckoning with Pinochet: The Memory Question in Democratic Chile, 1989–2006.* Durham: Duke University Press, 2010.

Sturken, Marita. *Tangled Memories: The Vietnam War, the AIDS Epidemic, and the Politics of Remembering.* Berkeley: University of California Press, 1997.

Sutton, John. *Philosophy and Memory Traces: Descartes to Connectionism.* Cambridge: Cambridge University Press, 1998.

———. "Constructive Memory and Distributed Cognition: Towards an Interdisciplinary Framework." In *Constructive Memory,* ed. Boicho Kokinov and William Hirst, 290–303. Sofia: New Bulgarian University, 2003.

———. "Distributed Cognition: Domains and Dimensions." *Pragmatics and Cognition* 14(2): 295–347, 2006.

Taylor, Charles. *Sources of the Self: The Making of the Modern Identity.* Cambridge: Harvard University Press, 1992.

Teitel, Ruti G. *Transitional Justice.* New York: Oxford University Press, 2002.

Terdiman, Richard. *Present Past: Modernity and the Memory Crisis.* Ithaca: Cornell University Press, 1993.

Thelen, David. "History after the Enola Gay Controversy: An Introduction." *Journal of American History* 82(3): 1029–35, 1995.

Theweleit, Klaus. *Male Fantasies.* Trans. Chris Turner, Stephen Conway, and Erica Carter. Cambridge: Polity Press, 1987.

Thompson, John B. *The Media and Modernity: A Social Theory of the Media.* Stanford: Stanford University Press, 1995.

Todes, Daniel P. *Pavlov's Physiology Factory: Experiment, Interpretation, Laboratory Enterprise.* Baltimore: Johns Hopkins University Press, 2001.

Todorov, Tzvetan. *Hope and Memory: Lessons from the Twentieth Century.* Trans. David Bellos. Princeton: Princeton University Press, 2003.

Topalov, Christian. "Maurice Halbwachs et les Villes (19808-1912): Une Enquête d'Histoire Sociale des Sciences Sociales." *Annales. Histoire, Sciences Sociales* 52(5): 1057–83, 1997.

———. "Maurice Halbwachs and Chicago Sociologists." *Revue Française de Sociologie* 49: 187–214, 2008.

Torpey, John. *Politics and the Past: On Repairing Historical Injustices.* Lanham: Rowman and Littlefield, 2003.

———. *Making Whole What Has Been Smashed: On Reparations Politics.* Cambridge: Harvard University Press, 2006.

Trouillot, Michel-Rolph. *Silencing the Past.* Boston: Beacon Press, 1997.

Tulving, Endel. *Elements of Episodic Memory.* New York: Oxford University Press, 1985.

Tumarkin, Nina. *Lenin Lives! The Lenin Cult in Soviet Russia.* Cambridge: Harvard University Press, 1997.

Van Dijck, José. *Mediated Memories: Personal Cultural Memory in the Digital Age.* Stanford: Stanford University Press, 2007.

Van Doren, Charles L. *The Idea of Progress.* Bel Air: F. A. Praeger, 1967.

Verdery, Katherine. *The Political Life of Dead Bodies: Reburial and Postsocialist Change.* New York: Columbia University Press, 1999.

Veyne, Paul. *Writing History: Essay on Epistemology.* Trans. Mina Moore-Rinvolucri. Middletown: Wesleyan University Press, 1984.

Vincent, George Edgar. *The Social Mind and Education.* Chicago: University of Chicago Press, 1897.

Vinitzky-Seroussi, Vered. "Commemorating a Difficult Past: Yitzhak Rabin's Memorial." *American Sociological Review* 67(1): 30–51, 2002.

Vromen, Suzanne. *The Sociology of Maurice Halbwachs.* PhD diss., New York University, 1975.

Vygotsky, Lev Semenovich. *Mind in Society.* Ed. Michael Cole and Sylvia Scribner. Cambridge: Harvard University Press, 1978.

Wagner-Pacifici, Robin, and Barry Schwartz. "The Vietnam Veterans Memorial: Commemorating a Difficult Past." *American Journal of Sociology* 97(2): 376–420, 1991.

Wallace, Mike. *Mickey Mouse History and Other Essays on American Memory.* Philadelphia: Temple University Press, 1996.

Walzer, Michael. *Exodus and Revolution.* New York: Basic Books, 1986.

Warburg, Aby. *The Renewal of Pagan Antiquity.* Trans. David Britt. Los Angeles: Getty Publications, 1999.

———. *Der Bilderatlas Mnemosyne.* Ed. Martin Warnke and Claudia Brink. Germany: Akademie Verlag, 2008.

Warner, W. Lloyd. *The Living and the Dead: A Study of the Symbolic Life of Americans.* New Haven: Yale University Press, 1959.

Weber, Eugen. *Peasants into Frenchmen: The Modernization of Rural France, 1870–1914.* Stanford: Stanford University Press, 1976.

Wertsch, James V. *Vygotsky and the Social Formation of Mind.* Cambridge: Harvard University Press, 1988.

———. *Voices of Collective Remembering.* Cambridge: Cambridge University Press, 2002.

Wetzel, Dietmar. *Maurice Halbwachs.* Konstanz: UVK, 2009.

Whitehead, Anne. *Memory.* Oxford: Routledge, 2008.

Wieviorka, Annette. *The Era of the Witness.* Trans. Jared Stark. Ithaca: Cornell University Press, 2006.

Winter, Jay. *Sites of Memory, Sites of Mourning: The Great War in European Cultural History.* Cambridge: Cambridge University Press, 1995.

———. "The Memory Boom in Contemporary Historical Studies." *Raritan* 21(1): 52–66, 2001.

———. *Remembering War: The Great War between Memory and History in the 20th Century.* New Haven: Yale University Press, 2006.

Winthrop-Young, Geoffrey. "Memories of the Nile: Egyptian Traumas and Communication Technologies in Jan Assmann's Theory of Cultural Memory." *New German Critique* 96: 103–33, 2005.

Wolf, Eric R. *Europe and the People without History.* Berkeley: University of California Press, 1982.

Wolf, Philipp. *Modernization and the Crisis of Memory: John Donne to Don DeLillo.* Amsterdam: Editions Rodopi, 2002.

Wood, Nancy. *Vectors of Memory: Legacies of Postwar Europe.* Oxford: Berg, 1999.

Wright, Patrick. *On Living in an Old Country: The National Past in Contemporary Britain.* London: Verso, 1985.

62 THE COLLECTIVE MEMORY READER

Wundt, Wilhelm. *Outlines of Psychology.* Trans. Charles Hubbard Judd. New York: G. E. Stechert, 1897.

———. *Principles of Physiological Psychology.* Trans. Edward Bradford Titchener. Periodicals Service Co., 1910.

———. *An Introduction to Psychology.* Trans. Rudolf Pinteb. New York: Macmillan, 1912.

Yates, Frances A. *The Art of Memory.* London: Routledge and Kegan Paul, 1966.

Yerushalmi, Yosef H. *Zakhor: Jewish History and Jewish Memory.* Seattle: University of Washington Press, 1996 [1982].

———. *Freud's Moses: Judaism Terminable and Interminable.* New Haven: Yale University Press, 1993.

Young, James E. *The Texture of Memory: Holocaust Memorials and Meaning.* New Haven: Yale University Press, 1993.

———. *At Memory's Edge: After-Images of the Holocaust in Contemporary Art and Architecture.* New Haven: Yale University Press, 2000.

Zelizer, Barbie. *Covering the Body: The Kennedy Assassination, the Media, and the Shaping of Collective Memory.* Chicago: University of Chicago Press, 1992.

———. "Reading the Past against the Grain: The Shape of Memory Studies." *Critical Studies in Mass Communication* 12: 214–39, 1995.

———. *Remembering to Forget: Holocaust Memory through the Camera's Eye.* Chicago: University of Chicago Press, 2000.

Zerubavel, Eviatar. "The Standardization of Time: A Sociohistorical Perspective." *American Journal of Sociology* 88: 1–23, 1982.

———. *The Seven Day Circle: The History and Meaning of the Week.* Chicago: University of Chicago Press, 1989.

———. "Calendars and History: A Comparative Study of the Social Organization of National Memory." In *States of Memory*, ed. Jeffrey K. Olick, 315–37. Durham: Duke University Press, 2003.

Zolberg, Vera. "Contested Remembrance: The Hiroshima Exhibit Controversy." *Theory and Society* 27: 565–90, 1998.

PART I

Precursors and Classics

Interest in memory, individual and collective, is as old as organized thought. But serious thinking about the social dimensions of memory took important new forms in the late nineteenth century, with the consolidation of European modernity. In this section, we present a variety of exemplars from the late nineteenth century and the first half of the twentieth that provide seminal formulations of the collective memory problematic, whether or not they employ the term.

Some of these are quite familiar in contemporary memory studies, for a wide range of reasons. For instance, Ernest Renan's statement on the role of remembering and forgetting in national identity, though certainly well enough known in its time and to scholars in the first decades of the twentieth century, was resurrected for contemporary scholars largely through Benedict Anderson's discussion in his famous book *Imagined Communities*. Friedrich Nietzsche's essay on antiquarian, monumental, and critical history is known not only to most historians but also to memory studies as a classic reference, though his argument is more general background, rather than active model, for contemporary work. And of course Maurice Halbwachs is considered the founding father of social memory studies, just as Frederic Bartlett is considered a classic—though more recently rediscovered—source for psychologists interested in social dimensions of remembering.

Others are often cited but for one reason or another not as widely read. Marc Bloch's and Charles Blondel's reviews of Halbwachs are presented here in English for the first time. Carl Becker's essay "Everyman His Own Historian" and Karl Mannheim's essay on generations are well cited in the field, but relatively difficult to find and not often framed in terms of social memory studies. Émile Durkheim was Halbwachs's intellectual father and the central progenitor of "collective memory," but his remarks on memory are contained deep within a rich argument about social time and the elementary forms of religious life, and for this reason perhaps stand out less well than they might; our edits aim to highlight those of Durkheim's remarks that pertain most directly to collective memory.

Some works—certainly those of Edmund Burke, Alexis de Tocqueville, Sigmund Freud, Karl Marx, Walter Benjamin, Theodor Adorno, E. E. Evans-Pritchard, and Claude Lévi-Strauss—are quite famous, though not necessarily for their insights on collective memory, and we present excerpts of their work here in the hope that they will become more common landmarks for, and within, social memory studies.

Other works are less well known, or known mostly within their disciplines (such as George Herbert Mead and Charles Horton Cooley to sociologists). Some are even more obscure, and we include them here so as not to miss their unique insights: Lev Vygotsky's cultural psychology, for instance, is a relatively forgotten—or only recently recovered (Wertsch 1985)—source for social approaches in contemporary psychology. Aby Warburg, whose work was quite fragmentary and difficult, has nevertheless been an inspiration to many contemporary scholars, particularly in Germany, but largely unknown outside of art history and some European strands of memory theory. Roger Bastide's unique insights into Halbwachs are cited occasionally but not nearly as often as they should be, in part because he writes about geographical areas too far from those that are dominant in contemporary social memory studies; but his important work provides a unique perspective on cultural syncretism as well as a trenchant revision of Halbwachs's approach. Finally, Lloyd Warner's Durkheimian analysis of the ritual life of an American city provides important insights into the generation of social solidarity through commemoration.

To be sure, there are many other relevant figures in the history of modern thought who are not included here but whose work could or should be known to contemporary memory scholars. These include Giambatista Vico and Georg Friedrich Hegel in philosophy, whose historicist thought in many ways defined an age; Mikhail Bakhtin's dialogical approach to genres, which links up with both poststructuralist literary theory and varieties of Russian psychology from the 1930s forward (not least that of Vygotsky); and psychologists like Wilhelm Wundt and Hermann Ebbinghaus, among others, who have perhaps not received the attention they deserve, along with Richard Semon, all of whose importance we discussed in the volume introduction. However, the works presented here are all part of our reconstruction of a more inclusive disciplinary narrative for contemporary work, which could indeed include a great number of other works as well.

REFERENCES

Wertsch, James V. *Vygotsky and the Social Formation of Mind.* Cambridge: Harvard University Press, 1985.

Edmund Burke (1729–1797)

Anglo-Irish political commentator and philosopher. Considered by many the founding father of political conservatism. Burke vigorously opposed the French Revolution, in part because, as he adumbrates here (1790), he believed strongly in the role of memory and tradition in sustaining social order. Burke's insights on the role of memory and tradition in social order influenced many subsequent thinkers, conservative and otherwise. See especially **Durkheim** and **Shils**.

From *Reflections on the Revolution in France*

The Revolution was made to preserve our ancient, indisputable laws and liberties, and that ancient constitution of government which is our only security for law and liberty. If you are desirous of knowing the spirit of our constitution, and the policy which predominated in that great period which has secured it to this hour, pray look for both in our histories, in our records, in our acts of parliament, and journals of parliament, and not in the sermons of the Old Jewry, and the afterdinner toasts of the Revolution Society. In the former you will find other ideas and another language. Such a claim is as illsuited to our temper and wishes as it is unsupported by an appearance of authority. The very idea of the fabrication of a new government is enough to fill us with disgust and horror. We wished at the period of the Revolution, and do now wish, to derive all we possess as an inheritance from our forefathers. Upon that body and stock of inheritance we have taken care not to inoculate any scion alien to the nature of the original plant. All the reformations we have hitherto made have proceeded upon the principle of reverence to antiquity: and I hope, nay I am persuaded, that all those which possibly may be made hereafter, will be carefully formed upon analogical precedent, authority, and example. . . .

Through the same plan of a conformity to nature in our artificial institutions, and by calling in the aid of her unerring and powerful instincts to fortify the fallible and feeble contrivances of our reason, we have derived several others, and those no small benefits, from considering our liberties in the light of an inheritance. Always acting as if in the presence of canonized forefathers, the spirit of freedom, leading in itself to misrule and excess, is tempered with an awful gravity. This idea of a liberal descent inspires us with a sense of habitual native dignity, which prevents that upstart insolence almost inevitably adhering to and disgracing those who are the first acquirers of any distinction. By this means our liberty becomes a noble freedom. It carries an imposing and majestic aspect. It has a pedigree and illustrating ancestors. It has its bearings and its ensigns armorial. It has its gallery of portraits; its monumental inscriptions; its records, evidences, and titles. We procure reverence to our civil institutions on the principle upon which nature teaches us to revere individual men; on account of their age, and on account of those from whom they are descended. All your sophisters cannot produce anything better adapted to preserve a rational and manly freedom than the course that we have pursued, who have chosen our nature, rather than our speculations, our breasts rather than our inventions, for the great conservatories and magazines of our rights and privileges.

You [*in France*-Ed.] might, if you pleased, have profited of our example, and have given to your recovered freedom a correspondent dignity. Your privileges, though discontinued, were not lost to memory. Your constitution, it is true, whilst you were out of possession, suffered waste and dilapidation; but you possessed in some parts the walls, and, in all, the foundations, of a noble and venerable castle. You might have repaired those walls; you might have built on those old foundations. Your constitution was suspended before it was perfected; but you had the elements of a constitution very nearly as good as could be wished. In your old states you possessed that variety of parts corresponding with the various descriptions of which your community was happily composed; you had all that combination, and all that opposition of interests, you had that action and counteraction, which, in the natural and in the political world, from the reciprocal struggle of discordant powers, draws out the harmony of the universe. These opposed and conflicting interests, which you considered as so great a blemish in your old and in our present constitution, interpose a salutary check to all precipitate resolutions. They render deliberation a matter not of choice, but of necessity; they make all change a subject of *compromise*, which naturally begets moderation; they produce *temperaments* preventing the sore evil of harsh, crude, unqualified reformations; and rendering all the headlong exertions of arbitrary power, in the few or in the many, for ever impracticable. Through that diversity of members and interests, general liberty had as many securities as there were separate views in the several orders; whilst by pressing down the whole by the weight of a real monarchy, the separate parts would have been prevented from warping, and starting from their allotted places.

You had all these advantages in your ancient states; but you chose to act as if you had never been moulded into civil society, and had everything to begin anew. You began ill, because you began by despising everything that belonged to you. You set up your trade without a capital. If the last generations of your country appeared without much lustre in your eyes, you might have passed them by, and derived your claims from a more early race of ancestors. Under a pious predilection for those ancestors your imaginations would have realized in them a standard of virtue and wisdom, beyond the vulgar practice of the hour: and you would have risen with the example to whose imitation you aspired. Respecting your forefathers, you would have been taught to respect yourselves. You would not have chosen to consider the French as a people of yesterday, as a nation of low born servile wretches until the emancipating year of 1789. In order to furnish, at the expense of your honour, an excuse to your apologists here for several enormities of yours, you would not have been content to be represented as a gang of

Maroon slaves, suddenly broke loose from the house of bondage, and therefore to be pardoned for your abuse of the liberty to which you were not accustomed, and ill fitted. Would it not, my worthy friend, have been wiser to
have you thought, what I, for one, always thought you, a generous and gal-
lant nation, long misled to your disadvantage by your high and romantic
sentiments of fidelity, honour, and loyalty; that events had been unfavour-
able to you, but that you were not enslaved through any illiberal or servile
disposition; in your most devoted submission, you were actuated by a principle of public spirit, and that it was your Country you worshipped, in the
person of your king? Had you made it to be understood, that in the delusion
of this amiable error you had gone further than your wise ancestors; that
you were resolved to resume your ancient privileges, whilst you preserved
the spirit of your ancient and your recent loyalty and honour; or if, diffident
of yourselves, and not clearly discerning the almost obliterated constitution
of your ancestors, you had looked to your neighbours in this land, who had
kept alive the ancient principles and models of the old common law of
Europe meliorated and adapted to its present state-by following wise examples you would have given new examples of wisdom to the world. You would
have rendered the cause of liberty venerable in the eyes of every worthy
mind in every nation. You would have shamed despotism from the earth, by
showing that freedom was not only reconcilable, but, as when well disciplined it is, auxiliary to law. You would have an unoppressive but a productive revenue. You would have had a flourishing commerce to feed it. You
would have had a free constitution; a potent monarchy; a disciplined army;
a reformed and venerated clergy; a mitigated but spirited nobility, to lead
your virtue, not to overlay it; you would have had a liberal order of com-
mons, to emulate and to recruit that nobility; you would have had a protected, satisfied, laborious, and obedient people, taught to seek and to
recognise the happiness that is to be found by virtue in all conditions; in
which consists the true moral equality of mankind, and not in that mon-
strous fiction, which, by inspiring false ideas and vain expectations into men
destined to travel in the obscure walk of laborious life, serves only to aggra-
vate and embitter that real inequality, which it never can remove; and which
the order of civil life establishes as much for the benefit of those whom it
must leave in an humble state, as those whom it is able to exalt to a condition more splendid, but not more happy. You had a smooth and easy career
of felicity and glory laid open to you beyond anything recorded in the history
of the world; but you have shown that difficulty is good for men.

Alexis de Tocqueville (1805–1859)

French political thinker and historian. Like Burke, Tocqueville was concerned about the effects of the transition from aristocratic to democratic politics. Tocqueville draws an interesting (and mostly forgotten) distinction between aristocratic societies as societies of memory and democratic societies as societies of forgetting. There are strong similarities between Tocqueville's observation here (1835) and those of later theorists, like **Halbwachs** and **Nora**, who emphasize the transition from a world suffused with memory to a world in which the relation to the past is problematic.

From *Democracy in America*

Historians who write in aristocratic ages are inclined to refer all occurrences to the particular will and character of certain individuals; and they are apt to attribute the most important revolutions to slight accidents. They trace out the smallest causes with sagacity, and frequently leave the greatest unperceived.

Historians who live in democratic ages exhibit precisely opposite characteristics. Most of them attribute hardly any influence to the individual over the destiny of the race, or to citizens over the fate of a people; but, on the other hand, they assign great general causes to all petty incidents. These contrary tendencies explain each other.

When the historian of aristocratic ages surveys the theater of the world, he at once perceives a very small number of prominent actors who manage the whole piece. These great personages, who occupy the front of the stage, arrest attention and fix it on themselves; and while the historian is bent on penetrating the secret motives which make these persons speak and act, the others escape his memory. The importance of the things that some men are seen to do gives him an exaggerated estimate of the influence that one man may possess, and naturally leads him to think that in order to explain the impulses of the multitude, it is necessary to refer them to the particular influence of some one individual.

When, on the contrary, all the citizens are independent of one another, and each of them is individually weak, no one is seen to exert a great or still less a lasting power over the community. At first sight individuals appear to be absolutely devoid of any influence over it, and society would seem to advance alone by the free and voluntary action of all the men who compose it. This naturally prompts the mind to search for that general reason which operates upon so many men's faculties at once and turns them simultaneously in the same direction.

I am very well convinced that even among democratic nations the genius, the vices, or the virtues of certain individuals retard or accelerate the natural current of a people's history; but causes of this secondary and fortuitous nature are infinitely more various, more concealed, more complex, less powerful, and consequently less easy to trace, in periods of equality than in ages of aristocracy, when the task of the historian is simply to detach from the mass of general events the particular influence of one man or of a few men. In the former case the historian is soon wearied by the toil, his mind loses itself in this labyrinth, and, in his inability clearly to discern or conspicuously to point out the influence of individuals, he denies that they have any. He prefers talking about the characteristics of race, the physical conformation of the country, or the genius of civilization, and thus abridges his own labors and satisfies his reader better at less cost.

M. de Lafayette says somewhere in his *Memoirs* that the exaggerated system of general causes affords surprising consolations to second-rate statesmen. I will add that its effects are not less consolatory to second-rate historians; it can always furnish a few mighty reasons to extricate them from the most difficult part of their work, and it indulges the indolence or incapacity of their minds while it confers upon them the honors of deep thinking.

For myself, I am of the opinion that, at all times, one great portion of the events of this world are attributable to very general facts and another to special influences. These two kinds of cause are always in operation; only their proportion varies. General facts serve to explain more things in democratic than in aristocratic ages, and fewer things are then assignable to individual influences. During periods of aristocracy the reverse takes place: special influences are stronger, general causes weaker; unless, indeed, we consider as a general cause the fact itself of the inequality of condition, which allows some individuals to baffle the natural tendencies of all the rest.

The historians who seek to describe what occurs in democratic societies are right, therefore, in assigning much to general causes and in devoting their chief attention to discover them; but they are wrong in wholly denying the special influence of individuals because they cannot easily trace or follow it.

The historians who live in democratic ages not only are prone to assign a great cause to every incident, but are also given to connect incidents together so as to deduce a system from them. In aristocratic ages, as the attention of historians is constantly drawn to individuals, the connection of events escapes them; or rather they do not believe in any such connection. To them, the thread of history seems constantly to be broken by the course of one man's life. In democratic ages, on the contrary, as the historian sees much more of actions than of actors, he may easily establish some kind of sequence and methodical order among the former.

Ancient literature, which is so rich in fine historical compositions, does not contain a single great historical system, while the poorest of modern literatures abound with them. It would appear that the ancient historians did not make sufficient use of those general theories which our historical writers are ever ready to carry to excess.

Those who write in democratic ages have another more dangerous tendency. When the traces of individual action upon nations are lost, it often happens that you see the world move without the impelling force being evident. As it becomes extremely difficult to discern and analyze the reasons that, acting separately on the will of each member of the community, concur in the end to produce movement in the whole mass, men are led to believe that this movement is involuntary and that societies unconsciously obey some superior force ruling over them. But even when the general fact that governs the private volition of all individuals is supposed to be discovered upon the earth, the principle of human free-will is not made certain. A cause sufficiently extensive to affect millions of men at once and sufficiently strong to bend them all together in the same direction may well seem irresistible, having seen that mankind do yield to it, the mind is close upon the inference that mankind cannot resist it.

Historians who live in democratic ages, then, not only deny that the few have any power of acting upon the destiny of a people, but deprive the people themselves of the power of modifying their own condition, and they subject them either to an inflexible Providence or to some blind necessity. According to them, each nation is indissolubly bound by its position, its origin, its antecedents, and its character to a certain lot that no efforts can ever change. They involve generation in generation, and thus, going back from age to age, and from necessity to necessity, up to the origin of the world, they forge a close and enormous chain, which girds and binds the human race. To their minds it is not enough to show what events have occurred: they wish to show that events could not have occurred otherwise. They take a nation arrived at a certain stage of its history and affirm that it could not but follow the track that brought it hither. It is easier to make such an assertion than to show how the nation might have adopted a better course.

In reading the historians of aristocratic ages, and especially those of antiquity, it would seem that, to be master of his lot and to govern his fellow creatures, man requires only to be master of himself. In perusing the historical volumes which our age has produced, it would seem that man is utterly powerless over himself and over all around him. The historians of antiquity taught how to command; those of our time teach only how to obey; in their writings the author often appears great, but humanity is always diminutive.

If this doctrine of necessity, which is so attractive to those who write history in democratic ages, passes from authors to their readers till it infects the whole mass of the community and gets possession of the public mind, it will soon paralyze the activity of modern society and reduce Christians to the level of the Turks.

Moreover, I would observe that such doctrines are peculiarly dangerous at the period at which we have arrived. Our contemporaries are only too prone to doubt of human free-will, because each of them feels himself confined on every side by his own weakness; but they are still willing to acknowledge the strength and independence of men united in society. Do not let this principle be lost sight of, for the great object in our time is to raise the faculties of men, not to complete their prostration.

I have shown how it is that in ages of equality every man seeks for his opinions within himself; I am now to show how it is that in the same ages all his feelings are turned towards himself alone. *Individualism* is a novel expression, to which a novel idea has given birth. Our fathers were only acquainted with *egoisme* (selfishness). Selfishness is a passionate and exaggerated love of self, which leads a man to connect everything with himself and to prefer himself to everything in the world. Individualism is a mature and calm feeling, which disposes each member of the community to sever himself from the mass of his fellows and to draw apart with his family and his friends, so that after he has thus formed a little circle of his own, he willingly leaves society at large to itself. Selfishness originates in blind instinct; individualism proceeds from erroneous judgment more than from depraved feelings; it originates as much in deficiencies of mind as in perversity of heart.

Selfishness blights the germ of all virtue; individualism, at first, only saps the virtues of public life; but in the long run it attacks and destroys all others and is at length absorbed in downright selfishness. Selfishness is a vice as old as the world, which does not belong to one form of society more than to another; individualism is of democratic origin, and it threatens to spread in the same ratio as the equality of condition.

Among aristocratic nations, as families remain for centuries in the same condition, often on the same spot, all generations become, as it were, contemporaneous. A man almost always knows his forefathers and respects them; he thinks he already sees his remote descendants and he loves them. He willingly imposes duties on himself towards the former and the latter, and he will frequently sacrifice his personal gratifications to those who went before and to those who will come after him. Aristocratic institutions, moreover, have the effect of closely binding every man to several of his fellow citizens. As the classes of an aristocratic people are strongly marked and permanent, each of them is regarded by its own members as a sort of lesser country, more tangible and more cherished than the country at large. As in aristocratic communities all the citizens occupy fixed positions, one above another, the result is that each of them always sees a man above himself whose patronage is necessary to him, and below himself another man whose co-operation he may claim. Men living in aristocratic ages are therefore almost always closely attached to something placed out of their own sphere, and they are often disposed to forget themselves. It is true that in these ages the notion of human fellowship is faint and that men seldom think of sacrificing themselves for mankind; but they often sacrifice themselves for other men. In democratic times, on the contrary, when the duties of each individual to the race are much more clear, devoted service to any one man becomes more rare; the bond of human affection is extended, but it is relaxed.

Among democratic nations new families are constantly springing up, others are constantly falling away, and all that remain change their condition; the woof of time is every instant broken and the track of generations effaced. Those who went before are soon forgotten; of those who will come after, no one has any idea: the interest of man is confined to those in close propinquity to himself. As each class gradually approaches others and mingles with them, its members become undifferentiated and lose their class identity for each other. Aristocracy had made a chain of all the members of the community, from the peasant to the king; democracy breaks that chain and severs every link of it.

As social conditions become more equal, the number of persons increases who, although they are neither rich nor powerful enough to exercise any great influence over their fellows, have nevertheless acquired or retained sufficient education and fortune to satisfy their own wants. They owe nothing to any man, they expect nothing from any man; they acquire the habit of always considering themselves as standing alone, and they are apt to imagine that their whole destiny is in their own hands.

Thus not only does democracy make every man forget his ancestors, but it hides his descendants and separates his contemporaries from him; it throws him back forever upon himself alone and threatens in the end to confine him entirely within the solitude of his own heart.

Friedrich Nietzsche (1844–1900)

German philosopher and philologist. From the second of his *Untimely Meditations* (1874), the distinctions Nietzsche draws here among monumental, antiquarian, and critical history characterize his skeptical attitude to both the nationalist's involvement with history and the historian's cool detachment from it. His comment that "the past has to be forgotten if it is not to become the gravedigger of the present" is a touchstone for many contemporary critics of the late twentieth-century "memory boom."

From "On the Uses and Disadvantages of History for Life"

Consider the cattle, grazing as they pass you by: they do not know what is meant by yesterday or today, they leap about, eat, rest, digest, leap about again, and so from morn till night and from day to day, fettered to the moment and its pleasure or displeasure, and thus neither melancholy nor bored. This is a hard sight for man to see; for, though he thinks himself better than the animals because he is human, he cannot help envying them their happiness—what they have, a life neither bored nor painful, is precisely what he wants, yet he cannot have it because he refuses to be like an animal. A human being may well ask an animal: 'Why do you not speak to me of your happiness but only stand and gaze at me?' The animal would like to answer, and say: 'The reason is I always forget what I was going to say'—but then he forgot this answer too, and stayed silent: so that the human being was left wondering.

But he also wonders at himself, that he cannot learn to forget but clings relentlessly to the past: however far and fast he may run, this chain runs with him. And it is a matter for wonder: a moment, now here and then gone, nothing before it came, again nothing after it has gone, nonetheless returns as a ghost and disturbs the peace a later moment. A leaf flutters from the scroll of time, floats away—and suddenly floats back again and falls into the man's lap. Then the man says 'I remember' and envies the animal, who at once forgets and for whom every moment really dies, sinks back into night and fog and is extinguished for ever. Thus the animal lives *unhistorically*: for it is contained in the present, like a number without any awkward fraction left over; it does not know how to dissimulate, it conceals nothing and at every instant appears wholly as what it is; it can therefore never be anything but honest. Man, on the other hand, braces himself against the great and ever greater pressure of what is past: it pushes him down or bends him sideways, it encumbers his steps as a dark, invisible burden which he can sometimes appear to disown and which in traffic with his fellow men he is only too glad to disown, so as to excite their envy. That is why it affects him like a vision of a lost paradise to see the herds grazing or, in closer proximity to him, a child which, having as yet nothing of the past to shake off, plays in blissful blindness between the hedges of past and future. Yet its play must be disturbed; all too soon it will be called out of its state of forgetfulness. Then it will learn to understand the phrase 'it was:' that pass-word which gives conflict, suffering and satiety access to man so as to remind him what his existence fundamentally is—an imperfect tense that can never become a perfect one. If death at last brings the desired forgetting, by that act it at the same time extinguishes the present and all existence and therewith sets the seal on the knowledge that existence is only an uninterrupted has-been, a thing that lives by negating, consuming and contradicting itself.

If happiness, if reaching out for new happiness, is in any sense what fetters living creatures to life and makes them go on living, then perhaps no philosopher is more justified than the Cynic: for the happiness of the animal, as the perfect Cynic, is the living proof of the rightness of Cynicism. The smallest happiness, if only it is present uninterruptedly and makes happy, is incomparably more happiness than the greatest happiness that comes only as an episode, as it were a piece of waywardness or folly, in a continuum of joy-lessness, desire and privation. In the case of the smallest or of the greatest happiness, however, it is always the same thing that makes happiness happi-ness: the ability to forget or, expressed in more scholarly fashion, the capacity to feel *unhistorically* during its duration. He who cannot sink down on the threshold of the moment and forget all the past, who cannot stand balanced like a goddess of victory without growing dizzy and afraid, will never know what happiness is—worse, he will never do anything to make others happy. Imagine the extremest possible example of a man who did not possess the power of forgetting at all and who was thus condemned to see everywhere a state of becoming: such a man would no longer believe in his own being, would no longer believe in himself, would see everything flowing asunder in moving points and would lose himself in this stream of becoming: like a true pupil of Heraclitus, he would in the end hardly dare to raise his finger. Forget-ting is essential to action of any kind, just as not only light but darkness too is essential for the life of everything organic. A man who wanted to feel histor-ically through and through would be like one forcibly deprived of sleep, or an animal that had to live only by rumination and ever repeated rumination. Thus: it is possible to live almost without memory, and to live happily more-over, as the animal demonstrates; but it is altogether impossible to *live* at all without forgetting. Or, to express my theme even more simply: *there is a degree of sleeplessness, of rumination, of the historical sense, which is harmful and ultimately fatal to the living thing, whether this living thing be a man or a people or a culture.*

To determine this degree, and therewith the boundary at which the past has to be forgotten if it is not to become the gravedigger of the present, one would have to know of exactly how great the *plastic power* of a man, a people, a culture is: I mean by plastic power the capacity to develop out of oneself in one's own way, to transform and incorporate into oneself what is past and foreign, to heal wounds, to replace what has been lost, to recreate broken moulds. There are people who possess so little of this power that they can perish from a single experience, from a single painful event, often and especially from a single subtle piece of injustice, like a man bleeding to death from a scratch; on the other hand, there are those who are so little affected by the worst and most dreadful disasters, and even by their own wicked acts, that they are able to feel tolerably well and be in possession of a kind of clear conscience even in the midst of them or at any rate very soon afterwards. The stronger the innermost roots of a man's nature, the more readily will he be able to assimilate and appropriate the things of the past; and the most powerful and tremendous nature would be characterized by the fact that it would know no boundary at all at which the historical sense began to overwhelm it; it would draw to itself and incorporate into itself all the past, its own and that most foreign to it, and as it were transform it into blood. That which such a nature cannot subdue it knows how to forget; it no longer exists, the horizon is rounded and closed, and there is nothing left to suggest there are people, passions, teachings, goals lying beyond it. And this is a universal law: a living thing can be healthy, strong and fruitful only when bounded by a horizon; if it is incapable of drawing a horizon around itself, and at the same time too self-centred to enclose its own view within that of another, it will pine away slowly or hasten to its timely end. Cheerfulness, the good conscience, the joyful deed, confidence in the future— all of them depend, in the case of the individual as of a nation, on the existence of a line dividing the bright and discernible from the unilluminable and dark; on one's being just as able to forget at the right time as to remember at the right time; on the possession of a powerful instinct for sensing when it is necessary to feel historically and when unhistorically. This, precisely, is the proposition the reader is invited to meditate upon: *the unhistorical and the historical are necessary in equal measure for the health of an individual, of a people and of a culture.* . . .

That life is in need of the services of history . . . must be grasped as firmly as must the proposition, which is to be demonstrated later, that an excess of history is harmful to the living man. History pertains to the living man in three respects: it pertains to him as a being who acts and strives, as a being who preserves and reveres, as a being who suffers and seeks deliverance. This three-fold relationship corresponds to three species of history—insofar as it is per-missible to distinguish between a *monumental,* an *antiquarian* and a *critical* species of history.

History belongs above all to the man of deeds and power, to him who fights a great fight, who needs models, teachers, comforters and cannot find them among his contemporaries. . . .

As long as the soul of historiography lies in the great *stimuli* that a man of power derives from it, as long as the past has to be described as worthy of imitation, as imitable and possible for a second time, it of course incurs the danger of becoming somewhat distorted, beautified and coming close to free poetic invention; there have been ages, indeed, which were quite incapable of distinguishing between a monumentalized past and a mythical fiction, because precisely the same stimuli can be derived from the one world as from the other. If, therefore, the monumental mode of regarding history *rules* over the other modes—I mean over the antiquarian and critical—the past itself suffers *harm:* whole segments of it are forgotten, despised, and flow away in an uninterrupted colourless flood, and only individual embellished facts rise out of it like islands: the few personalities who are visible at all have something strange and unnatural about them, like the golden hip which the pupils of Pythagoras supposed they saw on their master. Monumental history deceives by analogies: with seductive similarities it inspires the courageous to foolhardiness and the inspired to fanaticism; and when we go on to think of this kind of history in the hands and heads of gifted egoists and visionary scoundrels, then we see empires destroyed, princes murdered, wars and revolutions launched and the number of historical 'effects in themselves,' that is to say, effects without sufficient cause, again augmented. So much as a reminder of the harm that monumental history can do among men of power and achievement, whether they be good men or evil: what, however, is it likely to do when the impotent and indolent take possession of it and employ it! . . .

Sometimes this clinging to one's own environment and companions, one's own toilsome customs, one's own bare mountainside, looks like obstinacy and ignorance—yet it is a very salutary ignorance and one most calculated to further the interests of the community: a fact of which anyone must be aware who knows the dreadful consequences of the desire for expeditions and adventures, especially when it seizes whole hordes of nations, and who has seen from close up the condition a nation gets into when it has ceased to be faithful to its own origins and is given over to a restless, cosmopolitan hunting after new and ever newer things. The feeling antithetical to this, the contentment of the tree in its roots, the happiness of knowing that one is not wholly accidental and arbitrary but grown out of a past as its heir, flower and fruit, and that one's existence is thus excused and, indeed, justified—it is this which is today usually designated as the real sense of history. . . .

This always produces one very imminent danger: everything old and past that enters one's field of vision at all is in the end blandly taken to be equally worthy of reverence, while everything that does not approach this antiquity with reverence, that is to say everything new and evolving, is rejected and persecuted. . . .

When the senses of a people harden in this fashion, when the study of history serves the life of the past in such a way that it undermines continuing and especially higher life, when the historical sense no longer conserves life but mummifies it, then the tree gradually dies unnaturally from the top downwards to the roots—and in the end the roots themselves usually perish too. Antiquarian history itself degenerates from the moment it is no longer animated and inspired by the fresh life of the present. Its piety withers away, the habit of scholarliness continues without it and rotates in egoistic self-satisfaction around its own axis. Then there appears the repulsive spectacle of a blind rage for collecting, a restless raking together of everything that has ever existed. Man is encased in the stench of must and mould; through the antiquarian approach he succeeds in reducing even a more creative disposition, a nobler desire, to an insatiable thirst for novelty, or rather for antiquity and for all and everything; often he sinks so low that in the end he is content to gobble down any food whatever, even the dust of bibliographical minutiae.

But even when this degeneration does not take place, when antiquarian history does not lose the foundation in which alone it must be rooted if it is to benefit life, sufficient dangers remain should it grow too mighty and overpower the other modes of regarding the past. For it knows only how to *preserve* life, not how to engender it; it always undervalues that which is becoming because it has no instinct for divining it—as monumental history, for example, has. Thus it hinders any firm resolve to attempt something new, thus it paralyses the man of action who, as one who acts, will and must offend some piety or other. . . .

Here it becomes clear how necessary it is to mankind to have, beside the monumental and antiquarian modes of regarding the past, a *third* mode, the *critical:* and this, too, in the service of life. If he is to live, man must possess and from time to time employ the strength to break up and dissolve a part of the past: he does this by bringing it before the tribunal, scrupulously examining it and finally condemning it; every past, however, is worthy to be condemned—for that is the nature of human things: human violence and weakness have always played a mighty role in them. It is not justice which here sits in judgment; it is even less mercy which pronounces the verdict: it is life alone, that dark, driving power that insatiably thirsts for itself. Its sentence is always unmerciful, always unjust, because it has never proceeded out of a pure well of knowledge; but in most cases the sentence would be the same even if it were pronounced by justice itself. 'For all that exists is *worthy* of perishing. So it would be better if nothing existed.' It requires a great deal of strength to be able to live and to forget the extent to which to live and to be unjust is one and the same thing. Luther himself once opined that the world existed only through a piece of forgetful negligence on God's part: for if God had foreseen 'heavy artillery' he would not have created the world. Sometimes, however, this same life that requires forgetting demands a temporary suspension of this forgetfulness; it wants to be clear as to how unjust the existence of anything— a privilege, a caste, a dynasty, for example—is, and how greatly this thing deserves to perish. Then its past is regarded critically, then one takes the knife to its roots, then one cruelly tramples over every kind of piety. It is always a dangerous process, especially so for life itself: and men and ages which serve life by judging and destroying a past are always dangerous and endangered men and ages. For since we are the outcome of earlier generations, we are also the outcome of their aberrations, passions and errors, and indeed of their crimes; it is not possible wholly to free oneself from this chain. If we condemn these aberrations and regard ourselves as free of them, this does not alter the fact that we originate in them. The best we can do is to confront our inherited and hereditary nature with our knowledge, and through a new, stern discipline combat our inborn heritage and inplant in ourselves a new habit, a new instinct, a second nature, so that our first nature withers away. It is an attempt to give oneself, as it were *a posteriori*, a past in which one would like to originate in opposition to that in which one did originate:—always a dangerous attempt because it is so hard to know the limit to denial of the past and because second natures are usually weaker than first. What happens all too often is that we know the good but do not do it, because we also know the better but cannot do it. But here and there a victory is nonetheless achieved, and for the combatants, for those who employ critical history for the sake of life, there is even a noteworthy consolation: that of knowing that this first nature was once a second nature and that every victorious second nature will become a first. . . .

These are the services history is capable of performing for life; every man and every nation requires, in accordance with its goals, energies and needs, a certain kind of knowledge of the past, now in the form of monumental, now of antiquarian, now of critical history: but it does not require it as a host of pure thinkers who only look on at life, of knowledge-thirsty individuals whom knowledge alone will satisfy and to whom the accumulation of knowledge is itself the goal, but always and only for the ends of life and thus also under the domination and supreme direction of these ends. That this is the natural relationship of an age, a culture, a nation with its history—evoked by hunger, regulated by the extent of its need, held in bounds by its inherent plastic powers—that knowledge of the past has at all times been desired only in the service of the future and the present and not for the weakening of the present or for depriving a vigorous future of its roots: all this is simple, as the truth is simple, and will at once be obvious even to him who has not had it demonstrated by historical proof. . . .

The oversaturation of an age with history seems to me to be hostile and dangerous to life in five respects: such an excess creates that contrast between inner and outer which we have just discussed, and thereby weakens the personality; it leads an age to imagine that it possesses the rarest of virtues, justice, to a greater degree than any other age; it disrupts the instincts of a people, and hinders the individual no less than the whole in the attainment of maturity; it implants the belief, harmful at any time, in the old age of mankind, the belief that one is a latecomer and epigone; it leads an age into a dangerous mood of irony in regard to itself and subsequently into the even more dangerous mood of cynicism: in this mood, however, it develops more and more a prudent practical egoism through which the forces of life are paralyzed and at last destroyed. . . .

We know, indeed, what history can do when it gains a certain ascendancy, we know it only too well: it can cut off the strongest instincts of youth, its fire, defiance, unselfishness and love, at the roots, damp down the heat of its sense of justice, suppress or regress its desire to mature slowly with the counter-desire to be ready, useful, fruitful as quickly as possible, cast morbid doubt on its honesty and boldness of feeling; indeed, it can even deprive youth of its fairest privilege, of its power to implant in itself the belief in a great idea and then let it grow to an even greater one. A certain excess of history can do all this, we have seen it do it: and it does it by continually shifting horizons and removing a protective atmosphere and thus preventing man from feeling and acting *unhistorically*. . . .

With the word 'the unhistorical' I designate the art and power of *forgetting* and of enclosing oneself within a bounded *horizon*; I call 'suprahistorical' the powers which lead the eye away from becoming towards that which bestows upon existence the character of the eternal and stable, towards *art* and *religion*. *Science*—for it is science which would here speak of poisons—sees in these two forces hostile forces: for science considers the only right and true way of regarding things, that is to say the only scientific way, as being that which sees everywhere things that have been, things historical, and nowhere things that are, things eternal; it likewise lives in a profound antagonism towards the eternalizing powers of art and religion, for it hates forgetting, which is the death of knowledge, and seeks to abolish all limitations of horizon and launch mankind upon an infinite and unbounded sea of light whose light is knowledge of all becoming.

If only man could live in it! As cities collapse and grow desolate when there is an earthquake and man erects his house on volcanic land only in fear and trembling and only briefly, so life itself caves in and grows weak and fearful when the *concept-quake* caused by science robs man of the foundation of all his rest and security, his belief in the enduring and eternal. Is life to dominate knowledge and science, or is knowledge to dominate life? Which of these two forces is the higher and more decisive? There can be no doubt: life is the higher, the dominating force, for knowledge which annihilated life would have annihilated itself with it. Knowledge presupposes life and thus has in the preservation of life the same interest as any creature has in its own continued existence. Thus science requires superintendence and supervision; a *hygiene of life* belongs close beside science and one of the clauses of this hygiene would read: the unhistorical and the suprahistorical are the natural antidotes to the stifling of life by the historical, by the malady of history. It is probable that we who suffer from the malady of history will also have to suffer from the antidotes. But that we suffer from them is no evidence against the correctness of the chosen treatment.

Ernest Renan (1856–1892)

French philosopher and political writer. Due in part to the popularity of Benedict Anderson's (1983) book *Imagined Communities*, in which it was quoted prominently, Renan's
essay "What Is a Nation?" (1882) has become a standard reference not only in studies
of nationalism, but for memory studies as well. Rejecting assumptions that national
identities are natural or unquestionable, Renan called attention to the role of narrative,
in particular the balance between remembering and forgetting, in the ongoing production and reproduction of national identities.

From "What Is a Nation?"

Forgetting, I would even go so far as to say historical error, is a crucial factor in
the creation of a nation, which is why progress in historical studies often constitutes a danger for [the principle of] nationality. Indeed, historical enquiry
brings to light deeds of violence which took place at the origin of all political
formations, even of those whose consequences have been altogether beneficial.
Unity is always effected by means of brutality; the union of northern France
with the Midi was the result of massacres and terror lasting for the best part of
a century. Though the king of France was, if I may make so bold as to say,
almost the perfect instance of an agent that crystallized (a nation) over a long
period; though he established the most perfect national unity that there has
ever been, too searching a scrutiny had destroyed his prestige. The nation
which he had formed has cursed him, and, nowadays, it is only men of culture
who know something of his former value and of his achievements.

Yet the essence of a nation is that all individuals have many things in
common; and also that they have forgotten many things. No French citizen
knows whether he is a Burgundian, an Alan, a Taifale, or a Visigoth, yet every
French citizen has to have forgotten the massacre of Saint Bartholomew, or the
massacres that took place in the Midi in the thirteenth century. There are not
ten families in France that can supply proof of their Frankish origin, and any
such proof would anyway be essentially flawed, as a consequence of countless
unknown alliances which are liable to disrupt any genealogical system.

The modern nation is therefore a historical result brought about by a series
of convergent facts. Sometimes unity has been effected by a dynasty, as was the
case in France; sometimes it has been brought about by the direct will of provinces, as was the case with Holland, Switzerland, and Belgium; sometimes it
has been the work of a general consciousness, belatedly victorious over the
caprices of feudalism, as was the case in Italy and Germany. These formations
always had a profound *raison d'être*. Principles, in such cases, always emerge
through the most unexpected surprises.

But what is a nation? Why is Holland a nation, when Hanover, or the Grand
Duchy of Parma, are not? How is it that France continues to be a nation, when

the principle which created it has disappeared? How is it that Switzerland, which has three languages, two religions, and three or four races, is a nation, when Tuscany, which is so homogeneous, is not one? Why is Austria a state and not a nation? In what ways does the principle of nationality differ from that of races? These are points that a thoughtful person would wish to have settled, in order to put his mind at rest. The affairs of this world can hardly be said to be ruled by reasonings of this sort, yet diligent men are desirous of bringing some reason into these matters and of unravelling the confusions in which superficial intelligences are entangled.

If one were to believe some political theorists, a nation is above all a dynasty, representing an earlier conquest, one which was first of all accepted, and then forgotten by the mass of the people. According to the above-mentioned theorists, the grouping of provinces effected by a dynasty, by its wars, its marriages, and its treaties, ends with the dynasty which had established it. It is quite true that the majority of modern nations were made by a family of feudal origin, which had contracted a marriage with the soil and which was in some sense a nucleus of centralization.

It must therefore be admitted that a nation can exist without a dynastic principle, and even that nations which have been formed by dynasties can be separated from them without therefore ceasing to exist. The old principle, which only takes account of the right of princes, could no longer be maintained; apart from dynastic right, there is also national right. Upon what criterion, however, should one base this national right? By what sign should one know it? From what tangible fact can one derive it?

Several confidently assert that it is derived from race. The artificial divisions, resulting from feudalism, from princely marriages, from diplomatic congresses are, [these authors assert], in a state of decay. It is a population's race which remains firm and fixed. This is what constitutes a right, a legitimacy. The Germanic family, according to the theory I am expounding here, has the right to reassemble the scattered limbs of the Germanic order, even when these limbs are not asking to be joined together again. The right of the Germanic order over such-and-such a province is stronger than the right of the inhabitants of that province over themselves. There is thus created a kind of primordial right analogous to the divine right of kings; an ethnographic principle is substituted for a national one. This is a very great error, which, if it were to become dominant, would destroy European civilization. The primordial right of races is as narrow and as perilous for genuine progress as the national principle is just and legitimate.

What we have just said of race applies to language too. Language invites people to unite, but it does not force them to do so. The United States and England, Latin America and Spain, speak the same languages yet do not form single nations. Conversely, Switzerland, so well made, since she was made with the consent of her different parts, numbers three or four languages. There is something in man which is superior to language, namely, the will. The will of Switzerland to be united, in spite of the diversity of her dialects, is a fact of far greater importance than a similitude often obtained by various vexatious measures.

An honourable fact about France is that she has never sought to win unity of language by coercive measures. Can one not have the same sentiments and the same thoughts, and love the same things in different languages? I was speaking just now of the disadvantages of making international politics depend upon ethnography; they would be no less if one were to make it depend upon comparative philology. Let us allow these intriguing studies full freedom of discussion; let us not mix them up with matters which would undermine their serenity. The political importance attaching to languages derives from their being regarded as signs of race. . . .

A community of interest is assuredly a powerful bond between men. Do interests, however, suffice to make a nation? I do not think so. Community of interest brings about trade agreements, but nationality has a sentimental side to it; it is both soul and body at once; a *Zollverein* is not a *patrie*.

Geography, or what are known as natural frontiers, undoubtedly plays a considerable part in the division of nations. Geography is one of the crucial factors in history. Rivers have led races on; mountains have brought them to a halt. The former have favoured movement in history, whereas the latter have restricted it. Can one say, however, that as some parties believe, a nation's frontiers are written on the map and that this nation has the right to judge what is necessary to round off certain contours, in order to reach such and such a mountain and such and such a river, which are thereby accorded a kind of *a priori* limiting faculty? I know of no doctrine which is more arbitrary or more fatal, for it allows one to justify any or every violence. . . .

A nation is a soul, a spiritual principle. Two things, which in truth are but one, constitute this soul or spiritual principle. One lies in the past, one in the present. One is the possession in common of a rich legacy of memories; the other is present-day consent, the desire to live together, the will to perpetuate the value of the heritage that one has received in an undivided form. Man, Gentlemen, does not improvise. The nation, like the individual, is the culmination of a long past of endeavours, sacrifice, and devotion. Of all cults, that of the ancestors is the most legitimate, for the ancestors have made us what we are. A heroic past, great men, glory (by which I understand genuine glory), this is the social capital upon which one bases a national idea. To have common glories in the past and to have a common will in the present; to have performed great deeds together, to wish to perform still more—these are the essential conditions for being a people. One loves in proportion to the sacrifices to which one has consented, and in proportion to the ills that one has suffered. One loves the house that one has built and that one has handed down. The Spartan song— "We are what you were; we, will be what you are"—is, in its simplicity, the abridged hymn of every patrie.

More valuable by far than common customs posts and frontiers conforming to strategic ideas is the fact of sharing, in the past, a glorious heritage and regrets, and of having, in the future, [a shared] programme to put into effect, or the fact of having suffered, enjoyed, and hoped together. These are the kinds of things that can be understood in spite of differences of race and language. I spoke just now of "having suffered together" and, indeed, suffering in common unifies more than joy does. Where national memories are concerned, griefs are of more value than triumphs, for they impose duties, and require a common effort.

A nation is therefore a large-scale solidarity, constituted by the feeling of the sacrifices that one has made in the past and of those that one is prepared to make in the future. It presupposes a past; it is summarized, however, in the present by a tangible fact, namely, consent, the clearly expressed desire to continue a common life. A nation's existence is, if you will pardon the metaphor, a daily plebiscite, just as an individual's existence is a perpetual affirmation of life. That, I know full well, is less metaphysical than divine right and less brutal than so-called historical right. According to the ideas that I am outlining to you, a nation has no more right than a king does to say to a province: "You belong to me, I am seizing you." A province, as far as I am concerned, is its inhabitants; if anyone has the right to be consulted in such an affair, it is the inhabitant. A nation never has any real interest in annexing or holding on to a country against its will. The wish of nations is, all in all, the sole legitimate criterion, the one to which one must always return.

Sigmund Freud (1856–1939)

Viennese physician and founding father of psychoanalysis. Despite his principal association with psychology, Freud was a *social* thinker of the first order. Through a number of
major works, including "Group Psychology and the Analysis of the Ego" (1921) and *Civilization and Its Discontents* (1930), Freud explored sociological and anthropological
themes directly. In both *Totem and Taboo* (1913) and *Moses and Monotheism* (1939), from
which the following two excerpts are drawn, Freud addresses the issue of collective
memory, asking how repressed memories could be handed down in societies through
the ages rather than simply in individual minds over a lifetime, thus posing a central
problem for later theorists of cultural memory like **Yerushalmi** and **J. Assmann**, among
many others.

From *Totem and Taboo: Resemblances between the Psychic Lives of Savages and Neurotics*

Without the assumption of a mass psyche, or a continuity in the emotional life
of mankind which permits us to disregard the interruptions of psychic acts
through the transgression of individuals, social psychology could not exist at
all. If psychic processes of one generation did not continue to the next, if each
had to acquire its attitude towards life afresh, there would be no progress in
this field and almost no development. We are now confronted by two new questions: how much can be attributed to this psychic continuity within the series
of generations, and what ways and means does a generation use to transfer its
psychic states to the next generation? I do not claim that these problems have
been sufficiently explained or that direct communication and tradition, of
which one immediately thinks, are adequate for the task. Social psychology is
in general little concerned with the manner in which the required continuity in
the psychic life of succeeding generations is established. A part of the task
seems to be performed by the inheritance of psychic dispositions which, however, need certain incentives in the individual life in order to become effective.
This may be the meaning of the poet's words: Strive to possess yourself of what
you have inherited from your ancestors. The problem would appear more
difficult if we could admit that there are psychic impulses which can be so
completely suppressed that they leave no traces whatsoever behind them. But
that does not exist. The greatest suppression must leave room for distorted
substitutions and their resulting reactions. But in that case we may assume
that no generation is capable of concealing its more important psychic processes from the next. For psychoanalysis has taught us that in his unconscious
psychic activity every person possesses an apparatus which enables him to
interpret the reactions of others, that is to say to straighten out the distortions
which the other person has affected in the expression of his feelings. By this
method of unconscious understanding of all customs, ceremonies, and laws

which the original relation to the primal father had left behind, later generations may also have succeeded in taking over this legacy of feelings.

From *Moses and Monotheism*

I have more than once traced the events in Qadeš when the two components of
the later Jewish people combined in the acceptance of a new religion.
With those who had been in Egypt the memory of the Exodus and of the figure
of Moses was still so strong and vivid that it insisted on being incorporated
into any account of their early history. There might have been among them
grandsons of persons who themselves had known Moses, and some of them
still felt themselves to be Egyptians and bore Egyptian names. They had good
reasons, however, for "repressing" the memory of the fate that had befallen
their leader and lawgiver. For the other component of the tribe the leading
motive was to glorify the new God and deny his foreignness. Both parties were
equally concerned to deny that there had been an earlier religion and especially
what it contained. This is how the first compromise came about, which probably was soon codified in writing; the people from Egypt had brought with
them the art of writing and the fondness for writing history. A long time was to
elapse, however, before historians came to develop an ideal of objective truth.
At first they shaped their accounts according to their needs and tendencies of
the moment, with an easy conscience, as if they had not yet understood what
falsification signified. In consequence, a difference began to develop between
the written version and the oral report—that is, the tradition—of the same
subject-matter. What has been deleted or altered in the written version might
quite well have been preserved uninjured in the tradition. Tradition was the
complement and at the same time the contradiction of the written history. It
was less subject to distorting influences—perhaps in part entirely free from
them—and therefore might be more truthful than the account set down in
writing. Its trustworthiness, however, was impaired by being vaguer and more
fluid than the written text, being exposed to many changes and distortions as it
was passed on from one generation to the next by word of mouth. Such a tradition may have different outcomes. The most likely event would be for it to be
vanquished by the written version, ousted by it, until it grows more and more
shadowy and at last is forgotten. Another fate might be that the tradition itself
ends by becoming a written version. There are other possibilities which will be
mentioned later.

The phenomenon of the latency period in the history of the Jewish religion
may find its explanation in this: the facts which the so-called official written
history purposely tried to suppress were in reality never lost. The knowledge of
them survived in traditions which were kept alive among the people. According
to Ernst Sellin, there even existed a tradition concerning the end of Moses which
contradicted outright the official account and came far nearer the truth. The
same thing, we may suppose, happened with other beliefs that had apparently

found an end at the same time as Moses, doctrines of the Mosaic religion that had been unacceptable to the majority of Moses' contemporaries.

Here we meet with a remarkable fact. It is that these traditions, instead of growing weaker as time went on, grew more and more powerful in the course of centuries, found their way into the later codifications of the official accounts, and at last proved themselves strong enough decisively to influence the thought and activity of the people. What the conditions were that made such a development possible seems, however, far from evident.

This fact is indeed strange, so much so that we feel justified in examining it afresh. Within it our problem lies. The Jewish people had abandoned the Aton religion which Moses had given them and had turned to the worship of another god who differed little from the Baalim of the neighbouring tribes. All the efforts of later distorting influences failed to hide this humiliating fact. Yet the religion of Moses did not disappear without leaving any trace; a kind of memory of it had survived, a tradition perhaps obscured and distorted. It was this tradition of a great past that continued to work in the background, until it slowly gained more and more power over the mind of the people and at last succeeded in transforming the God Jahve into the Mosaic God and in waking to a new life the religion which Moses had instituted centuries before and which had later been forsaken. That a dormant tradition should exert such a powerful influence on the spiritual life of a people is not a familiar conception. There we find ourselves in a domain of mass psychology where we do not feel at home. We must look around for analogies, for facts of a similar nature even if in other fields. We shall find them I am sure.

When the time was ripening for a return of the religion of Moses, the Greek people possessed an exceptionally rich treasure of legends and myths of heroes. It is believed that the ninth or eighth century. B.C. saw the creation of the Homeric epics, which derived their material from this complex of myths. With our psychological knowledge of today we could long before Schliemann and Evans have put the question: Whence did the Greeks obtain all this material of myths and legends which Homer and the great Attic dramatists transformed into immortal works of art? The answer would have had to be: This people probably passed in its early history through a period of outward splendour and highly developed culture which ended in catastrophe—as, indeed, history tells—and of which a faint tradition lived on in these legends. Archæological research of our day has confirmed this suggestion, which if made earlier would surely have been considered too bold. It has discovered the evidence of the grandiose Minoan-Mycenæan culture, which had probably already come to an end on the Greek mainland by 1250 B.C. The Greek historians of a later period hardly ever refer to it. There is the remark that there was a time when the Cretans ruled the sea, a mention of the name of King Minos and his palace, and of the labyrinth; but that is all. Nothing remained of that great time but the traditions seized upon by the great writers.

Other peoples also possess such folk-epics—for example, the Indians, Finns, and Germans. It is for the literary historian to investigate whether the same conditions as with the Greeks applied there as well. I think that such an investigation

SIGMUND FREUD 87

would yield a positive result. The conditions we have specified for the origin of folk-epics are as follows: there exists a period of early history that immediately afterwards is regarded as eventful, significant, grandiose, and perhaps always heroic; yet it happened so long ago and belonged to time so remote that later generations receive intelligence of it only as an obscure and incomplete tradition. Surprise has been expressed that the epic as a literary form should have disappeared in later times. The explanation may be that the conditions for the production of epics no longer exist. The old material has been used up and, so far as later events are concerned, history has taken the place of tradition. The bravest heroic deeds of our days are no longer able to inspire an epic; Alexander the Great himself had grounds for his complaint that he would have no Homer to celebrate his life.

Remote times have a great attraction—sometimes mysteriously so—for the imagination. As often as mankind is dissatisfied with its present—and that happens often enough—it harks back to the past and hopes at last to win belief in the never forgotten dream of a Golden Age. Probably man still stands under the magic spell of his childhood, which a not unbiased memory presents to him as a time of unalloyed bliss. Incomplete and dim memories of the past, which we call tradition, are a great incentive to the artist, for he is free to fill in the gaps in the memories according to the behests of his imagination and to form after his own purpose the image of the time he has undertaken to reproduce. One might almost say that the more shadowy tradition has become, the more meet is it for the poet's use. The value tradition has for poetry, therefore, need not surprise us, and the analogy we have found of the dependence of epic poetry on precise conditions will make us more inclined to accept the strange suggestion that with the Jews it was the tradition of Moses that turned the Jahve-worship in the direction of the old Mosaic religion. The two cases, however, are very different in other respects. In the one the result is poetry, in the other a religion, and we have assumed that the latter—under the stimulus of a tradition—was reproduced with a faithfulness for which, of course, the epic cannot provide a parallel. Enough remains, therefore, of our problem to encourage a search for better analogies. . . .

I cannot reproduce here the contents of *Totem and Taboo*, but I must try to account for the long interval that took place between the events which I suggested happened in primeval times and the victory of monotheism in historical times. After the combination of brother clan, matriarchy, exogamy, and totemism had been established there began a development which may be described as a slow "return of the repressed." The term "repressed" is here used not in its technical sense. Here I mean something past, vanished, and overcome in the life of a people, which I venture to treat as equivalent to repressed material in the mental life of the individual. In what psychological form the past existed during its period of darkness we cannot as yet tell. It is not easy to translate the concepts of individual psychology into mass psychology, and I do not think that much is to be gained by introducing the concept of a "collective" unconscious—the content of the unconscious is collective anyhow, a general possession of mankind. So in the meantime the use of analogies must help us out. The processes we study here in the life of a people are very similar to those we know from psychopathology, but still they are not quite the same. We must conclude that the mental residue of those primeval times has become a heritage which, with each new generation, needs only to be awakened, not to be reacquired. We may think here of the example of speech symbolism, which certainly seems to be inborn. It originates in the time of speech-development, and it is familiar to all children without their having been specially instructed. It is the same in all people in spite of the differences in language. What we may still lack in certainty we may acquire from other results of psychoanalytic investigations. We learn that our children in a number of significant relationships do not react as their own experiences would lead us to expect, but instinctively, like animals; this is explicable only by phylogenetic inheritance.

Karl Marx (1818–1883)

German philosopher and political writer. First published in 1852, the essay from which these pages are drawn is hailed as Marx's most supple close reading of an historical event (the December 1851 coup of Louis Napoleon, nephew of the deposed emperor) and as evidence against the accusation that Marx was an historical determinist, particularly because of his statement here that "men make their own history, but they do not make it just as they please." Collective memory was not a central theme for Marx, though his analysis of commodities as social products that "forget their origins" has been taken by later theorists, for instance **Adorno**, as relevant to understanding the role of memory and forgetting in late capitalism. Marx's statement about "the tradition of all the dead generations," while something of a slogan, is also a pregnant insight for much subsequent political sociology of memory, among other enterprises.

From "The Eighteenth Brumaire of Louis Bonaparte"

Men make their own history, but they do not make it just as they please; they do not make it under circumstances chosen by themselves, but under circumstances directly found, given and transmitted from the past. The tradition of all the dead generations weighs like a nightmare on the brain of the living. And just when they seem engaged in revolutionising themselves and things, in creating something entirely new, precisely in such epochs of revolutionary crisis they anxiously conjure up the spirits of the past to their service and borrow from them names, battle slogans and costumes in order to present the new scene of world history in this time-honoured disguise and this borrowed language. Thus Luther donned the mask of the Apostle Paul, the Revolution of 1789 to 1814 draped itself alternately as the Roman Republic and the Roman Empire, and the Revolution of 1848 knew nothing better to do than to parody, in turn, 1789 and the revolutionary tradition of 1793 to 1795. In like manner the beginner who has learnt a new language always translates it back into his mother tongue, but he has assimilated the spirit of the new language and can produce freely in it only when he moves in it without remembering the old and forgets in it his ancestral tongue.

Consideration of this world-historical conjuring up of the dead reveals at once a salient difference. Camille Desmoulins, Danton, Robespierre, Saint-Just, Napoleon, the heroes, as well as the parties and the masses of the old French Revolution, performed the task of their time in Roman costume and with Roman phrases, the task of releasing and setting up modern *bourgeois* society. The first ones knocked the feudal basis to pieces and mowed off the feudal heads which had grown from it. The other created inside France the conditions under which free competition could first be developed, the parcelled landed property exploited, the unfettered productive power of the nation employed, and outside the French borders he everywhere swept the feudal formations away, so far as was necessary to furnish bourgeois society in France with a suitable up-to-date environment on the European Continent. The new social formation once established, the antediluvian Colossi disappeared and with them the resurrected Romans—the Brutuses, Gracchi, Publicolas, the tribunes, the senators and Caesar himself. Bourgeois society in its sober reality had begotten its true interpreters and mouthpieces in the Says, Cousins, Royer-Collards, Benjamin Constants and Guizots; its real military leaders sat behind the office desks, and the hogheaded Louis XVIII was its political chief. Wholly absorbed in the production of wealth and in the peaceful struggle of competition, it no longer comprehended that ghosts from the days of Rome had watched over its cradle. But unheroic as bourgeois society is, yet it had need of heroism, of sacrifice, of terror, of civil war and of national battles to bring it into being. And in the classically austere traditions of the Roman Republic its gladiators found the ideals and the art forms, the self-deceptions that they needed in order to conceal from themselves the bourgeois limitations of the content of their struggles and to keep their passion at the height of the great historical tragedy. Similarly, at another stage of development, a century earlier, Cromwell and the English people had borrowed speech, passions and illusions from the Old Testament for their bourgeois revolution. When the real aim had been achieved, when the bourgeois transformation of English society had been accomplished, Locke supplanted Habakkuk.

The awakening of the dead in those revolutions therefore served the purpose of glorifying the new struggles, not of parodying the old; of magnifying the given tasks in imagination, not of taking flight from their solution in reality; of finding once more the spirit of revolution, not of making its ghost walk again.

From 1848 to 1851 only the ghost of the old revolution walked, from Marrast, the *republicain en gants jaunes*, who disguised himself as the old Bailly, to the adventurer who hides his trivially repulsive features under the iron death mask of Napoleon. An entire people, which had imagined that by a revolution it had increased its power of action, suddenly finds itself set back into a dead epoch and, in order that no doubt as to the relapse may be possible, the old data again arise, the old chronology, the old names, the old edicts, which have long become a subject of antiquarian erudition, and the old henchmen, who had long seemed dead and decayed. The nation appears to itself like that mad Englishman in Bedlam, who fancies that he lives in the times of the ancient Pharaohs and daily bemoans the hard labour that he must perform in the Ethiopian mines as a gold digger, immured in this subterranean prison, a dimly burning lamp fastened to his head, the overseer of the slaves behind him with a long whip, and at the exits a confused mass of barbarian mercenaries, who understand neither the forced labourers in the mines nor one another, since they have no common speech. "And all this is expected of me," groans the mad Englishman, "of me, a free-born Briton, in order to make gold for the old Pharaohs." "In order to pay the debts of the Bonaparte family," sighs the French nation. The Englishman, so long as he was in his right mind, could not get rid of the fixed idea of making gold. The French, so long as they were engaged in revolution, could not get rid of the memory of Napoleon, as the election of December 10, 1848, proved. From the perils of revolution their longings went back to the flesh-pots of Egypt, and December 2, 1851, was the answer. They have not only a caricature of the old Napoleon, they have the old Napoleon himself, caricatured as he would inevitably appear in the middle of the nineteenth century.

The social revolution of the nineteenth century cannot draw its poetry from the past, but only from the future. It cannot begin with itself, before it has stripped off all superstition in regard to the past. Earlier revolutions required world-historical recollections in order to drug themselves concerning their own content. In order to arrive at its content, the revolution of the nineteenth century must let the dead bury their dead. There the phrase went beyond the content; here the content goes beyond the phrase.

Karl Mannheim (1893–1947)

Hungarian-German sociologist. A remarkably prolific scholar, credited as a founding father of the sociology of knowledge. Where Max Weber added status and party to Marx's class as fundamental units of social organization, here Mannheim articulates his seminal account of generations as social and cultural rather than biological units, the analysis of which is essential, Mannheim argues, to a complete sociological account. Generations, in his account, are constituted by memory of historical events experienced by those who were at formative ages during the event. As a result, different generations remember historical events differently. A central distinction for Mannheim is also between memories appropriated from earlier generations, and memories acquired personally. In this way, Mannheim draws a similar distinction to **Halbwachs**'s between autobiographical and historical memory, demonstrating that the field's conceptual history is more diverse than its memory has it.

From "The Sociological Problem of Generations"

The best way to appreciate which features of social life result from the existence of generations is to make the experiment of imagining what the social life of man would be like if one generation lived on for ever and none followed to replace it. In contrast to such a utopian, imaginary society, our own has the following characteristics:

(a) new participants in the cultural process are emerging, whilst
(b) former participants in that process are continually disappearing;
(c) members of any one generation can participate only in a temporally limited section of the historical process, and
(d) it is therefore necessary continually to transmit the accumulated cultural heritage;
(e) the transition from generation to generation is a continuous process.

These are the basic phenomena implied by the mere fact of the existence of generations. . . . With this as a beginning, let us then investigate the bearing of these elementary facts upon formal sociology. . . .

In contrast to the imaginary society with no generations, our own—in which generation follows generation—is principally characterized by the fact that cultural creation and cultural accumulation are not accomplished by the same individuals—instead, we have the continuous emergence of new age groups.

This means, in the first place, that our culture is developed by individuals who come into contact anew with the accumulated heritage. In the nature of our psychical make-up, a fresh contact (meeting something anew) always means a changed relationship of distance from the object and a novel approach in assimilating, using, and developing the proffered material. The phenomenon of "fresh contact" is, incidentally, of great significance in many social contexts;

the problem of generations is only one among those upon which it has a bearing. Fresh contacts play an important part in the life of the individual when he is forced by events to leave his own social group and enter a new one—when, for example, an adolescent leaves home, or a peasant the countryside for the town, or when an emigrant changes his home, or a social climber his social status or class. . . . In all these cases, however, the fresh contact is an event in one individual biography, whereas in the case of generations, we may speak of "fresh contacts" in the sense of the addition of new psycho-physical units who are in the literal sense beginning a "new life." Whereas the adolescent, peasant, emigrant, and social climber can only in a more or less restricted sense be said to begin a "new life," in the case of generations, the "fresh contact" with the social and cultural heritage is determined not by mere social change, but by fundamental biological factors. We can accordingly differentiate between two types of "fresh contact:" one based on a shift in social relations, and the other on vital factors (the change from one generation to another). The latter type is *potentially* much more radical, since with the advent of the new participant in the process of culture, the change of attitude takes place in a different individual whose attitude towards the heritage handed down by his predecessors is a novel one. . . .

The continuous emergence of new human beings certainly results in some loss of accumulated cultural possessions; but, on the other hand, it alone makes a fresh selection possible when it becomes necessary; it facilitates re-evaluation of our inventory and teaches us both to forget that which is no longer useful and to covet that which has yet to be won. . . .

The function of this second factor is implied in what has already been said. It serves the necessary social purpose of enabling us to forget. If society is to continue, social remembering is just as important as forgetting and action starting from scratch.

At this point we must make clear in what social form remembering manifests itself and how the cultural heritage is actually accumulated. All psychic and cultural data only really exist in so far as they are produced and reproduced in the present: hence past experience is only relevant when it exists concretely incorporated in the present. In our present context, we have to consider two ways in which past experience can be incorporated in the present:

(i) as consciously recognized models[1] on which men pattern their behaviour (for example, the majority of subsequent revolutions tended to model themselves more or less consciously on the French Revolution); or

---

1. This is not the place to enumerate all the many forms of social memory. We will therefore deliberately simplify the matter by limiting ourselves to two extreme alternatives. "Consciously recognized models" include, in the wider sense, also the body of global knowledge, stored in libraries. But this sort of knowledge is only effective in so far as it is continually actualized. This can happen in two ways—either intellectually, when it is used as a pattern or guide for action, or spontaneously, when it is "virtually present" as condensed experience.

Instinct, as well as repressed and unconscious knowledge, as dealt with in particular by Freud, would need separate treatment.

(ii)   as unconsciously "condensed," merely "implicit" or "virtual" patterns; consider, for instance, how past experiences are "virtually" contained in such specific manifestations as that of sentimentality. Every present performance operates a certain selection among handed-down data, for the most part unconsciously. That is, the traditional material is transformed to fit a prevailing new situation, or hitherto unnoticed or neglected potentialities inherent in that material are discovered in the course of developing new patterns of action.

At the more primitive levels of social life, we mostly encounter unconscious selection. There the past tends to be present in a "condensed," "implicit," and "virtual" form only. Even at the present level of social reality, we see this unconscious selection at work in the deeper regions of our intellectual and spiritual lives, where the tempo of transformation is of less significance. A conscious and reflective selection becomes necessary only when a semi-conscious transformation, such as can be effected by the traditionalist mind, is no longer sufficient. In general, rational elucidation and reflectiveness invade only those realms of experience which become problematic as a result of a change in the historical and social situation; where that is the case, the necessary transformation can no longer be effected without conscious reflec-tion and its technique of de-stabilization.

We are directly aware primarily of those aspects of our culture which have become subject to reflection; and these contain only those elements which in the course of development have somehow, at some point, become problematical. This is not to say, however, that once having become conscious and reflective, they cannot again sink back into the a-problematical, untouched region of vege-tative life. In any case, that form of memory which contains the past in the form of reflection is much less significant—e.g. it extends over a much more restricted range of experience—than that in which the past is only "implicitly," "virtually" present; and reflective elements are more often dependent on unreflective elements than *vice versa*.

Here we must make a fundamental distinction between *appropriated* mem-ories and *personally acquired* memories (a distinction applicable both to reflec-tive and unreflective elements). It makes a great difference whether I acquire memories for myself in the process of personal development, or whether I simply take them over from someone else. I only really possess those "mem-ories" which I have created directly for myself, only that "knowledge" I have personally gained in real situations. This is the only sort of knowledge which really "sticks" and it alone has real binding power. Hence, although it would appear desirable that man's spiritual and intellectual possessions should consist of nothing but individually acquired memories, this would also involve the danger that the earlier ways of possession and acquisition will inhibit the new acquisition of knowledge. That experience goes with age is in many ways an advantage. That, on the other hand, youth lacks experience means a light-ening of the ballast for the young; it facilitates their living on in a changing world. One is old primarily in so far as he comes to live within a specific, individually acquired, framework of useable past experience, so that every new experience has its form and its place largely marked out for it in advance. In youth, on the other hand, where life is new, formative forces are just coming into being, and basic attitudes in the process of development can take advantage of the moulding power of new situations. Thus a human race living on for ever would have to learn to forget to compensate for the lack of new generations. . . .

To be able to start afresh with a new life, to build a new destiny, a new framework of anticipations, upon a new set of experiences, are things which can come into the world only through the fact of new birth. All this is implied by the factor of social rejuvenation. The factor we are dealing with now, however, can be adequately analysed only in terms of the category of "similarity of location." . . .

Members of a generation are "similarly located," first of all, in so far as they all are exposed to the same phase of the collective process. This, however, is a merely mechanical and external criterion of the phenomenon of "similar location." For a deeper understanding, we must turn to the phenomenon of the "stratification"of experience (*Erlebnisschichtung*), just as before we turned to "memory." The fact that people are born at the same time, or that their youth, adulthood, and old age coincide, does not in itself involve similarity of location; what does create a similar location is that they are in a position to experience the same events and data, etc., and especially that these experiences impinge upon a similarly "stratified" consciousness. It is not difficult to see why mere chronological contemporaneity cannot of itself produce a common generation location. No one, for example, would assert that there was community of location between the young people of China and Germany about 1800. Only where contemporaries definitely are in a position to participate as an integrated group in certain common experiences can we rightly speak of community of location of a generation. Mere contemporaneity becomes sociologically significant only when it also involves participation in the same historical and social circumstances. Further, we have to take into consideration at this point the phenomenon of "stratification," mentioned above. Some older generation groups experience certain historical processes together with the young generation and yet we cannot say that they have the same generation location. The fact that their location is a different one, however, can be explained primarily by the different "stratification" of their lives. The human consciousness, structurally speaking, is characterized by a particular inner "dialectic." It is of considerable importance for the formation of the consciousness which experiences happen to make those all-important "first impressions," "childhood experiences"—and which follow to form the second, third, and other "strata." Conversely, in estimating the biographical significance of a particular experience, it is important to know whether it is undergone by an individual as a decisive childhood experience, or later in life, superimposed upon other basic and early impressions. Early impressions tend to coalesce into a *natural view* of the world. All later experiences then tend to receive their meaning from this original set, whether they appear as that set's verification and fulfilment or as its negation and antithesis.

Experiences are not accumulated in the course of a lifetime through a process of summation or agglomeration, but are "dialectically" articulated in the way described. We cannot here analyse the specific forms of this dialectical articulation, which is potentially present whenever we act, think, or feel, in more detail (the relationship of "antithesis" is only one way in which new experiences may graft themselves upon old ones). This much, however, is certain, that even if the rest of one's life consisted in one long process of negation and destruction of the natural world view acquired in youth, the determining influence of these early impressions would still be predominant. For even in negation our orientation is fundamentally centred upon that which is being negated, and we are thus still unwittingly determined by it. If we bear in mind that every concrete experience acquires its particular face and form from its relation to this primary stratum of experiences from which all others receive their meaning, we can appreciate its importance for the further development of the human consciousness. Another fact, closely related to the phenomenon just described, is that any two generations following one another always fight different opponents, both within and without. While the older people may still be combating something in themselves or in the external world in such fashion that all their feelings and efforts and even their concepts and categories of thought are determined by that adversary, for the younger people this adversary may be simply non-existent: their primary orientation is an entirely different one. That historical development does not proceed in a straight line—a feature frequently observed particularly in the cultural sphere— is largely attributed to this shifting of the "polar" components of life, that is, to the fact that internal or external adversaries constantly disappear and are replaced by others. . . .

Some structural facts which follow from this must at least be indicated here. To mention one problem only: a utopian, immortal society would not have to face this necessity of cultural transmission, the most important aspect of which is the automatic passing on to the new generations of the traditional ways of life, feelings, and attitudes. The data transmitted by conscious teaching are of more limited importance, both quantitatively and qualitatively. All those attitudes and ideas which go on functioning satisfactorily in the new situation and serve as the basic inventory of group life are unconsciously and unwittingly handed on and transmitted: they seep in without either the teacher or pupil knowing anything about it. What is consciously learned or inculcated belongs to those things which in the course of time have somehow, somewhere, become problematic and therefore invited conscious reflection. This is why that inventory of experience which is absorbed by infiltration from the environment in early youth often becomes the historically oldest stratum of consciousness, which tends to stabilize itself as the natural view of the world.

But in early childhood even many reflective elements are assimilated in the same "a-problematical" fashion as those elements of the basic inventory had been. The new germ of an original intellectual and spiritual life which is latent in the new human being has by no means as yet come into its own. The possibility of really questioning and reflecting on things only emerges at the point where personal experimentation with life begins—round about the age of 17, sometimes a little earlier and sometimes a little later. It is only then that life's problems begin to be located in a "present" and are experienced as such. That level of data and attitudes which social change has rendered problematical, and which therefore requires reflection, has now been reached; for the first time, one lives "in the present." Combative juvenile groups struggle to clarify these issues, but never realise that, however radical they are, they are merely out to transform the uppermost stratum of consciousness which is open to conscious reflection. For it seems that the deeper strata are not easily destabilized and that when this becomes necessary, the process must start out from the level of reflection and work down to the stratum of habits. The "up-to-dateness" of youth therefore consists in their being closer to the "present" problems . . . , and in the fact that they are dramatically aware of a process of de-stabilization and take sides in it. All this while, the older generation cling to the re-orientation that had been the drama of *their* youth.

From this angle, we can see that an adequate education or instruction of the young (in the sense of the complete transmission of all experiential stimuli which underlie pragmatic knowledge) would encounter a formidable difficulty in the fact that the experiential problems of the young are defined by a different set of adversaries from those of their teachers. Thus (apart from the exact sciences), the teacher-pupil relationship is not as between one representative of "consciousness in general" and another, but as between one possible subjective centre of vital orientation and another subsequent one. This tension appears incapable of solution except for one compensating factor: not only does the teacher educate his pupil, but the pupil educates his teacher too. Generations are in a state of constant interaction. . . .

The question now arises, what produces a generation unit? In what does the greater intensity of the bond consist in this case? The first thing that strikes one on considering any particular generation unit is the great similarity in the data making up the consciousness of its members. Mental data are of sociological importance not only because of their actual content, but also because they cause the individuals sharing them to form one group—they have a socializing effect. . . .

The data as such, however, are not the primary factor producing a group— this function belongs to a far greater extent to those formative forces which shape the data and give them character and direction. From the casual slogan to a reasoned system of thought, from the apparently isolated gesture to the finished work of art, the same formative tendency is often at work—the social importance of which lies in its power to bind individuals socially together. The profound emotional significance of a slogan, of an expressive gesture, or of a work of art lies in the fact that we not merely absorb them as objective data, but also as vehicles of formative tendencies and fundamental integrative attitudes, thus identifying ourselves with a set of collective strivings.

Fundamental integrative attitudes and formative principles are all-important also in the handing down of every tradition, firstly because they alone can bind groups together, secondly, and, what is perhaps even more important, they alone are really capable of becoming the basis of continuing practice. A mere statement of fact has a minimum capacity of initiating a continuing practice. Potentialities of a continued thought process, on the other hand, are contained in every thesis that has real group-forming potency; intuitions, feelings, and works of art which create a spiritual community among men also contain in themselves the potentially new manner in which the intuition, feeling, or work of art in question can be re-created, rejuvenated and re-interpreted in novel situations. That is why unambiguousness, too great clarity is not an unqualified social value; productive misunderstanding is often a condition of continuing life. Fundamental integrative attitudes and formative principles are the primary socializing forces in the history of society, and it is necessary to live them fully in order really to participate in collective life. . . .

To become really assimilated into a group involves more than the mere acceptance of its characteristic values—it involves the ability to see things from its particular "aspect," to endow concepts with its particular shade of meaning, and to experience psychological and intellectual impulses in the configuration characteristic of the group. It means, further, to absorb those interpretive formative principles which enable the individual to deal with new impressions and events in a fashion broadly pre-determined by the group.

The social importance of these formative and interpretive principles is that they form a link between spatially separated individuals who may never come into personal contact at all. Whereas mere common "location" in a generation is of only potential significance, a generation as an actuality is constituted when similarly "located" contemporaries participate in a common destiny and in the ideas and concepts which are in some way bound up with its unfolding. Within this community of people with a common destiny there can then arise particular *generation-units*. These are characterized by the fact that they do not merely involve a loose participation by a number of individuals in a pattern of events shared by all alike though interpreted by the different individuals differently, but an identity of responses, a certain affinity in the way in which all move with and are formed by their common experiences.

Walter Benjamin (1892–1940)

German cultural critic. For many of his readers, Benjamin was the philosopher of modernity par excellence, though his positions are difficult to pigeonhole, as they range from the politically radical to the religiously messianic. In this evocative essay (1936), Benjamin highlights the changing conditions of temporality, and hence of storytelling, with the rise of modern culture: we have moved, he writes, from a society that values wisdom to one that floods us with "information." With a refined Marxist undertone, he attributes this transformation to "the secular productive forces of history." He also writes here about the narrative and existential implications of trench warfare in World War I, after which "men returned from the battlefield grown silent—not richer but poorer in communicable experience." We also append here Benjamin's perhaps most famous aphorism, his ninth "Thesis on the Philosophy of History," in which he characterized "the angel of history" as one whose gaze is directed resolutely toward the wreckage it leaves in its wake, a rather dark inversion of Enlightenment hopes near the apogee of Benjamin's, and his society's, despair.

From "The Storyteller"

Familiar though his name may be to us, the storyteller in his living immediacy is by no means a present force. He has already become something remote from us and something that is getting even more distant. . . . This distance and this angle of vision are prescribed for us by an experience which we may have almost every day. It teaches us that the art of storytelling is coming to an end. Less and less frequently do we encounter people with the ability to tell a tale properly. More and more often there is embarrassment all around when the wish to hear a story is expressed. It is as if something that seemed inalienable to us, the securest among our possessions, were taken from us: the ability to exchange experiences.

One reason for this phenomenon is obvious: experience has fallen in value. And it looks as if it is continuing to fall into bottomlessness. Every glance at a newspaper demonstrates that it has reached a new low, that our picture, not only of the external world but of the moral world as well, overnight has undergone changes which were never thought possible. With the [First] World War a process began to become apparent which has not halted since then. Was it not noticeable at the end of the war that men returned from the battlefield grown silent—not richer, but poorer in communicable experience? What ten years later was poured out in the flood of war books was anything but experience that goes from mouth to mouth. And there was nothing remarkable about that. For never has experience been contradicted more thoroughly than strategic experience by tactical warfare, economic experience by inflation, bodily experience by mechanical warfare, moral experience by those in power. A generation that had gone to school on a horse-drawn streetcar now stood under the open sky in a countryside in which nothing remained unchanged but the clouds, and beneath these clouds, in a field of force of destructive torrents and explosions, was the tiny, fragile human body. . . .

An orientation toward practical interests is characteristic of many born storytellers. . . . This points to the nature of every real story. It contains, openly or covertly, something useful. The usefulness may, in one case, consist in a moral, in another, in some practical advice, in a third, in a proverb or maxim. In every case the storyteller is a man who has counsel for his readers. But if today "having counsel" is beginning to have an old-fashioned ring, this is because the communicability of experience is decreasing. In consequence we have no counsel either for ourselves or for others. After all, counsel is less an answer to a question than a proposal concerning the continuation of a story which is just unfolding. To seek this counsel one would first have to be able to tell the story. (Quite apart from the fact that a man is receptive to counsel only to the extent that he allows his situation to speak.) Counsel woven into the fabric of real life is wisdom. The art of storytelling is reaching its end because the epic side of truth, wisdom, is dying out. This, however, is a process that has been going on for a long time. And nothing would be more fatuous than to want to see in it merely a "symptom of decay," let alone a "modern" symptom. It is, rather, only a concomitant symptom of the secular productive forces of history, a concomitant that has quite gradually removed narrative from the realm of living speech and at the same time is making it possible to see a new beauty in what is vanishing. . . .

The earliest symptom of a process whose end is the decline of storytelling is the rise of the novel at the beginning of modern times. What distinguishes the novel from the story (and from the epic in the narrower sense) is its essential dependence on the book. The dissemination of the novel became possible only with the invention of printing. What can be handed on orally, the wealth of the epic, is of a different kind from what constitutes the stock in trade of the novel. What differentiates the novel from all other forms of prose literature—the fairy tale, the legend, even the novella—is that it neither comes from oral tradition nor goes into it. This distinguishes it from storytelling in particular. The storyteller takes what he tells from experience—his own or that reported by others. And he in turn makes it the experience of those who are listening to his tale. The novelist has isolated himself. The birthplace of the novel is the solitary individual, who is no longer able to express himself by giving examples of his most important concerns, is himself uncounseled, and cannot counsel others. To write a novel means to carry the incommensurable to extremes in the representation of human life. In the midst of life's fullness, and through the representation of this fullness, the novel gives evidence of the profound perplexity of the living. . . .

One must imagine the transformation of epic forms occurring in rhythms comparable to those of the change that has come over the earth's surface in the course of thousands of centuries. Hardly any other forms of human communication have taken shape more slowly, been lost more slowly. It took the novel, whose beginnings go back to antiquity, hundreds of years before it encountered in the evolving middle class those elements which were favorable to its flowering. With the appearance of these elements, storytelling began quite slowly to recede into the archaic; in many ways, it is true, it took hold of the new material, but it was not really determined by it. On the other hand, we recognize that with the full control of the middle class, which has the press as one of its most important instruments in fully developed capitalism, there emerges a form of communication which, no matter how far back its origin may lie, never before influenced the epic form in a decisive way. But now it does exert such an influence. And it turns out that it confronts storytelling as no less of a stranger than did the novel, but in a more menacing way, and that it also brings about a crisis in the novel. This new form of communication is information.

Villemessant, the founder of *Le Figaro*, characterized the nature of information in a famous formulation. "To my readers," he used to say, "an attic fire in the Latin Quarter is more important than a revolution in Madrid." This makes strikingly clear that it is no longer intelligence coming from afar, but the information which supplies a handle for what is nearest that gets the readiest hearing. The intelligence that came from afar—whether the spatial kind from foreign countries or the temporal kind of tradition—possessed an authority which gave it validity, even when it was not subject to verification. Information, however, lays claim to prompt verifiability. The prime requirement is that it appear "understandable in itself." Often it is no more exact than the intelligence of earlier centuries was. But while the latter was inclined to borrow from the miraculous, it is indispensable for information to sound plausible. Because of this it proves incompatible with the spirit of storytelling. If the art of storytelling has become rare, the dissemination of information has had a decisive share in this state of affairs.

Every morning brings us the news of the globe, and yet we are poor in noteworthy stories. This is because no event any longer comes to us without already being shot through with explanation. In other words, by now almost nothing that happens benefits storytelling; almost everything benefits information. Actually, it is half the art of storytelling to keep a story free from explanation as one reproduces it. . . . The most extraordinary things, marvelous things, are related with the greatest accuracy, but the psychological connection of the events is not forced on the reader. It is left up to him to interpret things the way he understands them, and thus the narrative achieves an amplitude that information lacks. . . .

The value of information does not survive the moment in which it was new. It lives only at that moment; it has to surrender to it completely and explain itself to it without losing any time. A story is different. It does not expend itself. It preserves and concentrates its strength and is capable of releasing it even after a long time. . . .

There is nothing that commends a story to memory more effectively than that chaste compactness which precludes psychological analysis. And the more natural the process by which the storyteller forgoes psychological shading, the greater becomes the story's claim to a place in the memory of the listener, the more completely is it integrated into his own experience, the greater will be his inclination to repeat it to someone else someday, sooner or later. This process of assimilation, which takes place in depth, requires a state of relaxation which is becoming rarer and rarer. If sleep is the apogee of physical relaxation, boredom is the apogee of mental relaxation. Boredom is the dream bird that hatches the egg of experience. A rustling in the leaves drives him away. His nesting places—the activities that are intimately associated with boredom—are already extinct in the cities and are declining in the country as well. With this the gift for listening is lost and the community of listeners disappears. For storytelling is always the art of repeating stories, and this art is lost when the stories are no longer retained. It is lost because there is no more weaving and spinning to go on while they are being listened to. The more self-forgetful the listener is, the more deeply is what he listens to impressed upon his memory. When the rhythm of work has seized him, he listens to the tales in such a way that the gift of retelling them comes to him all by itself. This, then, is the nature of the web in which the gift of storytelling is cradled. This is how today it is becoming unraveled at all its ends after being woven thousands of years ago in the ambience of the oldest forms of craftsmanship. . . .

It has seldom been realized that the listener's naïve relationship to the storyteller is controlled by his interest in retaining what he is told. The cardinal point for the unaffected listener is to assure himself of the possibility of reproducing the story. Memory is the epic faculty *par excellence*. Only by virtue of a comprehensive memory can epic writing absorb the course of events on the one hand and, with the passing of these, make its peace with the power of death on the other. . . .

Mnemosyne, the rememberer, was the Muse of the epic art among the Greeks. This name takes the observer back to a parting of the ways in world history. For if the record kept by memory—historiography—constitutes the creative matrix of the various epic forms (as great prose is the creative matrix of the various metrical forms), its oldest form, the epic, by virtue of being a kind of common denominator includes the story and the novel. When in the course of centuries the novel began to emerge from the womb of the epic, it turned out that in the novel the element of the epic mind that is derived from the Muse—that is, memory—manifests itself in a form quite different from the way it manifests itself in the story.

Memory creates the chain of tradition which passes a happening on from generation to generation. It is the Muse-derived element of the epic art in a broader sense and encompasses its varieties. In the first place among these is the one practiced by the storyteller. It starts the web which all stories together form in the end. One ties on to the next, as the great storytellers, particularly the Oriental ones, have always readily shown. In each of them there is a Scheherazade who thinks of a fresh story whenever her tale comes to a stop. This is epic remembrance and the Muse-inspired element of the narrative. But this should be set against another principle, also a Muse-derived element in a narrower sense, which as an element of the novel in its earliest form—that is, in the epic—lies concealed, still undifferentiated from the similarly derived element of the story. It can, at any rate, occasionally be divined in the epics, particularly at moments of solemnity in the Homeric epics, as in the invocations to the Muse at their beginning. What announces itself in these passages is the perpetuating remembrance of the novelist as contrasted with the short-lived reminiscences of the storyteller. The first is dedicated to *one* hero, *one* odyssey, *one* battle; the second, to *many* diffuse occurrences. It is, in other words, *remembrance* which, as the Muse-derived element of the novel, is added to reminiscence, the corresponding element of the story, the unity of their origin in memory having disappeared with the decline of the epic.

From "Theses on the Philosophy of History"

A Klee painting named "Angelus Novus" shows an angel looking as though he is about to move away from something he is fixedly contemplating. His eyes are staring, his mouth is open, his wings are spread. This is how one pictures the angel of history. His face is turned toward the past. Where we perceive a chain of events, he sees one single catastrophe which keeps piling wreckage upon wreckage and hurls it in front of his feet. The angel would like to stay, awaken the dead, and make whole what has been smashed. But a storm is blowing from Paradise; it has got caught in his wings with such violence that the angel can no longer close them. This storm irresistibly propels him into the future to which his back is turned, while the pile of debris before him grows skyward. This storm is what we call progress.

Ernst Gombrich (1909–2001) / Aby (Abraham Moritz) Warburg (1866–1929)

Aby Warburg is a remarkably complex figure in intellectual history. Warburg called his field "iconology," and his principal interest was in what he called the survival of the antique: the residues and "afterlives" of classical forms in subsequent art. Over the door to the library he founded in Hamburg, he placed the inscription "Mnemosyne," which indicated his understanding of art as a mnemonic record, though one whose "exchanges" and "migrations" were complex indeed. Perhaps Warburg's most significant project, never completed, was his *Mnemosyne Atlas*, which aimed at what he called an "art history without words" and involved juxtaposed and superimposed images that would demonstrate the complexities of the exchanges and migrations that constituted the iconographic memory. Given Warburg's emphasis on visuality in his scholarly project, the theoretical contributions, mostly in the form of notebook entries and aphorisms, come to us only reconstructed through the painstaking biographical work of the Austrian British art historian Ernst Gombrich. Through Gombrich's account of Warburg as a theorist of "social memory," Warburg's importance for social memory studies, particularly in Germany, has been enormous, though in ways that would perhaps require a Warburg to disentangle!

From *Aby Warburg: An Intellectual Biography*

The attentive reader will have noticed that Warburg's lecture on Rembrandt was novel for him not only in its subject-matter, but also in its psychological emphasis. The classical *pathos* Rembrandt resisted is here described as a memory to which the artist may succumb or which he can control. The *pathos formula* embodied in ancient sculpture and revived in the Baroque is really a deposit of an emotional experience which is derived from primitive religious attitudes. Western civilization must live with the heritage of these early experiences and must learn to dominate them as Rembrandt did. There is thus a direct parallelism between the artist's achievement of poise and the scientist's achievement of rational detachment. Both can be seen as victories over memories from that primitive stage which Vignoli and the evolutionists had postulated and which Warburg had dealt with once more in his lecture on the American Indians.

It was particularly from the next year onwards, that is from 1927, that Warburg's notes begin to turn on the role of memory in civilization. He never spelt out the theory as such in an ordered form, indeed it often has to be reconstructed from the type of mental shorthand he usually adopted when dealing with issues of this kind. But these cryptic utterances, examples of which will have to be quoted in this chapter, fall into place if we trace Warburg's terminology back to its sources.

Some notions of a 'racial' memory were so widespread in the nineteenth century that they passed almost unquestioned in the phraseology of historians, poets and critics. Thus Jacob Burckhardt, discussing Donatello's 'David,' seeks to explain its classical character through heritage rather than through direct imitation:

> If this work is indeed redolent of antiquity, this must really have happened by way of an invisible force, or through inheritance. Indeed one must never wholly forget . . . that the people of central Italy stem from the ancient population.

Among the poets and critics of the *fin de siècle*, speculations about the influence of racial memory were of course much in vogue. Warburg could hardly have read W. B. Yeats, who propounded such a theory in his essay on magic in 1901, nor is he likely to have come into contact with Samuel Butler's theories. Lafcadio Hearn was more popular on the continent of Europe, and whether Warburg knew him or not, the following formulation presents a surprising parallel to Warburg's position:

> When there is perceived some objective comeliness faintly corresponding to certain outlines of the inherited ideal, at once a wave of emotion ancestral bathes the long darkened image . . . the sense-reflection of the living objective becomes temporarily blended with the subjective phantasm—with the beautiful luminous ghost made of centillions of memories . . . and so the riddle resolves itself as Memory.

. . . It cannot be denied that our own period has become especially allergic to unsupported speculations on these lines because of the danger that they may give 'aid and comfort' to racialist creeds. . . .

Warburg's bias for the scientific, his moral valuation of rationality, had kept him apart from writings of this kind. Indeed problems of a 'collective' memory play little part in the theoretical notes of his student days, but there are indications that at that time he was interested in 'monistic' psychology. He also read a famous paper by the great psychologist Ewald Hering on 'Memory as a General Function of Organized Matter.'

In this lecture Hering proposed to reduce the two characteristics of living matter—memory and heredity—to one. Heredity is nothing but racial memory. Hering also touched upon the role of cultural traditions, of language and symbolism, in the 'memory' of mankind, but surmised that there must be some inherited dispositions which account for the force of certain traditions.

There is a fleeting allusion to Hering's ideas in Warburg's fragment on the 'Nympha'—'The memory of Antiquity as a function of organized matter' . . . but this was obviously dropped as unpromising. Even so there are indications that Warburg thought of expressive movement as due to impulses reaching the artist from the past. He speaks of unconscious inherited dispositions and regards art as an 'organ of social memory.' . . .

It must remain an open question how far these ideas may have been reinforced in Warburg through contacts he may have had, at the time of his illness,
with the doctrines of Jung. There is indeed a suggestive parallelism between
the system Warburg developed and Jung's ideas about archetypes and racial
memory. Nevertheless, Warburg never alluded to Jung's writings in his notes.
True to his 'monistic' bias, he turned to one of Hering's most passionate
followers, Richard Semon, whose book on *Mneme* he had bought in 1908.

Put in a nutshell, Semon's theory amounts to this: memory is not a property
of consciousness but the one quality which distinguishes living from dead
matter. It is the capacity to react to an event over a period of time; that is, a form
of preserving and transmitting energy not known to the physical world. Any
event affecting living matter leaves a trace which Semon calls an '*engram.*' The
potential energy conserved in this 'engram' may, under suitable conditions, be
reactivated and discharged—we then say the organism acts in a specific way
because it *remembers* the previous event. This goes for the individual no less
than for the species. It was this concept of mnemic energy, preserved in
'engrams,' but obeying laws comparable to those of physics which attracted
Warburg when he took up the theories of his youth on the nature of the symbol
and its function in the social organism. Taken together with Lamprecht's
notion of social psychology, in which the body social was treated very much like
the mind of the individual as a bundle of stimuli, the theory provided a framework for his historical psychology. . . .

In the life of civilizations it is the *symbol* which corresponds to Semon's
'engram.' In the symbol—in the widest sense of the term—we find preserved
those energies of which it is, itself, the result. These energies, which gave birth
to the symbols of civilization, were derived from the intense basic experiences
which also make up the life of primitive man. It was in these archaic strata of
the mind that Warburg sought the roots of the two basic aspects of civilization,
which he called 'expression' and 'orientation.'

Though Warburg does not appear to have said so explicitly, his theory of
expression remained wedded to Darwin's book on *The Expression of Emotions in
Animals and Men* which had made such an impression on him in his student
days. For Darwin, it will be remembered, human expression is best explicable
as a residue of animal reactions which were once part of the animal's useful
repertory of movements. The clenched fist was once ready to strike, the frown
once protected the eyes in a fight. What is now a symbolic action, an 'expression,' derives from a much stronger bodily movement. For man, to regress to
such movement is to succumb to madness; to bite or scratch is to surrender
human status. But without the attenuated memories of these ancestral
reactions, man would be devoid of expression altogether.

In Warburg's interpretation, . . . Darwin's animal state is all but fused with
the idea of the 'primitive.' For Warburg it is not the animal but primitive man
who surrenders totally to the emotions and passions which hold him in their
grip and who thus coined those highly charged symbols of basic reactions
which live on in tradition as the archetypes of human experience. It is, above

all, the waves of religious enthusiasm in primitive ritual and Dionysiac frenzy which crystallize in symbols or 'engrams' of permanent significance. Herein lies the importance of 'Dionysiac' Greek antiquity for our Western civilization. In its myth we find enshrined the extremes of emotion and self-abandon from which modern man must shrink in awe but which, as preserved in the symbols of art, contain those very moulds of emotion which alone make artistic expression possible. Without the primeval passion which was discharged in maenadic dances and Bacchantic frenzy, Greek art would never have been able to create those 'superlatives' of gesture with which the greatest of Renaissance artists expressed the deepest human values. . . .

[H]is researches into the concrete history of classical 'engrams' suggested to Warburg another mode of absorption: that of re-interpretation. The artist who uses the dangerous 'superlatives' of thiasotic origin may draw on the full energy of these symbols without at the same time giving rein to their archaic mentality. He can use them in a different context, 'invert' their original savage meaning, and yet benefit from their value as expressive formulae. . . .

Whatever the validity of Warburg's individual examples—and some of them are certainly open to criticism—they appeared to prove that, while the energy of past experience remains enshrined in the 'engrams' or symbols, this energy may be canalized into different themes of expression. It is here that Warburg's philosophy of polarity found its clearest application. The symbol or 'engram' is a charge of latent energy, but the way in which it is discharged may be positive or negative—as murder or rescue, as fear or triumph. . . . In this sense Warburg could describe the 'engrams' as 'neutral' in their charge. Only through contact with the 'selective will' of an age does it become 'polarized' into one of the interpretations of which it is potentially capable.

> The dynamograms of ancient art are handed down in a state of maximal tension but unpolarized with regard to the passive or active energy charge to the responding, imitating, or remembering artists. It is only the contact with the new age that results in polarization. This polarization can lead to a radical reversal (inversion) of the meaning they held for classical antiquity.
>
> Polarizing of the energies of images coined in the memory stores of ancient art as an elemental psychological process. . . .
>
> The polarizing of dynamograms through the memory of antiquity.
>
> The essence of thiasotic engrams as balanced charges in a Leyden bottle before their contact with the selective will of the age.
>
> The inherited consciousness of maximalized impressions stamped on the mind (engram) passes them on without taking cognizance of the direction of their emotional charge, simply as an experience of energy tensions; this unpolarized contiguum can also function as a continuum. The imparting of a new meaning to these energies serves as a protective screen.

In this way, Warburg could re-formulate his view of tradition as a neutral force. To be carried away by the symbols of the past with all their dark and sinister associations is a sign of weakness. The powerful personality can withstand the shock and turn the energy he derives from more primitive strata to good account in the service of enlightenment and humanization. In fact the role of the truly great man is precisely to undertake that act of sublimation by which the dangerous impulses of the past are brought under control and harnessed to the creation of serenity and beauty. . . .

Warburg . . . in fact developed his theory through a comparison with the banking system. He spoke of the gold reserves of suffering of which our civilization disposes and compared the ancient heritage to a mint or 'savings bank' whose issues were backed by the archaic passions of which they bore the stamp. . . .

> . . . one aspect of the development towards the Baroque was that expressive values were cut loose from the mint of real life in movement.

> Here the task of social memory as a 'mnemic function' emerges quite clearly: through renewed contact with the monuments of the past, the sap should be enabled, to rise directly from the subsoil of the past and imbue the classicizing form in such a way that a creation charged with energy should not become a calligraphic dynamogram.

. . . [I]t was up to the individual who came into contact with this part of our heritage to decide whether to succumb to the primitive associations which turned these symbols into demons who ruled over human life—or to resist the temptation and instead to turn the energy derived from these cosmic symbols to the business of orientation. To view the image as a mythological being means turning it into a monster. For the urge to interpret the signs of its being, and thus to use it as a 'hieroglyph' with which to explore the future, has resulted in more and more strange and illogical accretions to the pure outline of the Greek stellar symbols. Only by ridding itself of this pseudo-logic and seeing these images for what they are—conventional landmarks created to bring order into the chaos of impressions—could mankind learn to master the laws of the universe by means of mathematical calculation. . . .

The fate of the individual depends on the way in which he masters these messengers of a bygone form of existence, the traces of which are forever within us.

It is the artist and the historian who are most sensitive to these unseen influences from the past. Indeed Warburg sometimes speaks of the historian—including himself—in similar mechanical metaphors which also pervade his language about art. He is the 'seismograph' responding to the tremors of distant earthquakes, or the antenna picking up the wave from distant cultures. His equipment, his library, is a receiving station, set up to register these influences and in doing so to keep them under control. . . .

The note which he drafted for the concluding words of his next seminar shows once more to what an extent Warburg himself felt like a mystagogue initiating his hearers into the perilous secrets of the historian's vocation:

> It has been granted to us to linger for a moment in the uncanny vaults where we found the transformers which transmute the innermost stirrings of the human soul into lasting forms—we could not hope to find there the solution of the enigma of the human mind; only a new formulation of the eternal question as to why fate consigns any creative mind to the realm of perpetual unrest where it is left to him to choose whether to form his personality in the Inferno, Purgatorio or Paradiso.

Theodor W. Adorno (1903–1969)

German philosopher, musicologist, and sociologist. Influenced by, though critically refining, Freudian ideas about guilt, Adorno wrote extensively after the Holocaust about
the obligations, particularly for Germans but also for their victims, of "working through"
(a form of critical acknowledgment) rather than "mastering" (a form of repressing) the
past. In the following two passages, Adorno in many ways echoes, though as was usual
for him also struggles with, **Benjamin**'s thoughts about the disturbances of temporality
in modernity. Perhaps most famous here is Adorno's observation about the association
between the words "museum" and "mausoleum."

From "Valéry Proust Museum"

The German word, '*museal*' ['*museumlike*'], has unpleasant overtones. It
describes objects to which the observer no longer has a vital relationship and
which are in the process of dying. They owe their preservation more to historical respect them to the needs of the present. Museum and mausoleum are
connected by more than phonetic association. Museums are like the family
sepulchers of works of art. They testify to the neutralization of culture. Art
treasures are hoarded in them, and their market value leaves no room for
the pleasure of looking at them. Nevertheless that pleasure is dependent on the
existence of museums. Anyone who does not have his own collection (and the
great private collections are becoming rare) can, for the most part, become
familiar with painting and sculpture only in museums. When discontent with
museums is strong enough to provoke the attempt to exhibit paintings in their
original surroundings or in ones similar, in baroque or rococo castles, for
instance, the result is even more distressing than when the works are wrenched
from their original surroundings and then brought together. Sensibility wreaks
even more havoc with art then does the hodge-podge of collections. With music
the situation is analogous. The programmes of large concert societies, generally retrospective in orientation, have continullay more in common with
museums, while Mozart performed by candlelight is degraded to a costume
piece. In efforts to retrieve music from the remoteness of the performance and
put it into the immediate context of life there is not only something ineffectual
but also a tinge of industriously regressive spite. When some well-intentioned
person advised Mahler to darken the hall during the concert for the sake of the
mood, the composer rightly replied that a performance at which one didn't
forget about the surroundings was worthless. Such problems reveal something
of the fatal situation of what is called 'the cultural tradidition.' Once tradition
is no longer animated by a comprehensive, substantial force but has to be conjured up by means of citations because "It's . . . important to have tradition,"
then whatever happens to be left of it is dissolved into a means to an end. An
exhibition of applied art only makes a mockery of what it pretends to conserve.

Anyone who thinks that art can be reproduced in its original form through an act of the will is trapped in hopeless romanticism. Modernizing the past does it much violence and little good. But to renounce radically the possibility of experiencing the traditional would be to capitulate to barbarism out of devotion to culture. That the world is out of joint is shown everywhere in the fact that however a problem is solved, the solution is false.

From "In Memory of Eichendorff"

In a culture that has been resurrected on a false basis, one's relation to the cultural past is poisoned. Love for the past is frequently accompanied by resentment toward the present; by belief in the possession of a heritage that one loses the moment one imagines it cannot be lost; by a feeling of comfort in familiar things that have been handed down and under whose aegis those whose complicity helped pave the way for the horror hope to escape it. The alternative to all that seems to be an incisive gesture of "that's no longer acceptable." Sensitivity to the false happiness of a cozy security zealously seizes upon the dream of a true happiness, and heightened sensitivity to sentimentality contracts until it is focused on the abstract point of the mere present, in the face of which what once existed counts no more than if it had never existed. One might say that experience is the union of tradition with an open yearning for what is foreign. But the very possibility of experience is in jeopardy. The break in the continuity of historical consciousness that Hermann Heimpel saw results in a polarization: on the one hand, cultural goods that are antiquarian, and perhaps even shaped for ideological purposes; and on the other, a contemporary historical moment that, precisely because it is lacking in memory, is ready to subscribe to the status quo, even by mirroring it where it opposes it. The rhythm of time has become distorted. While the streets of philosophy are echoing with the metaphysics of time, time itself, once measured by the steady course of a person's life, has become alienated from human beings; this is probably why it is being discussed so feverishly. Something in the past that had truly been handed down would have been sublated in its opposite, in the most advanced form of consciousness; but an advanced consciousness that was in command of itself and did not have to worry about being negated by the most recent information would also have the freedom to love what is past. Great avant-garde artists like Schönberg did not have to prove to themselves that they had escaped from the spell of their forebears by experiencing anger toward those forebears. Having escaped and become emancipated, they could perceive the tradition as their equal instead of insisting on a distinction from tradition that only drowns out one's bondage to history in the demand for a radical and natural, as it were, new beginning. They knew that they were fulfilling the secret purpose of the tradition they were shattering. Only when one no longer breaks with tradition because one no longer senses it and hence does not try one's strength against it does one deny it; something that is different does not shrink from its affinity with its point of departure. It is not the timeless Now that would be contemporary but a Now saturated with the force of the past and therefore not needing to idolize it. It is up to advanced consciousness to correct the relationship to the past, not by glossing over the breach but by wresting what is contemporary away from what is transient in the past and granting no tradition authority. Tradition no longer has any more validity than does the converse belief that the living are right and the dead wrong, or that the world began when those now alive were born.

Lev Vygotsky (1896–1934)

Soviet-era psychologist. Emphasizing the role of "cultural mediation" in psychological development, Vygotsky is taken by many contemporary social psychologists (for instance, James Wertsch or Jerome Bruner) as a progenitor of a social and cultural approach to memory within psychology. Though he was not widely known to Western scholars until the 1970s, his work bears many similarities to the early-twentieth-century work of psychologists like **Mead** and **Bartlett**.

From *Mind in Society*

A comparative investigation of human memory reveals that, even at the earliest stages of social development, there are two, principally different, types of memory. One, dominating in the behavior of nonliterate peoples, is characterized by the nonmediated impression of materials, by the retention of actual experiences as the basis of mnemonic (memory) traces. We call this *natural memory*, and it is clearly illustrated in E. R. Jaensch's studies of eidetic imagery. This kind of memory is very close to perception, because it arises out of the direct influence of external stimuli upon human beings. From the point of view of structure, the entire process is characterized by a quality of immediacy.

Natural memory is not the only kind, however, even in the case of nonliterate men and women. On the contrary, other types of memory belonging to a completely different developmental line coexist with natural memory. The use of notched sticks and knots, the beginnings of writing and simple memory aids all demonstrate that even at early stages of historical development humans went beyond the limits of the psychological functions given to them by nature and proceeded to a new culturally-elaborated organization of their behavior. Comparative analysis shows that such activity is absent in even the highest species of animals; we believe that these sign operations are the product of specific conditions of *social* development.

Even such comparatively simple operations as tying a knot or marking a stick as a reminder change the psychological structure of the memory process. They extend the operation of memory beyond the biological dimensions of the human nervous system and permit it to incorporate artificial, or self-generated, stimuli, which we call *signs*. This merger, unique to human beings, signifies an entirely new form of behavior. The essential difference between it and the elementary functions is to be found in the structure of the stimulus-response relations of each. The central characteristic of elementary functions is that they are totally and directly determined by stimulation from the environment. For higher functions, the central feature is self-generated stimulation, that is, the creation and use of artificial stimuli which become the immediate causes of behavior. . . .

The memory of older children is not only different from the memory of younger children; it also plays a different role in the older child's cognitive activity. Memory in early childhood is one of the central psychological functions upon which all the other functions are built. Our analyses suggest that thinking in the very young child is in many respects determined by his memory, and is certainly not the same thing as the thinking of the more mature child. For the very young child, to think means to remember; at no time after very early childhood do we see such a close connection between these two psychological functions.

I will give three examples. The first is the definition of concepts in children, which are based on their recollections. If you ask a child to tell you what a snail is, he will say that it is little, it slithers, and it sticks out its foot; it you ask him to tell you what a grandmother is, he is likely to reply, "She has a soft lap." In both cases the child gives a very clear summary of the impressions which the topic has made upon him and which he recollects. The content of the thinking act in the child when defining such concepts is determined not so much by the logical structure of the concept itself as by the child's concrete recollections. It is syncretic in character and reflects the fact that the child's thinking depends first of all on his memory.

Another example is the development of visual concepts in very young children. Investigations of children's thinking when they are required to transpose a relation learned with one set of stimuli to a similar set have shown that their transfer is nothing more than remembering with respect to isolated instances. Their general representations of the world are based on the recall of concrete instances and do not yet possess the character of an abstraction.

The last example concerns the analysis of word meaning. Investigations in this area show that the connections underlying words are fundamentally different in the young child and in the adult. Children's concepts relate to a series of examples and are constructed in a manner similar to the way we represent family names. To name words for them is not so much to indicate familiar concepts as to name familiar families or whole groups of visual things connected by visual ties. In this way the experience of the child and the "unmediated" influence of the child's experience are documented in his memory and directly determine the entire structure of the young child's thought.

All these facts suggest that, from the point of view of psychological development, memory rather than abstract thought is the definitive characteristic of the early stages of cognitive development. However, in the course of development a transformation occurs, especially in adolescence. Investigations of memory at this age have shown that toward the end of childhood the interfunctional relations involving memory reverse their direction. *For the young child, to think means to recall; but for the adolescent, to recall means to think.* Her memory is so "logicalized" that remembering is reduced to establishing and finding logical relations; recognizing consists in discovering that element which the task indicates has to be found.

This logicalization is indicative of how relations among cognitive functions change in the course of development. At the transitional age all ideas and concepts, all mental structures, cease to be organized according to family types and become organized as abstract concepts.

There can be no doubt that to remember an item when thinking in concepts is a completely different task from thinking in complexes, although the processes are compatible with each other. Therefore, the development of children's memory must be studied not only with respect to changes happening within memory itself, but also with respect to the relation between memory and other functions.

When a human being ties a knot in her handkerchief as a reminder, she is, in essence, constructing the process of memorizing by forcing an external object to remind her of something; she transforms remembering into an external activity. This fact alone is enough to demonstrate the fundamental characteristic of the higher forms of behavior. In the elementary form something is remembered; in the higher form humans remember something. In the first case a temporary link is formed owing to the simultaneous occurrence of two stimuli that affect the organism; in the second case humans personally create a temporary link through an artificial combination of stimuli.

The very essence of human memory consists in the fact that human beings actively remember with the help of signs. It may be said that the basic characteristic of human behavior in general is that humans personally influence their relations with the environment and through that environment personally change their behavior, subjugating it to their control. It has been remarked that the very essence of civilization consists of purposely building monuments so as not to forget. In both the knot and the monument we have manifestations of the most fundamental and characteristic feature distinguishing human from animal memory.

Frederic Bartlett (1886–1969)

British experimental psychologist. In a chapter on institutional memory in her book *How Institutions Think*, anthropologist Mary Douglas takes Bartlett as an ironic example of institutional forgetting: Bartlett, she shows, introduced a social perspective to the psychology of memory decades before the contemporary rediscovery of "collective memory." The following excerpt bears out Douglas's claims quite convincingly.

From *Remembering: A Study in Experimental and Social Psychology*

The pathway to an understanding of the general mechanism of remembering is strewn with rejected theories; but concerning social memory proper there has been much less speculation. For the most part the arguments used have turned upon analogy. A more or less elaborate likeness has been drawn between the social group and the human individual, and on the basis of this, whatever is attributed to the latter has been ascribed to the former. This is certainly unsatisfactory. What is required is a direct study of social facts, and conclusions should be founded upon these facts alone. Speculations based upon analogy are bound to appear incomplete and unconvincing.

There are, it is true, a number of views regarding the social origin of memory. Prof. Pierre Janet has, for example, written upon this topic in his most persuasive and attractive manner. Human beings, he believes, confronted by a difficult world, have been forced to invent various special ways of dealing with adverse circumstances. The most important of these all concern the utilisation of absent objects. Many of the most significant biological advances, such as the development of distance receptor organs, are directly connected with this, and memory, which is something utterly different from conservation, is a triumphant solution of the problem. Now according to Janet the need for dealing with absent objects becomes acute only in a social situation; and this is why the development, or invention, of memory is in extricably bound up with some form of overt conduct and especially with the use of language.

Such a view is clearly, in some respects, in line with the one which I have adopted in the present book. I, also, believe that the development of remembering is in line with the growth of the distance reactions of the special senses. But there appears to me to be no adequate reason for specialising either of these to social situations. It is, of course, perfectly true that the remembering which we are in a position to study in any detail practically always does occur in some social setting, except, maybe, in the case of certain rather abstract psychological experiments. However, the same is true of every other reaction that can be investigated at a psychological level, and does not itself give us any sure ground in theory for holding that the absolute origin of recall is social. A solitary human being, since he is in any case a complex organisation of different tendencies, would again and again need, for his own sake, to be able to deal with what, from the point of view of any one, or any group, of these tendencies, is an absent object. Further, there seems to be no adequate reason for regarding remembering as in itself an entirely unique method of dealing with absent objects. Rather is it a combination of the image method and the 'schematic' method, although, like all such combinations, it gains characteristics of its own. Finally, I think we should be very chary of assigning the locus of absolute origin of any biological reaction, for to do this is most certainly to run beyond the limits of observable conditions.

And when all is said and done, this, or any other hypothesis of the same kind, is not a theory of social memory, but only of the social determination of remembering. Strictly speaking, a theory of social memory ought to be able to demonstrate that a group, considered as a unit, itself actually does remember, and not merely that it provides either the stimulus or the conditions under which individuals belonging to the group recall the past. . . .

Perhaps the best way of beginning to attack this question will be to consider the views of a psychologist who definitely and constantly uses the phrase "collective memory." Prof. Maurice Halbwachs has written a careful and attractive study of *Les Cadres Sociaux de la Mémoire*. He is considerably influenced by the views of Durkheim, who, as is well known, believes that the social group constitutes a genuine psychical unit, and is possessed of nearly all the characteristics of the human individual. Durkheim's views are not merely based upon easy analogy, but directly upon a patient and detailed study of social phenomena. This feature of his method is faithfully followed by Halbwachs, and it is interesting to consider some of the specific instances adduced by him. Halbwachs deals in particular with what he calls the "collective memory" of the family, of religious groups and of social classes.

In all well-established modern communities, says Halbwachs, every family has its own characteristic mental life (*esprit propre*); its memories which it alone cherishes; its secrets which are revealed to none but its own members. Moreover, these memories, like the religious traditions of the family group of earlier days, are no mere series of individualised images of the past. They may be this, but they are also models, examples, a kind of basis for education and development. In them is expressed the general attitude of the group, so that they do more than reproduce its history, they define its nature, its strength and its weakness. "When we say 'In our family we are long lived,' or, 'we are proud,' or 'we do not get rich,' we speak of some physical or moral property which we treat as inherent in the group and passing from it to its members. Sometimes it is the place or country of origin of the family, or again it may be some outstanding characteristic of one of its members, which becomes the more or less mysterious symbol of the common stock from which all the constituent individuals draw their peculiar qualities. Thus out of different elements of this kind, retained from its past history, the family memory (*mémoire familiale*) shapes a framework which it tends to keep intact, as it were a kind of traditional family armour. No doubt this framework is all made up of facts each of which had its date, of images each of which appeared and disappeared at a given time. But as it is to be found in the judgments which the family, and those that surround the family, have passed upon these facts and images, it partakes of the nature of those collective notions which have neither place nor definite moment, but which seem to set the direction of the stream of time."

It may be that we have occasion to recall some event or other of our family life which is "engraven upon our memory." If we then try to cut out all those traditional ideas and judgments which are a part of the family proper, practically nothing remains. Or rather, try how we will, we cannot make this kind of dissociation. We cannot distinguish, in our remembering of the particular event, between "the image which has but one place and time" and the notions which reflect in a general way "our experience of the acts and manner of life of our parents." . . .

Halbwachs gives in detail a number of instances which he describes and analyses in such a way as to show that the life of the family group may contribute to behaviour something which can come from no other source. If the family memory expresses itself, so to speak, through some particular person, that person must, no doubt, use words and images, but these all possess a halo of sentiment which is derived from the life of the group itself. "When the family remembers (*Quand la famille se souvient*) it certainly uses words and it certainly makes reference to events or images which were unique of their kind: but neither the words, which are only material movements, nor the events and images of the past, which are only virtual objects of sensory or thought processes, constitute the whole memory. A family memory must be something else; it must both orientate us towards the events and images referred to or used, and support itself upon the words which are its expression."

Certainly most of these remarks, in so far as it is possible to give them clear significance, seem to be both true and important. Certainly also Halbwachs is justified in going on to speak in a similar manner of memory in the religious group and in the social class. Yet he is still treating only of memory *in* the group, and not of memory *of* the group. As to the former, there need be no dispute whatever. Social organisation gives a persistent framework into which all detailed recall must fit, and it very powerfully influences both the manner and the matter of recall. Moreover, this persistent framework helps to provide those 'schemata' which are a basis for the imaginative reconstruction called memory. It is equally probable that the social creation and clash of interests aid in the development of the specific images which, as our study has repeatedly shown, may be present in individual recall. But we need to go far beyond this if we are to show that the social group itself possesses a capacity to retain and recall its own past. . . .

If we wish to know whether a man remembers anything, we ask him; and we generally take his word for it, even when he can give us but little detail. We cannot adopt this easy way with the social group, because, if it has a means of self-expression other than its contemporary movements and its social organisation, we do not know that means. We are therefore driven to see whether there is any mark of recall, considered as a form of behaviour, which definitely distinguishes it from all other possible reactions. If the general view of the nature of remembering which has been adopted here is correct, there is such a mark. Whenever an agent, be he man, animal, or social group, acts as if it were being predominantly determined by some distant event in its history, using this directly to help it to solve some immediate problem, it may be said to 'remember.' I have tried to show that mere serial recapitulation is different from 'schematic' reconstruction since the latter demands that items should be picked out of schemes, reshuffled, and used to aid adaptation towards conditions which have perhaps never occurred before. The items picked out are the distant events; the immediate situation sets the problems which they are to help to solve.

Can we find unequivocal evidence of the occurrence of this sort of behaviour in the social group? It is not easy to decide, but I do not think we can. When a group is faced with a threat of sudden crisis it often seems to adopt a form of response which runs counter to its recent social history, but is at the same time closely related to a more distant past. This happens in the contemporary political group, for example, when it goes to war, or reverses its fiscal policy, or suffers any other more or less violent revolution. But the case is not at all clear, because always, in such instances, there are individuals to adduce the required precedents and advise the course of behaviour that is based upon them. To get a clear case we must find a group acting upon a distant precedent, with at least considerable unanimity, when that precedent has not been formulated by any individual group member and put before the others.

It might possibly seem that the curious phenomena of social reversions, or social regressions, would give us what we require; but it is difficult to base any definite views upon them, both because there is always a chance that the disapproved customs, or views, may have been fairly continuously practised by a minority in the group, and because the principle of the 'fitness' of material to function means that if ever certain persistent human tendencies are stimulated certain features of contemporary social environment are sure to receive emphasis.

At first sight it looks as if a curious case of group suggestion discussed by W. H. R. Rivers might give us exactly the evidence needed. He reports that, in some of the relatively small groups of Polynesia and Melanesia, decisions are often arrived at and acted upon, although they have never been formulated by anybody. The white observer, listening to the proceedings of a native Council, realises after a while that, the original topic of dispute has changed. When he "has inquired when they were going to decide the question in which he was interested, he has been told that it had already been decided and that they had passed on to other business. The decision had been made with none of the processes by which our councils or committees decide disputed points. The members of the council have become aware at a certain point that they are in agreement, and it was not necessary to bring the agreement explicitly to notice."

This kind of case, assuming that it actually does occur, is susceptible of two explanations. We may assume that at some stage of the discussion a common conclusion spread rapidly throughout the group; or that, somehow, the group itself, literally as a unit, decided the issue. Since the decision is practically always governed by precedent, the second line of explanation would, if it could be maintained, perhaps give us a genuine instance of group memory.

But the actual facts are far from clear. Rivers gives scanty detail, even concerning the instances he observed himself, and he indicates no other authorities. I have myself been unable to find any clear evidence whatsoever, either in books, or in the field. Certainly this kind of group decision, without formulation, does not seem to occur among small groups of native races in Africa. At any rate, no observation, and no amount of most careful questioning of Basuto, Zulu and Swazi natives and residents on my part brought any case to light. There is, of course, no doubt that certain social conditions favour the rapid spread of decisions by suggestibility. But so far as my own observation goes, always, except where mere social habit or custom is concerned, somebody has to formulate the proposals which are eventually acted upon.

In fact, it seems entirely impossible to discover anywhere unequivocal evidence of group memory. Social direction and control of recalls—memory within the group—are obvious; but a literal memory *of* the group cannot, at present at least, be demonstrated. Equally it cannot be disproved, and consequently must not be dogmatically denied. Social grouping produces new properties both of behaviour and of experience. So far as we know these, we have to find them in the conduct and life of individual members of the group. Yet it is not theoretically impossible that the organisation of individuals into a group should literally produce a new mental unit which perhaps feels, knows and remembers in its own right. The main difficulty is that it seems as if the most unequivocal evidence of all the higher mental processes consists in their formulation in language by their possessors. When the only language accessible to the observer is gesture, there is always a great amount of ambiguity present. In some cases, especially where we are dealing with relatively isolated individuals on much the same level as ourselves, we can infer the mental process from the gesture with a fair amount of certainty; but the case of the social group is hopelessly complicated in this respect, owing to age and environmental overlap and the fact that every individual member has himself acquired to some extent the capacity of direct language formulation. It may be that social conventions, institutions and traditions formed by persistent group tendencies constitute 'group schemata;' just as the individual images, ideas and trains of thought formed by persistent personal interests constitute 'individual schemata.' If they do, these 'group schemata' still occupy a peculiar position. For whether they are known to the group or not, they certainly may be known by at least some of its individual members. Consequently, even if the group should in some manner be able to "turn round upon its own schemata" and to utilise them directly, we can never be quite sure that any results which may follow are not merely due to the fact that a similar use can be made of social 'schemes' by important group individuals. It appears that one thing only could resolve the difficulty, and that is the development of a direct group language accessible to members of the group. Some people seem to think that what is rather vaguely called group atmosphere, or group sentiment, provides the kind of language required. Clearly it does not. For it may be the result simply of affective modifications of individual experience due, no doubt, to social grouping, and hence the product of the group as a psychological unit, but not the possession of the group as a psychical unit. In fact, if there are groups which are psychical units, very likely only another group, with which they could directly communicate in some sort of group language, would ever for certain know. Thus, whether there are literally group images, group memories, and group ideas must remain a matter of interesting but uncertain speculation. We cannot affirm or deny them. Our views about them will be dictated, as, in fact, men's views concerning these matters always have been, by our beliefs in regard to the relative values of the individual and the group.

All these considerations, however, make no difference to the certainty that the group is a psychological unit. There are numberless ways of conduct and of thought that are the direct outcome of social organisation. Created by the group, they cease to be explicable the moment the group is ignored. Whether the social group has a mental life over and above that of its individual members is a matter for speculation and belief. That the organised group functions in a unique and unitary manner in determining and directing the mental lives of its individual members is a matter of certainty and of fact.

Carl Becker (1873–1945)

American historian. In his 1931 Presidential Address to the American Historical Association, from which the following excerpt is drawn, Becker introduces the "Everyman His Own Historian" trope to subsequent discourse, inspiring contemporary writers who challenge the sharp distinction academic historians frequently draw between what they and what ordinary people do with the past. See especially **Rosenzweig** and **Thelen**.

From "Everyman His Own Historian"

What then of us, historians by profession? What have we to do with Mr. Everyman, or he with us? More, I venture to believe, than we are apt to think. For each of us is Mr. Everyman too. Each of us is subject to the limitations of time and place; and for each of us, no less than for the Browns and Smiths of the world, the pattern of remembered things said and done will be woven, safeguard the process how we may, at the behest of circumstance and purpose.

True it is that although each of us is Mr. Everyman, each is something more than his own historian. Mr. Everyman, being but an informal historian, is under no bond to remember what is irrelevant to his personal affairs. But we are historians by profession. Our profession, less intimately bound up with the practical activities, is to be directly concerned with the ideal series of events that is only of casual or occasional import to others; it is our business in life to be ever preoccupied with that far-flung pattern of artificial memories that encloses and completes the central pattern of individual experience. We are Mr. Everybody's historian as well as our own, since our histories serve the double purpose, which written histories have always served, of keeping alive the recollection of memorable men and events. We are thus of that ancient and honorable company of wise men of the tribe, of bards and story-tellers and minstrels, of soothsayers and priests, to whom in successive ages has been entrusted the keeping of the useful myths. Let not the harmless, necessary word "myth" put us out of countenance. In the history of history a myth is a once valid but now discarded version of the human story, as our now valid versions will in due course be relegated to the category of discarded myths. With our predecessors, the bards and storytellers and priests, we have therefore this in common: that it is our function, as it was theirs, not to create, but to preserve and perpetuate the social tradition; to harmonize, as well as ignorance and prejudice permit, the actual and the remembered series of events; to enlarge and enrich the specious present common to us all to the end that "society" (the tribe, the nation, or all mankind) may judge of what it is doing in the light of what it has done and what it hopes to do.

History as the artificial extension of the social memory (and I willingly concede that there are other appropriate ways of apprehending human experience) is an art of long standing, necessarily so since it springs instinctively from the impulse to enlarge the range of immediate experience; and however camouflaged by the disfiguring jargon of science, it is still in essence what it has always been. History in this sense is story, in aim always a true story; a story that employs all the devices of literary art (statement and generalization, narration and description, comparison and comment and analogy) to present the succession of events in the life of man, and from the succession of events thus presented to derive a satisfactory meaning. The history written by historians, like the history informally fashioned by Mr. Everyman, is thus a convenient blend of truth and fancy, of what we commonly distinguished as "fact" and "interpretation." In primitive times, when tradition is orally transmitted, bards and story-tellers frankly embroider or improvise the facts to heighten the dramatic import of the story. With the use of written records, history, gradually differentiated from fiction, is understood as the story of events that actually occurred; and with the increase and refinement of knowledge the historian recognizes that his first duty is to be sure of his facts, let their meaning be what it may. Nevertheless, in every age history is taken to be a story of actual events from which a significant meaning may be derived, and in every age the illusion is that the present version is valid because the related facts are true, whereas former versions are invalid because based upon inaccurate or inadequate facts.

Never was this conviction more impressively displayed than in our own time—that age of erudition in which we live, or from which we are perhaps just emerging. Finding the course of history littered with the *debris* of exploded philosophies, the historians of the last century, unwilling to be forever duped, turned away (as they fondly hoped) from "interpretation" to the rigorous examination of the factual event, just as it occurred. Perfecting the technique of investigation, they laboriously collected and edited the sources of information, and with incredible persistence and ingenuity ran illusive error to earth, letting the significance of the Middle Ages wait until it was certainly known "whether Charles the Fat was at Ingelheim or Lustnau on July I, 887," shedding their "life-blood," in many a hard fought battle, "for the sublime truths of Sac and Soc." I have no quarrel with this so great concern and with hoti's business. One of the first duties of man is not to be duped, to be aware of his world; and to derive the significance of human experience from events that never occurred is surely an enterprise of doubtful value. To establish the facts is always in order, and is indeed the first duty of the historian; but to suppose that the facts, once established in all their fullness, will "speak for themselves" is an illusion. It was perhaps peculiarly the illusion of those historians of the last century who found some special magic in the word "scientific." The scientific historian, it seems, was one who set forth the facts without injecting any extraneous meaning into them. He was the objective man whom Nietzsche described— "a mirror: accustomed to prostration before something that wants to be known, . . . he waits until something comes, and then expands himself sensitively, so that even the light footsteps and gliding past of spiritual things may not be lost in his surface and film." . . . "It is not I who speak, but history which speaks through me," was Fustel's reproof to applauding students. "If a certain philosophy emerges from this scientific history, it must be permitted to emerge naturally, of its own accord, all but independently of the will of the historian." . . . Thus the scientific historian deliberately renounced philosophy only to submit to it without being aware. His philosophy was just this, that by not taking thought a cubit would be added to his stature. With no other preconception than the will to know, the historian would reflect in his surface and film the "order of events throughout past times in all places;" so that, in the fullness of time, when innumerable patient expert scholars, by "exhausting the sources," should have reflected without refracting the truth of all the facts, the definitive and impregnable meaning of human experience would emerge of its own accord to enlighten and emancipate mankind. Hoping to find something without looking for it, expecting to obtain final answers to life's riddle by resolutely refusing to ask questions—it was surely the most romantic species of realism yet invented, the oddest attempt ever made to get something for nothing!

That mood is passing. The fullness of time is not yet, over-much learning proves a weariness to the flesh, and a younger generation that knows not Von Ranke is eager to believe that Fustel's counsel, if one of perfection, is equally one of futility. Even the most disinterested historian has at least one preconception, which is the fixed idea that he has none. The facts of history are already set forth, implicitly, in the sources; and the historian who could restate without reshaping them would, by submerging and suffocating the mind in diffuse existence, accomplish the superfluous task of depriving human experience of all significance. Left to themselves, the facts do not speak; left to themselves they do not exist, not really, since for all practical purposes there is no fact until some one affirms it. The least the historian can do with any historical fact is to select and affirm it. To select and affirm even the simplest complex of facts is to give them a certain place in a certain pattern of ideas, and this alone is sufficient to give them a special meaning. However "hard" or "cold" they may be, historical facts are after all not material substances which, like bricks or scantlings, possess definite shape and clear, persistent outline. To set forth historical facts is not comparable to dumping a barrow of bricks. A brick retains its form and pressure wherever placed; but the form and substance of historical facts, having a negotiable existence only in literary discourse, vary with the words employed to convey them. Since history is not part of the external material world, but an imaginative reconstruction of vanished events, its form and substance are inseparable: in the realm of literary discourse substance, being an idea, is form; and form, conveying the idea, is substance. It is thus not the undiscriminated fact, but the perceiving mind of the historian that speaks: the special meaning which the facts are made to convey emerges from the substance-form which the historian employs to recreate imaginatively a series of events not present to perception.

In constructing this substance-form of vanished events, the historian, like Mr. Everyman, like the bards and story-tellers of an earlier time, will he conditioned by the specious present in which alone he can be aware of his world. Being neither omniscient nor omnipresent, the historian is not the same person always and everywhere; and for him, as for Mr. Everyman, the form and significance of remembered events, like the extension and velocity of physical objects, will vary with the time and place of the observer. After fifty years we can clearly see that it was not history which spoke through Fustel, but Fustel who spoke through history. We see less clearly perhaps that the voice of Fustel was the voice, amplified and freed from static as one may say, of Mr. Everyman; what the admiring students applauded on that famous occasion was neither history nor Fustel, but a deftly colored pattern of selected events which Fustel fashioned, all the more skillfully for not being aware of doing so, in the service of Mr. Everyman's emotional needs—the emotional satisfaction, so essential to Frenchmen at that time, of perceiving that French institutions were not of German origin. And so it must always be. Played upon by all the diverse, unnoted influences of his own time, the historian will elicit history out of documents by the same principle, however more consciously and expertly applied, that Mr. Everyman employs to breed legends out of remembered episodes and oral tradition.

Berate him as we will for not reading our books, Mr. Everyman is stronger than we are, and sooner or later we must adapt our knowledge to his necessities. Otherwise he will leave us to our own devices, leave us it may be to cultivate a species of dry professional arrogance growing out of the thin soil of antiquarian research. Such research, valuable not in itself but for some ulterior purpose, will be of little import except in so far as it is transmuted into common knowledge. The history that lies inert in unread books does no work in the world. The history that does work in the world, the history that influences the course of history, is living history, that pattern of remembered events, whether true or false, that enlarges and enriches the collective specious present, the specious present of Mr. Everyman. This is why the history of history is a record of the "new history" that in every age rises to confound and supplant the old. It should be a relief to us to renounce omniscience, to recognize that every generation, our own included, will, must inevitably, understand the past and anticipate the future in the light of its own restricted experience, must inevitably play on the dead whatever tricks it finds necessary for its own peace of mind. The appropriate trick for any age is not a malicious invention designed to take anyone in, but an unconscious and necessary effort on the part of "society" to understand what it is doing in the light of what it has done and what it hopes to do. We, historians by profession, share in the necessary effort. But we do not impose our version of the human story on Mr. Everyman; in the end it is rather Mr. Everyman who imposes his version on us—compelling us, in an age of political revolution, to see that history is past politics, in an age of social stress and conflict to search for the economic interpretation. If we remain too long recalcitrant Mr. Everyman will ignore us, shelving our recondite works behind glass doors rarely opened. Our proper function is not to repeat the past but to make use of it, to correct and rationalize for common use Mr. Everyman's mythological adaptation of what actually happened. We are surely under bond to be as honest and as intelligent as human frailty permits; but the secret of our success in the long run is in conforming to the temper of Mr. Everyman, which we seem to guide only because we are so sure, eventually, to follow it.

Neither the value nor the dignity of history need suffer by regarding it as a foreshortened and incomplete representation of the reality that once was, an unstable pattern of remembered things redesigned, and newly colored to suit the convenience of those who make use of it. Nor need our labors be the less highly prized because our task is limited, our contributions of incidental and temporary significance. History is an indispensable even though not the highest form of intellectual endeavor, since it makes, as Santayana says, a gift of "great interests . . . to the heart. A barbarian is no less subject to the past than is the civic man who knows what the past is and means to be loyal to it; but the barbarian, for want of a transpersonal memory crawls among superstitions which he cannot understand or revoke and among people whom he may hate or love, but whom he can never think of raising to a higher plane, to the level of a purer happiness. The whole dignity of human endeavor is thus bound up with historic issues, and as conscience needs to be controlled by experience if it is to become rational, so personal experience itself needs to be enlarged ideally if the failures and success it reports are to touch impersonal interests."

George Herbert Mead (1863–1931)

American philosopher, sociologist, and social psychologist. Developing a social psychology out of pragmatist philosophy, Mead is relevant for social memory studies mainly through his concept, articulated here, of the "specious present" and his argument that the socially relevant reality of the past exists only in the present: as such, "the past" is fundamentally malleable. Mead is thus taken as an exemplary "presentist" in memory studies, though he is surely more than that label implies.

From "The Nature of the Past"

The present is not the past and the future. The distinction which we make between them is evidently fundamental. If we spread a specious present so that it covers more events, as Whitehead suggests, taking in some of the past and conceivably some of the future, the events so included would belong, not to the past and the future, but to the present. It is true that in this present there is something going on. There is passage within the duration, but that is a present passage. The past arises with memory. We attach to the backward limit of the present the memory images of what has just taken place. In the same fashion we have images of the words which we are going to speak. We build out at both limits. But the images are in the present. Whitehead's suggestion that rendering these images sufficiently vivid would spread the specious present is quite beside the mark. No memory image, however vivid, would be anything but a memory image, which is a surrogate merely for what was or will be spoken.

The actual passage of reality is in the passage of one present into another, where alone is reality, and a present which has merged in another is not a past. Its reality is always that of a present. The past as it appears is in terms of representations of various sorts, typically in memory images, which are themselves present. It is not true that what has passed is in the past, for the early stages of a motion lying within a specious present are not past. They belong to something that is going on. The distinction between the present and the past evidently involves more than passage. An essential condition is its inclusion in some present in this representational form. Passage as it takes place in experience is an overlapping of one specious present by another. There is continuity of experience, which is a continuity of presents. In this continuity of experience there is distinction of happening. There is direction. There is dependence or conditioning. What is taking place flows out of that which is taking place. Not only does succession take place, but there is a succession of contents. What is going on would be otherwise if the earlier stage of the occurrence had been of a different character. It is always a passage of something. There is always a character which connects different phases of the passage, and the earlier stage of the happening is the condition of the later stage. Otherwise there would be no passage. Mere juxtaposition of events, if this is conceivable, would not constitute passage. The connection involves both identity and difference, and it involves that in the identity which makes the condition for that which follows. The immediate position of a moving body is conditioned by that which preceded it. Continuity is involved as a presupposition in passage in experience.

Although apparently sudden dislocations take place, back of these we imply continuities within which these dislocations could be resolved into continuities. The spatio-temporal connections which these continuities express involve the conditioning of any spatio-temporal position by a previous set of positions. This conditioning is not complete determination, but the conditions that are involved in the continuity of passage are necessary. That which is novel can emerge, but conditions of the emergence are there. It is this conditioning which is the qualitative character of the past as distinguished from mere passage. Mere passage signifies disappearance and is negative. The conditioning, spatio-temporally considered, is the necessity of continuity of relationship in space-time and of characters which are dependent upon space and time, such as velocities and momenta. The discontinuous is the novel. When a force is applied which is responsible for an acceleration, the moment at which that force is applied may be as respects its appearance an emergence from a continuous past, but the spatio-temporal continuities set conditions for the accelerations which result from the application of the force.

There are other continuities which we look for besides those of space-time. These are those of the so-called uniformities of nature. The embedding of any two successive events and their characters, however fortuitous they may seem, within a continuity of happening registers itself as carrying some conditioning of their happening in the succession within which they have appeared. The physical sciences push this conditioning into spatio-temporal form as far as it is possible. They attempt so to state the two happenings that the mere fact that one occurs at a certain place and time determines in some degree that which follows upon it. The ideal of this presentation is an equation between a situation at one moment and that at the next. We seek such a statement that the mere passage of experience will determine that which takes place. Where this can rigorously be carried out we reach what Whitehead calls the Aristotelian adjectives of events, but where it is impossible to so present the happenings that the continuity of passage determines what will take place we have in his terms pseudo-adjectives of events. But that the continuities of space-time do carry with them conditions of that which takes place is a fundamental presupposition of experience. The order within which things happen and appear conditions that which will happen and appear.

It is here that we find the function of the past as it arises in memory and the records of the past. Imagery is not past but present. It rests with what we call our mental processes to place these images in a temporal order. We are engaged in spreading backward what is going on so that the steps we are taking will be a continuity in the advance to the goals of our conduct. That memory imagery has in it characters which tend to identify it as belonging to the past is undoubtedly true, and these characters seem to be frequently independent of its place in a continuous order. A face or a landscape may flash upon the inward eye with seemingly intrinsic evidence of past experience, although we may have great difficulty in placing them. The evidence is not necessarily of an immediate character. There are certain sorts of images which belong to our pasts and we are confident of them because they fit in. And there are sorts of images which betray the operation of the imagination. A memory may be recognized as such by a method of exclusion, because it has not the fashion of the fancy—because we cannot otherwise account for it. The assurances which we give to a remembered occurrence come from the structures with which they accord.

What is, then, the immediate occasion for this building out of specious presents into a past? These presents themselves pass into each other by an overlapping process. There is no break except under what may be called pathological conditions. We do not build out into the past to preserve mere continuity, i.e., to fill out breaks in reality. But it is evident that we need to complete something that is lacking in that which is going on. The span of that which occupies us is greater than the span of the specious present. The "what it is" has a temporal spread which transcends our experience. This is very evident in the pasts which we carry around with us. They are in great part thought constructs of what the present by its nature involves, into which very slight material of memory imagery is fitted. This memory in a manner tests and verifies the structure. We must have arisen and eaten our breakfasts and taken the car, to be where we are. The sense of this past is there as in implication and bits of imperfect scenes come in at call—and sometimes refuse to arise. But even in this latter case we do not feel that the past is lost.

It may be said that the existence in experience of affairs that transcend our presents is the very past under discussion, and this is true, and what I am endeavoring to make evident. The past is an overflow of the present. It is oriented from the present. It is akin on the one side to our escape fancies, those in which we rebuild the world according to our hearts' desires, and on the other to the selection of what is significant in the immediate situation, the significant that must be held and reconstructed, but its decisive character is the pushing back of the conditioning continuities of the present. The past is what must have been before it is present in experience as a past. A past triumph is indefinitely superior to an escape fancy, and will be worn threadbare before we take refuge in the realm of the imagination, but more particularly the past is the sure extension which the continuities of the present demand. . . .

The inevitability of existence is betrayed in its continuity. What follows flows from what was. If there is continuity, then what follows is conditioned by what was. A complete break between events would remove the character of inevitability. . . . If there were bare replacement of one experience by another, the experience would not be that of passage. They would be different experiences each wrapped up in itself, but with no connection, no way of passing from one to the other. Even a geometrical demonstration involves passage from situation to situation. The final structure is a timeless affair in the sense that it is a completed structure which is now irrelevant to the passage by which it has arisen. Any passage is in so far inevitable as earlier stages condition later achievements, and the demonstration is the exhibition of the continuity of the passage. One route when it is once taken is as inevitable as another. The child's whimsical movements of the men upon the chessboard is as inevitable as the play of the expert. In the one case its inevitability is displayed by the psychologist and in the other by the logician. Continuity in the passage of events is what we mean by the inevitable.

But bare continuity could not be experienced. There is a tang of novelty in each moment of experience. . . . Without this break within continuity, continuity would be inexperienceable. The content alone is blind, and the form alone is empty, and experience in either case is impossible. . . . The continuity is always of some quality, but as present passes into present there is always some break in the continuity—within the continuity, not of the continuity. The break reveals the continuity, while the continuity is the background for the novelty.

The memory of the unexpected appearance of a supposedly far distant friend, or the memory of an earthquake can never recover the peculiar tang of the experience. I remember that there was a break which is now connected with just the phases of the experience which were unconnected. We recall the joy or the terror, but it is over against a background of a continuum whose discontinuity has been healed. Something was going on—the rising anger of a titan or the adjustment of the earth's internal pressures which resulted in that which was unexpected, but this was not the original experience, when there was no connection between the events before the occurrence and the sudden emergence. Even if no qualitative causal connection appears in the memory, the spatio-temporal connection is there to be developed as thought or imagination may refashion it.

Redintegration of the past can never bring back the unexpected. This is just the character of the past as distinguished from the passage of presents into each other. The primal break of novelty in passage is gone and the problem of bridging the contingent factors is before the mind, though it may go no further than the oppressive sense of chance or fate. The character of the past is that it connects what is unconnected in the merging of one present into another.

Charles Horton Cooley (1864–1929)

American sociologist. A leading figure of the first "Chicago school" in sociology, Cooley extended philosopher William James's idea of the "self" into a pragmatist social psychology, one in which social interaction in primary groups is highlighted more than abstract institutional forces. Here Cooley develops an interactionist perspective on fame and reputation that, like that of his associate **Mead**, sees the changing needs of the present as primary. Even more important for memory studies, Cooley highlights the social processes that, more than any intrinsic qualities of historical accomplishments, shape the chances of such accomplishments being remembered. As such, Cooley is a major inspiration for later theorists of reputation and fame. See especially **Ducharme** and **Fine** and **Lang** and **Lang** below.

From *Social Process*

It is noteworthy that what a man did for humanity in the past is not the chief cause of fame, and not sufficient to insure it unless he can keep on doing something in the present. The world has little or no gratitude. If the past contribution is the only thing and there is nothing presently animating in the living idea of a man, it will use the former, without caring where it came from, and forget the latter.

The inventors who made possible the prodigious mechanical progress of the past century are, for the most part, forgotten. . . . Some . . . are remembered for the fascination of their biography, their heroic persistence, strokes of good fortune or the like; and probably it is safe to conclude that few men of this class would be famous for their inventions alone.

As Doctor Johnson remarks in The Rambler, the very fact that an idea is wholly successful may cause its originator to be forgotten. "It often happens that the general reception of a doctrine obscures the books in which it was delivered. When any tenet is generally received and adopted as an incontrovertible principle, we seldom look back to the arguments upon which it was first established, or can bear that tediousness of deduction and multiplicity of evidence by which its author was forced to reconcile it to prejudice and fortify it in the weakness of novelty against obstinacy and envy." He instances "Boyle's discovery of the qualities of the air;" and I suppose that if Darwin's views could have been easily accepted, instead of meeting the bitter and enduring opposition of theological and other traditions, his popular fame would have been comparatively small. He is known to the many chiefly as the symbol of a militant cause.

It is, then, present function, not past, which is the cause of fame, and any change which diminishes or enhances this has a parallel effect upon reputation. . . .

It is because fame exists for our present use and not to perpetuate a dead past that myth enters so largely into it. What we need is a good symbol to help us think and feel; and so, starting with an actual personality which more or less meets this need, we gradually improve upon it by a process of unconscious adaptation that omits the inessential and adds whatever is necessary to round out the ideal. Thus the human mind working through tradition is an artist, and creates types which go beyond nature. In this way, no doubt, were built up such legendary characters as Orpheus, Hercules, or King Arthur, while the same factor enters into the fame of historical persons like Joan of Arc, Richard I, Napoleon, and even Washington and Lincoln. It is merely an extension of that idealization which we apply to all the objects of our hero-worship, whether dead or living.

And where a historical character becomes the symbol of a perennial ideal, as in the case of Jesus, his fame becomes a developing institution, changing its forms with successive generations and modes of thought, according to the needs of the human spirit. This, apparently, is the genesis of all life-giving conceptions of divine personality.

There are aspects of fame that cannot be understood without considering the special influence upon it of the literary class. This class has control of the medium of communication through which fame chiefly works, and so exerts a power over it somewhat analogous to the power of the financial class over trade; in both cases the forces of demand and supply are transformed by the interests of the mediating agent.

One result of this is that literary fame is, of all kinds, the most justly assigned. Candidates for it, of any merit, are rarely overlooked, because there is always a small society of inquiring experts eager and able to rescue from oblivion any trait of kindred genius. They are not exempt from conventionalism and party spirit, which may make them unjust to contemporaries, but a second or third generation is sure to search out anything that deserves to survive, and reject the unworthy. "There is no luck in literary reputation. They who make up the final verdict upon every book are not the partial and noisy readers of the hour when it appears; but a court as of angels, a public not to be bribed, not to be entreated, and not to be overawed, decides upon every man's title to fame. Only those books come down which deserve to last." In this way, by the reiterated selection of an expert class with power to hand on their judgments, there is a sure evolution of substantial fame. . . .

The popular judgment of the hour has little to do with the matter, one way or the other. An author may be a "best seller," . . . or almost unread, . . . and fare equally well with the higher court; though in this as in all departments of life most contemporary reputations prove transitory, because their "fitness" is to a special and passing phase of the human mind, and not to its enduring needs.

However, literary reputation also has its symbolism, and a name may come to be remembered as the type of a school or a tendency rather than strictly on its own merits. Sainte-Beuve, an authority on such a matter, remarks in his essay on Villon: "But the essential thing, I see clearly, even in literature, is to become one of those names convenient to posterity, which uses them constantly, which employs them as the *résumé* of many others, and which, as it becomes more remote, not being able to reach the whole extent of the chain, measures the distance from one point to another only by some shining link."

Democracy does not in the least alter the fact that literary fame is assigned by a small but perpetual group of experts. In one sense the process is always democratic; in another it is never so: there is democracy in that all may share in the making of fame who have discrimination enough to make their opinion count, but the number of these is always small, and they constitute, in this field, a kind of self-made aristocracy, not of professed critics alone, but of select readers intelligently seeking and enjoying the best. The fame of men of letters, philosophers, artists, indeed of nearly all sorts of great men, reaches the majority only as the people outside the grounds hear the names of the players shouted by those within. We know who it was that was great, but just why he was so we should, if put to it, be quite unable to tell.

This certainty and justice of literary fame, which distinguish it sharply from other kinds, depend not only upon the literary class but upon the precision of the record—the fact that the deed upon which the fame rests is imperishable and unalterable—and also upon the extremely personal and intimate character of the achievement itself, which makes it comparatively independent of external events, and capable of being valued for its own sake at any time and by anybody competent to appreciate it. It is more fortunate in this respect than political achievement, which is involved with transient institutional conditions.

For similar reasons the other and non-literary sorts of fame are certain and enduring very much in proportion as they interest the literary class. The latter, being artists or critics of art, have a natural predilection for other arts as well as their own, and cherish the fame of painters, sculptors, actors, and musicians. Actors, especially, whose art leaves no record of its own, would scarcely be remembered were it not for the enthusiasm of literary admirers. . . . As to painting or sculpture, thousands of us who have little direct knowledge or appreciation of the great names have learned to cherish them at second hand through the fascination of what has been written by admiring men of letters. On the other hand, the comparative neglect of inventors, engineers, and the captains of industry and commerce is due in great part to their not appealing strongly to the literary type of mind.

If one's work has no universal appeal to human nature, nor any special attraction for the literary class, it may yet survive in memory if there is a continuing technical group, with a recorded tradition, to which it is significant. Professions, like law, surgery, and engineering; . . . even traditional sports and pastimes, like golf . . . and football, have their special records in which are enshrined the names of heroes who will not be forgotten so long as the group endures. A tradition of this kind has far more power over time than the acclaim of all the newspapers of the day, which indeed, without the support of a more considerate judgment, is *vox et præterea nihil*.

I can see no reason to expect that the men of our day who are notable for vast riches, or even for substantial economic leadership in addition to riches, will be remembered long after their deaths. This class of people have been soon forgotten in the past, and the case is not now essentially different. They have no lasting spiritual value to preserve their names, nor yet do they appeal to the admiration and loyalty of a continuous technical group. Their services, though possibly greater than those of statesmen and soldiers who will be remembered, are of the sort that the world appropriates without much commemoration.

A group which is important as a whole, and holds the eye of posterity for that reason, preserves the names of many individual members of no great importance in themselves. They help each other to burn, like sticks in a heap, when each one by itself might go out. English statesmen and men of letters have a great advantage over American in this respect, because they belong to a more centralized and interrelated society. To know Burke and Goldsmith and Johnson is also to know Garrick and Boswell, and Mrs. Thrale, . . . and many others, who, like characters in a play, are far more taken together than the mere sum of the individuals. Indeed a culture group and epoch of this kind *is* a sort of play, appealing to a complex historical and dramatic interest, and animating personalities by their membership in the whole. We love to domesticate ourselves in it, when we might not care greatly for the individuals in separation.

So every "great epoch" . . . gives us a group of names which shine by the general light of their time. And in the same way a whole nation or civilization which has a unique value for mankind may give immortality to a thousand persons and events which might otherwise be insignificant. Of this the best illustration is, no doubt, the Hebrew nation and history, as we have it in the Bible, which unites patriarchs, kings, prophets, apostles and minor characters in one vast symbol.

Another influence of similar character is the knowledge and feeling that the fame in question is accepted and social, so that we are part of a fellowship to be moved by it. I take it that much of the delight that people have in reading Horace comes from the sense of being in the company not only of Horace but of hundreds of Horace-spirited readers. We love things more genially when we know that others have loved them before us.

The question whether fame is just, considered as a reward to the individual, must on the whole be answered: No, especially if, for the reasons already given, we except the literary class. Justice in this sense has little to do with the function of fame as a symbol for impressing certain ideas and sentiments and arousing emulation. What name best meets this purpose is determined partly by real service, but largely by opportuneness, by publicity, by dramatic accessories, and by other circumstances which, so far as the individual is concerned, may be called luck. "So to order it that actions may be known and seen is purely the work of fortune," says Montaigne, "'tis chance that helps us to glory. . . . A great many brave actions must be expected to be performed without witness, and so lost, before one turns to account; a man is not always on the top of a breach or at the head of an army, . . . a man is often surprised betwixt the hedge and the ditch; he must run the hazard of his life against a hen-roost, he must dislodge four rascally musketeers from a barn; . . . and whoever will observe will, I believe, find it experimentally true that occasions of the least lustre are ever the most dangerous." It is no less true, I suppose, in the wars of our day, and of a hundred soldiers equally brave and resourceful, only one gets the cross of honor. In a high sense this is not only for the man who happens to receive it, but for a company of nameless heroes of whom he is the symbol.

And so in all history; it is partly a matter of chance which name the myth crystallizes about, especially in those earlier times when the critical study of biography was unknown. We are not certain that Solomon was really the wisest man, or Orpheus the sweetest singer, . . . but it is convenient to have names to stand for these traits. In general, history is no doubt far more individual, more a matter of a few great names, than is accomplishment.

Mankind does things and a few names get the credit. Sir Thomas Browne expressed the truth very moderately when he said that there have been more remarkable persons forgotten than remembered.

We hear rumors of the decay of fame: it is said that "modern life . . . favors less and less the growth and preservation of great personalities;" but I see no proof of it and doubt whether such a decay is conformable to human nature. Other epochs far enough past to give time for selection and idealization have left symbolic names, and the burden of proof is upon those who hold that ours will not. I do not doubt there is a change; we are coming to see life more in wholes than formerly; but I conceive that our need to see it as persons is not diminished.

Has there not come to be a feeling, especially during the Great War, that the desire for fame is selfish and a little outgrown, that the good soldier of humanity does not care for it? I think so; but it seems to me that we must distinguish, as to this, between one who is borne up on a great human whole that lives in the looks and voices of those about him, like a soldier in a patriotic war, or a workman in the labor movement, and one who is more or less isolated, as are nearly all men of unique originality. The latter, I imagine, will always feel the need to believe in the appreciation of posterity; they will appeal from the present to the future and, like Dante, meditate *come l'uom s'elterna.*

The desire for fame is simply a larger form of personal ambition, and in one respect, at least, nobler than other forms, in that it reflects the need to associate ourselves with some enduring reality, raised above the accidents of time. "Nay, I am persuaded that all men do all things, and the better they are the more they do them, in hope of the glorious fame of immortal virtue; for they desire the immortal."

It is the "last infirmity of noble minds," if it be an infirmity at all, and few of the greatest of the earth have been without it. All of us would regard it as the mark of a superior mind to wish to *be* something of imperishable worth, but, social beings as we are, we can hardly separate this wish from that for social recognition of the worth. The alleged "vanity" of the desire for fame is vanity only in the sense that all idealism is empty for those who can see the real only in the tangible.

And yet it would be a finer thing to "desire the immortal" without requiring it to be stained with the color of our own mortality.

Émile Durkheim (1858–1917)

French sociologist. As one of the founding fathers of sociology, Durkheim's influence on social memory studies, particularly as manifested in the work of his student Maurice Halbwachs, cannot be overstated. In these excerpts from the last pages of *The Elementary Forms of Religious Life*, Durkheim describes the importance of commemorative ritual for social solidarity. Besides **Halbwachs**, see also **Warner** as an exemplar of Durkheim's influence.

From *The Elementary Forms of Religious Life*

The mythology of a group is the system of beliefs common to this group. The traditions whose memory it perpetuates express the way in which society represents man and the world; it is a moral system and a cosmology as well as a history. So the rite serves and can serve only to sustain the vitality of these beliefs, to keep them from being effaced from memory and, in sum, to revivify the most essential elements of the collective consciousness. Through it, the group periodically renews the sentiment which it has of itself and of its unity; at the same time, individuals are strengthened in their social natures. The glorious souvenirs which are made to live again before their eyes, and with which they feel that they have a kinship, give them a feeling of strength and confidence: a man is surer of his faith when he sees to how distant a past it goes back and what great things it has inspired. This is the characteristic of the ceremony which makes it instructive. . . .

But there are ceremonies in which this representative and idealistic character is still more accentuated.

In those of which we have been speaking, the dramatic representation did not exist for itself; it was only a means having a very material end in view, namely, the reproduction of the totemic species. But there are others which do not differ materially from the preceding ones, but from which, nevertheless, all preoccupations of this sort are absent. The past is here represented for the mere sake of representing it and fixing it more firmly in the mind, while no determined action over nature is expected of the rite. At least, the physical effects sometimes imputed to it are wholly secondary and have no relation with the liturgical importance attributed to it. . . .

So we have here a whole group of ceremonies whose sole purpose is to awaken certain ideas and sentiments, to attach the present to the past or the individual to the group. Not only are they unable to serve useful ends, but the worshippers themselves demand none. This is still another proof that the psychical state in which the assembled group happens to be constitutes the only solid and stable basis of what we may call the ritual mentality. The beliefs which attribute such or such a physical efficaciousness to the rites are wholly accessory and contingent, for they may be lacking without causing any alteration in the essentials of the rite. . . .

[T]here is something eternal in religion which is destined to survive all the particular symbols in which religious thought has successively enveloped itself. There can be no society which does not feel the need of upholding and reaffirming at regular intervals the collective sentiments and the collective ideas which make its unity and its personality. Now this moral remaking cannot be achieved except by the means of reunions, assemblies and meetings where the individuals, being closely united to one another, reaffirm in common their common sentiments; hence come ceremonies which do not differ from regular religious ceremonies, either in their object, the results which they produce, or the processes employed to attain these results. What essential difference is there between an assembly of Christians celebrating the principal dates of the life of Christ, or of Jews remembering the exodus from Egypt or the promulgation of the decalogue, and a reunion of citizens commemorating the promulgation of a new moral or legal system or some great event in the national life?

If we find a little difficulty to-day in imagining what these feasts and ceremonies of the future could consist in, it is because we are going through a stage of transition and moral mediocrity. The great things of the past which filled our fathers with enthusiasm do not excite the same ardour in us, either because they have come into common usage to such an extent that we are unconscious of them, or else because they no longer answer to our actual aspirations; but as yet there is nothing to replace them. We can no longer impassionate our selves for the principles in the name of which Christianity recommended to masters that they treat their slaves humanely, and, on the other hand, the idea which it has formed of human equality and fraternity seems to us to-day to leave too large a place for unjust inequalities. Its pity for the outcast seems to us too Platonic; we desire another which would be more practicable; but as yet we cannot clearly see what it should be nor how it could be realized in facts. In a word, the old gods are growing old or already dead, and others are not yet born. This is what rendered vain the attempt of Comte with the old historic souvenirs artificially revived: it is life itself, and not a dead past which can produce a living cult. But this state of incertitude and confused agitation cannot last for ever. A day will come when our societies will know again those hours of creative effervescence, in the course of which new ideas arise and new formulæ are found which serve for a while as a guide to humanity; and when these hours shall have been passed through once, men will spontaneously feel the need of reliving them from time to time in thought, that is to say, of keeping alive their memory by means of celebrations which regularly reproduce their fruits. We have already seen how the French Revolution established a whole cycle of holidays to keep the principles with which it was inspired in a state of perpetual youth. If this institution quickly fell away, it was because the revolutionary faith lasted but a moment, and deceptions and discouragements rapidly succeeded the first moments of enthusiasm. But though the work may have miscarried, it enables us to imagine what might have happened in other conditions; and everything leads us to believe that it will be taken up again sooner or later.

There are no gospels which are immortal, but neither is there any reason for believing that humanity is incapable of inventing new ones. As to the question of what symbols this new faith will express itself with, whether they will resemble those of the past or not, and whether or not they will be more adequate for the reality which they seek to translate, that is something which surpasses the human faculty of foresight and which does not appertain to the principal question.

Maurice Halbwachs (1877–1945)

French sociologist. Halbwachs, a protégé of Émile Durkheim and earlier a student of Henri Bergson, is the widely acknowledged founding father of social memory studies, though the reception history of his seminal ideas has been rather complicated.

Halbwachs's first major treatise on memory was his 1925 *Social Frameworks of Memory* (*Les Cadres sociaux de la mémoire*), which connected logically his work on Durkheim's theory of "collective representations" with his earlier studies of the working class, in which he had developed a Durkheimian take on what Marx had discussed in terms of class consciousness. The 1925 *Social Frameworks* was met with a mixed reception. Two of its most important critiques were from Halbwachs's associates, the historian **Marc Bloch** and the psychiatrist **Charles Blondel**. In 1941 Halbwachs published a second book on memory, a study he called *The Legendary Topography of the Holy Land*, which was at least partly a response to Bloch's call for Halbwachs "to one day study the errors in the collective memory." A third volume on memory by Halbwachs appeared posthumously under the title *The Collective Memory* and includes essays Halbwachs worked on throughout the 1930s and early 1940s; in many of these essays, Halbwachs engaged directly with the critique from Blondel, who argued that Halbwachs over-sociologized the neurological substratum of memory. These immediate critical contexts have been largely forgotten (though the Bloch review is frequently referenced), at least in part because neither essay, until now, has been translated into English.

The reception history of Halbwachs more generally in subsequent scholarship is even more complicated. The first translation of Halbwachs was anthropologist Mary Douglas's edition of *The Collective Memory*, which appeared in 1980 but quickly went, and still remains, out of print. In 1992, the sociologist Lewis Coser published in the University of Chicago Press *Heritage of Sociology* series a volume called *Maurice Halbwachs: On Collective Memory*. The Coser edition contained substantial portions of the 1925 *Social Frameworks* and the conclusion to *The Legendary Topography* (the remaining portions of both are still untranslated into English). The Coser volume, appearing at the beginning of the supposed memory boom, has become the standard reference for Anglophone scholars. In the process, the development of Halbwachs's thought on collective memory over time (that is, between his 1925 book and his later essay collection) has been neglected by many outside of France and Germany. Additionally, writing by scholars influenced by Halbwachs but writing before the memory boom, like **Bastide**, has often been overlooked.

Because Coser's excerpts from Halbwachs's first two books on memory remain easily available and widely known, and because they do not present the developed result of Halbwachs's dialogues with critics, we have chosen to present selections of our never-before-published translations of the Bloch and Blondel responses with selections from Halbwachs's most mature work, *The Collective Memory*.

From *The Collective Memory*

Often we deem ourselves the originators of thoughts and ideas, feelings and passions, actually inspired by some group. Our agreement with those about us is so complete that we vibrate in unison, ignorant of the real source of the vibrations. How often do we present, as deeply held convictions, thoughts borrowed from a newspaper, book, or conversation? They respond so well to our way of seeing things that we are surprised to discover that their author is someone other than ourself. "That's just what I think about that!" We are unaware that we are but an echo. The whole art of the orator probably consists in his giving listeners the illusion that the convictions and feelings he arouses within them have come not from him but from themselves, that he has only divined and lent his voice to what has been worked out in their innermost consciousness. In one way or another, each social group endeavors to maintain a similar persuasion over its members. How many people are critical enough to discern what they owe to others in their thinking and so acknowledge to themselves how small their own contribution usually is? Occasionally an individual increases the range of his acquaintances and readings, making a virtue of an eclecticism that permits him to view and reconcile divergent aspects of things. Even in such instances the particular dosage of opinions, the complexity of feelings and desires, may only express his accidental relationships with groups divergent or opposed on some issue. The relative value attributed to each way of looking at things is really a function of the respective intensity of influences that each group has separately exerted upon him. In any case, insofar as we yield without struggle to an external suggestion, we believe we are free in our thought and feelings. Therefore most social influences we obey usually remain unperceived.

But this is probably even more true for these complex states that occur at the intersection of several currents of collective thought, states we are wont to see as unique events existing only for ourself. A traveler suddenly caught up by influences from a milieu foreign to his companions, a child exposed to adult feelings and concerns by unexpected circumstances, someone who has experienced a change of location, occupation, or family that hasn't totally ruptured his bonds with previous groups—all are instances of this phenomenon. Often the social influences concerned are much more complex, being more numerous and interwoven. Hence they are more difficult and more confusing to unravel. We see each milieu by the light of the other (or others) as well as its own and so gain an impression of resisting it. Certainly each of these influences ought to emerge more sharply from their comparison and contrast. Instead, the confrontation of these milieus gives us a feeling of no longer being involved in any of them. What becomes paramount is the "strangeness" of our situation, absorbing individual thought enough to screen off the social thoughts whose conjunction has elaborated it. This strangeness cannot be fully understood by any other member of these milieus, only myself. In this sense it belongs to me and, at the moment of its occurrence, I am tempted to explain it by reference to myself and myself alone. At the most, I might concede that circumstances (that is, the conjunction of these milieus) have served as the occasion permitting the production of an event long ago incorporated in my individual destiny, the appearance of a feeling latent in my innermost person. I have no other means of explaining its subsequent return to memory, because others were unaware of it and have had no role in its production (as we mistakenly imagine). Therefore, in one way or another, it must have been preserved in its original form in my mind. But that is not the case at all. These remembrances that seem purely personal, since we alone are aware of and capable of retrieving them, are distinguished by the greater complexity of the conditions necessary for their recall. But this is a difference in degree only.

One doctrine is satisfied to note that our past comprises two kinds of elements. Certain elements we can evoke whenever we want. By contrast, others cannot simply be summoned and we seem to encounter various obstacles in searching for them in our past. In reality, the first might be said to belong to a common domain, in the sense that they are familiar or easily accessible to others as well as ourself. The idea we most easily picture to ourself, no matter how personal and specific its elements, is the idea others have of us. The events of our life most immediate to ourself are also engraved in the memory of those groups closest to us. Hence, facts and conceptions we possess with least effort are recalled to us from a common domain (common at least to one or several milieus). These remembrances are "everybody's" to this extent. We can recall them whenever we want just because we can base ourself on the memory of others. The second type, which cannot be recalled at will, are readily acknowledged to be available only to ourself because only we could have known about them. So we apparently end up in this strange paradox. The remembrances we evoke with most difficulty are our concern alone and constitute our most exclusive possession. They seem to escape the purview of others only at the expense of escaping ourself also. It is as if a person locked his treasure in a safe with a lock so complicated that he could not open it; he does not remember the combination and must rely on chance to remind him of it.

But there is an explanation at once simpler and more natural. The difference between remembrances we evoke at will and remembrances we seem to command no longer is merely a matter of degree of complexity. The former are always at hand because they are preserved in groups that we enter at will and collective thoughts to which we remain closely related. The elements of these remembrances and their relationships are all familiar to us. The latter are less accessible because the groups that carry them are more remote and intermittent in contact with us. Groups that associate frequently enable us to be in them simultaneously, whereas others have so little contact that we have neither intention nor occasion to trace their faded paths of communication. Now it is along such routes, along such sheltered pathways, that we retrieve those remembrances that are uniquely our own. In the same way, a traveler might consider as his own a spring, an outcropping of rock, or a landscape reached only by leaving the main thoroughfare and rejoining another via a rough and infrequently used trail. The starting points of such a short cut lie on the main routes and are common knowledge. But close scrutiny and maybe a bit of luck are required to find them again. A person might frequently pass by either without bothering to look for them, especially if he couldn't count upon passers-by to point them out, passers-by who travel one of these thoroughfares but have no concern to go where the other might lead. . . .

While the collective memory endures and draws strength from its base in a coherent body of people, it is individuals as group members who remember. While these remembrances are mutually supportive of each other and common to all, individual members still vary in the intensity with which they experience them. I would readily acknowledge that each memory is a viewpoint on the collective memory, that this viewpoint changes as my position changes, that this position itself changes as my relationships to other milieus change. Therefore, it is not surprising that everyone does not draw on the same part of this common instrument. In accounting for that diversity, however, it is always necessary to revert to a combination of influences that are social in nature.

Certain of these combinations are extremely complex. Hence their appearance is not under our control. In a sense, we must trust to chance. We must wait for the various systems of waves (in those social milieus where we move mentally or physically) to intersect again and cause that registering apparatus which is our individual consciousness to vibrate the same way it did in the past. But the type of causality is the same and could not be different from what it was then. The succession of our remembrances, of even our most personal ones, is always explained by changes occurring in our relationships to various collective milieus—in short, by the transformations these milieus undergo separately and as a whole.

Some may say how strange it is that our most personal remembrances, offering such a striking character of absolute unity, actually derive from a fusion of diverse and separate elements. First of all, reflection shows this unity to dissolve rapidly into a multiplicity. It has been claimed that one recovers, when plumbing the depths of a truly personal conscious state, the whole content of mind as seen from a certain viewpoint. But "content of mind" must be understood as all the elements that mark its relationships to various milieus. A personal state thus reveals the complexity of the combination that was its source. Its apparent unity is explained by a quite natural type of illusion. Philosophers have shown that the feeling of liberty may be explained by the multiplicity of causal series that combine to produce an action. We conceive each influence as being opposed by some other and thus believe we act independently of each influence since we do not act under the exclusive power of any one. We do not perceive that our act really results from their action in concert, that our act is always governed by the law of causality. Similarly, since the remembrance reappears, owing to the interweaving of several series of collective thoughts, and since we cannot attribute it to any single one, we imagine it independent and contrast its unity to their multiplicity. We might as well assume that a heavy object, suspended in air by means of a number of very thin and interlaced wires, actually rests in the void where it holds itself up. . . .

Collective memory differs from history in at least two respects. It is a current of continuous thought whose continuity is not at all artificial, for it retains from the past only what still lives or is capable of living in the consciousness of the groups keeping the memory alive. By definition it does not exceed the boundaries of this group. When a given period ceases to interest the subsequent period, the same group has not forgotten a part of its past, because, in reality, there are two successive groups, one following the other. History divides the sequence of centuries into periods, just as the content of a tragedy is divided into several acts. But in a play the same plot is carried from one act to another and the same characters remain true to form to the end, their feelings and emotions developing in an unbroken movement. History, however, gives the impression that everything—the interplay of interests, general orientations, modes of studying men and events, traditions, and perspectives on the future—is transformed from one period to another. The apparent persistence of the same groups merely reflects the persistence of external distinctions resulting from places, names, and the general character of societies. But the men composing the same group in two successive periods are like two tree stumps that touch at their extremities but do not form one plant because they are not otherwise connected.

Of course, reason sufficient to partition the succession of generations at any given moment is not immediately evident, because the number of births hardly varies from year to year. Society is like a thread that is made from a series of animal or vegetable fibers intertwined at regular intervals; or, rather, it resembles the cloth made from weaving these threads together. The sections of a cotton or silk fabric correspond to the end of a motif or design. Is it the same for the sequence of generations?

Situated external to and above groups, history readily introduces into the stream of facts simple demarcations fixed once and for all. In doing so, history not merely obeys a didactic need for schematization. Each period is apparently considered a whole, independent for the most part of those preceding and following, and having some task—good, bad, or indifferent—to accomplish. Young and old, regardless of age, are encompassed within the same perspective so long as this task has not yet been completed, so long as certain national, political, or religious situations have not yet realized their full implications. As soon as this task is finished and a new one proposed or imposed, ensuing generations start down a new slope, so to speak. Some people were left behind on the opposite side of the mountain, having never made it up. But the young, who hurry as if fearful of missing the boat, sweep along a portion of the older adults. By contrast, those who are located at the beginning of either slope down, even if they are very near the crest, do not see each other any better and they remain as ignorant of one another as they would be were they further down on their respective slope. The farther they are located down their respective slope, the farther they are placed into the past or what is no longer the past; or, alternatively, the more distant they are from one another on the sinuous line of time.

Some parts of this portrait are accurate. Viewed as a whole from afar and, especially, viewed from without by the spectator who never belonged to the groups he observes, the facts may allow such an arrangement into successive and distinct configurations, each period having a beginning, middle, and end. But just as history is interested in differences and contrasts, and highlights the diverse features of a group by concentrating them in an individual, it similarly attributes to an interval of a few years changes that in reality took much longer. Another period of society might conceivably begin on the day after an event had disrupted, partially destroyed, and transformed its structure. But only later, when the new society had already engendered new resources and pushed on to other goals, would this fact be noticed. The historian cannot take these demarcations seriously. He cannot imagine them to have been noted by those who lived during the years so demarcated, in the manner of the character in the farce who exclaims, "Today the Hundred Years War begins!" A war or revolution may create a great chasm between two generations, as if an intermediate generation had just disappeared. In such a case, who can be sure that, on the day after, the youth of society will not be primarily concerned, as the old will be, with erasing any traces of that rupture, reconciling separated generations and maintaining, in spite of everything, continuity of social evolution? Society must live. Even when institutions are radically transformed, and especially then, the best means of making them take root is to buttress them with everything transferable from tradition. Then, on the day after the crisis, everyone affirms that they must begin again at the point of interruption, that they must pick up the pieces and carry on. Sometimes nothing is considered changed, for the thread of continuity has been retied. Although soon rejected, such an illusion allows transition to the new phase without any feeling that the collective memory has been interrupted.

In reality, the continuous development of the collective memory is marked not, as is history, by clearly etched demarcations but only by irregular and uncertain boundaries. The present (understood as extending over a certain duration that is of interest to contemporary society) is not contrasted to the past in the way two neighboring historical periods are distinguished. Rather, the past no longer exists, whereas, for the historian, the two periods have equivalent reality. The memory of a society extends as far as the memory of the groups composing it. Neither ill will nor indifference causes it to forget so many past events and personages. Instead, the groups keeping these remembrances fade away. Were the duration of human life doubled or tripled, the scope of the collective memory as measured in units of time would be more extensive. Nevertheless, such an enlarged memory might well lack richer content if so much tradition were to hinder its evolution. Similarly, were human life shorter, a collective memory covering a lesser duration might never grow impoverished because change might accelerate a society "unburdened" in this way. In any case, since social memory erodes at the edges as individual members, especially older ones, become isolated or die, it is constantly transformed along with the group itself. Stating when a collective remembrance has disappeared and whether it has definitely left group consciousness is difficult, especially since its recovery only requires its preservation in some limited portion of the social body. . . .

In effect, there are several collective memories. This is the second character-istic distinguishing the collective memory from history. History is unitary, and it can be said that there is only one history. Let me explain what I mean. Of course, we can distinguish the history of France, Germany, Italy, the history of a certain period, region, or city, and even that of an individual. Sometimes his-torical work is even reproached for its excessive specialization and fanatic desire for detailed study that neglects the whole and in some manner takes the part for the whole. But let us consider this matter more closely. The historian justifies these detailed studies by believing that detail added to detail will form a whole that can in turn be added to other wholes; in the total record resulting from all these successive summations, no fact will be subordinated to any other fact, since every fact is as interesting as any other and merits as much to be brought forth and recorded. Now the historian can make such judgments because he is not located within the viewpoint of any genuine and living groups of past or present. In contrast to the historian, these groups are far from afford-ing equal significance to events, places, and periods that have not affected them equally. But the historian certainly means to be objective and impartial. Even when writing the history of his own country, he tries to synthesize a set of facts comparable with some other set, such as the history of another country, so as to avoid any break in continuity. Thus, in the total record of European history, the comparison of the various national viewpoints on the facts is never found; what is found, rather, is the sequence and totality of the facts such as they are, not for a certain country or a certain group but independent of any group judg-ment. The very divisions that separate countries are historical facts of the same value as any others in such a record. All, then, is on the same level. The histor-ical world is like an ocean fed by the many partial histories. Not surprisingly, many historians in every period since the beginning of historical writing have considered writing universal histories. Such is the natural orientation of the historical mind. Such is the fatal course along which every historian would be swept were he not restricted to the framework of more limited works by either modesty or short-windedness.

Of course, the muse of history is Clio. History can be represented as the universal memory of the human species. But there is no universal memory. Every collective memory requires the support of a group delimited in space and time. The totality of past events can be put together in a single record only by separating them from the memory of the groups who preserved them and by severing the bonds that held them close to the psychological life of the social milieus where they occurred, while retaining only the group's chronological and spatial outline of them. This procedure no longer entails restoring them to lifelike reality, but requires relocating them within the frameworks with which history organizes events. These frameworks are external to these groups and define them by mutual contrast. That is, history is interested primarily in differences and disregards the resemblances without which there would have been no memory, since the only facts remembered are those having the common trait of belonging to the same consciousness. Despite the variety of times and places, history reduces events to seemingly comparable terms, allowing their interrelation as variations on one or several themes. Only in this way does it manage to give us a summary vision of the past, gathering into a moment and symbolizing in a few abrupt changes or in certain stages undergone by a people or individual, a slow collective evolution. In this way it presents us a unique and total image of the past.

In order to give ourselves, by way of contrast, an idea of the multiplicity of collective memories, imagine what the history of our own life would be like were we, in recounting it, to halt each time we recalled some group to which we had belonged, in order to examine its nature and say everything we know about it. It would not be enough to single out just a few groups—for example, our parents, primary school, lycée, friends, professional colleagues, social acquaintances, and any political, religious, or artistic circles with which we have been connected. These major spheres are convenient, but they correspond to a still external and simplified view of reality. These groups are composed of much smaller groups, and we have contact with only a local unit of the latter. They change and segment continually. Even though we stay, the group itself actually becomes, by the slow or rapid replacement of its members, another group having only a few traditions in common with its original ones. Having lived a long time in the same city, we have old and new friends; even within our family, the funerals, marriages, and births are like so many successive endings and new beginnings. Of course, these more recent groups are sometimes only branches of a larger group growing in extent and complexity, to which new segments have been joined. Nevertheless, we discern distinct zones within them, and the same currents of thought and sequences of remembrances do not pass through our mind when we pass from one zone to another. That is, the great majority of these groups, even though not currently divided, nevertheless represent, as Leibnitz said, a kind of social material indefinitely divisible in the most diverse directions.

Let us now consider the content of these collective memories. In contrast to history or, if it is preferred, to the historical memory, I do not claim that the collective memory retains only resemblances. To be able to speak of memory, the parts of the period over which it extends must be differentiated in some way. Each of these groups has a history. Persons and events are distinguished. What strikes us about this memory, however, is that resemblances are paramount. When it considers its own past, the group feels strongly that it has remained the same and becomes conscious of its identity through time. History, I have said, is not interested in these intervals when nothing apparently happens, when life is content with repetition in a somewhat different, but essentially unaltered, form without rupture or upheaval. But the group, living first and foremost for its own sake, aims to perpetuate the feelings and images forming the substance of its thought. The greatest part of its memory spans time during which nothing has radically changed. Thus events happening within a family or to its members would be stressed in a written history of the family, though they would have meaning for the kin group only by providing clear proof of its own almost unaltered character, distinctive from all other families. Were a conflicting event, the initiative of one or several members, or, finally, external circumstances to introduce into the life of the group a new element incompatible with its past, then another group, with its own memory, would arise, and only an incomplete and vague remembrance of what had preceded this crisis would remain.

History is a record of changes; it is naturally persuaded that societies change constantly, because it focuses on the whole, and hardly a year passes when some part of the whole is not transformed. Since history teaches that everything is interrelated, each of these transformations must react on the other parts of the social body and prepare, in turn, further change. Apparently the sequence of historical events is discontinuous, each fact separated from what precedes or follows by an interval in which it is believed that nothing has happened. In reality, those who write history and pay primary attention to changes and differences understand that passing from one such difference to another requires the unfolding of a sequence of transformations of which history perceives only the sum (in the sense of the integral calculus) or final result. This viewpoint of history is due to its examining groups from outside and to its encompassing a rather long duration. In contrast, the collective memory is the group seen from within during a period not exceeding, and most often much shorter than, the average duration of a human life. It provides the group a self-portrait that unfolds through time, since it is an image of the past, and allows the group to recognize itself throughout the total succession of images. The collective memory is a record of resemblances and, naturally, is convinced that the group remains the same because it focuses attention on the group, whereas what has changed are the group's relations or contacts with other groups. If the group always remains the same, any changes must be imaginary, and the changes that do occur in the group are transformed into similarities. Their function is to develop the several aspects of one single content—that is, the various fundamental characteristics of the group itself.

Moreover, how would a memory be possible otherwise? It would be paradoxical to claim that the memory preserves the past in the present or introduces the present into the past if they were not actually two zones of the same domain and if the group, insofar as it returns into itself and becomes self-conscious through remembering and isolation from others, does not tend to enclose itself in a relatively immobile form. The group is undoubtedly under the influence of an illusion when it believes the similarities more important than the differences, but it clearly cannot account for the differences, because the images it has previously made of itself are only slowly transformed. But the framework may be enlarged or compressed without being destroyed, and the assumption may be made that the group has only gradually focused on previously unemphasized aspects of itself. What is essential is that the features distinguishing it from other groups survive and be imprinted on all its content. We might have to leave one of these groups for a long time, or the group may break up, its older membership may die off, or a change in our residence, career, or sympathies and beliefs may oblige us to bid it farewell. When we then recall all the times we have spent in the group, do these remembrances not actually come to us as a single piece? So much so that we sometimes imagine the oldest remembrances to be the most immediate; or, rather, they are all illuminated in a uniform light, like objects blending together in the twilight. . . .

Consider matters now from the point of view of the individual. He belongs to several groups, participates in several social thoughts, and is successively immersed in several collective times. The fact that people are not immersed, within a given time and space, in the same collective currents already permits an element of individual differentiation. Moreover, individuals vary in the speed at which and distance to which their thought goes into the past, or time, of each group. In this sense each consciousness may concentrate, in a given interval, on durations of differing extent. That is, in a given interval of lived social duration, each consciousness is occupied with a varying extent of represented time. The range of variation, of course, is quite large.

A quite different interpretation is provided by those psychologists who believe that each individual consciousness has a distinctive duration, irreducible to any other. They consider each consciousness a flood of thought with its own characteristic movement. First of all, however, time does not flow, but endures and continues to exist. It must do so, for otherwise how could memory reascend the course of time? Moreover, how could a representation of time common to more than one consciousness be derived if each of these currents is a unique and continuous sequence of states that unfolds with varying speed? In reality, the thoughts and events of individual consciousnesses can be compared and relocated within a common time because inner duration dissolves into various currents whose source is the group. The individual consciousness is only a passageway for these currents, a point of intersection for collective times.

Curiously enough, philosophers of time have hardly considered this conception until recently. They have continued to picture the individual consciousness as isolated and sealed within itself. The expression "stream of thought," or psychological flux or current, found in the writings of William James and Henri Bergson, translates with the help of an appropriate metaphor the feeling that each of us experiences when he is a spectator at the unfolding of his own psychic life. It is as if, within each of us, our states of consciousness follow one another in a continuous current, like so many waves pushing one after another. This is indeed true, as reflection confirms, of thinking that continually progresses from one perception or emotion to another. By contrast, memory characteristically forces us to stop and momentarily turn aside from this flux, so that we might, if not reascend, at least cut across a current along which appear numerous branchings off, as it were. Of course, thought is still active in memory, shifting and moving about. But what is noteworthy is that only in this instance can it be said that thought shifts and moves about in time. Without memory and apart from those moments when we remember, how could we ever be aware of being in time and of transporting ourselves through duration? Absorbed in our impressions, pursuing them as they appear and then disappear, we doubtless merge into one moment of duration after another. But how can we also represent time itself, that temporal framework that encompasses many other moments as well as this one? We can *be* in time, in the present, which is a part of time, and nevertheless not be capable of *thinking* in time, of taking ourselves back in thought to the near or more distant past. In other words, we must distinguish the current of impressions from the current of thought (properly so called), or memory. The first is rigidly linked to the body, never causes us to go outside ourself, and provides no perspective on the past. The second has its origins and most of its course in the thought of the various groups to which we belong.

Suppose now that we focus on groups and their representations, conceiving individual thought as a sequence of successive viewpoints on the thought of these groups. Then we will understand how a person's thought can go varying distances into the past, depending on the extent of the perspectives on the past provided by each collective consciousness in which he participates. One condition is necessary for this to be the case. Past time (a certain image of time) has to exist immobile in each collective consciousness and endure within given limits, which vary by group. This is the great paradox. On reflection, however, we realize it could not be otherwise. How could any society or group exist and gain self-awareness if it could not survey a set of present and past events, if it did not have the capacity to reascend the course of time and pass continually over traces left behind of itself? Every group—be it religious, political or economic, family, friends, or acquaintances, even a transient gathering in a salon, auditorium, or street—immobilizes time in its own way and imposes on its members the illusion that, in a given duration of a constantly changing world, certain zones have acquired a relative stability and balance in which nothing essential is altered.

Of course, how far we may so return into the past depends on the group. Consequently, individual thought, depending on the degree of its participation in a given collective thought, attains ever more distant remembrances. Beyond this moving fringe of time or, more correctly, of collective times, there is nothing more, for the time of the philosophers is an empty form. Time is real only insofar as it has content—that is, insofar as it offers events as material for thought. It is limited and relative, but it is plainly real. Moreover, it is large and substantial enough to offer the individual consciousness a framework within which to arrange and retrieve its remembrances.

Marc Bloch (1886–1944)

French historian, founding figure of the Annales school in French historiography. Though here we present only Bloch's direct engagement with **Halbwachs**'s 1925 *Social Frameworks of Memory*, Bloch himself also wrote extensively on collective memory, most explicitly in his book *Feudal Society*.

From "Mémoire collective, tradition et coutume: À propos d'un livre récent"

The extremely rich and suggestive work that I would like to present to the readers of *La Revue de Synthèse* originated with an observation that the author first made about himself and then confirmed in a study of the literature on dreams. As summarized . . . : "We are incapable of reliving our past while we dream; if our dreams bring to mind images that have the appearance of memories, they are only in fragments, in disconnected shreds of the scenes we experienced in real life . . . a scene that occurred in the past never appears, in full detail, in one's dreams." If Halbwachs, as these lines might lead us to believe, had written from the perspective of individual psychology, the historian writing this review would have limited his ambitions to reading the book, and certainly would not have been so rash as to review it. But Halbwachs, by trade and by avocation, is a sociologist. Accordingly, this initial observation led him to construct an entire theory of memory from the viewpoint of collective psychology—a theory which, as we will see, is two-fold. On the one hand, this author seeks to reveal "how the social enters into individual memories;" on the other hand, he studies collective memory proper, that is, the collection of memories common to an entire human group and their influence on social life. Following a natural scholarly progression, this last inquiry adds to Halbwachs' well-known work on the concept of social class.

Halbwachs argues for a sharp distinction between dreaming and remembering, posing a challenge to Bergsonian psychology. If it were true, as Bergson holds, that "true memory"—as opposed to habitual memory—"retains and organizes alongside each other all of our experiences as they progressively take place," and if, furthermore, we accepted that our past remains hidden to us most of the time because it is "inhibited by the necessities of present action," then how could we explain why, during sleep—the time when we are *least* interested in efficient action—our memory fails us the most? More to the point, any theory that depicts memory as a completely individual phenomenon will find itself forever incapable of explaining why our dreams do not consist purely of individual memories.

Without presuming to understand the nature of memory, let us instead undertake a detailed analysis of the nature of the dream. No one could deny that "it is in dreaming that the mind is furthest away from society." Could this be the precise reason why dreams are not made up of memories? A natural assumption, but for the moment an ungrounded one; we must subject it to the test of experience by studying the way in which the past is relived in our minds. According to Halbwachs, remembering is always an active process: to remember is not to sit back and watch, like a passive spectator, while images preserved in the unconscious are uncovered and brought into focus. On the contrary, to remember is to reconstruct the past. However, this reconstructive work is only possible because the individual mind has recourse to the group mind, which provides a framework for reconstructing the past. "Every memory, however personal, is linked with an entire set of notions that many others possess, with people, with groups, places, dates, words and forms of language, with thoughts and ideas, in other words with the entire material and moral life of the societies in which we participate and have participated." These social phenomena allow us to locate our images of the past within time and space, to name them, and to make sense of them. Is there—to give only one example—an activity more social than language? Who can't see that memory is to a large degree dependent upon internalized speech? The collective frameworks of memory never leave us entirely; even in sleep, some of them remain, because in dreaming, "the contact between us and society is never entirely gone; we still utter words, we still understand their meaning." Yet they remain few in number and in an imprecise form; that is why, in our dreams, the images of the past appear only in pieces, too disconnected from each other and from the rest of the social past to be recognized as memories. The things that we remember may be solely personal; the frameworks of memory, without which memories would not exist as such, are always furnished by society. Individual memory finds a point of reference, without which it would be meaningless, in the collective memory; in a certain sense, one could say that an individual memory is only "one part and one aspect of the group memory."

But an individual does not belong to only one group; each one of us is part of a considerable number of groups on which we depend, as we have just seen, even in our most seemingly intimate thought processes. This insight leads us to the second part of the book, the analysis of different genres of collective memory. Halbwachs focused his research on three specific types: family memory, religious memory, and class memory. He in no way claimed to exhaust all types of social memory; the different "memories" that he studied were simply chosen as particularly instructive examples. However, from this point of view, it is unfortunate that customary law was deliberately left out of the analysis. We will revisit this point later.

It would not be possible to trace out all the details of this three-part inquiry, which is far too rich in observation and reflection to be condensed into a review. One essential idea, however, emerges from the work. Every social group derives its spiritual unity from the traditions that constitute the specific content of the collective memory and from "the ideas and conventions that stem from the knowledge of the present." However, these two types of collective representation—the past and the present—do not, as many authors have argued, exist in opposition to each other; on the contrary, they exist only in reference to each other, as societies can interpret the past only through the lens of the present, and the present becomes meaningful only in light of the past. Let's take, for example, Christian groups: in this case, the beliefs of the faithful are nourished simultaneously by rites, continuously reenacted, and by memories, particularly those of the Savior. However, the majority of rites would be devoid of meaning if they did not commemorate the power of God or that of his saints, and by the same token, the historical legacy of Christianity is transmitted, from generation to generation, mainly through the intermediary of rites. In sum, one could say, pushing Halbwachs' theory to its limits, that for him the Mass is the social act par excellence because it permanently joins the commemoration of the Last Supper with an actual ritual of sacrifice. Along these lines, in a similar way, familial sentiment exists only through the somewhat abstract notion of kinship ties—that is my father, my brother, etc.—and the memories that allow each of us to look beyond these names of father or brother and see the reality of flesh and blood. Furthermore, every social class becomes conscious of itself through concrete shared activity in the present and through shared conceptions and sentiments provided by knowledge, more or less accurate, of the group's past. It should come as no surprise that, in the collective memory, the conditions of the present give rise to somewhat imperfect notions of the past. The collective memory, like the individual memory, does not preserve the past precisely; it is constantly reconstructing and reformulating in light of the present. Remembering is always a process.

One can easily see the fruitfulness of this line of thought. In particular, readers familiar with Halbwachs's great work which seeks to define the working class will find a bold extension of his thought in his new book, which develops without contradiction. For as he continues to believe—with good reason, no doubt—that "in urban societies, what distinguishes the working class from other groups is that industrial workers are put, by the nature of their work, in contact with things, not with men," he would presumably shrink from studying this class today by ignoring in its members all representation of the traditional order. Moreover, this reconciliation, if we can call it that, of tradition with the present seems to imply certain conclusions of a political and practical order, which he does not speak a word of, except for his explicit refusal to engage with these matters. But precisely because this reconciliation is so general, a view of this kind should never be discussed without testing particular cases. We are permitted, in this review, to primarily consider it as a direct call to historians, notably to those who have the courage to undertake the study, until now too neglected, of social class. Now I would like to offer some comments on the work, in no particular order.

How are memories passed down from generation to generation within a group? The answer obviously varies according to the group, but the question is too important to leave unanswered. Halbwachs, it seems to me, scarcely addresses this question, most often limiting himself to explanations of a certain finality and, if I may be so bold, to a slightly vague anthropomorphism. He writes, "The group tends to erase from its memory everything that could divide individuals;" the group is, at certain times, "obligated to adopt new values, to emphasize new traditions that are more in accordance with its present-day needs." Such an omission, from an author so well-informed about social life, is surprising enough to tempt one to fix the blame on something external to him, on certain styles or conventions of language. I would also be tempted to hold Durkheimian language, which is characterized by its use of terms designed for individual psychology in conjunction with the epithet "collective." It is not that I have any objection to speaking of "collective memory," just as we speak of collective representations or collective consciousness. These terms are important and expressive, and their use is entirely legitimate, but on one condition: that we do not automatically subsume all of the realities that we label "individual memory" under the name of "collective memory." How does an individual retain or recover his memories? How does a group retain or recover its memories? Traditional psychology certainly considered the first of these questions to be independent from the second; Halbwachs, on the contrary, clearly shows us that the idea of an individual memory completely separate from the social memory is merely an abstraction, nearly devoid of any meaning. His book adds to an entire series of work which, in the last few years, has prompted us to seek out the social within the individual. The influence of Durkheim today seems to have been particularly successful within studies that would normally be strictly psychological. However, while they may be closely linked, the two questions that I mentioned above are nonetheless in a certain sense distinct, and their constitutive elements are different. For a social group that exists longer than the life of one man to have a memory, it is not enough that the members at one point in time hold in their minds the representations of the group's past. It is also necessary that the oldest members of the group transmit these representations to the youngest. We are free to use the term "collective memory," but we must remember that at least a part of what we are referring to is simply everyday communication between individuals.

An example can illustrate more clearly why it is important to study memory transmission. In reference to family memory, Halbwachs offers the following analysis of grandparents: "It is only in fragments, occasionally interspersed with the immediate family, that grandparents pass their memories down to their grandchildren." It seems to me that in many cases, the role of grandparents is infinitely more important and interesting than that. Consider, for instance, the case of rural societies. Normally, during the day while the father is at work in the fields and the mother is occupied by endless housework, young children rest in the care of their grandparents. It is from them, as much as or more so than from their parents, that children learn about all sorts of customs and traditions. Indeed, one must question whether, in these rural societies before the age of newspapers, primary school, and military service, the education of the youngest generation by the oldest generation could have been responsible for the perpetuation of the traditional way of life. In towns, on the other hand, the conditions of professional and domestic life did not demand so much of parents, and thus, this atmosphere was more favorable to the development of intellectual curiosity and change.

Studying religious collective memory, Halbwachs writes the following: "In the beginning, sacred rites undoubtedly responded to the need to commemorate a religious memory, for example, Passover among Jews and Communion among Christians." Is this accurate? Without a doubt, pious Jews have for a long time celebrated the memory of their ancestors who fled Pharaoh, just as Christians have slowly learned the mysteries of their religion by watching the priest raise the host and declare, "this is my body . . . this is my blood." These are irrefutably the present meanings attached to these rites; but do these present meanings mirror the original ones? Few religious historians would concur. On the contrary, it must be emphasized that the idea of Holy Communion has nothing specifically Christian about it; in the first century a.d. it was a ritual of the common patrimony on the banks of the Mediterranean. Thus, Communion does not stem from the Last Supper; rather, we can only explain the Last Supper in reference to older traditions. In the same vein, the Passover meal was only later attached to the story that justifies it today, and I must point out that the fit between the ritual and the story is not a perfect one. What we have here are false memories. Is Halbwachs going to one day study the errors in the collective memory?

He would have inevitably been forced to do so, if he had not, as I previously indicated, neglected the study of customary law; this omission is all the more regrettable since many useful historical works could have paved the way for him. Medieval societies can provide important case studies for sociologists. For several centuries in Western Europe, law had no basis other than custom; legal rules were considered legitimate solely because they had been in place for as long as anyone could remember. When a dutiful judge, a St. Louis for example, had to search for the true meaning of a law, his first inclination was to turn to the past and ask himself: what did those before me do? Under these conditions, it seems that the law would have remained nearly immutable over long periods of time; yet, on the contrary, we know that it evolved dramatically and rapidly during these centuries. In the name of tradition, a vast array of novelties was introduced into the law. Isn't this a curious phenomenon, worthy of the attention of a psychologist preoccupied by the study of the collective consciousness? During this same time period, we can also find examples of this phenomenon outside the law, in the religious domain. For example, between the Peace of the Church and the Reformation, Christianity transformed more profoundly than Halbwachs imagines. Seemingly traditionalist, medieval societies believed that they lived from memory, but this memory was in many respects a false one.

The chapter dedicated to social class evidently suffered from the extreme lack of historical work on the subject. I am not sure if Halbwachs sufficiently took into account the relatively recent character—if one dares apply the word "recent" to the twelfth and thirteenth centuries—of what we refer to as the "noble class." In addition, I am not entirely convinced by his explanation of the rule—also relatively recent—which holds that the nobility could not take up certain professions because "a fortune whose sources are too visible . . . loses some of its prestige." On the contrary, there was always a source of noble fortunes that was both perfectly legitimate and perfectly visible—war—and if Halbwachs doubts that war was considered openly, and even cynically, as a source of profit, then he needs only to turn to the poetry of Bertrand de Born for some examples. In addition, the existence of a functional nobility appears to me to be much older than Halbwachs supposes; the medieval nobility has its origin, at least partly, in the Carolingian civil servant. . . . But all of these questions are infinitely complex, and it would be absurd to presume to touch on any of them more than in passing here. We do not have good histories of the nobility; as soon as we have one, Halbwachs will be the first to modify some of his developments. In return, the historian of the nobility, whoever he may be, will certainly profit from Halbwachs' work. It is only through intellectual debates of this kind that we can hope to advance the social sciences. There is no greater danger than a narrow dogmatism, which would lead historians and sociologists to ignore each other or to dismiss each other's work. For this reason, I have reviewed this remarkable work. Independent of its philosophical scope, which I have obviously not done justice to (we must not forget that some of the great metaphysical doctrines of our time have been formulated by Halbwachs), independent as well of all its insightful observations, this work does us a great service that no one better than a historian—too often isolated by the necessities of his work, lost in the details of erudition—could appreciate: he pushes us to reflect on the conditions of the historical development of humanity; indeed, what would this development look like without "collective memory"?

—Translated by Jennifer Marie Silva

Charles Blondel (1876–1939)

French psychiatrist, psychologist, and philosopher, known widely for his work on shell shock. Blondel challenged **Halbwachs**'s effort to sociologize psychology and for downplaying memory's somatic foundation.

From "Revue critique: M. Halbwachs *Les cadres sociaux de la mémoire*"

[D]espite the range and seriousness of Halbwachs' demonstration, one feels a certain concern over his elimination, or near elimination, of any glimmer of sensory intuition, which does not, of course, constitute all perception, but which is, all the same, the indispensable preamble to and the condition *sine qua non* of memory.

I do not wish to dispute that we reconstruct our past in large part through the use of materials which are collective and, almost, anonymous. However, in order to not confuse the reconstruction of our own past with our neighbor's, in order for this empirically, logically, socially possible past to appear to correspond to our real past, it is necessary that this reconstruction consist, at least partly, of something more than commonly shared materials. I know that I once went to school for the first time, but I do not remember it, and what seems like a memory in my mind is entirely secondary to my knowledge. But I do remember, as a child, exploring an abandoned house and suddenly sinking waist-deep in a hole filled with water in the middle of a dark room, and I can more or less easily piece together where and when this happened; here, my knowledge is entirely secondary to my memory. In this case, I might need to reconstruct the environment of my memory, but I have no need to reconstruct the memory itself. It truly seems that in memories of this type, we have—ignoring for the moment how this operates—a direct contact with the past which precedes and conditions its historical reconstruction. We come across an old friend from high school. He brings up the past. He tells stories, to which we sometimes respond, "That's true, I remember," and sometimes respond, "Really, do you think so? I don't remember that anymore." How could we conceive of the difference between the evocations that stimulate a recollection within us and those that stimulate nothing, if all memories are purely reconstructions of the past created in the present with the aid of collective images and ideas? In brief, we are not always reduced to judging the authenticity of our reconstitutions solely on the basis of their plausibility. Most often, on the contrary, our reconstructions strike us with some kind of signal that reveals to us that our goal of rediscovering our past has been achieved. What could this difference between our reconstructions that evoke nothing and our reconstructions that evoke something mean, other than the possibility of judging or not judging them according to their original, in the persistence, or the disappearance, of our initial sensory intuitions?

—Translated by Jennifer Marie Silva

Roger Bastide (1898–1974)

French anthropologist. Part of the mythology of collective memory research is that a long period of silence followed **Halbwachs**'s seminal work, which awaited rediscovery in the late 1980s and 1990s. This genealogy is clearly inaccurate. One of the most important direct engagements with Halbwachs's work was by the structuralist anthropologist Roger Bastide. In his book *The African Religions of Brazil* (1960), Bastide extends and revises Halbwachs's ideas on religious memory. According to a strict reading of Halbwachs, religious meanings should be lost when they are unmoored from the social frameworks of their original contexts. But, as Bastide shows, the syncretic African religions of Brazil provide much evidence to the contrary. This was because, Bastide argues in this excerpt, Halbwachs was too committed to **Durkheim**'s theory of collective consciousness and thus neglected the autonomy of individuals in the process of mnemonic transmission. The study of collective memory, Bastide argues here, must include not just a stark choice between remembering and forgetting, but also an account of the metamorphosis of collective memories.

From *The African Religions of Brazil: Toward a Sociology of the Interpenetration of Civilizations*

All religion is a tradition—a dual tradition of stereotyped actions and rites and of mental images and myths. It has often been claimed that the two elements are inseparable, myths being a definition or justification of the ceremonial actions. And it is true that myth does seem to constitute a model to be reproduced, an account of a past event that took place at the dawning of the world and that must be continually repeated lest the world collapse into nothingness. Myth is not simply monologue or "precedent," as Lévy-Bruhl termed it. It is already an oral action intimately bound up with a manual one. Nevertheless those who perform the rite are not always completely cognizant of the underlying myth. There are various degrees of initiation, and only the top priests in the hierarchy are privy to the whole heritage of divine lore. Rite is encaged in the matrix of muscular capacity; its range is narrowly limited by the body. The scope of myth, on the other hand, is the almost infinite one of the creative imagination. It is capable of all kinds of proliferation—the unpredictable flowering of dreams. Bergson distinguished two types of memory: motor memory as a bodily function, and the memory of pure images capable of self-crystallization. This distinction is helpful in comprehending the difference between what is commonly accepted as rite and what is commonly accepted as myth, as well as the gap between the two.

This gap will help us to understand why the various elements of religious life in Brazil have shown varying degrees of resistance to change or oblivion. The rites have held out much more tenaciously than the myths. . . .

Myth now survives only through its connection with ritual. In passing from one generation to the next, from mouth to mouth, it has lost its original richness of detail and been reduced to a mere explanation of certain actions. The transplanting of African civilization across the ocean was a process antithetical to the one Bergson studied in *The Two Sources of Morality and Religion*: the process of decrystallization, nonproliferation, and loss of all poetic substance. It would be incorrect to say that the myths have died out. . . .

[T]he fact is that myth now survives only as a definition of rite. Only by allying itself with actions or with the rules of divination did it save itself from extinction. Only to the extent that Bergsonian pure memories are able to attach themselves to the more substantial motor mechanisms, which are less easily forgotten because they operate within the living organism, have the stories of the gods been able to survive—and even then not without losing some of their color, poetic vigor, and richness.

Perhaps we can now take a step forward and ask what has been lost to myth and why. Although myth may shift events back into a mysterious past, it still depicts a certain society. It reflects the structure of lineages, the emergence of chiefhoods, the laws of communal life. As we have seen, slavery destroyed the organization of Negro society. It is true that in Brazil this society was able to rebuild itself, and in doing so it certainly reinterpreted some of the more resistant archaic customs like polygamy or respect for old age. But it naturally rebuilt itself according to the norms and models of the surrounding Luso-Brazilian society. By applying to Brazil a test used by Clémence Ramnoux to study the transmission of legends but using it on a sociological rather than psychological plane, I determined that what is lost when one moves from one social group to another is the collective representations characteristic of the archaic social structures, the parts of the legend connected with ancient forms of marriage or exchanges—in short, everything that is no longer meaningful to the Western world. I concluded that the vital elements in oral transmission are "the structures of contemporary society . . . as well as the changes in collective values, social representations, and ideals resulting from these morphological upheavals. This explains why we immediately try to rationalize and justify according to our own mentality anything that appears at all strange and why these strange elements are the first to be swept away into oblivion because we can no longer fit them into the social frameworks of memory."

The allusion in the last sentence to Halbwachs's famous book is not a casual one. After all, it was he who established (with the help of other data) that "social thought is essentially memory, and . . . its content consists entirely of collective memories. But only those memories survive—and only that part of any one memory—that society, operating within its existing frameworks, is able to reconstruct at any given time." The impoverishment of African myths is not the result of real forgetting of a psychological nature, induced by the destructive action of time, but of the lack of landmarks to which memories can attach themselves. Societal change, not erosion, is responsible for the loss of images.

This test may explain the impoverishment of myth, but having been designed to study change, not survival, it does not explain what preserves it. How are we to account for what survives? Arthur Ramos devoted half of his book *O Negro Brasileiro* to a psychoanalytical interpretation of African myths based on matriarchy, the murder of the father, the birth of the hero, and the twin nature of the human personality. . . . Taking Ramos's hypothesis as a point of departure, the part of myth that survives is the part that best meets the inmost leanings of the black soul. To uphold this explanation one would have to accept that acquired characteristics can be inherited (which is controversial), that we are dealing with a black unconscious different from the racial unconscious of other peoples and possessing its own archetypes (which Jung would not admit), or that the social conditions in which Brazilian blacks live are a continuation of the original African ones. . . . Nevertheless, if psychoanalysis is to elucidate certain aspects of the survivals, it ultimately has to call upon sociology. What survive are the complexes of the collective unconscious that are upheld by contemporary social conditions, and in the end these conditions are the essential factor. . . .

In contrast, da Costa Eduardo winds up with a sociological explanation for the survival of memories: "The process of memory is socially determined and is therefore to be explained in terms of attitudes, feelings, and collective conventions on the part of groups of individuals."

This sociology is a functionalist one. Legend preserves anything that fulfills a useful function within the community. The black, first a slave and later relegated to the lower levels of society, defends himself against his white master or against people of greater social prestige through the story of rabbits outwitting brute force by guile and intelligence. . . . While I do not deny the importance of this function, our problem, the preservation of African elements, requires an investigation of other factors too. After all, the same function could have been served by the legends of Renard the Fox just as well as by stories of the African rabbit.

Their survival is explained not so much by the function of the stories as by the carry-over of the African social frameworks in the Maranhão communities. . . . Collective memory does not come into play unless the ancestral institutions have been preserved. Memories are so much a part of interpersonal relations, constituted groups, or human associations that they spring to life again only where these sociological phenomena are perpetually operative. Thus the functionalist thesis and the psychoanalytical one lead to the same conclusion: the primary importance of social frameworks in collective memory.

Halbwachs's strong insistence on this point, that the individual cannot remember without recourse to group thought and that forgetting is caused by the disappearance of the old social frameworks, makes further elaboration unnecessary. For one thing, Halbwachs was too firmly committed to the Durkheimian dilemma of the individual and the group—the group becoming aware of its identity in the course of time and the individual remembering only through his membership in a group. He was also too committed to the theory of collective consciousness, which led him to distinguish as many types of memory as there are groups in society. He forgot that every group is structured and is in the process of either destructuring or restructuring. To be more accurate, he did at one point (in a little article on the memory of musicians, each of whom plays a different role in the orchestra) recognize the importance of the respective places of individuals in an organized whole, but he never revised his earlier theses in the light of this article. Yet to understand the reason for survivals or disappearances in African religious traditions we must concentrate on the structure of groups rather than on groups per se.

Religious rites are not performed by just anyone but by actors carefully chosen for each particular ceremony. The ceremonies themselves are distributed among the various social categories: the moieties or clans, sex or age groups, those qualified to handle what is sacred and the rank and file of the sect, family and community heads, farmers and the artisan castes. Each category has a special function quite distinct from all others, although all functions are complementary and seek the well-being of the community as a whole. . . .

The assertion that religious ceremonies create great emotional exaltation through the massing of individuals has created an extraordinarily false impression. They have been interpreted as a re-creation of primeval chaos through the momentary abolition of all taboos and rules, through sexual license, and through an anarchic jumbling of classes and sexes, ranks and roles. Nothing is further from the truth. Even in its apparent madness the festival is always controlled. . . . If exaltation occurs, it is a controlled exaltation, . . . It has nothing in common with the madness of modern crowds. The ceremony is the image of the group and hence is structured like the group. While I do not wish to equate the social role with a theatrical one, we are nonetheless dealing with a kind of spectacle in which each actor has certain lines to speak and certain actions to perform. But these lines make sense only within the total dialogue; the actions acquire significance only when they connect with those of the other actors. Social continuity thus depends on structural continuity, and if the latter were for some reason to be broken, the tradition would be in instant danger of crumbling. In short, collective memory can indeed be regarded as a group memory provided we add that it is a memory articulated among the members of the group. . . .

The religious tradition can be seen in two different aspects: as constraint and as structure. The former aspect has been stressed most frequently because the pressure of the older generations on the younger was regarded as the elementary process of social continuity. But this constraint operates within a certain division of social labor, and apprenticeship to the past changes with the make-up of the community. It is the structure of the group rather than the group itself that provides the frameworks of collective memory; otherwise it would be impossible to understand why individual memory needs the support of the community as a whole. If we need someone else in order to remember, it is because our memories are articulated together with the memories of others in the well-ordered interplay of reciprocal images. . . . This explains why African survivals maintained themselves infinitely more vigorously in the towns than in the country. If tradition were merely the force of the past, mere group constraint, it would simply have assumed the form of individual initiations, the handing on by the oldest members of the group to the youngest of a heritage of images, or the conversion of a few Bantu to the Yoruba religion. But when that did happen, only two or three roles were interiorized; the totality of the liturgical drama (and of the mythology, which is linked to it) disappeared. In the city, though, the old structure could more easily find many of its actors, if not the entire cast, so that the memories could be reconstituted almost in full.

But in Africa the different sectors of society, each of which retains memories that complement the memories of other sectors . . . are also geographic sectors. The sanctuaries of the deities are scattered about a space that thus itself becomes structured. This brings us to another theme in Halbwachs's theory. Since memories are psychic by nature, if they are to survive they must survive in something durable; they must be attached to a permanent material base of some kind. Psychologists seek this material base in the brain; sociologists seek it in nature. The localization of memories in material objects that endure in social time is the exact equivalent, it seems to me, of cerebral localizations in psychological theory. The transplantation of blacks from Africa to America and the consequent loss of certain sectors of society pose a problem analogous to the problem of the destruction of, or of lesions in, certain convolutions of the brain and the subsequent formation of new memory centers. When Halbwachs studies the topography of Palestine and shows the Crusades trying to localize the collective representations of the Christian church in a country profoundly modified since the death of Christ and the Arab invasion, he comes close to the problem we are dealing with here: the problem of the memory of a religious group establishing new material centers to which to attach its mental images. . . .

The foregoing arguments show that collective memory is a set of mental images linked on the one hand to the motor mechanisms of rites (although going beyond them) and on the other hand to morphological and social structures. Hence remembrance is precipitated whenever the assembled African community regains its structure and reactivates, in the linking of roles, the ancestral motor mechanisms. Place, society, actions, and memory now become one. . . .

An analogous phenomenon occurs in individual memory. Every memory partakes of both the past and the present and, inasmuch as it belongs to the present, is part of the total stream of consciousness. It is therefore modified in response to changing affectivity or central interests. Halbwachs's observation that not all traditional images are resurrected but only those that fit the present, an observation by which he explains the evolution of the Catholic mystique, underlines the importance of the phenomenon I am alluding to: the penetration of the past by the present or, to rephrase it in terms of structure, dual participation in two different social worlds: the past-oriented African sects and the perpetually changing global Brazilian society.

The study of collective memory must therefore include, besides an explanation of retaining and forgetting, an explanation of the metamorphosis of collective memories. . . .

Collective memories, . . . are attached to groups, and the degree of their resistance depends on the nature of those groups. But we also see that if the present affects the past, it is always along the line marked out by the past. Nothing is created; a selection is simply made among memories. . . . So the present acts primarily as a kind of sluice gate that lets through only what can adapt itself to the new environment or at any rate what does not conflict with it, while holding back irreconcilable representations. Perhaps the present might also be compared to the Freudian censor, which represses in the unconscious anything that conflicts with the customs and ethics of the social environment. There is, however, one difference, a difference that stems from the twofold distinction between affective and intellectual memory and between the individual and the group—namely that the repressed libido goes on working while collective myths or representations that have fallen into desuetude are gradually forgotten. . . .

Certain general conclusions concerning the sociological problems of memory can be drawn from this study of the gods.

1. There are two kinds of memory—motor and intellectual. The more closely collective representations and myths are interwoven in the web of actions, the more resistant to change they will be.

2. It is not the group itself that explains the phenomena of the preservation or forgetting of memories so much as the group's structure or organization. More generally, I have distinguished three operative structures: the sect, the sacred space, and the secret. Since memories are localized in specific separate yet complementary sectors, the presence or absence of these sectors in Brazil as related to Africa accounts for survivals and gaps in the collective memory.

3. Memories inherited from the ancestors survive only insofar as they can insinuate themselves into the existing frameworks of society. If the collective African memory persists in the new land, it is because the African sects "work." And because they work in symbiosis with the global Brazilian society, whatever is no longer in accord with the new environmental values is forgotten.

4. Although myth retains a certain richness of detail, it tends to decrystallize, to become schematized. Its principal function is now to justify or explain rites or the forms and types of sacrifices, taboos, and ceremonial sequences.

W. Lloyd Warner (1898–1970)

American anthropologist. Yet another demonstration that post-Durkheimian interest in collective memory was alive and well between Halbwachs and the "memory boom" of the 1980s–1990s. In a series of five books, Warner and colleagues undertook an exhaustive ethnography of a small American city. The fifth volume, *The Living and the Dead*, studies the commemorative structures of "Yankee City," including the integrative powers of Memorial Day and other cults of the dead, which constitute essential symbol systems organizing individual and group memories.

From *The Living and the Dead: A Study of the Symbolic Life of Americans*

The Memorial Day rites of Yankee City and hundreds of other American towns . . . are a modern cult of the dead and conform to Durkheim's definition of sacred collective representations. They are a cult because they consist of a system of sacred beliefs and dramatic rituals held by a group of people who, when they congregate, represent the whole community. They are sacred because they ritually relate the living to sacred things. They are a cult because the members have not been formally organized into an institutionalized church with a defined theology, but depend on informal organization to order their sacred activities. They are called a cult here because this term, though more narrowly used in common parlance, accurately places them in a class of social phenomena clearly identified in the sacred behavior of other societies.

The cult system of sacred belief conceptualizes in organized form sentiments common to everyone in the community about death. These sentiments are composed of fears of death which conflict with the social reassurances our culture provides us to combat such anxieties. These assurances, usually acquired in childhood and thereby carrying some of the authority of the adults who provided them, are a composite of theology and folk belief. The deep anxieties to which we refer include anticipation of our own deaths, of the deaths or possible deaths of loved ones, and—less powerfully—of the deaths or possible deaths of the wise of our generation—those who have taught us—and of men in general.

Each man's church provides him and those of his faith with a set of beliefs and a mode of action to face these problems, but his church and those of other men do not equip their respective members with a common set of social beliefs and rituals which permit them to unite with all their fellows to confront this common and most feared of all enemies. The Memorial Day rite and other subsidiary rituals connected with it form a cult which partially satisfies this need for common action on a common problem. It dramatically expresses the sentiments of unity of all the living among themselves, of all the living with all the dead, and of all the living and dead as a group with God. God, as worshiped by Catholic, Protestant, and Jew, loses sectarian definition, limitations, and foreignness as between different customs and becomes the common object of worship for the whole group and the protector of everyone.

The unifying and integrating symbols of this cult are the dead. The graves of the dead are the most powerful of the visible emblems which unify all the activities of the separate groups of the community. The cemetery and its graves become the objects of sacred rituals which permit opposing organizations, often in conflict, to subordinate their ordinary opposition and cooperate in collectively expressing the larger unity of the total community. The rites show extraordinary respect for all the dead, but they pay particular honor to those who were killed in battle "fighting for their country." The death of a soldier in battle is believed to be a "voluntary sacrifice" by him on the altar of his country. To be understood, this belief in the sacrifice of a man's life for his country must be judged first with our general scientific knowledge on the nature of all forms of sacrifice. It must then be subjected to the principles which explain human sacrifice whenever and wherever found. More particularly, this belief must be examined with the realization that these sacrifices occur in a society whose Deity was once incarnate as a man who voluntarily sacrificed his life for all men.

The Memorial Day rite is a cult of the dead but not just of the dead as such, since by symbolically elaborating sacrifice of human life for the country through, or identifying it with, the Christian Church's sacred sacrifice of the incarnate God, the deaths of such men also become powerful sacred symbols which organize, direct, and constantly revive the collective ideals of the community and the nation. . . .

As long as the cemetery is being filled with a fresh stream of the recently dead it stays symbolically a live and vital emblem, telling the living of the meaning of life and death. But when the family, the kindred, and other members of the community gradually discontinue burying their loved ones there, the cemetery, in a manner of speaking, dies its own death as a meaningful symbol of life and death, for it ceases to exist as a living sacred emblem and, through time, becomes an historical monument. As a symbolic object it, too, is subject to the meaning of time. Its spirituality then resides in a different context, for it becomes an object of historical value in stable communities rather than a sacred collective representation effectively relating the dead to the living.

The active cemetery, funerals, and mourning symbols ritually look to the sacred life of the future while marking the secular end of the lifetime of the individual, while the "dead" cemeteries look backward to the life of the past. Their grave stones are not so much symbols of a man's death as the fact that he and the others once lived and constituted in their aggregate a way of life and a society. If a cemetery holds no future for *our own* deaths to mark our passage from the living to the dead—if we cannot project the life of our time into it— then its dead belong to the *life* of the past. The gravestones become artifacts that refer to the past; the cemetery becomes a symbol speaking of the people of the past to those of the present and stands for the regard of the present for its own past. But man's hope for immortality, his hope for the future, cannot be evoked by such historical symbols. They must be projected into cemeteries and into other symbols which represent man's beliefs and feelings about himself. . . .

When cemeteries no longer receive fresh burials which continue to tie the emotions of the living to the recently dead and thereby connect the living in a chain of generations to an early ancestry, the graveyards must lose their sacred quality and become objects of historical ritual. The lifetime of individuals and the living meanings of cemeteries are curiously interdependent, for both are dependent on an ascription of sacred meaning bestowed upon them by those who live. The symbols of death say what life is and those of life define what death must be. The meanings of man's fate are forever what he makes them. . . .

Whenever several symbols of the same or different kinds, with the same or different functions, are coordinated into a recognizable unity they constitute a symbol system. The many ancient and recently invented symbol systems our society possesses, although recognizably unitary, clearly interpenetrate each other. In a symbol system such as an Easter ritual, literary and art systems are integral parts of the ceremony. Gesture, word, song, and emblematic systems intermingle with a prescribed choreography. Each of these separate symbol-assemblages may be integral parts of several other systems, yet be functioning parts of, let us say, an Easter service. The identification of such systems depends partly upon who is recognizing them, the circumstances under which they are being used, and the purposes of the observer. Some of the conventionally and more generally recognized systems are the various forms of art and popular culture: drama, radio, television, the comics, news stories, novels; play and games, ceremony, dogma, creed, sacred and secular ideologies, etiquette; as well as vague and more implicit forms such as reveries, daydreams, and dreams during sleep.

Symbol systems function in part to organize individual and group memories of the immediate and distant past and their expectancies of the future, and by so doing strengthen and unify the persistent life of each. Those symbols which evoke memories of past events for the individual or the group are greatly con-tracted and condensed, often modified beyond the power of the individual or group to recognize what their full references are. Such condensed systems arouse the emotions of individuals and the sentiments of the group; the emotions and sentiments aroused range from overwhelming intensity to slight feelings with only minimal significance to those who have them. They may range from the indifference of an onlooker passing a highway sign in a swiftly moving car to the devoted involvement of the initiate holding the Communion cup.

Generally speaking, living symbols which direct the attention of the individual or group to the past and relate him to it tend to be non-rational and evocative rather than rational and referential. Often for the individual they express memories of past events which are deeply buried in the transpositions of "condensation." [sic] This statement, properly modified, also seems true for the society. The symbols used to arouse memories of Armistice Day and Memorial Day, for example, carry a charge directly connected with the emotions of World Wars I and II and the Civil War, but convey only a blurred, condensed notion of what those events were felt to be by those who directly experienced them. In being related to the whole body of past experience which makes up the life of the group at the time, to be continually modified by the new experience of the group and individuals who compose it, much of a symbol's original meaning—both evocative and referential—while transmitted by the older generation into the minds, thoughts, feelings, and expectancies of the younger, is condensed and transformed. The social relations involved in this transmission, including those of parents and children, sex and age groupings, the economic and political orders, and the society generally, each with its own needs, values, and previously acquired symbols, refashion and sometimes transfigure the words, signs, and meanings of original events in the symbols used for them, which come to have a new significance, functioning to produce new and different effects in the individual and the society.

Symbols which evoke *sentiments* proper for contemporary ritual recognition of the memories of an occasion often have little to do with recreating the beliefs and ideas involved in the actual event. They become condensed versions of much that we have felt and thought about ourselves and the experiences we have in living together. But the *effect* of what has been forgotten remains a powerful part of the collective life of the group.

Such basic groupings as the family order transform and store traditional meanings as part of the physical conditioning of the organisms which are members of the interactive group. The conscious and "unconscious" symbols we retain are present expressions of past experiences, related and adapted to the ongoing life of the species, the society, and each individual.

At the time it is taken, a family photograph of a young mother and father and their several small children may be a representation of what they are in so far as a camera can represent them as human, physical, and social objects. But to the children grown old, with the parents long since dead, the picture may be no longer a representation but a memento, now acting as a fetish does in ritual life to arouse conscious and unconscious feelings and beliefs they have about themselves and their family. To *their* own children, it may evoke at most only feelings of family solidarity and pride. The once representational and referential "individuals" in the photograph may to their great grandchildren become symbolic figures which arouse, portray, and focus the new generation's values, feelings, and beliefs about themselves in the manner of the inward, non-visible images of a dream. They portray a reality of feeling and social value for what the person viewing the photograph in himself is, rather than what the individuals once were to whom the picture refers.

These statements are *not* meant to imply that there is a *racial* unconscious. They do indicate that part of the non-rational symbolic life of the "far away and long ago" world of past generations—forever refreshed in the same kind of mold from which it came—continues and lives in the present.

Every interpretative act is but one momentary event in an infinite series. The flow of evocative meanings of hate, fear, pity, and love, of confident hope and anxious dread and all the other meanings of men is forever being transformed in the present minds of those who interpret; yet, being the ongoing symbolic activity of the human species, it remains fundamentally the same. Tomorrow's meanings are prepared by those of today; those of the present are firmly founded on the meanings of yesterday. The meaning of an interpretative act must always be sought in the present, as the past is momentarily caught, rushing into a previously structured future.

E. E. Evans-Pritchard (1902–1973)

British anthropologist. In his famous book *The Nuer* (1940), Evans-Pritchard drew a distinction between ecological time (natural and regular) and structural time (social and variable) and found that the genealogical capacity of premodern societies like the Nuer is limited to about six generations, beyond which earlier ancestors are absorbed in a timeless mythology. This is important for memory studies because, in his account, Evans-Pritchard shows that such mythic structures, more a means of coordinating relationships than of coordinating events, are the projection of actual social relations into the past.

From *The Nuer: A Description of the Modes of Livelihood and Political Institutions of a Nilotic People*

In describing Nuer concepts of time we may distinguish between those that are mainly reflections of their relations to environment, which we call oecological time, and those that are reflections of their relations to one another in the social structure, which we call structural time. Both refer to successions of events which are of sufficient interest to the community for them to be noted and related to each other conceptually. The larger periods of time are almost entirely structural, because the events they relate are changes in the relationship of social groups. Moreover, time-reckoning based on changes in nature and man's response to them is limited to an annual cycle and therefore cannot be used to differentiate longer periods than seasons. Both, also, have limited and fixed notations. Seasonal and lunar changes repeat themselves year after year, so that a Nuer standing at any point of time has conceptual knowledge of what lies before him and can predict and organize his life accordingly. A man's structural future is likewise already fixed and ordered into different periods, so that the total changes in status a boy will undergo in his ordained passage through the social system, if he lives long enough, can be foreseen. Structural time appears to an individual passing through the social system to be entirely progressive, but, as we shall see, in a sense this is illusion. Oecological time appears to be, and is, cyclical. . . .

Oecological time-reckoning is ultimately, of course, entirely determined by the movement of the heavenly bodies, but only some of its units and notations are directly based on these movements, e.g. month, day, night, and some parts of the day and night, and such points of reference are paid attention to and selected as points only because they are significant for social activities. It is the activities themselves, chiefly of an economic kind, which are basic to the system and furnish most of its units and notations, and the passage of time is perceived in the relation of activities to one another. Since activities are dependent on the movement of the heavenly bodies and since the movement of the heavenly bodies is significant only in relation to the activities one may often refer to either in indication of the time of an event. . . . The movements of the heavenly bodies permit Nuer to select natural points that are significant in relation to activities. Hence in linguistic usage nights, or rather 'sleeps,' are more clearly defined units of time than days, or 'suns,' because they are undifferentiated units of social activity, and months, or rather 'moons,' though they are clearly differentiated units of natural time, are little employed as points of reference because they are not clearly differentiated units of activity, whereas the day, the year, and its main seasons are complete occupational units.

Certain conclusions may be drawn from this quality of time among the Nuer. Time has not the same value throughout the year. Thus in dry season camps, although daily pastoral tasks follow one another in the same order as in the rains, they do not take place at the same time, are more a precise routine owing to the severity of seasonal conditions, especially with regard to water and pasturage, and require greater co-ordination and co-operative action. On the other hand, life in the dry season is generally uneventful, outside routine tasks, and oecological and social relations are more monotonous from month to month than in the rains when there are frequent feasts, dances, and ceremonies. When time is considered as relations between activities it will be understood that it has a different connotation in rains and drought. In the drought the daily time-reckoning is more uniform and precise while lunar reckoning receives less attention. . . . The pace of time may vary accordingly, since perception of time is a function of systems of time-reckoning. . . .

Though I have spoken of time and units of time the Nuer have no expression equivalent to 'time' in our language, and they cannot, therefore, as we can, speak of time as though it were something actual, which passes, can be wasted, can be saved, and so forth. I do not think that they ever experience the same feeling of fighting against time or of having to co-ordinate activities with an abstract passage of time, because their points of reference are mainly the activities themselves, which are generally of a leisurely character. Events follow a logical order, but they are not controlled by an abstract system there being no autonomous points of reference to which activities have to conform with precision. Nuer are fortunate.

Also they have very limited means of reckoning the relative duration of periods of time intervening between events, since they have few, and not well-defined or systematized, units of time. Having no hours or other small units of time they cannot measure the periods which intervene between positions of the sun or daily activities. It is true that the year is divided into twelve lunar units, but Nuer do not reckon in them as fractions of a unit. They may be able to state in what month an event occurred, but it is with great difficulty that they reckon the relation between events in abstract numerical symbols. They think much more easily in terms of activities and of successions of activities and in terms of social structure and of structural differences than in pure units of time.

We may conclude that the Nuer system of time-reckoning within the annual cycle and parts of the cycle is a series of conceptualizations of natural changes, and that the selection of points of reference is determined by the significance which these natural changes have for human activities. . . .

In a sense all time is structural since it is a conceptualization of collateral, co-ordinated, or co-operative activities: the movemeats of a group. Otherwise time concepts of this kind could not exist, for they must have a like meaning for every one within a group. Milking-time and meal-times are approximately the same for all people who normally come into contact with one another, and the movement from villages to camps has approximately the same connotation everywhere in Nuerland, though it may have a special connotation for a particular group of persons. There is, however, a point at which we can say that time concepts cease to be determined by oecological factors and become more determined by structural interrelations, being no longer a reflection of man's dependence on nature, but a reflection of the interaction of social groups.

The year is the largest unit of oecological time. Nuer have words for the year before last, last year, this year, next year, and the year after next. Events which took place in the last few years are then the points of reference in time-reckoning, and these are different according to the group of persons who make use of them: joint family, village, tribal section, tribe, &c. One of the commonest ways of stating the year of an event is to mention where the people of the village made their dry season camps, or to refer to some evil that befell their cattle. A joint family may reckon time in the birth of calves of their herds. Weddings and other ceremonies, fights, and raids, may likewise give points of time, though in the absence of numerical dating no one can say without lengthy calculations how many years ago an event took place. Moreover, since time is to Nuer an order of events of outstanding significance to a group, each group has its own points of reference and time is consequently relative to structural space, locally considered. This is obvious when we examine the names given to years by different tribes, or sometimes by adjacent tribes, for these are floods, pestilences, famines, wars, &c., experienced by the tribe. In course of time the names of years are forgotten and all events beyond the limits of this crude historical reckoning fade into the dim vista of long long ago. Historical time, in this sense of a sequence of outstanding events of significance to a tribe, goes back much farther than the historical time of smaller groups, but fifty years is probably its limit, and the farther back from the present day the sparser and vaguer become its points of reference.

However, Nuer have another way of stating roughly when events took place; not in numbers of years, but by reference to the age-set system. Distance between events ceases to be reckoned in time concepts as we understand them and is reckoned in terms of structural distance, being the relation between groups of persons. It is therefore entirely relative to the social structure. . . . [W]e cannot accurately translate a reckoning in sets into a reckoning in years, but . . . we can roughly estimate a ten-year interval between the commencement of successive sets. There are six sets in existence, the names of the sets are not cyclic, and the order of extinct sets, all but the last, are soon forgotten, so that an age-set reckoning has seven units covering a period of rather under a century.

The structural system of time-reckoning is partly the selection of points of reference of significance to local groups which give these groups a common and distinctive history: partly the distance between specific sets in the age-set system; and partly distances of a kinship and lineage order. Four generation-steps (kath) in the kinship system are linguistically differentiated relations, grandfather, father, son, and grandson, and within a small kinship group these relationships give a time-depth to members of the group and points of reference in a line of ascent by which their relationships are determined and explained. Any kinship relationship must have a point of reference on a line of ascent, namely a common ancestor, so that such a relationship always has a time connotation couched in structural terms. Beyond the range of the kinship system in this narrow sense the connotation is expressed in terms of the lineage system. . . .

We have remarked that the movement of structural time is, in a sense, an illusion, for the structure remains fairly constant and the perception of time is no more than the movement of persons, often as groups, through the structure. Thus age-sets succeed one another for ever, but there are never more than six in existence and the relative positions occupied by these six sets at any time are fixed structural points through which actual sets of persons pass in endless succession. Similarly, . . . Nuer system of lineages may be considered a fixed system, there being a constant number of steps between living persons and the founder of their clan and the lineages having a constant position relative to one another. However many generations succeed one another the depth and range of lineages does not increase unless there has been structural change. . . .

Beyond the limits of historical time we enter a plane of tradition in which a certain element of historical fact may be supposed to be incorporated in a complex of myth. Here the points of reference are the structural ones we have indicated. At one end this plane merges into history; at the other end into myth. Time perspective is here not a true impression of actual distances like that created by our dating technique, but a reflection of relations between lineages, so that the traditional events recorded have to be placed at the points where the lineages concerned in them converge in their lines of ascent. The events have therefore a position in structure, but no exact position in historical time as we understand it. Beyond tradition lies the horizon of pure myth which is always seen in the same time perspective. One mythological event did not precede another, for myths explain customs of general social significance rather than the interrelations of particular segments and are, therefore, not structurally stratified. Explanations of any qualities of nature or of culture are drawn from this intellectual ambient which imposes limits on the Nuer world and makes it self-contained and entirely intelligible to Nuer in the relation of its parts. The world, peoples, and cultures all existed together from the same remote past.

It will have been noted that the Nuer time dimension is shallow. Valid history ends a century ago, and tradition, generously measured, takes us back only ten to twelve generations in lineage structure, and if we are right in supposing that lineage structure never grows, it follows that the distance between the beginning of the world and the present day remains unalterable. Time is thus not a continuum, but is a constant structural relationship between two points, the first and last persons in a line of agnatic descent. How shallow is Nuer time may be judged from the fact that the tree under which mankind came into being was still standing in Western Nuerland a few years ago!

Beyond the annual cycle, time-reckoning is a conceptualization of the social structure, and the points of reference are a projection into the past of actual relations between groups of persons. It is less a means of co-ordinating events than of co-ordinating relationships, and is therefore mainly a looking-backwards, since relationships must be explained in terms of the past.

Claude Lévi-Strauss (1908–2009)

French anthropologist. In one of his best-known books, *The Savage Mind*, Lévi-Strauss replaces what he sees as a "clumsy distinction between 'peoples without history' and others" with one between what he calls "hot" and "cold" societies. In this way, he argues, we can understand better the "savage mind's" veneration of ancestors, who seem to exist in a "flattened out" plane of timelessness, in comparison to the contemporary preoccupation with the archive, which puts us "in touch with pure historicity."

From *The Savage Mind*

I have suggested elsewhere that the clumsy distinction between 'peoples without history' and others could with advantage be replaced by a distinction between what for convenience I called 'cold' and 'hot' societies: the former seeking, by the institutions they give themselves, to annul the possible effects of historical factors on their equilibrium and continuity in a quasi-automatic fashion; the latter resolutely internalizing the historical process and making it the moving power of their development. . . . Several types of historical sequences will still need to be distinguished. Some, while existing in duration, are of a recurrent nature; the annual cycle of the seasons, for instance, or that of individual life or that of exchanges of goods and services within the social group. These sequences raise no problem because they are periodically repeated in duration without their structure necessarily undergoing any change; the object of 'cold' societies is to make it the case that the order of temporal succession should have as little influence as possible on their content. No doubt they do not succeed perfectly; but this is the norm they set themselves. Apart from the fact that the procedures they employ are more efficacious than some contemporary ethnologists (Vogt) are willing to admit, the real question is not what genuine results they obtain but rather by what lasting purpose they are guided, for their image of themselves is an essential part of their reality.

It is tedious as well as useless, in this connection, to amass arguments to prove that all societies are in history and change: that this is so is patent. But in getting embroiled in a superfluous demonstration, there is a risk of overlooking the fact that human societies react to this common condition in very different fashions. Some accept it, with good or ill grace, and its consequences (to themselves and other societies) assume immense proportions through their attention to it. Others (which we call primitive for this reason) want to deny it and try, with a dexterity we underestimate, to make the states of their development which they consider 'prior' as permanent as possible. It is not sufficient, in order that they should succeed, that their institutions should exercise a regulating action on the recurrent sequences by limiting the incidence of demographic factors, smoothing down antagonisms which manifest themselves within the group or between groups and perpetuating the framework in which individual and collective activities take place. It is also necessary that these non-recurrent chains of events whose effects accumulate to produce economic and social upheavals, should be broken as soon as they form, or that the society should have an effective procedure to prevent their formation. We are acquainted with this procedure, which consists not in denying the historical process but in admitting it as a form without content. There is indeed a before and an after, but their sole significance lies in reflecting each other. . . .

Mythical history . . . presents the paradox of being both disjoined from and conjoined with the present. It is disjoined from it because the original ancestors were of a nature different from contemporary men: they were creators and these are imitators. It is conjoined with it because nothing has been going on since the appearance of the ancestors except events whose recurrence periodically effaces their particularity. It remains to be shown how the savage mind succeeds not only in overcoming this twofold contradiction, but also in deriving from it the materials of a coherent system in which diachrony, in some sort mastered, collaborates with synchrony without the risk of further conflicts arising between them.

Thanks to ritual, the 'disjoined' past of myth is expressed, on the one hand, through biological and seasonal periodicity and, on the other, through the 'conjoined' past, which unites from generation to generation the living and the dead. This synchro-diachronic system has been well analysed by Sharp, . . . who divides the rites of the Australian tribes of the Cape York Peninsula into three categories. The *rites of control* are positive or negative. They aim to increase or restrict species or totemic phenomena, sometimes for the benefit of, sometimes to the detriment of the group, by fixing the quantity of spirits or spirit-substance allowed to emanate from the totemic centres established by the ancestors at various points in the tribal territory. The commemorative or *historical rites* recreate the sacred and beneficial atmosphere of mythical times— the 'dream age,' as the Australians call it— mirroring its protagonists and their great deeds. The *mourning rites* correspond to an inverse procedure: instead of charging living men with the personification of remote ancestors, these rites assure the conversion of men who are no longer living men into ancestors. It can thus be seen that the function of the system of ritual is to overcome and integrate three oppositions: that of diachrony and synchrony; that of the periodic or non-periodic features which either may exhibit; and, finally, within diachrony, that of reversible and irreversible time, for, although present and past are theoretically distinct, the historical rites bring the past into the present and the rites of mourning the present into the past, and the two processes are not equivalent: mythical heroes can truly be said to return, for their only reality lies in their personification; but human beings die for good. . . .

[W]hy do we set such store by our archives? The events to which they relate are independently attested, in innumerable ways: they survive in the present and in our books; in themselves they are devoid of meaning; they acquire it entirely through their historical repercussions and the commentaries which explain them by relating them to other events. Paraphrasing an argument of Durkheim's, we might say of archives that they are after all only pieces of paper. They need only all have been published, for our knowledge and condition to be totally unaffected were a cataclysm to destroy the originals. We should, however, feel this loss as an irreparable injury that strikes to the core of our being. . . . [O]ur past would not disappear if we lost our archives: it would be deprived of what one is inclined to call its diachronic flavour. It would still exist as a past but preserved in nothing but contemporary or recent books, institutions, or even a situation. So it too would be exhibited in synchrony.

The virtue of archives is to put us in contact with pure historicity. As I have already said about myths concerning the origin of totemic appellations, their value does not lie in the intrinsic significance of the events evoked: these can be insignificant or even entirely absent, if what is in question is a few lines of autograph or a signature out of context. But think of the value of Johann Sebastian Bach's signature to one who cannot hear a bar of his music without a quickening of his pulse. As for events themselves, I have pointed out that they are attested otherwise than by the authentic documents, and generally better. Archives thus provide something else: on the one hand they constitute events in their radical contingence (since only interpretation, which forms no part of them, can ground them in reason), and, on the other, they give a physical existence to history, for in them alone is the contradiction of a completed past and a present in which it survives, surmounted. Archives are the embodied essence of the event.

By this approach we recover, at the very centre of the savage mind, that pure history to which we were already led by totemic myths. It is not inconceivable that some of the events they relate are genuine, even if the picture they paint of them is symbolic and distorted. . . . However, this is not at issue, for all historical events are to a large extent the products of the historian's choice of categories. Even if mythical history is false, it at least manifests in a pure and accentuated form (the more so, one might say, because it *is* false) the characteristic traits of an historical event. These depend on the one hand on its contingent status (the ancestor appeared in such and such a spot; he went here, then there; he performed this and that deed . . .) and on the other on its power of arousing intense and varied feelings. . . .

When it is noted that these events and sites are the same as those which furnished the materials of the symbolic systems to which the previous chapters were devoted, it must be acknowledged that so-called primitive peoples have managed to evolve not unreasonable methods for inserting irrationality, in its dual aspect of logical contingence and emotional turbulence, into rationality. Classificatory systems thus allow the incorporation of history, even and particularly that which might be thought to defy the system. For make no mistake: the totemic myths which solemnly relate futile incidents and sentimentalize over particular places are comparable only to minor, lesser history: that of the dimmest chroniclers. Those same societies, whose social organization and marriage rules require the efforts of mathematicians for their interpretation, and whose cosmology astonishes philosophers, see no solution which would maintain continuity between the lofty theorizing to which they devote themselves in these domains and a history which is that not of a Burckhardt or Spengler but of a Lenôtre and a La Force. . . . And nothing in our civilization more closely resembles the periodic pilgrimages made by the intiated Australians, escorted by their sages, than our conducted tours to Goethe's or Victor Hugo's house, the furniture of which inspires emotions as strong as they are arbitrary. . . . [T]he main thing is not that the bed is the self-same one on which it is proved Van Gogh slept: all the visitor asks is to be shown it.

PART II

History, Memory, and Identity

In the volume introduction, we quoted James Joyce's Stephen Dedalus, who asserts that "I, entelechy, form of forms, am I by memory." The term "entelechy" traces back to Aristotle, who coined it to describe an essence or principle realized in the world. "Entelechy" appeared again in Hegel, as well as elsewhere (for instance in Karl Mannheim's work), to characterize a process of becoming, a principle of growth and self-realization that takes place only over the course of time. As Joyce asserts, memory is essential because the "I" is "under ever-changing forms." How is the self of yesterday connected to the self of today and of tomorrow? Only by memory. As the contemporary Aristotelian philosopher Alisdair MacIntyre (1984: 204) puts it, similarly to Joyce, modernity partitions our lives into segments, "so that life comes to appear as nothing but a series of unconnected episodes." As a result, modernity requires "a concept of self whose unity resides in the unity of a narrative which links birth to life to death as narrative beginning to middle to end" (205). However, despite our apparent isolation, MacIntyre argues (216), "the key question for men is not about their own authorship; I can only answer the question 'What am I to do?' if I can answer the prior question 'Of what story or stories do I find myself a part?'" And as the German hermeneutical philosopher Hans-Georg Gadamer shows in the excerpt below, this storytelling is an ongoing act of continuous reconstruction.

As we discussed in the volume introduction, Halbwachs's approach highlighted what he called the "social frameworks of memory," which can be understood as related to this process of the individual finding him- or herself in the stories of his or her group. By the same token, groups as well as individuals are constituted by the stories they tell. Without shared stories about the past of the group, there would be no group identities, or at least they would be fleeting. So where Marx saw a class consciousness developing out of shared interests at a particular point in time, Halbwachs highlighted the role of shared memory in constituting group identities (including the identities of the working class) over time. But these identities must be activated in rituals of solidarity—commemoration, as Edward Casey shows, is a prime mode—if they are not to die or become what Halbwachs called "dead memory."

Finally, Halbwachs famously associated "dead memory" with history, the study of which was to be contrasted to collective memory, a sense of the past to which we bear an organic and living relation. To be sure, Halbwachs's distinction between history as dead memory and collective memory as the living past was overdrawn. As Yosef Yerushalmi eloquently asserts in the passage presented here, a history that does not aspire to be memorable can become "a rampant growth." In a different way, Nietzsche, too, was concerned with the debilitating effects of too much history, which he believed could become "the gravedigger of the present." Nevertheless, since the beginning of historical writing, historians have debated the role of their enterprise. Is history a form of memory, an enterprise that can—and should—underwrite identities? It is not by accident, after all, that the rise of professional history coincided with the consolidation of nationalistic states in the late nineteenth century. Or is history distinct, perhaps radically so, from memory, because it has different aims, namely, as the historians' dictum of Leopold Ranke put it, to determine "what actually happened"? Where memory might be driven by authenticity and the desire for identity, moreover, it is notoriously variable and unreliable. History, on the other hand, is driven by "facts" and by a desire for accuracy; history that is in the service of, or that draws on, memory thus risks corruption.

Nevertheless, as we discussed in the volume introduction, these two last issues are distinct—whether history can serve identity and is thus a form of memory, and whether history can draw on memory as evidence. The latter point is more easily resolved than the former: history can refuse to draw on the unreliable record of memory and nonetheless contribute to identity. But as shown in readings by Peter Burke, Allan Megill, and Alon Confino, and culminating in the historically and philosophically reflexive statement by Yerushalmi, the debate has been complex and hard-fought indeed. Included for other reasons in a later part of the Reader, Patrick Hutton's important argument in his aptly titled book—*History as an Art of Memory*—is also clearly important in this context. It is against this background, moreover, that Jan Assmann's work comes as a real innovation. Assmann, relatively unknown in Anglo-American discourse in part because his work has been slow to be translated into English, and in part because his contributions to memory studies emerged originally from the province of Egyptology, is surely now a (perhaps *the*) major contemporary figure in memory studies, and his concept of cultural memory has inspired significant new research across a number of disciplines. In the present context, however, his effort to transcend the "history versus memory" debate by introducing the idea of "mnemohistory" is particularly interesting.

In some ways unlike historians, sociologists and their intellectual kin, who follow Halbwachs more than historians do, have often been more comfortable exploring the role of collective memory in constituting group identities. The cluster of readings including those from Peter Berger, Eviatar Zerubavel, Jeffrey Olick, and Robert Bellah et al. provides a range of concepts for studying, and insights into, the role of collective memory in constituting communal identities, while works by Anthony Smith, Yael Zerubavel, and Barry Schwartz pay particular attention to the utility of memory for national modes of identification. As such they form a central strand in the contemporary sociology of collective memory and group identity.

REFERENCES

MacIntyre, Alisdair. *After Virtue: A Study in Moral Theory.* 2nd ed. Notre Dame: University of Notre Dame Press, 1984.

Hans-Georg Gadamer (1900–2002)

German philosopher. Gadamer is the major figure in contemporary hermeneutical philosophy, an approach centered on understanding tradition as an ongoing process of
interpretation. Problems arise, Gadamer argues, when we view our relationship to the
past as either radically discontinuous or as a matter of identity. Rather, as he argues
here, the prerequisite for historical thinking is for it to take into account its own historicity. The relevance of this argument in the context of memory studies, which often sees
memory as produced *either* in the present *or* in the past, is clear: memory is not a special
function but our way of being in time and, as such, is an ongoing project.

From *Truth and Method*

The meaning of the connection with tradition, i.e. the element of tradition in
our historical, hermeneutical attitude, is fulfilled in the fact that we share
fundamental prejudices with tradition. Hermeneutics must start from the
position that a person seeking to understand something has a relation to the
object that comes into language in the transmitted text and has, or acquires, a
connection with the tradition out of which the text speaks. On the other hand,
hermeneutical consciousness is aware that it cannot be connected with this
object in some self evident, questioned way, as is the case with the unbroken
stream of a tradition. There is a polarity of familiarity and strangeness on
which hermeneutic work is based: only that this polarity is not to be seen, psychologically, with Schleiermacher, as the tension that conceals the mystery of
individuality, but truly hermeneutically, i.e. in regard to what has been said: the
language in which the text addresses us, the story that it tells us. Here too there
is a tension. The place between strangeness and familiarity that a transmitted
text has for us is that intermediate place between being an historically intended
separate object and being part of a tradition. The true home of hermeneutics is
in this intermediate area.

It follows from this intermediate position in which hermeneutics operates
that its work is not to develop a procedure of understanding, but to clarify the
conditions in which understanding takes place. But these conditions are not of
the nature of a 'procedure' or a method, which the interpreter must of himself
bring to bear on the text, but rather they must be given. The prejudices and
fore-meanings in the mind of the interpreter are not at his free disposal. He is
not able to separate in advance the productive prejudices that make understanding possible from the prejudices that hinder understanding and lead to
misunderstandings.

This separation, rather, must take place in the understanding itself, and
hence hermeneutics must ask how it happens. But this means it must place in
the foreground what has remained entirely peripheral in previous hermeneutics: temporal distance and its significance for understanding. . . .

Every age has to understand a transmitted text in its own way, for the text is part of the whole of the tradition in which the age takes an objective interest and in which it seeks to understand itself. The real meaning of a text, as it speaks to the interpreter, does not depend on the contingencies of the author and whom he originally wrote for. It certainly is not identical with them, for it is always partly determined also by the historical situation of the interpreter and hence by the totality of the objective course of history. . . .

This concept of understanding undoubtedly breaks right out of the circle drawn by romantic hermeneutics. Because what we are now concerned with is not individuality and what it thinks, but the objective truth of what is said, a text is not understood as a mere expression of life, but taken seriously in its claim to truth. That this is what is meant by 'understanding' was once self-evident (we need only recall Chladenius).

But this dimension of the hermeneutical problem was discredited by historical consciousness and the psychological turn that Schleiermacher gave to hermeneutics, and could only be regained when the impasses of historicism appeared and led finally to the new development inspired chiefly, in my opinion, by Heidegger. For the hermeneutic importance of temporal distance could be understood only as a result of the ontological direction that Heidegger gave to understanding as an 'existential' and of his temporal interpretation of the mode of being of there-being.

Time is no longer primarily a gulf to be bridged, because it separates, but it is actually the supportive ground of process in which the present is rooted. Hence temporal distance is not something that must be overcome. This was, rather, the naive assumption of historicism, namely that we must set ourselves within the spirit of the age, and think with its ideas and its thoughts, not with our own, and thus advance towards historical objectivity. In fact the important thing is to recognise the distance in time as a positive and productive possibility of understanding. It is not a yawning abyss, but is filled with the continuity of custom and tradition, in the light of which all that is handed down presents itself to us. Here it is not too much to speak of a genuine productivity of process. Everyone knows that curious impotence of our judgment where the distance in time has not given us sure criteria. Thus the judgment of contemporary works of art is desperately uncertain for the scientific consciousness. Obviously we approach such creations with the prejudices we are not in control of, presuppositions that have too great an influence over us for us to know about them; these can give to contemporary creations an extra resonance that does not correspond to their true content and their true significance. Only when all their relations to the present time have faded away can their real nature appear, so that the understanding of what is said in them can claim to be authoritative and universal.

It is this experience that has led to the idea in historical studies that objective knowledge can be arrived at only when there has been a certain historical distance. It is true that what a thing has to say, its intrinsic content, first appears only after it is divorced from the fleeting circumstances of its actuality. The positive conditions of historical understanding include the self-contained quality of an historical event, which allows it to appear as a whole, and its distance from the opinions concerning its import with which the present is filled. The implicit prerequisite of the historical method, then, is that the permanent significance of something can first be known objectively only when it belongs within a self-contained context. In other words, when it is dead enough to have only historical interest. Only then does it seem possible to exclude the subjective involvement of the observer. . . . It is true that certain hermeneutic requirements are automatically fulfilled when a historical context has become of no more than historical interest. Certain sources of error are automatically excluded. But it is questionable whether this is the end of the hermeneutical problem. Temporal distance has obviously another meaning than that of the quenching of our interest in the object. It lets the true meaning of the object emerge fully. But the discovery of the true meaning of a text or a work of art is never finished; it is in fact an infinite process. Not only are fresh sources of error constantly excluded, so that the true meaning has filtered out of it all kinds of things that obscure it, but there emerge continually new sources of understanding, which reveal unsuspected elements of meaning. The temporal distance which performs the filtering process is not a closed dimension, but is itself undergoing constant movement and extension. And with the negative side of the filtering process brought about by temporal distance there is also the positive side, namely the value it has for understanding. It not only lets those prejudices that are of a particular and limited nature die away, but causes those that bring about genuine understanding to emerge clearly as such.

It is only this temporal distance that can solve the really critical question of hermeneutics, namely of distinguishing the true prejudices, by which we understand, from the false ones by which we misunderstand. Hence the hermeneutically trained mind will also include historical consciousness. It will make conscious the prejudices governing our own understanding, so that the text, as another's meaning, can be isolated and valued on its own. The isolation of a prejudice clearly requires the suspension of its validity for us. For so long as our mind is influenced by a prejudice, we do not know and consider it as a judgment. How then are we able to isolate it? It is impossible to make ourselves aware of it while it is constantly operating unnoticed, but only when it is, so to speak, stimulated. The encounter with a text from the past can provide this stimulus. For what leads to understanding must be something that has already asserted itself in its own separate validity. Understanding begins, as we have already said above, when something addresses us. This is the primary hermeneutical condition. We now know what this requires, namely the fundamental suspension of our own prejudices. But all suspension of judgments and hence, a fortiori, of prejudices, has logically the structure of a question.

The essence of the question is the opening up, and keeping open, of possibilities. If a prejudice becomes questionable, in view of what another or a text says to us, this does not mean that it is simply set aside and the other writing or the other person accepted as valid in its place. It shows, rather, the naiveté of historical objectivism to accept this disregarding of ourselves as what actually happens. In fact our own prejudice is properly brought into play through its being at risk. Only through its being given full play is it able to experience the other's claim to truth and make it possible for he himself to have full play. . . .

. . . True historical thinking must take account of its own historicality. Only then will it not chase the phantom of an historical object which is the object of progressive research, but learn to see in the object the counterpart of itself and hence understand both. The true historical object is not an object at all, but the unity of the one and the other, a relationship in which exist both the reality of history and the reality of historical understanding. A proper hermeneutics would have to demonstrate the effectivity of history within understanding itself. I shall refer to this as 'effective-history.' Understanding is, essentially, an effective-historical relation.

Edward Casey (contemp.)

American philosopher. Casey is a phenomenologist, thus one who seeks to describe the essential properties of subjective experience. Here Casey makes clear that commemoration is not a derivative mode of memory but an integral part of it. A focus on commemoration highlights the participatory and bodily aspects of memory: to remember, he argues, is to commemorate the past. While he does not explicitly discuss anthropological analyses of the ritual dimension of memory, his connections to such analyses (see, for instance, **Durkheim** and **Warner**) are easy to see, as are his links to others that emphasize bodily experience, like **Connerton**.

From *Remembering: A Phenomenological Study*

We have yet to confront what might be termed the "functional essence" of commemoration. This is *participation*. Commemorating, by its very structure, encourages and enhances participation on the part of those who engage in it. The primary participation is in the *commemorandum*, the commemorated object, person, or event. This participation occurs via the mediating presence of various *commemorabilia*, material or psychical; we remember *through* these translucent media; but we could just as well say that we participate *with* them in honoring a common *commemorandum*. In ceremonial commemoration, we also participate with other persons, forming with them a "horizontal," participatory *communitas* that lies perpendicular to the "vertical" community which the commemorator (or group of commemorators) establishes with the *commemorandum* proper. On certain occasions, the two communities—the two kinds of participation—coincide. In mourning, for example, the dyadic community of myself-as-griever and the other-as-grieved is at once horizontal and vertical. Here, participation is unusually intense: not only is there incorporation of the other into myself (as also occurs in the Eucharist and in totem meals) but a con-fusion of self and other thanks to identification, itself a form of inter-psychic participation. . . . For a Western philosophical mind, the single most striking aspect of participation is its freedom from the constraints of contradiction. Thanks to participation, things can be simultaneously themselves and *not* themselves, here and also there, past as well as present. The metaphysical basis for participation is "a mystical community of essence between beings," beings which enjoy an "essential identity." Thus, identity of the members of one's clan "results from participation in the invisible and timeless essence of the group." The totem of such a clan *is* its essence. As a consequence, there is "a similar identity between the individuals of a totemic group and their totem" [Lévy-Bruhl].

Participation is not, however, limited to horizontal and vertical communities as these relate to a totem. Lévy-Bruhl was struck by the sheer multiplicity of types of participation. For the primitive, there is a profound participation between himself and his "appurtenances," that is, any part of himself or his life with which he could be said to be identical: e.g., clothes, fingernails, excreta, footprints. These appurtenances do not merely represent or simply "belong to" a particular person. They *are* him: hence the respect with which they must be treated. There is also participation between humans and non-totemic animals; between an individual and his or her ancestors (mythical and real); between a person and what he or she eats. In the end, everything is swept up into participation: "All objects and beings are involved in a network of mystical participations and exclusions." . . .

. . . . If commemoration has everything to do with participation—if its functional essence is to solicit and sustain participation between commemorators and that to which they pay homage, often by means of *co*-participation in special communities and just as often by sharing in *commemorabilia* through which the *commemorandum* is made present—then by the same token commemoration has to do with overcoming the separation from which otherwise unaffiliated individuals suffer. Still more radically, commemoration suggests that such separation is a sham. If it is true that *"to be is to participate,"* the beings who participate cannot be atomic entities who are merely gathering to commemorate out of a motive of repetition, guilt, piety, or fellow feeling. The commemorators are *already* deeply conjoined, bonded at the most profound level. . . .

Separatism itself presupposes collective roots of various kinds: from language to class, from gender identity to personal identity, from shared history to shared tradition. And it is just because of the reality of such deeply interpersonal roots that commemoration assumes unusual importance in our culture—and doubtless in *every* culture. *For commemoration promotes participation even as it thrives on it.* Commemorating calls upon us not as separate beings but as always already intertwined; it calls on us in our strictly social being.

But more than this is at stake. Commemorating also creates new forms of sociality, new modes of interconnection: between past and present, self and other, one group and another, one form of thinking or acting or speaking and another, one sex and another, one art form and another. In these ways commemorating brings about "a mystical community of essence between beings," constituting a shared identity more lasting and more significant than would be possible in an uncommemorated existence. Commemorating does more than pay tribute to honorable actions undertaken in the past and at another place. It constructs the space, and continues the time, in which the commendably inter-human will be perduringly appreciated. Rather than looking back only, commemoration concerns itself with "what, lasting, comes toward us."

From this view of commemoration as a thoroughly conjoint participation in a project of continuing connection with the *commemorandum*—whether this be effected by ritual or text or by psychic identification—we may dervie three corollary insights:

1. Commemoration cannot be accomplished by representations alone, however accurate or adept or dramatic these may be. . . . Whenever we become engaged in commemorative activity—whether this occurs in a dyadic or a polyadic context—representation *cedes place to participation.*

2. The participatory element in commemoration is so extensive that it includes not only minds or psyches but aspects of body and place as well. In a circumstance of commemoration, body, place, and psyche become more fully participatory. They commingle with one another intimately, and they invite other factors to join in. . . .

. . . In comparison with body memory in this most highly participatory mode—and in a significantly commemorative setting—recollection presents itself as a secondary formation, as a superstructure of memory. This suggests that just as representation supervenes upon and presupposes participation, so recollection is parasitic on body memory and the commemoration which it helps to realize.

3. Commemoration is not separable in the end from body memory—or from place memory either. Each is an essential component, an equiprimordial part, in remembering that goes beyond—perhaps we should also say *under*—mind. Moreover, far from being a momentary affair, something restricted to particular ceremonial occasions, commemorating is continually occurring. We can even say that *all remembering has a commemorative component.* . . .

. . . Even when commemoration bears straightforwardly on something that is ending—e.g., "the end of an era"—it still may not be directed at anything simply terminal. On the contrary, the commemorating may itself serve to *prolong* the ending, giving to it (and to its origin) a species of after-life. If "what has been brings about futural approaching," this is all the more true in the case of commemorating, which is capable of transforming something "frozen in the finality of *rigor mortis*" into a re-living presence, alive in the minds and bodies of its commemorators. In mourning, the dead or absent other is transmogrified into an active internal presence; thus something that has come to an end in terms of world-time acquires an ongoing end*ing* in and through commemoration. Insofar as such ending is not yet concluded, it will be going on in the future. Commemorating here exhibits its Janusian ability to look at once forward and backward: or more exactly, to look ahead in looking back. . . .

If commemoration is indeed a way of coming to terms with ending and if it succeeds to the extent that it refuses to succumb to the sheer pastness of the past—its facticity, its "frozen finality," its severe "It was"—then it must consist in an action of carrying the past forward through the present so as to perdure in the future. But the past can be carried forward in this fashion only if it has attained a certain consistent selfsameness in the wake of the perishing of the particulars by which it had once presented itself. This selfsameness is what Whitehead calls "objective immortality:" "actual entities 'perpetually perish' subjectively, but are immortal objectively." Commemoration not only looks forward in looking back, thereby transmitting deferred effects of the past, it affirms the past's selfsameness in the present by means of a consolidated re-enactment, thus assuring a continuation of remembering into the future. Whether this re-enactment is by text or ritual, or whether it occurs within the psyche, it connects past with present in a genuinely perduring way. And if commemoration brings about a circumstance in which "what has been offers future to itself," it does so less *from* the future—as Heidegger holds—than from the present. In this present, where commemorating is bound to occur, a memorialization of the past is brought forth which, as ritualistic, textual, or intrapsychic, allows for the past to be borne forward rememoratively into the future. Ultimately, we remember *through* such a memorialization, which defies reduction to the separatist categories of 'matter' or 'psyche'—indeed, to 'self' and 'other,' or even to 'past' and 'present.' In this memorialization all such metaphysically determined dyads begin to dissolve, and the inner connection of their respective members—their intimate participation in each other—becomes apparent.

It is usual to regard commemoration (when commemoration is considered at all) as a merely derivative mode of memory. But I have been suggesting that, on the contrary, commemorating is an "intensified remembering" and that it is integral to remembering, as inherent in it as are body memory and place memory. Memory is always memorializing—however fleetingly, inconsistently, or inadequately on a given occasion. To remember is to commemorate the past. It is to redeem the perishing of particulars in a selfsameness that conspires in the present to persist into the future.

Whitehead cites a Latin inscription on ancient sundials: *Pereunt et imputantur,* "the hours perish and are laid to account." Commemoration can be considered the laying to account of perishings, the consolidating and continuing of endings. It is the creating of memorializations in the media of ritual, text, and psyche; it enables us to honor the past by carrying it intact into new and lasting forms of alliance and participation.

Peter Burke (contemp.)

British historian. A central issue for historians has been the relationship between history and memory as modes of apprehending the past. Here Peter Burke offers what has become a classic statement of moderation, one that preserves the distinctive contribution of historiography but sees it nonetheless as a kind of social memory. This issue is also taken up in the following selections by **Megill** and **Yerushalmi**, among others.

From "History as Social Memory"

The traditional view of the relation between history and memory is a relatively simple one. The historian's function is to be a 'remembrancer,' the custodian of the memory of public events which are put down in writing for the benefit of the actors, to give them fame, and also for the benefit of posterity, to learn from their example. History, as Cicero wrote in a passage which has been quoted ever since, is 'the life of memory' (*vita memoriae*). . . .

This traditional account of the relation between memory and written history, in which memory reflects what actually happened and history reflects memory, now seems rather too simple. Both history and memory are coming to appear increasingly problematic. Remembering the past and writing about it no longer seem the innocent activities they were once taken to be. Neither memories nor histories seem objective any longer. In both cases we are learning to take account of conscious or unconscious selection, interpretation and distortion. In both cases this selection, interpretation and distortion is socially conditioned. It is not the work of individuals alone. . . .

Halbwachs made a sharp distinction between collective memory, which was a social construct, and written history, which he considered—in a somewhat old-fashioned positivist way—to be objective. However, current studies of the history of historical writing treat it much as Halbwachs treated memory, as the product of social groups such as Roman senators, Chinese mandarins, Benedictine monks, university professors and so on.

It is becoming commonplace to point out that in different places and times, historians have considered different aspects of the past to be memorable (battles, politics, religion, the economy and so on) and that they have presented the past in very different ways (concentrating on events or structures, on great men or ordinary people, according to their group's point of view).

It is because I share this latter, relativist view of the history of history that I chose the title 'history as social memory' for this piece, using the term as a convenient piece of shorthand which sums up the complex process of selection and interpretation in a simple formula and stresses the homology between the ways in which the past is recorded and remembered.

The phrase 'social memory' and the term 'relativism' do raise awkward problems, so I had better try to state my position, as follows. The analogies between individual and group thought are as elusive as they are fascinating. If we use terms like 'social memory' we do risk reifying concepts. On the other hand, if we refuse to use such terms, we are in danger of failing to notice the different way in which the ideas of individuals are influenced by the groups to which they belong. As for historical relativism, my argument is not that any account of the past is just as good (reliable, plausible, perceptive . . .) as any other; some investigators are better-informed or more judicious than others. The point is that we have access to the past (like the present) only via the categories and schemata (or as Durkheim would say, the 'collective representations') of our own culture. . . .

Historians are concerned, or at any rate need to be concerned, with memory from two different points of view. In the first place, they need to study memory as a historical *source*, to produce a critique of the reliability of reminiscence on the lines of the traditional critique of historical documents. This enterprise has in fact been under way since the 1960s, when historians of the twentieth century came to realize the importance of 'oral history.' Even those of us who work on earlier periods have something to learn form the oral history movement, since we need to be aware of the oral testimonies and traditions embedded in many written records.

In the second place, historians are concerned, or should be concerned, with memory as a historical phenomenon, with what might be called the social history of remembering. Given the fact that the social memory, like the individual memory, is selective, we need to identify the principles of selection and to note how they vary form place to place or from one group to another and how they change over time. Memories are malleable, and we need to understand how they are shaped and by whom. These are topics which for some reason attracted the attention of historians only in the late 1970s; but now there seem to be books and articles and conferences about them everywhere. . . .

Memories are affected by the social organization of transmission and the different media employed. Consider for a moment the sheer variety of these media, five in particular.

1. . . . Oral traditions . . . [C]hanges . . . have taken place in the discipline of history in the last generation, notably the decline of positivism and the rise of interest in symbolic aspects of narrative.

2. The traditional province of the historian, memoirs and other written records (another term related to remembering, *ricordare* in Italian). We need of course to remind ourselves . . . that these records are not innocent acts of memory, but rather attempts to persuade, to shape the memory of others. . . . [Moreover] as we read the writings of memory, it is easy to forget that we do not read memory itself but its transformation through writing.

3. Images, pictorial or photographic, still or moving. . . . [M]aterial images have long been constructed in order to assist the retention and transmission of memories. . . . Historians of the nineteenth and twentieth centuries in particular have been taking an increasing interest in public monuments in the last

few years, precisely because these monuments both expressed and shaped the national memory.

4. Actions transmit memories as they transmit skills, from master to apprentice for example. Many of them leave no traces for later historians to study but ritual actions in particular are often recorded, including rituals of 'commemoration.' . . . These rituals are reenactments of the past, acts of memory, but they are also attempts to impose interpretations of the past, to shape memory. They are in every sense collective re-presentations.

5. One of the most interesting observations in the study of the social framework of memory by Maurice Halbwachs concerned the importance of a fifth medium in the transmission of memories: space. He made explicit a point implicit in the classical and Renaissance art of memory; the value of 'placing' images that one wishes to remember in particular locations such as memory palaces or memory theatres. . . .

There is an obvious question for a historian to ask at this point. Why do myths attach themselves to some individuals (living or dead) and not to others? . . . The existence of oral or literary schemata, or more generally of perceptual schemata, does not explain why these schemata become attached to particular individuals, why some people are, shall we say, more 'mythogenic' than others. Nor is it an adequate answer to do what literal-minded positivist historians generally do and describe the actual achievements of the successful rulers or saints, considerable as these may be, since the myth often attributes qualities to them which there is no evidence that they ever possessed. . . .

In my view, the central element in the explanation of this mythogenesis is the perception (conscious or unconscious) of a 'fit' in some respect or respects between a particular individual and a current stereotype of a hero or villain—ruler, saint, bandit, witch, or whatever. This 'fit' strikes people's imagination and stories about that individual begin to circulate, orally in the first instance. In the course of this oral circulation, the ordinary mechanisms of distortion studied by social psychologists, such as 'levelling' and 'sharpening,' come into play. These mechanisms assist the assimilation of the life of the particular individual to a particular stereotype from the repertoire of stereotypes present in the social memory in a given culture. . . .

But of course this explanation of the process of hero-making in terms of the media is insufficient. To offer it as a complete explanation would be politically naive. I have still to consider the function of the social memory. . . .

As a cultural historian, I find it helpful to approach the question of the uses of social memory by asking why some cultures seem to be more concerned with recalling their past then others. It is commonplace to contrast the traditional Chinese concern for their past with the traditional Indian indifference to theirs. Within Europe, contrasts of this kind are also apparent. . . .

Why is there such a sharp contrast in attitudes to the past in different cultures? It is often said that history is written by the victors. It might also be said that history is forgotten by the victors. They can afford to forget, while the losers are unable to accept what happened and are condemned to brood over it, relive it, and reflect how different it might have been. Another explanation might be given in terms of cultural roots. When you have them you can afford to take them for granted but when you lose them you search for them. . . .

The later nineteenth century has been provocatively described as the age of the 'invention of tradition.' It was certainly an age of a search for national traditions, in which national monuments were constructed, and national rituals (like Bastille Day) devised, while national history had a greater place in European schools than ever before or since. The aim of all this was essentially to justify or 'legitimate' the existence of the nation-state; whether in the case of new nations like Italy and Germany, or of older ones like France, in which national loyalty still had to be created, and peasants turned into Frenchmen.

The sociology of Emile Durkheim, with its emphasis on community, consensus and cohesion, itself bears the stamp of this period. It would be unwise to follow Durkheim and his pupil Halbwachs too closely in this respect, and to discuss the social function of the social memory as if conflict and dissent did not exist. . . . Given the multiplicity of social identities, and the coexistence of rival memories, alternative memories (family memories, local memories, class memories, national memories, and so on), it is surely more fruitful to think in pluralistic terms about the uses of memories to different social groups, who may well have different views about what is significant or 'worthy of memory.'

. . . It might be useful to think in terms of different 'memory communities' within a given society. It is important to ask the question, who wants whom to remember what, and why? Whose version of the past is recorded and preserved?

Disputes between historians presenting rival accounts of the past sometimes reflect wider and deeper social conflicts. . . . Official and unofficial memories of the past may differ sharply and the unofficial memories, which have been relatively little studied, are sometimes historical forces in their own right. . . . Without invoking social memories it would be hard to explain the geography of dissent and protest, the fact that some villages, for example, take part in different protest movements century after century, while others do not. . . .

[T]o understand the workings of the social memory it may be worth investigating the social organization of forgetting, the rules of exclusion, suppression or repression, and the question of who wants whom to forget what, and why. Amnesia is related to 'amnesty,' to what used to be called 'acts of oblivion,' official erasure of memories of conflict in the interests of social cohesion.

Official censorship of the past is all too well known, and there is little need to talk about the various revisions of the *Soviet Encyclopaedia*. Many revolutionary and counter-revolutionary regimes like to symbolize their break with the past by changing the name of streets, especially when these names refer to the date of significant events. . . .

The official censorship of embarrassing memories is well known. What is in need of investigation is their unofficial suppression or repression, and this topic raises once more the awkward question of the analogy between individual and collective memory. Freud's famous metaphor of the 'censor' inside each individual was of course derived from the official censorship of the Habsburg Empire. . . . But between these two censors, public and private, there is space for a third, collective but unofficial. Can groups, like individuals, suppress what it is inconvenient to remember? If so, how do they do it? . . .

It is often quite easy to show major discrepancies between the image of the past shared by members of a particular social group, and the surviving records of that past. . . .

Generally speaking, what happens in the case of . . . myths is that differences between past and present are elided, and unintended consequences are turned into conscious aims, as if the main purpose of these past heroes had been to bring about the present—our present.

Writing and print are not powerful enough to stop the spread of myths of this kind. What they can do, however, is to preserve records of the past which are inconsistent with the myths, which undermine them—records of a past which has become awkward and embarrassing, a past which people for one reason or another do not wish to know about, though it might be better for them if they did. It might, for example, free them from the dangerous illusion that past, present and future may be seen as a simple struggle between heroes and villains, good and evil, right and wrong. Myths are not to be despised, but reading them literally is not to be recommended. Herodotus thought of historians as the guardians of memory, the memory of glorious deeds. I prefer to see historians as the guardians of awkward facts, the skeletons in the cupboard of the social memory.

Allan Megill (contemp.)

Intellectual historian. Whereas **Becker**, **Burke**, **Yerushalmi**, and others emphasize the continuities between history and memory, the following excerpt from Allan Megill offers a nuanced defense of a relatively "separatist" position, seeing memory as "an other that continually haunts history."

From "History, Memory, Identity"

The terms *identity* and *memory* are in wide and contentious circulation at the present moment. Identity has been turned into a site of commitment and also of dispute and uncertainty. Not unconnectedly, memory has been seen as a privileged discourse having peculiar claims to authenticity and truth. What can the uncertainties that surround memory and identity teach us about the project of historical understanding? Conversely, what can history teach us about memory and identity?

Historical research and writing are caught between commitment to the universal and the claims made by particular identities. This seems to be one manifestation of the unresolving tension or dialectic that characterizes all truthful history. The universal dimension of historical research and writing is rooted in the commitment of historians to a set of procedures designed to maximize the chances of arriving at justified historical claims and to minimize the chances of error. The particularistic dimension, which has gained some outspoken advocates in the wake of Michel Foucault and other theorists who equate knowledge with cultural power, attaches itself to the good cause in the present (we are expected to know at each moment *which* cause that is). Since historical particularism is often articulated in the language of memory, a tension is set up between history and memory. On the one hand, "history" appears as a pseudo-objective discourse that rides roughshod over particular memories and identities, which claim to have an experiential reality and authenticity that history lacks. On the other hand, memory appears as an unmeasured discourse that, in the service of desire, makes claims for its own validity that cannot be justified.

How can we square this circle? We cannot: the dialectic does not resolve. But we can arrive at some clarity concerning the history-memory tension and concerning the relation of both to identity. This chapter examines certain salient features of the history-memory-identity relation. My aim is less to be definitive about the matter—for no single theory can satisfactorily embrace everything that is in conflict here—than it is to show where the crosscuts lie. It is not a question of a simple opposition: history vs. memory. Nor is it a question of another simple opposition: discipline vs. desire. Rather, it is a matter of both writing and living in a situation in which some certainty can be achieved, but in which, finally, a background of uncertainty persists. Let us now explore these points in a manner that is more concrete and specific, and hence more capable of being grasped and retained. . . .

A memory wave has swept through much of contemporary culture. Its most important site, although far from the only one, has been the United States. Appearing in the 1980s and reaching something of a peak in the mid-1990s, memory invaded a wide variety of fields, often in the company of its evil twin, amnesia. By the end of the 1990s some of the more extreme forms of memory preoccupation had retreated, but in many respects memory continues as a major preoccupation in contemporary culture. . . . The common feature under-pinning most contemporary manifestations of the memory craze seems to be an insecurity about identity. In a world in which opposing certainties constantly come into conflict with each other and in which a multitude of possible iden-tities are put on display, insecurity about identity may be an inevitable by-product. Such a situation provides ample reason for "memory" to come to the fore. We might postulate a rule: when identity becomes uncertain, memory rises in value. . . .

In the presence of the conviction that the new identity is authorized by God, there is perhaps no need to support the new identity with the claim that it already implicitly existed before the turn: in any case, the old identity is seen as unredeemed, tied to a world dominated by sin. However, in contemporary culture a different linguistic and conceptual move seems more prevalent. . . . Here the memory of having always been an X supports an identity that might otherwise seem insufficiently justified. When such a move is made, issues of "memory" and "history" come directly into play.

A sense of weak or threatened identity seems to be a common feature uniting evocations of "memory" in ethnic conflict, in the recall of deeply troubling com-munal events, and in the recovery of traumatic or supposedly traumatic events of personal life. In short, there seems to be a fact here, and there also seems to be *prima facie* justification for regarding the fact as significant. The phenom-enon of self-designation is in no way incompatible with the sense that identity is weak or threatened: on the contrary, an identity that has been brought into visibility by means of self-designation would be all the more likely to need justification of the sort that "memory" can bring. The memory wave and uncer-tainty concerning identity go together. . . .

The question now arises of the relation between current concerns with iden-tity and memory and the project of historical understanding. There exists a large literature on history and memory, one that has burgeoned since its begin-nings in the late 1970s. But while the literature has cast much light on the history-identity-memory relation, it has largely failed to explore the relation of historical understanding to the problematizing of identity. The literature has focused much more on how history and memory have functioned to consoli-date and carry forward identities already assumed to exist. It has not much considered the possible volatility of these identities. . . .

Crucially, the Halbwachsian model holds that memory is determined by an identity (collective or individual) *that is already well established.* Halbwachs's work on memory—both his account of memory in general and his account of historical memory—is primarily about the construction of memory by such identities. His account of historical memory deals with how an identity, whose integrity at a certain moment is assumed, goes about inventing a past congruent with that identity. . . .

In contrast, the most characteristic feature of the contemporary scene is a lack of fixity at the level of identity, leading to the project of constructing memory with a view to constructing identity itself. The appropriate model for understanding such a context is less Halbwachs's than Benedict Anderson's. In Anderson's evocative phrase, it is a matter of "imagined communities;" we might think of imagined communities as imagined identities. Of course, every community beyond a very small group is in some strong sense "imagined." The more a community is imagined, the more it finds that "memory" is necessary to it—and so is "forgetting." Conversely, the less rooted the community is in extant and well-functioning practices—that is, the more problematic its identity—the more constitutive for it is its "remembered" past.

It is important to note what the "memory" in question is not. First, it is not nostalgia. For purposes of the present analysis, let us define *nostalgia* as attraction to—a homesickness for—a real or imagined past. . . . The difference between nostalgia and memory, as here defined, is that whereas nostalgia is oriented outward *from* the subject (the individual person; the group), focusing attention on a real or imagined past, memory is oriented *toward* the subject and is concerned with a real or imagined past only because that past is perceived as crucial for the subject, even constitutive of it. Whereas memory, as understood here, is connected with insecurities concerning the present-day identity constructing those memories, nostalgia is connected with a sense of complacency about the present-day identity bearing the nostalgia. . . .

Second, memory as understood here is also not quite tradition. Let us here define *tradition* as an objectively existing set of cultural artifacts or articulations. Adherents of a tradition that is confident of its own validity are unlikely to make an appeal to memory: instead, when required to defend the tradition, they characteristically appeal to nonsubjective factors—to a canon, to a set of philosophical or religious truths, to alleged historical events, to an existing institutional structure. An identity that solidly exists has little need for an explicit, thematized appeal to memory. When memory approximates to tradition, it approximates to *weak* tradition. In other words, an appeal to memory— that is, an appeal to what is subjective and personal—is likely to arise only when objectively existing supports are felt to be inadequate. . . .

Consequently, at a deep, experiential level, memory is crucial to us. As noted above, we are terrified by Alzheimer's disease. We are morbidly fascinated by memory disorders of the sort that the psychiatrist Oliver Sacks has described. We treasure family photographs. None of this has much to do with "science," but it has a lot to do with our sense of ourselves. A high valuation of memory tends to enter into historiography (and into public interest in history) at those points where historical events and circumstances intersect with personal and familial experience. Our personal experience with history is a matter of "memory." Familial experience with history—say, the experience of grandparents who escaped the Holocaust, now narrated to and passed on by their descendants—is often designated as "memory," although in a strict sense it is not. The literary critic Geoffrey Hartman has written of the desirability of changing history into memory. The point here is not whether one agrees or disagrees with Hartman, but that, in calling for such a change, he acknowledges and participates in the high valuing of memory (and likewise the focus on identity) in contemporary culture. . . .

. . . It is easy to imagine that we ought to *remember* the past. But we do not remember the past. It is the present that we remember: that is, we "remember" what remains living within our situations *now*. We *think* the past: that is, we construct or reconstruct it on the basis of certain critical procedures. The relevant motto is: "Remember the present, think the past." "Je me souviens" ("I remember," the motto of Québec) relates to subjectivity that is present, not to a past that is thought. Almost invariably, when historical understanding is described as "remembering," we can infer that we are confronting an attempt to promote some presumably desirable collective identity in the present. . . .

The notion of a zone of incomprehensibility helps us to unravel the difficult relations between memory and history by suggesting another horizon that lies behind *both* memory and history. It is a mistake to see memory and history as continuous with each other: a mistake, for example, to think of memory as the raw material of history. It is likewise a mistake to think that history is simply the sum of all possible memories: *pace* Tolstoy, the Battle of Waterloo is not to be reconstructed by bringing together all memories of it. But it is equally a mistake to see history and memory as simply opposed to each other. On the one hand, far from being history's raw material, memory is an Other that continually haunts history. Memory is an image of the past constructed by a subjectivity in the present. It is thus by definition subjective; it may also be irrational and inconsistent. On the other hand, history as a discipline has the obligation to be objective, unified, orderly, justified. Yet it cannot entirely be so, for there is always a residue of incomprehensibility behind what is known, and an engagement with subjectivity that cannot be eliminated. . . .

It may be that memory has emerged in part as a response to an anxiety arising from the failure of modernity, with its focus on the pursuit of the new, to provide an adequate account of what is past yet continues to haunt the present. . . .

In its demand for proof, history stands in sharp opposition to memory. History reminds memory of the need for evidence coming from eyewitnesses (*autopsy*) and from material remains. Memory is a domain of obscurity: it is not to be trusted. Yet one should not think that history is by this token the domain of light, for along with the relative light of history and the relative darkness of memory, we must acknowledge a vast domain of historical unknowability. This lesson arises from the uncertainty of identity in our time, for in undermining the notion that a single authoritative perspective exists to which we can have access, the uncertainty of identity also undermines the arrogance of *both* history and memory: on the one hand, the arrogance of definitiveness; on the other, the arrogance of authenticity.

The limits of history and of memory are perhaps most clearly manifested in an important twentieth-century phenomenon, namely, trials of alleged perpetrators of state-sponsored brutality, when the trials are intended both to arrive at truth/justice and to help in shaping a new collective identity through the formation of collective memory. What is striking is the simultaneous necessity and impossibility of the dual project that is envisaged: how can it be done? How can it *not* be done? Courts and commissions seeking at the same time to discover historical truth and to reconstruct collective identity are relevant in the present context as a manifestation of the general theoretical points that I have tried to articulate, which can be put in the form of several propositions:

1. The uncertainties of history, identity, and memory are mutual.
2. History and memory are sharply different, as manifested above all in the radically different histories that different people or groups remember.
3. The boundaries between history and memory nonetheless cannot be precisely established.
4. In the absence of a single, unquestioned authority or framework, the tension between history and memory cannot be resolved.

In the time of grand narrative, the presence of History meant that history could always conquer memory: History trumped "histories." In the time of grand narrative's collapse, this is no longer so. Thus it is hard to know how the tension between the historical and the mnemonic can ever be overcome. It is certain that the sum of memories does not add up to history. It is equally certain that history does not *by itself* generate a collective consciousness, an identity, and that when it gets involved in projects of identity-formation and promotion, trouble results. Thus a boundary remains between history and memory that we can cross from time to time but that we cannot, and should not wish to, eliminate. Perhaps the more disturbing tendency in our time is the tendency to eliminate oppressive history in favor of authentic memory. But truth and justice, or whatever simulacra of them remain to us, require at least the *ghost* of History if they are to have any claim on people at all. What is left otherwise is only what feels good (or satisfyingly bad) at the moment.

Alon Confino (contemp.)

Israeli-American historian. A sympathetic critic of memory studies, Confino argues against the reduction of memory to politics, which neglects the richer roots of memory studies in the "history of mentalities." For Confino, studying memory entails drawing "the mental horizon of an age," which depends on recognizing that "the first task of the history of memory is to historicize memory." This argument is relevant not only to the role of memory in historiography, but also to questions about the politics of memory, taken up below under "politics and contestation."

From "Collective Memory and Cultural History: Problems of Method"

One of the significant contributions of memory studies has been to explore how the construction of the past, through a process of invention and appropriation, affected the relationship of power within society. The "politics of memory" (at times, "the politics of identity") has emerged as a leading theme in the growing body of literature about memory. Memory is viewed here as a subjective experience of a social group that essentially sustains a relationship of power. Simply stated, it is who wants whom to remember what, and why. This theme is no doubt illuminating to our understanding of the functions and meanings of collective memory. But it seems to me only partially illuminating, for one consequence of it is the tendency to reduce memory, which is fundamentally a concept of culture, to the political.

The problem with memory defined in terms of politics and political use is that it becomes an illustrative reflection of political development and often is relativized to ideology. . . .

More important, the result of memory being sacrificed to an analysis of politics and political use is, often, to ignore the category of the social. In this case, representations of the past derive from and are mainly used to explain relationships of a political nature, but they are considerably silent about the effect of memory on the organization, hierarchization, and arrangements of social and cultural relationships. . . .

By sanctifying the political while underplaying the social, and by sacrificing the cultural to the political, we transform memory into a "natural" corollary of political development and interests. Consequently, we are the poorer in method and theory to analyze crucial memory issues that cannot be reduced to the political: the relations between modernity (and postmodernity) and memory; the obsession with and/or neglect of memory, forgetting, and conservation in modern and premodern societies. Furthermore, one unfortunate side effect of treating memory as a symptom of politics is the lack of explorations of power in areas that are not politically evident. Consequently, a search for memory traces is made mostly among visible places and familiar names, where memory construction is explicit and its meaning palpably manipulated, while in fact we should look for memory where it is implied rather than said, blurred rather than clear, in the realm of collective mentality. We miss a whole world of human activities that cannot be immediately recognized (and categorized) as political, although they are decisive to the way people construct and contest images of the past. We can think of the family, voluntary association, and workplace but should also include practices such as tourism and consumerism.

Interestingly enough, by sacrificing the cultural to the political, memory studies—and by extension cultural history—has reproduced a model of society that is, in a sense, not dissimilar from that of the social history of the 1960s and 1970s. According to classic social history, cultural cleavages necessarily reflected social differences constructed beforehand; the social structure identified and explained cultural originations that subsequently needed only to be characterized. The underlying assumption was that culture can only be explained by its relation to social structural preconditions, thus changes in the formation of culture are explained by earlier changes in social relation. Cultural history has justifiably demolished the validity of this approach by arguing that culture shapes, as much it is shaped by, the social structure. But if social history reduced the cultural to the social, cultural history often reduces the cultural to the political. Memory cleavages reflect political differences constructed beforehand. Political differences identify and explain memory origination. Memory thus becomes a prisoner of political reductionism and functionalism.

There is another significant consequence to the sacrificing of the cultural to the political, namely that we tend to ignore the issue of reception, that ogre that awaits every cultural historian. Many studies of memory are content to describe the representation of the past without bothering to explore the transmission, diffusion, and, ultimately, the meaning of this representation. The study of reception is not an issue that simply adds to our knowledge. Rather, it is a necessary one to avoid an arbitrary choice and interpretation of evidence. . . .

. . . One result of the separate narratives of evolution and reception . . . is that the evolution of memory stands like a foundational story against which reception is measured. The separate narratives thus assume levels of analysis and explanations: we must first construct the evolution of memory in order to understand its meaning as revealed in reception. But this, of course, is an artificial separation, for the meaning of memory's evolution commingles with, and is dependent on, the story of its reception. . . .

[T]he history of memory [m]ust be more rigorous theoretically in articulating the relationship between the social, the political, and the cultural and, at the same time, more anarchical and comprehensive in using the term memory as an explanatory device that links representation and social experience. There exists in memory studies the danger of reducing culture to politics and ideology, instead of broadening the field from the political to the social and the experiential, to an everyday history of memory. And there exists the danger of reducing culture to some vague notion of memory, whereby memory is separated from other memories in society and from the culture around it. That a given memory exists, that it has a symbolic representation and a political significance is obvious, but in itself it explains little if we do not place this memory within a global network of social transmission and symbolic representations. . . .

There are many ways of doing memory, and while my critique raises some problems in current approaches, it simultaneously emphasizes the open-endedness of the notion. The beauty of memory is that it is imprecise enough to be appropriated by unexpected hands, to connect apparently unrelated topics, to explain anew old problems. Among the many roads open for scholars, one, I believe, is especially fruitful in the current state of the field: to write the history of memory. We have to distinguish between memory as a heuristic device and memory as part of the mental equipment of a society, of an age. It is not always clear whether "memory" is used as an imposed methodological tool to analyze how a given society constructed a past (similar to using "class" to understand seventeenth-century Eruope) or whether "memory" was indeed a contemporary metaphor to understand the past (like class in twentieth-century Europe). Thus the memory, say, of World War II in a given society cannot be separated from the development after 1945 of the term "memory" itself into a leading concept used by people to understand the past, private and public, personal and national. For if the study of memory focuses creatively on how people construct a past through a process of appropriation and contestation, is the real problem not, perhaps, that people construct the past by using the term "memory" at all?

To write a history of memory, we need to draw the mental horizon of an age. When and why did memory become a habit of mind shared by people to give meaning to the past? One can imagine that it is the kind of historical problem Warburg and Bloch would have been delighted to pose, and perhaps to begin to answer. And so, perhaps the first task of the history of memory is to historicize memory.

Yosef Hayim Yerushalmi (1932–2009)

American Jewish historian. From ritual and recital, canon and commentary, to historiography and reconstruction, Yerushalmi eloquently illustrates in these pages the contrast between biblical and rabbinical conceptions of historical time and contemporary Jewish historiography. Beyond providing intriguing historical details in this history of memory, Yerushalmi concludes with the crucial reminder that "a historiography that does not aspire to be memorable is in peril of becoming a rampant growth."

From *Zakhor: Jewish History and Jewish Memory*

For those reared and educated in the modern West it is often hard to grasp the fact that a concern with history, let alone the writing of history, is not an innate endowment of human civilization. Many cultures past and present have found no particular virtue in the historical, temporal dimension, of human existence. Out of a mass of ethnographic materials from around the world anthropologists and historians of religion have gradually clarified the extent to which, in primitive societies, only mythic rather than historical time is "real," the time of primeval beginning and paradigmatic first acts, the dream-time when the world was new, suffering unknown, and men consorted with the god. Indeed, in such cultures the present historical moment possesses little independent value. It achieves meaning and reality only by subverting itself, when, through the repetition of a ritual or the recitation or re-enactment of a myth, historical time is periodically shattered. . . .

Herodotus, we are told, was the "father of history," . . . until fairly recently every educated person knew that the Greeks had produced a line of great historians who could still be read with pleasure and empathy. Yet neither the Greek historians nor the civilization that nurtured them saw any ultimate or transcendent meaning to history as a whole; indeed, they never quite arrive at a concept of universal history, of history "as a whole." Herodotus wrote with the very human aspiration of—in his own words—"preserving from decay the remembrance of what men have done, and of preventing the great and wonderful actions of the Greeks and the barbarians from losing their due need of glory." For Herodotus the writing of history was first and foremost a bulwark against the inexorable erosion of memory engendered by the passage of time. In general, the historiography of the Greeks was an expression of that splendid Hellenic curiosity to know and to explore which can still draw us close to them, or else it sought from the past moral examples or political insights. Beyond that, history had no truths to offer, and thus it had no place in Greek religion or philosophy. If Herodotus was the father of history, the fathers of meaning in history were the Jews.

It was ancient Israel that first assigned a decisive significance to history and thus forged a new world-view whose essential premises were eventually appropriated by Christianity and Islam as well. "The heavens," in the words of the psalmist, might still "declare the glory of the Lord," but it was human history that revealed his will and purpose. This novel perception was not the result of philosophical speculation, but of the peculiar nature of Israelite faith. It emerged out of an intuitive and revolutionary understanding of God, and was refined through profoundly felt historical experience. However it came about, in retrospect the consequences are manifest. Suddenly, as it were, the crucial encounter between man and the divine shifted away from the realm of nature and the cosmos to the plane of history, conceived now in terms of divine challenge and human response. The pagan conflict of the gods with the forces of chaos, or with one another, was replaced by a drama of different and more poignant order: the paradoxical struggle between the divine will of an omnipotent Creator and the free will of his creature, man, in the course of history; a tense dialectic of obedience and rebellion. The primeval dream-time world of the archetypes, represented in the Bible only by the Paradise story in Genesis, was abandoned irrevocably. With the departure of Adam and Eve from Eden, history begins, historical time becomes real, and the way back is closed forever. East of Eden hangs "the fiery ever-turning sword" to bar re-entry. Thrust reluctantly into history, man in Hebrew thought comes to affirm his historical existence despite the suffering it entails, and gradually, ploddingly, he discovers that God reveals himself in the course of it. Rituals and festivals in ancient Israel are themselves no longer primarily repetitions of mythic archetypes meant to annihilate historical time. Where they evoke the past, it is not the primeval but the historical past, in which the great and critical moments of Israel's history were fulfilled. Far from attempting a flight from history, biblical religion allows itself to be saturated by it and is inconceivable apart from it. . . .

Only in Israel and nowhere else is the injunction to remember felt as a religious imperative to an entire people. . . .

If the command to remember is absolute, there is, nonetheless, an almost desperate pathos about the biblical concern with memory, and a shrewd wisdom that knows how short and fickle human memory can be. Not history, as is commonly supposed, but only mythic time repeats itself. If history is real, then the Red Sea can be crossed only once, and Israel cannot stand twice at Sinai, a Hebrew counterpart, if you wish, to the wisdom of Heraclitus. Yet the covenant is to endure forever. . . . It is an outrageous claim. Surely there comes a day "when your children will ask you in time to come, saying: What mean you by these stones? Then you shall say to them: Because the waters of the Jordan were cut off before the ark of the covenant of the Lord when it passed through the Jordan" (Josh. 4:6–7). Not the stone, but the memory transmitted by the fathers, is decisive if the memory embedded in the stone is to be conjured out of it to live again for subsequent generations. If there can be no return to Sinai, then what took place at Sinai must be borne along the conduits of memory to those who were not there that day.

The biblical appeal to remember thus has little to do with curiosity about the past. Israel is told only that it must be a kingdom of priests and a holy people;

nowhere is it suggested that it become a nation of historians. Memory is, by its nature, selective, and the demand that Israel remember is no exception. . . .

Memory flowed, above all, through two channels: ritual and recital. Even while fully preserving their organic links to the natural cycles of the agricultural year (spring and first fruits), the great pilgrimage festivals of Passover and Tabernacles were transformed into commemorations of the Exodus from Egypt and the sojourn in the wilderness. . . .

Yet although the continuity of memory could be sustained by such means, and while fundamental biblical conceptions of history were forged, not by historians, but by priests and prophets, the need to remember overflowed inevitably into actual historical narrative as well. In the process, and within that varied Hebrew literature spanning a millennium which we laconically call "the Bible," a succession of anonymous authors created the most distinguished corpus of historical writing in the ancient Near East.

It was an astonishing achievement by any standard applicable to ancient historiography, all the more so when we bear in mind some of its own presuppositions. With God as the true hero of history one wonders at the very human scale of the historical narratives themselves. . . .

Yet if biblical history has, at its core, a recital of the acts of God, its accounts are filled predominantly with the actions of men and women and the deeds of Israel and the nations. Granted that historical writing in ancient Israel had its roots in the belief that history was a theophany and that events were ultimately to be interpreted in light of this faith. The result was, not theology, but history on an unprecedented scale. . . .

Obviously much more could still be said about the place and function of history in ancient Israel. . . . But if we really seek to understand what happened later, then we may already have touched on something that can prove of considerable help, and should therefore be reformulated explicitly. We have learned, in effect, that meaning in history, memory of the past, and the writing of history are by no means to be equated. In the Bible, to be sure, the three elements are linked, they overlap at critical points, and, in general, they are held together in a web of delicate and reciprocal relationships. In post-biblical Judaism, . . . they pull asunder. Even in the Bible, however, historiography is but one expression of the awareness that history is meaningful and of the need to remember, and neither meaning nor memory ultimately depends upon it. The meaning of history is explored more directly and more deeply in the prophets than in the actual historical narratives; the collective memory is transmitted more actively through ritual than through chronicle. Conversely, in Israel as in Greece, historiography could be propelled by other needs and considerations. There were other, more mundane, genres of historical writing, apparently quite unrelated to the quest for transcendent meanings. . . .

If Joshua, Samuel, Kings, and the other historical books of the Bible were destined to survive, that is because something quite extraordinary happened to them. They had become part of an authoritative anthology of sacred writings. . . .

With the sealing of the biblical canon by the rabbis at Yabneh, the biblical historical books and narratives were endowed with an immortality to which no subsequent historian could ever aspire and that was denied to certain historical works that already existed. . . .

That which was included in the biblical canon had, so to speak, a constantly renewable lease on life, and we must try to savor some of what this has meant. For the first time the history of a people became part of its sacred scripture. The Pentateuchal narratives, which brought the historical record up to the eve of the conquest of Canaan, together with the weekly lesson form the prophets, were read aloud in the synagogue from beginning to end. . . .

Every generation of scribes would copy and transmit the historical texts with the reverent care that only the sacred can command. An unbroken chain of scholars would arise later to explicate what had been recorded long ago in a constantly receding past. With the gradual democratization of Jewish learning, both the recitals of ancient chroniclers and the interpretations of prophets long dead would become the patrimony, not of a minority, but of the people at large. . . .

A problem of a very different sort is posed by the meager attention accorded in rabbinic literature to post-biblical events. While we can accept the aggadic transfigurations of biblical history as forms of commentary and interpretations, we may still ask, tentatively at least, why the rabbis did not see fit to take up where biblical history broke off. . . .

. . . If the rabbis, wise men who had inherited a powerful historical tradition, were no longer interested in mundane history, this indicates nothing more than that they felt no need to cultivate it. Perhaps they already knew of history what they needed to know. Perhaps they were even wary of it. . . .

[I]n rabbinic Judaism, which was to permeate Jewish life the world over, historiography came to a long halt even while belief in the meaning of history remained. We can freely concede, moreover, that much in the rabbinic (and even the biblical) heritage inculcated patterns and habits of thought in later generations that were, from a modern point of view, if not anti-historical, then at least ahistorical. Yet these factors did not inhibit the transmission of a vital Jewish past from one generation to the next, and Judaism neither lost its link to history nor its fundamentally historical orientation. The difficulty in grasping this apparent incongruity lies in a poverty of language that forces us, *faute de mieux*, to apply the term "history" both to the sort of past with which we are concerned, and to that of Jewish tradition. . . .

The modern effort to reconstruct the Jewish past begins at a time that witnesses a sharp break in the continuity of Jewish living and hence also an ever-growing decay of Jewish group memory. In this sense, if for no other, history becomes what it had never been before—the faith of fallen Jews. For the first time history, not a sacred text, becomes the arbiter of Judaism. Virtually all nineteenth-century Jewish ideologies, from Reform to Zionism, would feel a need to appeal to history for validation. Predictably, "history" yielded the most varied conclusion to the appellants. . . .

There is an inherent tension in modern Jewish historiography even though most often it is not felt on the surface nor even acknowledged. To the degree that this historiography is indeed "modern" and demands to be taken seriously, it must at least functionally repudiate premises that were basic to all Jewish conceptions of history in the past. In effect, it must stand in sharp opposition to its own subject matter, not on this or that detail, but concerning the vital core: the belief that divine providence is not only an ultimate but an active causal factor in Jewish history, and the related belief in the uniqueness of Jewish history itself.

It is the conscious denial, or at least the pragmatic evasion, of these two cardinal assumptions that constitutes the essence of the secularization of Jewish history on which modern Jewish historiography is grounded. . . .

[T]he notion that Jewish history is on the same level of reality as any other history, subject to the same kind of causality and accessible to the same types of analysis, did not find its way into actual historical writing until the nineteenth century. Long after an essentially secular view of world history had permeated ever-widening European circles, a providential view of Jewish history was still held tenaciously, albeit for very different reasons, by Jews and Christians alike. Indeed, it has far from disappeared even now. The reason for the lag is apparent. Of all histories, that of the Jewish people has been the most refractory to secularization because this history alone, as a national history, was considered by all to be sacred to begin with. The point has been made forcefully by Karl Löwith:

> There is only one particular history—that of the Jews—which as a political history can be interpreted strictly religiously. . . .
>
> Christians are not an historical people. Their solidarity all over the world is merely one of faith. In the Christian view the history of salvation is no longer bound up with a particular nation, but is internationalized because it is individualized. . . . From this it follows that the historical destiny of Christian peoples is no possible subject for a specifically Christian interpretation of political history, while the destiny of the Jews *is* a possible subject of a specifically Jewish interpretation.

. . . If the secularization of Jewish history is a break with the past, the historicizing of Judaism itself has been an equally significant departure. It could hardly be otherwise. Western man's discovery of history is not a mere interest in the past, which always existed, but a new awareness, a perception of a fluid temporal dimension from which nothing is exempt. The major consequence for Jewish historiography is that it cannot view Judaism as something absolutely given and subject to *a priori* definition. Judaism is inseparable from its evolution through time, from its concrete manifestations at any point in history. . . . [T]he historical outlook has by no means enjoyed an unqualified triumph within Jewry. . . .

Only in the modern era do we really find, for the first time, a Jewish historiography divorced from Jewish collective memory and, in crucial respects, thoroughly at odds with it.

To a large extent, of course, this reflects a universal and ever-growing modern dichotomy. The traditions and memories of many peoples are in disarray. At the same time, national history in the nineteenth-century sense has yielded increasingly to other thematic structures. . . .

There are many within Jewry today who deplore the widespread decay of Jewish memory even while, perhaps symptomatically, sharing no real consensus as to its original or ideal content. Who, then, can be expected to step into the breach, if not the historian? Is it not both his chosen and appointed task to restore the past to us all? Though he did not have the Jewish historian in mind, Eugen Rosenstock-Huessay's description of the historical vocation might almost seem, fortuitously, to pose a particular challenge to him. "The historian," he wrote, "is the physician of memory. It is his honor to heal wounds, genuine wounds. As a physician must act, regardless of medical theories, because his patient is ill, so the historian must act under a moral pressure to restore a nation's memory, or that of mankind."

Yet those who would demand of the historian that he be the restorer of Jewish memory attribute to him powers that he may not possess. Intrinsically, modern Jewish historiography cannot replace an eroded group memory which . . . never depended on historians in the first place. The collective memories of the Jewish people were a function of the shared faith, cohesiveness, and will of the group itself, transmitting and recreating its past through an entire complex of interlocking social and religious institutions that functioned organically to achieve this. The decline of Jewish collective memory in modern times is only a symptom of the unraveling of that common network of belief and praxis through whose mechanisms. . . . the past was once made present. Therein lies the root of the malady. Ultimately Jewish memory cannot be "healed" unless the group itself finds healing, unless its wholeness is restored or rejuvenated. But for the wounds inflicted upon Jewish life by the disintegrative blows of the last two hundred years the historian seems at best pathologist, hardly a physician.

That much is, or should be, obvious, and can be laid aside. It is when we approach the historian with more modest and sober expectations, within his proper sphere, so to speak, that a deeper rift is revealed.

Memory and modern historiography stand, by their very nature, in radically different relations to the past. The latter represents, not an attempt at a restoration of memory, but a truly new kind of recollection. In its quest for understanding it brings to the fore texts, events, processes, that never really became part of Jewish group memory even when it was at its most vigorous. With unprecedented energy it continually recreates an ever more detailed past whose shapes and textures memory does not recognize. But that is not all. The historian does not simply come in to replenish the gaps of memory. He constantly challenges even those memories that have survived intact. Moreover, in common with historians in all fields of inquiry, he seeks ultimately to recover a total past—in this case the entire Jewish past—even if he is directly concerned with only a segment of it. No subject is potentially unworthy of his interest, no document, no artifact, beneath his attention. We understand the rationales for this. The point is that all these features cut against the grain of collective memory which . . . is drastically selective. Certain memories live on; the rest are winnowed out, repressed, or simply discarded by a process of natural selection which the historian, uninvited, disturbs and reverses. The question remains whether, as a result, some genuine catharsis or reintegration is foreseeable.

Certainly at the present moment the very opposite seems to be the case. Gone is that optimistic assurance . . . that the whole of Jewish history can yield, if only in secular terms, a meaningful unified structure or a clear pattern of development. . . .

An anti-historical attitude of a very different kind is expressed by those who have experienced modern Jewish existence as something so totally new that it demands the past be either forgotten or demolished. . . .

. . . When I spoke earlier of the coincidence of the rise of modern Jewish historiography and the decay of Jewish memory, I had in mind a specific kind of memory of the past, that of Jewish tradition. But hardly any Jew today is without some Jewish past. Total amnesia is still relatively rare. The choice for Jews as for non-Jews is not whether or not to have a past, but rather—what kind of past shall one have. . . .

Today Jewry lives a bifurcated life. As a result of emancipation in the diaspora and national sovereignty in Israel Jews have fully re-entered the mainstream of history, and yet their perception of how they got there and where they are is most often more mythical than real. Myth and memory condition action. There are myths that are life-sustaining and deserve to be reinterpreted for our age. There are some that lead astray and must be redefined. Others are dangerous and must be exposed.

The burden of building a bridge to his people remains with the historian. I do not know for certain that this will be possible. I am convinced only that first the historian must truly desire it and then try to act accordingly. . . . What historians choose to study and write about is obviously part of the problem. The notion that everything in the past is worth knowing "for its own sake" is a mythology of modern historians, as is the lingering suspicion that a conscious responsibility toward the living concerns of the group must result in history that is somehow less scholarly or "scientific." Both stances lead, not to science, but to antiquarianism. How historians write is also germane. What I have in mind need not involve us in the now tiresome debate as to whether history is an "art" or a "science," which merely perpetuates the fallacy that the content of an historical work can be separated from the form in which the historian presents it. The divorce of history from literature has been as calamitous for Jewish as for general historical writing, not only because it widens the breach between the historian and the layman, but

because it affects the very image of the past that results. Those who are alienated from the past cannot be drawn to it by explanation alone; they require
evocation as well.

Above all, the historian must fully confront a contemporary Jewish reality if
he is to be heard at all. . . .

[M]odern Jewish historiography can never substitute for Jewish memory.
But I am equally convinced that a historiography that does not aspire to be
memorable is in peril of becoming a rampant growth.

Jan Assmann (contemp.)

German Egyptologist. Jan Assmann's work (along with that of his wife, **Aleida Assmann**) is still not well-known in Anglo-American contexts, at least in part because his 1992 magnum opus, *Das kulturelle Gedächtnis: Schrift, Erinnerung und politische Identität in frühen Hochkulturen* (*The Cultural Memory: Writing, Remembering, and Political Identity in Early Civilizations*), has not yet been translated. This is particularly unfortunate because his theories and concepts have achieved predominance in European (especially German) discourse; Assmann is both the major legatee of the Halbwachsian tradition and its most potent critical reconstructor. Drawing on figures like **Gadamer**, **Warburg**, **Benjamin**, and **Freud**, among others, Assmann outlines the field of memory studies' task as what he calls "mnemo-history," the aim of which is "not to ascertain the possible truth of traditions . . . but to study these traditions as phenomena of collective memory." In response to Halbwachs's concept of "collective memory," however, Assmann distinguishes between what he calls "communicative memory" (images of the past negotiated and handed down within groups from grand-parents to grandchildren and in everyday communication, within limited time horizons, and thus malleable and changing) and "cultural memory" (accumulated residues of often distant pasts that constitute "the store of knowledge from which a group derives awareness of its unity and peculiarity"); this distinction has defined numerous research programs and projects, and indeed the term "cultural memory" is probably now more widely used in Germany and elsewhere in Europe than "collective memory;" for Assmann and many of his followers, cultural memory is a more compelling topic than communicative memory, or at least they resist what they see as the prevalent focus on communicative memory in Halbwachs-inspired studies of "collective memory," which they see as resulting from the ahistoricism of sociology or the narrow focus of oral history.

From *Moses the Egyptian: The Memory of Egypt in Western Monotheism*

Unlike history proper, mnemohistory is concerned not with the past as such, but only with the past as it is remembered. It surveys the story-lines of tradition, the webs of intertextuality, the diachronic continuities and discontinuities of reading the past. Mnemohistory is not the opposite of history but rather is one of its branches or subdisciplines, such as intellectual history, social history, the history of mentalities, or the history of ideas. But it has an approach of its own in that it deliberately leaves aside the synchronic aspects of what it is investigating. It concentrates exclusively on those aspects of significance and relevance which are the product of memory—that is, of a recourse to a past—and which appear only in the light of later readings. Mnemohistory is reception theory applied to history. But "reception" is not to be understood here merely in the narrow sense of transmitting and receiving. The past is not simply "received" by the present. The present is "haunted" by the past and the past is modeled, invented, reinvented, and reconstructed by the present. . . .

The aim of a mnemohistorical study is not to ascertain the possible truth of traditions . . . but to study these traditions as phenomena of collective memory. Memories may be false, distorted, invented, or implanted. This has been sufficiently shown in recent discussions in the fields of forensic psychiatry, psychoanalysis, biography, and history. Memory cannot be validated as a historical source without being checked against "objective" evidence. This is as true of collective memory as of individual memory. . . . But for a historian of memory, the "truth" of a given memory lies not so much in its "factuality" as in its "actuality." Events tend to be forgotten unless they live on in collective memory. The same principle applies to fundamental semantic distinctions. There is no meaning in history unless these distinctions are remembered. The reason for this "living on" lies in the continuous relevance of these events. This relevance comes not from their historical past, but from an ever-changing present in which these events are remembered as facts of importance. Mnemohistory analyzes the importance which a present ascribes to the past. The task of historical positivism consists in separating the historical from the mythical elements in memory and distinguishing the elements which retain the past from those which shape the present. In contrast, the task of mnemohistory consists in analyzing the mythical elements in tradition and discovering their hidden agenda. . . .

Looming large in this debate is the infelicitous opposition between history and myth, leading to an all-too antiseptic conception of "pure facts" as opposed to the egocentrism of myth-making memory. History turns into myth as soon as it is remembered, narrated, and used, that is, woven into the fabric of the present. The mythical qualities of history have nothing to do with its truth values. For example, Masada is both a complex of uncontested historical facts and a powerful component of modern Israel's national mythology. Its mythological function does not in the least invalidate its historicity, nor would its demythization enlarge our historical knowledge. . . . All of this does not, however, affect the historicity of the events themselves in the least. The historical study of the events should be carefully distinguished from the study of their commemoration, tradition, and transformation in the collective memory of the people concerned.

Seen as an individual and as a social capacity, memory is not simply the storage of past "facts" but the ongoing work of reconstructive imagination. In other words, the past cannot be stored but always has to be "processed" and mediated. This mediation depends on the semantic frames and needs of a given individual or society within a given present.

If "We Are What We Remember," the truth of memory lies in the identity that it shapes. This truth is subject to time so that it changes with every new identity and every new present. It lies in the story, not as it happened but as it lives on and unfolds in collective memory. If "We Are What We Remember," we are the stories that we are able to tell about ourselves. "We have, each of us, a life-story, an inner narrative—whose continuity, whose sense, is one's life. It might be said that each of us constructs and lives, a 'narrative,' and that this narrative is us, our identities" [Oliver Sacks]. The same concept of a narrative organization of memory and self-construction applies to the collective level. Here, the stories are called "myths." They are the stories which a group, a society, or a culture lives by. Myths in the sense of traditional narratives play a very important role in the formation of ethnic identities ("ethnogenesis"). Ethnogenetic movements typically derive their dynamics from some master narratives which act as a "mythomoteur." As far as contemporary events are experienced and interpreted by contemporaries in the light of such metanarratives, history (in the sense of *res gestae*) is already imbued with narrative, quite independently of its being told or written in the form of narrative. Narrative structures are operative in the organization of action, experience, memory, and representation. . . . Mnemohistory investigates the history of cultural memory. The term "cultural memory" is merely a translation of the Greek name Mnemosyne. Since Mnemosyne was the mother of the nine Muses, her name came to stand for the totality of cultural activities as they were personified by the different Muses. By subsuming these cultural activities under the personification of memory, the Greeks were viewing culture not only as based on memory but as a form of memory in itself. The memory-line I am concerned with is, however, much more specific. It is just one of the many *Wanderstrassen* of cultural memory, as Aby Warburg called it. Further, its investigation involves a methodology of its own which must not be confounded with the much more general concerns of mnemohistory. This is the history of discourse. By "discourse" I understand something much more specific than what this term has come to refer to in the wake of Michel Foucault and others. I am referring to a concatenation of texts which are based on each other and treat or negotiate a common subject matter. In this vein, discourse is a kind of textual conversation or debate which might extend over generations and centuries, even millennia, depending on institutionalizations of permanence such as writing, canonization, educational and clerical institutions, and so forth.

Discourse (in this restricted sense of debate) is organized by a thematic frame and a set of (unwritten) rules as to how to deal both with antecedent texts and with the subject matter. These include rules of conversation, argumentation, quotation, verification, and many others. A mnemohistorical discourse analysis investigates this concatenation of texts as a vertical line of memory and seeks out the threads of connectivity which are working behind the texts; the intertextuality, evolution of ideas, recourse to forgotten evidence, shifts of focus, and so forth. In dealing with a specific topic within the general frame of imagining Egypt in European cultural memory (Mozart's *Magic Flute* and its Egyptian associations), Siegfried Morenz spoke of the "*Lebenszusammenhang* [vital coherence] of Egypt-Antiquity-Occident." This term is not very illuminating; indeed, it is somewhat mystifying. Cultural memory is the principle that organizes a "vital coherence," and one of its forms is "discourse." . . .

Metaphorically speaking, a discourse has a life of its own which reproduces itself in those who are joining in it. It is this "life of its own" that might be related to the mythical aspect of discourse in Lévi-Strauss's sense. Behind, beside, and beneath the discourse that takes place in the realm of the written word, there is the myth of Egypt, which transcends this realm and which works its "mythomotoric" spell from behind the stage. In the eighteenth century one would have personified this mythomotoric fascination as the "genius of the discourse." For us, this kind of helpful mystification is, of course, illicit and so is the use of unanalyzed concepts like "discourse" and "cultural memory." I can only hope that the forgoing remarks have sufficiently clarified my use of the terms.

From "Collective Memory and Cultural Identity"

The specific character that a person derives from belonging to a distinct society and culture is not seen to maintain itself for generations as a result of phylogenetic evolution, but rather as a result of socialization and customs. The "survival of the type" in the sense of a cultural pseudo-species is a function of the cultural memory. According to Nietzsche, while in the world of animals genetic programs guarantee the survival of the species, humans must find a means by which to maintain their nature consistently through generations. The solution to this problem is offered by cultural memory, a collective concept for all knowledge that directs behavior and experience in the interactive framework of a society and one that obtains through generations in repeated societal practice and initiation.

We define the concept of cultural memory through a double delimitation in that distinguishes it:

1. from what we call "communicative" or "everyday memory," which in the narrower sense of our usage lacks "cultural" characteristics;
2. from science, which does not have the characteristics of memory as it relates to a collective self-image. For the sake of brevity, we will leave aside this second delimitation which Halbwachs developed as the distinction between memory and history and limit ourselves to the first: the distinction between communicative and cultural memory. . . .

For us the concept of "communicative memory" includes those varieties of collective memory that are based exclusively on everyday communications. These varieties, which M. Halbwachs gathered and analyzed under the concept of collective memory, constitute the field of oral history. Everyday communication is characterized by a high degree of non specialization, reciprocity of roles, thematic instability, and disorganization. Typically, it takes place between partners who can change roles. Whoever relates a joke, a memory, a bit of gossip, or an experience becomes the listener in the next moment. There are occasions which more or less predetermine such communications, for example train rides, waiting rooms, or the common table; and there are rules—"laws of the market"—that regulate this exchange. There is a "household" within the confines of which this communication takes place. Yet beyond this reigns a high degree of formlessness, willfulness, and disorganization. Through this manner of communication, each individual composes a memory which, as Halbwachs has shown, is (a) socially mediated and (b) relates to a group. Every individual memory constitutes itself in communication with others. These "others," however, are not just any set of people, rather they are groups who conceive their unity and peculiarity through a common image of their past. Halbwachs thinks of families, neighborhood and professional groups, political parties, associations, etc., up to and including nations. Every individual belongs to numerous such groups and therefore entertains numerous collective self-images and memories.

Through the practice of oral history, we have gained a more precise insight into the peculiar qualities of this everyday form of collective memory, which, with L. Niethammer, we will call communicative memory. Its most important characteristic is its limited temporal horizon. As all oral history studies suggest, this horizon does not extend more than eighty to (at the very most) one hundred years into the past, which equals three or four generations or the Latin *saeculum*. This horizon shifts in direct relation to the passing of time. The communicative memory offers no fixed point which would bind it to the ever expanding past in the passing of time. Such fixity can only be achieved through a cultural formation and therefore lies outside of informal everyday memory. . . .

Just as the communicative memory is characterized by its proximity to the everyday, cultural memory is characterized by its distance form the everyday. Distance from the everyday (transcendence) marks its temporal horizon. Cultural memory has its fixed point; its horizon does not change with the passing of time. These fixed points are fateful events of the past, whose memory is maintained through cultural formation (texts, rites, monuments) and institutional communication (recitation, practice, observance). We call these "figures of memory." . . .

Our theory of cultural memory attempts to relate all three poles—memory (the contemporized past), culture, and the group (society)—to each other. We want to stress the following characteristics of cultural memory:

1) *"The concretion of identity"* or the relation to the group. Cultural memory preserves the store of knowledge from which a group derives an awareness of its unity and peculiarity. The objective manifestations of cultural memory are defined through a kind of identificatory determination in a positive ("We are this") or in a negative ("That's our opposite") sense.

Through such a concretion of identity evolves what Nietzsche has called the "constitution of horizons." The supply of knowledge in the cultural memory is characterized by sharp distinctions made between those who belong and those who do not, i.e., between what appertains to oneself and what is foreign. Access to and transmission of this knowledge are not controlled by what Blumenberg calls "theoretical curiosity," but rather by a "need for identity" as described by Hans Mol.

Connected with this is

2) *Its capacity to reconstruct.* No memory can preserve the past. What remains is only that "which society in each era can reconstruct within its contemporary frame of reference" [Halbwachs]. Cultural memory works by reconstructing, that is, it always relates its knowledge to an actual and contemporary situation. True, it is fixed in immovable figures of memory and stores of knowledge, but every contemporary context relates to these differently, sometimes by appropriations, sometimes by criticism, sometimes by preservation or by transformation. Cultural memory exists in two modes: first in the mode of potentiality of the archive whose accumulated texts, images, and rules of conduct act as a total horizon, and second in the mode of actuality, whereby each contemporary context puts the objectivized meaning into its own perspective, giving it its own relevance.

3) *Formation.* The objectivation or crystallization of communicated meaning and collectively shared knowledge is a prerequisite of its transmission *in the culturally institutionalized heritage of a society.*

"Stable" formation is not dependent on a single medium such as writing. Pictorial images and rituals can also function in the same way. One can speak of linguistic, pictorial, or ritual formation and thus arrives at the trinity of the Greek mysteries: legomenon, dromenon, and deiknymenon. As far as language is concerned, formation takes place long before the invention of writing. The distinction between the communicative memory and the cultural memory is *not* identical with the distinction between oral and written language.

4) *Organization.* With this we mean a) the institutional buttressing of communication, e.g., through formulization of the communicative situation in ceremony and b) the specialization of the bearers of cultural memory. The distribution and structure of participation in the communicative memory are diffuse. No specialists exist in this regard. Cultural memory, by contrast, always depends on a specialized practice, a kind of "cultivation." In special cases of written cultures with canonized texts, such cultivation can expand enormously and become extremely differentiated.

5) *Obligation.* The relation to a normative self-image of the group engenders a clear *system of values and differentiations in importance* which structure the cultural supply of knowledge and the symbols. There are important and unimportant, central and peripheral, local and interlocal symbols, depending on how they function in the production representation, and reproduction, of this self-image. Historicism is positioned firmly against this perspectival evaluation of a heritage, which is centered on cultural identity. . . .

The binding character of the knowledge preserved in cultural memory has two aspects: the *formative* one in its educative, civilizing, and humanizing functions and the *normative* one in its function of providing rules of conduct.

6) *Reflexivity*. Cultural memory is reflexive in three ways:

a) it is practice-reflexive in that it interprets common practice in terms through proverbs, maxims, "ethno-theories," to use Bourdieu's term, rituals (for instance, sacrificial rites that interpret the practice of hunting), and so on.

b) It is self-reflexive in that its draws on itself to explain, distinguish, reinterpret, criticize, censure, control, surpass, and receive hypoleptically.

c) It is reflexive of its own image insofar as it reflects the self-image of the group through a preoccupation with its own social system.

The concept of cultural memory comprises that body of reusable texts, images, and rituals specific to each society in each epoch, whose "cultivation" serves to stabilize and convey that society's self-image. Upon such collective knowledge, for the most part (but not exclusively) of the past, each group bases its awareness of unity and particularity.

The content of such knowledge varies from culture to culture as well as from epoch to epoch. The manner of its organization, its media, and its institutions, are also highly variable. The binding and reflexive character of a heritage can display varying intensities and appear in various aggregations. One society bases its self-image on a canon of sacred scripture, the next on a basic set of ritual activities, and the third on a fixed and hieratic language of forms in a canon of architectural and artistic types. The basic attitude toward history, the past, and thus the function of remembering itself introduces another variable. One group remembers the past in fear of deviating from its model, the next for fear of repeating the past: "Those who cannot remember their past are condemned to relive it" [George Santayana]. The basic openness of these variables lends the question of the relation between culture and memory a cultural-topological interest. Through its cultural heritage a society becomes visible to itself and to others. Which past becomes evident in that heritage and which values emerge in its identificatory appropriation tells us much about the constitution and tendencies of a society.

Peter Berger (contemp.)

American (émigré) sociologist. In their famous book *The Social Construction of Reality: A Treatise in the Sociology of Knowledge*, Peter Berger and Thomas Luckmann provide a phenomenological perspective on tradition, which they characterize as the sedimentation of experience; these sediments can be transmitted only when they are objectified in sign systems, the most common of which is language. In the following excerpt from his book *An Invitation to Sociology: A Humanist Perspective*, Berger characterizes the past as an ongoing reconstruction—whether biographically by an individual or historically for a collectivity—in the present, arguing that the commonsense view that the past is fixed and immutable is mistaken. In particular, Berger highlights the relevance of turning points and other such chronological markers, though he also stresses that the identification of certain moments as turning points can happen at those moments, or be reevaluated later not to have been a turning point, or that a moment not recognized at the time as a turning point can be identified as such later, within the revised narrative frame. This is a manifestation of Berger's phenomenology—his characterization of commonsense as an ongoing accomplishment.

From *Invitation to Sociology: A Humanistic Approach*

The commonsense view would have it that we live through a certain sequence of events, some more and some less important, the sum of which is our biography. To compile a biography, then, is to record these events in chronological order or in the order of their importance. But even a purely chronological record raises the problem of just what events should be included, since obviously not everything the subject of the record ever did could be covered. In other words, even a purely chronological record forces one to raise questions concerning the relative importance of certain events. This becomes especially clear in deciding on what historians call "periodization." Just when in the history of Western civilization should one consider the Middle Ages to have begun? And just when in the biography of an individual can one assume that his youth has come to an end? Typically, such decisions are made on the basis of events that the historian or the biographer considers to have been "turning points." . . . However, even the most optimistic historians and biographers have moments of doubts as to the choice of these particular events as the truly decisive ones. . . . The decision for one as against another event obviously depends on one's frame of reference.

This fact is not altogether hidden from commonsense thinking. It is taken care of by the notion that a certain maturity is required before one can really understand what one's life has been all about. The mature consciousness of oneself is then the one that has, so to speak, an epistemologically privileged position . . . Maturity is the state of mind that has settled down, come to terms with the *status quo*, given up the wilder dreams of adventure and fulfillment. It is not difficult to see that such a notion of maturity is psychologically functional in giving the individual a rationalization for having lowered his sights. . . . In other words, we would contend that the notion of maturity really begs the question of what is important and what unimportant in one's biography. What may look like mellow maturity from one point of view may be interpreted as cowardly compromise from another. To become older, alas, is not necessarily to become wiser. And the perspective of today has no epistemological priority over the one of last year. Incidentally, it is this same recognition that makes most historians today wary of any notion of progress or evolution in human affairs. It is too easy to think that our own age is the epitome of what men have achieved so far, so that any past period can be judged on a scale of progress in terms of its closeness to or distance from the point at which we now stand. . . .

But to return from such metaphysical speculation to the problems of biography, it would seem, therefore, that the course of events that constitute one's life can be subjected to alternate interpretations. Nor can this be done only by the outside observer, so that after we're dead rival biographers may quarrel over the real significance of this or that thing we have done or said. We ourselves go on interpreting and reinterpreting our own life. As Henri Bergson has shown, memory itself is a reiterated act of interpretation. As we remember the past, we reconstruct it in accordance with our present ideas of what is important and what is not . . . This means that in any situation, with its near infinite number of things that could be noticed, we notice only those things that are important for our immediate purposes. The rest we ignore. But in the present these things that we have ignored may be thrust upon our consciousness by someone who points them out to us. Unless we are literally mad we shall have to admit that they are there, although we may emphasize that we are not interested in them very much. But the things in the past that we have decided to ignore are much more helpless against our annihilating nonremembrance. They are not here to be pointed out to us against our will, and only in rare instances (as, for example, in criminal proceedings) are we confronted with evidence that we cannot dispute. This means that common sense is quite wrong in thinking that the past is fixed, immutable, invariable, as against the ever changing flux of the present. On the contrary, at least within our own consciousness, the past is malleable and flexible, constantly changing as our recollection reinterprets and re-explains what has happened. Thus we have as many lives as we have points of views. We keep reinterpreting our biography very much as the Stalinists kept rewriting the Soviet Encyclopedia, calling forth some events into decisive importance as others were banished to ignominious oblivion.

We can safely assume that this process of reshaping the past . . . is as old as *homo sapiens*, if not his hominoid ancestors, and that it helped to while away the long millennia in which men did little but dully bang away with their fist-axes. Every rite of passage is an act of historical interpretation and every wise old man is a theorist of historical development. But what is distinctively modern is the frequency and rapidity with which such reinterpretation often occurs in the lives of many individuals, and the increasingly common situation in which different systems of interpretation can be chosen in this game of re-creating the world. . . .

People on the move physically are frequently people who are also on the move in their self-understanding. Take the amazing transformations of identity and self-image that can be the result of a simple change of residence. . . . What was proper before is improper after, and vice versa. What used to be tabu becomes *de rigueur*, what used to be obvious becomes laughable, and what used to be one's world becomes that which must be overcome. Obviously going through such a transformation involves a reinterpretation of one's past, and a radical one at that. One now realizes that the great emotional upheavals of the past were but puerile titillations, that those whom one thought important people in one's life were but limited provincials all along. The events of which one used to be proud are now embarrassing episodes in one's prehistory. They may even be repressed from memory if they are too much at variance with the way in which one wants to think of oneself now. . . . We go through life refashioning our calendar of holy days, raising up and tearing down again the signposts that mark our progress through time toward ever newly defined fulfillments. For it will be clear by now that no magic *is so strong* that it may not be overcome by a newer brand. . . . The "true" understanding of our past is a matter of our viewpoint. And, obviously, our viewpoint may change. "Truth," then, is not only a matter of geography but of the time of day. Today's "insight" becomes tomorrow's "rationalization," and the other way around.

Social mobility (the movement from one level of society to another) has very similar consequences, in terms of the reinterpretation of one's life as geographical mobility. Take the way in which a man's self-image changes as he moves up the social ladder. Perhaps the saddest aspect of this change is the way in which he now reinterprets his relationships to the people and events that used to be closest to him. . . .

Instances of geographical and social mobility merely illustrate more sharply a process that goes on throughout society and in many different social situations. The confessing husband who reinterprets the love affairs of his past to bring them into a line of ascent culminating in his marriage, the newly divorced wife who reinterprets her marriage *ab initio* in such a way that each stage of it serves to explain the final fiasco. . . . [A]ll these are engaged in the same perennial pastime of correcting fortune by remaking history. Now, in most of these cases, the process of reinterpretation is partial and at best half-conscious. One rectifies the past where one has to, leaving untouched what one can incorporate into one's present self-image. And these continuous modifications and adjustments in one's biographical *tableau* are rarely integrated in a clear, consistent definition of oneself. Most of us do not set out deliberately to paint a grand portrait of ourselves. Rather we stumble like drunkards over the sprawling canvas of our self-conception, throwing a little paint here, erasing some lines there, never really stopping to obtain a view of the likeness we have produced. In other words, we might accept the existentialist notion that we create ourselves if we add the observation that most of this creation occurs haphazardly and at best in half-awareness.

There are some cases, however where the reinterpretation of the past is part of a deliberate, fully conscious and intellectually integrated activity. This happens when the reinterpretation of one's biography is one aspect of conversion to a new religious or ideological *Weltanschauung,* that is, a universal meaning system, *within which* one's biography can be located. . . . Classic statements of this would be Augustine's *Confessions.* . . . [I]n other words, conversion is an act in which *the past* is dramatically transformed. . . .

Psychoanalysis provides for many people in our society a similar method of ordering the discrepant fragments of their biography in a meaningful scheme. This method is particularly functional in a comfortable middle-class society, too "mature" for the courageous commitment demanded by religion or revolution. Containing within its system an elaborate and supposedly scientific means of explaining all human behavior, psychoanalysis gives its adherents the luxury of a convincing picture of themselves without making any moral demands on them and without upsetting their socioeconomic applecarts. This is evidently a technological improvement in conversion management as compared with Christianity or Communism. Apart from that, the reinterpretation of the past proceeds in analogous fashion. Fathers, mothers, brothers, sisters, wives and children are thrown one by one into the conceptual cauldron and emerge as metamorphosed figures of the Freudian pantheon. . . .

The experience of conversion to a meaning system that is capable of ordering the scattered data of one's biography is liberating and profoundly satisfying. Perhaps this has its roots in a deep human need for order, purpose and intelligibility. However, the dawning recognition that this or any other conversion is not necessarily final, that one could be reconverted and re-reconverted, is one of the most terrifying ideas the mind can have. The experience of what we have called "alternation" (which is precisely the perception of oneself in front of an infinite series of mirrors, each one transforming one's image in a different potential conversion) leads to a feeling of vertigo, a metaphysical agoraphobia before the endlessly overlapping horizons of one's possible being. . . .

[W]e change our world views (and thus our interpretations and reinterpretations of our biography) as we move from one social world to another. Only the madman or the rare case of genius can inhabit a world of meaning all by himself. Most of us acquire our meanings from other men and require their constant support so that these meanings may continue to be believable. Churches are agencies for the mutual reinforcement of meaningful interpretations. The beatnik must have a beatnik subculture, as must the pacifist, the vegetarian and the Christian Scientist. But the fully adjusted, mature, middle-of-the-road, sane and sensible suburbanite also requires a specific social context that will approve and sustain his way of life. Indeed, every one of these terms—"adjustment," "maturity," "sanity," and so on— refers to socially relative situations and becomes meaningless when divorced from these. One adjusts to a particular society. One matures by becoming habituated to it. One is sane if one shares its cognitive and normative assumptions.

Individuals who change their meaning systems must, therefore, change their social relationships. The man who redefines himself by marrying a certain woman must drop the friends that do not fit this self-definition. . . .

[T]he experience of relativity and "alternation" is not only a global historical phenomenon but a real existential problem in the life of the individual. . . . Sociological consciousness moves in a frame of reference that allows one to perceive one's biography as a movement within and through specific social worlds, to which specific meaning systems are attached. This by no means solves the problem of truth. But it makes us a little less likely to be trapped by every missionary band we encounter on the way.

Eviatar Zerubavel (contemp.)

Israeli-American sociologist. A student of Erving Goffman, though also an avid reader of Georg Simmel, Zerubavel is a founding father of what has come to be known as "cognitive sociology." Divisions of temporality, and divisions of groups in terms of their relations to temporality, are thus major themes in Zerubavel's work. Zerubavel's writings related to collective memory have included studies of the calendar, commemorative attention, the structure of denial, and ways of distinguishing between past and present. Here Zerubavel distinguishes the sociological approach to memory from the psychological (characterizing the sociological as in many ways primary) and articulates the very useful concepts of mnemonic socialization and mnemonic communities (on the latter see also **Bellah et al.**).

From "Social Memories: Steps towards a Sociology of the Past"

The work on memory typically generated by psychologists might lead one to believe that the act of remembering takes place in a social vacuum. The total lack of attention to the social context within which memory is actually situated supports a vision of "mnemonic Robinson Crusoes" whose memories are virtually free of any social influence or constraint.

Such a naive vision is quite inappropriate even within the synthetic context of the psychological laboratory, where most of the research on memory actually takes place. It is even less appropriate, however, within the context of real life.

Consider, for example, the role of others as witnesses whose memories help corroborate our own. . . . No wonder courts rarely accept uncorroborated testimony as admissible evidence. Indeed, most of us feel reassured that what we remember actually happened when other people verify our recollections. The frustrating experience of recalling events that no one else remembers resembles that of seeing things or hearing sounds which no one else does.

In fact, other people sometimes have even better access to certain parts of our past than we ourselves and can therefore help us recall people and events which we have forgotten. A wife, for example, may remind her husband about an old friend he had once mentioned to her yet has since forgotten. Parents, grandparents, and older siblings, of course, often remember people and events from our own childhood that we cannot. In fact, many of our earliest "memories" are actually recollections of stories we heard from them about our childhood. In an odd way, they remember them for us!

Yet such "mnemonic others" can also block our access to certain events in our own life, thereby preventing them from becoming memories in the first place. This is especially critical in the case of very young children, who still depend on others to define for them what is real (as well as memorable) and what is not. A 35-year-old secretary whose boss tells her to "forget this ever happened" will probably be psychologically independent enough to be able to store that forbidden memory in her mind anyway. However, a five-year-old boy whose mother flatly denies that an event they have just experienced together ever took place will most likely have a much harder time resisting her pressure to suppress it from his consciousness and may thus end up repressing it altogether.

The extent to which our social environment affects the way we remember the past becomes even clearer when we realize that much of what we "remember" is actually filtered (and therefore inevitably distorted) through a process of interpretation that usually takes place within particular social surroundings. Such distortion affects the actual facts we recall as well as the particular "tone" in which we recall them. . . .

The reason we often need to spend so much mental effort trying to reclaim our own personal recollections from parents or older siblings is that, as the very first thought community in which we learn to interpret our own experience, the family plays a critical role in our *mnemonic socialization*. In fact, all subsequent interpretations of our early "recollections" are only reinterpretations of the way they were originally experienced and remembered within the context of our family. Yet the process of mnemonic socialization also continues beyond the family, and entering a new thought community (such as when we get married, start a new job, convert to another religion, or emigrate to another country) usually entails reinterpreting our personal recollections in light of some new *mnemonic tradition*. . . .

The notion of a tradition of remembering (most commonly manifested in the form of required history classes in school) underscores the normative dimension of memory, which is by and large ignored by cognitive science. Remembering, after all, is more than just a spontaneous personal act. It is also regulated by unmistakably social *rules of remembrance* that tell us quite specifically what we should remember and what we can or must forget.

Such rules determine, for example, how far back we remember. Just as society delineates the scope of our attention and concern, it also delimits our mental reach into the past by setting certain historical horizons beyond which past events are basically regarded as irrelevant and, as such, often forgotten altogether. . . .

[T]he remarkable power of society to relegate the past to irrelevance (and thereby to practical oblivion) is the aptly-named statute of limitations, the ultimate institutionalization of the idea that it is time to put something "behind us." The very notion of such a statute implies that even events that we all agree happened can nonetheless be mentally banished by society to some "pre-historical" past that is officially forgotten.

The extent to which our social environment affects the "depth" of our memory is also manifested somewhat more tacitly in the way we convention-ally begin historical narratives. . . . After all, by defining a certain moment in history as the actual beginning of a particular historical narrative, it implicitly also defines for us everything that preceded it as mere "pre-history" which we can practically forget. Thus, when sociologists say, as many often do, that sociology was "born" in the 1830s with the work of Auguste Comte, they are implicitly also saying that their students need not read the work of Aristotle, Hobbes, or Rousseau, which is, after all, only "pre-sociological." . . .

Nowhere is the social partitioning of the past into a memorable "history" and a practically forgettable "pre-history" more blatantly evident than in the case of "discoveries," When the *New York Times,* for example, offers its readers a brief historical profile of Mozambique that begins with its "discovery" by the Portuguese in 1498 and fails to remind them that that particular moment marks only the beginning of the *European* chapter in its history, it implicitly relegates that country's entire pre-European past to official oblivion. . . .

The division of the past into a memorable "history" and a practically forget-table "pre-history" is neither logical nor natural. It is an unmistakably social, normative convention. One needs to be mnemonically socialized to view Columbus's first voyage to the Caribbean as the beginning of American history. One needs to be taught to regard everything that had happened in America prior to 1492 as a mere prelude to its "real" history. Only then can one forget "pre-Columbian" America.

The extent to which our memory is affected by our social environment is also evident from the unmistakably conventional formulaic "plot structures" we normally use to narrate the past. Thus, for example, it is hardly surprising that someone who grows up in a highly traditionalistic family who tends to embellish and romanticize the past would come to "remember" one's great-grandfather as a larger-than-life, almost mythical figure, just as the great social upheavals of the 1960s and 1970s are likely to be remembered quite differently by children who grow up today in liberal and conservative homes, respectively. . . .

The sociology of memory also highlights the impersonal aspect of our recollections, reminding us that what we "remember" includes more than just what we have *personally* experienced. In doing so, it also reminds us that the study of memory must include more than what experimental psychologists usually do in their laboratories.

I was already forty-three when I first saw Venice, yet I soon realized that it was actually quite familiar to me. The majestic Grand Canal, for example, was something I had already "seen" on the cover of an album of brass concerti by Venetian composer Antonio Vivaldi when I was eighteen. . . .

Stored in my mind are vivid "recollections" not only of the meeting I attended last week or the shower I took this morning, but also of the Crucifixion (the way I first "saw" it in Nicholas Ray's film *The King of Kings* when I was twelve), and Ferdinand Magellan's first voyage around the world (the way I first envisioned it when I read Stefan Zweig's biography *Magellan* as a teenager). . . .

In fact, neither are my recollections of most of the historical events that have taken place during my own lifetime entirely personal. What I usually remember is the way they were actually experienced by others. Thus, for example, I "remember" the French pullout from Algeria, the Soviet invasion of Prague, and the war in Biafra mainly through the way they were reported at the time in the newspapers. I likewise "recall" the Eichmann trial, the Cuban missile crisis, the Profumo affair, and the landing of Apollo 11 on the moon mainly through radio and television reports.

In fact, much of what we remember we did not experience personally. We do so as members of particular families, organizations, nations, and other *mnemonic communities*. . . .

Indeed, being social presupposes the ability to experience events that had happened to groups and communities to which we belong long before we joined them as if they were part of our own past, as manifested in the traditional Jewish claim, explicitly repeated every Passover, that "*we* were slaves to Pharaoh in Egypt, and God brought *us* out of there with a mighty hand." (On Passover, Jews also recite the following passage from the Haggadah: "In every generation, a man should see himself *as though he* had gone forth from Egypt. As it is said: 'And you shall tell your son on that day, it is because of what God did for *me* when I went forth, from Egypt.'") Such existential fusion of our own personal biography with the history of the groups or communities to which we belong is an indispensable part of our social identity as anthropologists, Mormons, Native Americans, Miami Dolphins fans, or Marines.

Such *sociobiographical memory* also accounts for the sense of pride, pain, or shame we sometimes experience with regard to events that had happened to groups and communities to which we belong long before we joined them. Consider, for example, the national pride of present-day Greeks, much of which rests on the glorious accomplishments of Greek scholars, artists, and philosophers twenty-four centuries ago. . . . Consider also the long tradition of pain and suffering carried by many present-day American descendants of nineteenth-century African slaves, or the great sense of shame that pervades the experience of many young Germans who feel personally guilty about the atrocities of the Nazi regime despite the fact that they were born long after its collapse.

Indeed, familiarizing new members with its past is an important part of a community's effort to incorporate them. Business corporations, army battalions, colleges, and law firms, for example, often introduce new member to their history as part of their general "orientation." Children whose parents came to the United States from Portugal, Vietnam, or Guatemala are likewise taught in school to remember Paul Revere and the *Mayflower* as part of their own past.

Given its highly impersonal nature, social memory need not be stored in the minds of individuals. Indeed, there are some unmistakably impersonal "sites" of memory. . . .

Jeffrey K. Olick (contemp.)

American sociologist. In a 1998 article, Olick and his coauthor Joyce Robbins provided a relatively early synthesis of "social memory studies," proposing to reconceptualize "collective memory" as an umbrella term for distinct varieties of "mnemonic practices." Subsequent work on "the politics of regret" in postwar Germany and elsewhere led to an account of mnemonic practices as "dialogical," highlighting the ways in which commemoration responds not only to the past being commemorated but to earlier commemorations, and hence enacts a "memory of memory." The following excerpt articulates an ontological and methodological distinction that has often divided scholars of memory, particularly, but not only, psychologists from sociologists, namely that between individualistic and collectivistic understandings of social memory. Its purpose was to lay the foundation for a rapprochement, or at least greater dialogue, between the two perspectives.

From "Collective Memory: The Two Cultures"

"Collective memory" . . . indicates at least two distinct, and not obviously complementary, sorts of phenomena: socially framed individual memories and collective commemorative representations and mnemonic traces. . . .

The problem is that these two sorts of phenomena . . . seem to be of radically distinct ontological orders and to require different epistemological and methodological strategies. . . .

The first kind of collective memory is that based on individualistic principles: the aggregated individual memories of members of a group. Surely, work of this sort does not preclude that some transformations may occur when individual memories are aggregated, through the activities either of the people involved or of the social scientists "collecting" or "measuring" their memories. But the fundamental presumption here is that individuals are central: only individuals remember, though they may do so alone or together, and any publicly available commemorative symbols are interpretable only to the degree to which they elicit a reaction in some group of individuals. This ontology of memory does not exclude the possibility that different rememberers are valued differently in the group, that the memories of some command more attention than those of others, but some of the research strategies here function either technically democratically (surveys that assign the same value to every respondent) or even redistributively (such as oral history projects, which often aim at recovering the lost or neglected memories of those who have been disenfranchised). From the point of view of what I would call the "collected" memory approach, notions of collective memory as objective symbols or deep structures that transcend the individual risk slipping into a metaphysics of group mind. There is no doubt, from this perspective, that social frameworks shape what individuals remember, but ultimately it is only individuals who do the remembering.

And shared symbols and deep structures are only real insofar as individuals (albeit sometimes organized as members of groups) treat them as such or instantiate them in practice. It does not make sense from an individualist's point of view to treat commemorative objects, symbols, or structures as having a "life of their own:" only people have lives. . . .

Because it locates shared memories in individual minds and sees collective outcomes as aggregated individual processes . . . the collected memory approach is formally open to the investigation of psychological or even neurological factors in social memory outcomes, though its behaviorist approach—manifest in survey methodology or in the oral historian's interest in merely giving play to neglected voices—tends to treat the human mind as something of a black box. In substantive but not formal contrast, cognitive, behavioral, and even physical psychologists have highlighted the roles of both mind and brain in individual and, by extension, social memory processes. Perhaps the greatest advantage of the collected memory approach, then, is that it leaves open the possibility of dialogue among the physical, behavioral, and social sciences. With this formal opening, we have the opportunity to move beyond the apparent mutual irrelevance of neurological and psychological studies of memory on the one hand and sociological and cultural approaches on the other. . . .

An individualist approach to memory thus has a great deal of potential for producing insights about social memory outcomes. One problem with much of the psychological work that has been done, however, is that it works within a very strict independent-dependent variable format, in which the ability to recall is the dependent variable. Social contexts thus remain undertheorized. Aggregate outcomes, moreover, are largely irrelevant to the physical or cognitive psychologist, whose job it is to explain individual behavior. And yet, the ways in which individual brains and minds work clearly have an effect on aggregate outcomes. Race and class may affect . . . memories, but it is also possible that . . . memories shape the salient group identities. . . . And not only do the psychological processes of powerful individuals—such as political leaders—affect their broadly consequential acts. Common psychological dispositions can shape the way large groups of people react to shared experiences: documented tendencies toward cognitive consistency, for instance, perhaps in part based on neurological and cognitive organization, might constrain certain collective courses of action or the appeal of particular political programs (though we clearly have vast capacities—some psychological, others cultural—for bypassing such constraints), while psychologically based analogical reasoning and typification clearly play a great role in how groups of people interpret new situations in common. . . .

Nevertheless, the collective—as opposed to collected—memory tradition offers a number of powerful arguments that demonstrate the inadequacy of a purely psychological (individual or aggregated) approach. Three major varieties of argument are relevant here. First, certain patterns of sociation not reducible to individual psychological processes are relevant for those processes. . . .

This is a version of Halbwachs's "social frameworks" approach: groups provide the definitions, as well as the divisions, by which particular events are subjectively defined as consequential; these definitions trigger different cognitive and neurological processes of storage. Moreover, as many political historians of memory have demonstrated, contemporary circumstances provide the cues for certain images of the past. Quite consistent with the neuro-psychological image of remembering as an active and constructive process rather than as a reproduction, sociologists have demonstrated the ways the past is remade in the present for present purposes. . . . These more sociological observations are thus quite assimilable to the individualist perspective, though their focus is somewhat different. Other arguments, however, depend on a more radical ontological break between individualist and collectivist perspectives.

A great deal of work, for instance, has argued that symbols and their systems of relations have a degree of autonomy from the subjective perceptions of individuals. Of course, the nature and degree of that autonomy vary greatly depending on the approach. . . . [I]t is fairly common to assert that collectivities have memories, just like they have identities, and that ideas, styles, genres, and discourses, among other things, are more than the aggregation of individual subjectivities; while discourses are instantiated in individual utterances, such a perspective views it as a trivial truism to say that there are no ideas without thinking individuals. More extreme versions of this approach have certainly produced extravagant metaphors that have often been misunderstood—and sometimes even foolishly intended—such as that texts write authors. But clearly there is something to the argument that ideas and institutions are subject to pressures and take on patterns that cannot be explained by the interests, capacities, or activities of individuals except in the most trivial sense.

It is on the basis of such arguments, mostly implicit, that many scholars and commentators have employed the concept of collective memory. From this perspective, the collected memory approach to memory misses a great deal of what is going on. Indeed, in this way, one might argue that survey research on social memory excludes much of what is genuinely social about memory. In the first place, there are well-documented aggregation effects that cannot be predicted from individual responses: groups, for instance, tend to act more extremely than individuals. Additionally, there are clearly demonstrable long-term structures to what societies remember or commemorate that are stubbornly impervious to the efforts of individuals to escape them. Powerful institutions clearly value some histories more than others, provide narrative patterns and exemplars of how individuals can and should remember, and stimulate memory in ways and for reasons that have nothing to do with the individual or aggregate neurological records. Without such a collective perspective, we are both unable to provide good explanations of mythology, tradition, heritage, and the like either as forms or in particular, as well as risk reifying the individual. In regard to the latter, collectivist approaches to memory challenge the very idea of an individual memory. It is not just that we remember as members of groups, but that we constitute those groups and their members simultaneously in the act (thus re-member-ing). Robert Bellah and colleagues have therefore referred to "genuine communities as communities of memory" and have highlighted the role of "constitutive narratives." Individual and collective identity, in this view, are two sides of a coin rather than different phenomena.

There is an additional argument for collective as opposed to collected memory that does not necessarily abut such metaphysical and ontological matters, which I call the technologies of memory argument. Quite simply, there are mnemonic technologies other than the brain. Historians of memory, for instance, have demonstrated the importance of various forms of recording for our mnemonic capacities. These affect both individual rememberers as well as societies. For individuals, being able to write a note or record a message or take a photograph vastly extends the capacity to "remember," not simply by providing storage space outside of the brain but by stimulating our neurological storage processes in particular ways; in this manner, we have become genuine cyborgs with what several authors have called "prosthetic" memories. And this implies no particular attachment to modern computer technology: medieval orators are legendary for their mnemonic capacities, which depended on conceptual devices collectively known as *ars memoriae*, the arts of memory. . . .

At the societal level, moreover, different forms of social organization have clearly depended on different technologies of memory. There is the famous sociological argument about the importance of double-entry bookkeeping for the development of commercial society. Particular forms of record keeping are obviously associated with the possibility of an administrative state. Nineteenth-century European states increased their power and legitimacy vastly by developing new mnemonic forms like the museum, the archive, and indeed professional historiography itself. . . . Our current concern with memory in political contexts is thus in direct ways a result of technologies of memory outside of the brain.

Robert Bellah, Richard Madsen, William M. Sullivan, Ann Swidler, and Steven M. Tipton (contemp.)

American sociologists. In this classic statement by latter-day Tocquevillians, Bellah et al. speak of the constitutive role memory plays in maintaining communities. "A real community," they write, is a "community of memory, one that does not forget its past." Central to this role is the act of storytelling, the articulation and repetition of "constitutive narratives." From this functionalist perspective, "constitutive narratives" are to be understood as "practices of commitment," sources of social solidarity. On the role of narrative, see also **Ricoeur** and **Hervieu-Léger**, among others.

From *Habits of the Heart: Individualism and Commitment in American Life*

Communities . . . have a history—in an important sense they are constituted by their past—and for this reason we can speak of a real community as a "community of memory," one that does not forget its past. In order not to forget that past, a community is involved in retelling its story, its constitutive narrative, and in so doing, it offers examples of the men and women who have embodied and exemplified the meaning of the community. These stories of collective history and exemplary individuals are an important part of the tradition that is so central to a community of memory.

The stories that make up a tradition contain conceptions of character, of what a good person is like, and of the virtues that define such character. But the stories are not all exemplary, not all about successes and achievements. A genuine community of memory will also tell painful stories of shared suffering that sometimes creates deeper identities than success. . . . And if the community is completely honest, it will remember stories not only of suffering received but of suffering inflicted—dangerous memories, for they call the community to alter ancient evils. The communities of memory that tie us to past also turn us toward *the future as communities of hope.* They carry a context of meaning that can allow us to connect our aspirations for ourselves and those closest to us with the aspirations of a larger whole and see our own efforts as being, in part, *contributions to a common good.*

Examples of such genuine communities are not hard to find in the United States. There are ethnic and racial communities, each with its own story and its own heroes and heroines. There are *religious communities* that recall and reenact their stories in the weekly and annual cycles of their ritual year, remembering the scriptural stories that tell them who they are and the saints and martyrs who define their identity. There is the national community, defined by its history and by the character of its representative leaders. . . . Families can be communities, remembering their past, telling the children the stories of parents' and grandparents' lives, and sustaining hope for the future—though without the context of a larger community that sense of family is hard to maintain. Where history and hope are forgotten and community means only the gathering of the similar, community degenerates into lifestyle enclave. The temptation toward that transformation is endemic. . . .

People growing up in communities of memory not only hear the stories that tell how the community came to be, what its hopes and fears are, and how its ideals are exemplified in outstanding men and women; they also participate in the practices—ritual, aesthetic, ethical—that define the community as a way of life. We call these "practices of commitment" for they define the patterns of loyalty and obligation that keep the community alive.

Anthony Smith (contemp.)

British (émigré) nationalism scholar. Through a number of influential works, Smith has attempted to avoid both the modernist and primordialist positions on nationalism (the idea that nations are uniquely modern phenomena versus the idea that modern nations are expressions of primordial allegiances). In some ways redolent of **Renan**, Smith's position is that national identities are supported by a sense of a shared past. Here, however, Smith has much in common with sociologists who debate the relative influence of the present and the past on present images of the past when he argues that one can distinguish between empty and full pasts and that the past is often fuller than is convenient for nationalists who seek to advance a particular view of the past; as a result, and in some ways the inverse of **Hobsbawm**'s emphasis on "invention," Smith points out that nationalists in fact have to "prune" the past a great deal of the time to accomplish their goals. See also **Y. Zerubavel**.

From *The Ethnic Origins of Nations*

One of the paradoxes of contemporary society is its appetite for innovation coupled with a deep nostalgia for the past. Great numbers of men and women today, however committed to social change and new ideas, cling to traditions and values that embody personal and collective memories of a former way of life from which they are loath to be wholly sundered, and to some aspects of which they even yearn to return. This can be seen in the swift succession of 'revivals' in literature, art, music and fashion, all of which recreate for us 'lost worlds' of childhood memory. Though many people have lost this sense of the past, these successive revivals and fashions, though fed by commercialism, these revivals of *art nouveau* and Victoriana, the nostalgia for country life and a vanished aristocracy, the fascination with archeology and ancient monuments, all point to a deeper and more widespread attachment to past epochs and their values.

How can this widespread nostalgia for irrecoverable pasts be explained? Is it something that flourishes only today, when materialism and commerce render so much of the past obsolete? One answer is the need to control the pace and scope of social change. All societies have to legitimate their innovations, and the rate of contemporary change makes it all the more necessary to appeal to the past for precedents. That is why we find so many Third World leaders looking into the pasts of their peoples for sanction for their new policies and innovations; archaizing is the concomitant of rapid change. But this only begs the question: why *do* societies need to legitimate their innovations by returning to the past, and why 'their' particular pasts? In a 'traditional' society, too, one might expect a concern with precedent and custom; but why the pressing need for it in 'modernizing' innovative societies?

. . . One could even say that *ethnie* and ethnicity itself contain an element of 'nostalgia,' a desire to revert to the simpler ways of an alleged golden age in an earlier life-style, one which has been irretrievably lost. This suggests a more universal need, or at any rate one that goes beyond the modern era and its need for 'legitimations.'

There is another standard reply to the questions about nostalgia for tradition and the past that has gone. This is that modern conditions, notably capitalism and bureaucracy, have corroded individuality and induced powerful feelings of estrangement and homelessness. The social structure of modern industrial capitalism, too, is one of alienation; our own products and creations, like our work, become alien 'objects' standing over against us and inducing feelings of fragmentation. Alternatively, modern societies are regarded as peculiarly liable to *anomie:* rapid change deregulates our lives and throws our passions out of line with our opportunities. Hence, the urgent need for antidotes, which will reintegrate and re-root us in a satisfying social framework, one that preserves liberty and individuality while anchoring both in social justice and solidarity. This means, in turn, linking a modern type of society and social order with collective traditions and native habitats: in other words, with a group's history and homeland.

The difficulty here is that 'native history' hardly encourages satisfaction of the need for both social integration and individual liberty. Nor is it clear why any vision of social justice and solidarity needs to be confined to local habitats; revolution knows no borders. One answer to these problems has been provided by Regis Debray: the nation with its stress on a beginning and flow in time, and a delimitation in space, raises barriers to the flood of meaninglessness and absurdity that might otherwise engulf human beings. It tells them that they belong to ancient associations of 'their kind' with definite boundaries in time and space, and this gives their otherwise ambiguous and precarious lives a degree of certainty and purpose. But, then, this means that the problem of alienation becomes universalized. In *this* sense, nations or human associations bounded in space and time have always existed in varying degrees, and this would suggest a more or less universal need to overcome meaninglessness, which is by no means confined to modern times.

There is another possibility. Nostalgia for the past, especially the ethnic past of 'one's own' people, has indeed been a feature of society in all ages and continents, because people have always sought to overcome death and the futility with which death threatens mortals. By linking oneself to a 'community of history and destiny,' the individual hopes to achieve a measure of immortality which will preserve his or her person and achievements from oblivion; they will live on and bear fruit in the community. Now, as long as the community was seen as a vessel and embodiment of a religious way of life, linked to the attainment of salvation (usually in the next world), nostalgia for an ethnic past only surfaced in periods of acute crisis, when the values and life-style of the religious community were under threat. As long as the individual, by living according to communal traditions, could hope to attain salvation in another world or state of being, the need to revive the past was muted. Besides, in a 'traditional' society, one was expected to fashion one's life-style and ambitions in terms of collective traditions, so that there was little need to yearn for a past that was being continued. Only when new developments within or pressures from outside undermined that practice and sense of continuity, was there any need for 'ethnic revival.'

But the rise of science, utilitarian philosophies and acquisitive materialism, have eroded traditions and promoted a secular conception of history. With the waning of beliefs in heaven and hell, the privatization of beliefs and the reaction against 'meaningless rituals,' the ethnic past of the community has been sundered from its religious anchorage; and men and women have had to look elsewhere for that immortality which so many desire. Many have found it in the idea of posterity. It is in and through offspring that deeds live on and memories are kept alive. But these deeds and memories only 'make sense' within a chain of like deeds and memories, which stretch back into the mists of obscure generations of ancestors and forward into the equally unknowable generations of descendants. Perhaps this accounts for both the quest for family roots and the yearning for communal histories and destinies, so characteristic of our otherwise matter-of-fact modernity. In any case, nostalgia for one's ethnic past has become more acute and more widespread and persistent in the modern era, with the decline of tradition and salvation religions. In this sense, ethnic nationalism becomes a 'surrogate' religion which aims to overcome the sense of futility engendered by the removal of any vision of an existence after death, by linking individuals to persisting communities whose generations form indissoluble links in a chain of memories and identities.

The virtue of this approach is that it does justice to both pre-modern instances of 'ethnic' nostalgia and the more widespread modern examples of 'national' nostalgia. The causal difference between these two forms lies in the transformation of our conceptions of time and space as a result of the decline of religious beliefs and traditions concerning an after-life or a reality beyond our empirical universe. Earlier implicit beliefs in such supra-empirical realities relativized mundane events and experiences, including death itself, by placing them in an 'eternal' and 'space-less' perspective which was felt to constitute a more genuine form of 'reality.' This conferred a measure of identity and security on individuals and groups alike, by locating them confidently in metaphysical realities or a divine plan. In this way, they became integral parts of the cosmos and no longer alone.

But secularization of beliefs and the introduction of new conceptions of finite space and homogenous, calendrical time, have undermined this cosmic solidarity and returned individuals to their 'pre-religious' isolation. Their identities are now threatened by a lack of continuity between their earthly and supernatural existences, and their sense of security is destroyed by the seeming finality of death. All that is left is memory and hope, history and destiny. But these memories and hopes are collective and inter-generational; they are 'our' history and 'our' destiny. Nostalgia is so often linked with utopia; our blueprints for the future are invariably derived from our experiences of our pasts, and as we travel forward, we do so looking backwards to a past that alone seems knowable and intelligible and which alone can 'make sense' of a future that is forever neither. . . .

But is the 'past' really so intelligible? Are we faced by a single coherent past, or by multiple pasts which we must reconstruct? Or is the 'past' we yearn for a mere invention designed to meet our present needs? . . .

[D]oes nationalism write its history as it pleases, or is it also constrained by tradition and the 'past' which it records? Is that past, in other words, 'full' or 'empty'? It seems to me fuller than is often thought; sometimes so full, nationalists must prune it for their purposes and use a very selective memory for the tale they wish to impart. There are, of course, straightforward bits of pure invention—in the sense of fabrication—as in all periods of history. . . . But in most cases, the mythologies elaborated by nationalists have not been fabrications, but recombinations of traditional, perhaps unanalysed, motifs and myths taken from epics, chronicles, documents of the period, and material artefacts. As inventions are very often such novel recombinations of existing elements and motifs, we may, in this restricted sense, call the nationalist mythologies 'inventions.' Such novel recombinations are pre-eminently the work of intellectuals in search of their 'roots.'

Yet, there are very clear and very specific limits to their activities. These are provided both by the existing criteria of historiography of the time, and by the texture and inner coherence of the myths and motifs themselves. In other words, a recombination must be 'in character.' It must intuitively 'belong to,' or cohere with, a particular traditional past and its peculiar flavour. That is why we can immediately tell Greek history and the Greek past from the French past and its history. The type of hero-figures, the degree of sacredness, the atmosphere of key events, the aroma of the habitat, all differ systematically; together they form a specific 'historical configuration,' a constellation which, while susceptible of valid comparison analytically, nevertheless is quite distinctive in quality and flavour.

Here an important qualification needs to be made. History is 'full' where the *ethnie* is fortunate enough to have retained its memories and records in sufficient quantity. This sounds tautological, but it leads to the vital point that historically 'full' *ethnie* are the pace-setters and models for historically 'drained' ones. . . . In other words, the 'past' that is to serve modern purposes must not only be 'full,' it must be well preserved'—or it must be 'reconstructed.'

We may therefore usefully distinguish between those *ethnie* with full and well-preserved pasts and those whose pasts are either lacking or hidden from view by subsequent accretions. In the first case, it is more a case of selective memory 'rediscovering' the past; in the second, a more conjectural 'reconstruction' of the past from such motifs and myths as can be unearthed. So, that, depending upon the state of preservation of the ethnic past, we can speak of either historical 'rediscovery' or 'reconstruction.' Only in rare cases need we speak of pure fabrication.

There is a further point to be made about such rediscoveries and reconstructions. In the nature of things, the 'past' that is handed down is multi-layered and susceptible of different interpretations. It also often contains quite different strands of tradition. Very rarely is it possible to speak of a 'single' past of any *ethnie*; rather, each *ethnie* possesses a series of pasts, which modern secular intellectuals attempt to interrelate in a coherent and purposive manner. The fact that they rarely achieve their goals, at least in the eyes of significant sections of the population, testifies to the 'multiple' nature of the 'past' with which they grapple. Indeed, there are significant and systematic variations of interpretation and of tradition which intellectuals from different strata and regions may select for their needs and purposes. . . .

Creating nations is a recurrent activity, which has to be renewed periodically. It is one that involves ceaseless re-interpretations, rediscoveries and reconstructions; each generation must re-fashion national institutions and stratification systems in the light of the myths, memories, values and symbols of the 'past,' which can best minister to the needs and aspirations of its dominant social groups and institutions. Hence that activity of rediscovery and re-interpretation is never complete and never simple; it is the product of dialogues between the major social groups and institutions within the boundaries of the 'nation,' and it answers to their perceived ideals and interests.

At the same time, this 'nation-building' activity operates within a definite tradition; it is not made over entirely anew by each generation, but inherits the mythologies and symbolisms of previous generations. A new generation may come to reject the interpretation of its predecessor, and question its values, myths and symbols, forsaking its holy sites for new ones and replacing its golden ages and heroes by others; but all this questioning and replacement is carried on within definite emotional and intellectual confines, which constitute far more powerful and durable barriers to the outside than any physical boundaries. This is because a social magnetism and psychological charge attaches to the 'myth-symbol complexes' of particular *ethnie* which in turn form the basis of a nation's core heritage. It is not only a question of their often considerable antiquity, though that is potent, but of their proven capacity to create bonds and generate a 'society' in the past, through the mythical and emotional union of kin groups sharing a common 'history and destiny.'

Each generation, therefore, constructs its own social maps and chooses its special ethnic moralities, but it does so within a limited matrix formed by a strong social attachment to specific 'myth-symbol complexes,' particular landscapes and unique ranges of epochs and personages, for these constitute the intrinsic ethnicity of particular *ethnie*. Hence, it is not only necessary to become conversant with the histories of particular *ethnie* if we wish to gauge their range of map-making and moralities in our era; we need also to grasp the histories of their successive rediscoveries and reconstructions, to see what each generation has made of the heritage it received.

All this powerfully qualifies the 'modernity' of nations. Not only must nations be founded upon ethnic cores, if they are to endure; they must also have, or find, a living past into which successive social circles of the educated may re-enter and whose legends and landscapes can locate the nation and direct its future. In this recurrent activity, successive generations of intellectuals and intelligentsia, often frustrated in their status ambitions, are drawn back to reconstructions of 'the past' which exert a strong fascination and provide an antidote to their arid professionalism. The images they piece together and disseminate through the education system and media become the often unconscious assumptions of later generations in whose social consciousness they form a kind of rich sediment. . . .

This brings me back to my point of departure. The return to the past is necessary because of our need for immortality through the memory of posterity which the seeming finality of death threatens. In our descendants' memory lies our hope. That requires our story to be set down, to become 'history,' like the stories of our fathers before us. In this sense, history is the precondition of destiny, the guarantee of our immortality, the lesson for posterity. Since we must live through *our* posterity, the offspring of our families, that history and its lesson must belong to us and tell our collective tale. Hence our myths, memories and symbols must be constantly renewed and continually re-told, to ensure our survival. The nation becomes the constant renewal and re-telling of our tale by each generation of our descendants.

Yael Zerubavel (contemp.)

Israeli American Jewish Studies scholar. In her book *Recovered Roots*, from which the present excerpt is drawn, Zerubavel provides a detailed historical account of the deployment of memory in the construction of Israeli nationhood and of national mythologies in general. Here she develops the concept of "master commemorative narratives," deep structures that, she argues, underwrite the generation of particular accounts in different settings; in particular, she highlights the role of these master narratives in defining turning points. See also **Berger** and **Smith**.

From *Recovered Roots: Collective Memory and the Making of Israeli National Tradition*

Each act of commemoration reproduces a *commemorative narrative*, a story about a particular past that accounts for this ritualized remembrance and provides a moral message for the group members. In creating this narrative, collective memory clearly draws upon historical sources. Yet it does so selectively and creatively. Like the historical narrative, the commemorative narrative differs from the chronicle because it undergoes the process of narrativization. As Hayden White observes, the selection and organization of a vast array of chronicled facts into a narrative form requires a response to concerns that are essentially literary and poetic. This fictional dimension, which he points out with regard to the historical narrative, is even more pronounced in the case of the commemorative narrative, which more easily blurs the line between the real and the imagined. The creativity of the commemorative narrative within the constraints of the historical narrative, its manipulation of the historical record with deliberate suppressions and imaginative elaborations, is explored throughout this work.

Each commemoration reconstructs a specific segment of the past and is therefore fragmentary in nature. Yet these commemorations together contribute to the formation of a *master commemorative narrative* that structures collective memory. With this concept I refer to a broader view of history, a basic "story line" that is culturally constructed and provides the group members with a general notion of their shared past.

To fully appreciate the meaning of individual commemorations, then, it is important to examine them within the framework of the master commemorative narrative. The study of the collective memory of a particular event thus calls for the examination of the history of its commemoration as well as its relation to other significant events in the group's past. . . . The formation of such analogies or contrasts between major historical periods and events is in itself a part of the construction of collective memory.

The master commemorative narrative focuses on the group's distinct social identity and highlights its historical development. In this sense it contributes to the formation of the nation, portraying it as a unified group moving through history. This general thrust often implies a linear conception of time. Yet the master commemorative narrative occasionally suspends this linearity by the omission, regression, repetition, and the conflation of historical events. The holiday cycle, the annual calendar, and the liturgical cycle typically disrupt the flow of time by highlighting recurrent patterns in the group's experiences. Indeed, the tension between the linear and cyclical perceptions of history often underlies the construction of collective memory. . . . [T]he commemorative narratives of specific events often suggest their unique character, while their examination within the context of the master commemorative narrative indicates the recurrence of historical patterns in the group's experience.

Since collective memory highlights the group's distinct identity, the master commemorative narrative focuses on the event that marks the group's emergence as an independent social entity. The commemoration of beginnings is clearly essential for demarcating the group's distinct identity vis-à-vis others. The emphasis on a "great divide" between this group and others is used to dispel any denial of the group's legitimacy. The commemoration of beginnings justifies the group's claim as a distinct unit, often by demonstrating that its roots go back to a distant past. European national movements displayed keen interest in peasants' folklore since they believed that it provided evidence of a unique national past and traditions preserved by this folk. Similarly, more modern nations attempted to recover or invent older traditions to display their common roots in a distant past.

Pierre Nora comments that modern nations celebrate "birth" rather than "origins" to articulate a sense of historical discontinuity. Indeed, birth symbolizes at one and the same time a point of separation from another group and the beginning of a new life as a collective entity with a future of its own. A shift in the commemoration of beginnings can also serve as a means of transforming a group's identity. The more recent emphasis by African Americans on their African origins is a case in point. While the term "negro" is associated with their past as slaves in America, a greater desire to embrace their earlier African origins has contributed to the recasting of their identity as "African Americans."

Collective memory provides an overall sense of the group's development by offering a system of periodization that imposes a certain order on the past. Like other aspects of collective memory, this periodization involves a dialogue between the past and the present, as the group reconstructs its own history from a current ideological stance. Drawing upon selective criteria, collective memory divides the past into major stages, reducing complex historical events to basic plot structures. The power of collective memory does not lie in its accurate, systematic, or sophisticated mapping of the past, but in establishing basic images that articulate and reinforce a particular ideological stance.

The tendency to provide extreme images in the construction of collective memory accentuates the contrast between different periods and encourages the formation of unambiguous attitudes toward different stages of the group's development. Thus, it highlights certain periods as representing important developments for the group while defining others as historical setbacks. Nations typically portray eras of pioneering, conquest, or struggle for independence as "positive periods;" in contrast, they are likely to define those periods when they were part of a larger empire as essentially negative, denying the full realization of their legitimacy as separate political entities.

The mapping of the past through the construction of a master commemorative narrative also designates its *commemorative density*, which is the function of what Lévi-Strauss calls "the pressure of history." Commemorative density thus indicates the importance that the society attributes to different periods in its past: while some periods enjoy multiple commemorations, others attract little attention, or fall into oblivion. The commemorative density thus ranges from periods or events that are central to the group memory and commemorated in great detail and elaboration to ones that remain unmarked in the master commemorative narrative. Such periods or events that collective memory suppresses become subjects of *collective amnesia*. Thus, the construction of the master commemorative narrative exposes the dynamics of remembering and forgetting that underlie the construction of any commemorative narrative: by focusing attention on certain aspects of the past, it necessarily covers up others that are deemed irrelevant or disruptive to the flow of the narrative and ideological message. Bernard Lewis points out the phenomenon of recovering a forgotten past. Yet it is no less important to note that such a recovery may lead to the covering up of other aspects of the past. Remembering and forgetting are thus closely interlinked in the construction of collective memory. . . .

Through the restructuring of the past, the commemorative narrative creates its own version of historical time as it elaborates, condenses, omits, or conflates historical events. By using these and other discursive techniques, the narrative transforms historical time into *commemorative time*. Thus, a highly elaborate reference to the past is likely to expand historical time, and conversely, a brief and generalized commemoration symbolically shrinks it within the framework of the narrative.

Although historical changes usually occur over a period of time and as a result of a process rather than a single event, collective memory tends to select particular events and portrays them as symbolic markers of change. The choice of a single event clearly provides a better opportunity for ritualized remembrance than a gradual process of transition does. The master commemorative narrative thus presents these events as *turning points* that changed the course of the group's historical development and hence are commemorated in great emphasis and elaboration. In turn, the selection of certain events as turning points highlights the ideological principles underlying the master commemorative narrative by dramatizing the transitions between periods.

The high commemorative density attributed to certain events not only serves to emphasize their historical significance. It may also elevate them beyond their immediate historical context into symbolic texts that serve as paradigms for understanding other developments in the group's experience. Thus, collective memory can transform historical events into *political myths* that function as a lens through which group members perceive the present and prepare for the future. Because turning points often assume symbolic significance as markers of change, they are more likely to transform into myths. As such they not only reflect the social and political needs of the group that contributed to their formation but also become active agents in molding the group's needs.

Their highly symbolic function of representing historical transitions grants the turning points more ambiguity than events that the master commemorative narrative clearly locates within a particular period. Indeed, the ambiguity stems from their liminal location between periods, presenting a pattern of separation and reincorporation typical of rites of passage in general. As Victor Turner observes: "Liminal entities are neither here nor there; they are betwixt and between the positions assigned and arrayed by law, custom, convention and ceremonial. As such, their ambiguous and indeterminate attributes are expressed by a rich variety of symbols in the many societies that ritualize social and cultural transitions."

Like other rites of passage, the commemoration of these turning points is imbued with sacredness but also with tensions. This symbolic state of liminality, of being between and betwixt historical periods, contributes to the ambiguity of turning points on the one hand, and to their ability to function as political myths subject to different interpretations, on the other hand. The ambiguity may be less apparent within a single performance of commemoration that attempts to emphasize a certain meaning of the past and suppress other possible interpretations. But the comparative study of various commemorative performances relating to the same event makes it possible to observe these tensions and the amazing capacity of the myth to mediate between highly divergent readings of the past.

This capacity may help explain why certain events can continue to occupy a central place in the group's memory in spite of the tensions underlying their commemorations. The liminal position of the turning point allows for different interpretations, obscuring the tensions between them, and thereby protecting the sacredness of these events as well as their place within the master commemorative narrative. In some cases, however, a fragile coexistence between divergent interpretations breaks down, and the myth can no longer contain those tensions. At such points the past becomes openly contested, as rival parties engage in a conflict over its interpretation.

The alternative commemorative narrative that directly opposes the master commemorative narrative, operating under and against its hegemony, thus constitutes a *countermemory*. As the term implies, countermemory is essentially oppositional and stands in hostile and subversive relation to collective memory. If the master commemorative narrative attempts to suppress alternative views of the past, the countermemory in turn denies the validity of the narrative constructed by the collective memory and presents its own claim for a more accurate representation of history. This challenge not only addresses the symbolic realm, but obviously has direct political implications. The master commemorative narrative represents the political elite's construction of the past, which serves its special interests and promotes its political agenda. Countermemory challenges this hegemony by offering a divergent commemorative narrative representing the views of marginalised individuals or groups within the society. The commemoration of the past can thus become a contested territory in which groups engaging in a political conflict promote competing views of the past in order to gain control over the political center or to legitimize a separatist orientation.

While this conception of countermemory shares Foucault's emphasis on its oppositional and subversive character, it departs from his insistence on the fragmentary nature of countermemory. Countermemory is not necessarily limited to the construction of a single past event; it can be part of a different commemorative framework forming an alternative overview of the past that stands in opposition to the hegemonic one. In fact, even when countermemory challenges the commemoration of a single event, it is considered highly subversive precisely because the implications of this challenge tend to go beyond the memory of that particular event, targeting that master commemorative narrative. . . .

The existence of such tensions ultimately forges change in collective memory and makes it a dynamic cultural force rather than a body of "survivals" that modern societies simply tolerate. Acts of commemoration recharge collective memory and allow for its transformation. The pressure of countermemory too can contribute to this vitality by encouraging further commemorative activity in response to its challenge. Collective memory can successfully suppress an oppositional memory or hold it in check; but countermemory may also gain momentum and, as it increases in popularity, lose its oppositional status. In such cases countermemory is transformed into a collective memory. The French and the Bolshevik revolutions provide examples of attempts to obliterate older commemorative systems by force, transforming what was previously a countermemory into an official memory, supporting those governments' new political, social, and economic orders.

Barry Schwartz (contemp.)

American sociologist. Early in his career an associate of **Shils**, in many ways Barry Schwartz is the father of collective memory studies in contemporary American sociology, having revived and extended Halbwachs's insights in a series of seminal papers beginning in the early 1980s. Throughout his work, Schwartz articulates, and seeks to overcome, what he sees as a dichotomy between "presentist" and "essentialist" positions on collective memory (the view that the past is made and remade in the present for present purposes versus the view that the past defines identities and constrains action in the present). Schwartz is particularly skeptical, however, of presentist positions that reduce collective memory to politics. For him, memory is a "cultural system" rather than simply a resource and serves as both "a mirror and a lamp." In studies of George Washington, Abraham Lincoln, and Christopher Columbus, among others, Schwartz's work also makes signal contributions to the study of historical reputations; see also **Fine** and **Lang** and **Lang**.

From *Abraham Lincoln and the Forge of American Memory*

In the theory of the politics of memory, pronouncements about the past, whether in the form of historical or commemorative statements, are placed against a background of political struggle. No perspective that reduces social experience to politics can be very true to reality, yet the theory of the politics of memory is no straw man whose shortcomings make alternatives look more convincing. Indeed, no perspective on collective memory would be more difficult to discredit; no perspective has done more to align collective memory study to the conditions of a new kind of society, one where the minorities and the powerless enjoy more dignity and rights than ever before.

The theoretical coherence of the politics of memory, the clarity of its concepts, and the boldness with which these enter into propositions about reality make it a good point of departure for developing knowledge of how collective memory works. . . .

Research on the politics of memory . . . is exemplified in many fine works, including that of Eric Hobsbawm and Terence Ranger . . . on the invention of public rituals and spectacles as modes of social control during Europe's democratic revolutions and John Bodnar . . . on official and vernacular memories in the Unites States. These two works are exemplary because they articulate so clearly the constructionist position that this book seeks to qualify.

For Hobsbawm and Ranger, the void left by the decline of traditional political structures has led to invented traditions that symbolize societal cohesion, legitimize new institutions, statuses, and relations of authority, and inculcate new beliefs and values. These social forms are "invented" in the sense of being deliberately designed and produced with a view to sustaining order. Tradition, commonly defined as a conception or practice unwittingly transmitted across generations, becomes a conscious strategy adopted by political regimes to reinforce their authority. . . .

The richest and most coherent application of this approach to American studies is John Bodnar's *Remarking America*. . . . Bodnar develops the agenda of the politics of memory by distinguishing between "official memory"—state-sponsored commemorations of familiar national events, including the American Revolution and the Civil War; and "vernacular memory"—ethnic, local, and regional communities' recollection of subnational pasts. Official and vernacular memories erode one another, but the battle is uneven: commemorative resources have always been controlled by the dominant class (Protestant middle-class businessmen of the nineteenth century; professionals, editors, and government officials of the twentieth), whose official "programmers" are "disciplining authorities" seeking to promote loyalty to the state and its leaders. The great narratives and symbols of official memory, from the best-selling high school history texts to Fourth of July celebrations and the Washington Monument, are means by which America's elite class beguiles and imposes its own values on the rest of society and preserves the institutions in which it has a personal stake. Do planners and organizers of the ethnic past play a similar role? Are they "disciplining authorities" who promote loyalty to the ethnic community and obedience to its leaders? No; they are too busy defending their culture against the state. Only the custodians of the national past seek hegemony.

Bodnar's approach, emphasizing the profane motives that go into the preservation and commemoration of the past, is ideologically driven, for it is never applied to memories cherished by minorities. Bodnar offers no account of what Charles Maier . . . calls the American "Holocaust industry," no account of the political wrangling associated with memorials to African American heroes or inflated Native American claims. The theory of the politics of memory, given its affinity for postmodernism, multiculturalism, and hegemony theory, focuses on the social construction of the *official* past because the retention of state hegemony depends on control over the way that past is represented. . . .

If social change is conceived in terms of the redistribution of power, the theory of the politics of memory is also a theory of "the history of memory," or, more precisely, a theory of how political changes revise understandings of the past. The most systematic studies in this tradition show how memories of particular *subjects* change across generations. . . . Images of past events and their participants change as time passes and political actors replace one another.

Conceiving the past as a political fact, made and remade in the service of new power arrangements, leads to an atemporal concept of collective memory, one that makes the past precarious, its contents hostage to the political conditions of the present. All events, including progressive challenges to the status quo, are insidious efforts to deepen the oppression of the powerless. This claim has become monotonous. True, the past is always transmitted through lines of authority. The American Revolution, the Civil War, and the two world wars were defined for us by adults while we were still children and adolescents, we did not determine for ourselves what to make of them. This defining does not mean that our instructors were consciously or unconsciously manipulating us. It does not mean that officials planned commemorative celebrations in order to get us to do their bidding or to make us loyal to a political system against which we would have otherwise rebelled. Collective memory is in truth an effective weapon in contemporary power struggles, but the battlefield image of society, taken alone, distorts understanding of collective memory's sources and functions, leaving out, as it does, the cultural realm within which the politics of memory is situated. . . .

The politics of memory produces little understanding of collective memory as such—only of its causes and consequences. How the past is symbolized and how it functions as a mediator of meaning are questions that go to the heart of collective memory, but they have been skirted. Now is the time to engage them.

It has been said that humans, because of their psychological constitution, cannot live without attachment to some object that transcends and survives them, that there is a human craving for meaning that appears to have the force of instinct, and that people are "congenitally compelled to impose a meaningful order upon reality" [Berger]. . . . This need for incorporation into something that transfigures individual existence may or may not be based on genetic realities, but it is basic to an understanding of what collective memory is. Ever since Max Weber designated "the problem of meaning" as the key problem of human culture, different investigators have shown, in different ways, how symbolic frameworks enable us to make sense of the world. Connecting past events to one another and to the events of the present, collective memory is part of culture's meaning-making apparatus. How this apparatus works is, to say the least, problematic; that we depend on it as part of the nature of things is certain. How collective memory establishes an image of the world so compelling as to render meaningful its deepest perplexities remains to be investigated.

Efforts to work through this problem must build on Clifford Geertz's semiotic interpretation of culture. Geertz's inquiries into selected articulations of culture—"Ideology as a Cultural System," . . . "Religion as a Cultural System," . . . "Art as a Cultural System," . . . and "Common Sense as a Cultural System"—define culture as an organization of symbolic patterns on which people rely to make sense of their experience. Articulating a symbolic pattern of commemoration, memory becomes a meaning-conferring cultural system.

Collective memory, like all cultural systems, is a pattern of "inherited conceptions expressed in symbolic forms by means of which men communicate, perpetuate, and develop their knowledge about and attitudes toward life." . . . Since collective memory is never a simple act of power but a symbolic filter through which experience—political and otherwise—is apprehended, it consists of the construction and manipulation of symbol systems, which are employed as models of other systems, physical, organic, social, psychological, and so forth, in such a way that the structure of these other systems . . . is, as we say, "understood." Thinking, conceptualization, formulation, comprehension, understanding [and memory] consists not of ghostly happenings in the head but of a matching of the states and processes of symbolic models against the states and process of the wider world [Geertz]. . . .

Understanding memory, then, is a matter of knowing not only why the past is interpreted but also how it is interpreted.

The past is matched to the present as a model *of* society and a model *for* society. As a model *of* society, collective memory reflects past events in terms of the needs, interests, fears, and aspirations of the present. As a model *for* society, collective memory performs two functions: it embodies a *template* that organizes and animates behavior and a *frame* within which people locate and find meaning for their present experience. Collective memory affects social reality by *reflecting, shaping,* and *framing* it.

Collective memory reflects reality by interpreting the past in terms of images appropriate and relevant to the present; it shapes reality by providing people with a program in terms of which their present lines of conduct can be formulated and enacted; it frames reality through standards in terms of which the effectiveness and moral qualities of their conduct can be discerned.

The distinction between memory as a model *of* and a model *for* social reality is an analytic, not an empirical, one: both aspects are realized in every act of remembrance. Memories must express current problems before they can program ways to deal with them, for we cannot be oriented by a past in which we fail to see ourselves. This is what Charles Horton Cooley . . . meant when he observed: "the function of the great and famous man is to be a symbol, and the real question in our minds is not so much, What are you? as, What can I believe that you are? How far can I use you as a symbol in the development of my instinctive tendency?" . . . On the other hand, the programming the framing functions of memory are what make its reflexive function significant, for we have no reason to look for ourselves in a past that does not already orient our lives. In Cooley's words: "The mind, having energy, must work, and requires a guide, a form of thought, to facilitate its working. . . . Therefore, we feed our characters, while they are forming, upon the vision of admired models." . . .

Cooley's formulation of the past's dependence on the present makes sense, but he makes no less sense in suggesting that "personal fames are the most active part of the social tradition," and that the famous name must appeal "not one time only, but again and again, and to many persons, until it has become a tradition.". . . Cooley never wrote about commemoration and tradition as succinctly as Durkheim, or as richly as Shils and Schudson. He never understood how, through commemorative symbol and ritual, the relevance of the past is solidified. Yet in his commentary titled "Fame" (the "extended leadership," as he called it), Cooley displayed great sensitivity to the tension organizing the commemorative process. He recognized society's dual need to sustain appreciation of past heroes by keeping their images intact and by revising them to match changing conditions and tastes. . . .

[B]ut there is a limit to how far collective memory can diminish. . . . Many students of memory . . . believe that all aspect of the past lose relevance when social conditions change. This belief is neither unprecedented nor confined to adherents of one perspective. Maurice Halbwachs asked: "How can currents of collective thought whose impetus lies in the past be re-created, when we can grasp only the present[?]" . . . The radical element in this formulation, prefiguring those of present-day constructionists, is not only its focus on present relevance as a condition for remembering but also the assumption that the past endures only if society remains unchanged; different generations entertaining different conceptions of the past must be alien to one another, "like two tree stumps," as Halbwachs put it, "that touch at their extremities but do not form one plant because they are not otherwise connected." . . . Halbwachs assumes that social changes altering perception of the past are reconstructive changes. When these changes occur, the past is replaced rather than built upon or modified. Thus, collective memory undergoes basic revision as new values and social structures replace the old. Theorists of the politics of memory believe, with Lowenthal, that under such conditions "the past is a foreign country." . . .

Understanding social change as a cumulative process, one superimposing new social and symbolic structures on old ones, explains how structural transformation occurs without altering basic values. . . . This cumulative process makes it easier to go beyond the politics of memory and understand how early conceptions of the past are sustained across time. . . . In collective memory's change and continuity inheres the broader question of how culture's need for stability and revision reconcile themselves to one another and to society. Alfred North Whitehead spoke to this question many years ago when he noted that

> [T]he art of free society consists in the maintenance of the symbolic code; and secondly in fearlessness of revision, to secure that the code serves those purposes which satisfy an enlightened reason . . .

Society's memory of its great people is one part of this "symbolic code." Emphasizing its revisions and discontinuities, constructionists like Bodnar, Alonzo, and Hobsbawm make this code seem more precarious than it actually is. Stressing the continuities of collective memory, essentialists like Durkheim and Shils—who believe in society as an entity *sui generis* (self-generating and self-maintaining)—underestimate the extent to which the code adapts to society's changing needs and tendencies. . . .

Since permanent and changing visions of the past are part of one another, separate theories of collective memory—one to explain variation in what is remembered; another to explain persistence in what is remembered—are unfeasible. . . . The present is constituted by the past, but the past's retention, as well as its reconstruction, must be anchored in the present. As each generation modifies the beliefs presented by previous generations, an assemblage of old beliefs coexists with the new, including old beliefs about the past itself. . . .

The theory of the politics of memory properly anchors collective memory in the present. Its error is to underestimate the present's carrying power by failing to recognize that the same present can sustain different memories and the different presents can sustain the same memory. Once this error is corrected, collective memory's role in human experience appears with greater clarity. . . . The past, then, is a familiar rather than a foreign country, its people different, but not strangers to the present.

PART III

Power, Politics, and Contestation

As the readings in part II demonstrate, collective memory is a constitutive feature of collective identities and, as such, underwrites contemporary political projects and cultural practices. By the same token, many of the readings in this section show how memory is continually made and remade in the present from present perspectives and for present purposes. Taking this as their starting point, many scholars have thus advanced an "instrumentalist" approach to collective memory, emphasizing not what memory does, but what we do with memory. Collective memory, it turns out, is an extraordinarily useful tool of politics and is also continually subject to it.

At the heart of instrumentalist perspectives is the recognition that collective memory is essentially contested: there is a great deal at stake in how we represent the past, and different groups in societies struggle to advance their own view of the past and its meanings. As the Czech novelist Milan Kundera (1983: 3) put it—and as memory scholars frequently quote—"The struggle of man against power is the struggle of memory against forgetting." Recognizing that meanings of the past are essentially contested, many scholars thus highlight the different versions of the past articulated in reaction to official or otherwise dominant views, and they frequently do so with recourse to the idea of the competition between official memories and "counter-memories," a term credited to Michel Foucault. The main point of "counter-memory" approaches, however, including those of the Popular Memory Group and Raphael Samuel below, is not simply an exploration of alternate sources of memory—"official" and "vernacular," as the excerpt from John Bodnar puts it—but is often a suspicion of the motives and mechanisms of official memory. Heeding the resultant call to engage in reception studies, Roy Rosenzweig and David Thelen report on an extensive survey largely confirming the notion that memories deemed by elites to be central to national self-understanding are not as pervasive among the public as previously assumed.

The tension between official and public memory is also famously represented by Eric Hobsbawm's concept of the "invention of tradition." In some versions, Hobsbawm's approach—which can be used to debunk putatively venerable practices by showing that their ancientness is a bogus deception in the present—can lead to cynicism, in which the task of memory studies involves a sort of continuous unmasking. But Hobsbawm and his colleague Terence Ranger's development of the "invention of tradition" concept also shows how it is not only particular traditions that are invented, but the very idea of traditionalism. Moreover, simply identifying historical misrepresentations of a practice's ancientness begs the question of why such inventions work so well in the first place, how they remain obscure to those exposed to them, and why they sometimes endure even after they have been unmasked. Two excellent examples of these complex processes are Richard Sennett's analysis of memories of career failure in an economic downturn, and Orlando Patterson's discussion of what he calls "natal alienation" as a mechanism for the social and cultural control of slaves. In a more general discussion, Michael Schudson usefully articulates the theoretical terms by which images of the past both are subject to instrumental efforts to change them and resist such efforts because of more obdurate features of their social structure.

In this part, we also include an additional cluster of readings on a very different area in which power, politics, and contestation play out, namely the sociology of reputations. Reputations are an important and intriguing site of the kinds of contestation discussed here. Earlier works on the celebration of heroes have called attention to the importance of the representation of individuals as icons for and screens on which to project collective identity. By employing a social memory approach, Lori Ducharme and Gary Alan Fine provide a unique perspective on reputations (of both heroes and villains), asking why and how we remember the people we do, and why and how images of those figures change over time. Along with canons and collections, moreover, reputational processes are well explained from the perspective of social memory studies, as is clearly illustrated in the work of Gladys and Kurt Lang on artistic reputations. But that does not exhaust their relevance, for reputation, canon, and knowledge systems can themselves be understood as memory systems, as well as central loci for the mnemonic activities and constitution of groups and societies. We will return to some of these issues in the following section on media and modes of transmission. We include these selections here for their contribution of concepts such as memory entrepreneurship and contestation, issues central to the critical sociological perspective suggested by dialogue (accepting or rejecting) with the Hobsbawm tradition.

Finally, we place three excerpts on the concept of "cultural trauma" at the end of this section, though to be sure they fit equally well elsewhere in the volume. The concept of "cultural trauma" is one of the most interesting and complex developments in recent discourse. As Wulf Kansteiner argues, however, it may be that applying the term "trauma"—originally developed to refer to an individual-level process—to the collective level can be seen as a "category mistake." By the same token, Ron Eyerman and Jeffrey Alexander make a strong case for the value of the concept to the discourse on collective memory, showing not only how cultural trauma operates at the level of collective memories but also how the traumatic form of cultural memory in the present is in many ways a paradigm of the contemporary age. These excerpts can thus be read both as addressing the issues of what is lost or covered up in the politics of memory and counter-memory and as part of the epochal diagnosis addressed by many of the readings in the final section.

REFERENCE

Kundera, Milan. *The Book of Laughter and Forgetting.* Trans. Michael Henry Heim. London: Penguin, 1983.

Michel Foucault (1926–1984)

French historian, philosopher, and social critic. Foucault is perhaps the major contemporary legatee of **Nietzsche**, and virtually all of his work is shot through with a concern for the divisions of time and the structures of temporality. However, his writings directly on memory are few and, as in his essay "Nietzsche, Genealogy, History," often rather elliptical. Nevertheless, Foucault is the major referent for subsequent theorists of "counter-memory," alternative and subterranean forms of remembering that resist, or come between, official, dominant versions of the past; related to counter-memory is the category of popular memory Foucault articulated here, in a relatively hard-to-find, yet frequently cited, 1974 interview that originally appeared in *Cahiers du Cinema* and was translated and published in *Radical Philosophy*, from which the following passages are drawn.

From "Film in Popular Memory: An Interview with Michel Foucault"

[T]he history of the war, and what took place around it, has never really been written except in completely official accounts. These official histories are to all intents and purposes centered on Gaullism, which, on the one hand, was the only way of writing this history in terms of an honourable nationalism; and, on the other hand, the only way of introducing the Great Man, the man of the right, the man of the old 19th century nationalism, as an historical figure.

It boils down to the fact that France was exonerated by de Gaulle, while the right (and we know how it behaved at the time of the war) was purified and sanctified by him.

What has never been described is what was going on in the very heart of the country from 1936, and even from the end of the 1914 war, up until Liberation. . . .

. . . There's a real fight going on. Over what? Over what we can roughly describe as *popular memory*. It's an actual fact that people—I'm talking about those who are barred from writing, from producing their books themselves, from drawing up their own historical accounts—that these people nevertheless do have a way of recording history, or remembering it, of keeping it fresh and of using it. This popular history was, to a certain extent, even more alive, more clearly formulated in the 19th century, where, for instance, there was a whole tradition of struggles which were transmitted orally, or in writing or songs, etc.

Now, a whole number of apparatuses have been set up ("popular literature," cheap books and the stuff that's taught in school as well) to obstruct the flow of this popular memory. And it could be said that this attempt has been pretty successful. The historical knowledge the working class has of itself is continually shrinking. If you think, for instance, of what workers at the end of the

19th century knew about their own history, what the trade union tradition (in the strict sense of the word) was like up until the 1914 war, it's really quite remarkable. This has been progressively diminished, but although it gets less, it doesn't vanish.

Today, cheap books aren't enough. There are much more effective means like television and the cinema. And I believe this was one way of reprogramming popular memory, which existed but had no way of expressing itself. So people are shown not what they were, but what they must remember having been.

Since memory is actually a very important factor in struggle (recall, in fact, struggles develop in a kind of conscious moving forward of history), if one controls people's memory, one controls their dynamism. And one also controls their experience, their knowledge of previous struggles. Just what the Resistance was, must no longer be known. . . .

. . . There's a battle for and around history going on at this very moment which is extremely interesting. The intention is to reprogramme, to stifle what I've called the "popular memory;" and also to propose and impose on people a framework in which to interpret the present. Up to 1968, popular struggles were part of folklore. For some people, they weren't even a part of their immediate concept of reality. After 1968, every popular struggle, whether in South America or Africa, has found some echo, some sympathetic response. So it's no longer possible to keep up their separation, this geographical "cordon sanitaire." Popular struggles have become for our society, not part of the actual, but of the possible. So they have to be set at a distance. How? Not by providing a direct interpretation of them, which would be asking to be exposed. But by offering an historical interpretation of those popular struggles which have occurred in France in the past, in order to show that they never really happened! Before 1968, it was: "It won't happen here because it never has done! Take something like the Resistance even, this glorious past you've talked about so much, just look at it for a moment. . . Nothing. It's empty, a hollow façade!" It's another way of saying, "Don't worry about Chile, it's no different; the Chilean peasants couldn't care less. And France, too: the bulk of the population isn't interested in anything a few malcontents might do". . . .

As soon as you start seeing pictures of war every evening, war becomes totally acceptable. That's to say, thoroughly tedious, you'd really love to see something else. But when it becomes boring, you put up with it. You don't even watch it. So how is this particular reality on film to be reactivated as an existing, historically important reality?

Popular Memory Group (contemp.)

British cultural theorists. The so-called Popular Memory Group met at the Center for Contemporary Cultural Studies at the University of Birmingham (U.K.) in 1979–1980 and strove to reassess the tradition of Marxist historical scholarship. Historical consciousness, they argue here, is not just the gift of professional historiography but is produced through a variety of media and institutions. However, in self-proclaimed contrast to efforts by various radical and democratic scholars who are interested in recovering the lost pasts of the historiographically disenfranchised, the authors here argue that such efforts at recuperation must be expanded to include a "relational" analysis of how popular historical consciousness does not only arise outside or beyond the purview of conventional historiography but is affected by it in politically relevant ways.

From "Popular Memory: Theory, Politics, Method"

What do we mean by "popular memory"? . . . We define popular memory first as an *object of study*, but, second, as a *dimension of political practice*. . . . The first move in defining popular memory is to extend what we mean by history-writing. . . .

[T]o expand the idea of historical production well beyond the limits of academic history-writing, we must include *all* the ways in which a sense of the past is constructed in our society. These do not necessarily take a written or literary form. Still less do they conform to academic standards of scholarship or canons of truthfulness. Academic history has a particular place in a much larger process. We will call this "the social production of memory." In this collective production everyone participates, though unequally. Everyone, in this sense, is a historian. As Jean Chesneaux argues, professionalized history has attempted to appropriate a much more general set of relationships and needs: "the collective and contradictory relationship of our society to its past" and the "collective need" for guidance in the struggle to make the future. We have a similar stress in Christopher Hill's work: the recognition of a larger social process in which "we ourselves are shaped by the past" but are also continually reworking the past which shapes us. The first problem in the pursuit of "popular memory" is to specify the "we" in Hill's formulation or "our society" in Chesneaux's. What *are* the means by which social memory is produced? And what practices are relevant especially outside those of professional history-writing?

It is useful to distinguish the main ways in which a sense of the past is produced: through public representations and through private memory (which, however, may also be collective and shared). The first way involves a public "theatre" of history, a public stage and a public audience for the enacting of dramas concerning "our" history, or heritage, the story, traditions and legacy. . . . This public stage is occupied by many actors who often speak from contradictory scripts, but collectively we shall term the agencies which construct this public historical sphere and control access to the means of publication "the historical apparatus." We shall call the products of these agencies, in their aggregate relations and combinations at any point of time, "the field of public representations of history." In thinking about the ways in which these representations affect individual or group conceptions of the past, we might speak of "dominant memory." This term points to the power and pervasiveness of historical representations, their connections with dominant institutions and the part they play in winning consent and building alliances in the processes of formal politics. But we do not mean to imply that conceptions of the past that acquire a dominance in the field of public representations are either monolithically installed or everywhere believed in. Not all the historical representations that win access to the public field are "dominant." The field is crossed by competing constructions of the past, often at war with each other. Dominant memory is produced in the course of these struggles and is always open to contestation. We do want to insist, however, that there are real processes of domination in the historical field. Certain representations achieve centrality and luxuriate grandly; others are marginalized or excluded or reworked. Nor are the criteria of success here those of truth: dominant representations may be those that are most ideological, most obviously conforming to the flattened stereotypes of myth.

Historical constructions are most obviously public when linked to central state institutions. The governmental and parliamentary system . . . are historical apparatuses in their own right. . . .

Other institutions, though linked to the national or local state, have a greater degree of autonomy, operating with high-cultural, educational, preservational or archival purposes. We include here the whole world of museums, art galleries, record offices, the Department of the Environment's official preservation orders, the "National" Trust, the "National" Theatre, and in general the sphere of history as "cultural policy". . . . Perhaps the educational system itself belongs here too. . . . In this "cultural" field, the relations between scholarly and dominant historiographies are especially intimate; the historian's criteria of truthfulness are more likely to prevail here than in the more overtly politicized versions.

History is also business. It is important for the whole range of publishing activity, especially since historical writing retains much more of an amateur or "lay" public than other social sciences. Best-seller lists commonly contain items that are marketed as "historical," especially biographies and autobiographies, historical fictions and military histories. . . . To popular fiction and the modern form of the glossy illustrated documentary book, we have to add the historical movies, somewhat displaced in the block-buster market by the contemporary salience of science fiction. More interesting because less remarked on is the massive contemporary growth of "historical tourism." We mean the way in which historically significant places become a resource, physically or ideologically, for the leisure and tourist industries. . . .

The public media too – especially radio, television and the press – are a principal source of historical constructions. We include the intersections of history, journalism and documentary, but also the media arts, especially historical drama. The media certainly produce their own historical accounts – they produce a contemporary history daily, for instance, in the form of "news." But they also select, amplify and transform constructions of the past produced elsewhere. They increasingly draw, for example, from oral history and "yesterday's witness." They give a privileged space to conceptions of the past which accompany the party-political battles. Of all parts of the historical apparatus the electronic media are perhaps the most compelling and ubiquitous. Access here may often be decisive in gaining currency for an historical account.

More removed from the patronage of state and of capital are the voluntary associations of the world of history. Most counties and many towns have their own historical and archaeological societies, often with a long nineteenth-century pedigree. Like the Historical Association which links schoolteachers and academics, these societies draw on a fund of amateur historical enthusiasm, bounded by a strong sense of locality. . . . The growth of "oral history," and of the History Workshop movement has added whole layers, sometimes of a radically new kind, to these local and participatory forms.

As this last set of examples suggests, the various sites and institutions do not act in concert. To make them sing, if not in harmony at least with only minor dissonances, involves hard labour and active intervention. Sometimes this has been achieved by direct control (censorship for example) and by a violent recasting or obliteration of whole fields of public history. More commonly today, in the capitalist West, the intersections of formal political debates and the public media are probably the crucial site. Certainly political ideologies involve a view of past and present and future. Ranged against powers such as these, what price the lonely scholar, producing (also through commercial channels) the one or two thousand copies of the latest monograph?!

There is a second way of looking at the social production of memory which draws attention to quite other processes. A knowledge of past and present is also produced in the course of everyday life. There is a common sense of the past which, though it may lack consistency and explanatory force, nonetheless contains elements of good sense. Such knowledge may circulate, usually without amplification, in everyday talk and in personal comparisons and narratives. It may even be recorded in certain intimate cultural forms: letters, diaries, photograph albums and collections of things with past associations. It may be encapsulated in anecdotes that acquire the force and generality of myth. If this is history, it is history under extreme pressures and privations. Usually this history is held to the level of private remembrance. It is not only unrecorded, but actually silenced. It is not offered the occasion to speak. In one domain, the modern Women's Movement well understands the process of silencing and is raising the "hidden" history of women's feelings, thoughts and actions more clearly to view. Feminist history challenges the very distinction "public"/"private" that silences or marginalizes women's lived sense of the past. But similar processes of domination operate in relation to specifically working-class experiences, for most working-class people are also robbed of access to the means of publicity and are equally unused to the male, middle-class habit of giving universal or "historic" significance to an extremely partial experience. But we are only beginning to understand the class dimensions of cultural domination, partly by transferring the feminist insights. Nor is this only a question of class or gender positions. Even the articulate middle-class historian, facing the dominant memory of events through which he has actually lived, can also be silenced (almost) in this way. . . .

It is this kind of recovery that has become the mission of the radical and democratic currents in oral history, popular autobiography and community-based publishing. . . .

[W]e wish to stress first that the study of popular memory cannot be limited to this level alone. It is a necessarily *relational* study. It has to take in the dominant historical representations in the public field as well as attempts to amplify or generalize subordinated or private experiences. Like all struggles it must needs have two sides. Private memories cannot, in concrete studies, be readily unscrambled from the effects of dominant historical discourses. It is often these that supply the very terms by which a private history is thought through. Memories of the past are, like all common-sense forms, strangely composite constructions, resembling a kind of geology, the selective sedimentation of past traces. As Gramsci put it, writing about the necessity of historical consciousness for a Communist politics, the problem is "knowing thyself" as a product of the historical process to date which has deposited in you an infinity of traces, without leaving an inventory." Similarly the public discourses live off the primary recording of events in the course of everyday transactions and take over the practical knowledges of historical agents. It is for these reasons that the study of "popular memory" is concerned with *two* sets of relations. It is concerned with the relation between dominant memory and oppositional forms across the whole public (including academic) field. It is also concerned with the relation between these public discourses in their contemporary state of play and the more privatized sense of the past which is generated within a lived culture. . . .

[M]emory is, by definition, a term which directs our attention not to the past but to *the past–present relation*. It is because "the past" has this living active existence in the present that it matters so much politically. As "the past"— dead, gone or only *subsumed in* the present – it matters much less. This argument may be clarified if we compare a number of approaches to the political significance of history. . . .

We may . . . [distinguish] three main approaches to the political relevance of history. The first approach, while retaining in a strong form the notion that the object of history is "the past," seeks to link past and present in the form of salutary "lessons." These may have a negative force, warning, for instance, against returns to past disasters. . . . But this argument may also work more positively, typically by identifying "traditions" which then become a resource for present struggles . . . The link between past and present, between history-writing and the construction of historical futures today, is in essence an exhortatory one.

A second way of conceiving the past-present relation is to employ historical perspectives and methods as an element in strategic analysis. We start from the need to understand contemporary political problems. We seek to examine the conditions on which contemporary dilemmas rest. In looking at the nature and origins of current oppressions, we trace their genesis as far back as it is necessary to go. Here the relation between past and present is necessarily more organic, more internal. The past *is* present today in particular social structures with determinate origins and particular histories. . . .

A stress on popular memory adds something to both these conceptions, though it does not displace them. The construction of traditions is certainly *one* way in which historical argument operates as a political force though it risks a certain conservatism; similarly any adequate analysis of the contemporary relations of political force has to be historical in form as well as reaching back to more or less distant historical times. It must also attempt to grasp the broader epochal limits and possibilities in terms of a longer history of capitalist and patriarchal structures.

What we may insist on in addition is that all political activity is intrinsically a process of historical argument and definition, that all political programmes involve some construction of the past as well as the future, and that these processes go on every day, often outrunning, especially in terms of period, the preoccupations of historians. Political domination involves historical definition. History—in particular popular memory—is a stake in the constant struggle for hegemony. The relation between history and politics, like the relation between past and present, is, therefore, an *internal* one: it is about the politics of history and the historical dimensions of politics. . . .

It is oral history—the evocation and recording of individual memories of the past – which seems, at first sight, nearest to the popular memory perspective, or one aspect of it. In fact the term oral history embraces a very large range of practices only tenuously connected by a "common" methodology. What interests us most about oral history is that it is often the place where the tension between competing historical and political aims is most apparent: between professional procedures and amateur enthusiasm, between oral history as recreation (in both senses) and as politics, between canons of objectivity and an interest, precisely, in subjectivity and in cultural forms. . . .

But it is arguable that the most significant development has been the growth of community history, popular autobiography and working-class writing more generally, where the terms of authorship have been more completely changed. In one sense, *all* these texts and projects are evidence for the forms of popular memory; they are all about the relation of past to present, whether self-consciously "historical" or not. . . .

The first set of difficulties is epistemological in character. They arise from the ways in which "historical" objects of study are defined. They revolve around the empiricism of orthodox historical practice. They are not purely technical matters for philosophers to adjudicate. The historian's empiricism is a real difficulty. It blocks political progress. That is why it is so important to return to these questions once more, showing the political effects of this persistently empiricist stance.

The second set of difficulties derive initially from the form in which the "raw material" of oral history or popular autobiography first arises; the *individual* testimony, narrative or autobiography. This poses, in a very acute form, the problem of the individual subject and his or her broader social context. In what sense is individual witness evidence for larger social changes? How can these changes themselves be understood, not as something that evades human action, but also as the product of human labour, including this individual personality? This difficulty runs through the oral history method and through the autobiographical form. It is also reflected in larger divisions of genres: history, autobiography, fiction (with its particular experiential truth). Such divisions in turn encapsulate hierarchies of significance. The oral-historical witness or the autobiographer, unless held to be a personage of exceptional public power, speaks only for herself. . . .

We have already touched on a third set of difficulties: the tendency to identify the object of history as "the past." This largely unquestioned feature of historical common sense has extremely paradoxical results when applied to oral history or popular autobiography. Indeed it shows us that this definition cannot be held without a radical depoliticization of the practice of research. What is interesting about the forms of oral-historical witness or autobiography are not just the nuggets of "fact" about the past, but the whole way in which popular memories are constructed and reconstructed as part of a *contemporary* consciousness. . . .

The fourth set of difficulties is more fundamental. It concerns not just the manifest intellectual and theoretical blockages, but the social relations which these inhibitions express. In oral history and in similar practices the epistemologic problem—how historians are going to use their "sources"—is also a problem of human relationships. The practice of research actually conforms to (and may in practice deepen) social divisions which are also relations of power and of inequality. It is cultural power that is at stake here, of course, rather than economic power or political coercion. Even so research may certainly construct a kind of economic relation (a balance of economic and cultural benefits) that is "exploitative" in that the returns are grossly unequal ones. On the one hand there is "the historian," who specializes in the production of explanations and interpretations and who constitutes himself as the most active, thinking part of the process. On the other hand, there is a "source" who happens in this case to be a living human being who is positioned in the process in order to yield up information. The interviewee is certainly subject to the professional power of the interviewer who may take the initiative in seeking her out and questioning her. Of course, the problem may be solved rhetorically or at the level of personal relations: the historian may assert that he has "sat at the feet of working-class witnesses" and has learnt all he knows in that improbable and uncomfortable posture. It is, however, *he* that produces the final account, *he* that provides the dominant interpretation, *he* that judges what is true and not true, reliable or inauthentic. It is his name that appears on the jacket of his monograph and his academic career that is furthered by its publication. It is he who receives a portion of the royalties and almost all the "cultural capital" involved in authorship. It is his *amour propre* as "creator" that is served here. It is his professional standing among his peers that is enhanced in the case of "success." In all this, at best, the first constructors of historical accounts—the "sources" themselves—are left untouched, unchanged by the whole process except in what they have given up—the telling. They do not participate, or only indirectly, in the educational work which produces the final account. They may never get to read the book of which they were part authors, nor fully comprehend it if they do.

Raphael Samuel (1934–1996)

British Marxist historian. In the late 1970s and 1980s, British intellectuals debated the causes and effects of what was frequently called "the heritage industry," which included the restoration of aristocratic manors, a rise in heritage tourism, the reclamation of urban cores, a wave of historical museum building, and an array of other activities, many sponsored by the British National Trust. How was this wave of "nostalgia" to be assessed? Was it a cultural throwback, a regressive strategy of distraction à la **Hobsbawm's** "invented traditions," the result of a politically conservative program of reaction to the government's failure to respond adequately to social transformations and the needs of the working class? Here, in an excerpt from his book *Theaters of Memory*, Samuel illuminates various aspects of the debate and works toward a more nuanced position. See also **Davis** and **Boym**.

From *Theatres of Memory*

When Patrick Wright launched his attack on "heritage," he accused it of reactionary chic and argued that it represented the triumph of aristocratic and reactionary nostalgia over the levelling tendencies of the Welfare State: it was Evelyn Waugh's posthumous revenge on Clement Attlee. Robert Hewison, more crudely, puts the appearance of "heritage" down to an aristocratic plot hatched, it seems, by the beleaguered owners of country houses in 1975. Faced with the prospect of a wealth tax and an incoming and unsympathetic Labour government, they mounted a high-level lobby, raising the cry of "heritage in danger," and enlisting the support of the House of Lords, the National Trust and the Victoria and Albert Museum. . . .

If in one set of discriminations heritage is accused of being crypto-feudal—a vast system of outdoor relief for decayed gentlefolk—in another it is charged with being "deeply capitalist,' albeit in a postmodern rather than a proto-industrial vein. In a consumer-led society, in which everything has its price, and market values are unchallenged, it "traffics" in history and "commodifies" the past. It turns real-life suffering into tourist spectacle, while at the same time creating simulacra of a past that never was. Museums are particularly suspect. They are "part of the leisure and tourist business," and thus intimately linked to the Disneylands and theme parks. . . . In either of these two cases heritage is an expressive totality, a seamless web. It is conceptualized as systemic, projecting a unified set of meanings which are impervious to challenge—what Umberto Eco calls "hyper-reality." In essence it is conservative, even when it takes on, or co-opts, popular themes. It brings the most disparate materials together under a singler head. It is what one critic defines as a "closed story," i.e. a fixed narrative which allows for neither subtext nor counter-readings. Its biases are more or less consistent, its messages coded, its meanings clear. Politics, culture and economics are all of a piece, reinforcing one another's influence, reciprocating one another's effects.

Heritage is also seen by its critics as a "project," if not a conspiracy or plot then at the very least a strategy, "a complex and purposefully selective process of historical recollection." It is a "bid for hegemony," a way of using knowledge in the service of power. It shores up national identity at a time when it is beset by uncertainties on all sides. It is a way of compensating for the collapse of British power.

Chronology alone would put these symmetries in doubt, quite apart from the fact that the country cottage has played an inconceivably greater part in the idea of "lost England" than the country house. It might suggest that there was not one moment but many from which current retrieval projects and strategies could trace their origin. . . .

Chronology would also call into question association of heritage with conservative reaction. It might suggest that the cry of "Heritage in danger," or at any rate that sentiment, crystallized, in the first place, in a recoil from the modernizations of the 1950s, rather than as a reflex of economic decline. The post-war mechanization of agriculture, the dieselization of the tractor, and the disappearance of the horseman, might appear as the inspiration, albeit a negative one, for the growth of the idea of the "folk" or "working farm," museum—an innovation of the late 1950s and early 1960s. The steam preservation mania of the 1950s is more obviously related to the dieselization of railways, the rationalization of services and the diminution of branch lines. So far as the built environment is concerned, it was arguably the astonishing increase in car ownership—a feature of the "affluent society" of the 1950s—which set the alarm bells ringing and changed preservation from a rural to an urban cause.

Many of heritage's enthusiasms were in place long before 1975, the year when in Britain, as in the other countries involved in European Architectural Heritage Year, the term entered general circulation. Railway antiquarianism is almost as old as the railways themselves. . . .

Economics, and especially economic history, might also put the moment of 1974–75 into question, by drawing attention to the long gestation period of many conservationist projects, and the changes in the material conditions of existence which allowed them to enter the realm of the thinkable. Statistics of car ownership—2 million in 1949, 17.5 million in 1980—might help to account for the growth of historic tourism, while attendance figures . . . might dispose of the absurd idea that open-air museums are a great magnet to foreign tourists. In another sphere the spread of that most labour-saving and comfort-making of modern household devices, central heating, which can be logged, quinquennium by quinquennium from 1960, might appear as the ghost-in-the-machine of restoration, and the extraordinary increase in the number of "listed" historic buildings which began in 1967. At a stroke it converted draughty Victorian mansions, fit only for conversion to flats, into desirable period residences.

Economics, disaggregating such abstracts as "capital" and "consumerism" and inquiring into their heterogenous and promiscuous components, might also serve as a useful corrective to those top-down accounts of the heritage industry which see it as a kind of ruling-class conspiracy or plot, or imply that there is some directive intelligence at work. While paying due regard to the ways in which business has been able to profit from, or accommodate itself to, the rehabilitation of old property, or to latch onto notions of "period" in commodity marketing and design, it might draw attention to those more molecular processes in which any cultural politics takes shape. In heritage-ware, to judge by those who take up the stands when the gift trade holds its annual fairs, the typical entrepreneurs seem to be one-man businesses, female-run franchises and husband-and-wife (or gay) partnerships; the business corporation is a conspicuous absence. Heritage supports and is supported by chains of charity shops and armies of flea-market stallholders. Organic farms make some contribution to it; so do the health and whole-food co-operatives.

Heritage puts a premium on the labour and services of the craftsman-retailer, and the maintenance of artisanal skills. . . . It has often given short-life tenancies to craftsmen while properties are awaiting rehabilitation, or in the protracted period when building work is in progress. It has provided premises or work-space at peppercorn rents for absolute beginners, one basis for the crafts revival of the 1970s. And it supports, at any given moment, a mass of short-life businesses. . . . Mention might be made here of those unemployed historians who scratch a small livelihood conducting historical walks, or those penny capitalists who have been developing murder tours. . . .

A sociological perspective on heritage, which took into account the hybridization of contemporary social identities, the mixing and mingling of what were formerly class preserves, or a Marxist one which looked for a dialectical relationship between the imaginary and the real, rather than a reductive and reflective one, might be even more unsettling to currently accepted negative stereotypes than an economic one. It could begin by pointing out that the rise of the heritage industry, if one chooses to take 1975 as a significant date, so far from heralding an epoch of feudal reaction, coincides, rather, in Britain, as in other European countries, with political dealignment and a collapse of two-camp class divides. . . .

One way of attempting to account for the popularity of heritage, as also the rapidity with which it has spread, is to see it as an attempt to *escape* from class. Instead of heredity it offers a sense of place, rather as environmentalism offers the activist and the reformist an alternative to the worn-out routines of party politics. . . . It encourages white-collar workers and middle-class men, getting up steam from the boiler, to try their hand at being mechanics; landlubbers, sailing before the mast, to play at being mariners. Heritage offers an ideal home which is defined not by pedigree but by period, and which can be decked out with make-believe family heirlooms. Still more pertinent, through the medium of family history it gives us a second identity and allows the most humdrum and ordinary, so far as present occupation is concerned, to indulge in a romance of otherness.

Heritage might also be aligned with the emergence in the 1960s of what Frank Parkin has called, in another context, "middle-class radicalism." It is a familiar feature of the universities in the 1960s, of such newly radicalized groups as social workers and of the new-wave charities of the 1960s. But might it not be applied equally to the formation of amenity societies and "ginger" groups, the staging of single-issue campaigns, such as those who in London defeated the motorway box, the growth of the country wildlife trusts, and not least the appearance, for the first time, of mass membership environmental campaigning organizations?

John Bodnar (contemp.)

American historian. Though Bodnar is not strictly a Foucauldian or a Birmingham cultural theorist (see **Popular Memory Group**), there is at least a loose similarity between those approaches to popular memory and Bodnar's description here of the relations between "official" and "vernacular" memory, as well as his account of commemorative politics. For a critique of Bodnar as a representative of a "politics of memory" approach, see **Schwartz**.

From *Remaking America: Public Memory, Commemoration and Patriotism in the Twentieth Century*

Public memory emerges from the intersection of official and vernacular cultural expressions. The former originates in the concerns of cultural leaders or authorities at all levels of society. Whether in positions of prominence in small towns, ethnic communities, or in educational, government, or military bureaucracies, these leaders share a common interest in social unity, the continuity of existing institutions, and loyalty to the status quo. They attempt to advance these concerns by promoting interpretations of past and present reality that reduce the power of competing interests that threaten the attainment of their goals. Official culture relies on "dogmatic formalism" and the restatement of reality in ideal rather than complex or ambiguous terms. It presents the past on an abstract basis of timelessness and sacredness. . . . Normally official culture promotes a nationalistic, patriotic culture of the whole that mediates an assortment of vernacular interests. But seldom does it seek meditation at the expense of ascendency.

Vernacular culture, on the other hand, represents an array of specialized interests that are grounded in parts of the whole. They are diverse and changing and can be reformulated from time to time by the creation of new social units such as soldiers and their friends who share an experience in war or immigrants who settle a particular place. They can even clash with one another. Defenders of such cultures are numerous and intent on protecting values and restating views of reality derived from firsthand experience in small-scale communities rather than the "imagined" communities of a large nation. Both cultures are championed by leaders and gain adherents from throughout the population, and individuals themselves can support aspects of both cultures at once. But normally vernacular expressions convey what social reality feels like rather than what it should be like. Its very existence threatens the sacred and timeless nature of official expressions.

Public memory is produced from a political discussion that involves not so much specific economic or moral problems but rather fundamental issues about the entire existence of a society: its organization, structure of power, and the very meaning of its past and present. This is not simple class or status politics, although those concerns are involved in the discussion, but it is an argument about the interpretation of reality; this is an aspect of the politics of culture. It is rooted not simply in a time dimension between the past and the present but is ultimately grounded in the inherent contradictions of a social system: local and national structures, ethnic and national cultures, men and women, young and old, professionals and clients, workers and managers, political leaders and followers, soldiers and commanders. Its function is to mediate the competing restatements of reality these antinomies express. Because it takes the form of an ideological system with special language, beliefs, symbols, and stories, people can use it as a cognitive device to mediate competing interpretations and privilege some explanations over others. Thus, the symbolic language of patriotism is central to public memory . . . because it has the capacity to mediate both vernacular loyalties to local and familiar places and official loyalties to national and imagined structures.

Public memory is a body of beliefs and ideas about the past that help a public or society understand both its past, present, and by implication, its future. It is fashioned ideally in a public sphere in which various parts of the social structure exchange views. The major focus of this communicative and cognitive process is not the past, however, but serious matters in the present such as the nature of power and the question of loyalty to both official and vernacular cultures. Public memory speaks primarily about the structure of power in society because that power is always in question in a world of polarities and contradictions and because cultural understanding is always grounded in the material structure of society itself. Memory adds perspective and authenticity to the views articulated in this exchange; defenders of official and vernacular interests are selectively retrieved from the past to perform similar functions in the present.

Adherents to official and vernacular interests demonstrate conflicting obsessions. Cultural leaders orchestrate commemorative events to calm anxiety about change or political events, eliminate citizen indifference toward official concerns, promote exemplary patterns of citizen behavior, and stress citizen duties over rights. They feel the need to do this because of the existence of social contradictions, alternative views, and indifference that perpetuate fears of societal dissolution and unregulated political behavior.

Ordinary people, on the other hand, react to the actions of leaders in a variety of ways. At times they accept official interpretations of reality. Sometimes this can be seen when an individual declares that a son died in defense of his country or an immigrant ancestor emigrated to build a new nation. Individuals also express alternative renditions of reality when they feel a war death was needless or an immigrant ancestor moved simply to support his family. Frequently people put official agendas to unintended uses as they almost always do when they use public ritual time for recreational purposes or patriotic symbols to demand political rights.

Most cultural leaders in the United States come from a broad group of middle-class professionals—government officials, editors, lawyers, clerics, teachers, military officers, and small businessmen. They are "self-conscious purveyors" of loyalty to larger political structures and existing institutions. Their careers and social positions usually depend upon the survival of the very institutions that are celebrated in commemorative activities. The boundaries of the leadership group are permeable, however, and can be crossed by rich and very influential individuals. Seldom are they crossed by factory workers, home-makers, millhands, farmers, and others whose work and social position allow them little time and access to the organizations that shape most public commemorative events.

The term "ordinary people" best describes the rest of society that partici-pates in public commemoration and protects vernacular interests. They are a diverse lot, are not synonymous with the working class, and invariably include individuals from all social stations. They are more likely to honor pioneer ancestors rather than founding fathers and favor comrades over patriots. . . . They acknowledge the ideal of loyalty in commemorative events and agree to defend the symbol of the nation but often use commemoration to redefine that symbol or ignore it for the sake of leisure or economic ends. There is certainly patriotism in much of what they honor, but they do not hesitate to privilege the personal or vernacular dimension of patriotism over the public one. They are less interested than cultural leaders in exerting influence or control over others, and are preoccupied, instead, with defending the interests and rights of their respective social segments.

Because numerous interests clash in commemorative events they are inevi-tably multivocal. They contain powerful symbolic expressions—metaphors, signs, and rituals—that give meaning to competing interpretations of past and present reality. In modern America no cultural expression contains the multi-vocal quality of public commemorations better than the idea of the nation-state and the language of patriotism. On a cultural level it serves as a symbol that "coerces" the discordant interests of diverse social groups and unites them into a "unitary conceptual framework" which connects the ideal with the real. Officials use it as a powerful metaphor that stimulates ideals of social unity and civic loyalty. And its very real structure of local, regional, and national government constantly seeks loyalty and respect. But the component parts of the nation-state—its families, classes, ethnic groups, and regions—also attract loyalty and devotion. Citizens view the larger entity of the nation through the lens of smaller units and places that they know firsthand. And they frequently see the nation as a defender of their rights rather than simply a source of obligation. The symbols of the nation-state and the patriot do what all symbols do: they mediate both official and vernacular interests. By themselves they do not privilege one interest over another. That task is performed admirably by men and women living in space and time.

Public commemorations usually celebrate official concerns more than vernacular ones. This does not mean that cultural differences are removed from the discussion over memory. Most citizens can honor the basic political structure of the nation, for instance, and still vigorously disagree with cultural leaders about what the nation stands for and what type of devotion it merits. They often express this disagreement not in violent terms but in more subtle expressions of indifference or inventive historical constructions of their own.

Because the expression of patriotic and nationalistic texts, moreover, reflects both the interests of cultural leaders and ordinary people, it does not follow that an equitable compromise is reached. Negotiation and cultural mediation do not preclude domination and distortion. Usually it is the local and personal past that is incorporated into a nationalized public memory rather than the other way around. Local, regional, class, and ethnic interests are sustained in one form or another in the final product, but the dominant meaning is usually nationalistic. And this does not seem to be particularly wrong to most citizens. In fact, it appears to be "fundamentally true." As Maurice Godelier argues, it is when ideologies do not appear to the "exploited" as illusions or as instruments of their exploitation that they contribute effectively to persuading people to accept them. They can only do this if they incorporate—as the symbols of the pioneer and patriot do—meanings dear to a number of social groups that participate in the memory debate.

Roy Rosenzweig (1950–2007) and David Thelen (contemp.)

American historians. In the tradition of **Becker** and other scholars of popular memory, Rosenzweig and Thelen conducted survey research to determine what and how "ordinary" people know about and relate to the past. They found that their respondents avoid collective frameworks like ethnicity, class, and religion, as well as the triumphal nationalist narratives of textbook writers, and instead see the shared past in highly personal terms.

From *The Presence of the Past: Popular Uses of History in American Life*

To learn about the bridges people constructed between their personal pasts and larger historical stories, we asked respondents to name an event from the past that had affected them. Among public historical events, the most frequent choice was World War II—selected by 26 of the 358 respondents who answered the question. Though some of them spoke about the futility of war or man's inhumanity to man, a much larger group—almost half of those who cited World War II—reflected on the war in more personal terms. A 71-year-old Philadelphia woman said she learned self-reliance from the war: "My husband was in that. It was a lot of heartache with both of us being young and him being away in his early twenties. I learned how to be independent and how to take care of myself." What they didn't talk about was the narrative most familiar to us from high school history books and popular culture: the war as a story of victory over fascism or as a key moment in a patriotic narrative of the nation-state.

Respondents rarely mentioned the triumphal national narrative favored by those who write textbooks or advocate history as a means of teaching patriotism and civics. Instead, like the Philadelphia woman, they placed national events within their familial stories or made national personages into familiar figures in personal narratives. Or they talked about national events as disconnected incidents not linked to a larger narrative, and about national figures and events in distant and attenuated terms, rather than the rich terms they used for describing moments in their personal and family histories. Or they did all of these. Our respondents did not reject or ignore national history; they simply rejected the textbook narratives of national greatness that they had been forced to passively consume and regurgitate in school.

Conservatives may be alarmed at how rarely our respondents referred to patriotic narratives. Liberals and leftists (especially historians) may be unsettled by another of our survey findings: when Americans think and talk about the past, many of them avoid collective frameworks like ethnicity, class, region, and gender—categories close to the hearts of professional history practitioners. Some of our respondents did reach more directly for pasts beyond the world of their family and friends. Religious communities and religious narratives, for example, turned out to be a powerful way of understanding and using the past. And respondents also offered larger narratives of change and continuity about crime, discipline, and popular culture. But these popular historical narratives veered off in different directions from the textbook narratives of linear progress associated with capital "H" history. Americans engaged larger pasts on their own terms.

Several subgroups put distinctive spins on the process of making connections beyond the intimate past. Most white Americans kept their historical narratives focused on the family: when they discussed public events, they usually personalized them. African Americans, American Indians, and evangelical Christians drew upon and constructed a much wider set of usable pasts, building ties to their communities as well as their families. African American and American Indians were also more likely to create narratives of group progress, while white Americans tended to talk about decline. . . .

Mexican Americans . . . occupy a figurative borderland—white European Americans on one side, American Indians and African Americans on the other. Mexican Americans share some modes and assumptions of each of the other groups, but translate them into a rich and vigorous historical narrative that is distinctly their own.

Eric Hobsbawm (contemp.)

British Marxist historian. In one of memory studies' landmark texts, Hobsbawm here introduces the term "the invention of tradition," which has become the calling card of the "politics of memory" approach: in other words, one that sees images of the past as produced for (often cynical) reasons in the present. Hobsbawm's concept, however, is much richer than this description implies, for it is not just the invention of particular traditions that the term allows us to unmask, but the invention of "tradition" and "traditionalism" itself: traditionalism implies the self-conscious adherence to a status quo (even a bogus one), which is to be contrasted to a world of custom, in which the legacies of the past are more fluid. As such, Hobsbawm's approach can profitably be compared to that of **Marx Nora**, **Giddens**, and **Hutton**, among other theorists of memory in modernity.

From "Introduction: Inventing Traditions"

"Traditions" which appear or claim to be old are often quite recent in origin and sometimes invented. . . .

The term "invented tradition" is used in a broad, but not imprecise sense. It includes both "traditions" actually invented, constructed and formally instituted and those emerging in a less easily traceable manner within a brief and dateable period—a matter of a few years perhaps–and establishing themselves with great rapidity. . . . It is evident that not all of them are equally permanent, but it is their appearance and establishment rather than their chances of survival which are our primary concern.

"Invented tradition" is taken to mean a set of practices, normally governed by overtly or tacitly accepted rules and of a ritual or symbolic nature, which seek to inculcate certain values and norms of behaviour by repetition, which automatically implies continuity with the past. In fact, where possible, they normally attempt to establish continuity with a suitable historic past. . . .

The historic past into which the new tradition is inserted need not be lengthy, stretching back into the assumed mists of time. Revolutions and "progressive movements" which break with the past, by definition, have their own relevant past, though it may be cut off at a certain date, such as 1789. However, insofar as there is such reference to a historic past, the peculiarity of "invented" traditions is that the continuity with it is largely factitious. In short, they are responses to novel situations which take the form of reference to old situations, or which establish their own past by quasi-obligatory repetition. It is the contrast between the constant change and innovation of the modern world and the attempt to structure at least some parts of social life within it as unchanging and invariant, that makes the "invention of tradition" so interesting for historians of the past two centuries.

"Tradition" in this sense must be distinguished clearly from "custom" which dominates so-called "traditional" societies. The object and characteristics of "traditions," including invented ones, is invariance. The past, real or invented, to which they refer imposes fixed (normally formalized) practices, such as repetition. "Custom" in traditional societies has the double function of motor and fly-wheel. It does not preclude innovation and change up to a point, though evidently the requirement that it must appear compatible or even identical with precedent imposes substantial limitations on it. What it does is to give any desired change (or resistance to innovation) the sanction of precedent, social continuity and natural law as expressed in history. . . . "Custom" cannot afford to be invariant, because even in "traditional" societies life is not so. Customary or common law still shows this combination of flexibility in substance and formal adherence to precedent. The difference between "tradition" and "custom" in our sense is indeed well illustrated here. "Custom" is what judges do; "tradition" (in this instance invented tradition) is the wig, robe and other formal paraphernalia and ritualized practices surrounding their substantial action. The decline of "custom" inevitably changes the "tradition" with which it is habitually intertwined.

A second, less important, distinction that must be made is between "tradition" in our sense and convention or routine, which has no significant ritual or symbolic function as such, though it may acquire it incidentally. It is evident that any social practice that needs to be carried out repeatedly will tend, for convenience and efficiency, to develop a set of such conventions and routines, which may be de facto or de jure formalized for the purposes of imparting the practice to new practitioners. This applies to unprecedented practices . . . as much as to long-familiar ones. Societies since the industrial revolution have naturally been obliged to invent, institute or develop new networks of such convention or routine more frequently than previous ones. Insofar as they function best when turned into habit, automatic procedure or even reflex action, they require invariance, which may get in the way of the other necessary requirement of practice, the capacity to deal with unforeseen or inhabitual contingencies. This is a well-known weakness of routinization or bureaucratization, particularly at the subaltern levels where invariant performance is generally considered the most efficient.

Such networks of convention and routine are not "invented traditions" since their functions, and therefore their justifications, are technical rather than ideological. . . . They are designed to facilitate readily definable practical operations, and are readily modified or abandoned to meet changing practical needs, always allowing for the inertia which any practice acquires with time and the emotional resistance to any innovation by people who have become attached to it. The same applies to the recognized "rules" of games or other patterns of social interaction, where these exist, or to any other pragmatically based norms. Where these exist in combination with "tradition," the difference is readily observable. Wearing hard hats when riding makes practical sense, like wearing crash helmets for motor-cyclists or steel helmets for soldiers; wearing a particular type of hard hat in combination with hunting pink makes an entirely different kind of sense. If this were not so, it would be as easy to change the "traditional" costume of fox-hunters as it is to substitute a differently shaped helmet in armies—rather conservative institutions—if it can be shown to provide more effective protection. Indeed, it may be suggested that "traditions" and pragmatic conventions or routines are inversely related. "Tradition" shows weakness when, as among liberal Jews, dietary prohibitions are justified pragmatically, as by arguing that the ancient Hebrews banned pork on grounds of hygiene. Conversely, objects or practices are liberated for full symbolic and ritual use when no longer fettered by practical use. . . .

Inventing traditions, it is assumed here, is essentially a process of formalization and ritualization, characterized by reference to the past, if only by imposing repetition. The actual process of creating such ritual and symbolic complexes has not been adequately studied by historians. Much of it is still rather obscure. It is presumably most clearly exemplified where a "tradition" is deliberately invented and constructed by a single initiator. . . . Perhaps it is almost as easily traced in the case of officially instituted and planned ceremonials, since they are likely to be well documented. . . . It is probably most difficult to trace where such traditions are partly invented, partly evolved in private groups (where the process is less likely to be bureaucratically recorded), or informally over a period of time as, say, in parliament and the legal profession. The difficulty is not only one of sources but also of techniques, though there are available both esoteric disciplines specializing in symbolism and ritual, such as heraldry and the study of liturgy, as well as Warburgian historic disciplines for the study of such subjects. Unfortunately neither are usually familiar to historians of the industrial era.

There is probably no time and place with which historians are concerned which has not seen the "invention" of tradition in this sense. However, we should expect it to occur more frequently when a rapid transformation of society weakens or destroys the social patterns for which "old" traditions had been designed, producing new ones to which they were not applicable, or when such old traditions and their institutional carriers and promulgators no longer prove sufficiently adaptable and flexible, or are otherwise eliminated: in short, when there are sufficiently large and rapid changes on the demand or the supply side. Such changes have been particularly significant in the past 200 years, and it is therefore reasonable to expect these instant formalizations of new traditions to cluster during this period. This implies, incidentally, against both nineteenth-century liberalism and more recent "modernization" theory that such formalizations are not confined to so-called "traditional" societies, but also have their place, in one form or another, in "modern" ones. Broadly speaking this is so, but one must beware of making the further assumptions, firstly that older forms of community and authority structure, and consequently the traditions associated with them, were unadoptable and became rapidly unviable, and secondly that "new" traditions simply resulted from the inability to use or adapt old ones. . . .

More interesting, from our point of view, is the use of ancient materials to construct invented traditions of a novel type for quite novel purposes. A large store of such materials is accumulated in the past of any society, and an elaborate language of symbolic practice and communication is always available.

Sometimes new traditions could be readily grafted on old ones, sometimes they could be devised by borrowing from the well-supplied warehouses of official ritual, symbolism and moral exhortation—religion and princely pomp, folklore and freemasonry (itself an earlier invented tradition of great symbolic force).

Terence Ranger (contemp.)

British African historian. In 1993, ten years after the publication of his edited volume with **Hobsbawm** on the "invention of tradition," Ranger revisited the concept and its applicability in non-Western settings. In his updated view, the original work overemphasized the instrumental and planned qualities of invention, and saw invention as too much of a once-and-for-all event; in contrast, Ranger here favors Benedict Anderson's term "imagining" and argues that "the history of modern tradition has been much more complex than we have supposed."

From "The Invention of Tradition Revisited: The Case of Colonial Africa"

[I]nsistences on the invented character of ethnicity, language, law, religion—of "tradition" itself—have naturally posed severe problems for historians of precolonial Africa. How can one get back to the realities behind these inventions? Can one still talk of continuous "charters" or "cultural archives" which give continuous identity to African societies throughout all upheavals?

In 1990 two leading ethno-historians, Jan Vansina and Steven Feierman, addressed themselves to these problems. Vansina understands the impulses behind a book like the *Invention of Tradition*. Commenting on it, he writes:

> Traditions are historical phenomena which occur everywhere. Historians, however, have tended to shy away from them. . . . The popular use of the term in the sense of "lack of change" irritates historians whose avocation is to discover change. . . . In addition "tradition" is often invoked to designate the historical consciousness of a particular group and more often than not the term is just a flag of convenience to legitimate a position held on other grounds.

Thus it is natural and even useful for historians to challenge the notion of tradition, especially (as we shall see) in colonial Africa. Nevertheless, Vansina insists that "traditions are not just in the minds of observers." They are "out there" . . . "phenomena with their own characteristics." . . . Vansina . . . uses the term in an archaeological or cultural anthropological sense:

> The past of equatorial Africa exemplified the workings of a powerful endogenous process, a cultural tradition that had its roots some 4000–5000 years ago, and that maintained itself by perennial rejuvenation, until it withered as a result of the colonial conquest. . . . Historians and anthropologists have, on the whole, shunned the study of such phenomena that stretch over thousands of years and span vast regions. . . . [Yet] the main outline of the past in equatorial Africa is a story about tradition.

Vansina's insistence on the "perennial rejuvenation" of Equatorial African tradition makes his book a study, one might say, of "invention *by* tradition rather than the invention *of* tradition. He speaks with indignation of a western scholarship which saw African traditions as unchanging; how hurtful it is, he says, to Equatorial Africans "to be told by foreign scholars that, in earlier days, the ingenuity of your forebears was so constrained by 'cultural tradition' that people were condemned to repeat themselves endlessly, to be stuck in the same rut for time immemorial." In fact, cultural tradition is "both continuity and yet change," a great ancestral repository of values and solutions which allows for a wide range of elaborations and innovations within its terms. Indeed, he asserts, "all the social innovations . . . were but an elaboration of the social legacy of the ancestral tradition," even though these innovations encompassed chiefs, kings, brotherhoods, matriliny, patriliny, and so on. Even at the great crises of external incursion and the slave trade, "the tradition was not defeated. It adapted. It invented new structures."

Working from this dynamic and fundamental definition of precolonial tradition, Vansina goes further than any previous author in his scathing characterisation of colonial inventions. The colonial conquest of Equatorial Africa, he says, took only forty years "to destroy the equatorial tradition." It did so partly by imposing its own invented constructs:

> The conquest prevented the tradition from inventing new structures to cope with a new situation. Instead the colonial government invented them. Its agents preserved some old practices but the whole structure made sense only in the cognitive realm of the Europeans, not in the equatorial tradition. . . . The cognitive part of the old tradition, its very core, went into irreversible crisis. . . . The Europeans first built their own cognitive view of rural African society and then imposed it on daily life. . . . The only concession to the equatorial way of life was to preserve some cultural flotsam and jetsam, and to erect a structure labeled customary law, which was utterly foreign to the spirit of the former tradition. Customary law was the headstone on its grave.

The result of all this was disastrous. "Traditions are processes. They must continually change to stay alive. . . . Traditions need autonomy. The peoples who carry them must have the power of self-determination." Yet the recovery of political self-determination with national independence offered no solution. With independence, "insecurity exploded. . . . There was no turning back to an age of unsullied tradition." Instead there was a new sort of pluralism, featuring "variants of neo African tradition" but "without the guidance of a basic tradition." Today the people of Equatorial Africa are "still bereft of a common mind or purpose."

Steven Feierman takes a quite different route towards reconciling the idea of colonial invention with the idea of a long standing cultural tradition. In his marvellous *Peasant Intellectuals: Anthropology and History in Tanzania* Feierman argues that "long-term continuity and active creation are in fact compatible." But he remarks that the study of "long-term durations" may

> lead to the mystification of cultural continuities—to a sense that the continuity of a cultural form is unexceptional and expected, that it is passively accepted by the people who use it. [Yet] when people select a particular form of

discourse . . . this is by no means a passive act. . . . Long-term continuities in political language are the outcome of radical social change and of struggle within peasant society.

This plainly is not a criticism of Vansina's dynamic definition of "the tradition." Yet Feierman's approach is nevertheless very different from Vansina's. For Vansina, as we have seen, the pluralism of twentieth-century Africa implies the end of the great tradition and the inevitable impotence of modern African thought. But, for Feierman, pluralism is the essence of creativity. . . .

[T]here are . . . serious drawbacks to the term "invention." It implies too one-sided a happening. An invention presupposes an inventor—and in my chapter in *The Invention* the inventors were mainly colonial administrators or missionaries, working admittedly with African collaborators but with these playing the role of laboratory assistants rather than of scientists. . . .

Moreover, invention is too once-for-all an event. An invention may take some time to develop but, once made by the individual or team who have been working on it, all that is left is to apply for a patent. It is a term which makes little allowance for process, for the constant reworking of identities and the steady transformation of institutions. . . .

Hence I have come to think that the defects of the term "invention" compromise not only my chapter but also some of the later work on colonial custom. The idea can be a foreclosing one. It emphasises, and emphasises rightly, a contrast between precolonial fluidity and the reification of colonial classification, between mobile custom and static tradition. But, however codi-fied and static colonial tradition was intended to be, it could never end there. To focus on the innovation of a tradition is certainly to approach it historically, but to approach it fully historically means also to study its subsequent development and the conflict over its meaning. Moreover, to say that "invented tradition was a product of the ideological needs of colonialism" foreshortens colonialism as well as tradition.

Brief as it was in the overall history of Africa, the colonial period was long enough for a shifting history of hegemony. My chapter and the subse-quent literature is strong on early colonialism and on the 1930s but much weaker on the period of the Second World War and after, when other legiti-mations and innovations were required. The continuation in Africa of the invented traditions of Europe, long after they had become irrelevant to gov-ernance at home . . . was real but deceptive. Things had changed in colonial Africa too.

So the word "invention" gets in the way of a fully historical treatment of colonial hegemony *and* of a fully historical treatment of African participation and initiative in innovating custom. I have come to prefer Benedict Anderson's word from his *Imagined Communities*. Some traditions in colonial Africa really *were* invented by a single colonial officer for a single occasion. But customary law and ethnicity and religion and language were *imagined*, by many different people and over a long time. These multiple imaginations were in tension with each other and in constant contestation to define the meaning of what had been imagined—to imagine it further. Traditions imagined by whites were re-imagined by blacks; traditions imagined by particular black interest groups were re-imagined by others. The history of modern tradition has been much more complex than we have supposed.

Above all, I like the word "imagining" because, much more than the term "invention," it lays stress upon ideas and images and symbols. However politically convenient they were, the new traditions were, after all, essentially about identity and identity is essentially a matter of imagination. It is good that the growing focus on colonial ideology is beginning to be matched by an interest in African ideas.

Orlando Patterson (contemp.)

Jamaican-American sociologist. Slavery, according to Patterson's extensive study, is essentially a form of social death. One of the most significant mechanisms of this social death is what Patterson describes with the concept "natal alienation," the severing of slaves from their rights to an ancestry (and legacy); alienation from one's patrimony is a central mechanism of establishing the nonpersonhood essential to slavery.

From *Slavery and Social Death: A Comparative Study*

Perhaps the most distinctive attribute of the slave's powerlessness was that it always originated (or was conceived of as having originated) as a substitute for death, usually violent death. . . . Archetypically, slavery was a substitute for death in war. But almost as frequently, the death commuted was punishment for some capital offense, or death from exposure or starvation.

The condition of slavery did not absolve or erase the prospect of death. Slavery was not a pardon; it was, peculiarly, a conditional commutation. The execution was suspended only as long as the slave acquiesced in his powerlessness. The master was essentially a ransomer. What he bought or, acquired was the slave's life, and restraints on the master's capacity wantonly to destroy his slave did not undermine his claim on that life. Because the slave had no socially recognized existence outside of his master, he became a social nonperson.

This brings us to the second constituent element of the slave relation: the slave's natal alienation. Here we move to the cultural aspect of the relation, to that aspect of it which rests on authority, on the control of symbolic instruments. This is achieved in a unique way in the relation of slavery: the definition of the slave, however recruited, as a socially dead person. Alienated from all "rights" or claims of birth, he ceased to belong in his own right to any legitimate social order. All slaves experienced, at the very least, a secular excommunication.

Not only was the slave denied all claims on, and obligations to, his parents and living blood relations but, by extension, all such claims and obligations on his more remote ancestors and on his descendants. He was truly a genealogical isolate. Formally isolated in his social relations with those who lived, he also was culturally isolated from the social heritage of his ancestors. He had a past, to be sure. But a past is not a heritage. Everything has a history, including sticks and stones. Slaves differed from other human beings in that they were not allowed freely to integrate the experience of their ancestors into their lives, to inform their understanding of social reality with the inherited meanings of their natural forebears, or to anchor the living present in any conscious community of memory. That they reached back for the past, as they reached out for the related living, there can be no doubt. Unlike other persons, doing so meant struggling with and penetrating the iron curtain of the master, his community, his laws, his policemen or patrollers, and his heritage. . . .

When we say that the slave was natally alienated and ceased to belong independently to any formally recognised community, this does not mean that he or she did not experience or share informal social relations. A large number of works have demonstrated that slaves in both ancient and modern times had strong social ties among themselves. The important point, however, is that these relationships were never recognized as legitimate or binding. Thus American slaves, like their ancient Greco-Roman counterparts, had regular sexual unions, but such unions were never recognized as marriages; both groups were attached to their local communities, but such attachments had no binding force; both sets of parents were deeply attached to their children, but the parental bond had no social support.

The refusal formally to recognize the social relations of the slave had profound emotional and social implications. In all slaveholding societies slave couples could be and were forcibly separated and the consensual "wives" of slaves were obliged to submit sexually to their masters; slaves had no custodial claims or powers over their children, and children inherited no claims or obligations to their parents. And the master had the power to remove a slave from the local community in which he or she was brought up.

Even if such forcible separations occurred only infrequently, the fact that they were possible and that from time to time they did take place was enough to strike terror in the hearts of all slaves and to transform significantly the way they behaved and conceived of themselves. . . .

The independent constituent role of natal alienation in the emergence of slavery is vividly illustrated by the early history of slavery in America. Winthrop D. Jordan has shown that in the early decades of the seventeenth century there were few marked differences in the conception of black and white servitude, the terms "slave" and "servant" being used synonymously. The power of the master over both black and white servants was near total: both could be whipped and sold.

Gradually there emerged, however, something new in the conception of the black servant: the view that he did not belong to the same community of Christian, civilized Europeans. The focus of this "we-they" distinction was at first religious, later racial. "Enslavement was captivity, the loser's lot in a contest of power. Slaves were infidels or heathens." But as Jordan argues, although the focus may have changed, there was really a fusion of race, religion and nationality in a generalized conception of "us"—white, English, free—and "them"—black, heathen, slave. "From the first, then, vis-á-vis the Negro the concept embedded in the term Christian seems to have conveyed much of the idea and feeling of *we* as against *they*: to be Christian was to be civilized rather than barbarous, English rather than African, white rather than black." The strangeness and seeming savagery of the Africans, reinforced by traditional attitudes and the context of early contact, "were major components in that sense of *difference* which provided the mental margin absolutely requisite for placing the European on the deck of the slave ship and the Negro in the hold."

Although using different symbolic tools, much the same sense of apartness, of not belonging, emerged in other cultures to differentiate the genuine slave from other forms of involuntary servants over whom almost total power was exercised. Yet the natal alienation of the slave was not necessarily expressed in religious, racial, or even ethnic terms. Among primitives, . . . alienation from one's natal ties was all that was necessary. Sometimes law alone, superimposed on the slave's sense of not belonging, was sufficient. Indeed, it was Moses Finley, drawing on the Greco-Roman experience, who was among the first to emphasize what he called the "outsider" status of the slave as a critical attribute of his condition. He did not make the mistake that Henri Lévi-Bruhl had earlier made, of generalizing from the Roman experience to the conclusion that the social alienation of the slave was necessarily an ethnic one. Insofar as Roman slaves were foreigners, Finley argued, they were outsiders twice over, clearly allowing for the reduction of locally recruited slaves to the status of outsiders.

I prefer the term "natal alienation," because it goes directly to the heart of what is critical in the slave's forced alienation, the loss of ties of birth in both ascending and descending generations. It also has the important nuance of a loss of native status, of deracination. It was this alienation of the slave from all formal, legally enforceable ties of "blood," and from any attachment to groups or localities other than those chosen for him by the master, that gave the relation of slavery its peculiar value to the master. The slave was the ultimate human tool, as imprintable and as disposable as the master wished. And this is true, at least in theory, of all slaves, no matter how elevated. . . .

The incapacity to make any claims of birth or to pass on such claims is considered a natural injustice among all peoples, so that those who were obliged to suffer it had to be regarded as somehow socially dead. . . .

How, we may ask, could persons be made to accept such natural injustice? The question applies not only to the victims but to those third parties not directly involved in the slave relation who stood by and accepted it. Denying the slave's humanity, his independent social existence, begins to explain this acceptance. Yet it is only a beginning, for it immediately poses the further question: how was the slave's social death, the outward conception of his natal alienation, articulated and reinforced? . . .

[T]he master's authority was derived from his control over symbolic instruments, which effectively persuaded both slave and others that the master was the only mediator between the living community to which he belonged and the living death that his slave experienced.

The symbolic instruments may be seen as the cultural counterpart to the physical instruments used to control the slave's body. In much the same way that the literal whips were fashioned from different materials, the symbolic whips of slavery were woven from many areas of culture. Masters all over the world used special rituals of enslavement upon first acquiring slaves: the symbolism of naming, of clothing, of hairstyle, of language, and of body marks. And they used, especially in the more advanced slave systems, the sacred symbols of religion.

Natal alienation has one critical corollary that is an important feature of slavery, so important indeed that many scholars have seen it as the distinguishing element of the relation. This is the fact that the relation was perpetual and inheritable. James Curtis Ballagh's assessment sums this up for many scholars: "The distinguishing mark of the state of slavery is not the loss of liberty, political or civil, but the perpetuity and almost absolute character of that loss, whether voluntary or involuntary." . . .

Ballagh was wrong, however, in his assumption that the inheritability of slavery was the "natural consequence" of the life bondage of the slave. . . . [I]t is easy to show in purely empirical terms that neither absolute power nor lifetime selection to such power necessarily imply the inheritability of such status. . . .

The hereditary factor only entered in when the servant lost his natal claims to his own parents and community. Having no natal claims and powers of his own, he had none to pass on to his children. And because no one else had any claim or interest in such children, the master could claim them as his own essentially on the grounds that whatever the parents of such children expended in their upbringing incurred a debt to him. Not by virtue, then, of his lifetime power over the slave did the master claim the latter's issue, but by virtue of the absence of any third party's interest in the child, the absence of the child's capacity to assert a claim on any such third parties, and the claim that necessarily accrued to the master with the parent's expenditures for childrearing.

Richard Sennett (contemp.)

British American sociologist. **Halbwachs**, it is often forgotten, came to collective memory at least in part through his study of working-class consciousness. Ironically, however, and despite the popularity of the "popular memory" concept, few scholars have followed up on this connection. Richard Sennett's contribution here is thus unusual in the literature. Based on his study of laid-off computer programmers at IBM, Sennett finds that capitalism encourages such workers to individualize their failures and thus to fail to "remember well."

From "Disturbing Memories"

Memory is consciousness of time which has passed. In the Darwinian time-frame, our memories are trivial records; we cannot, obviously, summon to consciousness the millions of years which formed us as a species. But the conflictual, competitive Darwinian order of time obviously troubles also those acts of recovered time in which we are able to engage. Rather than a halcyon recovery of a golden age, of an Edenic pastoral, a more accurate act of memory reveals to us an unending record of pains and struggles which has formed us into the creatures we now are. Truthful memory opens wounds which forgetting cannot heal; the traces of conflict, failure and disaster are never erasable in time. The science of evolutionary reconstruction seemed to offer testimony to those ineradicable traces. There is no solace in the truths of memory.

Karl Marx came independently to this view in his studies of the revolutions of 1848. He detected revolutionary nostalgia, evinced by insurgents that year for the Great Revolution of 1789, and his later reading of Darwin strengthened him in his hatred of nostalgia—which is, Marx said, memory's lie. Sigmund Freud, who as a young man was an avid reader of Darwin, learned from Charcot that the gates of memory shut when the inner warfare described by Charcot becomes unbearable; truthful memory of the past requires courage as nostalgia does not, since the collage of conscious pain only becomes thicker when we remember well.

Yet if *what* we remember offers no solace, *how* we remember these wounds seemed to many of Darwin's heirs to offer some release. Like Freud, Marcel Proust came to that view of the work of memory in the final volume of *À la Recherche du Temps Perdu*: remembered pain or conflict can be objectified as present pain cannot be. In my own field of sociology, a similar emphasis on how we remember has shaped the study of collective memory.

That study began with Émile Durkheim. When families or communities share their memories, he argued, they draw closer together; they create a sense of solidarity through remembering together, even if what they remember is traumatic, like a war or an economic disaster. That is, collective memory is a source of social strength. Durkheim knew enough to recognize that these collectively shared memories might be anything but objective and factual; the degree of group solidarity might instead depend on their mythic properties. Yet he continued to hope that, by sharing rather than privatizing memories, communities might find a way to tell the truth about themselves. The question is, how? For Durkheim, the more varied the voices engaged in that common dialogue, the more likely the accuracy of what would be recalled: he is the first liberal theorist of memory.

I have been thinking about Darwin's age and legacy in trying to understand a set of social problems which may seem unrelated to the ways in which people today make sense of a new chapter in the history of capitalism, a chapter creating a fexible economy and undoing the protections and supports of the welfare state. Certainly social Darwinism of a sort has reappeared in this new order, which emphasizes the survival of the fittest in terms of those with technical skills and flexible (i.e. adaptive) behaviour patterns in their work. What has struck me is the difficulty people have in making an accurate record of what has happened to them in the course of this political-economic change: the denials of injuries sustained in the course of recent experience. The tendency of communally shared memories to generate myth rather than accurate histories.

I believe that people can indeed deal with the wounds of memory in their life histories only by remembering well (that is, by becoming more objective) and I am convinced that Durkheim's liberal faith remains compelling. Remembering well a shared injury is something which people cannot do by themselves, but must be shared by a group of diverse voices. However, the organization of the modern economy seems to work against people remembering well together; it does not support them in their efforts. . . .

. . . Remembering well requires reopening wounds in a particular way, one which people cannot do by themselves; remembering well requires a social structure in which people can address others across the boundaries of difference. This is the liberal hope for collective memory.

This may seem highly idealistic; common sense, that most fallible of guides, tells us, for instance, that people shy away from conflict. But in fact people dwell in this state all the time. Not only business competitors but lawyers, diplomats, and labour negotiators live off debating contrary narratives and are stimulated by it. The sociologist Lewis Coser long ago showed how verbal conflict in fact creates social bonds between disputants. Arguing supposes you care what the other side thinks, and the verbal process itself—its feints, shifts of argument, offers of compromise—gradually knits people together.

So the problem is why, in the kinds of economic experience of unemployment and premature uselessness . . . those conflictual relations are not taking form, why collective memory of shared injury can become a detour rather than a confrontation with capitalism's current pains. . . .

There are a host of institutional reasons for this detour. The modern economic system is intensely individualizing; as it strips away collective supports and defences against economic dislocation, it forces people to behave as isolated entrepreneurs, even when they work in large organizations. The very character of work has become redefined as a task unrelated to past performance or to future embedding within a bureaucratic structure. . . . All this means that the narrative of a life is no longer a tight, well-made story.

Institutional, individualizing insecurity makes subjective life itself highly unstable and uncertain. Shoring up the sense of self in a world without reliable institutions thus becomes urgent psychological business, as the economy deforms the coherence and continuity of lived time. And here, I think, is where the work of memory enters.

The final stage of memory among the unemployed computer programmers yielded them a sense of subjective solidarity. I want to argue that, by extension, under current conditions the work of memory, much more than momentary sensation or the operations of deductive reasoning, holds out the promise of making inner life feel definite and solid. It is through memory that we seem to possess ourselves. Put another way, memory becomes like a form of private property, to be protected from challenge and conflict—a property of the self which those exchanges might erode.

Modern capitalism encourages such feelings about memory as private property. In their emerging forms of growth, chameleon institutions such as IBM are undoing their own institutional memories; the businesses want to change rapidly, and fear being stuck in the past. They thus shy away from rewarding length of service or experience. Debureaucratized institutions instead reward people not prone to institutional attachments; in the computer business, for example, employers now put a greater premium on hiring those who have moved from place to place than upon those who have remained steadily at one firm. Institutional loyalty is seen as a portent of personal dependency, a lack of enterprise; people with long institutional memories are a drag on change.

Under these conditions, a negative value is placed on the work of recall. Unlike the bureaucratic dinosaurs which rigidly graded length of service and operated by seniority, a new-style corporation has no interest in its own history, save as a caution about what needs to change. It certainly has no interest in provoking its employees to remember; it is not an interlocutor of time. And for this reason, memory has become increasingly subjective and internal, the *longue durée* of personal private experience.

Given these realities, it becomes indeed reasonable to see the domain of memory instead as a private matter, an archive one wants to protect from the violations of the competitive world. People will express their memories in a way which empowers and solidifies their remembering; by sharing those reminiscences they will create bonds of trust and loyalty missing in the corporate world. I would never say of the dismissed computer programmers I know that they have acted irrationally; rather, self-destructively. A business magazine recently reported the 45,000 employees who would be dismissed by the AT&T corporation in 1996 were taking their imminent redundancy with resignation rather than anger. Shared memories do not protect the workers I have interviewed against the world. They acknowledge this in an inverted way, by speaking of themselves as "past it," by focusing on what they should have done when there still was time.

My claim is that people do not remember well because the modern economy does not encourage it. Defence lies not in repression of the past, but in narratives which empower the remembering subject, and this private empowerment is an act in which people can collectively collude. Durkheim's and Halbwachs' liberal dream has been defeated by the denials of time in the economy and, perversely, by the freedom of the narrating subject. . . .

This, at least as I understand it, is a large part of the crisis of liberal culture in modern capitalism. It is a complicated story in which people's sense of time is victimized both by an economy with no interest in duration, stability, or continuity, and by the way people construct these values of time for themselves.

In a way we have returned to the problem Darwin posed to his contemporaries: how can we make the time that we have lived matter in the conduct of our lives? In Darwin's era, the length of biological time seemed to make experienced time insignificant; in our era, the shortness of economic time seems to result in the same sense of insignificance.

Michael Schudson (contemp.)

American sociologist. First published in 1993, Michael Schudson's book *Watergate in American Memory* appeared relatively early in the current wave of collective memory research in sociology. In an earlier article (1989), from which the following excerpts are drawn, Schudson sorts out his theoretical perspective on collective memory, providing a clear model of how present interests are constrained by the reality of the past being remembered.

From "The Past in the Present versus the Present in the Past"

Where the creation of a sense of the past is not in the hands of professional historians, it is all the more likely that the past will be used as a resource for legitimating rather than as an avenue toward truth. . . .

But the recollection of the past does not always serve present interests. The past is in some respects, and under some conditions, highly resistant to efforts to make it over. It cannot be made over at will—which is not to say that people don't try. People and organizations and nations do make their own pasts, to paraphrase Karl Marx, but they do not do so in conditions of their own choosing, with materials of their own making, or even with their memories acting entirely under their own volition.

The full freedom to reconstruct the past according to one's own present interests is limited by three factors: the structure of available pasts, the structure of individual choices, and the conflicts about the past among a multitude of mutually aware individuals or groups. . . .

Individuals, groups, organizations, nations, and societies do not have all possible materials available to them from which to construct a past. From the viewpoint of the individual seeking legitimation from the past, there are just so many things to work with; the available materials are far from infinite. Of course, within what is available, there is much that can still be done to bend interpretation to one's will—but the available materials still set limits. . . .

That is precisely what I mean by a structure of available pasts. There are features of our own pasts that become part of the givens of our lives, whether they are convenient or not. English writers of the past several centuries have been free to take different attitudes to the English literary heritage, but they have not been free to ignore it and its illustrious reputation. Goethe said that he was glad to be German so as not to have had Shakespeare to compete with; English authors, in contrast, have deeply felt what one critic has called "the burden of the past". . . .

In the long passage of time, everything fades. It would be impossible now to rewrite the history of the 20th century and claim that the 1930s was a time of great prosperity. But if I claimed that the 1830s was a time of great prosperity, only professional historians would be equipped to dispute me or emotionally engaged enough with the panic of 1837 to bother. The salience of the past declines. . . .

Not only are people's reconstructions of the past generally confined to the experiences in their own traditions, then, but they are further limited to those elements of the tradition that have emerged, over time, as especially salient. There is what I will call a rhetorical structure to social organisation that gives prominence to some facets of the past and not others. Once commemoration gets underway, it picks up steam; it operates by a logic and force of its own. Not only are records kept, diaries saved, and news accounts written, but statues are built, museums are endowed, brass plaques are engraved and placed in sidewalks and on the walls of buildings. Certainly the statues can be destroyed, the museum exhibits redone, the plaques removed—but this is not easy to do and may well create public controversy that revives rather than erases memory. . . .

By the rhetorical structure of social organization, I do not refer exclusively to physical or material implantation of memory, museums and statues and the like. Take the question of how a novel becomes a "classic" that is treated as a great work of art and canonized in school curricula, examination questions, anniversary editions, scholarly conferences, and so forth. Recent studies make it clear that this is far from a matter of pure aesthetic judgment. The political, economic, and social relations of the author (or sometimes the author's friends, publishers, and heirs) have a great deal to do with the establishment of a reputation as a "classic" or "great" art . . .). My point, however, is not that social power is required to enshrine a work but that, once enshrined, the work accumulates a self-perpetuating rhetorical power. It gathers partisans, partisans beget schools, schools beget cultural authority, cultural authority begets an established tradition, the tradition embeds itself not only in formal institutions but in our very language. . . .

This happens in science as well as in art. Robert Merton has called it the "Matthew effect"—those that have, shall get. . . . He observes that co-authored articles in science are usually credited to the more famous author, whether the work is primarily his (or hers) or not. Readers recognize and assimilate the more famous name (whether it is listed first or last does not matter very much), not that of the up-and-coming graduate student or colleague. A "Matthew effect" exists not only in the crediting of work but in the giving of grants and other central processes in the distribution of goods and reputations. . . .

Given that people can choose only from the available past and that the available past is limited, are individuals free to choose as they wish? Far from it. There are a variety of ways in which the freedom to choose is constrained. . . .

Traumas, as I use the term here, are past experiences people (or organizations or nations) cannot ignore even when they would like to, cannot divert their attention from without courting anxiety, fear, and pain. Not only must Americans confront slavery, not only must Germans face the Holocaust, but they must do so repeatedly, obsessively, necessarily, whether they like it or not. . . .

The past becomes part of us; and shapes us, it influences our consciousness, whether we like it or not. In the pathological, but familiar, form, people become entrapped by their old wounds. . . .

People react not only to extreme conditions in their own lives but to extreme conditions in the lives of others. . . .

They do so not because of some traumatic experience they themselves have undergone but because they are aware of stories of others in similar situations. . . .

We might call "vicarious trauma" simply "lessons" since it is the task of much of education to instill in newcomers (children, new recruits to an organization, new immigrants to an established community) not only information about the past but appropriate emotional orientations to it. It should be clear that this includes not only aspects of the past regarded with horror but other aspects regarded with pride. . . .

There are some facets of the past we cannot ignore because we do not have enough energy to escape their inertial pull. . . . A key feature that shapes how a community responds to conflict will be, quite simply, how the community has responded to conflict in the past. . . .

[E]ven rare events, even unique events, may have extraordinary influence on people and organizations long after the fact. There is, in particular, great power to originating events, the character of "founding fathers" or constitutional documents. As anyone who has ever been a member of a committee knows, there is frequently a need for orientation, for a starting point to deal with a new problem or issue, and a search for precedent ensues. . . .

There are some facets of the past we cannot ignore or forget without feeling the loss of some part of ourselves. Not only does the past, as Freud says, live in people's mental life; people's mental life lives in the past. A person is constituted by a train of events and experiences. People make commitments, make promises, forge ties, establish loyalties, invest in lines of action, and these become defining for the person of what he or she is. A person comes to have a commitment in him or her self—in what is called identity or character or, with a more social aspect emphasized, reputation. These are then difficult to let go of—even if rational self-interest (if the word "self-interest" can be said to have any meaning in this context) would so advise. . . .

So long, then, as individuals, groups, organizations, and societies undergo traumatic experiences—experiences that truly leave a mark and engender the formation of "preemptive metaphors" for better (loyalties and commitments) or for worse (neurosis), so long as they seek to minimize the expenditure of effort in confronting new tasks and problems, so long as they seek to maintain a continuous, stable sense of identity, they will not, because they cannot, reconstruct the past entirely in their own "interest." It follows that the structure of available pasts and the rhetorical structure of available pasts and the rhetorical structure of social organization that makes some facets of the past more salient than others will necessarily be powerful influences on how an individual or organization thinks and acts and constructs or reconstructs a history from which to act. . . .

Finally, people's ability to reconstruct the past just as they wish is limited by the crucial social fact that other people within their awareness are trying to do the same thing. Different reconstructions clash. Control over the past is disputed and the past becomes contested terrain. Some individuals, organizations, classes, and nations have more power than others to claim the territory of memory. There is a politics of memory that requires study. Certainly political leaders of both powerful and aspiring groups recognise that the mobilization of memory is often a vital political resource. But as for the idea that people and groups and nations rewrite the past to legitimate the present, this observation cuts two ways. Yes, individuals and groups try to co-opt memory for their own purposes; but no, they do not do so with a free hand so long as success in even convincing oneself requires non-contradiction by others. . . .

There is plenty of evidence that people rewrite history—and this is deeply important, but it should not lead to loose talk that suggests it is the whole story. The present shapes our understanding of the past, yes. But this is half the truth, at best, and a particularly cynical half-truth, at that. It is the other half of the truth I call attention to here—that the past shapes the present, even when the most powerful people and classes and institutions least want it to.

Gladys Lang and Kurt Lang (contemp.)

American sociologists. In this seminal article for reputation studies (see also **Cooley**), the Langs develop a sociological perspective on reputational dynamics, comparing the different conditions for the establishment and survival of reputations in different fields like art, music, politics, and science, as well as the impact of different factors like age, position in an art world, being survived by a spouse, and so on. They point out that "small and nonmeasurable differences in lifetime recognition can result in significant disparities in posthumous recognition."

From "Recognition and Renown: The Survival of Artistic Reputation"

[T]he surviving residue of records always gives a less than perfect account of past activity. Not everything is preserved. The chances for survival improve where a large number of copies in a durable medium are widely distributed and valued by contemporaries.

In quantity, printmakers have an obvious advantage over other artists. The survival prospects of work by productive etchers with access to market channels are good, even though an image on paper is more vulnerable than one chiseled in stone or painted on a wall or canvas. But number and distribution do not assure the preservation (and identification) of the requisite oeuvre unless some value attaches to it. Thus, of the hundreds of copies of the *New England Primer* printed in the colonies before 1727, not one has ever been located because, unlike family Bibles from the same period, they were not treasured as heirlooms. . . . Although the initial impetus to preservation may come from a bereaved widow or loving daughter, moved by her loss to assemble the creations, papers, and other ephemera of the deceased, this is no more than a first step. There must be others who share this interest. What obviously matters most in the long run is the proximity of the deceased to institutions with organized arrangements for the archiving and restoration of the historical evidence. Particularly those who enjoyed power and esteem in their lifetimes are also more likely to have had friends with influence and connections to archives.

As to what it is that has to survive, there is in the visual arts no substitute for the original. Pictures are valued not just for what they portray but for the authentic touch of the artist, believed to be irretrievably lost in a copy, no matter how difficult it is for the naked eye to detect the difference. This does not hold for texts in the form of notations that must first be translated into words or sound before their meaning can be assimilated. In these cases, the original manuscript is of no interest, except as a source document. Certainly, no one would claim that the appeal and "value" of a literary work was diminished when printed in a large edition on poor paper and weakly bound—even if the edition is pirated. The reputation of the writer can be sustained as long as there is at least one legible copy available for duplication. A theatrical script or a musical score survives through the interpretations of performers.

Given that the work, or at least an acceptable facsimile, has been preserved, the collective memory is further influenced by the means available for dissemination. In the past, the more enterprising painters relied on engravers to copy their work and make it known to a larger public. But engravings are not duplications but generalized, abstract reports about iconography and compositions. . . . They cannot accurately render the surface, brush strokes, and nuances through which the personality of the artist is revealed. As the color print (or slide) becomes the preferred medium through which paintings are copied and remembered, the visibility of artists who paint in flat tones that lend themselves to reproduction in greater verisimilitude will increase. . . . The suitability of a theater for the revival of certain genres of plays . . . or of the musical instrumentation and specialization of orchestras for a particular musical repertoire . . . similarly affects the accessibility of these works and hence the reputations of their creators. Blaukopf . . . suggests that the advent of the technically perfected stereo record promoted the music of Gustav Mahler by making it possible for the first time to realize fully the "considered spatial pattern of sound" contained in the technical directives of the composer's musical notations for his Eighth Symphony, where the sound of a church organ is combined with the voices of singers and the strains of the orchestra. Recordings can also transmit in permanent form what once could only be experienced as a live performance.

Another influence is "measurement." In modern sport, more than anywhere else, an increasingly precise technology for scoring and preserving performance has given rise to a new concept of record that invites comparison in nearly every kind of athletic competition. . . . Achievement, in the sense of "winning," tends to be overlooked unless written in an official record book, which then becomes the basis for bestowing recognition through awards and commemorative devices. . . . Though records are forever being surpassed, some record holders stand a better chance of surviving in memory, having passed some kind of "natural" marker, like the four-minute mile; Roger Bannister, the first to break this barrier, is still better remembered than several who have since been clocked at even faster times.

Clear and presumably "objective" criteria in the presence of authentic records, such as exist more often in sport than in art, leave little room for judgment. In science, where the prime objective is not to surpass others but to extend knowledge, the distribution of rewards turns on priority, on being the first to come up with a pathbreaking discovery. In fact, however, posterity has considerable leeway in bestowing credit with regard to a class of "accidental discoveries" by researchers who, so to speak, stumble onto a previously unknown phenomenon that at first they do not fully understand. The class includes such breakthroughs as the discovery of oxygen and the principle of the conservation of energy, where the full import of laboratory observations by several scientists emerged only gradually as the full range of contemporary ideas was brought to bear on them. . . . How lack of documentation and other related factors may adversely affect who is remembered is evident in the case of Gregor Mendel, who must, by any objective standard, rate with the far better-known Charles Darwin as one of the discoverers of evolution. Unlike Darwin, who gained instantaneous fame with the publication of *The Origin of Species*, the first edition of which quickly sold out, Mendel received recognition only belatedly and after his observations had been independently verified. Except in his native Czechoslovakia, the centennial of his death in 1984 went completely unnoticed outside the world of science. . . . Meanwhile, the name of Darwin remains a household word associated with the idea of evolution, which he did not even invent but only made popular by contributing an explication of the mechanism of natural selection, and here also Alfred Wallace and Edward Blythe, two contemporaries, had come close to understanding this same process. What is more, Darwin had actually observed Mendelian ratios in snapdragons but failed to draw the appropriate conclusions. His preeminence over Mendel can be attributed to the large residue of information about him. Darwin left an autobiography, scientific sketches, and hundreds of letters on just about every subject, all of them grist for the academic mill. No comparable source material exists about Mendel, nearly all of whose notes were burned at his death.

In the assessment of presidential reputations, and those of others in public life, the "impossibility of agreeing on yardsticks" . . . is an even greater stumbling block. The powers and responsibilities of the office have changed, and its occupants have had to cope with vastly different contingencies. But every administration has generated truckloads of records through the normal institutional processes on which the reputation of the chief executive will ultimately rest. Presidential reputations, like those of artists, are affected by the circumstances of death. Some live long enough to produce memoirs to influence their reputations or to take a hand in setting up a library not only to house their papers but also to serve as a permanent monument. Theodore Roosevelt actually wrote "posterity letters." The success of such personal initiatives toward image building is apt to be limited since, as Schwartz . . . has pointed out, the selection of public figures for commemoration derives less from the past than from their relevance to contemporary issues.

The art that survives from the past is likewise viewed through the eyes of contemporaries. The works themselves are not the locus of a single value known as "beauty;" they are, as George Boas. . . . puts it, "multivalent. . . . Certain of their values are experienced by some people, others by others." There is no a priori method, other than by fiat, for determining which of the many values are properly "aesthetic." Even the reputation of *Mona Lisa*, a universally recognized masterpiece, has undergone change. Similarly, Tompkins . . . shows how the stories that made Nathaniel Hawthorne great in the eyes of his contemporaries are not the same as the ones most admired today and that some have been considered "great" for quite different reasons. This kind of "posthumous editing" . . . is taken for granted in the performing arts, where each director or conductor puts his own stamp on the work. In this respect, musicians are in the worst position, observed Gustav Mahler in 1905. Everyone can read (and supposedly everyone can make out what there is in a picture) but "a musical score is a sealed book. Even the conductors who can decipher it present it to the public imbued with their varying conceptions. The important thing is to create a tradition," . . . which is exactly what Mahler set out to do, using his position with the Vienna Court Opera to give performances of his own work all over Europe.

The strategies by which one gains renown are beyond the scope of this article. We observe only, as others have before us, that the name attached to a work of art functions much like a brand label. The imprimatur of the creator, living or dead, validates the quality, value, and—where relevant—the price of the work. Good things without recognized signatures are often overlooked. . . . Moreover, the advantages of a favorable entry into memory tend to be cumulative not only for etchers but for all artists. Curators and collectors will vie with one another for the contents of a newly deceased artist's studio, if he is already famous, while things left by another who is equally talented will disappear because they have no value. The same goes for authors not in the mainstream. . . . However, those whose names once were household words, as judged by the frequency of mentions in press reviews, continue to receive publicity even after they die and the style in which they wrote has been superseded. . . . Conductors and players can be as crucial as reviewers. Because of the cost of rehearsal time, orchestras are inclined to stick to "classics" that their members already know how to play. . . . Once bypassed, composers regain a place in the repertoire only with difficulty. As yet unknown composers encounter the same obstacle.

Such disparities are further aggravated by the tendency to resolve ambiguities with regard to authorship in favor of the more renowned. The phenomenon has been elucidated by Merton . . . for scientists. When two researchers collaborate and publish their results jointly, notes Merton, the greater credit usually goes to the senior. Perhaps, it is only realistic to assume that innovative ideas come only from seasoned scientists with known track records, but this cannot be universally true. And once a name becomes attached to a discovery, others who paved the way cease to hold interest save perhaps for the historian. The parallel in art of such a "misallocation of credit" rests on the manifestly false assumption that any unidentified masterpiece must be the work of a renowned master. On this premise, Rembrandt scholars have, at least until recently, attributed any painting that looked at all Rembrandtesque to Rembrandt himself. . . . Endeavors to correct this bias have resulted in reattributions and shrunk his oeuvre by nearly one-half. Reduced in size, what remains of it becomes even more valuable. But the Dutch virtuoso had about 100 pupils, all of whom strove to produce paintings like those of their master, yet their names, having been lost, are doomed to be lost forever. Identifications like "follower of" or "in the school of" Rembrandt continue to evoke the great painter's name and attest to his influence.

To return to etching. Here, as in other areas of activity, small and nonmeasurable differences in lifetime recognition can result in significant disparities in posthumous acclaim. The etcher's achievement is refracted through initiatives taken in the artist's lifetime, through survivors' acting as links to posterity, through networks that bring his or her work into the museums and archives, and through the artist's availability as a symbolic focus for a variety of sentiments that may have nothing to do directly with art. Peculiar to etching as a form of printmaking is that the much-admired images, unlike those of painters, exist in multiples that are neither copies nor fakes. Each impression is a unique original, different in at least some minor way from all other prints yielded by the same plate. For the *amateur d'estampes*, on whom the marketability of etchings and the reputations of their creators ultimately depend, the mystique of the print lies in the opportunity to hold in one's hand a true original that gives a sense of communication with the artist, and across time. In this precise sense, the persona of the artist as well as the work itself comes to be etched in memory.

Lori Ducharme and Gary Alan Fine (contemp).

American sociologists. Through a series of connected papers, many collected in his book *Difficult Reputations*, Gary Fine has elaborated a program of research on reputations, good and bad. Here Fine and his coauthor highlight the _polarization effect,_ in which, similar to how successful figures are heroized, failures and rogues are demonized and denied their personhood. This view is similar to **Halbwachs**'s observation that collective memory often whittles the past down to _"imagos;"_ it can also be associated with _"labeling theory"_ in the study of deviant behavior, which highlights the process whereby individuals who participate in "deviant" behaviors are labeled deviant and, as a result, take on deviant identities.

From "The Construction of Nonpersonhood and Demonization: Commemorating the 'Traitorous' Reputation of Benedict Arnold"

To uncover the values for which a society stands, one need only look at its heroes, and at the mechanisms through which those heroes are commemorated and celebrated. . . . The memory of heroic identities and events reveals the ideals upon which social solidarity rests. Celebration of the remembered past enhances collective commitment to those ideals. Communities benefit from the endurance of heroic events in the collective representations found within individual memory. . . . But might not a society's villains reveal as much about its values as its heroes? Might not the creation and preservation of negative images benefit the community as well?

✳ The notion that the commemoration of negative events and identities may be beneficial to a community seems, at least on the surface, to go against commonsense notions of what is valuable and worth preserving. Durkheim . . . argues that the celebration of *positive* memories reaffirms the collective conscience. But elsewhere Durkheim . . . notes the functional consequences of deviance for the affirmation of social solidarity, and here he provides a clue to the benefits of commemorating negative events. Particularly in societies characterized by mechanical solidarity, the public reaction to deviance provides an outlet for collective moral outrage, and dramatically publicizes social rules of acceptable behavior. . . . In this sense, the public response to negative images defined as deviant behavior can also fulfill society's need for integration by defining boundaries. . . . If heroic figures represent the power of the morally sacred, villains reflect the danger of the profane. By warning against deviant acts, creating folk devils, and drawing boundaries, society reaffirms normative behavior and communal integration.

Communities solidify the reputations of their villains in collective memory through dramatic public reactions to activities that offend shared values. The public response often is expressed through a process akin to an extended degradation ceremony . . . in which the identity of the offender is transformed into that of a deviant and outcast, and becomes defined as evil. Largely irreversible, successful status degradation processes relegate the offenders, and their reputations, to the area outside society's moral boundaries. Although tarnished reputations may shed some of their stigma over time when the moral terrain of society changes . . . it is difficult, if not impossible, for them to shed the deviant label altogether. In the language of social control, such ceremonies dramatize "where the line is drawn" between deviance and acceptability. . . . The perpetuation of evil in collective memory exemplifies the mechanisms by which a society regulates the flow of human traffic across its moral boundaries. . . .

But historical reputations are as much *products* of shifting moral boundaries as they are illustrative of them. . . . Particularly under conditions of mechanical solidarity, the presence of external threats to social organization influences the tightening or loosening of moral boundaries, and, as a result, the rejection or toleration of deviance. . . . Under threat from outside, societies often increase their rejection of internal deviance. Collective reactions against deviance ultimately foster increased social solidarity. . . . Thus, the punishment of deviance may not be strictly a factor of the inherent negative qualities of the act; punishment may itself depend on externally provoked shifts in the society's moral boundaries.

Negative events and identities yield increased integration for society only to the extent that they are preserved in collective memory. It is insufficient to suggest that such memories are constructed simply because they have a particular effect or result. Just how is this construction accomplished? We contend that historical reputations (particularly negative reputations) result from two basic processes: (1) the reconstruction of biography, through selective emphasis on historical events . . . and (2) the evaluation of motives, that is, the process by which accounts are presented, challenged, honored, ascribed and assessed. . . .

Evil is potentially a difficult construct in a society given to tolerance and moral relativism. Yet, on some occasions, evil is robust and consensually agreed upon, as in the memorialization of the Nazi leaders associated with the Holocaust. On other occasions, evil can be contested, as the memories of Watergate . . . or the Alger Hiss trial attest. In still other cases, there are figures (e.g., traitors) or events (e.g., the Vietnam conflict) whose remembrance combines both positive and negative characteristics. On these occasions, society faces a challenge, for any commemoration must adequately address both the object's virtue and its depravity. When heroism and glory cannot be ignored, they may be discounted, such that these characteristics seem accidental or irrelevant. Or these same characteristics may be used to magnify the evil also found in the event, as when heroism and treason are juxtaposed to show the extent of an individual's fall from grace. In such instances, society segments or splits the image of the actor or event, thereby permitting the simultaneous preservation of positive and negative characteristics.

On the one hand, the identities of heroic individuals may be commemorated, while the greater purpose of their actions is suppressed or redefined.

Such has been the case with the formal commemoration of the Vietnam conflict in the Vietnam Veterans Memorial, where the identities and heroic sacrifices of fallen soldiers are remembered, but the broader political context of their actions (on which American society lacks moral consensus) is quietly ignored. . . . On the other hand, a virtuous act may be recalled, but the villainous actor is ignored as the animator of the deed. In memorialization, the actor is transformed into a nonperson.

While similarities exist among all forms of commemoration, differences occur in the specific processes by which heroic acts and villainy are remembared. We examine two related processes, which we term demonization and the transformation into nonpersonhood. Demonization refers to a process in which ambiguities of moral character are erased, so that the commemorated figure is seen as fully, intensely, and quintessentially evil. While heroes may have their virtues magnified and their flaws overlooked, the transformation of a sinner into a demon, and the erasure of all personal virtue, may be a more significant transformation. Thus in commemorating villains, demonization works in conjunction with a process of disidentification. The process is especially visible in the case of a prominent figure who has had a seemingly virtuous career prior to his or her villainy, where the moral heroic aspect of the self must be discarded.

Unlike heroes, most villains are known for a single highly condemned act. When these actors are persons of some prominence, they will likely also possess some virtuous characteristics or have to their credit numerous meritorious or otherwise seemingly contradictory acts that historians and the public must confront in the process of commemoration. The construction of villainous reputations depends upon society's ability to negate positive actions and characteristics and to see only those deeds and qualities that confirm the malefactor's transformed identity. In this transformation, the self is essentialized, so all that remains from the public's perspective is the evil core. "Nonpersonhood" describes, not the erasure of the whole person, but the denial of the virtuous aspects of self in the villain's commemoration . . .

The construction of negative identities is both similar to and different from the creation of heroic figures. In both cases, the establishment of character and total identities extends beyond bounds of time and place. The creation of historical reputation is not a discrete event, but a continuous, enduring, and potentially contested process; it is a means of perpetual labeling, transforming a person into an object, a moral identity. Since evaluation continues over time, with repeated ascription of motives and honoring (and dishonoring) of accounts, a pivotal identity persists as a historical reputation. Commemoration is the mechanism by which historical events are processed and contradictions are resolved.

However, the commemorative process for malefactors is not identical to that for heroic figures. A collective memory cannot permit a highly differentiated view of events and persons; complexity must be reduced for collective meaning. While the faults of heroes can be explained away as proof of their "humanity," virtuous elements in the biographies of villains cannot be so neatly explained. Such actors must be made totally evil, and all hints of virtue must be excised. The portrayal of the actor must be tightly controlled; much of the villain's identity must be treated as nonexistent to emphasize the demonic activity. Thus demonization and the construction of nonpersonhood provide the basis for collective remembrance of evildoers. . . .

Yet there is an intellectual danger in romanticizing and magnifying evil; it can be made to appear larger than life. The "evil" acts of those who have been labeled villains may have been routinized, logical, and "banal". . . . Acts that would seem incredibly wicked in retrospect may have been conducted to achieve socially legitimated goals; selling military secrets to achieve a comfortable lifestyle is one such example.

Societal reaction to deviance may foster cohesion, but the strength of social control inherent in the reaction is weakened to the extent that society values behavioral freedom and upholds a zone of privacy. Evil is deviance made concrete, permanent, and absolute. It provides a social system with an outer, nonporous boundary. Societies will have many deviants who may function as reminders to behave properly, but they need only a few villains to provoke deeper emotions and stronger responses and to teach moral lessons where there might not otherwise be much consensus on values. In this regard, villains are granted a measure of celebrity; villainy suggests that one's actions have been sufficiently dramatic as to be publicly notable and the basis for collective memory.

Wulf Kansteiner (contemp.)

German-American historian. A sympathetic but tough critic of social memory studies, Kansteiner here makes the important point that the field too readily asserts an identity between individual and collective memory processes. Individual and collective memory dynamics are distinct and require distinct analytical frameworks. Perhaps most important, Kansteiner applies this critique to the associated extension from psychological to cultural trauma. See also **Alexander**.

From "Finding Meaning in Memory: A Methodological Critique of Collective Memory Studies"

The impressive unanimity among psychological, sociological, historical, and artistic perspectives on human memory seems to confirm Halbwachs, who had already argued in 1925 that "the idea of an individual memory, absolutely separate from social memory, is an abstraction almost devoid of meaning." But the fact that individual memory cannot be conceptualized and studied without recourse to its social context does not necessarily imply the reverse, that is, that collective memory can only be imagined and accessed through its manifestation in individuals. At the very least, we have to differentiate between different types of "social" memory, autobiographical memory on the one hand and collective memory on the other. For lack of such differentiation, many inquiries into collective memories commit a tempting yet potentially grave methodological error: they perceive and conceptualize collective memory exclusively in terms of the psychological and emotional dynamics of individual remembering.

Since the threshold between the individual and the collective is often crossed without any adjustments in method, collectives are said to remember, to forget, and to repress the past; but this is done without any awareness that such language is at best metaphorical and at worst misleading about the phenomenon under study. Historians rationalize this conflation and sidestep the theoretical and methodological challenge of thinking in terms of collectives as distinct from individuals by emphasizing the role of human agency in the construction of collective memories. They focus on acts of memorialization, for instance in museum design, assuming the realized object and its meaning is prescribed by its maker's conscious or unconscious objectives.

These category mistakes stem from a subtle but decisive confusion of the difference between "collected memory" and "collective memory." A collected memory is an aggregate of individual memories which behaves and develops just like its individual composites, and which can therefore be studied with the whole inventory of neurological, psychological, and psychoanalytical methods and insights concerning the memories of individuals. Unfortunately, collective memories do not behave according to such rules, but have their own dynamics for which we have to find appropriate methods of analysis.

For instance, it might make sense to argue with Freud that an individual's failure to work through his or her past results in unwanted symptoms of psychological unhealth, that the self relies on a sense of continuity that makes it impossible to repress the past without having to pay a psychological price for this repression. But on a collective scale, especially on the scale of larger collectives, such assumptions are misleading. Nations *can* repress with psychological impunity; their collective memories can be changed without a "return of the repressed." Therefore, "when speaking of social forgetting, we are best advised to keep psychological or psychoanalytical categories at bay and to focus, rather, on the social, political, and cultural factors at work" [Iwona Irwin-Zarecka].

Reservations about the use of psychoanalytical methods in collective memory studies extend to the concept of trauma, which has particular relevance for our understanding of the legacy of collective catastrophes. However, unlike the concepts of the unconscious and repression that inappropriately individualize and psychologize collective memory processes, the use of the concept of trauma has had an opposite yet equally misleading effect. Some recent works in trauma theory invoke the example of the Holocaust as illustration of a more general postmodern claim about the undecidability of the nature of our historical experience and our representations of it. The very specific and unusual experiences and memory challenges of survivors—who find that their memories of the "Final Solution" form a volatile, independent realm of memory that remains painfully irreconcilable with subsequent experiences—are offered as proof of the general traumatic characteristics of the postmodern condition. In this vein Cathy Caruth has argued with regard to the Holocaust that such "a crisis of truth extends beyond the question of individual cure and asks how we in this era can have access to our own historical experience, to a history that is in its immediacy a crisis to whose truth there is no simple access." Not surprisingly, such obliteration of historical specificity has met with determined criticism, even from theorists who are very sympathetic to the use of psychoanalytical methods in memory studies. Dominick LaCapra, who has systematically and extensively worked on trauma and memory, has pointed out that "there is a great temptation to trope away from specificity and to generalize hyperbolically, for example, through an extremely abstract mode of discourse that may at times serve as a surrogate for a certain form of deconstruction, elaborate an undifferentiated notion of all history (or at least all modernity) as trauma, and overextend the concept of victim and survivor."

I would go even further in my criticism to suggest that though specific visions of the past might originate in traumatic experiences they do not retain that quality if they become successful collective memories. The concept of trauma, as well as the concept of repression, neither captures nor illuminates the forces that contribute to the making and unmaking of collective memories. Even in cases of so-called delayed collective memory (as in the case of the Holocaust or Vietnam), the delayed onset of public debates about the meaning of negative pasts has more to do with political interest and opportunities than the persistence of trauma or with any "leakage" in the collective unconscious.

Small groups whose members have directly experienced such traumatic events (veterans' or survivors' groups) only have a chance to shape the national memory if they command the means to express their visions, and if their vision meets with compatible social or political objectives and inclinations among other important social groups, for instance, political elites or parties. Past events can only be recalled in a collective setting "if they fit within a framework of contemporary interests" [Nancy Wood].

Still, although collective memories have no organic basis and do not exist in any literal sense, and though they involve individual agency, the term "collective memory" is not simply a metaphorical expression. Collective memories originate from shared communications about the meaning of the past that are anchored in the life-worlds of individuals who partake in the communal life of the respective collective. As such, collective memories are based in a society and its inventory of signs and symbols: "[M]emory seems to reside not in perceiving consciousness but *in the material*: in the practices and institutions of social or psychic life, which function within us, but, strangely, do not seem to require either our participation or our explicit allegiance" [Richard Terdiman]. Such collective memories exist on the level of families, professions, political generations, ethnic and regional groups, social classes, and nations. These examples indicate that we are always part of several mnemonic communities, and that collective remembering can be explored on very different scales; it takes place in very private settings as well as in the public sphere. On one side of the spectrum we might pursue collective memories of small groups such as families whose members weave a common vision of the family's origin and identity. On the other side, we are beginning to consider supranational collective memories as in the case of the (still dubious) entity, a European collective memory. On any level, however, "[c]ollective memory works by subsuming individual experiences under cultural schemes that make them comprehensible and, therefore, meaningful" [Barry Schwartz].

Methodologically speaking, memories are at their most collective when they transcend the time and space of the events' original occurrence. As such, they take on a powerful life of their own, "unencumbered" by actual individual memory, and become the basis of all collective remembering as disembodied, omnipresent, low-intensity memory. This point has been reached, for instance, with regard to the memory of the Holocaust in American society. As a result, millions of people share a limited range of stories and images about the Holocaust although few of them have any personal link to the actual events. For many consumers the stories and images do not constitute particularly intense or overpowering experiences, but they nevertheless shape people's identities and worldviews.

Concern with low-intensity collective memories shifts the focus from the politics of memory and its excess of scandal and intrigue to rituals and representations of the past that are produced and consumed routinely without causing much disagreement. Most groups settle temporarily on such collective memories and reproduce them for years and decades until they are questioned and perhaps overturned, often in the wake of generational turn-over. These repetitive representations form the backbone of collective memories. They represent the common denominator in questions of historical taste that are widely and frequently-enough disseminated to create and maintain group identities.

The study of memory routines can certainly profit from psychological models that help explain their reproduction. However, in this context the work of Bergson might prove a better point of departure than the insights of Freud, especially Bergson's concept of "habit memory;" his understanding of "the physical being as incarnation of all the possibilities of acting out the past in the present" seems to be well-suited to bridge the methodological gap between individual and collective memory. The concept has, for instance, significantly improved our understanding of rituals of commemoration as collective memory processes.

Ron Eyerman (contemp.)

American sociologist. In his book on slavery and the formation of African-American identity, Ron Eyerman elaborates multiple paths whereby past traumas are transmitted— and persist as ongoing traumas—generations after the initial traumatic events. Here Eyerman offers a concise description of the "cultural trauma" concept that he has developed with colleagues Jeffrey Alexander, Neil Smelser, Piotr Sztompka, and Bernhard Giesen. For a critical view of the concept in general, see **Kansteiner**.

From "The Past in the Present: Culture and the Transmission of Memory"

Like memory, the notion of trauma, or deeply felt emotional response to some occurrence, has both individual and collective connotation. Alexander . . . speaks of a cultural trauma:

> . . . when members of a collective feel they have been subjected to a horrendous event that leaves indelible marks upon their group consciousness, marking their memories forever, and changing their future identity in fundamental and irrevocable ways.

Most often trauma is conceptualized on the individual level through psychological and psychoanalytical frameworks. . . . We sought a more cultural notion that would help us account for the emergence of new collective identities in times of social crisis, so deep as to undermine established identities. The aim was modest, not to construct a general theory, but one restricted to the emergence of collective identities in times of crisis.

As opposed to psychological or physical trauma which involves a wound and the experience of great emotional anguish by an individual, cultural trauma refers to a dramatic loss of identity and meaning, a tear in the social fabric, affecting a group of people who have achieved some degree of cohesion. In this sense, the trauma need not necessarily be felt by everyone in a group or have been directly experienced by any or all. While it may be necessary to establish some event or occurrence as the significant "cause," its traumatic meaning must be established and accepted, a process which requires time, as well as mediation and representation. A cultural trauma must be understood, explained and made coherent through public reflection and discourse. Here, in modern societies, mass-mediated representations play a decisive role. Alexander . . . calls this process "a meaning struggle" and "a trauma process," and we sometimes called it a "trauma drama," when, with the help of mass mediation, collective representation, the collective experience of massive disruption and social crisis becomes a crisis of meaning and identity. Let me offer the more formal definition of cultural trauma provided by Neil Smelser: . . .

A memory accepted and publicly given credence by a relevant membership group and evoking an event or situation which is (a) laden with negative affect, (b) represented as indelible, and (c) regarded as threatening a society's [or group's] existence or violating one or more of its fundamental cultural presuppositions.

The point here is that collective identity formation, which is intimately linked with collective memory, may be grounded in loss and crisis, as well as in triumph. In fact, one way of dealing with loss is by attempting to turn tragedy into triumph, something which is one of the common themes or processes in our collaborative studies of cultural trauma. . . . This process may take time, especially if the group in question is in a marginal or subordinate position, as is the case with American blacks. . . .

As already mentioned, sociologists seldom speak about memory, except perhaps disparagingly as nostalgia. Modernity is characterized by the "tradition of the new," by future, rather than past, orientation. Central to modernity and to one classical sociological narrative is not only the idea of progress, but also that of freeing individual and society from the shackles of the past. As Marx put it with respect to the events of 1848, the burden of the past weighs heavily on the present. Memory is usually left to psychologists and biologists and now to the newly developed cognitive science. But memory in the form of history and tradition is central to what we mean by society and to all social interaction, which was exactly the point Marx wished to make. Memory provides individuals and collectives with a cognitive map, helping orient who they are, why they are here and where they are going. Memory in other words is central to individual and collective identity. . . .

From this perspective, the past is a collectively shaped, if not collectively experienced, temporal reference point, which is formative of a collective and which serves to orient those individuals within it. The past becomes present through symbolic interactions, through narrative and discourse, with memory itself being a product of both, "called upon to legitimate identity, to construct and reconstruct it." . . . While the "past" may be embodied in material objects, in the way a town or city is structured, or the arrangements in a museum which are laid out to recall aspects of the "past" in a particular way, what the past means is recounted, understood and interpreted and transmitted through language and through dialogue. These dialogues are framed as stories, narratives which structure their telling and influence their reception. All nations and groups have founding myths, stories which tell who we are through recounting where we came from. Such narratives form "master frames" and are passed on through traditions, in rituals and ceremonies, public performances which reconnect a group, and where membership is confirmed. Within this process, "we" are remembered and "they" are excluded.

These founding narratives can be compared to discourse in the sense of Foucault, especially as developed in *The Archaeology of Knowledge*. . . . Where Foucault's discourses, at least as developed in this work, impose order from above and outside through disciplinary knowledge, narratives are less institutionalized, more open and malleable. Discourses offer what Stuart Hall and others in the Birmingham School called the "preferred readings" of texts, in that they structure possible telling and impose interpretation: producing the object of which they speak, thus linking discourse with established power and thus with ideology. Discourses, in this sense, unify, and legitimate a diverse set of practices, "establishing" a "system of relations". . . . Even in literary fields or in popular culture, discourses can be silently at work in terms of selectivity, sorting out those authors/texts that express the ideologies and values of the dominant culture. It is these that are more likely to get published, to be read and talked about.

Both narrative and discourse have in common that they are framing structures which include and exclude, voice and silence, conditioning what can be seen and said and by whom. As opposed to Foucaultian discourse, however, collective narratives leave more room for individual agency even as they provide the framework through which individual stories gain wider meaning. While discourses are exercises in power and empower those rightly positioned, narratives can provide means for a "counter-story" for a minority or an oppressed group, in which some of the central concepts of a dominating discourse can be appropriated and given new meaning. An example is the concept of "race," which was appropriated and revalued by American blacks in their struggle to redefine their standing in society. Even here, however, those more powerful 'representatives' of a marginalized group can exert a discursive influence in seeking to define how their groups should be represented.

In many instances founding narratives involve a dramatic, traumatic, occurrence from which the collective is said to emerge. In this, such narratives might be compared to myths, but they lack the all-embracing and ontological scope with which myth is usually associated. This "primal scene" is usually given positive connotation, but it can also be negative. In all cases, however, it is powerful in the sense of being emotionally compelling. Founding narratives are about creating, constituting, a collective subject as much as they are about creating an "imagined community". . . .

Cultural trauma calls attention to the negotiated recollection of events and to the role of representation. There is power involved here as well, the power of political elites, for example, of mass media in selecting what will be represented, thus affecting what will be forgotten as well as remembered. In the case of extremely powerful occurrences, like civil wars, there may be additional factors at work. Interpreting events may take time and distance. Where there are winners and losers, the losers may never get their side told, or they may have to wait, sometimes even generations.

Jeffrey Alexander (contemp.)

American sociologist. In contrast to accounts that see trauma as a "natural" category inhering in events, Alexander offers a general theory of cultural trauma as an ascription of meaning to events. He also outlines a sociological theory of the factors affecting that ascription, most importantly "carrier groups" and their role in creating a compelling framework for classifying the event and its participants.

From "Toward a Cultural Theory of Trauma"

Cultural trauma occurs when members of a collectivity feel they have been subjected to a horrendous event that leaves indelible marks upon their group consciousness, marking their memories forever and changing their future identity in fundamental and irrevocable ways. . . .

It is by constructing cultural traumas that social groups, national societies, and sometimes even entire civilizations not only cognitively identify the existence and source of human suffering but "take on board" some significant responsibility for it. Insofar as they identify the cause of trauma, and thereby assume such moral responsibility, members of collectivities define their solidary relationships in ways that, in principle, allow them to share the sufferings of others. Is the suffering of others also our own? In thinking that it might in fact be, societies expand the circle of the we. By the same token, social groups can, and often do, refuse to recognize the existence of others' trauma, and because of their failure they cannot achieve a moral stance. By denying the reality of others' suffering, people not only diffuse their own responsibility for the suffering but often project the responsibility for their own suffering on these others. In other words, by refusing to participate in what I will describe as the process of trauma creation, social groups restrict solidarity, leaving others to suffer alone.

Throughout the twentieth century, first in Western societies and then, soon after, throughout the rest of the world, people have spoken continually about being traumatized by an experience, by an event, by an act of violence or harassment, or even, simply, by an abrupt and unexpected, and sometimes not even particularly malevolent, experience of social transformation and change. People also have continually employed the language of trauma to explain what happens, not only to themselves, but to the collectivities to which they belong as well. We often speak of an organization being traumatized when a leader departs or dies, when a governing regime falls, when an organization suffers an unexpected reversal of fortune. Actors describe themselves as traumatized when the environment of an individual or a collectivity suddenly shifts in an unforeseen and unwelcome manner.

We know from ordinary language, in other words, that we are onto something widely experienced and intuitively understood. . . .

The trick is to gain reflexivity, to move from the sense of something commonly experienced to the sense of strangeness that allows us to think sociologically. For trauma is not something naturally existing; it is something constructed by society. . . . (thinking of victim narratives)

[W]e maintain that events do not, in and of themselves, create collective trauma. Events are not inherently traumatic. Trauma is a socially mediated attribution. The attribution may be made in real time, as an event unfolds; it may also be made before the event occurs, as an adumbration, or after the event has concluded, as a post-hoc reconstruction. Sometimes, in fact, events that are deeply traumatizing may not actually have occurred at all; such imagined events, however, can be as traumatizing as events that have actually occurred. . . .

Traumatic status is attributed to real or imagined phenomena, not because of their actual harmfulness or their objective abruptness, but because these phenomena are believed to have abruptly, and harmfully, affected collective identity. Individual security is anchored in structures of emotional and cultural expectations that provide a sense of security and capability. These expectations and capabilities, in turn, are rooted in the sturdiness of the collectivities of which individuals are a part. At issue is not the stability of a collectivity in the material or behavioral sense, although this certainly plays a part. What is at stake, rather, is the collectivity's identity, its stability in terms of meaning, not action.

Identity involves a cultural reference. Only if the patterned meanings of the collectivity are abruptly dislodged is traumatic status attributed to an event. It is the meanings that provide the sense of shock and fear, not the events in themselves. Whether or not the structures of meaning are destabilized and shocked is not the result of an event but the effect of a sociocultural process. It is the result of an exercise of human agency, of the successful imposition of a new system of cultural classification. This cultural process is deeply affected by power structures and by the contingent skills of reflexive social agents. . . .

At the level of the social system, societies can experience massive disruptions that do not become traumatic. . . . For traumas to emerge at the level of the collectivity, social crises must become cultural crises. Events are one thing, representations of these events quite another. Trauma is not the result of a group experiencing pain. It is the result of this acute discomfort entering into the core of the collectivity's sense of its own identity. Collective actors "decide" to represent social pain as a fundamental threat to their sense of who they are, where they came from, and where they want to go. . . .

Carrier groups are the collective agents of the trauma process. Carrier groups have both ideal and material interests, they are situated in particular places in the social structure, and they have particular discursive talents for articulating their claims—for what might be called "meaning making"—in the public sphere. Carrier groups may be elites, but they may also be denigrated and marginalized classes. They may be prestigious religious leaders or groups whom the majority has designated as spiritual pariahs. A carrier group can be

generational, representing the perspectives and interests of a younger generation against an older one. It can be national, pitting one's own nation against a
putative enemy. It can be institutional, representing one particular social sector
or organization against others in a fragmented and polarized social order. . . .

Representation of trauma depends on constructing a compelling framework
of cultural classification. In one sense, this is simply telling a new story. Yet this
storytelling is, at the same time, a complex and multivalent symbolic process
that is contingent, highly contested, and sometimes highly polarizing. For the
wider audience to become persuaded that they, too, have become traumatized
by an experience or an event, the carrier group needs to engage in successful
meaning work. . . .

"Experiencing trauma" can be understood as a sociological process that
defines a painful injury to the collectivity, establishes the victim, attributes
responsibility, and distributes the ideal and material consequences. Insofar as
traumas are so experienced, and thus imagined and represented, the collective
identity will become significantly revised. This identity revision means that
there will be a searching re-remembering of the collective past, for memory is
not only social and fluid but deeply connected to the contemporary sense of the
self. Identities are continuously constructed and secured not only by facing the
present and future but also by reconstructing the collectivity's earlier life.

Once the collective identity has been so reconstructed, there will eventually
emerge a period of "calming down." The spiral of signification flattens out,
affect and emotion become less inflamed, preoccupation with sacrality and
pollution fades. Charisma becomes routinized, effervescence evaporates, and
liminality gives way to reaggregation. As the heightened and powerfully
affecting discourse of trauma disappears, the "lessons" of the trauma become
objectified in monuments, museums, and collections of historical artifacts.
The new collective identity will be rooted in sacred places and structured in
ritual routines. . . .

In this routinization process, the trauma process, once so vivid, can become
subject to the technical, sometimes desiccating attention of specialists who
detach affect from meaning. This triumph of the mundane is often noted with
regret by audiences that had been mobilized by the trauma process, and it is
sometimes forcefully opposed by carrier groups. Often, however, it is welcomed
with a sense of public and private relief. Intended to remember and commemorate the trauma process, efforts to institutionalize the lessons of the trauma
will eventually prove unable to evoke the strong emotions, the sentiments of
betrayal, and the affirmations of sacrality that once were so powerfully associated with it. No longer deeply preoccupying, the reconstructed collective identity remains, nevertheless, a fundamental resource for resolving future social
problems and disturbances of collective consciousness.

The inevitability of such routinization processes by no means neutralizes
the extraordinary social significance of cultural traumas. Their creation and
routinization have, to the contrary, the most profound normative implications for the conduct of social life. By allowing members of wider publics to

participate in the pain of others, cultural traumas broaden the realm of social understanding and sympathy, and they provide powerful avenues for new forms of social incorporation. . . .

[F]ailures to recognize collective traumas, much less to incorporate their lessons into collective identity, do not result from the intrinsic nature of the original suffering. This is the naturalistic fallacy that follows from lay trauma theory. The failure stems, rather, from an inability to carry through what I have called here the *trauma process*.

[F]or both social structural and culture reasons, carrier groups have not emerged with the resources, authority, or interpretive competence to powerfully disseminate these trauma claims. Sufficiently persuasive narratives have not been created, or they have not been successfully broadcast to wider audiences. Because of these failures, the perpetrators of these collective sufferings have not been compelled to accept moral responsibility, and the lessons of these social traumas have been neither memorialized nor ritualized. New definitions of moral responsibility have not been generated. Social solidarities have not been extended. More primordial and more particularistic collective identities have not been changed.

PART IV

Media and Modes of Transmission

Conventional images of memory portray it as a kind of storage and retrieval. But memory is more a crucible of meaning than a vessel of truth. As such, many contemporary social memory scholars have highlighted both the role of memory as a medium of identity and the role of various technological media in the transmission of memory. In this part, we present a number of different perspectives on the material and technological substrata of individual and social memory as well as works on the various material forms in and through which the past can be represented and transmitted to the present. Recognition of the media of memory is especially important because social memory studies begins from the premise that there is an important interaction between brains and cultures and that brains are not the only or even the most important technologies of memory.

We begin with a cluster of works addressing the long-term shifts in technologies and meanings of memory, including those of André Leroi-Gourhan, Jack Goody, and Merlin Donald, all of whom in their ways limn the outlines of a media history for memory (among other important works, one might also have included here those of Walter Ong and Eric Havelock, to say nothing of Mircea Eliade's). Many writers have referred to a so-called orality-literacy problem in anthropology—the ways in which the move from oral cultures to literate ones has been associated with a shift from circular to linear temporalities. This group of excerpts, followed directly by Aleida Assmann's important discussion of canon and archive as modes of transmission, provides keen insights into the orality-literacy divide and related issues from the perspective of memory studies. We also include here the seminal work of Paul Connerton, who addresses the neglected corporeal dimension of memory, the quite literal embodiment of attitudes toward and about the past.

As many writers, including Halbwachs, Freud, and Mannheim, have noted, one of the principle loci for the transmission of memory is intergenerational storytelling, particularly in families. The sociological concept of generations, as most famously elaborated by Mannheim in the excerpt we included in part I, is a rich and complex one indeed and has contributed to important work in social memory studies (e.g., that of the sociologist Howard Schuman and colleagues [Schuman and Scott 1989; Schuman and Corning 2000], who have empirically redeemed Mannheim's insights that momentous historical events can be formative of generations and that events experienced at a formative age are remembered as more momentous than events experienced later). In different readings presented here—namely those of Harald Welzer and Marianne Hirsch—we gain insight into other dimensions of intergenerational transmission of memory. Welzer highlights the blind spots in the reception of such memories, while Hirsch directs our attention to the complex aftereffects of vital experiences beyond the first generation, a process she calls "postmemory."

In these ways, generations and families are media of memory. More conventionally, of course, the term "media" implies the mass media, such as journalism and television. Excerpts from the work of John Thompson, Barbie Zelizer, Daniel Dayan and Elihu Katz, and George Lipsitz outline the role of the mass media and popular culture in shaping collective memory, as well as the ways in which changes in mass media are connected to changes in memory. "Mass media," of course, does not exhaust the meaning of media, which also implies the wide variety of other forms in which images of the past are embodied and through which they are transmitted. In an extension of this thread, we include here an excerpt from the work of Danièle Hervieu-Léger on religion as a chain of memory, though this perhaps lies beyond a tight definition of media and modes of transmission. Works by Reinhart Koselleck and James Young examine the shapes and roles of monuments and memorials in the context of changing political and cultural sensibilities about war and atrocity from the French Revolution to the twentieth century. Commemoration is also the center of Vered Vinitzky-Seroussi's excerpt, in which she highlights the fragmented nature of commemorative activities in a time of difficult pasts. M. Christine Boyer's excerpt explores the mnemonic dimensions that are contained in urban contexts. In a piece that could be connected not only to Aleida Assmann's work on canon and archive but also to the excerpts on artistic reputation included in part III, a short piece by Harald Weinrich from his book *The Art of Forgetting* addresses science as a medium of memory as well. Finally, Robin Wagner-Pacifici takes the broadest meaning of mediation when she characterizes memory itself as a medium, namely of our existence in time.

REFERENCES

Eliade, Mircea. *The Myth of the Eternal Return: Cosmos and History.* Trans. Willard R. Trask. Princeton: Princeton University Press, 1971.
Havelock, Eric A. *The Muse Learns to Write: Reflections on Orality and Literacy from Antiquity to the Present.* New Haven: Yale University Press, 1988.

Ong, Walter. *The Presence of the Word*. New Haven: Yale University Press, 1967.

Schuman, Howard, and Jacqueline Scott. "Generations and Collective Memories." *American Sociological Review* 54 (1989): 359–81.

Schuman, Howard, and Amy D. Corning. "Collective Knowledge of Public Events: The Soviet Era from the Great Purge to Glasnost." *American Journal of Sociology* 105 (2000): 913–56.

André Leroi-Gourhan (1911–1986)

French archaeologist, paleontologist, and anthropologist. From the sweeping viewpoint of paleo-archaeology, Leroi-Gourhan here constructs a megahistorical account of the impact of changing basic technologies on memory. His five-stage account of the history of mnemonic technologies has been quite influential for later theorists like Jacques LeGoff and can be compared to those of **Goody** and **Donald**.

From *Gesture and Speech*

The history of the collective memory can be divided into five periods: that of oral transmission, that of written transmission using tables or an index, that of simple index cards, that of mechanography, and that of electronic serial transmission. . . .

A group's body of knowledge is the basic constituent of its unity and its personality. The transmission of this intellectual capital is the necessary precondition for the group's material and social survival. Transmission is effected through the same hierarchy as operating sequences.

Mechanical operating sequences are part and parcel of the common memory of families. They are performed in all material and moral episodes of daily life and are recorded in the personal memory of individuals during childhood by means of processes in which the role of language is not necessarily the most important. The same cannot be said of less frequent or exceptional practices that, in all societies without writing, are stored in the memory of specialists—elders, bards, priests, who in traditional human groups discharge the highly important function of maintaining the group's cohesion.

The recording of knowledge is connected with the development of oral literature and of figurative representation in general. . . . In the most general sense practical, technical, and scientific knowledge is rarely recorded in literature of any kind, although it normally forms part of a context in which magical and religious matters are not clearly separated from practical ones. In agricultural societies and so far as artisanal tasks are concerned, the social structuring of crafts plays an important role: This applies as much to the blacksmiths of Africa and Asia as to European corporations before the seventeenth century. The training of apprentices and the preservation of craft secrets are taken care of within each of the ethnic group's social cells. At this level, which is that of primitive peoples as well as of quite recent agricultural societies, the contents of technical memory are not systematically organized in any way. To put it more precisely, each group of operating sequences—or each sequence—forms a more or less independent whole including actions to be copied as well as oral instructions. . . .

Writing did not spring into existence by chance; after thousands of years of maturing in systems of mythographic representation, linear notation of thought emerged together with metals and slavery. . . . Nor were the initial contents of linear notation a matter of chance: They were accounts, records of debts owed to gods or to others, series of dynasties, oracular pronouncements, lists of penalties. The limited and very poorly documented nature of the earliest texts is a constant source of disappointment to the ethnologist: How much more we would know if the Sumerians had left us some cookery recipes, hints on etiquette or woodworking, or metalworking manuals! But in point of fact it is unimaginable that writing should have been invented for such purposes, traditionally consigned to oral memory. The first concern of evolution is with the new, and in order to be felt as "new," early metallurgy itself would have had to fall completely outside the scope of existing mechanical practices. It would have had to be an exceptional operation unconnected with any established gestural sequence, which a manufacturing technique clearly could not be. Or else writing would have had to mature without an object for centuries in order to acquire the means of recording what had only recently become suitable material for notation, as unlikely a hypothesis as the earlier one. The collective memory would not have broken out of its traditional cycle at the birth of writing except in order to deal with matters that in a nascent social system were felt to be of an exceptional kind. Therefore it is not by chance that what was written down was not what is made or experienced in the normal course of events bur what constitutes the very bones of an urbanized society where the nodal point of the autonomic system is the interchange between producers—be they celestial or human—and rulers. Innovation was concerned with the upper end of the system and selectively encompassed financial and religious acts, dedications, genealogies, the calendar—all those things within the new structures of the city that could not be completely consigned to memory either through gesture sequences or through products.

Only a few characteristic elements of science in its infancy were consigned to written memory. The earliest references of this order, whether in Mesopotamia, Egypt, China, or Precolumbian America, relate to the calendar and to distances. Primitive peoples before the settlement of agriculture did not lack knowledge about time and space, but both of these took on a new meaning from the moment when the capital city became the pivot of the celestial world and of humanized space.

As the instrument for storing words and phrases in the memory of generations became more efficient, the keeping of records developed and spread to deeper strata of knowledge. But even in classical antiquity, the sum total of facts that could be transmitted to future generations was limited by the hierarchy of social values to certain well-defined areas: religious, historical, and geographical texts, together with philosophy, accounted for the main bulk of written material. In other words, the basic theme was the connection between the divine and the human, and within that framework the material to be committed to memory concerned the threefold problem of time, space, and the human being. Agriculture cropped up in poems whose main subjects were the seasons, and architecture in descriptions where cosmic space was identified with palaces and temples. Mathematics and music, emerging at the same time as medicine, were the first scientific subjects in the full sense of the word, but they too were haloed with magic and religion.

Until the invention of printing, in the West as in China, the distinction between oral and written transmission is difficult to draw. The main body of knowledge was buried in oral practices and in techniques. Only the uppermost part of knowledge, its framework unchanged since antiquity, was set down in writing, to be learned by heart. During the centuries that lay between Homer or Yu the Great and the first western or oriental printed manuscripts, the concept of reference developed together with the growing mass of recorded facts. But each piece of writing was a compact sequence, rhythmically broken up by seals and marginal notes, around which the readers found their way like primitive hunters—by following a trail rather than by studying a plan. The spoken word had not yet been converted into a system of orientation tables. We saw earlier that the conversion of the two-dimensional mythogram not reducible to a phonetic phrase into a linear series of alphabetic signs represented the freeing of speech and at the same time a certain restriction of the individual's symbolizing power. With the advent of printing a further conversion, soon to become indispensable because of the abundance of texts, began to take place.

The texts set down in ancient or medieval manuscripts were intended to be committed to the reader's memory for life, at least firmly enough to enable readers to find their way around the manuscript with ease. There was also of course written material of a more mundane kind—letters and contracts, just as in the earliest days of writing but involving larger sections of the population—but these were kept in the possession of the persons concerned or of notaries, and practical problems of orientation did not arise. The same is by no means true of printed matter, which soon went beyond the range of traditional subjects. Readers not only obtained access to an enormous collective memory whose entire contents they could not possibly register but were also frequently confronted with new material. A process of exteriorization of the individual memory then began to take place. The work of finding one's way around printed material was done from outside. For centuries, dictionaries and glossaries had offered some possibilities of orientation; Chinese writing with its phoneticized mythograms, as well as the Greek and Latin scripts, had provided readers with means of orienting themselves along the traditional thread of successive ideographic or phonetic signs. But the dictionary provides only a narrow outlet for written memory, a form of knowledge that is both linearized and fragmented and therefore incompatible with the processes of sustained thought.

The eighteenth century in Europe marked the end of the ancient world in printing as well as in technology. It saw the old tradition at its richest as well as the first stirrings of the process of change still going on today. Within the space of a few decades the social memory had engulfed in books the whole of antiquity, the history of the great peoples, the geography and ethnography of a world now definitely acknowledged to be round, philosophy, law, the sciences, the arts, the study of technics, and a literature translated from twenty different languages. The ever-widening stream still flows today, but at no moment in human history did the collective memory dilate more rapidly than in the eighteenth century in Europe. This is why all possible methods of equipping readers with a preconstituted memory were already to be found at that time.

The dictionary reached its limits with the encyclopedias of every kind that were published for the use of manufacturers or artisans as well as of pure scholars. In the latter half of the eighteenth century, technical literature began to flourish. Every subject was explored, and the descriptive vocabulary still in use today began to form. The dictionary is a highly developed form of external memory in which thought is broken down into an infinity of fragments; the "Great Encyclopedia" of 1751 is a series of short manuals encased in a dictionary. The level of the art of documentation was then as high as that of mechanical animation: The automaton reached its peak when actuated by separate cams that endowed each of its organs with a fraction of memory; the encyclopedia is a fractional alphabetically arranged memory each of whose isolated mechanisms contains an animated part of the whole of memory. The relationship between Vaucansson's automaton and the French encyclopedia—its contemporary—was the same as that between today's electronic machine and integrated memory.

In sequentially arranged works the eighteenth century made use of practically every known method, in particular the medieval method of the marginal note (which still survives today) in order either to sum up a paragraph or to provide references, with the latter being more often consigned to footnotes. An alphabetic index at the end of the volume, already fairly common in the sixteenth century, became an almost standard feature.

The most interesting development from our point of view was the direct opposite of alphabetical indexing and affected the contents of the work as a whole. As early as the Middle Ages, and more or less universally from the sixteenth century onward, the margins of a book had served to provide summaries of the contents of each page or paragraph, and a brief list of contents had been supplied (without pagination) at the beginning of the volume. Little by little book presentation began to be organized in such a way as to help readers find their way around an unfamiliar volume. That is exactly the function of an external memory. The process took place along two tracks, each developing until the early twentieth century. One consisted in having each chapter preceded by a summary, the other in including a table of contents before or after the main body of the work. The former was a residue of the old attitude whereby a considerable personal memory input was expected from readers and, barring a few exceptions, has today disappeared. A summary at the head of each chapter after a list of contents at the head of the volume was a logical stage in the detailed discovery of the volume's contents, but the trend has been to turn the table of contents into something resembling a mythogram—a significant assembly of symbols in which the eye and the intelligence are not obliged to follow the rectilinear progress of the written text. To achieve this status, the table of contents has had to divest itself of all syntactic elements and now contains only freestanding words that serve as signposts for readers. In the sphere of printed matter, we have not gone any further than this point, first reached two centuries ago. As in all other spheres the spearhead of evolution has shifted; it is no longer in the book, which survives as the documentary infrastructure, but in documentary material freed from any context. . . .

By the nineteenth century the collective memory had expanded to such proportions that the individual memory could no longer be expected to store the contents of whole libraries. The need became apparent to organize the inert "thought" contained in the printed "brain" of the collective by means of an additional fabric upon which a highly simplified picture of the contents could be projected. Above all else, the constituent cells of this new fabric had to be capable of indefinite enrichment and reconstruction in a manner appropriate to every type of documentary research. The eighteenth and part of the nineteenth century had still made do with notebooks and catalogs. These methods were succeeded by the card index, which did not begin to be properly organized until the early twentieth century. In its most rudimentary form it already represents a real exteriorized cerebral cortex: A simple set of bibliographical index cards will lend itself to many adaptations in the hands of its user, becoming an author or subject index, a geographical or a chronological one with every possible permutation to meet requirements as particular as the place of publication or the dimensions of inset plates. This is still more obvious in the case of card indexes containing scientific information, where each documentary component can be rearranged at will in relation to all other components. Actually the parallel with the cerebral cortex is in some respects misleading, for if a card index is a memory in the strict sense, it is a memory lacking its own means of recollection and has to be brought into the researcher's visual and manual operating field before it can go into action. . . .

A further step forward was taken by making the card index contain several sets of cards, perhaps of different colors, so that a second network of references was added to the first basic one, or—better still—by using punched cards. Books in their "raw" state are comparable to hand tools: However sophisticated their presentation, the reader's full technical participation is still required. A simple card index already corresponds to a hand-operated machine: Some of the operations have been transformed and are now contained in potential form in the index cards, which are the only things the reader needs to activate. Punched index cards represent yet another stage, comparable to that of early automatic machines. Whether they are cards with marginal perforations that have to be activated by hand or cards of some other kind requiring mechanical or electronic sorting, the principle of the punched-card index is always the same: The data are converted by means of a binary code (positive = no perforation, negative = open perforation), and a sorting device separates the cards according to a set of questions, releasing only those that produce an affirmative response. The principle is that of the Jacquard loom, and it is curious to note that documentary material waited for more than a century to follow in the footsteps of weaving. But although the mechanism is the same, the degree to which it is exploited is entirely different. The punched strips of the weaving loom express answers, whereas each perforated index card corresponds to a possible question. A punched card index is a memory-collecting machine. It works like a brain memory of unlimited capacity that is endowed with the ability—not present in the human brain—of correlating every recollection with all others.

No progress beyond this stage has so for been made except in the matter of proportions. The electronic brain, although it employs different and more subtle processes, operates on the same principles. Theoretically devices using perforations or integrators (generally associated with the former) can compete with the brain in terms of the ability to compare. They can—on a gigantic scale and within a negligible period of time—process a mountain of data to achieve a well-defined end, and they can produce every possible answer. If provided with the data needed for an oriented choice, they can weigh those answers and enrich such preestablished weightings with judgments based on experience drawn from precedents stored in their memory. The electronic integrator's superiority over the card index is derived from the amount of data it can process within a very short period through the simultaneous action of several selection centers capable of checking and correcting their own output, whereas the most efficient cards in existence, having a data density of 20,000 per card or 10,000,000 per 500 cards, still require the operator's direct participation and considerably more time. The artificial brain of course is still in its infancy, but we can already be sure that it will be more than just a nine days' wonder with limited applications. To refuse to see that machines will soon overtake the human brain in operations involving memory and rational judgment is to be like the Pithecanthropus who would have denied the possibility of the biface, the archer who would have laughed at the mere suggestion of the crossbow, most of all like the Homeric bard who would have dismissed writing as a mnemonic trick without any future. We must get used to being less clever than the artificial brain that we have produced, just as our teeth are less strong than a millstone and our ability to fly negligible compared with that of a jet aircraft.

The tradition that holds the human brain responsible for human achievements is a very old one. The human species adjusted with equanimity to being overtaken in the use of its arms, its legs, and its eyes because it was confident of unparalleled power higher up. In the last few years the overtaking has reached the cranial box. Looking facts in the face, we may wonder what will be left of us once we have produced a better artificial version of everything we have got. We already know, or will soon know, how to construct machines capable of remembering everything and of judging the most complex

320 MEDIA AND MODES OF TRANSMISSION

situations without error. What this means is that our cerebral cortex, however admirable, is inadequate, just as our hands and eyes are inadequate; that it can be supplemented by electronic analysis methods; and that the evolution of the human being—a living fossil in the context of the present conditions of life—must eventually follow a path other than the neuronic one if it is to continue. Putting it more positively, we could say that if humans are to take the greatest possible advantage of the freedom they gained by evading the risk of organic overspecialization, they must eventually go even further in exteriorizing their faculties.

Jack Goody (contemp.)

British anthropologist. The so-called orality-literacy question is one of long standing for anthropologists (see, for instance, **Evans-Pritchard** and **Lévi-Strauss**). Here Jack Goody, one of the leading figures in this debate, traces out some implications for memory.

From "Memory in Oral and Literate Traditions"

I decided to start by discussing memory in oral cultures, which is what I call those without writing. Unlike many other scholars, I use the phrase "oral tradition" to refer to what is transmitted orally in literate cultures. The two forms of oral transmission in societies with and without writing are often conflated. . . .

Oral performance in literate societies is undoubtedly influenced to different degrees by the presence of writing and should not be identified with the products of purely oral cultures. . . .

Communication in oral cultures takes place overwhelmingly in face-to-face situations. Basically, information is stored in the memory, in the mind. Without writing there is virtually no storage of information outside the human brain and hence no distance communication over space and over time.

Plato decided that writing would ruin the memory and that oral man remembered much better than his literate counterparts. From Plato's time onwards we often hear tales of the phenomenal feats of memory in such cultures, of remembrancers who recalled the complexities of tribal histories, of bards who recited long myths or epics.

Those tales have continued to be told. In 1956, the American sociologist David Riesman claimed that members of oral cultures must have had good memories merely because nothing could be written down. That common assumption had even been made over twenty years earlier by Frederic Bartlett, author of a well-known book called *Remembering*, when he claimed that non-literate Africans had a special facility for low-level "rote representation." It is true that such societies are largely dependent on internal memory for transmitting culture, for the handing down of knowledge and customs from one generation to the next. However, they do not remember everything in a perfect form, that is, verbatim, by heart. I have known many people quite unable to give a consecutive account of the complex sequence of funeral or initiation rites. But, when the ceremonies actually start, one act leads to another until all is done; one person's recollection will help another. A sequence such as a burial also has a logic of its own. At times visual clues may jog the memory, as when an individual is finding his or her way from one place to another; as in a paperchase, one clue paints to the rest.

However, other more critical observers have found rather poor verbatim memories in oral cultures. They attribute these to a lack of the general mnemonic skills and strategies that come with literacy and schooling, because non-literates performed badly in standard psychological memory experiments.

But what are these standard tests measuring? In psychologists' terms, memory in the tests means exact, verbatim recall. . . .

I do not doubt there may be some occasions on which a member of an oral culture might find it useful to be able to recall items in this way (a list of trees for example) but from my own experience they are very few and far between. It is simply not a skill of any great value to people in oral cultures; that comes with schooling. . . .

Many experiences are placed in memory store, but we do not need to keep most of these in a precise form. Indeed in oral cultures the notion of verbatim recall is hard to grasp. . . .

All cultural knowledge in oral cultures is stored in the mind, largely because there is little alternative. When we congratulate the members of oral cultures on their good memories, on one level we are simply saying that they have no other storage option. In contrast we can pull down books from our library shelves and consult them to find the reference for a quotation we vaguely remember, or to discover the name of a bird we did not know.

What is clear is that much oral knowledge is not stored in the precise way we think of in literate cultures when we talk of memory. In fact non-literates are often in the state of having a vague recollection in their heads, but of being unable to refer to a book in the way that we do. Hence they may just have to create new knowledge or new variants to fill the gap. . . .

Visual mnemonics provide some exceptions to this dependence on internal memory. However, mnemonics serve merely to jog the internal memory; they are no substitute for it, unlike a book or a computer. These mnemonics are material objects and sometimes graphic signs that fall short of fully fledged writing because they do not record linguistic expressions per se but only loosely refer to them.

We should be quite clear about the difference between a mnemonic system in oral cultures and the kind of recall that full writing permits and encourages. At one level they may be seen as equivalent, especially to Jacques Derrida and other post-modernists who are anxious to stress the relativity of cultures, and effectively deny hierarchical or evolutionary differences. But their position neglects cultural history, since culture does have a developmental history in which changes in the mode of communication are as important as those in the mode of production. For the information stored in mnemonic systems is rarely verbatim, word for word. Mnemonic systems present you with an object or a grapheme to remind you of an event or a recitation which you then elaborate. It is true that if I recite a short tale and offer you a mnemonic, you may be able to repeat it almost exactly. But such reproduction depends upon my telling you the tale and showing you the mnemonic. No one else can read it off directly from the object. There is no precise distance communication as there is with writing, which provides a fixed, society-wide code enabling us to establish more or less perfect linguistic communication over distance in time and space with people we may have never met but who have learnt the code. . . .

It is a mistake to view the handing down of culture as the exact counterpart of genetic transmission, a kind of cultural mimesis; genetic reproduction is largely self-replicating, but human learning involves generative processes, what has been called "learning to know." Some changes in the corpus take place because of pressures from the outside, forcing or encouraging adjustment; others occur because of deliberately creative acts which have little to do with adjustments of this kind. . . .

In fact customary behaviour changes, like the dialects of a language, gradually over a large region. Dialects can change only because memory, mimesis, imitation, is imperfect; forgetting may occur but in many cases perfect reproduction is not even aimed at. That is the same with other features of human cultures. In the absence of centralized mechanisms of control which inhibit change, differences in behaviour constantly emerge in this way: there is little of the precise replication involved in verbatim memory.

Oral memory is of course simply experience reworked. Only in the light of such a notion can we explain how neighbouring oral cultures, even very small ones, display these differences; the world offers us enormous diversity even in the simplest societies. Written cultures manage more easily to establish relatively stable internal norms, and in certain areas inhibit but do not prevent diversity. It is only in literate cultures such as those of Cambridge colleges that we find people reciting the same prayer every evening of the week, whatever the weather, whatever the national events, without any thought of innovation.

In other areas as well, writing encourages diversity, hence the high degree of turnover in the artistic world and the increased speed of the accumulation of knowledge. But in some situations writing establishes a conformity, an orthodoxy, as with Religions of the Book which endure unchanged over the centuries. . . .

I do not mean to imply that in oral cultures people are incapable of exact reproduction from memory store. As we have seen, mimesis has to occur for children to be able to learn a language when there is little room for imprecise reproduction. That continues to be the case with other pieces of communication, short events such as proverbs and songs (where the rhythms help). It also occurs with short narrative sequences such as those found in folk-tales. . . .

As I have indicated, it is really with literacy and schooling that the task of having to recall exactly vast quantities of data (often half uncomprehendingly) is seen as necessary to keep culture going. . . . [A]t the moment that writing had provided a storage system that did not require one to memorize, scholarship insisted upon exact verbatim memory, as if, anticipating Platonic fears, it distrusted what the new medium would do to people's mental processes. . . .

I have tried to refute a number of "myths" about memory in oral cultures. Exact verbatim recall is in general more difficult than in written ones, partly because there is often no call for word-for-word repetition of a recitation like the Bagre. Every performance is also a creative act and there is no distinct separation between performer and creator; that dichotomy does not exist. For, *pace* Jacques Derrida, there is no archive in oral cultures of the same kind as our Public Record Office or the early libraries at Ebla or Alexandria. Of course a greater part of culture is carried in the mind, especially language, but not always in a fixed archival way; hence dialects proliferate. Like all cultures, oral ones depend on stored knowledge; however, much of this is stored in a way that cannot be recalled precisely, in the manner we usually relate to the psychological operation of memory. It is, as I have said, reworked experience. . . .

[I]t is dangerous to speak of a collective memory in oral cultures. An oral culture is not held in everybody's memory store (except for language, which largely is). Memories vary as does experience. Bits may be held by different people. They prompt one another regarding what to do at a marriage or a funeral and in so doing create cultural events anew. The notion of the static nature of oral cultures may, unlike ours, be partly true for the technological aspects. But for others there is greater flexibility. It is literate societies that proliferate mnemonic devices, not only in verse but of the spatial kind discussed by Frances Yates in her well-known book *The Art of Memory*. The limitations of memory in oral cultures, the role of forgetting and the generative use of language and gesture mean that human diversity is in a state of continuous creation, often cyclical rather than cumulative, even in the simplest of human societies.

Merlin Donald (contemp.)

Canadian cognitive neuroscientist. In this relatively unknown work for social memory studies, Donald describes the significant transformations in human societies that resulted from the introduction and development of what he calls "external memory systems," which provide unlimited storage capacity. With this understanding of memory as something that transcends the brain in more than just metaphorical ways, Donald makes clear that sharp distinctions between individual and social or collective memory are not appropriate even for the most scientific approaches. The distinction he employs between engrams and exograms, indicating the location of memories in brains versus outside them, has been quite influential in social and cognitive psychology, for instance in **Welzer**.

From *Origins of the Modern Mind: Three Stages in the Evolution of Culture and Cognition*

A distinction should be made between memory as contained within the individual and memory as part of a collective, external storage system. The first is biologically based, that is, it resides in the brain, so we will refer to it as *biological memory*. The second kind of memory may reside in a number of different external stores, including visual and electronic storage systems, as well as culturally transmitted memories that reside in other individuals. The key feature is that it is external to the biological memory of a given person. Therefore we will refer to it as *external memory*.

External memory media—especially written records but also many other forms of symbolic storages—are a major factor in human intellectual endeavor; few people would dispute this. But do they deserve to be treated as an integral part of cognitive architecture? In the traditional view of psychologists, the mind has clear biological boundaries. "External storage" might be seen as just another term for the culture or civilization within which the individual exists. The individual picks and chooses, acquires skills and knowledge from society, but nevertheless exists as an easily identifiable unit within that society. In this view, while society influences memory and thought, memory and thought occur only in the individual mind or brain and therefore are to be regarded as attributes of the individual, and studied in the individual. Consequently, the proper approach to the study of memory, language, and thought is to study the individual. The literature of experimental psychology testifies to our adherence to this tradition; it is composed mostly of studies of individual performance or competence and the variables that influence it.

But external memory is not simply coextensive with culture in general, or with civilization. Culture and civilization are broader concepts, including material products, such as technologies and cities, and many aspects of human life that are not cognitive. External memory is best defined in functional terms:

it is the *exact* external analog of internal, or biological memory, namely, a storage and retrieval system that allows humans to accumulate experience and knowledge. We do not possess any ready theoretical frameworks in psychology from which to view external memory. Fortunately, there is an excellent point of comparison in the field of computing science: networks.

Computing scientists are able to specify exactly what hardware a given computer possesses and what software. The "cognitive capacity" of a specific computer can be described in terms of its hardware features (such as memory size, central processing unit speed, and peripheral devices) and its software features (such as its operating system and available programming support). In detailing the two types of features, the machine would have been described as thoroughly as we know how. A comparable approach to the human individual would be to proceed in roughly the same manner, as is commonly the case in psychology: study the hardware (the nervous system) and describe the software (the skills, language, and knowledge carried by the individual).

However, the metaphor should be carried to its logical conclusion. If a computer is embedded in a network of computers, that is, if it interacts with a "society" of other computers, it does not necessarily retain the same "cognitive capacity." That is, the powers of the network must also be taken into account when defining and explaining what a computer can do. This is because networking involves a structural change; the processor and memory of the computer are now part of a larger network computational resource. As part of a network, the computer can now delegate computations beyond its own internal capacity. It can also assign priorities within the larger system. It can store its outputs anywhere in the network, that is, in external memory sources. It can even be assigned the role of controller of the system. The point is, in a true network the resources of the system are shared, and the system functions as a unit larger than any of its individual components.

Another relevant analogy might be the addition of magnetic tape or disk storage to a computer. The RAM (Random-Access Memory) of a computer is somewhat analogous to biological memory inasmuch as it lives and dies with the machine. A computer with no hard external memory medium has to rely on its own internal RAM capacity entirely. The only way to expand its capabilities without adding external memory would be to expand RAM memory; but this could not go on indefinitely, and would be extremely wasteful. In biological terms, a similar expansion of individual memory could not go on without running into the physical limitations imposed by factors such as energy requirements and metabolic functions. Just as the invention of hard storage was an economical and flexible, in fact essential, feature in expanding the powers of computers, external storage was an extremely important and efficient innovation in the history of human cognition.

Historically, culture is conventionally regarded as software, not hardware. There is some surface validity to this view. Learning a particular language will not alter basic memory skills or extend short-term memory and appears to leave basic cognitive skills unaffected. Similarly, many other aspects of culture that might be classified as software do not bear greatly on basic cognition. But some cultural artifacts are in fact hardware changes and not software changes. Visuographic inventions of all kinds should be classified as hardware changes. They have produced a collective memory bank as real, in terms of hardware, as any external memory device for a computer. And because they are not bound by time and space, they transport the very limited capabilities of the individual into realms that would not be remotely reachable by an isolated mind.

Individuals in possession of reading, writing, and other visuographic skills thus become somewhat like computers with networking capabilities; they are equipped to interface, to plug into whatever network becomes available. And once plugged in, their skills are determined by both the network and their own biological inheritance. Humans without such skills are isolated from the external memory system, somewhat like a computer that lacks the input/output devices needed to link up with a network. Network codes are collectively held by specified groups of people; those who possess the code, and the right of access, share a common source of representations and the knowledge encoded therein. Therefore, they share a common memory system; and as the data base in that system expands far beyond the mastery of any single individual, the system becomes by far the greatest determining factor in the cognitions of individuals.

The memory system, once collectivized into the external symbolic storage system, becomes virtually unlimited in capacity and much more robust and precise. Thought moves from the relatively informal narrative ramblings of the isolated mind to the collective arena, and ideas thus accumulate over the centuries until they acquire the precision of continuously refined exterior devices, of which the prime example is modern science. But science, ubiquitous though it is at present, is atypical in historical terms. Human cultural products have usually been stored in less obviously systematic forms: religions, rituals, oral literary traditions, carvings, songs—in fact, in any cultural device that allows some form of enduring externalized memory, with rules and routes of access. The products of this vast externalized culture have gradually become available to more people, who are limited only by their capacity to copy (understand) them.

Individuals connected to a cultural network can access an exterior memory bank, read its codes and contents, store new contributions in permanent form, and interact with other individuals who employ the same codes and access routes. If cultural technology is not easily seen as hardware, it is probably because our links with our own culture cannot be described in obviously physical terms. Human minds float freely, without any apparent physical tie-in, either temporary or permanent, to cultural devices. This is more apparent than real, however. Our collective memory devices are undoubtedly physical in nature. A written tablet or book or papyrus is a physical artifact. So is a totem pole, a mask, a costume, a poster, a traffic sign, or an affidavit. So, more obviously, is an electronic memory device. Our links with these devices are physical: they respond to and emit energy, whether electromagnetic or mechanical. The hardware links of computers to networks will undoubtedly become more subtle as technology progresses, and even now they too do not always require a direct physical attachment: satellite linkages can be regarded as hardware devices even though the components may be thousands of miles apart from one another.

External memory is a critical feature of modern human cognition, if we are trying to build an evolutionary bridge from Neolithic to modern cognitive capabilities or a structural bridge from mythic to theoretic culture. The brain may not have changed recently in its genetic makeup, but its link to an accumulating external memory network affords it cognitive powers that would not have been possible in isolation. This is more than a metaphor; each time the brain carries out an operation in concert with the external symbolic storage system, it becomes part of a network. Its memory structure is temporarily altered; and the locus of cognitive control changes. . . .

In a network, memory can reside anywhere in the system. For example, a program running a computer may not "reside" there; or it may reside there wholly or in part. In terms of the execution of the algorithm, these things do not matter; the system functions as a unified system, for whatever period it is defined as a system. The roles assumed by individual components in the system depend entirely on two things: system demands and the limitations of each component in the network. The key to control, or power, in the network, for an individual component, depends on the level of access to certain crucial aspects of the operating system and on preset priorities. Any component that cannot handle key aspects of either the operating system or the programming language, or that cannot execute long enough or complex enough programs, is automatically limited in the role it plays and eliminated from assuming a central role in the system. . . .

Given a compatible network, the powers of an element may become that of the entire network. For example, a single computer might be positioned to delegate priorities and assign roles to others in the system. It could drive many peripheral devices, delegate very large or complex computations to larger but less well-located machines, "piggy-back" excessively large operations on other devices, and so on. And simply by reassigning priorities, it may be relegated to a lesser role, even reduced to the level of a terminal peripheral to the network.

Individual humans, utilizing their biological memories, may interact with their collective memory apparatus in approximately similar ways. Of course, it is historically more accurate to reverse the metaphor and say that, in constructing computers, we have unreflectively emulated this feature of human society. The locus of memory is everywhere or anywhere in the system at any given moment, depending upon the flow of information, access, and priorities. The biologically encapsulated mind might be called a *monad*, after Giordano Bruno . . . and Leibniz. . . . Monads may form temporary connections with specific nodes in the external symbolic system, disconnecting and reconnecting at will in various configurations. A node may be defined simply as a particular location within a network; thus a specific scientific paper in a clearly defined area of the ESS might be considered a node, whereas the entire collection of journal and reference works in the area constitutes an information network. The annual report of a specific corporation might constitute another node, which could form part of several cross-referenced networks; for instance, it might be part of various networks of annual reports organized by region, economic sector, corporate size, growth rate, and so on. . . .

Given the enormity of modern information technology, and the amount of information collected and disseminated daily in society, monads can hold only a very small fraction of what the ESS contains. The major locus of stored knowledge is *out there*, not within the bounds of biological memory. Biological memories carry around the code, rather than a great deal of specific information. Monads confronted with a symbolic information environment are freed from the obligation to depend wholly on biological memory; but the price of this freedom is interpretative baggage. The reason other mammals cannot appreciate the symbolic environment of humans is not that they cannot hear, see, remember, and occasionally use symbols; it is that they cannot interpret them. They lack the various levels of semantic reference systems, and the encoding strategies, that are essential to the extensive use of symbols by humans. . . .

Single entries in the ESS [external symbolic storage] might be called *exograms*, after Lashley's term engram, which referred to a single entry in the biological memory system. An exogram is simply an external memory record of an idea. In both engrams and exograms there are retrievable traces of past experience that can be used to determine future interpretations of the world. Similarly, exograms and engrams are both interpretable only by the individual mind, which must provide the referential basis for understanding the memory record. Exograms, however, are inherently very different from engrams. Whereas engrams are built-in devices, genetically limited to the format and capacity of the human central nervous system, exograms are virtually unlimited in both format and capacity. Engrams are impermanent, at best lasting only as long as the life of a single individual; exograms can be made permanent, outlasting individuals and, at times, entire civilizations. Unlike engrams, systems of exogram storage are infinitely expandable, lending themselves to virtually any system of access, cross-indexing, cataloging, and organization. They also lend themselves to maximum flexibility and can be reformatted over and over in a variety of media and custom-designed for various purposes. Thus, a cognitive system containing exograms will have very different memory properties from a purely biological system. . . .

The most important feature of exograms as storage devices is their capacity for continuous refinement. Exograms are *crafted*; that is, they are symbolic inventions that have undergone a process of iterative examination, testing, and improvement. To a degree this may also be said of biological memory—for instance, a procedural skill like violin playing, or acting, or rhetoric may be rehearsed and improved, and individuals may employ mnemonic devices—but the conceptual products of cognition themselves cannot undergo extensive refinement in a purely oral tradition. Only in elaborate exographic systems, such as written histories or mathematical or physical theorems, can the products of thinking be frozen in time, held up to scrutiny at some future date, altered, and re-entered into storage, in a repetitive, iterative process of improvement.

Exograms also have unique *retrieval* features. Their position in the retrieval hierarchy, and the cues which access them, are a question of design and are entirely arbitrary, a matter of convention. This is not generally true of biological memory; episodic and procedural skills have highly constrained retrieval paths, time-constrained in the former case and structurally constrained (by the performance sequence itself) in the latter. Semantic memory has a highly fluid structure in modern humans, but as observed above, it is likely that its present internal structure is at least partially due to the influence of the external symbolic storage system, whereby the culture tends to restructure the individual's biological memory in its own image. . . .

The existence of exograms eventually changed the role of biological memory in several ways. Human memory had, from its inception, expanded the range of primate memory. The earliest form of hominid culture, mimetic culture, depended on an expansion in the self-representational systems of the brain and created the initial base for semantic memory storage, which consisted initially of representational action scenarios reflected in mime, gesture, craft, and skill. With the evolution of speech and narrative ability, there were even greater increases in the load on biological memory, adding not only the storage networks for phonological rules and the lexicon in its entirety but also a very large store of narrative conceptual knowledge. . . .

The expandability of the ESS also meant a great increase in the number of symbolically encoded things that could be known. This trend became particularly evident after urbanization and literacy, but it was already apparent in ancient Egypt and Mesopotamia, at least among the literate elite. Compared with the monotony and redundancy of the hunting-gathering lifestyle, these early centers of graphic invention exploded with symbolically encoded things to be mastered. Large state libraries were already a reality in ancient Babylon, and by the time of the Greeks ESS products had been systematically collected and stored in several world centers of learning. At this point in human history, standardized formal education of children was needed for the first time, primarily to master the increasing load on visual-symbolic memory. In fact, *formal education was invented mostly to facilitate use of the ESS*. Scribes were trained extensively; fully 15 percent of the more than 100,000 cuneiform tablets in existence are lexical lists for training scribes. . . .

The expansion of the ESS can be seen not only in the total number of entries but in the type of entry as well. The ESS introduced a completely new dimension into the human cognitive picture: large-scale memory management, including selectivity and the setting of priorities. How does human biological memory deal with its inherent capacity limits, when confronted with an expanding, virtually limitless ESS? It has first and foremost to learn how to search, locate, and choose items from the potential sets of items available. But how can it do this? The archaic strategies of biological memory simply do not apply here; there are too many possible routes, too many possible methods of classifying and structuring items. Temporal codes and phonological codes, the two retrieval workhorses of episodic and oral memory, are largely irrelevant to managing the ESS. In the ESS, it doesn't much matter what items sound like, or when, or in what order or juxtaposition, they were acquired. Once items are entered into the ESS, information about time of acquisition or physical contiguity may or may not be retained and may or may not be made relevant to their retrieval.

One requirement for successful use of the ESS is a *map* of its contents. Thus, biological memory must contain information about the structure and access routes of the ESS, as well as its retrieval codes. These skills are necessary, above and beyond the decoding skills needed to understand ESS entries, in order to find the appropriate information when needed. A significant percentage of the knowledge contained in the literate brain falls into this category; this is particularly true of scholars and administrators, whose familiarity with their "field" or the "levers of power" usually translates into the possession of a good cognitive map of the ESS entries relevant to some highly specific pursuit, for instance medieval Iberian history or Pacific Rim banking policy. The skilled user of the ESS does not try to carry around too much fine detail in biological memory but has learned to be very adept in accessing and utilizing the relevant parts of the external symbolic storage system. This has been true since the earliest great bureaucracies: a Chinese bureaucrat of the Han dynasty (roughly contemporary with Imperial Rome) spent a lifetime training for, and immersed in, the ESS.

Narrative memories—the elaborate semantic constructs that were enabled by speech—would have been a more immediately useful aspect of biological memory and must have served as the basis for interpreting and constructing ESS structure in some fields. In certain areas, therefore, biological memory exported its own organization; narrative versions of events are organized according to thematic codes, and classifications of themas are still useful in accessing, interpreting, and structuring certain areas of the ESS, particularly historical and literary items. But even here, the ESS product is far more refined and detailed than anything in biological memory, and there are many more items to recognize, analyze, store, and comprehend. The problem of selective biological storage from unlimited archives of ESS items thus possibly extends even more to the literary realm than to science.

When confronted with the modern electronic expansion of the ESS, the problem of accessing the system takes on a different complexion. It is fair to say that humans have not developed a strategy for dealing with the magnitude of the twentieth-century ESS. Children have to be trained for many years just to be able to master parts of some highly specialized, narrow area of the ESS. There is no longer any question of extensive crossing of linguistic or disciplinary lines; survival demands great specialization. But what are the children taught? Many of the skills being taught in schools now are really memory-management skills; maps, flags, and pointers are three appropriate computer-related terms that throw light on what students must learn. The map of the ESS is its overall structure; by exposing students to a wide variety of fields at the entry level, they become acquainted with the general geography of ESS-stored knowledge. Flags are priority markers that alert the biological memory to the relative importance of various items and access routes. Pointers are necessary direction markers that signal the addresses of relevant items at appropriate times. In addition, students have to be able to find a variety of ESS entry addresses, and therefore they must master a huge number of category labels. Biological memory is now necessarily cluttered with such items; however, for the most part they are empty of content and are concerned primarily with memory management: where to find things, how to scan them, how to assign their importance or priority.

The controlling structures of the modern mind must depend heavily, in modern humans, on this sort of information. The allocation of selective attention in an extensive ESS environment is ultimately a function of flags, pointers, and priorities, rather than simple front-end perceptual or motor selectivity. Much of ESS-oriented biological memory, then, is necessarily filled with directional information, address categories, and a general framework, or map, of that part of the ESS to which the individual has access.

The implicit assumption of modern education is that ESS devices will be a regular feature of most cognitive operations and that biological memory must be equipped primarily to deal with them, rather than to carry around a great deal of finely detailed information. This reflects a real change in the importance of the ESS. The mnemonic arts and rote learning, once a major part of education, . . . have receded into the background as the reliance on biological memory for storage has faded. In earlier human societies many fewer items were in external memory, and thus fewer ESS-related skills had to be mastered. For example, in ancient Egypt, very few people expected to be able to read hieroglyphics—Davies . . . estimates less than 10 percent of the population—and for those who could, the only ESS items encoded in a form they could comprehend were inscriptions and sculptures in ceremonial buildings and systems of numeration used in trade. By our standards, even professional scribes would have had very few inscriptions and manuscripts to read and remember. Biological memory would have exceeded in size and influence, by far, the useful contents of the ESS (except for lists of trade and government records such as censuses).

In such an environment, the ESS was a secondary player, the servant of a fundamentally oral-mythic society, dominated by ritual and tradition. In modern society this has changed; a great deal of public life takes place through ESS media, whether printed or electronic. Even illiterate people depend upon exographic channels of experience, provided by television or some other medium. There is much less dependence on biological memory. Even episodic experience depends upon electronic media. The great events—D-day, the first moon landing—are vicariously experienced and interpreted through the ESS. In modern society, it is not only the technological and bureaucratic aspects of life that are ESS-dominated; public life itself is lived through the ESS, whether in the print arena of periodicals or the newsrooms of network television. The biological memories of individuals are supplemented by photographs, school yearbooks, diaries, and innumerable symbolic artifacts collected over a lifetime. Even personal identities are stored, refreshed, elaborated, and sustained with the aid of ESS entries.

Aleida Assmann (contemp.)

German cultural theorist. Along with her husband, Jan Assmann, Aleida Assmann is one of the most prolific and influential cultural memory theorists writing today. Unfortunately, many of her works are not available in English, not least her 1999 magnum opus, *Erinnerungsräume: Formen und Wandlungen des kulturellen Gedächtnisses* (*Spaces of Remembering: Forms and Transformations of Cultural Memory*), which offers a wide-ranging account of the role of technologies of memory, particularly writing, canon, and archive, among many other topics. The handbook essay from which the following excerpts are drawn is the most concise, yet broadest, overview of her work in her own words, in English or otherwise.

From "Canon and Archive"

When thinking about memory, we must start with forgetting. The dynamics of individual memory consists in a perpetual interaction between remembering and forgetting. . . . In order to remember some things, other things must be forgotten. Our memory is highly selective. Memory capacity is limited by neural and cultural constraints such as focus and bias. It is also limited by psychological pressures, with the effect that painful or incongruent memories are hidden, displaced, overwritten, and possibly effaced. On the level of cultural memory, there is a similar dynamic at work. The continuous process of forgetting is part of social normality. As in the head of the individual, also in the communication of society much must be continuously forgotten to make place for new information, new challenges, and new ideas to face the present and future. Not only individual memories are irretrievably lost with the death of their owners, also a large part of material possessions and remains are lost after the death of a person when households are dissolved and personal belongings dispersed in flea markets, trashed, or recycled.

When looking more closely at these cultural practices, we can distinguish between two forms of forgetting, a more active and a more passive one. *Active* forgetting is implied in intentional acts such as trashing and destroying. Acts of forgetting are a necessary and constructive part of internal social transformations; they are, however, violently destructive when directed at an alien culture or a persecuted minority. Censorship has been a forceful if not always successful instrument for destroying material and mental cultural products. The *passive* form of cultural forgetting is related to non-intentional acts such as losing, hiding, dispersing, neglecting, abandoning, or leaving something behind. In these cases the objects are not materially destroyed; they fall out of the frames of attention, valuation, and use. What is lost but not materially destroyed may be discovered by accident at a later time in attics and other obscure depots, or eventually be dug up again by more systematic archaeological search. . . .

If we concede that forgetting is the normality of personal and cultural life, then remembering is the exception, which—especially in the cultural sphere—requires special and costly precautions. These precautions take the shape of cultural institutions. As forgetting, remembering also has an active and a passive side. The institutions of active memory preserve the *past as present* while the institutions of passive memory preserve the *past as past*. The tension between the pastness of the past and its presence is an important key to understanding the dynamics of cultural memory. These two modes of cultural memory may be illustrated by different rooms of the museum. The museum presents its prestigious objects to the viewers in representative shows which are arranged to catch attention and make a lasting impression. The same museum also houses storerooms stuffed with other paintings and objects in peripheral spaces such as cellars or attics which are not publicly presented. In the following, I will refer to the actively circulated memory that keeps the past present as the *canon* and the passively stored memory that preserves the past past as the *archive*. . . .

Cultural memory contains a number of cultural messages that are addressed to posterity and intended for continuous repetition and re-use. To this active memory belong, among other things, works of art, which are destined to be repeatedly re-read, appreciated, staged, performed, and commented. This aspiration, of course, cannot be realized for all artistic artifacts; only a small percentage acquire this status through a complex procedure which we call canonization. At the other end of the spectrum, there is the storehouse for cultural relicts. These are not unmediated; they have only lost their immediate addressees; they are de-contextualized and disconnected from their former frames which had authorised them or determined their meaning. As part of the archive, they are open to new contexts and lend themselves to new interpretations. . . .

The institutions of passive cultural memory are situated halfway between the canon and forgetting. The archive is its central and paradigmatic institution; to understand this dimension of cultural memory, it is necessary to explore the history and function of the archive. In literary studies, the archive is a concept that, just like trauma, has moved into the center of poststructuralist and postcolonial discourse: in this career, however, it is often disconnected from the empirical institution and used in metaphorical ways as a highly suggestive trope. According to a famous statement by Foucault, the archive is "the law that determines what can be said". . . . To bring this statement closer to the level of empirical institutions, it can be rephrased in the following way: The archive is the basis of what can be said in the future about the present when it will have become the past. . . .

The objects in the historical archive have lost their original "place in life" . . . and entered a new context which gives them the chance of a second life that considerably prolongs their existence. What is stored in historical archives is materially preserved and cataloged; it becomes part of an organizational structure, which allows it to be easily sourced. As part of the passive dimension of cultural memory, however, the knowledge that is stored in the archive is inert. It is stored and potentially available, but it is not interpreted. . . . The archive, therefore, can be described as a space that is located on the border between forgetting and remembering; its materials are preserved in a state of latency, in a space of intermediary storage (*Zwischenspeicher*). Thus, the institution of the archive is part of cultural memory in the passive dimension of preservation. It stores materials in the intermediary state of "no longer" and "not yet," deprived of their old existence and waiting for a new one. . . .

The selection criteria for what is to be remembered and circulated in the active cultural memory and what is to be merely stored are neither clear nor are they uncontested. In the modern print age of libraries, science, and the growth of encyclopedic knowledge, the storage capacity of the archive has by far exceeded that which can be translated back into active human memory. In the age of digital media, the growing rift between the amount of externalized information and internalizable knowledge becomes ever more dramatic. As the capacity of computers is doubled every two years, the external storage capacity of the digital age has expanded even further, while the human capacity for memory remains the same due to its neural constraints. Already at the beginning of the twentieth century, Georg Simmel had referred to this uncontrollable process as "the tragedy of culture."

According to Plato, the "tragedy of culture" started with the introduction of (alphabetic) writing, because this technique of notation separated the knower from the known and made knowledge available to the non-initiated. Plato argued that writing does not transmit memory but produces a memory ersatz. Though already inherent in the introduction of writing itself as a form of externalizing knowledge, the distinction between a cultural working memory and a cultural reference memory has been considerably exacerbated with the new institution of the historical archive. In Western democracies, these two functions of cultural memory have come to be more and more separated. But they are, contrary to Simmel's (or Nietzsche's) apprehensions, in no way unrelated. The two realms of cultural memory are not scaled against each other. On the contrary, they interact in different ways. The reference memory, for instance, provides a rich background for the working memory, which means that elements of the canon may be "estranged" and reinterpreted by framing them with elements of the archive (which is the method of New Historicism). Elements of the canon can also recede into the archive, while elements of the archive may be recovered and reclaimed for the canon. It is exactly this interdependence of the different realms and functions that creates the dynamics of cultural memory and keeps its energy flowing.

Although we cannot imagine a culture without an active cultural memory, we can well imagine a culture without a passive storing memory. In oral cultures in which the cultural memory is embodied and transmitted through performances and practices, material relics do not persist and accumulate. In such cultures, the range of the cultural memory is coextensive with the embodied repertoires that are performed in festive rites and repeated practices.

Cultures that do not make use of writing do not produce the type of relicts that are assembled in archives. Nor do they produce a canon that can be enshrined in museums and monuments. . . .

In totalitarian states, there is also no storing memory, but for very different reasons. In such a state, as Orwell has shown in his novel 1984, every scrap that is left over from the past has to be changed or eliminated because an authentic piece of evidence has the power to crush the official version of the past on which the rulers base their power. . . .

In order . . . to remember anything one has to forget; but what is forgotten need not necessarily be lost forever. The canon stands for the active working memory of a society that defines and supports the cultural identity of a group. . . . It is highly selective and built on the principle of exclusion. The function of the archive, the reference memory of a society, provides a kind of counterbalance against the necessarily reductive and restrictive drive of the working memory. It creates a meta-memory, a second-order memory that preserves what has been forgotten. The archive is a kind of "lost-and-found office" for what is no longer needed or immediately understood. The historical archive helps us to position ourselves in time; it affords us the possibility of comparison and reflection for a retrospective historical consciousness. We must acknowledge, however, that archives are selective as well. They are in no way all-inclusive but have their own structural mechanisms of exclusion in terms of class, race, and gender. . . . Luckily, there is not only intentional but also accidental preservation when hidden deposits are discovered. They are what involuntary memory is to voluntary memory. But even counting in accidental discoveries, the past remains, as Thomas Carlyle once put it, a "miserable, defective shred". . . .

Both the active and the passive realms of cultural memory are anchored in institutions that are not closed against each other but allow for mutual influx and reshuffling. This accounts for the dynamics within cultural memory and keeps it open to changes and negotiations. . . . [T]he archive is an institution with a history and specific functions. Like the recognition of human rights, the archive is an important achievement of civil society and perhaps not the least by which we may judge its strength.

Paul Connerton (contemp.)

British sociologist. Paul Connerton's 1989 *How Societies Remember* is a landmark text of contemporary social memory studies. Drawing not only on **Halbwachs** but also on theorists like Norbert Elias and Mikhail Bakhtin, Connerton highlights the neglected bodily dimensions of remembering. In these selections, Connerton elaborates his distinction between incorporated memory and inscribed memory, an idea that can be compared profitably to similar notions in the work of A. **Assmann**, **Hacking**, and others.

From *How Societies Remember*

What . . . is being remembered in commemorative ceremonies? Part of the answer is that a community is reminded of its identity as represented by and told in a master narrative. This is a collective variant of . . . personal memory, that is to say a making sense of the past as a kind of connective autobiography, with some explicitly cognitive components. But rituals are not just further instances of humanity's now much touted propensity to explain the world to itself by telling stories. A ritual is not a journal or memoir. Its master narrative is more than a story told and reflected on; it is a cult enacted. An image of the past, even in the form of a master narrative, is conveyed and sustained by ritual performances. And this means that what is remembered in commemorative ceremonies is something in addition to a collectively organised variant of personal and cognitive memory. For if the ceremonies are to work for their participants, if they are to be persuasive to them, then those participants must be not simply cognitively competent to execute the performance: they must be habituated to those performances. This habituation is to be found in the bodily substrate of the performance. . . .

[I]f there is a such a thing as social memory, we are likely to find it in commemorative ceremonies. Commemorative ceremonies prove to be commemorative (only) in so far as they are performative. But performative memory is in fact much more widespread than commemorative ceremonies which are—though performance is necessary to them—highly representational. Performative memory is bodily. Therefore, I want to argue, there is an aspect of social memory which has been greatly neglected but is absolutely essential: bodily social memory. . . .

We preserve versions of the past by representing it to ourselves in words and images. Commemorative ceremonies are pre-eminent instances of this. They keep the past in mind by a depictive representation of past events. They are re-enactments of the past, its return in a representational guise which normally includes a simulacrum of the scene or situation recaptured. Such re-enactments depend for much of their rhetorical persuasiveness, as we have seen, on prescribed bodily behaviour. But we can also preserve the past deliberately without explicitly re-presenting it in words and images. Our bodies, which in commemorations stylistically re-enact an image of the past, keep the past also in an entirely effective form in their continuing ability to perform certain skilled actions. We may not remember how or when we first learned to swim, but we can keep on swimming successfully—remembering how to do it—without any representational activity on our part at all; we consult a mental picture of what we should do when our capacity to execute spontaneously the bodily movements in question is defective. Many forms of habitual skilled remembering illustrate a keeping of the past in mind that, without ever adverting to its historical origin, nevertheless re-enacts the past in our present conduct. In habitual memory the past is, as it were, sedimented in the body.

In suggesting more particularly how memory is sedimented, or amassed, in the body, I want to distinguish between two fundamentally different types of social practice.

The first type of action I shall call an *incorporating* practice. Thus a smile or a handshake or words spoken in the presence of someone we address, are all messages that a sender or senders impart by means of their own current bodily activity, the transmission occurring only during the time that their bodies are present to sustain that particular activity. Whether the information imparted by these actions is conveyed intentionally or unintentionally, and whether it is carried by an individual or a group. I shall speak of such actions as incorporated.

The second type of action I shall call an *inscribing* practice. Thus our modern devices for storing and retrieving information, print, encyclopedias, indexes, photographs, sound tapes, computers, all require that we do something that traps and holds information, long after the human organism has stopped informing. Occasionally this imparting may be unintentional, as when we have our telephone tapped, but mostly it is intentional. I shall speak of all such actions as inscribing.

The memorisation of culturally specific postures may be taken as an example of incorporating practices. In a culture where the characteristic postures of men and women are nearly identical, there may be very little teaching of posture and very little conscious learning of posture. But whenever postural differences are introduced, for example, between the postures appropriate for ceremonial occasions and for everyday activities or between the modes of sitting appropriate for males and females, some awareness of postural appropriateness is involved. . . . Postural behaviour may be very highly structured . . . and completely predictable, even though it is neither verbalised nor consciously taught and may be so automatic that it is not even recognised as isolatable pieces of behaviour. The presence of living models, the presence, that is, of men and women actually sitting "correctly," is essential to the communication in question.

The importance of postures for communal memory is evident. Power and rank are commonly expressed through certain postures relative to others; from the way in which people group themselves and from the disposition of their bodies relative to the bodies of others, we can deduce the degree of authority which each is thought to enjoy or to which they lay claim. . . .

There will of course be disparities between cultures in the meanings ascribed to some postures, but, in all cultures, much of the choreography of authority is expressed through the body. Within this choreography, there is an identifiable range of repertoires through which many postural performances become meaningful by registering meaningful inflections of the upright posture. Such inflections recall a pattern of authority to performers and observers, and they are in turn recalled to mind in many of our verbal conventions. This is evident in our common metaphors. When we speak of someone as being "upright" we may use the expression descriptively and literally to mean that they are standing on their own feet, or we may use it evaluatively and metaphorically to express admiration and praise of someone whom we judge to be honest and just, to be loyal to friends in difficulties, to stand by their own convictions, and in general not to stoop to low or unworthy actions. . . . Nor are such metaphoric turns of phrase ad hoc; they remind us of patterns of authority because they form not simply individual metaphoric turns of phrase but whole systems of metaphoric expression. . . . Culturally specific postural performances [thus] provide us with a mnemonics of the body.

The alphabet may be cited, by contrast, as an example of an inscribing practice. It is a practice that exists by virtue of a systematic transfer from the temporal properties of the human voice to the spatial properties of the inscribed marks: that is, to replicable features of their form, position, actual distances, order and linear disposition. Other writing systems—pictograms, hieroglyphics and ideograms—exhibit the same characteristic; but their methods of spatial encoding are radically incomplete because they are still dependent on a direct inscription of meanings. That is why pictograms, for instance, are so deficient as mnemonic systems: a vast number of signs are needed to represent all the objects in the culture; the simplest sentence requires an elaborate series of signs; and only a limited number of things can be said. . . . The phonetic principle marks a decisive break with all such procedures. What distinguishes it from all other writing systems is the fact that the twenty-two components out of which the system is constructed have in themselves no intrinsic meaning. . . . When the component units of the system were in this way voided of any independent meaning, they were transformed into a mechanical mnemonic device. This device imposed a habit of recognition on the brain in the developmental phase before puberty while the oral language code was being acquired. The two codes needed for speaking and then for reading combine together at a time when mental resources are still extremely malleable, so that the acts of reading and writing become an unconscious reflex. The cultural break established by the phonetic principle thus has decisive ontogenetic significance.

The impact of writing on social memory is much written about and evidently vast. The transition from an oral culture to a literate culture is a transition from incorporating practices to inscribing practices. The impact of writing depends upon the fact that any account which is transmitted by means of inscriptions is unalterably fixed, the process of its composition being definitively closed. The standard edition and the canonic work are the emblems of this condition. This fixity is the spring that releases innovation. When the memories of a culture begin to be transmitted mainly by the reproduction of their inscriptions rather than by "live" tellings, improvisation becomes increasingly difficult and innovation is institutionalised. . . .

Phonetic writing generates cultural innovation by promoting two processes: economisation and scepticism. Economisation: because the form of communal memory is freed from its dependence on rhythm. Scepticism: because the content of communal memory is subjected to systematic criticism. With regard to economisation, we may note that in oral cultures most of the formal recollection of happenings takes the form of performances repeatedly recited by the custodians of memory to those who hear of it. These large-scale performative utterances have to be cast in a standardised form if there is to be any chance of their being repeated by successive generations; and the rhythms of oral verse are the privileged mechanisms of recall because rhythm enlists the co-operation of a whole series of bodily motor reflexes in the work of remembrance. But rhythm sets drastic limits to the verbal arrangement of what might be said and thought. Phonetic writing breaks down these limitations. By substituting a visual record for an acoustic one, the alphabet frees a society from the constraints of a rhythmic mnemonics. Particular statements need no longer be memorised but can lie around as artefacts and be consulted as required. This economisation of memory releases extensive mental energies previously invested in the construction and preservation of mnemonic systems; hence it encourages the production of unfamiliar statements and the thinking of novel thoughts. With regard to scepticism, we may note that in oral cultures much of the informal recollection of happenings takes the form of face-to-face conversation. This necessarily impedes the articulation of a sense of inconsistency or even incoherence in the fabric of the cultural inheritance. It is true that oral societies often make a distinction between the folktale, the myth, and the historical legend. But even if inconsistency occurs between or within such genres, it is unlikely that the sense of inconsistency will generate a permanent cultural impact. Scepticism is particular, not culturally accumulative; it generates titular disputes, but not a deliberate interpretation of the cultural inheritance. The distinction between what was held to be mythical and what was considered to be historical came into being when it became possible to set one fixed account of the world beside another so that the contradictions within and between them could literally be seen. Through criticism as well as through economisation, the substance of communal memory is changed by the transformation in the technology of preserved communication. . . .

Inscribing practices have always formed the privileged story, incorporating practices the neglected story, in the history of hermeneutics. . . .

The fact that incorporating practices have for long been backgrounded as objects of explicit interpretive attention is due not so much to a peculiarity of hermeneutics as rather to a defining feature incorporating practices themselves. For these practices . . . cannot be well accomplished without a diminution of the conscious attention that is paid to them. The study of habit teaches us this. Any bodily practice, swimming or typing or dancing, requires for its proper execution a whole chain of interconnected acts, and in the early performances of the action the conscious will has to choose each of the successive events that make up the action from a number of wrong alternatives; but habit eventually brings it about that each event precipitates an appropriate successor without an alternative appearing to offer itself and without reference to the conscious will. . . .

Incorporating practices therefore provide a particularly effective system of mnemonics. In this there is an element of paradox. For it is true that whatever is written, and more generally whatever is inscribed, demonstrates, by the fact of being inscribed, a will to be remembered and reaches as it were its fulfilment in the formation of a canon. It is equally true that incorporating practices, by contrast, are largely traceless and that, as such, they are incapable of providing a means by which any evidence of a will to be remembered can be "left behind." In consequence, we commonly consider inscription to be the privileged form for the transmission of a society's memories, and we see the diffusion and elaboration of a society's systems of inscription as making possible an exponential development of its capacity to remember.

Yet it would be misleading, on this account, to underestimate the mnemonic importance and persistence of what is incorporated. Incorporating practices depend for their particular mnemonic effect on two distinctive features: their mode of existence and their mode of acquisition. They do not exist "objectively," independently of their being performed. And they are acquired in such a way as not to require explicit reflection on their performance. It is important to notice that the relatively informal sets of actions I have referred to as culturally specific bodily practices enjoy significant features in common with the relatively more formal sets of actions I have called commemorative ceremonies. For commemorative ceremonies also are preserved only through their performance; and, because of their performativity and their formalisation, they too are not easily susceptible to critical scrutiny and evaluation by those habituated to their performance. Both commemorative ceremonies and bodily practices therefore contain a measure of insurance against the process of cumulative questioning entailed in all discursive practices. This is the source of their importance and persistence as mnemonic systems. Every group, then, will entrust to bodily automatisms the values and categories which they are most anxious to conserve. They will know how well the past can be kept in mind by a habitual memory sedimented in the body.

Harald Welzer (contemp.), Sabine Moller, Karoline Tschuggnall, Olaf Jensen, and Torsten Koch

German social psychologists. While the Assmanns and most of their followers have been more interested in cultural memory than communicative memory—the latter of which they see as Halbwachs's chief concern along with oral historians—Welzer and his colleagues have explored in depth the patterns and mechanisms of memory transmittal, particularly in families. Elsewhere, Welzer has advanced the same language that writers like **Donald** have employed about endograms versus exograms. But in his book *"Opa war kein Nazi"* (*"Grandpa Wasn't a Nazi"*), Welzer explores how memory of the Nazi past is shaped by family dynamics, finding that even when particular pasts are explicitly acknowledged by grandparents, grandchildren do not always assimilate that knowledge into their conception of history or into their familial identity. The transits of communicative memory are complex indeed. In highlighting here how memory is an ongoing process of complex construction and reconstruction, his argument is not entirely alien in some regards to **Gadamer's** or to **J. Assmann's** notion of "mnemohistory."

From, *"Opa war kein Nazi:" Nationalsozialismus und Holocaust im Familiengedächtnis*

The identity of a community of memory is tied to recurrent acts of self-commemoration, and the fictional unity of this identity consists in the continuity of the social praxis of self-commemoration. What Paul Ricoeur has established for individual narrative also applies for the social praxis of representing the past: that it would be utterly inadequate to see this praxis as a mere sequence of episodes. For every commemorative situation has a "configurational dimension," in which the communicative acts—stories, extensions, commentaries, questions—are organized through narrative conventions, expectations of causality and plausibility, and so on in such a way that it creates a meaningful story for all participants (a story that upon closer inspection breaks up into as many versions as there are speakers and listeners present).

In this way, the same thing applies to the group that Donald Polkinghorne had in mind when he spoke about identity as "a configuring of personal events into a historical unity which includes not only what one has been but also anticipations of what one will be." The social process of consolidating the past operates in all three temporal frames—in the past which is being told about, in the present in which the we-group is marking its past, and in the future toward which the coherence of the group is directed: This is how things will be in this and other mnemonic situations, or, put differently, this is how it will be in the future because this is how it is now and how it always was. No situation of recollection is like any other that has occurred: in the meantime, time has passed, perhaps someone has died in the interval, perhaps someone has joined, perhaps new aspects have entered the mnemonic situation from the dominant social discourses about the past—in each case, all the participants are entering the collective discussion from a different vantage point.

In the process, the past is also necessarily transformed, the way in which it is constituted, for it now appears in a new configuration. And here the situation for a community of memory is analogous to that of the remembering individual: memory always involves re-inscription. What is supposed to remain in memory requires consolidation through repeated re-thinking and re-feeling of the same event (or what one considers to be the same).

However, this has far reaching consequences for the evaluation of the authenticity of memories. For in a new process of consolidation the context in which the recollection takes place is "co-written and connected to the new memory. It therefore cannot be ruled out that the old memory is embedded in new context and thus is actively transformed" [Wolf Singer]. This is exactly what happens in the situation of recollection in the family: a paradoxical process in which stories that are apparently the same are retold, but changed in such a way that they appear the same as the old ones and can thus relate to the by now changed fictive unity of the family memory. And this explains the permanent transformation not only of individual but of collective remembering, as well as how the continuous fine-tuning of the family memory that can be seen in conversational transcripts also necessarily subtly changes the memory of the individual members. In this sense, nobody leaves the situation with the same implied fiction of a shared memory with which he entered it—but it is precisely this dynamic which ensures that the memory of the group remains coherent, guaranteeing that the group persists as a group.

We have tried to show in the case of the Meier family what happens when the fictive unity of family memory is threatened if a member of the mnemonic community, in this case the great-grandfather, emerges posthumously as someone with whom "wrong" memories are associated. Adapting to the new situation turned out to be very difficult, especially for the generation of the grandchildren. They had come to know him at a different point in time than his children did, and this more intimate generational relationship between grandparents and grandchildren, not shaped by separation conflicts, generated more powerful reactions to the reversal of images and conceptions than among the children's generation. But that too will become a new element in the Meier's family memory—the great-grandfather will in the future be remembered in light of his posthumously discovered "chronicle," which significantly altered the shared conceptions of him.

Memory, one could say, is after all always the event and the memory of its recollection. This, by the way, distinguishes cognitive memory contents from those that carry emotional significance: A historical date, like 1848, which is learned without any affective relation as the date of a failed revolution, does not change its meaning when it is recalled; a date like November 9, 1989, the day of the opening of the Wall, will constantly change its meanings for the people who were in any way involved in this event—depending on the context in which the event is subsequently perceived and remembered.

At this point it is necessary to mention the context in which memories are actualized: Both the interview as well as the family conversation are events for the participants. To tell lived autobiographical experiences is itself an autobiographical experience. It takes place at a particular time, at a particular place and with the participation of specific people—and all this, in turn, can at a later point be retold and remembered. If indeed memory is always the event and the recollection of its memory, then the interviews and family conversations about the experience of National Socialism and their transmission are themselves part of an interactively lived history—which will have an effect on how the interviewees will tell their stories in the future. In this sense, the communicative transmission of history is always a form of the reanimation of history, which in the process never remains as it was.

—*Translated by Daniel Levy and Jeffrey K. Olick*

Marianne Hirsch (contemp.)

American literary critic. Extensive research into individual and cultural trauma documents the effect of horrible events on individuals and societies. But it is not just individuals who suffer aftereffects: their children do as well. In this excerpt, Hirsch, a scholar who has written extensively on photography and other media of memory, introduces the concept of "postmemory" to describe the relationship that the generation after those who experienced trauma directly bears to those experiences. The second generation "remembers" not because they were there, but through stories, images, and behaviors that transmit the traumas of the first generation to their offspring. In Hirsch's account, however, postmemory is not only a quality of intergenerational transmission; rather, it characterizes the entire contemporary age, an age of postmemory. See also **Eyerman**, **Alexander**, and **Welzer**.

From "The Generation of Postmemory"

If "memory" as such a capacious analytic term and "memory studies" as a field of inquiry have grown exponentially in academic and popular importance in the last decade and a half, they have, in large part, been fueled by the limit case of the Holocaust and by the work of (and about) what has come to be known as "the second generation" or "the generation after." "Second generation" writers and artists have been publishing art works, films, novels, and memoirs, or hybrid "postmemoirs" (as Leslie Morris . . . has dubbed them), with titles like "After Such Knowledge," "The War After," "Second-Hand Smoke," "War Story," "Lessons of Darkness," "Losing the Dead," "Dark Lullabies," "Fifty Years of Silence," "After," "Daddy's War," as well as scholarly essays and collections like "Children of the Holocaust," "Daughters of the Shoah," "Shaping Losses," "Memorial Candles," "In the Shadow of the Holocaust," and so on. The particular relation to a parental past described, evoked, and analyzed in these works has come to be seen as a "syndrome" of belatedness or "post-ness" and has been variously termed "absent memory," . . . "inherited memory," "belated memory," "prosthetic memory," . . . "mémoire trouée," . . . "mémoire des cendres," . . . "vicarious witnessing," . . . "received history," . . . and "postmemory." These terms reveal a number of controversial assumptions: that descendants of survivors (of victims as well as of perpetrators) of massive traumatic events connect so deeply to the previous generation's remembrances of the past that they need to call that connection *memory* and thus that, in certain extreme circumstances, memory *can* be transmitted to those who were not actually there to live an event. At the same time—so it is assumed—this received memory is *distinct* from the recall of contemporary witnesses and participants. Hence the insistence on "post" or "after" and the many qualifying adjectives that try to define both a specifically inter- and transgenerational act of transfer and the resonant aftereffects of trauma. If this sounds like a contradiction, it is, indeed, one, and I believe it is inherent to this phenomenon.

Postmemory is the term I came to on the basis of my autobiographical readings of works by second generation writers and visual artists. The "post" in "postmemory" signals more than a temporal delay and more than a location in an aftermath. Postmodern, for example, inscribes both a critical distance and a profound interrelation with the modern; postcolonial does not mean the end of the colonial but its troubling continuity, though, in contrast, postfeminist *has* been used to mark a sequel to feminism. We certainly are, still, in the era of "posts," which continue to proliferate: "post-secular," "post-human," "postcolony," "post-white." Postmemory shares the layering of these other "posts" and their belatedness, aligning itself with the practice of citation and mediation that characterize them, marking a particular end-of-century/turn-of-century moment of looking backward rather than ahead and of defining the present in relation to a troubled past rather than initiating new paradigms. Like them, it reflects an uneasy oscillation between continuity and rupture. And yet postmemory is not a movement, method, or idea; I see it, rather, as a *structure* of inter- and trans-generational transmission of traumatic knowledge and experience. It is a *consequence* of traumatic recall but (unlike post-traumatic stress disorder) at a generational remove.

As Hoffman . . . writes: "The paradoxes of indirect knowledge haunt many of us who came after. The formative events of the twentieth century have crucially informed our biographies, threatening sometimes to overshadow and overwhelm our own lives. But we did not see them, suffer through them, experience their impact directly. Our relationship to them has been defined by our very 'post-ness' and by the powerful but mediated forms of knowledge that have followed from it." Postmemory describes the relationship that the generation after those who witnessed cultural or collective trauma bears to the experiences of those who came before, experiences that they "remember" only by means of the stories, images, and behaviors among which they grew up. But these experiences were transmitted to them so deeply and affectively as to *seem* to constitute memories in their own right. Postmemory's connection to the past is thus not actually mediated by recall but by imaginative investment, projection, and creation. To grow up with such overwhelming inherited memories, to be dominated by narratives that preceded one's birth or one's consciousness, is to risk having one's own stories and experiences displaced, even evacuated, by those of a previous generation. It is to be shaped, however indirectly, by traumatic events that still defy narrative reconstruction and exceed comprehension. These events happened in the past, but their effects continue into the present. This is, I believe, the experience of postmemory and the process of its generation.

John B. Thompson (contemp.)

British sociologist. In this exploration of the relationship between tradition and the mass media, Thompson provides a compelling technologically driven account of what he calls the "unmooring" and "remooring" of tradition in late modernity. As such, he rejects simplistic arguments that the role of mediatization involves a straightforward "de-traditionalization." See also **Giddens** and **Huyssen**.

From "Tradition and Self in a Mediated World"

If we wish to understand the relation between tradition and the media, we must put aside the view that exposure to the media will lead invariably to the abandonment of traditional ways of life and to the adoption of modern life-styles. Exposure to the media does not entail, in and by itself, any particular stance vis-à-vis tradition. But if the development of the media has not led to the demise of tradition, in what ways have traditional beliefs and practices been affected by the emergence and growth of mediated forms of communication?. . .

Prior to the development of the media, most people's sense of the past and of the world beyond their immediate milieu was shaped primarily by the symbolic content exchanged in face-to-face interaction. For most people, the sense of the past, of the world beyond their immediate locales, and of the socially delimited communities to which they belonged, was constituted primarily by oral traditions that were produced and reproduced in the social contexts of everyday life. With the development of the media, however, individuals were able to experience events, observe others and, in general, learn about worlds—both real and imaginary—that extended well beyond the sphere of their day-to-day encounters. They were increasingly drawn into networks of communication and forms of interaction that were not face-to-face in character.

We can distinguish two forms or types of interaction which were (and remain) particularly important in this regard—what I describe as "mediated interaction" and "mediated quasi-interaction." By "mediated interaction" I mean forms of interaction such as letter-writing, telephone conversations and so on. By "mediated quasi-interaction" I mean the kinds of social interaction created by the media of "mass communication," such as books, newspapers, radio and television. Both mediated interaction and mediated quasi-interaction involve the use of a technical medium (paper, electrical wires, electromagnetic waves, etc.) which enables information or symbolic content to be transmitted to individuals who are remote in space, in time or in both. Unlike face-to-face interaction, which takes place in a particular spatial-temporal locale, mediated interaction and quasi-interaction are stretched across space and time, and they therefore establish social relations between individuals who do not share the same spatial-temporal context. But whereas mediated interaction is dialogical in character, in the sense that it generally involves a two-way flow of information and communication, mediated quasi-interaction is largely monological or one-way. The viewer of a television programme, for instance, is primarily the recipient of a symbolic form whose producer does not require (and generally does not receive) a direct and immediate response.

Before the early modern period in Europe, and until quite recently in some other parts of the world, the exchange of information and symbolic content was, for most people, a process that took place exclusively within the context of face-to-face interaction. Communication networks depended largely on nodal exchanges that were face-to-face in character. Forms of mediated interaction and quasi-interaction did exist, but they were restricted to a relatively small sector of the population. To participate in mediated interaction or quasi-interaction required special skills—such as the capacity to write or read—which were predominantly the preserve of political, commercial or ecclesiastical elites. But, with the rise of the printing industry in fifteenth- and sixteenth-century Europe and its subsequent development elsewhere, and with the emergence of various types of electronic media in the nineteenth and twentieth centuries, face-to-face interaction was increasingly supplemented by forms of mediated interaction and quasi-interaction. To an ever-increasing extent, the exchange of information and symbolic content took place through mediated forms of interaction, rather than in contexts of face-to-face interaction between individuals who shared a common locale.

Viewed from the perspective of the individual, the historical rise of mediated interaction had far-reaching consequences. As individuals gained access to media products, they were able to keep some distance from the symbolic content of face-to-face interaction and from the forms of authority which prevailed in the shared locales of everyday life. For the purposes of forming a sense of self and of the possibilities open to them, individuals came to rely less and less on symbolic materials transmitted through face-to-face interaction. Increasingly they gained access to what we may describe, in a loose fashion, as "non-local knowledge." They also acquired the capacity to experience phenomena which they were unlikely ever to encounter in the locales of their daily lives; with the development of the media (and especially television), the capacity to experience was increasingly disconnected from the activity of encountering. The process of self-formation became more reflexive and open-ended, as individuals were able to draw increasingly on symbolic materials transmitted through the media to inform and refashion the project of the self.

How did these developments affect the nature of tradition? They did not undermine tradition—indeed, in some respects, traditions were largely untouched. Orally transmitted traditions continued to play an important role in the daily lives of many individuals, for example. In other respects, however, traditions were gradually and fundamentally transformed, as the symbolic content of tradition was increasingly inscribed in forms of communication which were not face-to-face in character. This in turn had several consequences; let me emphasize three.

(1) Since many forms of mediated communication involve some degree of fixation of symbolic content in a material substratum, they endow this content with a temporal permanence which is generally lacking in the communicative exchanges of face-to-face interaction. In the absence of material fixation, the maintenance of tradition over time requires the continual reenactment of its symbolic content in the activities of day-to-day life. Practical repetition is the only way of securing temporal continuity. But with the fixation of symbolic content in a material substratum of some kind, the maintenance of tradition over time can be separated to some extent from the need for practical and continual re-enactment. The cultivation of traditional values and beliefs becomes increasingly dependent on forms of interaction which involve media products; the fixing of symbolic content in media products (books, films etc.) provides a form of temporal continuity which diminishes the need for re-enactment. Hence, the decline of some of the ritualized aspects of tradition (such as church attendance) should not necessarily be interpreted as the decline of tradition as such: it may simply express the fact that the maintenance of tradition over time has become less dependent on ritualized re-enactment. Tradition has, in effect, become increasingly *de-ritualized*.

The de-ritualization of tradition does not imply that *all* elements of ritual will be eliminated from tradition, nor does it imply that tradition will become entirely divorced from the face-to-face interaction which takes place in shared locales. While the symbolic content of tradition may become increasingly fixed in media products, many traditions remain closely tied to the practical encounters of daily life (for example, within the family, the school and other institutional settings). Moreover, media products are commonly appropriated within contexts of face-to-face interaction, and hence the renewal of tradition may involve a constantly changing mixture of face-to-face interaction and of mediated quasi-interaction. This is evident to parents and teachers, who come to rely more and more on books, films and television, programmes to convey to children the main themes of a religious or other tradition, and who see their own role more in terms of elaboration and explication than in terms of the cultivation of tradition from scratch.

(2) To the extent that the transmission of tradition becomes dependent on mediated forms of communication, it also becomes detached from the individuals with whom one interacts in day-to-day life—that is, it becomes *depersonalized*. Once again, this process of de-personalization is never total, since the transmission of tradition remains interwoven with face-to-face interaction. But as mediated forms of communication acquire an increasing role, so the authority of tradition is gradually detached from the individuals with whom one interacts in the practical contexts of daily life. Tradition acquires a certain autonomy and an authority of its own, as a set of values, beliefs and assumptions which exist and persist independently of the

individuals who may be involved in transmitting them from one generation to the next.

The de-personalization of tradition is not, however, a uniform and unambiguous process, and we can see that, with the development of electronic media and especially television, the conditions are created for a renewal of the link between the authority of tradition and the individuals who transmit it. But the nature of this link is new and unprecedented: it is a link which is established and sustained largely within the framework of mediated quasi-interaction. For most people, individuals such as Billy Graham and Oral Roberts are known only as TV personalities. They are individuals one can witness and observe, watch and listen to (credulously or not, as the case may be); but they are not individuals with whom one is ever likely to interact in day-to-day life. Hence, while such individuals may succeed in "repersonalizing" tradition, it is a quite distinctive kind of personalization: it lacks the reciprocity of face-to-face interaction and it is dissociated from the individuals encountered in the shared locales of everyday life. It is a form of what I would describe as "non-reciprocal intimacy at a distance."

(3) As the transmission of tradition becomes increasingly linked to communication media, traditions are also increasingly detached from their moorings in particular locales. Prior to the development of the media, traditions had a certain rootedness: that is, they were rooted in the spatial locales within which individuals lived out their daily lives. Traditions were integral parts of communities of individuals who interacted—actually or potentially—with one another. But with the development of the media, traditions were gradually uprooted; the bond that tied traditions to specific locales of face-to-face interaction was gradually weakened. In other words, traditions were gradually and partially de-localized, as they became increasingly dependent on mediated forms of communication for their maintenance and transmission from one generation to the next.

The uprooting or "de-localization" of tradition had far-reaching consequences. . . . It enabled traditions to be detached from particular locales and freed from the constraints imposed by oral transmission in circumstances of face-to-face interaction. The reach of tradition—both in space and in time—was no longer restricted by the conditions of localized transmission. But the uprooting of traditions from particular locales did not lead them to wither away, nor did it destroy altogether the connection between traditions and spatial units. On the contrary, the uprooting of traditions was the condition for the re-embedding of traditions in new contexts and for the re-mooring of traditions to new kinds of territorial units that exceeded the limits of shared locales. Traditions were de-localized but they were not de-territorialized: they were refashioned in ways that enabled them to be re-embedded in a multiplicity of locales and re-connected to territorial units that exceed the limits of face-to-face interaction.

George Lipsitz (contemp.)

American cultural studies scholar. Tracing the history of popular culture and its effects on memory, Lipsitz highlights here and throughout his trenchant writing on mass media and popular culture the creative spaces that emerge even under the influence of homogenizing mass culture and the repressions of commercialized leisure.

From *Time Passages: Collective Memory and American Popular Culture*

The presence of sedimented historical currents within popular culture illumines the paradoxical relationship between history and commercialized leisure. Time, history, and memory become qualitatively different concepts in a world where electronic mass communication is possible. Instead of relating to the past through a shared sense of place or ancestry, consumers of electronic mass media can experience a common heritage with people they have never seen; they can acquire memories of a past to which they have no geographic or biological connection. This capacity of electronic mass communication to transcend time and space creates instability by disconnecting people from past traditions, but it also liberates people by making the past less determinate of experiences in the present.

History and commercialized leisure appear to be polar opposites—the former concerned with continuities that unite the totality of human experience, the latter with immediate sense gratifications that divide society into atomized consumers. But both the variants of history and the forms of commercialized leisure familiar to us originated at the same time and for the same reasons. Both developed in the nineteenth century in response to extraordinary technological and social changes. Recognition of the common origins of history and commercialized leisure can explain the seemingly paradoxical tensions within Roland Kirk's music, while also helping to explain how the "remembering" of history and the "forgetting" of commercialized leisure form parts of a dialectical totality. . . .

As literary critic Richard Terdiman has demonstrated, nineteenth-century industrialization and state-building entailed a massive disruption of traditional forms of memory. The instrumental mentality capable of building the political and industrial machines of that century had to countenance the destruction of tradition—the enclosure of farm lands, massive migrations to industrial cities, the construction of an interchangeable work force, and a consumer market free from the constraints of tradition. A sense of disconnection from the past united an otherwise fragmented and stratified polity, and consequently the study of the past took on new meaning. Terdiman notes that "history became the discipline of memory," whose task was to uncover "the crisis which inevitably entailed disconnection with the past as a referent." Michelet, Dilthey, Bancroft, and the other great historians of the nineteenth century emerged to provide a sense of continuity and connection with the past in societies riddled with the ruptures and dislocations of modernity.

The beginnings of the electronic mass media in the form of the telegraph exacerbated the nineteenth-century crisis of memory. The telegraph enabled simultaneous communication for the first time, dissolving previous barriers of time and space. But that very simultaneity favored the agenda of ascendant industrial capitalism. The telegraph innately privileged the transmission of isolated facts like prices or recent events; it did little to convey context or continuity. Newspapers took on a new role with the stimulus of the telegraph, but it was a role geared toward commerce and change rather than to the preservation of cultural memory. The daily newspaper naturalized a kind of confusion in which the world seemed structured by isolated and discrete events; news became synonymous with change and more important than tradition.

A new kind of commercialized leisure emerged as a corollary to the telegraph in the United States during the late nineteenth century. Previously, churches, lodge halls, and community centers had served as sites for theatrical productions designed to mark festive occasions like weddings and holidays. But urban taverns, dance halls, amusement parks, and theaters brought new meanings to culture. The new commercial theaters, and later variety, vaudeville, and motion-picture halls, needed no special occasions and no association with ritualized activities to justify plays, skits, and music. They carved away a new kind of social space for working-class people—buildings devoted exclusively to leisure activities. Theatrical performances became commodities sold to strangers for an agreed upon price rather than collective creations by communities enacting rituals essential to group identity and solidarity.

Of course, commercialized theater had existed since the sixteenth century in Europe. Jean-Christophe Agnew, among others, has delineated the complicated connections between the assumptions of theater and the values central to the capitalist marketplace, but in nineteenth-century America, theater, medicine shows, circuses, taverns, dance halls, amusement parks, and vaudeville-variety houses intervened in culture and society in especially important ways. They helped Americans make a decisive break with Victorian restraints, while at the same time blending an ethnically diverse working class into an "audience" with a unified language and sign-system.

The success of popular theater in nineteenth-century America aggravated the crisis of historical memory by further detaching culture from tradition. It institutionalized a kind of dissembling, one feared by philosophers as far back as Plato. To speak someone else's words or to wear someone else's cloths meant hiding one's own identity. In a world where ancestry, locality, and vocation determined social status and identity, the inherent disguise of acting threatened core values. Role playing in the theater suggested that identities could be changed, that one was not bound by bloodliness, nationality, or occupation. This contained the essence of egalitarian and utopian thought by challenging the legitimacy of static identities inherited from the past, but it also threatened a sense of authentic self-knowledge and created the psychic preconditions for the needy narcissism of consumer desire. On stage, actors deliberately speak and act inauthentically, off stage everyone learns to act, because everyone needs to take on ever-changing roles as a consumer and worker. As literary scholar Michael Bristol points out about the cultural crises posed by theater in Elizabethan England, "An actor is not just someone whose speech is "dissembling;" the deeper problem is that he is most valued for his ability to dissemble convincingly." As commercialized theaters in nineteenth-century America helped destroy connections to the past, historical tableaux and dramas became common features within them, offering a fictive representation of what was being destroyed in reality. Thus the contents of theatrical productions sometimes ministered to the very wounds that their forms had helped to open.

Along with the telegraph and the daily newspaper, the theater helped reshape cultural memory and consciousness. Its role on behalf of the emergent industrial order helped mold a diverse population into a unified working and consuming force, but it also raised anxieties about the moral costs of disconnection from the past. To many critics, the "dissembling" of theater presented a challenge to established order and morality. These critics feared that nothing genuine or refined could come from a sphere of activity devoted to false representations and masked identities. Furthermore, they recognized that theatrical "time" presented an alternative to work time, pitting the pleasures of leisure against the responsibilities of labor. Theater attendance enabled individuals to play out fictive scenarios of changed identities, to escape from the surveillance and supervision of moral authorities and institutions. The fantasy world of the theatrical stage encouraged audiences to pursue personal desires and passions at the expense of their socially prescribed responsibilities

Yet audiences embraced the new possibilities presented by commercial theater with enthusiasm. Unlike the wedding celebration or the community festival, the theater assembled an audience with no shared history, with no reciprocal responsibilities and obligations. Theatergoers in nineteenth-century America shared intimate and personal cultural moments with strangers. The unfamiliarity of the crowd with each other provided a kind of protective cover—a "privacy in public" whereby personal feelings and emotions could be aired without explanation or apology. Women especially utilized the new popular culture as a way of escaping parental surveillance and patriarchal domination. Using the borrowed legitimacy of theater's status as a form of cultural refinement, audiences flocked to the melodramas, vaudeville and variety shows, and later to motion pictures for decidedly unrefined productions and performances. In the theater, they encountered a world momentarily liberated from the sexual and emotional repressions of the nineteenth century. Theatrical performances provided an outlet for expression of the needs and desires for pleasure long suppressed by the normative constraints of Victorian America.

The sexual repressions of the Victorian era created powerful anxieties and tensions that could not be confronted directly by "respectable" citizens. But theater productions offered audiences an opportunity to view the forbidden and to contemplate the unthinkable. This "freedom" came less in the form of true sexual emancipation, however, than through a redirection of frustrations. The unfilled desires and unconsummated lusts of theater audiences made them good customers for sexually suggestive images, no matter how coded, coy, or indirect. The theater offered immediate but transitory gratification. It turned sexual impulses and desires into symbolic commodities to be purchased from others. One bought a theater ticket to see a performance that depicted happiness and pleasures missing from one's own life. Pleasure itself could not be purchased as a commodity—at least not legally—but the image of pleasure represented in the theater could be obtained for a small price. Similarly, theatrical productions evoked other desires—for intimacy, for recognition, for connection to the past. But the very forms of commercial theater aggravated rather than salved the wounds they pretended to heal.

Yet the theater did encompass a kind of free space for the imagination—an arena liberated from old restraints and repressions, a place where desire did not have to be justified or explained. By establishing commodity purchases as symbolic answers to real problems, the theater also helped lay the groundwork for the consumer-commodity culture of our own day wherein advertisers and entrepreneurs offer products that promise to bring pleasure and fulfillment. The nineteenth-century theater may have emerged in part as a rebellion against sexual repression, but its greatest long-term significance lay in shaping the psychic and material preconditions for Americans to shift from a Victorian industrial economy to a hedonistic consumer-commodity economy. It would not be the last time that the commercial matrix in which popular culture was embedded worked to undermine its potential for educational or social transcendence.

Melodramas, vaudeville and variety shows, and motion pictures taught Americans to make a break with the discipline, sobriety, thrift, and sexual repression that formed the core of Victorian culture. Appropriate to an industrializing economy, Victorian values provided necessary preconditions for economic growth during the nineteenth century. They stressed the work ethic, personal responsibility, punctuality, and willingness to defer gratification necessary for life as an industrial worker. But by the 1890s, it appeared that Victorian culture had done its work all too well. The hard-working Americans who internalized Victorian values helped build a powerful industrial economy that produced more products than the domestic market could consume. Overproduction and underconsumption threatened the very survival of industrial capitalism in the 1880s and 1890s, as business failures led to massive unemployment and repeated financial panics. The "false promise" of the Victorian code, that sober self-management would lead to upward mobility, helped provoke general strikes and other forms of "aggressive festivity" among workers. To solve their many problems, business leaders had to move away from the production of capital goods like railroads and locomotives and start producing consumer goods for the domestic market. But as long as Victorian repressions inhibited desires for immediate gratification, consumers lacked the psychological makeup necessary for an economy oriented around ever-increasing purchases of commodities by individuals.

Commercialized leisure evolved out of the contradictions in late nineteenth-century capitalism. As I. C. Jarvie notes, motion pictures not only served as renewable commodities in themselves, but they also helped legitimate the consciousness necessary for purchasing other renewable commodities. The specialization of industrial capitalism requires individuals "detachable from tradition, family, and ascription." Jarvie argues that motion pictures encouraged people to see themselves as detached and autonomous consumers by replacing ritualistic community celebrations with leisure that could be purchased as a commodity and shared with strangers. Between 1890 and 1930 American society underwent extraordinary changes, from a Victorian culture of thrift to a consumer-oriented culture of spending. By the 1920s, production of renewable commodities like automobiles and appliances played a more important role in the U.S. economy than production of nonrenewable capital goods like heavy equipment and machinery. Economic historians have long understood the logic of this change for the interests of capital; building factories and locomotive engines brought enormous immediate profits, but the market for them became saturated rather quickly. Consumer goods did not need to last—indeed advertisers worked very diligently to see to it that considerations of fashion and style would render old goods obsolete and engender a demand for new ones.

Scholars examining the transition from Victorianism to consumerism in the U.S. have concentrated on the idea of leisure as contested terrain. Drawing upon the research of E. P. Thompson and Herbert Gutman, they have emphasized the ways in which the transition from agrarian to industrial life gave new meanings to work and play. In pre-industrial society, agrarian labor could be done at one's own pace and for one's own benefit. In the industrial workplace, factory time replaced natural time, and unremitting labor measured by the time-clock replaced the task-oriented work of the farm. No longer could leisure be mixed in with work, and work itself became a more prominent and a more alienating part of human existence. Just as the centralized industrial work site replaced home labor, so commercial establishments devoted to leisure-time pursuits replicated in the arena of play the capitalist division of labor. Intense resistance against these practices fueled strikes, sabotage, and other forms of working-class self-activity throughout the era of industrialization, but religious, medical, and legal authorities attempted to prevent revolt by inculcating Victorian values within the character structure of the work force, values championing repression, denial, thrift, chastity, sobriety, and hard work. But like most forms of ideological legitimation, they contained severe internal contradictions. When workers *internalized* Victorian norms, their labor produced a surplus of goods that could not be consumed by a domestic market filled with poorly paid thrifty self-denying individuals like themselves. When workers *resisted*

Victorian norms, their repressions and anger drove them toward the only available source of pleasure—the illicit vices offered for sale by the underworld.

Thus commercialized leisure both facilitated the triumphs of industrial capitalism and focused attention on their psychic and emotional costs. Commercial culture sought credibility with its audiences by promising at least the illusion of connection with the past. But the gap between lived experience and the false promises of popular culture always created the possibility for counter-memories, for ethnic, class, and regional music, art, speech, and theater. Culture itself contributed to retraining and reshaping the masses to serve the interests of capital, but also to articulating unfilled desires and expressing disconnection from the past. British cultural studies theorist Stuart Hall notes the contradictions in this process as well as the centrality of tradition as a contested category in the nineteenth century.

> Capital had a stake in the culture of the popular classes because the constitution of a whole new social order around capital required a more or less continuous, if intermittent, process of re-education. And one of the principal sites of resistance to the forms through which this "reformation" of the people was pursued lay in popular tradition. That is why popular culture is linked, for so long, to questions of tradition, of traditional forms of life—and why its "traditionalism" has been so often misinterpreted as a product of a merely conservative impulse, backward looking and anachronistic.

The transformations in behavior and collective memory fueled by the contradictions of the nineteenth century have passed through three major stages in the United States. The first involved the establishment and codification of commercialized leisure from the invention of the telegraph to the 1890s. The second involved the transition from Victorian to consumer-hedonist values between 1890 and 1945. The third and most important stage, from World War II to the present, involved extraordinary expansion in both the distribution of consumer purchasing power and in the reach and scope of the electronic mass media. The dislocations of urban renewal, suburbanization, and deindustrialization accelerated the demise of tradition in America, while the worldwide pace of change undermined stability elsewhere. The period from World War II to the present marks the final triumph of commercialized leisure, and with it an augmented crisis over the loss of connection to the past. Popular culture has played an important role in creating this crisis of memory, but it has also been one of the main vehicles for the expression of loss and the projection of hopes for reconnection to the past.

Barbie Zelizer (contemp.)

American media scholar. In an early contribution to the wave of contemporary memory studies in sociology and related fields, Zelizer's 1992 book *Covering the Body: The Kennedy Assassination, the Media, and the Shaping of Collective Memory* provides a unique and nuanced account of the role of journalists in shaping much more recent collective memory of the Kennedy assassination in its immediate aftermath. In the following excerpts, Zelizer convincingly exhorts the field to pay more attention to the mutual relevance of media studies—particularly studies of journalism—and memory studies.

From "Why Memory's Work on Journalism Does Not Reflect Journalism's Work on Memory"

Memory and journalism resemble two distant cousins. They know of each other's existence, acknowledge their shared environment from time to time and proceed apace as autonomous phenomena without seeming to depend on the other. And yet neither reaches optimum functioning without the other occupying a backdrop. Just as journalism needs memory work to position its recounting of public events in context, so too does memory need journalism to provide one of the most public drafts of the past. . . .

To say that memory work depends in part on journalism is to state a truism that should be obvious to memory scholars though it is not necessarily recognized by journalists. In that the work of memory draws from a wide range of sources—performances, testimonies, standards of conduct and material artifacts, to name a few—the accounts provided by journalists constitute an important source of information about practices, issues and events of a given time period. The relevance of journalists' work to understanding the past, however, is not necessarily admitted by journalists, who neither explicitly speak of the past nor consider the past as part of their obvious purview. As purveyors of the present, they tend instead to display both obliviousness and disregard for what is in effect their unstated role as agents of memory. . . .

[E]ven today, decades into the systematic scholarly study of collective memory, there is still no default understanding of memory that includes journalism as one of its vital and critical agents. One of the key lessons of contemporary memory studies is that vast and intricate memory work is being accomplished all the time in settings having little to do with memory per se. While the scholarly understanding of other key institutions—religion, the educational system, the political system, to name a few—has produced a picture that includes practices and conventions associated with an unarticulated but patterned treatment of the past, such has not been the case with journalism. . . .

For as long as journalism has been around, the popular assumption has been that it provides a first, rather than final, draft of the past, leaving to the historians the final processing of journalism's raw events. Against such a division of labor, journalism has come to be seen as a setting driven more by its emphasis on the here-and-now than on the there-and-then, restricted by temporal limitations associated with rapidly overturning deadlines. Journalists distinguish themselves from those dealing with the past by aspiring to a sense of newsworthiness that draws from proximity, topicality and novelty, and they are motivated by an ongoing need to fill a depleting news-hole despite high stakes, a frantic pace and uncertain resources. In this regard, the past seems somewhat beyond the boundaries of what journalists can and ought to do in accomplishing their work goals. . . .

For their part, historians have generally agreed with journalism's rendering of the past to others. Often less interested in the variations and contradictions that arise in the record over time than they have been in securing a durable, accurate and reliable recounting of the past, historians have valued journalists' address to events as a present-oriented treatment. That address has tended to provide, at least explicitly, a durable record associated with "history's first draft" and a respect for truth, facts and reality. . . . But although historians regularly rely on news accounts of the past to establish the facts of what happened in a given time period, even among historians, journalism's treatments have been suspect. . . .

Journalism's alignment with the past reflects a more complicated dynamic and invested relationship than that suggested by traditional notions of history. Journalists have set their collective recollections and reconstructions of the past in place by attending to their own agendas. . . .

In recounting events, journalists deliver news stories by combining content and form in ways conventionalized by news organizations. By and large, journalists pride themselves on content, first and foremost, following the news story and playing to occurrences that are interesting, timely, and important, regardless of the form in which they are told. This has produced a gravitation toward simplistic narratives, a tendency to record without context, and a minimization of nuance and the grey areas of a phenomenon, all of which restrict journalism's ability to account for the past. While the focus on content makes journalism's status as memory work problematic, the forms of relay that journalists regularly use suggest a picture that is far more aligned with the work of memory than its content would suggest. In fact, the particular forms of journalistic relay bring memory work directly into the foreground of journalism.

Journalistic form takes on numerous guises in association with the past. In that the past offers a point of comparison, an opportunity for analogy, an invitation to nostalgia and a redress to earlier events, journalism's look to the past suggests some attendance to memory, though journalists do not insist on or even necessarily recognize its presence. Once journalists begin to make decisions about which stories play in which medium and using which tools for relay, they find themselves squarely in the realm of memory's work.

This makes form a leading sign of memory's presence, even if journalists do not admit as much. In this regard, the ascendance of the past in journalism enhances the possibility for journalists to act as sleuths of the past. . . .

Form incorporates memory into journalism in three main ways. At times, the coverage itself is structured formalistically in a way that insists on an engagement with the past; in these cases, form necessitates memory. Other times, the coverage is structured in a way that invites engagement with the past but keeps a footing in the present; in these cases, form invites memory. And finally, at times, coverage includes an address to the past so as to better treat an event in the past, though such treatment is neither necessary nor even clear; in such cases, form indulges memory. . . .

When form necessitates memory, journalists produce obits, rewrites and revisits to old events as typical of commemorative and anniversary journalism. In such cases, journalists would not have a story were they not to go back in time. Looking backward, then, is what makes the journalistic treatment newsworthy. . . .

When form invites memory, journalism uses the past so as to engage with the present. Neither necessary nor central to the journalistic coverage that ensues, journalism in this instance produces a variety of journalistic forms that allow for the present and past to be discussed in some kind of simultaneous relay. Included here would be historical analogues, direct comparisons between present and past, and investigations of seemingly "historical" events. . . .

When form indulges memory, the past is brought into a news story as an aside or afterthought. Though memory and the past are neither necessary nor critical to understanding the contemporary news story, here journalists produce investigations of the present that are illuminated by some foray into the past. The inclusion of the past helps illuminate the centrality that the past plays in helping journalists make sense of the present.

Daniel Dayan and Elihu Katz (contemp.)

Israeli and American media scholars. In this excerpt, Dayan and Katz outline the implications watching "historic" events on television has for collective memory, namely that media events serve as electronic monuments, provide frames for the unfolding of history, signal beginnings and endings, edit and re-edit collective memory, and compete with other versions of history.

From *Media Events: The Live Broadcasting of History*

The most obvious difference between media events and other formulas or genres of broadcasting is that they are, by definition, not routine. In fact, they are *interruptions* of routine; they intervene in the normal flow of broadcasting and our lives. Like the holidays that halt everyday routines, television events propose exceptional things to think about, to witness, and to do. Regular broadcasting is suspended and preempted as we are guided by a series of special announcements and preludes that transform daily life into something special and, upon the conclusion of the event, are guided back again. In the most characteristic events, the interruption is *monopolistic*, in that all channels switch away from their regularly scheduled programming in order to turn to the great event, perhaps leaving a handful of independent stations outside the consensus. Broadcasting can hardly make a more dramatic announcement of the importance of what is about to happen.

Moreover, the happening is *live*. The events are transmitted as they occur, in real time. . . . They are therefore unpredictable, at least in the sense that something can go wrong. . . . Typically, these events are *organized outside the media*, and the media serve them in what Jakobson . . . would call a phatic role in that, at least theoretically, the media only provide a channel for their transmission. By "outside" we mean both that the events take place outside the studio in what broadcasters call "remote locations" and that the event is not usually initiated by the broadcasting organizations. This kind of connection, in real time, to a remote place—one having major importance to some central value of society . . .—is credited with an exceptional value, by both broadcasters and their audiences. . . .

The organizers, typically, are public bodies with whom the media cooperate, such as governments, parliaments (congressional committees, for example), political parties (national conventions), international bodies (the Olympics committee), and the like. These organizers are well within the establishment. They are part of what Shils . . . calls the center. They stand for consensual values and they have the authority to command our attention. . . .

These events are *preplanned,* announced and advertised in advance. Viewers—and, indeed, broadcasters—had only a few days notice of the exact time of Sadat's arrival in Jerusalem; Irish television advertised the Pope's

362   MEDIA AND MODES OF TRANSMISSION

visit to Ireland a few weeks in advance; the 1984 Los Angeles Olympics were heralded for more than four years. Important for our purpose is that advance notice gives time for anticipation and preparation on the part of both broadcasters and audiences. There is an active period of looking forward, abetted by the promotional activity of the broadcasters.

The conjunction of *live* and *remote*, on the one hand, and *interrupted* but *preplanned*, on the other, takes us a considerable distance toward our definition of the genre. Note that live-and-remote excludes routine studio broadcasts that may originate live, as well as feature programs such as "Roots" or "Holocaust." The addition of interruption excludes the evening news, while preplanned excludes major news events—such as the attempted assassination of a pope or a president, the nuclear accident at Three Mile Island, and, at first glance (but we shall reconsider this), the so-called television revolutions in Romania and Czechoslovakia. In other words, our corpus is limited to ceremonial occasions. . . .

[W]e find that these broadcast events are presented with *reverence* and *ceremony*. The journalists who preside over them suspend their normally critical stance and treat their subject with respect, even awe. . . .

Of course, the very flow of ceremonial events is courtly and invites awe. There is the playing of the national anthem, the funereal beat of the drum corps, the diplomatic ceremony of being escorted from the plane, the rules of decorum in church and at Senate hearings. The point is that in media events television rarely intrudes: it interrupts only to identify the music being played or the name of the chief of protocol. It upholds the definition of the event by its organizers, explains the meaning of the symbols of the occasion, only rarely intervenes with analysis and almost never with criticism. . . .

Even when these programs address conflict—as they do—they celebrate not conflict but *reconciliation*.

This is where they differ from the daily news events, where conflict is the inevitable subject. Often they are ceremonial efforts to redress conflict or to restore order or, more rarely, to institute change. They call for a cessation of hostilities, at least for a moment. . . .

These events applaud the *voluntary* actions of great personalities. They celebrate what, on the whole, are establishment initiatives that are therefore unquestionably *hegemonic*. They are proclaimed *historic*.

These ceremonials *electrify very large audiences*—a nation, several nations, or the world. They are gripping, enthralling. They are characterized by a *norm of viewing* in which people tell each other that it is mandatory to view, that they must put all else aside. The unanimity of the networks in presenting the same event underlines the worth, even the obligation, of viewing. They cause viewers to *celebrate* the event by gathering before the television set in groups, rather than alone. Often the audience is given an active role in the celebration. Figuratively, at least, these events induce people to dress up, rather than dress down, to view television. These broadcasts *integrate* societies in a collective heartbeat and evoke a *renewal of loyalty* to the society and its legitimate authority. . . .

1. *Media events are electronic monuments.* They are meant to live in collective memory through association with either the traumas to which they are responses or the exceptional nature of the gratifications they provide. The memory of President Kennedy will forever evoke the image of the funeral as seen on television. One of the most important effects of "response ceremonies" is that they become so firmly sutured to the situations in which they arise that they ultimately come to represent them, retrospectively mediating or even displacing our experience of them.

2. *Media events endow collective memory not only with a substance but with a frame: they are mnemonics* for organizing personal and historical time. To members of the same generation, media events provide shared reference points, the sense of a common past, bridges between personal and collective history. People who watched the moon landing can still tell you where they were and what they were doing when the broadcast took place. Olympics viewers associate events in their lives with different Olympic Games.

3. *Media events are interruptions marking breaks in time, sometimes signaling the beginnings and ends of an "era."* Like wars, they disrupt existing calendars. Thus, presidential inaugurations may or may not succeed as media events, depending on the transitions they mark; the end of the Carter presidency and the beginning of Reagan's *was* a media event. Media events may be counted as "catastrophic time"—a decisive and meaningful intervention in history—rather than as the regularized progression from minor crisis to minor crisis which Braudy calls "soap opera time." The "end of an era" was the immediate meaning assigned to the intervention of state-run television on the side of the revolutionaries in Czechoslovakia and Romania. The disruptive nature of such events, it should be noted, enhances their mnemonic function.

4. *Media events edit and reedit collective memory.* Often serving the same functions as religious holidays, they "quote" from earlier events. Thus Nixon's resignation echoed other tragic partings, such as Kennedy's. By the same token, Kennedy's funeral recalled Lincoln's, but not Garfield's or McKinley's—who had also died at the hands of assassins. Media events also refer and give meaning to current events; the moon landing of Christmas 1968 was experienced as solace for the traumas (Vietnam, the assassinations, the riots) of the year then ending. Each serves as a discursive center which gives perspective to ongoing history.

5. *Thus media events and their narration are in competition with the writing of history* in defining the contents of collective memory. Their disruptive and heroic character is indeed what is remembered, upstaging the efforts of historians and social scientists to perceive continuities and to reach beyond the personal. Moreover, ceremonial events are constantly quoted in edited or fictionalized form within television itself, finding their way into films, historical miniseries, or contemporary serials. One thinks of films such as *All the President's Men* (Watergate), *Chariots of Fire* (Olympics), *The Right Stuff* (moon landing). The

coronation was quoted in the televised version of the "Forsyte Saga;" the royal
wedding in "Coronation Street;" Kennedy's death and King's "I had a dream"
speech in "Kennedy." A series was devoted to Sadat; one to Jesse Owens. This
alliance of ritualization and fictionalization makes it even more evident that the
professional recording of history is not synonymous with what is remembered.

Reinhart Koselleck (1923–2006)

German historian. Koselleck was one of the founding fathers of "conceptual history" (*Begriffsgeschichte*), an encyclopedic effort to unpack the basic conceptual structure of modernity's self-understanding. As part of this project, Koselleck developed an influential account of the role of "temporalization," the vast expansion of "horizons of expectation" beyond the confines of "spaces of experience," that he saw underlying the novel structure of modernity. This project is in some ways analogous to those of **Foucault**, **Warburg**, and **Benjamin**, though there are, to be sure, substantial differences among these authors. Here Koselleck contributes to the analysis of memorialization as part of yet another encyclopedic study, this time of war memorials, tracing out the transformations from the nineteenth century through the mid-twentieth.

From "War Memorials: Identity Formations of the Survivors"

Memorials to the dead are certainly as old as human history. They correspond to a fundamental state of being, pregiven to human beings, in which death and life intertwine in whatever ways they are referred to one another. Innocent III formulated the nearness of life and death in the following well-known words: "Morimur ergo semper dum vivimus, et tunc tantum desinimus mori cum desinimus vivere" (Therefore while we are living we are always dying, and we cease to die only then, when we cease to live). Whether consciously or not, memorials to the dead presuppose this—what Heidegger later analyzed as "Being toward death."

But it is different with war memorials because they are supposed to recall violent death at the hands of human beings. In addition to remembrance, the question of the justification of this death is also evoked. Here, factors of arbitrariness, freedom, and voluntariness, as well as factors of coercion and violence, come into play. Over and above natural death, so to speak, such deaths stand in need of legitimation and obviously are, therefore, especially worthy of remembrance. The dictum of Innocent III thus ought to be altered: human beings live so long as they are not killed, and only when they can no longer be killed have they stopped living . . . The thesis that I want to demonstrate from history is this: The only identity that endures clandestinely in all war memorials is the identity of the dead with themselves. All political and social identifications that try to visually capture and permanently fix the "dying for" . . . vanish in the course of time. For this reason, the message that was to have been established by a memorial changes. . . .

As the biological causes of death have been scientifically explained and, with such explanations, life expectancies increased, the ways of dying (likewise thanks to the natural sciences) have multiplied and death rates have risen with the violent killing of human beings. That certainly holds true for the last two centuries, whose death statistics can be readily surveyed. It is also during this time that the emergence and spread of war memorials has taken place with such memorials appearing in almost every community in Europe.

War memorials offer identifications in ways that could not have been offered before the French Revolution. For the time being, let me therefore start by giving two references to monuments to the dead in the prerevolutionary period. First, the otherworldly beyond of death was indicated figuratively, with death being interpreted not as an end but as a passageway. Secondly, in this outlook upon the world, the represented death remained differentiated by estate, even though death became increasingly individualized. Both findings, which roughly involve the period between the twelfth and eighteenth centuries, in no way stand in contradiction to one another. The late medieval *danse macabre* initially was not directed in a revolutionary manner against the existing estates. Each estate is judged individually in terms of its human quality that becomes visible before death, the great equalizer. The diversity of the estates is marked in this world before the equality of death swallows it up in the next.

This becomes especially clear with the gradual spread of double tombs . . . in France, England, and Germany during the fifteenth and sixteenth centuries. The worldly but transpersonal official position is indicated on the upper level where the ruler is represented lying down in his official dress, adorned with the insignia of power. Below, his body deteriorates so as to release the individual soul to eternal judgment. As a ruler, he represents his office which is not subject to mortality, but the ruler is also representative as a human being—for human mortality, for everyone.

Such tombs, which present the official position and the individual separately or sometimes blended together, were reserved for rulers and the rich. Until the eighteenth century, soldiers appear everywhere on victory monuments but not on war memorials. Within the society of estates, mercenaries or soldiers recruited by the state remained relegated to the lowest level, unworthy of a monument. . . . However, in places where commemorative monuments or memorial chapels for the fallen were erected, for example those that have come down to us from the Thirty Years' War, such monuments stood as tokens of expiation for human crimes. Thus the Christian transcendence of death and the estate-based leveling of empirical death were connected with one another. Death was a link between this world and the next; this allowed death to be defined both in its earthly sense and in its otherworldly context. Here a tension prevailed in which great personages were monumentally transfigured, but for the masses of fallen mercenaries, buildings could be erected as tokens of expiation without the death of individuals having to be remembered.

The shift to modernity can likewise be conceptualized in two ways. First, while the transcendental sense of death fades or is lost, the inner-worldly claims of representations of death grow. Notwithstanding the point that Christian images of death also always had an inner-worldly function (one need only to think of the tombs of the archbishops of Mainz), the definition of commemorative monuments now begins to change. Their inner-worldly function turns into an end in itself. The bourgeois memorial cult emerges, and within this cult, there originates the independent genre of the war memorial. Since the French Revolution and the Wars of Liberation (1813–14), the number of memorials dedicated to soldiers killed in action has steadily increased. Not only do they stand in churches and cemeteries, but they have also moved from the churches into open spaces and into the landscape. It is not only the death of soldiers itself that serves political purposes, but the remembrance of it is also put to political service. The war memorial is intended to fulfill this task. It shifts the memory of the death of soldiers into an inner-worldly functional context that aims only at the future of the survivors. The decline of a Christian interpretation of death thus creates a space for meaning to be purely established in political and social terms.

Second, as war memorials become more widespread, they are divested more and more of the traditional differences of the society of estates. The physical memorial, previously reserved for great personages, was to include everyone and to do so in the name of all. The individual soldier killed in action becomes entitled to a memorial. Democratization is brought together with functionalization. With this, the equality of death, formerly only related to the Christian world to come, also gains an egalitarian claim on the political entity in whose service death was met. The names of all the dead become individually inscribed, or at least the number of dead noted, on memorial plaques and monuments to soldiers killed in action, so that in the future no one sinks into the past. This kind of democratization includes all the states in the European community of culture and tradition, regardless of their particular constitutional forms.

Compulsory military service certainly furthered the general entitlement of all those killed in action to a memorial, but it was not a necessary prerequisite. This is shown in Great Britain, a land without conscription by the numerous memorials erected to honor heroes in overseas wars and wars in the colonies, culminating in Boer War memorials, which prefigured the type of memorials of the world wars.

The process of functionalization and democratization thus characterizes the historical succession of war memorials. They are supposed to attune the political sensibility of surviving onlookers to the same cause for whose sake the death of the soldiers is supposed to be remembered. This can certainly only be described as a long-term process, which is ramified in many different ways according to national and denominational patterns and can only be shown with many Christian overtones, accoutrements, signs of renewal, or relics.

But methodologically, it is especially difficult to distinguish the Christian and the national elements from one another. The recourse to the classical and Egyptian arsenal of forms, customary since the Renaissance, and later the use of natural and geometrical signs, gains a claim to exclusiveness in the late Enlightenment, figuratively countermanding the Christian interpretation of death. If, in the nineteenth century, numerous Christian symbols surface again, this iconographic finding can nevertheless refer to a context that is to be read differently in iconological terms. The context of classical figural elements in the baroque period is usually purely Christian, while the context of Christian figural elements in the nineteenth century can point in a different direction, primarily at the safeguarding of identity for a national future. In other words, the icono-graphically visible finding permits no immediate conclusion with regard to its iconological interpretation. In any case, war memorials themselves are already a visual sign of modernity (*Neuzeit*). . . .

The increasing thematization of mourning on tombs is part of the visual signature of the new age. . . . Since then, the meaning of death is forced back to the survivors; since then, non-Christian symbols rival Christian symbols, com-pletely eclipsing them in some places. The representation of subjective mourning is only the private mode of expression for a reinterpretation of death, a reinterpretation that allows death to be placed fully in the service of particular units of action in the political world of images. . . .

The transition from a monarchical memorial to a memorial for the people . . . finds its counterpart in the increase in the politically motivated layout of graves. Taken as a whole, the representative grave for the ruler is first complemented by the representative war grave, then—temporally speaking—overtaken by it. On the consecrated tombs, the identity of political protagonists—first of the dynasties and then of the nation to be created—was supposed to find its mani-fest expression. Not only do the living vouch for the dead in front of the memo-rial, but the dead are also supposed to vouch for life. Which life is politically intended is delimited by the layout of the grave, the memorial, and the cult attached to it. . . .

[W]ar graves and the soldiers' entitlement to a memorial owe their origin to a revolutionary impulse initially directed against the estates-monarchic tradition. . . .

The political cult of the dead, to the extent that it depends on the building of war memorials, remains under the victors' control—as long as they are in a position to exercise their power. But irrespective of the changing political situa-tion, the demand for equality for all war memorials has gained acceptance since the revolution. In addition, the same visual tone is sounded regardless of forms of government. The tombs of the "unknown soldier"—one for all—are the last step in this democratization of death. Some of the visual documents testifying to this path will be traced below. . . .

Almost all the memorials of World War I distinguish themselves by the fact that they compensate for helplessness by pathos. The death of hundreds of thou-sands on a few square miles of contested earth left an obligation to search for justifications that were hard to create with traditional metaphors and concepts. The desire to salvage continuities or identities that were everywhere torn apart by death all too easily fell short. . . .

World War II brought with it a transformation in the iconographic landcape of memorials that also changed political sensibility. The simple expansion of memorials by the addition of plaques for those who died between 1939–45 was still a fresh and generally customary tradition. . . .

Finally, during the Vietnam war, Edward Kienholz created the anti-memo-rial, a parody of the victory monument in Arlington. He constructed an ordi-nary scene within which a portable war memorial is placed. Next to it there is a plaque upon which, depending on the new beginning of a war, the dead can be recorded with chalk so that the memorial is not blamed for the oblivion of death but rather human beings who shirk the memory of the dead. Although not everywhere and not universally, a tendency has thus grown in the Western world to represent death in foreign or civil war only as a question and no longer as an answer, only as demanding meaning and no longer as establishing meaning. What remains is the identity of the dead with themselves; the capability of memorializing the dead eludes the formal language of political sensibility. . . .

The history of European war memorials testifies to a common visual signature of modernity. But it just as much attests to an optical transformation of experience. This transformation involves social and political sensibility, which has its own history and has had a productive as well as receptive effect on the language of memorials.

The connection between a demand for meaning in political and social terms and its visual expression is established by the formal language of memorials that is supposed to reach the sensibility of observers. Both the forms and the sensibility are subject to historical transformation, but they apparently change along different temporal rhythms. Hence the identities that a memorial is intended to evoke melt away—in part because sensory receptivity eludes the formal language presented and in part because the forms, once shaped, begin to speak another language than the one from which they were initially fashioned. Memorials, like all works of art, have a surplus potential to take on a life of their own. For this reason, the original meaning of countless memorials is no longer recognizable without recourse to inscriptions or other empirically comprehensible reference signals.

Since the French Revolution, the historical experience begins to emerge that war memorials lose their original emphasis with the passing of the generations responsible for their construction. Numerous memorials from the nineteenth century have not only acquired an external patina; they have fallen into oblivion, and if they are maintained and visited, then only rarely is it to reassert their original political sense. Even in the victor countries of 1918, the celebration of the armistice of November 11 draws fewer and fewer people. The political cult at the old war memorials dries up as soon as the last survivors pass away. One might trace this result back to the natural succession of generations, without having to call upon the fast pace of the modern age. Political experiences or messages can only be passed down beyond the death of a particular generation with great effort. To this end, societal institutions are required. In any case, the memorial, the supposed guarantor of sensory transmission beyond death, does not appear to be capable of achieving this task by itself. A conscious adoption of the message is always necessary.

For this reason, there are exceptions, especially where national memorials are concerned. Their maintenance is taken care of by particular political associations. In this case, it becomes possible for the cultic acts of which they are the focus to last for a longer time.

The dismantling of memorials testifies to how long the inscriptions and signatures of war memorials speak to future generations. Such dismantlings take place for the most part when the founding generation has neither entirely passed away nor can be fought as a direct political opponent. In 1918, after a half century had gone by, the French were able to afford to leave untouched the German war memorials of 1870–71 in Alsace-Lorraine—as monuments of those who were now the defeated. Memorials are taken down when they are felt to be a threat or when a tradition that is still living is intended to be suppressed. . . .

Memorials long outlasting their immediate occasion may be preserved for historical or traditional reasons, but, even then, their expressive power gradually changes. All over Europe, there is a diachronic line of victory memorials whose formal similarity holds out regardless of particular countries and victors. They move together structurally. It is, then, only victory as such, no longer any particular victory, that is brought to mind. The formal language specific to war memorials is obsolete without ceasing to speak. Evidently, this language outlives its unique, politically and socially determined causes, so that the signs are no longer understood politically but remain comprehensible nonetheless. This difference, this gap, is filled, so to speak, by aesthetics; it interrogates the forms in terms of their own "statement." In other words, the "aesthetic" possibilities for a statement, connected to the sensory receptivity of observers, outlast the political demands for identification that they were supposed to establish. If one investigates war memorials by asking which "aesthetic" signals have outlasted their immediate occasion and which signs have endured throughout the changes in form, one is clearly referred back to symbols of death. Whether dressed in hope or cloaked in grief, symbols of death last longer than any individual case. Although the individual case of death may fade, death is nonetheless still in store for every observer.

James E. Young (contemp.)

American literary and cultural critic. Young's influential work on memorials, particularly of the Holocaust, as media of memory, examines the variety of different ways in which the same past can be represented in different sculptural and other forms. In this essay on memory and counter-memory, Young explores whether the rhetoric of monuments has in fact exhausted itself in the post-Holocaust era.

From *At Memory's Edge: After-Images of the Holocaust in Contemporary Art and Architecture*

Among the hundreds of submissions in the 1995 competition for a German national "memorial to the murdered Jews of Europe," one seemed an especially uncanny embodiment of the impossible questions at the heart of Germany's memorial process. Artist Horst Hoheisel, already well known for his negative-form monument in Kassel, proposed a simple, if provocative antisolution to the memorial competition: blow up the Brandenburger Tor, grind its stone into dust, sprinkle the remains over its former site, and cover the entire memorial area with granite plates. How better to remember a destroyed people than by a destroyed monument?

Rather than commemorating the destruction of a people with the construction of yet another edifice, Hoheisel would mark one destruction with another destruction. Rather than filling in the void left by a murdered people with a positive form, the artist would carve out an empty space in Berlin by which to recall a now absent people. . . .

In fact, perhaps no single emblem better represents the conflicted, self-abnegating motives for memory in Germany today than the vanishing monument.

Of course, such a memorial undoing will never be sanctioned by the German government, and this, too, is part of the artist's point. Hoheisel's proposed destruction of the Brandenburg Gate participates in the competition for a national Holocaust memorial, even as its radicalism precludes the possibility of its execution. At least part of its polemic, therefore, is directed against actually building any winning design, against ever finishing the monument at all. Here he seems to suggest that the surest engagement with Holocaust memory in Germany may actually lie in its perpetual irresolution, that only an unfinished memorial process can guarantee the life of memory. For it may be the *finished* monument that completes memory itself, puts a cap on memory-work, and draws a bottom line underneath an era that must always haunt Germany. Better a thousand years of Holocaust memorial competitions in Germany than any single "final solution" to Germany's memorial problem.

Like other cultural and aesthetic forms in Europe and North America, the monument—in both idea and practice—has undergone a radical transformation over the course of the twentieth century. As intersection between public art and political memory, the monument has necessarily reflected the aesthetic and political revolutions, as well as the wider crises of representation, following all of the century's major upheavals—including both World Wars I and II, the Vietnam War, the rise and fall of communist regimes in the former Soviet Union and its Eastern European satellites. In every case, the monument reflects both its sociohistorical and its aesthetic context: artists working in eras of cubism, expressionism, socialist realism, earthworks, minimalism, or conceptual art remain answerable to the needs of both art and official history. The result has been a metamorphosis of the monument from the heroic, self-aggrandizing figurative icons of the late nineteenth century celebrating national ideals and triumphs to the antiheroic, often ironic, and self-effacing conceptual installations that mark the national ambivalence and uncertainty of late twentieth-century postmodernism. . . .

It is as if once we assign monumental form to memory, we have to some degree divested ourselves of the obligation to remember. In the eyes of modern critics and artists, the traditional monument's essential stiffness and grandiose pretensions to permanence thus doom it to an archaic, premodern status. Even worse by insisting that its meaning is as fixed as its place in the landscape, the monument seems oblivious to the essential mutability in all cultural artifacts, the ways the significance in all art evolves over time. In this way, monuments have long sought to provide a naturalizing locus for memory, in which a state triumphs and martyrs, its ideals and founding myths are cast as naturally true as the landscape in which they stand. These are the monument's sustaining illusions, the principles of its seeming longevity and power. But in fact, as several generations of artists—modern and postmodern alike—have made scathingly clear, neither the monument nor its meaning is everlasting. Both a monument and its significance are constructed in particular times and places, contingent on the political, historical, and aesthetic realities of the moment.

The early modernist ambivalence toward the monument hardened into outright hostility in the wake of World War I. Both artists and some governments shared a general distaste for the ways the monument seemed formally to recapitulate the archaic values of a past world now discredited by the slaughter of the war. A new generation of cubists and expressionists, in particular, rejected traditional mimetic and heroic evocations of events, contending that any such remembrance would elevate and mythologize events. In their view, yet another classically proportioned Prometheus would have falsely glorified and thereby redeemed the horrible suffering they were called upon to mourn. The traditional aim of war monuments had been to valorize the suffering in such a way as to justify, even redeem, it historically. But for these artists, such monuments would have been tantamount to betraying not only their experience of the Great War but also their new reasons for art's existence after the war: to challenge the world's realities, not affirm them.

As Albert Elsen has noted, modern and avant-garde sculptors between the wars in Europe were thus rarely invited to commemorate either the victories or losses, battles or war dead of World War I. And if figurative statuary were demanded of them, then only antiheroic figures would do, as exemplified in the pathetic heroes of German sculptor Wilhelm Lehmbrück's *Fallen Man* and *Seated Youth* (both 1917). As true to the artists' interwar vision as such work may have been, however, neither public nor state seemed ready to abide memorial edifices built on foundations of doubt instead of valor. The pathetic hero was thus condemned by emerging totalitarian regimes in Germany and Russia as defeatist for seeming to embody all that was worth forgetting—not remembering—in the war. Moreover, between the Nazi abhorrence of abstract art—or what it called *entartete Kunst* (decadent art)—and the officially mandated socialist realism of the Soviet Union, the traditional figurative monument even enjoyed something of a revival in totalitarian societies. Indeed, only the figurative statuary of officially sanctioned artists, like Germany's Arno Breker, or styles like the Soviet Union's socialist realism, could be trusted to embody the Nazi ideals of "Aryan race" or the Communist Party's vision of a heroic proletariat. In its consort with two of this century's most egregiously totalitarian regimes, the monument's credibility as public art was thus eroded further still.

Fifty-five years after the defeat of the Nazi regime, contemporary artists in Germany still have difficulty separating the monument there from its fascist past. German memory-artists are heirs to a double-edged postwar legacy: a deep distrust of monumental forms in light of their systematic exploitation by the Nazis and a profound desire to distinguish their generation from that of the killers through memory. In their eyes, the didactic logic of monuments—their demagogical rigidity and certainty of history—continues to recall too closely traits associated with fascism itself. How else would totalitarian regimes commemorate themselves except through totalitarian art like the monument? Conversely, how better to celebrate the fall of totalitarian regimes than by celebrating the fall of their monuments? A monument against fascism, therefore, would have to be monument against itself: against the traditionally didactic function of monuments, against their tendency to displace the past they would have us contemplate—and finally, against the authoritarian propensity in monumental spaces that reduces viewers to passive spectators. . . .

[O]ne of the most intriguing results of Germany's memorial conundrum has been the advent of what I would call its "countermonuments:" memorial spaces conceived to challenge the very premise of the monument. For a new generation of German artists, the possibility that memory of events so grave might be reduced to exhibitions of public artistry or cheap pathos remains intolerable. They contemptuously reject the traditional forms and reasons for public memorial art, those spaces that either console viewers or redeem such tragic events, or indulge in a facile kind of *Wiedergutmachung* or purport to mend the memory of a murdered people. Instead of searing memory into public consciousness, they fear, conventional memorials seal memory off from awareness altogether; instead of embodying memory, they find that memorials may only displace memory. These artists fear rightly that to the extent that we encourage monuments to do our memory-work for us, we become that much more forgetful. They believe, in effect, that the initial impulse to memorialize events like the Holocaust may actually spring from an opposite and equal desire to forget them. . . .

For an American watching Germany's memorial culture come to terms with the Holocaust, the conceptual torment implied by the countermonument holds immense appeal. As provocative and difficult as these monuments may be, no other memorial form seems to embody so well both the German memorial dilemma and the limitations of the traditional monument. The most important "space of memory" for these artists has not been the space in the ground or above it but the space between the memorial and the viewer, between the viewer and his or her own memory: the place of the memorial in the viewer's mind, heart, and conscience. To this end, they have attempted to embody the ambiguity and difficulty of Holocaust memorialization in Germany in conceptual, sculptural, and architectural forms that would return the burden of memory to those who come looking for it. Rather than creating self-contained sites of memory, detached from our daily lives, these artists would force both visitors and local citizens to look within themselves for memory, at their actions and motives for memory within these spaces. In the cases of disappearing, invisible, and other countermonuments, they have attempted to build into these spaces the capacity for changing memory, places where every new generation will find its own significance in this past.

In the end, the countermonument reminds us that the best German memorial to the fascist era and its victims may not be a single memorial at all—but simply the never-to-be-resolved debate over which kind of memory to preserve, how to do it, in whose name, and to what end. That is, what are the consequences of such memory? How do Germans respond to current persecutions of foreigners in their midst in light of their memory of the Third Reich and its crimes? Instead of a fixed sculptural or architectural icon for Holocaust memory in Germany, the debate itself—perpetually unresolved amid ever-changing conditions—might now be enshrined.

The status of monuments in the twentieth century remains double-edged and is fraught with an essential tension: outside of those nations with totalitarian pasts, the public and governmental hunger for traditional, self-aggrandizing monuments is matched only by the contemporary artists' skepticism of the monument. As a result, even as monuments continue to be commissioned and designed by governments and public agencies eager to assign singular meaning to complicated events and people, artists increasingly plant in them the seeds of self-doubt and impermanence. The state's need for monuments is acknowledged, even as the traditional forms and functions of monuments are increasingly challenged. Monuments at the end of the twentieth century are thus born resisting the very premises of their birth. Thus, the monument has increasingly become the site of contested and competing meanings, more likely the site of cultural conflict than one of shared national values and ideals.

Vered Vinitzky-Seroussi (contemp.)

Israeli sociologist. Vinitzky-Seroussi's early work on American high school reunions as "autobiographical occasions" provided a micro-sociological perspective on memory in groups and over the life-course. Her more recent work has focused on the dynamics of commemoration, particularly of the assassination of Israeli prime minister Yitzhak Rabin. The following excerpt builds on Robin Wagner-Pacifici and Barry Schwartz's well-known article on the Vietnam Veterans Memorial, which identified "dissensual" commemorations as responses to "difficult pasts." In this contribution to the sociology of commemoration, Vinitzky-Seroussi identifies "fragmented" commemorations as an alternative possibility and develops a model of when and where each type is likely to occur.

From "Commemorating a Difficult Past: Yitzhak Rabin's Memorials"

The notion of social memory, and of commemoration as its tangible public presentations, have haunted "ordinary people," political and social elites, and scholars from diverse disciplines over the last two decades. . . .

The preoccupation with the past is, however, less about a paradise lost than skeletons in the closet. The past threatens to penetrate the contemporary social and political scene, to change the hegemonic narrative, to encourage new voices, to demand justice and recognition. In the political sphere, democratic nations see fewer politicians who believe in their ability to win campaigns or maintain world-wide popularity without apologizing for their "fathers' sins." . . . Commemorations of the "good old days" seem to be disappearing in favor of acknowledgments of "difficult pasts." These are not necessarily more tragic than other commemorated past events; what constitutes a difficult past is an inherent moral trauma. . . .

The literature deals . . . with the question posed by Wagner-Pacifici and Schwartz: "How is commemoration without consensus, or without pride, possible?" Wagner-Pacifici and Schwartz have suggested a dissensual or, in Kertzer's terms, multivocal commemoration. A multivocal commemoration is about a shared space. . . . a shared time, or a shared text that carries diverse meanings and thus can be peopled by groups with different interpretations of the same past . . . [However], by no means does a multivocal commemoration exhaust all the possible ways of commemorating a difficult past. . . . A fragmented commemoration includes multiple commemorations in various spaces and times where diverse discourses of the past are coined and aimed at disparate audiences. . . .

. . . . [A] multivocal type of commemoration is more likely to emerge in a consensual political culture, when the commemorated past is no longer part of the present agenda, and when agents of memory have limited power and resources. In contrast, a fragmented type will be engendered in a conflictual political culture, when a strong link exists between the past and present debates, and in the presence of powerful agents of memory. Around a multi-vocal commemoration, heterogeneous groups may share the same time and space but they do not necessarily share the same meaning and interpretations of the past. Around a fragmented commemoration, homogenous groups may gather and share the interpretation, but such consensus is limited to those groups alone. . . .

Narratives are never mere lists—assemblages of dates or facts—put together without logic or motivation. Rather they are selective accounts with beginnings and endings, constructed to create meanings, interpret reality, organize events in time, establish coherency and continuity, construct identities, enable social action, and to construct the world and its moral and social order for its audience. Precisely because narratives are rarely naïve, how they are constructed is especially pertinent when considering . . . the planning and enactment of the commemorative practices of a difficult past.

Commemorative narratives, particularly the ones of painful pasts, can be understood as consisting of three components: (1) the protagonist(s) being commemorated, (2) the event itself, and (3) the event's context.

. . . Narratives also contain time structures—beginnings and endings—that help construct a context, thus reflecting and affecting the way in which a collective perceives the past and itself. . . .

The importance of the suggested analytic framework lies not only in its ability to detect the roots of potential social dissensus but also in its ability to illuminate the ways in which it can be dealt with. [T]he more tightly a mnemonic practice is restricted to include only the protagonist and/or the event, the larger the collective that can share the commemoration. Concentrating on the contextual component may draw a smaller collective that can share the moment.

While societies are of course never entirely consensual or dissensual, and while it is hard to discuss political culture without essentializing it, some societies are nonetheless characterized by a more or less consensual political culture. . . . To be sure, the issue of political culture may not be conceived independently of the nature of the event itself. . . . Traumatic events may even fix a political culture that in turn will affect the commemorative forms. Even so, political culture alone, which more often than not goes way beyond a specific event and may even explain it, cannot account for the emergence of a specific type of commemoration. It is only the combination of the variables that can do so. Moreover, for an event to affect political culture, it has to be commemorated in a specific way (e.g., fragmented).

. . . Both types of commemoration (multivocal and fragmented) do not serve to resolve social conflicts but rather to represent and express them. A multivocal commemoration has the potential of attracting people with diverse views of the past to remember in a shared space or time, and thus is about building and enhancing social solidarity despite disagreement. In contrast, a fragmented commemoration that consists of multiple and diverse times and spaces, and in which different discourses . . . appeal to diverse groups, does not enhance social solidarity. And more than representing social conflicts, it may sharpen them by offering contentious collectives what they scarcely could have laid claim to before the monuments were erected and the memorial days were set: a place to meet, a time to share, and a discourse to cherish. . . .

. . . To a significant degree, political culture, timing, and agency affect the type of commemoration from which memory will later be transformed, maintained, or lose its significance altogether. It is vital to uncover the social conditions that affect its emergence, not only because commemoration is a cultural agent in its own right and thus may strengthen or weaken social solidarity, but also because any future cultural production will have to take it into account.

M. Christine Boyer (contemp.)

American urban historian. Inspired by the "Arcades Project," **Benjamin**'s effort to view Paris as the layered remains of accumulated pasts, Boyer explores in this excerpt the modern city as a text and context of collective memory, in which and on which multiple pasts and multiple presents commingle.

From *The City of Collective Memory: Its Historical Imagery and Architectural Entertainments*

For many who lived in its whirl, the nineteenth century represented a world of ruins and fragments, emptied of meaningful traditions and authentic memories that once connected the present to the past. In such a world, everything seemed to be collectible: treasures transferred to the museums of culture, reprints and copies relocated as souvenirs in domestic interiors, city views and architectural monuments reconstructed and preserved as the landscapes of heritage. Walter Benjamin believed that a deep and pervasive memory crisis haunted the nineteenth century. Memory after all was a regressive gesture, holding onto a past that had been torn asunder by the hurricane winds of progress emanating from the nineteenth century's political, industrial, and urban revolutions. Benjamin thought in contradistinction that memory springing from the natural chains of tradition should be like an epiphany, flashing up in ephemeral moments of crisis, searching to exhibit at that particular time the way of the world in order to direct one's pathway toward the future. In the nineteenth century, however, this natural, traditional sense of memory was forgotten, replaced by a constructed linear series of events, a continuum of time, entitled "official history." This God's-eye view of history, Benjamin argued, was built on a false memory or dream from which the twentieth century must be awakened. For Benjamin believed that historical insight was like a scale, one side weighted with the past, the other with the present—many insignificant and unobtrusive events might be assembled on the side of the past, but the present should be weighted with only a few graspable and important events. If not evenly balanced in this manner, as happened in the nineteenth century, then historical insight would be biased by neohistoricist empathy.

So today we might say that the pervasive appearance of historic districts in our Western cities, the nostalgically designed theme parks and historically coded styles of life, have tilted the scale toward a contemporary form of memory crisis. Ripping fragments of buildings or artifacts from their original contexts and then collecting and preserving them in nineteenth-century museums is not that distinct an act from attempts to transform our present-day cities into outdoor museums whose architectural streetscapes and spatial stratas become privileged landscapes to explore in pleasure or dismay. If the nineteenth century sought stabilizing roots and permanent values in rare and treasured works of art, hoping to quell the explosions of progress and revolution: if the material value of these artifacts was enhanced as monetary value dematerialized in that century's creation of newfangled credit systems and speculative stock markets, then this act of collecting and retaining remnants from the past in face of increasing change and immateriality only added to that century's pervasive sense of flux and uncertainty. Because the museum's collection is built on this essential paradox—both closure and openness—it produces more anxiety than it absorbs. Thus our contemporary memory crisis with its attendant rash of commemorative acts may be based less on the production of synthetic memories that the migration of history into advertising and the nostalgia industry seems to affect and more on the paradoxical assumptions embedded within the methodology of curatorship and the ideology of the collection.

The museum's paradox stems from the nineteenth century and is cleverly outlined in Michel Foucault's famous comparison: "Flaubert is to the library what Manet is to the museum. They both produced works in a self-conscious relationship to earlier paintings or texts—or rather to the aspect in painting or writing that remains indefinitely open. They erect their art within the archive." So, Foucault believed, Flaubert was the first author of the nineteenth century to realize that imagination grew out of reading, among signs, from book to book stored within a library [fiction's labyrinthian web of textuality], while Manet's "Déjeuner sur "Herbe" or "Olympia" were the first paintings to be visualized in comparison to the network of paintings organized into periods and styles within the museum's collection. By internalizing the external world within the storehouse of the library or museum, these nineteenth-century institutions focused on the reader or spectator rather than the essential meaning of books or works of art in themselves. They inverted what Hegel called the aim of art "to strip the world of its inflexible foreignness . . . to make it into something the mind can recognize as its own product, its own image, so that man can enjoy in the shape of things an external realization of himself."

Librarians and curators dream of complete collections even while they acknowledge that every act of totalization can only be partial, a fragment of universal knowledge or a part of the history of art. Because the collector's series can never be closed—there is always another book to be written, another object of art to examine—the series necessarily opens an endless desire for an imaginary collection where all series of objects will form complete sets, a perfect representation, starting with their primitive origins and advancing to their final stage of mature development. Within the confining walls of the museum, in particular, the spatial juxtaposition of heterogeneous and arbitrarily associated artifacts is miraculously transformed into a carefully studied and ordered display. It assumes that the curator can create a rational organization of works of art that are simultaneously deprived of their spatial and temporal contexts and estranged from their origin and function. This is the fiction on which the museum is built: by asking that a fragment stand in for the whole or that a set of series produce an adequate representation of the history of art, it demands that the spectator cover over the voids left out of the imagined totality. Take away the fabulations of the curator and the museum's collection may simply disintegrate into a random display of bric-a-brac and assorted objects. Thus the paradox becomes apparent as it is acknowledged that the museum may at best be only a memory device based on fictional images drawn up by museum directors, art historians, archeologists, and antiquarians.

The museum offers the viewer a particular spatialization of knowledge—a storage device—that stems from the ancient art of memory. Since classical times, as Frances Yates explained, the art of memory depended on developing a mental construction that formed a series of places or "topoi" in which a set of images were stored: images that made striking impressions on the mind. Using this device, an orator trying to remember a speech, for example, located specific images as cues to parts of his speech in the rooms of his imaginary place system. The formation of the sequence of spaces, like the rooms of a house or the streets and places of a city, was essential, for the same set of places would be used repetitively as a memory prompt for different material. To recall specific facts, or to remember the parts of a speech, the orator visited the imaginary rooms, passing through the house in sequence and demanding of each location its specific contents. By the nineteenth century, the museum had become such a memory device: its rooms or "topoi" were places to stop and to look around, to visually observe the common and contrasting features, the arbitrary analogical relationships that arranged the history of art into self-enclosed periods, schools, and styles. The path through the sequence of rooms narrated the evolutionary development of history and simultaneously walled in the heterogeneity of time.

Thus within the museum's paradox there is as well a fundamental distinction to be made between history and memory that neither the collector, the archeologist, nor the antiquarian appears to address. Maurice Halbwachs drew a distinction in his writings on "Collective Memory" in the 1920s, noting that where tradition ends, history begins. As long as memory stays alive within a group's collective experience, he argued, there is no necessity to write it down or to fix it as the official story of events. But when distance appears, conferring its distinctions and exclusions, opening a gap between the enactments of the past and the recall of the present, then history begins to be artificially recreated. History divides the continuum of time into static periods and didactic stages, when in reality time exhibits undemarcated and irregular boundaries. History whips a disparity of details and fragments into a unitary whole, relocating these within newly erected frameworks. And these frameworks in turn enable the historian to establish comparisons and contrasts, thereby recomposing the variety of times and places into a uniform pattern of thematic shifts and minor variations, while leaving a range of inquiry outside of its posited mold. With this illusory structure, however, a universal history or a summary vision of the past is erected, tipping the scales toward historicism as it did in the nineteenth century. . . .

Yet as Walter Benjamin noted, revolutionary classes always believe they are exploding this linear continuum of time and this false sense of historicism. As a consequence, they immediately inaugurate a new calendar functioning as "a historical time-lapse camera," where flashes of memory are supposed momentarily to arrest the flow of time, leaving behind blank spaces as days of remembrance or handles on memory. Blank spaces enabled a community to withdraw from their activities of work, allowing them time to relax and to focus attention on rituals and traditions. "They [the blank spaces, the heterogeneous fragments of time] are days of recollection, . . . not marked by any experience . . . They are not concerned with other days but stand out from time." Nevertheless, these collective days of remembrance, Benjamin found, had been quickly secularized in the nineteenth century, becoming leisure events: the melancholic empty time of public holidays and dreadfully boring weekends. All the monuments and a marks of memory, just like the days of celebratory remembrance, were hollowed out of lived experiences and loaded instead with wishful dreams and anxious moments. What Benjamin called that whore, the eternal "once-upon-a-time" residing in "the brothel of historicism," erased every trace of authentic experience, seducing random and scattered events into its universalizing panorama. Experience became fragmented and the unity of community irretrievably lost.

Danièle Hervieu-Léger (contemp.)

French sociologist. Ostensibly a contribution to the sociology of religion and a response to the assumption that religion disappears with modernity, Hervieu-Léger's book *Religion as a Chain of Memory* (originally *Religion pour mémoire*) is little-noted in memory studies. This is unfortunate, given both the intriguing relation between religion and collective memory it theorizes and the rich and suggestive account it gives of collective memory in the process. Defining religion as a "chain of memory" that links past, present, and future, Hervieu-Léger is particularly concerned with the loss of interest in such chains of memory in modern societies, which she sees as amnesiac.

From *Religion as a Chain of Memory*

By placing tradition, that is to say reference to a chain of belief, at the centre of the question of religion, the future of religion is immediately associated with the problem of collective memory. The possibility that a group—or an individual—sees itself as part of a chain or lineage depends, to some extent at least, on mention of the past and memories that are consciously shared with and passed on to others. Yet one of the chief characteristics of modern societies is that they are no longer societies of memory, and as such ordered with a view to reproducing what is inherited. However wary one may be of making a rigid distinction between societies of memory and societies of change, it is perfectly reasonable to point out how the evidence of social, cultural and psychological continuity is eroded through the effect of change. Change, which is a function of modernity itself, has resulted in modern societies being less and less able to nurture the innate capacity of individuals and groups to assimilate or imaginatively to project a lineage of belief.

The empirical sociology of religious phenomena has long insisted on the significance of this characteristic discontinuity in modern societies. With theorists of secularization—especially those influenced by the opposition between community and society in Tönnies's classic formulation—preoccupations are similar, given the consequences of disappearing natural communities, such as families and villages, on religious socialization and, further, on the likelihood of a genuine religious sociability taking shape in modern societies. But theories of secularization, which have tended to view the relations between religion and modernity from the perspective of rationalization, have seldom placed the question of memory at the centre of their analysis. Yet there are grounds for thinking that consideration of the contemporary transmutation of memory, related to commitment to a chain of belief which is specific to believing in the religious sense, may be at least equally fruitful in the analysis of religious modernity.

In the perspective that we have adopted, all religion implies that collective memory is mobilized. In traditional societies where the domain of religious symbolism is structured entirely by a myth of creation, which accounts for the origin of both the world and the group, collective memory is given: it is totally contained within the structures, organization, language and everyday observances of tradition-based societies. In the case of differentiated societies where established religions prevail and where distinctive communities of faith emerge, collective religious memory is subject to constantly recurring construction, so that the past which has its source in the historical events at its core can be grasped at any moment as being totally meaningful. To the extent that the entire significance of the experience of the present is supposed to be contained, potentially at least, in the foundational events, the past is symbolically constituted as an immutable whole, situated "outside time," that is outside history. In the Jewish and Christian traditions, the religious wresting of the past from history is given privileged significance by the core events being magnified in time: and this at once opens up the possibility of the utopian anticipation of the end of time. The symbolic integration of time takes on other forms in different traditions (in eastern religions, for instance), but all of them have at their base the essentially *normative* character of religious memory.

This normative dimension to memory is not of itself specific to religious memory. It characterizes any collective memory which forms and endures through the processes of selective forgetting, sifting and retrospectively inventing. Of its essence fluid and evolutionary, collective memory functions as a regulator of individual memory at any one moment. It even takes the place of individual memory whenever it passes beyond the memory of a given group and the actual experience of those for whom it is a reference. This cultural memory which is more extensive than the memory of any particular group incorporates—and constantly reactivates and reconstructs—the currents of thought which have outlasted past experiences and which are newly actualized in the present. In the interpretation given by Halbwachs, this inseparably creative and normative dynamic function of collective memory is engendered by society itself.

In the case of religious memory, the normativity of collective memory is reinforced by the fact of the group's defining itself, objectively and subjectively, as a *lineage* of belief. And so its formation and reproductiveness spring entirely from the efforts of memory feeding this self-definition. At the source of all religious belief, as we have seen, there is belief in the continuity of the lineage of believers. This continuity transcends history. It is affirmed and manifested in the essentially religious act of recalling a past which gives meaning to the present and contains the future. The practice of *anamnesis*, of the recalling to memory of the past, is most often observed as a rite. And what characterizes a religious rite in relation to all other forms of social ritualization is that the regular repetition of a ritually set pattern of word and gesture exists in order to mark the passage of time (as well as the transience of each individual life incorporated in the chain) with the recall of the foundational events that enabled the chain to form and/or affirm its power to persist through whatever vicissitudes have come, and will still come, to threaten it.

The cycle of Jewish feasts clearly provide a paradigm of the specific nature of religious ritual. But the point needs making that the ritualized practice of an-amnesis is not only a feature of traditional religions; it also gives a religious dimension to secular ritual insofar as this (always potential) dimension is actu-alized. Thus, the ritual element in politics takes on a specifically religious di-mension whenever it assumes the function of reimbuing the routine experience of politics with the presence of the glorious memory of its source. . . .

The normativity specific to religious memory with regard to every experi-ence of the present is inherent in the structure of the religious group. It acquires substance mostly in the unequal relationship that binds the simple believers—ordinary dependent participants in such remembrance—to the authorized producers of collective memory. Authorized memory develops and is passed on in different ways. It legitimates itself differently in accordance with the type of religious sociality proper to the group in question, and in ac-cordance with the type of domination that prevails. The management of memory—if one takes Troeltsch's categories—differs with a church, a sect or a mystical group. The controlled mobilization of memory by a priesthood who are so ordained by a establishment differs from the charismatic mobilization of memory initiated by a prophet. But in all instances it is the recognized ability to expound the true memory of the group that constitutes the core of religious power.

This is not to say that religious memory presents a greater degree of unity and coherence than do other collective forms of memory—family, local, national and so on. Indeed, Halbwachs has insisted on the highly conflictual character of religious memory, combining, as it always does, a plurality of collective memories in a state of tension one with another. In his opinion, the main cause of conflict lies in the opposition between a rational, dogmatic type of memory (which he calls theological memory) and memory of a mystical nature. The two do not order the relationship with the foundational narrative in which the chain of belief is rooted in the same way. According to Halbwachs, whose position appears to be much influenced by Catholicism, the dogma of a religious group is nothing other than the culmination of a deliberate drive to achieve a unified religious memory:

> it [dogma] results from the superimposition and fusion of a series of successive layers and, as it were, so many phases of collective thinking; thus theological thought projects . . . successive views it has formed into the past. It reconstructs the edifice of religious truths on a number of planes, as if its work had been carried out on one single plane.

By continuously homogenizing the various syntheses of memory already effected in the past, theological memory ensures the unity of religious memory in time and its actualization in the present, elements that are indispensable to the subjective realization of the chain of belief. At the same time it protects the chain from the disturbances caused by mystical memory and its pretension to reinstate the foundational event, the point of origin, in the immediate present through direct contact with the divine. One of the advantages of Halbwachs's analysis of religious memory is to give prominence to the process of rationalization that accompanies the unifying effort of authorized memory. Further, it illuminates the dialectic that develops between the emotive and symbolic evocation of the chain (secured particularly in the liturgy) and the elaboration of a body of belief, adherence to which is the formal condition of access to and participation in the chain. The emotional intensity and symbolic richness in the ritual evocation of the chain may vary considerably, in the same way as does the degree of explicitness and formality of shared beliefs in the community of the faithful in which the chain is actualized. But this dialectic, which one can see as tradition in the act of becoming itself, constitutes in our opinion the central dynamic of all religion. . . .

The question is to know whether this dynamic can still function in a society in which the acceleration of change obliterates what might remain of "integrated memory, dictatorial and unconscious of itself, organizing and all-powerful, spontaneously actualizing," for which Pierre Nora reminds us, "so-called primitive or archaic societies constituted the model and took away the secret." For comprehensive social memory the crisis came with the emergence and historical development of modernity. The affirmation of the autonomous individual, the advance of rationalization breaking up the "sacred canopies," and the process of institutional differentiation denote the end of societies based on memory. The fact of being able to differentiate between a family memory, a religious memory, a national memory, a class memory and so on is already a token of having left behind the pure world of tradition. The growth of secularization and the loss of total memory in societies without a history and without a past coincide completely; the dislocation of the structures of religion's plausibility in the modern world works in parallel with the advance of rationalization and successive stages in the crumbling of collective memory.

The differentiation of a specialized religious field, the gradual pluralization of institutions, communities and systems of religious thought historically—and exactly—correspond to the differentiation of total social memory into a plurality of specialized circles of memory. Industrialization, urbanization, the spread of trade and interchange mark the waning of the social influence of religion and the piecemeal destruction of communities, societies and even ideologies based on memory; Pierre Nora signals their final eclipse under the impact of globalization in all its forms, together with democratization, the coming mass societies and media encroachment. The more advanced societies are those in which one no longer finds even a minimal continuum of memory, those currents of thought in which Halbwachs identified the continuation in diluted form of the concrete living memory of multiple groups of humans and which he thought could still be reactivated in certain circumstances. In fact, the disintegration of collective memory in modern societies is the consequence of the conjunction of two trends that are only apparently contradictory. . . .

The first is a tendency towards the expansion and homogenization of memory, resulting from the eclipse of the idiosyncrasies rooted in the collective memory of differentiated concrete groups. For Maurice Halbwachs, this amplification is closely linked to the advent of the bourgeoisie and the modern capitalist economy. The triumph of the bourgeoisie introduced a new fluidity, a liberty, into society, yet implied the destruction of a social framework that assured the transmission of collective memories from one generation to the next. "Through growth based on every type of input, the bourgeoisie lost the power to establish itself as a hierarchy and set up a system of cadres in which future generations could find a place. The collective memory of the bourgeoisie lost in depth—in length—of memory what it gained in extent."

According to Halbwachs, the advent of capitalism and technology also signified the gradual alignment of all spheres of social life on the sphere of production, which itself only aroused technical, functionalized and neutral, memories; so that at the end of this homogenizing, functionalizing process, the memory of modern societies took on the aspect of surface memory, dull memory, whose normative, creative capacity seemed to have dissolved. The loss of depth in collective memory which Halbwachs linked to the advance of the modern industrial economy is far more marked in image-fed societies with their developed systems of mass communication. The overabundance of information available at any moment tends to obliterate a meaningful continuity that would make such information intelligible. The image enables any event of any catastrophe wherever it occurs to be instantly available to all and in the process immediately neutralizes whatever preceded it, such is the effect of saturation. The immediacy of communication singles out the occurrence and inhibits its being brought into context.

The complexity of the world shown in the vast incoherent mass of available information is decreasingly amenable to being ordered in the more or less impromptu way that collective memory was able to achieve by finding explanatory links. Such links, it is true, contained much that was illusory or mistaken; they constituted the essence of the preconceptions which science in its analysis of reality was bound to cast out; but with all their frailty at least they afforded an immediate and effective basis for developing individual and collective systems of meaning. When this interpretative process collapsed under the onslaught of the scientific method, it was replaced by a rational system which rendered the world more intelligible; thus did the scientific mind gradually triumph over the illusions and reconstructions of legendary memory.

In a wider focus, one must allow that a fundamental provision of modernity lies in the formidable social liberation induced by the advance of critical reasoning, which by its systematic unravelling of official memories, as well as of what was self-evident in the common stock of memory, bearing in mind the tyranny both exercised, called into question the contributory role each played in the pattern of social domination which dictated their preparation. Nevertheless, a consideration of the potential for alienation inherent in the omnipotence of memory in traditional societies need not preclude an examination of the socially and psychologically damaging effects of the fragmentation of memory in the modern world of mass communication. The spontaneously generated interpretative process mentioned above dissolved under the weight of image-fed information only to be replaced by anomic memory, made up of isolated recollection and scraps of information which are increasingly incoherent.

This process of homogenizing collective memory further creates the conditions for a second tendency to develop, that of the limitless fragmentation of individual and group memory. In modern societies each individual belongs to a number of groups. The functional dissociation of the experience he or she undergoes forbids access to a unified memory, which in any case is beyond the power of any single group to construct, restricted as each is by its specialization. The contemporary fragmentation of space, time and institutions entails the fragmentation of memory, which the speed of social and cultural change destroys almost as soon as it is produced. The collective memory of modern societies is composed of bits and pieces. The recurring debate on the growing ignorance of young people concerning history or the scale of their supposed lack of culture (especially where religion is concerned) assumes an altered significance when put in the context of the twin process of the homogenization and fragmentation of collective memory. For the problem is not that of the amount of information stored by the younger generations, which (thanks to television) is probably greater than that of previous generations. What is at issue is whether young people have the ability to organize this mass of information by relating it to a lineage to which they spontaneously see themselves as belonging. The problem of transmission, whether in culture or religion, is not primarily a problem of failure to adjust to the educational methods used to transmit a body of knowledge. It is structurally linked to the collapse of the framework of collective memory which provided every individual with the possibility of a link between what comes before and his or her own actual experience.

A recurring prospect in Maurice Halbwachs's mind was that a society "which can only live if there exists a sufficient unity of views among the groups and individuals composing it" might be able to reconstitute such unity beyond and in spite of the dissolution of its collective memory. The question of social ties clearly underlies the question of the future of religion in modernity. The question of secularization here takes on a new form, namely that of the possibility, and plausibility, of a group being able, within a context of memory reduced to fragments and made instantaneous, to recognize itself as a link in a chain of belief and entrusted with the task of extending that chain into the future.

Harald Weinrich (contemp.)

German classicist. Among the important loci of collective memory are not only canon, archive, journalism, reputation, and the city but also science. The American sociologist Robert Merton wrote extensively on the sociology of science and scientific reputations in the middle of the last century. Here we present a somewhat different take on science as a medium of memory, and memory as a medium of science—a study on the balance between remembering and forgetting, Mnemosyne and Lethe—in this excerpt from Weinrich's essay on forgetting. Echoes of **Nietzsche**, among many others, abound.

From *Lethe: The Art and Critique of Forgetting*

Setting aside distinctions specific to particular disciplines, scholarly and scientific activity, as it is practiced today all over the world, can be described as an enterprise involving many people and that in accord with regulated and intersubjectively verifiable procedures (1) makes true discoveries concerning the world, (2) disseminates them through publication, and (3) keeps them available through documentation. For contemporary science, it is now beyond question that these first three phases, which can perhaps be formulated simply as seeking, writing, and storing, correspond at the same time to levels of decreasing scientific prestige. The researcher who *seeks* scientific knowledge (and one may hope, *finds* it) attracts almost all the public attention and recognition, and thus the functions of writing and storing are rewarded with only modest applause—or none at all.

In earlier periods, for example in the Middle Ages, things were different. It seemed to scientists—there were far fewer of them than today—that the fundamental knowledge concerning God and the world was given, either through divine revelation or through the unsurpassable wisdom of the ancients, so that the primary task for humanity was the preservation of this knowledge. To this task were subordinated those of writing and particularly of discovery. This kind of knowledge was thus defined above all through its close association with memory. We can call it the "memorialism" of ancient science. . . .

[T]he cultural memory of Europe was overtaken and finally surpassed by a moralistic and enlightened critique of memory, and at the same time lost little by little its scientific prestige. This movement culminates toward the end of the seventeenth century, when the *ars inveniendi,* especially in Leibniz, developed from a rhetorical art of finding what was already there (which could still operate within a given body of knowledge) into a philosophical art of discovering something new (whose field of knowledge lay open before it). It was just this that introduced the new rights and privileges of "research" and has since provided the impetus for its legions of "researchers" (*Forscher, chercheurs, ricercatori, investigadores,* etc.) to seek scientific truth not in its past but in its future.

No one can doubt that science redefined in this way has become a success story on the grand scale. It has changed the world. Whether it has changed it for the better, I shall not attempt to decide here. However, no present-day person who has grown up in this world shaped by science would want to return to a society that was not addicted to research. We have long since internalized the self-evident value of research and discovers, and at the same time complacently trivialized its results in the form of countless "achievements."

The question now is what modern science, which has shifted the polarity from storage to research, has done with memory after it was deprived of its earlier leading role. Is its old alliance with memory still in effect? This question requires a differentiated answer. On one hand, the memory achievements produced by modern science have considerably increased in comparison with earlier times. Thus scientific libraries, as every user of them knows, have long since become impressive information and documentation centers whose comprehensive data banks and rapid retrieval systems have been greatly improved by means of all sorts of electronic and photographic procedures. There are in fact few grounds for complaint about present-day possibilities for storage of human knowledge.

On the other hand, however, there is a serious flip side to the question. For instance, any young scientist who is embarking on the enterprise of research and has learned the craft of collecting information quickly encounters—no matter what his discipline and with respect to almost any subject—such an overwhelming mountain of information that he requires years to scale it. When he has arrived finally at its summit and is ready to begin his own process of research and discovery, he cannot avoid noting that while he was working through the "current state of research," another mountain of materials that have to be taken into account has accumulated. Hundreds of thousands of scientists produce millions of books, journal articles, and other sources of information that extend unforeseeably far beyond the capacity of any individual person.

Every genuine research project presupposes a complete review of all the preceding "research literature" on the subject: in science this rule, which stems from the period of "memorialism" and reflects the ancient ethos of knowledge, still holds true—or has at least never been formally invalidated. Anyone who infringes this comprehensive demand for documentation may be exposing himself to the harsh criticism that "he does not even know. . . ." And thus we see many young scientists who have not yet sufficiently reflected on the extent of the available information and who, even after years of collecting material for their dissertations, still feel that they are standing at the foot of this mountain of information and look upward at "leading-edge research" with fear and trembling. It is clear that anyone who cannot wrest himself free in time, even if recklessly, will be oppressed by the mass of available information to the point that he will no longer be able to participate actively in the research process.

What can be done about this? First of all, every introduction to scientific activity should include, in addition to the indispensable techniques of information collecting, instruction in the subtle art of rejecting information. Contemporary science is no longer practicable without a significant component of forgetting. There is no need to feel guilty about this if we consider that if all the mountains of data that rain down from the annual millions of publications really consisted of genuinely new discoveries, as the principle of originality theoretically requires, this would be profoundly disturbing. No society can, without losing its identity, work through as many innovations as are offered it today in the form of information. Therefore it is comforting to explain to oneself and to others that not merely *some* but fortunately *much* scientific information is not really new. Often one can neglect it with slight risk (but not without any risk!).

How does one find, among the excess of information concerning almost any subject that our libraries and documentation centers offer on demand, the few—and perhaps very few—bits of information that really advance thought? That is precisely the art of forgetting that every scientist has to master if his research activity is not to be crippled by chronic overinformation. In the following we shall call this ability to reject information in a rational way "scientific oblivionism."

Scientific oblivionism does not need to be newly discovered here; it has long been practiced, with special success, by "leading-edge researchers." This is clearest in the natural sciences. Take for example the case of the biochemists James Watson and Francis Click, who in 1953 published their fundamental discovery of the structure of DNA in an article with the unprepossessing title "Molecular Structure of Nucleic Acids," on a single page with six footnotes, in the respected journal *Nature*—an article that immediately won for them a Nobel prize. By examining this article along with a few later papers we can see that scientific forgetting, which these researchers exemplify, functions more or less according to the following rules of procedure:

1. Forget anything published in a language other than English.
2. Forget anything published in any genre other than the journal article.
3. Forget anything not published in the respected journals x, y, and z.
4. Forget anything published more than about five years ago.

If one wants to determine more precisely the conditions of their validity, each of these four rules of behavior obviously requires various qualifications whose details can also be differentiated in accord with specific disciplines. Thus, for example, the use of the English language (rule #1) is not equally uncontested in all the natural sciences; it is particularly prominent in the scientific fields for which Nobel prizes are given. The journal article (rule #2), which acquired its dominant status through the academies of science established in London, Paris, and Berlin toward the end of the seventeenth century, has increasingly proven not sufficiently flexible to ensure that research results are reported in a timely and unambiguous manner. Many researchers therefore have more and more frequently resorted to other forms of accelerated publication. As a "short communication," Watson and Crick's contribution already stood on the boundary of the journal article. Moreover, which scientific journals are the ones read exclusively by the club of leading-edge researchers (rule #3) naturally varies from one discipline to another, and sometimes from one country to another. One simply has to *know* which journals these are and does not need even to glance at others in order to ignore them. The rule of forgetting that concerns "older" literature (rule #4), that is, literature more than about five years old, is of special importance. Obviously one cannot claim that Watson and Crick have forgotten the whole of ancient science from Aristotle to Röntgen just because they do not cite these predecessors. The knowledge associated with these and other great, learned men of the past has been deposited in the everyday practice of research or in its technical application and has thereby become inconspicuous or "latent." This historical memory is nonetheless revived on official occasions, when it is represented by specialists to whom the history of the discipline has been entrusted. Thus contemporary research involves a conscious, methodically controlled forgetting of its historical conditions and presuppositions. In making the ascent to the summits where leading-edge research is practiced, one carries a light pack.

Scientific forgetting must therefore not be confused with scientific falsificationism. The latter is based, as we know, on the sophism promoted by Karl Popper and his followers, according to which research, in accord with its inner logic, advances less from truth to truth than from falsehood to falsehood overcome, so that truth can hardly be distinguished from the sum of falsehoods constantly overcome.

In contrast to this conception, no assertions regarding right or wrong are contained in statements about scientific forgetting. Naturally, voluntary forgetting facilitates the conclusion—justified or not—that some previous opinion is wholly or partly false, but in any case it is in the carefully considered interest of research to forget much that is right, so that at a given time it can be rediscovered with pride and emotion; this is more likely to maintain the researcher's motivation than would making him aware that much of what he is researching has long been known in one form or another.

Moreover, scientific forgetting must not be confused with the revolutionism associated with Thomas S. Kuhn. Kuhn is probably right in using numerous examples drawn from the history of research to show that knowledge does not build up its discoveries stone by stone, laboriously, until at some mythical end of research the edifice of human knowledge is unveiled in its splendid perfection. It is in any case clear that the evolution of the sciences, like many processes of biological evolution in nature, proceeds by stages, shifting from one paradigm to another, as Kuhn initially was wont to say, or rushing from revolution to revolution, as Kuhn preferred to put it in his later writings addressed to a more general audience—with the problematic and almost laughable result that every self-respecting scientist would rather attack paradigms than slavishly support "normal science."

To understand scientific forgetting we can, without necessarily adopting all the assumptions and implications of Kuhn's theory of the development of science, take from it at least this much: every "shift" in scientific evolution, whether it represents an advance or a retreat or both at once, disburdens scientific memory in a significant way. The paradigm that has been surpassed can be—forgotten. To that extent every collapse of a paradigm, no matter what its utility or disadvantage for the history of human knowledge may be, is always at the same time a forgetting of great importance for the economy of science. Taking Kuhn and Popper together and limiting both of them, we can also say that science, which must make economical use of its memory, moves forward from forgetting to forgetting toward other discoveries that will, if we are lucky, be better ones.

However, since I do not want to evade the important question of the quality of scientific research, and above all the question of truth, I should now like to add to the four rules of scientific forgetting formulated and briefly commented on above a fifth that has two alternative variants relative to the quality of the research and the truth of its results. Both of these variants concern "mainstream" research. The first is:

Follow the mainstream of research—yon can forget the rest.

The second is:

Mainstream research, which everyone follows—you can forget that.

The plausibility of the second rule is suggested by the fact that the mainstream of research may be only a tributary of the Lethe.

The question whether what has been said here about scientific forgetting can be extended to the humanistic and social sciences is by its very nature not easy to answer. It is well known that the latter disciplines usually have a stronger historical component. The four rules of procedure formulated above are based on the natural sciences; they are not necessarily valid for other disciplines, and they must be qualified more or less as follows: in the humanistic and social sciences one must *not* forget scholarship in languages other than English; one must *not* forget the many other kinds of scholarly literature that exist alongside the scholarly article; one must *not* forget the countless journals and monograph series disseminated nationally, regionally, or locally; and especially, one must *not* forget older scholarly literature, from which Aristotle or Averroës or Lauther or Leibniz may suddenly appear in a brand new form. For these reasons a mainstream of research is not so easy to recognize in the humanistic and social sciences. These disciplines are distinguished from most of the natural sciences above all by the fact that they have no clearly defined, relatively unambiguous forefront of research. It is simply that everything, from the most sublime to the most trivial, even forgetting, can suddenly emerge as a subject of research. These disciplines must therefore be prepared to deal with the unexpected and cannot allow themselves, no matter how convenient it would be, to move forward with little memory-baggage and operate in a correspondingly nimble way. In other words, the humanistic and social sciences cannot be practiced without historical experience as insurance against all kinds of unpleasant surprises. Therefore, without falling back into the memorialism of ancient sciences, they still have to deal with memory. On the other hand, however, the humanistic and social sciences, precisely because they have to keep in step with the progress of time, are subject to the rules and language games of scientific forgetting. The trick here is to unite both of these, in spite of the principle of contradiction. To succeed in doing so we have to sacrifice—with measured polytheism—on the altars of two divinities: Mnemosyne and Lethe.

Robin Wagner-Pacifici (contemp.)

American sociologist. Memory is mediated through a wide array of cultural carriers and forms. But memory is also, or perhaps preeminently, a medium itself, the form of our existence in time. As this excerpt makes clear, collective memory thus "vibrates—it is existentially committed to being provisional," which is not the same thing as asserting, from the perspective of the politics of memory, that it is infinitely malleable.

From "Memories in the Making: The Shape of Things That Went"

Collective memory vibrates—it is existentially committed to being provisional, whether or not the memorizers in any given case are aware of this. Memory's uncertainty . . . does not derive primarily from the *inability* of a society to recall events or eras with specificity and accuracy. . . . Nor does the uncertainty derive from any philosophical precept of ultimate relativism. The root of memory's uncertainty lies rather in the necessary *embodiment* of collective memory as, and in, cultural forms. This is not the same thing as saying that collective memory is essentially and utterly relative in nature. It is rather drawing attention to the social acts of formal translation that encapsulate events that have occurred in the ever quickly receding past of social time and cultural space. . . .

Memories are never formless. They come to us as narratives, pictorial images, textbooks, pamphlets, legal charters, wills, diaries and statues. And the forms do more than simply present the collective memory in each case. . . . Textured, three-dimensional forms embody the memory in a socially recognizable way, one that is simultaneously cerebral and sensual. . . .

There is no natural dialogue between content and form. Everything waits to be decided. Whether or not some event takes on the forms of collective memory and what forms it may take cannot be known a priori. Some events, however, may be viewed as intrinsically important and meaningful; battles, strikes, natural disasters, discoveries, accidents, etc. These are events that can be viewed as breaking into "normal" time by stopping the flow of the everyday. They can also be viewed as foregrounding the usual environmental backdrop by pointing to our intimate involvement with such basic elements as water, land, air and fire, or such cyclical experiences as the seasons, the years, and the days and nights. Such events make us notice what is constantly at stake but just as constantly forestalled or buffered by the necessary routinization of the everyday. . . .

But even such "ordering" . . . events must await the "moral entrepreneur" who has the energy and memorializing discourse to give them collective shape. . . .

First, there is the question of the event itself, What, beyond the intuitive, can be said about the nature of events that *are* adopted and adapted for collective memorization? . . . [M]ust "naturally" memorizable events be of a certain scale; must they affect a certain number of people? . . .

One way of looking at this is to think of certain events as seeking out cultural encodings (just as, in their turn, extant cultural encodings and genres can be thought of as seeking out events) with a kind of combined moral, political and aesthetic categorical imperative. . . . A good fit still needs an entrepreneur to make things happen, but the event/code fit is existentially, if not chronologically prior. . . .

The issue of salience leads to the next analytical aspect of collective memorization. For it is one thing to consider whether or not a given event or process makes it into the collective memory and quite another to consider its cultural depth, breadth, and resonance. This raises the question of the characteristics of intensely . . . memorized events as opposed to those events less intensely evoked. Of course, such intensity or vagueness has many possible grounds, only one of which is the nature of the event itself. Whole historical periods may or may not resonate for a given society. Thus events that occur during one period rather than another may be given a kind of categorical advantage, regardless of their intrinsic qualities. . . .

[Barry] Schwartz's analysis highlights the distinctive and compelling memorializing attention given to historical moments of revolution, conflict, and contradiction. Here are events that literally could have gone either way—toward the founding of a new nation or the reassertion of a colonial identity. This finding brings me back to the issue of provisionality, an issue that engages my analysis of collective memory at every level. Given that reality, I am led to wonder if historical moments and events that are fraught with conflict and contradiction provide the kernel for some of the most resonant and compelling of collective memories? From this perspective, even the glorious past that a Durkheimian analysis would highlight as the natural source of collective memory, can legitimately be viewed as contradictory. For glorious, heroic moments always leave casualties and sacrifices in their paths. The Durkheimian attention to glorious events and the post-modernist attention to contradictory "incidents" *both* identify events that seem to have some intrinsic draw on us.

Another ground for registering the intensity as well as the valence of the embodied event is that of the genre of presentation. Thus we must also attend to the question of the particular genre brought to bear on the selected event. Is the genre of memorization appropriate to the event? Does seriousness at the level of event match up with seriousness of generic form? May a tragic event be collectively engaged by a comic form, and do so with conviction and persuasion? Further, what happens when the forms themselves mutate over time and cross-culturally?

Finally, the analyst must pay attention to the range and timbre of voices that effect the translation of event into collective memory through forms. This might actually be a more interesting and more deeply textured way of looking at power relations than a "hegemony" analysis would provide. Further, following Barry Schwartz's insight that, "'Collective memory' is a metaphor that formulates society's retention and loss of information about its past in the familiar terms of individual remembering and forgetting,'" the seemingly integral notion of hegemony ought to be opened up and complicated by the supplemental issue of what it really means to remember something. What I have in mind here is an image of a collectivity that, rather than simply being dominated by the world-view and imagery of the ruling classes, is perhaps "merely" not being encouraged to remember certain things that, at one point, everybody "knew." How many scandals . . . were "known" about long before there was ever an official, publicly choreographed and institutionalized (through the media or the courts) revelation? Or, alternatively, one might imagine a collectivity that does indeed know some truth about the past but is, for a variety of possible reasons (including a certain diffidence about offending certain members of the group), not saying as much during moments of commemoration etc. . . . [F]inally, a collectivity may have been actively prevented from knowing some historical truth and cannot, or chooses not, to question. All of these combinations of knowing, not knowing, remembering and forgetting are, it seems to me, a more useful mode of thinking about power relations than the term hegemony captures. . . .

[W]ho owns collective memories? If they are stored in official forms, does that grant title to the originating source of the form? Can they be simultaneously and rightly owned by both individuals, the collectivity, and the official representatives of the state? Here, as well, the focus on forms can be helpful as analysts attempt to locate those form/content combinations that best (or worst) provide for simultaneous individual, collective and state ownership. Certain forms may elicit participation from several constituencies simultaneously. . . . To get at the possible causes of such participation, it will be important to look at the intersections of design and event, authoritative and vernacular translators, as well as memory and history.

By attending to the social realities of empirical events, the cultural realities of modes of generic encodings, and the political and aesthetic realities of the work of translators, analysts of collective memory can begin to locate the mechanism by which collective memories are formed and reformed. . . .

[A]re collective memories only powerful and evocative when they are in the business of working through contradictions? In the terms I am establishing here, the question aims at gauging the resonance of *provisionality*, provisionality understood as itself inevitably, if variably, linked with contradiction. First, let me elaborate on my notion of provisionality, establishing its parameters within a four-fold analytic grid of cultural styles and temporal duration.

The first opposing pair of such an analytic grid is that of the conventional and the anomalous. Certain monuments, buildings, ceremonies, paintings, park designs and designations, etc., are conventional in the sense that they match expectations for "that sort of thing," either in terms of what they look like, where they are, or who is performing/using them. Other such forms of commemoration are anomalous in that the public doesn't quite recognize them as belonging to the set of established generic monuments, buildings, ceremonies etc. In this case, a kind of cognitive/aesthetic/moral dissonance announces itself. . . . Anomalous forms of commemoration are thus provisional in the sense of the implied risk that the form will not "take." In such cases, provisionality is part of the negotiation around the central issue of appropriateness, an issue that can never be completely disregarded, even, and especially, by the most radical of genres or images. As well, the whole point of anomalies is that they are experiments—novel forms applied to familiar content or familiar forms put to novel uses. The question of their "like" being successfully repeated is a significant one, for the whole point of an anomaly is that it is unique. Anomalies become conventional through repetition. Thus the cultural profile of the successful anomaly . . . is like that of a virtuoso performer. "Knock-offs" are derisively viewed as derivative and, usually, unevocative.

Conventional images do not have this burden. In fact, in some sense, the closer a conventional image comes to the "original" or the ideal-typical, the better. This does not, however, ensure their permanence, as some conventional images are also provisional. . . .

This short-lived, conventional representation points to the second opposing pair relevant to provisionality: the temporary and the permanent. Conventional commemorations may . . . be intentionally temporary. These are purposely provisional, not expected to cast a permanent shadow over the relevant group's collective memory map. Anomalous commemorations may also be temporary by design, matching a historical moment or empirical reality explicitly recognized to be provisional. . . .

[S]ymbolic forms that combine anomaly and ephemerality point to a socially unique phenomenon. When provisionality itself becomes an acknowledged genre, and plays a central, symbolic role in a particular society at a particular historical moment, something significant is at work. Here the form/content match-up is quite neat, as provisional events engage provisional forms. Indeed, one might expect no less (or more) from a historical period of relativism and dispersed subjectivities. On the other hand, I don't think one need attribute all of the engaging impact of the provisional collective memory to post-modernity. There may be . . . some kind of process of social cognition that is wired in the (apparently) alternating directions of glory and contradiction. . . .

Provisionality is as important as it might be transient. That which is provisional represents an experiment; let's try this on for awhile and see what happens. In a sense, while all collective memories are provisional. . . . Provisionality points to breakaway events, events that confound expectations and events that are rife with contradictions. . . . It also points to breakaway genres, genres in the process of expanding or contracting. . . . Finally, it points perhaps most explicitly to the interactive work of the various translators who struggle with events and formal vocabularies to solder "shared significance embodied in form."

PART V

Memory, Justice, and the Contemporary Epoch

As we discussed in the volume introduction, the contemporary interest in memory is in many ways—though not exclusively—tied up with significant transformations in Western and other societies since about World War II. However, these transformations also include broad epochal conditions like the move from the predominance of modernity to postmodern culture, from a faith in ever-expanding progress to pessimism about the powers of the state, from a fascination with the future to a preoccupation with the past. By the same token, it is also clear that since the Second World War we have moved to new ways of contemplating historical justice, reparations, and the "ethics of memory." The excerpts in this part address the epochal contours of the present as well as the issues that have been raised in new ways in this period.

Edward Shils directs our attention to the changing social functions of tradition, that is, the integrative and meaningful attributes the past carries for members of a collective in a given time. Ian Hacking focuses on the transformation of memory from a source of spirituality to a scientific category for the organization of knowledge. Patrick Hutton's excerpt from his book that appeared at the beginning of the "memory boom"—and which has not, in our opinion, received the attention it deserves—provides an excellent service by summarizing how epochal transformations mirror mnemonic practices and vice versa. Anthony Giddens's focus on "reflexivity" and David Gross's reading of "non-contemporaneity" exemplify central features of modernity as well, though from different perspectives in each.

The following group of readings, in many ways the broadest in the entire volume, seeks a general theoretical assay of what Jean-Francois Lyotard (1984) called "the postmodern condition," articulating the role of collective memory within it in a way not addressed in Lyotard's (anti-)foundational treatise. This cluster provides a variety of perspectives on the contemporary interest in memory and on the role of memory in contemporary culture more generally. For Jay Winter, the role of war and its commemoration is central to the contemporary interest in memory, which is not entirely salutary. For Andreas Huyssen, in contrast, the blurring of genres and intermixing of temporalities in postmodernity—which give memory its central role—invite creativity and new forms of engagement, artistic, intellectual, and political. Perhaps the most famous landmark work in contemporary memory studies, of course, is Pierre Nora's 1989 essay elaborating his distinction between *lieux* and *milieux* of memory and arguing that we focus so much today on memory because we have so little of it left (Nora 1989). Nora's magisterial encyclopedia on French "lieux de mémoire" (Nora 1984–1992) generated significant controversy: was it a neonationalist fantasy or, as Patrick Hutton put it, a postmodern autopsy? Because Nora's essay is so well known and easily obtainable, among other reasons, however, we have opted instead for Nora's much later reflection on the sources of the "memory boom," of which his work was such a significant part. Charles Maier's notion of a "surfeit of memory" provides another related take on the proliferation of mnemonic and commemorative activities.

The next group of excerpts addresses the concept of nostalgia, which was originally a medical diagnosis characterizing a melancholic longing for a lost home; it was formulated in 1688 by Johannes Hofer to describe the pathologies suffered by mercenaries fighting in distant lands. In contemporary discourse, however, nostalgia refers not to a homesickness but to a time-sickness, a yearning for a past that is no longer, or perhaps never was. Nostalgia, then, is a form of memory—perhaps not traumatic, but neurotic nonetheless. And, as the excerpts from Fred Davis and Svetlana Boym make clear, nostalgia is not merely inscribed in and caused by our contemporary culture but is also emblematic of it.

A final group of essays addresses the political and ethical issues raised under the rubric of "transitional justice" and the "ethics of memory," subfields related to memory studies, though not identical to it. What are the obligations of memory, and what are our obligations to it? What institutions are best able to handle the more toxic legacies of the past—the murders and murderers in our midst? What is to be done about the past, now so often seen as horrific rather than heroic? Michel-Rolph Trouillot offers a critical view on the political significance of public and official apologies. He treats apologies as "abortive rituals" that carry no restorative benefits for the party (i.e. the victims) for which they are intended but instead primarily serve as symbolic redemption for those seeking forgiveness. While some scholars, such as Trouillot, have thus dismissed the politics of regret as ritualistic and inconsequential, Daniel Levy and Natan Sznaider point to the potential implications memories of past human rights abuses carry for a global memory culture.

For Mark Osiel, restitutive rituals, especially when enacted in the arena of legal trials, are politically consequential and culturally significant. Operating within a Durkheimian framework, Osiel views the nexus of memory and law as an important foundation for social cohesion. Avishai Margalit too believes that the political and cultural salience of memory is related to group cohesion, but he sees the significance of memory as largely dependent on the cohesion of the group rather than as constituting it. Finally, Marc Augé and Paul Ricoeur remind us that forgetting is often an important prerequisite for stable social identities and political relations. Addressing questions about the political salience of the past for questions of justice and democratic stability, these readings show, is a pressing task for the future of the field and its contributions to politics.

REFERENCES

Lyotard, Jean-François. *The Postmodern Condition: A Report on Knowledge*. Trans. Geoff Bennington and Brian Massumi. Theory and History of Literature 10. Minneapolis: University of Minnesota Press, 1984.

Nora, Pierre, ed. *Les lieux de mémoire*. 7 vols. Paris: Gallimard, 1984–1992.

———. "Between Memory and History: Les Lieux de Mémoire." Trans. Marc Roudebush. *Representations* 26 (1989): 7–24.

Edward Shils (1911–1995)

American sociologist. First published in 1981, Shils's book *Tradition* reacted to the embedded political opposition between tradition and progress, maintaining that skepticism and rejection of tradition is at the very heart of tradition. In the conservative tradition of sociology, Shils's book explores the role of tradition in social stability and change, arguing that the loss of contact with ancestors is injurious and demoralizing, though also pleading that "traditions should be considered as constituents of the worthwhile life." There are strong ties between the views expressed here and those of **Burke**; see also **Schwartz**.

From *Tradition*

There is an order in the cosmos but it is not immediately apparent. It requires hard thought and prolonged study to discern it and to construct an image of it. There are many orders below this cosmic order and they too are difficult to discern. The orders of human society are not only difficult to discern; they are also difficult to maintain in the course of all the multifarious activities of practical life. The disorders of human societies are caused by the actions and beliefs of human beings.

Yet human beings, at least most of them, much of the time do not fare well in a disordered world. They need to live within the framework of a world of which they possess a chart. They need categories and rules: they need criteria of judgment. They cannot construct these for themselves. This is one of the limits to the ideal of total emancipation and total self-regulation. Authorities in family, church, community, educational institutions, army, and factory cannot construct all of this chart, and those rudiments of the chart which they can present are limited in their range and their acceptance depends on the legitimacy of their promulgators. Human beings need the help of their ancestors; they need the help which is provided by their own biological ancestors and they need the help of the ancestors of their communities and institutions, of the ancestors of their societies and their institutions.

The destruction or discrediting of these cognitive, moral, metaphysical, and technical charts is a step into chaos. Destructive criticism which is an extension of reasoned criticism, aggravated by hatred, annuls the benefits of reason and restrained emancipation.

The loss of contact with the accomplishments of ancestors is injurious because it deprives subsequent generations of the guiding chart which all human beings, even geniuses and prophets, need. They cannot create these for themselves in a stable and satisfying way. They lose something more when they lose contact with their ancestors' accomplishments. Scarcely less of an impoverishment is it to be without an image of ancestry. They lose the sense of being members of a collectivity which transcends themselves and which transcends their contemporaries. The acknowledgment of the unity of the past and present states of society is faint in many of the members of contemporary Western societies.

There is a demoralization arising from the loss of contact with ancestors. There is always a crisis among immigrants to another society when they feel the loss of what their ancestors offered them and have not acquired what the host society has accomplished. Their offspring are in danger of lying in a trough between the lost accomplishments of their ancestral society and the unacquired accomplishments of the society into which they have come as immigrants. It is not so bewildering to give up one's own linguistic and social ancestors if one is acquiring new ancestors through assimilation into the new society. To have experienced the disappearance of one's own biological and cultural ancestors in this sense without the compensating acquisition of new ones confines a person in his own generation. This is not easily borne although the sources of the unease are not perceived because the vocabulary available to describe this experience is very poor. The vocabulary to describe this phenomenon is poor because modern societies in the West have been trying to make it appear that the affirmation of dependence on the past is a defect. "Ancestor worship" is the derogatory polemical counterpart to the positive principle that a human being should be estimated for what he can accomplish by the exercise of his own efforts or that he should be rewarded the same as anyone else regardless of his accomplishments and simply for the property of being alive.

There was much that was morally reprehensible in the monopoly of opportunity for the wellborn. A large society is not made up only of families and the ranks or classes into which they are clustered. These are parts of the civil society which has to have a past which is the past of the whole society. The civil ancestry is a matter of gradual growth and acquisition, not formal promulgation. There are many things which stand in the way of its formation and there are many things which disrupt it once it begins to form. It is very vulnerable, but individual members of the society need it for their own lives and for the lives of their descendants. . . .

A society is a "trans-temporal" phenomenon. It is not constituted by its existence at a single moment in time. It exists only through time. It is temporally constituted. It has a temporal integration as well as spatial integration. To be cut off from the past of one's society is as disordering to the individual and to the society as being cut off in the present. *Anomie* has a temporal dimension.

Those who are constantly recommending innovation have never thought about this aspect of things. They are as dangerous to society as those who think that their "class" or "race" should dominate in every sphere, that it should monopolize all that society has produced, that it has no obligations to a society which includes but is not constituted by each of its "classes" or "races." "Civil amnesia" is as dangerous to society as the argument that the government should preempt the resources of society for the benefit of a particular "class" or "race." It is as untenable as are the arguments of those who assert that society should consist of wholly emancipated individuals whose sole concern should be the "fulfillment" of their own "individuality" and that governmental power should be increased in order to serve that end.

The connection which binds a society to its past can never die out completely; it is inherent in the nature of society, it cannot be created by governmental fiat or by a "movement" of citizens that aims at specific legislation. A society would not be a society if this bond were not there in some minimal degree. The strength or efficacy of the link can vary considerably, just as can the state of integration of a society at any point in time.

Our Western societies have taken too much to heart the command to innovate and emancipate. It is not that these commands should not have been taken seriously or that their execution has not brought notable benefits. The mistake lay in regarding them as the only goals to be pursued; it also lay in not giving thought to the consequences of the pursuit which caused the already accomplished to be neglected. One of the consequences has been the attenuation of the matrix of rules and standards of conduct in which individuals should live.

It would be a mistake to think that this matrix was always thick or strong enough to resist all the strains produced by impulse, interest, and reason. Nor would it be correct to think that where it was in effect, it was always benign. Not all traditions are benign; not all of them merit survival. Nonetheless, the fact that a practice or belief has persisted for an extended period is an argument for its retention. The mere fact of existence is generally an argument for continued existence. It should not be regarded as the sole argument to be taken into account. Other arguments might go against it and the case for its retention be thereby weakened or overcome. Not all traditions should be clung to although the heavens fall. But they should never have been dismissed as lightly as they have been. . . .

The fact that certain beliefs, institutions, and practices existed indicates that they served those who lived in accordance with them. The human beings who lived in accordance with them in the past were not fundamentally different from those who lived in succeeding generations or who are alive now. They did not arrive arbitrarily at their beliefs; the institutions in which they lived were not forced upon them from the outside. These institutions had to make sense to them, if they took them seriously. These traditions were not so crippling that human beings could not live under them. Nor did they prevent the human race from accomplishing great things. Rather the opposite! They enabled many great things to be accomplished by individuals in a dramatic form and by collectivities working much more gradually and silently. They should be dealt with more respectfully, perhaps even reverently. Gratitude for the human achievements which went before us and respect for the efforts of countless individuals, known and unknown, to carry out their various responsibilities in keeping their societies, their families, and their churches and kingdoms afloat around the miseries and catastrophes of existence calls for patience with the traditions which are offered to us. It is not only that the rightful place of piety in human life requires acknowledgment and that a life without piety, including piety to the past, courts grief and does damage to the life of the living individual. The respectful treatment of traditions is also enjoined on us by awareness that to refuse a tradition is not a guarantee that it will be well replaced. It might be replaced by a pattern of conduct or belief which is a poorer thing.

It should be remembered that, once a particular tradition of belief or conduct is jettisoned and has remained in relegation or suppression for an extended period, it might fade away entirely or nearly so, leaving an unfilled place, which will be felt as a gap and then replaced by a poorer belief or practice. Specific traditions may be lost forever or retained only in the record of physical artifacts. A tradition once it has receded from regular usage cannot be deliberately restored. The conditions and motives to say nothing of the memories of those of later times who would restore it are unsuited for the task. What will appear will be a fanatical distortion of the receded tradition, a distortion which cannot last if it is reimposed because those to whom it is offered or on whom it is imposed will not find it congenial to their circumstances and tastes. It will be an ideological reconstruction, and an ideological fervor does not last. Traditions cannot be dealt with experimentally; they cannot be suspended for a trial period during which something presumably better will be tried and after which the tradition will be restored if the replacement turns out to fall short of expectations.

Restorations are doomed to failure; traditionalistic movements are doomed to failure because long-existing traditions—traditions which are continuous into the present—cannot be wholly extirpated. This is one of the reasons for moderation in policy; all policy is ultimately, and often immediately, about traditions. Immediate advantages are often expected to follow the institution of a policy which puts aside a tradition. The advantages may be genuine and long-lasting, although just as often they are not. What will be renounced is generally not sufficiently considered, particularly with regard to its effects on substantive traditions.

The fact is that our knowledge of future events is very poor and very unreliable. All actions are oriented in some respect towards future events and towards the future consequences of present actions. This cannot be avoided. Actions have to be taken in conditions which are nearly always partly unprecedented. This cannot be avoided either. Practically all actions entail some deviation from or some independence of tradition. There is nothing intrinsically bad and nothing intrinsically good about this—although sometimes a new and great good results from an action of courageous innovation. What is important about these circumstances and these decisions is that tradition is always involved and is always affected by the actions attending them. What I would like to emphasize here is that great circumspection should be exercised and that traditions should be taken into account not just as obstacles or inevitable conditions. The renunciation of tradition should be considered as a cost of a new departure; the retention of traditions should be considered as a benefit of a new departure. Not that cost-benefit analysis could ever be applied except very vaguely. I wish to stress that traditions should be considered as constituents of the worthwhile life. A mistake of great historical significance has been made in modern times in the construction of a doctrine which treated traditions as the detritus of the forward movement of society. It was a distortion of the truth to assert this and to think that mankind could live without tradition and simply in the light of immediately perceived interest or immediately experienced impulse or immediately excogitated reason and the latest stage of scientific knowledge or some combination of them. It was wrong then, however admirable the motives for the mistake and whatever the benefits which the mistake helped to bring about. The Enlightenment was a very great accomplishment and it has become part of our tradition. It would be an exercise in the discriminating appreciation of traditions to discern what is living and what is dead in the tradition of the Enlightenment. Much of the overgrowth has lost its vitality and is an encumbrance. What is vital in it merits persistence. Substantive traditionality merits persistence, active cultivation, and solicitous care. To amalgamate some of the traditions of the Enlightenment and some of those which its heirs have attempted to discard is a task for patient watchfulness and tact of the utmost delicacy.

Ian Hacking (contemp.)

Canadian philosopher of science. In his book, *Rewriting the Soul*, of which this excerpt is a précis, Hacking focuses on a topic seemingly far at the individualist end of memory studies: repressed memory syndrome. Nevertheless, he explores the broadest social forces that explain the emergence of this question and the array of disciplines involved in addressing it. The question of repressed memory, he argues, is the result of the peculiar constellation of sciences of memory that developed through the nineteenth century, themselves tied up with a transformation in the way we think about the past, from knowing from the past *how* to do things to knowing about the past *that* things happened. His work thus fits well with other accounts of the transformations in historical consciousness in late modernity.

From "Memory Sciences, Memory Politics"

One feature of the modern sensibility is dazzling in its implausibility: the idea that what has been forgotten is what forms our character, our personality, our soul. To grasp this we need to reflect on how knowledge about memory became possible late in the nineteenth century. What were the new sciences of memory trying to do? I claim that they emerged as surrogate sciences of the soul, empirical sciences, positive sciences that would provide new kinds of knowledge in terms of which to cure, help, and control the one aspect of human beings that had hitherto been resistant to positivist science. If we address only the surface facts about memory, the politicization of memory will seem only a curious accident. But if we think of how the very idea of such facts came into being, the battles may seem almost inevitable. . . .

Philosophers of my stripe speak of the soul not to suggest something transcendental or eternal, but to invoke character, reflective choice, self-understanding, values that include honesty to others and oneself, and several types of freedom and responsibility. Those are intellectual conceits, powerful but abstract. Love, passion, envy, tedium, regret, and quiet contentment are the stuff of the soul. The gentle soul cares for others not from duty but from affection and affinity. The soul nevertheless remains self-centered because it means that we do have a center. This is not to say that the soul is eternal, or that the soul is a fixed point that somehow explains character. The soul (as I understand it) stands for whatever strange mix of things is, at some time, imaged as inner—a thought not contradicted by Wittgenstein's dictum, that the body is the best picture of the soul.

These ideas of the soul are in no way universal. But they do permeate the European background from which memoro-politics emerged. Other peoples don't have anything like this idea. They do not talk about the soul. Good for them. They don't have memoro-politics either. Within various bits and pieces of what is called the Western tradition conceptions of the soul have certainly been used to maintain a great many hierarchies, and have played a central role in power plays. The soul has been a way of internalizing the social order, of putting into myself those very virtues and cruelties that enable my society to survive. . . .

Memoro-politics is a power struggle founded upon a depth knowledge. That came into being fairly late in the nineteenth century as a way to study the soul. The depth knowledge was the knowledge that there are underlying truths about memory. The surface knowledge is constituted by the several sciences of memory that came into being at that time. One among the many reasons that we are now so uncomfortable speaking about the soul is that the sciences of memory have become surrogates for the soul. We prefer all sorts of abstract nonsense nouns—the self, the subject—to what does make sense, the soul. . . .

With "anatomo-" and "bio-," Foucault directed our attention to the body and kinds of people. I am proposing a third pole, memory. But I have to make two more observations. One is a stark reminder less of the intertwining of material from each pole, than of straightforward transfer from one pole to another. . . .[T]he normal and the pathological—concepts of medicine, physiology, and the organs of the body—were transferred to the species, collectivities, kinds of people. Normalcy, which is the cardinal meta-concept of bio-politics, was lifted straight from physiology. I call normalcy a meta-concept because no thing or person is simply "normal" or "abnormal." They are normal in some group of respects or other, as the age at which a child first walks, or the age at which an older person first begins have trouble recalling proper names.

. . . . As I sharpen my focus on memoro-politics, I shall increasingly attend to memories of trauma, cruel and painful experiences that corrupt or destroy one's sense of oneself. But just as "normal" comes from medical pathology, so "trauma" means wound (a cut, lesion, or break in the body produced by an outside force or agent). The word "trauma" was not a word of common English when it was in the hands of surgeons treating mutilated soldiers; it was one of those fancy words that lay people don't use, and often do not even understand. But now "traumatic experience" and all the rest are standard English. From that it might seem as if my distinction between three "poles" just collapses. I think not. These profound transfers, of "normality" or "trauma," always occur at the level of metaphor, which becomes dead metaphor. No one now looking at technical uses of the expression "normal distribution" (i.e. the Gaussian, bell-shaped, probability curve) ever thinks of pathology or diseased (as opposed to healthy) organs of the body, although that is where our modern idea of the normal comes from. . . .

Likewise, I have found that few people outside of the medical profession easily recall that "trauma" meant a physical wound, a cut or break. . . . The physical theory of memory, of unremovable brain traces of events that had been experienced, worked at the level of the body. But now we had bad events that could work on the soul. Instead of the remembering being what affected us, it was the forgotten. That strange transmutation was helped by an anatomical theory of memory, that everything that happened was preserved in some little spot of the brain. If it were forgotten, it was still there, and hence could act in potent ways. . . .

The body, the species, and the memory vie with each other for control of the soul, like the bean plants at the top of the apex, each twisting for the other's light, trying to put the other in the shade. Physiology, in the forms of the different types of anatomo-psychology, got there before Freud, whether in Wundt's laboratory or with localizing neurosurgeons after the Franco-Prussian war. Both needed the 1914–18 War. Intelligence testers defined techniques to sort a cohort of American conscripts, one of the most successful mobilizations of science of all time. The brain surgeons did their work on the field or when the boys came home. Memory was driven by war away from the mind. Perhaps the Freudians, some of whom opted out or were kept out of the mobilization, kept memoro-politics going. Those who were involved in treating shell-shocked soldiers, such as Ferenczi or Abraham, thought deeply about the causes of hysterical symptoms. It was not in lost events of childhood, but in terror of battle and its surroundings. That terror might be repressed, remembered, or distorted. . . . There was more than a change in the psychotrauma that produced the neurosis. There was also a change in emotional tone. The patients of the *Studies in Hysteria* by Breuer and Freud had, in the end, felt guilty about their childhood sexual experiences. In war there was no room for guilt. There was only fear. And here we get the seeds of the transition to a more recent conception of the effect of sex in childhood. We are not to think of it as guilt but as fear. We are victims. There are perpetrators who have terrified us. . . .

I don't mean that we began to think about memory only late in the nineteenth century. I claim that before that time there was no conception of a scientific knowledge about memory. We are concerned with a generation or so, the last quarter of the century; direct and self-conscious ancestors do not go back much before 1800. That was when the depth knowledge, that there are facts about memory, came into being. Why did it come into being then? Because the sciences of memory could serve as the public forum for something of which science could not openly speak. There could be no science of the soul. So there became a science of memory. . . .

First I should corroborate my assertion that the sciences of memory were truly new. Here we have a fortunate contrast between art and science. No art was more carefully studied, from Plato until the Enlightenment, than the Art of Memory, or, perhaps we had better say, the art of memorizing. Because of Michel Foucault's careful talk of technologies of the self, his imitators love to use the word "technology" for things that are not technologies. The word is supposed to invoke power and knowledge; its use is thought to be daring. In fact it is often boring. But we can instructively talk about technologies of the memory. I mean the Art of Memory, *De arte memorativa, memoria technica,* mnemonics. . . .

Three things will be noticed. First, the Art of Memory had a central role in both the ancient world and the Renaissance. Expertise conferred great stature; it was, in truth, a political asset. Doctors of the Church, who relied on the Art of Memory, were regarded as more reliable than the imperfect copies of manuscripts scattered across Europe. Gutenberg changed all that. Mnemonics will always be with us, but they are little more than parlor tricks today. This technology of memory, *memoria technica*, entirely antedates the desire to know about memory that came into being in the nineteenth century.

Secondly, the Art of Memory is truly a *techne*, a knowing how, and not a knowing that. It was not *scientia*, not knowledge about an entity, the memory. It was not knowledge about memory at all, but knowledge of how to improve it. Third, the Art of Memory was altogether outer-directed. It was at most incidentally concerned with one's own experiences. It aimed at nearly instant recall of any set of desired facts. One was to arrange external material in a vivid picture in one's mind, to which one has direct access. There is some truth in the thought that what we call computer memory, and its numerous technologies, are the lineal descendant of the Art of Memory. . . .

Why did memoro-politics emerge in the nineteenth century? Is it because the systematic recording of the lives of truly uninteresting people began in the mid-century, with the lives of criminals being recorded, lives of men who usually lied about their past? Is that it, plus the telling of the lives of the mildly deranged? Could that be what so transformed modern mores, our present conception of who we are and what made us? Certainly such events are not irrelevant, but they are not central either. . . . Forgetting may have been set up by new genres of biography, the medical case and the criminal record, and the recording of memories of deviant people. But it required something else to put forgetting in place: the sciences of memory.

Patrick Hutton (contemp.)

American historian. In his wide-ranging intellectual history of scholarly interest in memory, Hutton places **Halbwachs** in the context of numerous other theorists, including Giambattisto Vico, William Wordsworth, **Freud**, the historian of mentalities Philippe Aries, **Gadamer**, and others. In this summary of his argument, Hutton provides a concise account of the major issues underlying contemporary memory studies.

From *History as an Art of Memory*

I build my argument around four major themes. . . . :

1. *the interplay between repetition and recollection as the foundation of any consideration of the memory/history problem.* I argue that history is an art of memory because it mediates the encounter between two moments of memory: repetition and recollection. Repetition concerns the presence of the past. It is the moment of memory through which we bear forward images of the past that continue to shape our present understanding in unreflective ways. One might call them habits of mind; they are the stuff of the collective memories that we associate with living traditions. Recollection concerns our present efforts to evoke the past. It is the moment of memory with which we consciously reconstruct images of the past in the selective way that suits the needs of our present situation. It is the opening between these two moments that makes historical thinking possible.

Historical thinking mimics the operations of memory in its consideration of these moments, though typically they are characterized as an exchange between received tradition and critical historical interpretation. What has changed in the history of Western historiography is the historians' understanding of the relationship between the two. Historiography in its ancient beginnings was heavily dependent on repetition. Historical understanding was literally immersed in collective memory, which continuously invoked the presence of the past. Since then, history has always in some measure been concerned with that presence, for it is mementos issuing from the living traditions of the past that inspire the historians' curiosity. Generally speaking, though, the trend of modern (and more emphatically postmodern) historiography has been away from reliance on the authority of received tradition. Modern historical understanding reflects the values of modern culture, which displays less reverence for the past, and invests greater hope in innovations for the future. Though we know more about the past than did our ancestors, the weight of its authority on us is not as heavy, and its appeal is more easily manipulated. In our own time, we have come to speak of the uses rather than the influences of the past, and its mementos are often little more than signatures employed to underscore our present concerns.

2. *the orality/literacy problem and historically changing conceptions of the meaning of memory.* My study pays considerable attention to scholarship dealing

with changing technologies of communication (oral, chirographic, typographic, electronic), for it is an essential background to the rise and transformation of historical understanding. It would be an exaggeration to say that the possibility of history is tied to the rise of literacy. One could argue as does Vico, that literacy was present from the beginnings of civilization in hieroglyphics and other symbolic markings. Still, before the emergence of manuscript culture, knowledge of the past was largely conveyed through oral traditions that continually updated the past to reflect present circumstances. Change, although real, often passed unperceived or was integrated into the cycles of mythological time. Correspondingly, particular events were conflated into the archetypes of legend. Manuscript literacy therefore, contributed powerfully to the exteriorization of collective memory. Memory transposed into script seemingly made time stand still, permitting a specificity in recollection that had not been possible in oral culture. Memories—fluid, dynamic, and ever-changing in the repetition of oral tradition—could thenceforth be framed in more enduring representations of the past. In this way, accounts about the past rendered in script became places of memory, static simulacra that could nonetheless inspire the particular recollections that we have come to call history.

The trend in modern print culture was to democratize access to the historians' representations of the past. The literacy of manuscript culture, after all, did little to make exteriorized memory available to anyone outside a tiny intellectual elite. One could make a practical case for the proposition that the distinguishing feature of the historiography that we characterize as modern was its capacity to make available printed explications of less accessible manuscripts housed in archives and libraries. Our present-day electronic culture has intensified and deepened this trend toward easier access to representations of the past. In the computer, for example, not only can memory be exteriorized but it may also be instantaneously retrieved. In these circumstances, the imagery of representation is more easily manipulated. Factual information ironically becomes more malleable, for the contexts in which it may be located have grown exponentially, dissolving the once close relationship between specific places and particular memories. Historians today speak less of invoking the past, and more of using it. The point is that history as a memory problem concerns not only the recollection of images but also the modes of their representation. Changing technologies of communication, therefore, present an historical problem in understanding how over time the relationship between memory and history has been reconceived.

3. *the historicizing of collective memory in the eighteenth and nineteenth centuries as the foundation of modern historical scholarship.* The heart of my argument turns on the proposition that the art, one might say the beauty of modern historical scholarship lay in its striving to capture memory and history in equipoise—as an interplay between tradition's repetitions and history's recollections. The work of nineteenth-century historians was continually marked by their sympathetic understanding of the traditions they wished to explicate. Much of this scholarship concerned the recollection of particular traditions, notably

those identified with the rise of the modern nation-state or the advancement of the conception of progress derived from the culture of the Enlightenment. From our postmodern historiographical perspective, historians used such scholarship to confirm these traditions as official memories for the modern world.

The grounding of modern historiography in memory was often hidden beneath a facade of scientific objectivity, although its scholarship did display discerning standards for gathering, verifying, and discriminating among evidentiary sources, not to mention meticulous documentation in appendices to historical narratives. Still, modern historical scholarship was presented as a "new science" (a term coined by Vico), different in its methods and purposes from the natural sciences whose authority it strove to emulate. Modern historiography found its philosophical justification in the doctrine of historicism. Historicism was based upon the proposition that humankind, having created its own experience, can re-create it. The historians' task, the doctrine proposed, is to reenter the mind-set of the historical actors they would examine, however strange and alien that mind-set might be, with a view to understanding the challenges of their particular circumstances and even to thinking through their problems as they would have themselves. In effect, the historicists called on the historians to re-create the historical imagination. Recollecting the world as it was once perceived became the goal of their endeavor.

As a theory of history, therefore, historicism was in fact a problem of memory, for imagination and memory deal in images that are interchangeable. The historiographical issue was how images derived from the past might be invoked for the present age. The modern historians adopted a range of positions on what the relationship between repetition (images received from living tradition) and recollection (images retrieved from a forgotten past) ought to be. . . . There were some (particularly among the romantic historians of the early nineteenth century) who put their emphasis on the moment of repetition. They believed that the historians' task is to resurrect the mentality of the past, literally to reaffirm tradition by making its images live again. But most historians (particularly as the century wore on) acknowledged that this is an impossible task and accordingly shifted their emphasis to the moment of recollection. What historians can do, they contended, is to reconstruct images as they must once have existed, beyond the bounds of their own living memories. Thereby they maintain connections with the past by integrating its imagination into their own.

4. *the fading of the collective memories bequeathed by the traditions of modern culture to our own postmodern age as the source of the current historiographies interest in the memory/history problem.* Having rejected or lost touch with the nineteenth-century traditions in which modern historiography was formed, historians today have become interested in a more detached and reflective way in how these now-fragmenting traditions took shape. The critique of the traditions of modern historiography has surfaced across the spectrum of present-day historical inquiry. To that end, postmodern historians examine old

traditions not to reconstruct their imaginary conceptions but rather to de-construct their modes of publicity and their strategies for exercising power. In doing so, they have exposed the weakness of modern historiography in its naïveté about its own conceptual foundations. In place of the search to enliven memories that once sustained political ideals, they study the forms of the politics of commemoration.

One could argue that postmodern historians are not rejecting the traditions of modern history but are only appealing to others that have been too long neglected or forgotten. In opposition to the official memories enshrined in modern historiography, they contend, postmodern historiography poses new lines of historical inquiry in the guise of counter-memories: social history as an alternative to political history; the history of collective mentalities (attitudes toward everyday life) to that of the history of ideas (elite culture); women's history to that of men's history; non-Western history to that of European history; global history to that of national history. But the difficulty lies deeper, for the tendency of postmodern historiography is to see memory and history as sharply opposed in their purposes. In this view, memory is not the hidden ground of history, as it was in the historicist conceptions of modern historiography, but rather an internal activity of the living mind that can never be recovered. The imagery of the past establishes barriers beyond which we cannot go. Historians cannot hope to return to the sources of the protean images of living memory, the postmodern argument goes. But they can describe the way in which the remembered past has been inscribed over time in memorial forms. The recovery of memory in its material representations ("words and things," as Foucault characterized them) has therefore become a project over which postmodern historians believe they can exercise some mastery, even if they must, set aside the historicists' more ambitious claims. They may not be able to bring alive the thoughts of the actors of history, as the historicists proposed they could. But they can write histories of the changing ways in which the past has been portrayed in commemorative forms over time. If the modern historicists saw their task as using the recollective techniques of history to recover the repetitive truths of tradition, their postmodern counterparts focus almost exclusively on the material leavings once designed to inspire recollection. Historical memory, in their view, is a function of the power to determine the way in which the past is to be presented. Ultimately the problem of history is a problem of the politics of commemoration, that is, of identifying and inventorying those events, ideas, or personalities chosen by the power brokers of an earlier age for remembrance. . . .

But the postmodern perspective has its limitations, for no culture can sustain itself with autopsies of the institutional forms and modes of discourse of its discarded past. In the end, therefore, I want to reaffirm my conviction that even these days history is best appreciated as an art of memory. It is not enough to describe the past through its representations, for such an approach presupposes a detachment alien to the lived experiences that memory bears into the present. Historians neglect the moment of repetition at their peril, for living memory ultimately remains the ground of their interest in the past, just as it was once the foundation of the identity of the historical actors they seek to understand. Memory prompts our inquiries as historians, just as the search for that which has been forgotten focuses them. The past as it was experienced, not just the past as it has subsequently been used, is a moment of memory we should strive to recover. . . .

Research on the nature and uses of memory today is being pursued with newfound interest and intensity. The study of the representations of the past (the past as it was once imagined) promises to reconstruct patterns in the use of rhetoric in the past that parallel those devised earlier to place its events (the past as it actually transpired). It has added a new dimension to historiography by revealing the myriad ways in which memory inspires and directs the course of historical inquiry. In this respect, I do not see the study of memory's relationship to history as a cumulative enterprise, as do some of its practitioners. The positivist quest for certainty in our collective memory of the past is likely to remain an unrealized goal, just as memory itself is likely to remain an elusive topic. Interest in it crops up when we need to reflect on its power, as we do these days when so many historical certainties are being called into question. For us as historians, thinking about memory in a critical way confirms the power of the past and the depth of our attachments to it. It teaches us humility about what we may know of a past that forms us in countless ways still hidden, while providing us with the imaginative resources to speculate on what the future may hold.

Anthony Giddens (contemp.)

British sociologist. A principal architect of the theory of "reflexive modernization," among many other things, Giddens here outlines the place of tradition and detradition-alization in reflexive modernization. Following **Hobsbawm**, Giddens warns not against tradition per se but against the repressiveness of traditionalism.

From "Living in a Post-Traditional Society"

In the post-traditional order, even in the most modernized of societies today, traditions do not wholly disappear; indeed, in some respects, and in some contexts, they flourish. In what sense, however, or in what guises, do traditions persist in the late modern world? On a schematic level, the answer can be given as follows. Whether old or new, traditions in the modern world exist in one of two frameworks.

Traditions may be discursively articulated and defended—in other words, justified as having value in a universe of plural competing values. Traditions may be defended in their own terms, or against a more dialogical background; here reflexivity may be multilayered, as in those defences of religion which point to the difficulties of living in a world of radical doubt. A discursive defence of tradition does not necessarily compromise formulaic truth, for what is most consequential is a preparedness to enter into dialogue while suspending the threat of violence.

Otherwise, tradition becomes *fundamentalism*. There is nothing mysterious about the appearance of fundamentalism in the late modern world. "Fundamentalism" only assumes the sense it does against a background of the prevalence of radical doubt; it is nothing more or less than "tradition in its traditional sense," although today embattled rather than in the ascendant. Fundamentalism may be understood as an assertion of formulaic truth without regard to consequences.

In the concluding section I shall return to a discussion of the implications of these observations. For the moment, again in a rather schematic way, let me indicate some of the relations between tradition and quasi-traditional traits of the post-traditional society. I hope the reader will accept that such a relatively cursory account passes over a great deal which in another context would need to be unpacked—especially if a direct confrontation were to be made with some of the claims of postmodernism.

In the present day, the destruction of the local community, in the developed societies, has reached its apogee. Little traditions which either survived, or were actively created, during earlier phases of modern social development have increasingly succumbed to forces of cultural evacuation. The division between great and little traditions, which in some premodern civilizations survived for thousands of years, has today almost completely disappeared.

Distinctions between "high and low culture" of course still exist, and are associated with the persistence of a certain classicism in the former as compared to the latter; but this has only marginal connections with tradition as I have defined it.

The dissolution of the local community, such as it used to be, is not the same as the disappearance of local life or local practices. Place, however, becomes increasingly reshaped in terms of distant influences drawn upon in the local arena. Thus local customs that continue to exist tend to develop altered meanings. They become either *relics* or *habits*.

Habits may be purely personal forms of routinization. . . . They are individual routines of one kind or another, which have a certain degree of binding force simply by virtue of regular repetition. The psychological significance of such routines should not be underestimated. They are of basic importance for ontological security because they provide a structuring medium for the continuity of life across different contexts of action. In a post-traditional order habits are regularly infused with information drawn from abstract systems, with which also they often clash. A person might resolutely stick to a certain type of diet, for instance, even though a good deal of medical opinion condemns it. However, he or she may effectively be forced to shift if, as in the case of the ice-cube tray, manufacturing or design processes change.

Many personal habits effectively become collective as they are shaped by commodification, or as a result of generalizable influences of institutional reflexivity. Local customs are more genuinely collective habits when they are created by influences within an area or community; but those that are remnants of more traditional practices are likely to devolve into items in what some have called the *living museum*. Whether they are personal traits or more closely connected with social customs, habits have lost all tie with the formulaic truth of tradition. Their brittle character is indicated by the fuzzy boundary which separates them from compulsive behaviour; their compelling force can devolve into compulsive ritual, in specific instances into the obsessional neuroses which Freud was one of the first to describe and try to account for.

Artefacts once associated with both great and little traditions in the post-traditional order tend to become relics, although "relic" should be extended to cover more than only physical objects. A relic, as I use the word here, covers any item in a living museum. Relics are not just objects or practices which happen to live on as a residue of traditions that have become weakened or lost; they are invested with meaning as exemplars of a transcended past. Consider the story of Wigan pier. George Orwell's *The Road to Wigan Pier*, first published in 1937, described Wigan as a dilapidated area which bore witness to the evils of industrialism. The road to Wigan pier was a personal journey but also described a downward trajectory of modern civilization. Orwell's account of the town was so scathing that it in fact aroused a great deal of local resentment.

Orwell was disappointed to find that Wigan pier no longer existed when he got to the town. The pier was not actually a walkway, still less was it anywhere near the sea; the term referred to an iron frame employed to empty coal into barges along a canal. It had been scrapped several years before Orwell arrived there. In the 1980s, however, the pier was rebuilt. The surrounding dock and warehouses were cleaned up and refitted, trees planted, and the area designated as a "heritage centre." The centre harks back not to the 1930s but to 1900; an exhibition, which recreates a mine and miners' cottages, occupies part of it. It invites the visitor to experience "the way we were." Ironically, Orwell has been drummed into service as part of the very "heritage" he found so distasteful: visitors can take a drink in the Orwell pub.

Relics are signifiers of a past which has no development, or at least whose causal connections to the present are not part of what gives them their identity. They are display items in a showcase, and Wigan pier is in this respect no different from "true monuments," such as ruins preserved or refurbished palaces, castles and country homes. A material relic might seem to be something which literally "stays in place"—which remains untouched by the vagaries of change around it. It would be more correct to say the opposite. A relic has no effective connection with the area in which it exists, but is produced as a visible icon for observation by whosoever happens to wish to visit. Like other museum pieces, it may be on the site where it originated, but whether it is or not has little relevance to its nature, which is as a signifier of difference. A relic is like a memory-trace shorn of its collective frameworks.

A living museum is any collage of such "memory traces" presented for public display. In so far as they do not become habits, customs may fall into this category. The point about relics today is that only their association with a lapsed past gives them any significance. Relics were (and are) common in religious traditions, but there they had quite a different significance; they derived their importance not from simple connection with the past but from the fact that they participated in the domain of the sacred. As Durkheim pointed out, the sacred is indivisible; a small piece of Christ's cloak is as holy as any other seemingly more impressive religious object or practice.

The advent of modernity plainly does not spell the disappearance of collective ritual. Sometimes such ritual is proclaimed to go back for centuries, or even millennia; more commonly it is a relatively recent invention in the Hobsbawm mode. Max Gluckman makes a useful distinction between "ritualism" and the "ritualization of social relations" which has some purchase here. "Ritualism" exists where ritual activities are bound up with "mystical notions," or what I would call formulaic truth. The "ritualization of social relations" is where social interaction has a standardized form adopted as a way of defining the roles that people have on ceremonial occasions. Ritualism persists, or becomes revised, in some contexts, but in most instances has been displaced by ritualization (the two can come into conflict where, say, a person who never attends church wishes to have a church wedding). Ritualism and therefore tradition continue to exist and even flourish wherever formulaic truth forms a means of constructing interpretations of past time.

At about the same date as *The Road to Wigan Pier* was published, a crowd of some one hundred thousand people gathered just outside Pretoria, in South Africa, to celebrate the laying of the foundation stone for the Voortrekker Monument. Men and women turned out in the Voortrekker dress, fires were lit and *Die Stem*, the Afrikaner anthem, was sung. The Monument was built to celebrate the anniversary of the Great Trek undertaken by the Boers a hundred years before and the victory of the covered wagons over the massed forces of the Zulu army. The ritual, and the construction of the memorial building, were not just continuations of pre-existing traditions; they actually helped create a new version of Afrikaner nationalism.

Such examples demonstrate that tradition is not just about celebrating an unchangeable past or defending the *status quo*. South Africa at that point was still under the colonial control of the British; the Afrikaners looked forward to the time at which they would govern an independent country. In the words of one Afrikaner political leader: "The Great Trek gave our people its soul. It was the cradle of our nationhood. It will always show us the beacons on our path and serve as our lighthouse in our night."

Tradition, plainly, is bound up with power; it also protects against contingency. Some have argued that the sacred is the core of tradition, because it invests the past with a divine presence; from this point of view political rituals have a religious quality. However, one should rather see formulaic truth as the property which links the sacred with tradition. Formulaic truth is what renders central aspects of tradition "untouchable" and confers integrity upon the present in relation to the past. Monuments turn into relics once formulaic truths are disputed or discarded, and the traditional relapses into the merely customary or habitual.

David Gross (contemp.)

American historian. In this excerpt, Gross explores the theme of "noncontemporaneity," the modern idea that there can be things out of historical sync with the present—that some times, places, and practices can be "behind the times." Distinguishing absolute, relative, and enduring noncontemporaneity, Gross argues that playing with different temporal locations can be a source for critique and creativity; not all reference to the past is regressive.

From *Lost Time: On Remembering and Forgetting in Late Modern Culture*

Certainly there is much to be said in favor of forgetting the collective past. . . . [S]uch forgetting can free one from traditions of acrimony and prejudice which once burdened or impaired previous generations that remembered all too well. Given that many wars and conflicts have begun as a result of some group's need to right remembered wrongs, often to the detriment of all involved, it would seem that such forgetting must be counted a good thing. Forgetting also allows one to see one's present condition with fresh eyes, unencumbered by old legacies or interpretations, and this in turn appears to make one better able to appreciate and effectively engage the world as it actually is, "warm with life and immediately around us." Equally important, forgetting can help an individual perceive future possibilities in a present situation, for by letting go of the past, one necessarily becomes more cognizant of existing or emerging opportunities that lie directly at hand. As advocates of forgetting have long contended, it is these opportunities and possibilities that should be the primary focus of one's attention, since that which is coming into being will in the long run be more important for the individual than what has already passed away.

Each of these alleged benefits of forgetting seems convincing on its own terms, which may be one reason why the pro-forgetting outlook appears to be the prevalent one in the Western world today. But precisely because a stance favorable to forgetting has perhaps been too facilely and unquestioningly embraced by so many, it may be all the more imperative that we take a second look at what might be called the gains of collective remembering over those of collective forgetting. Two such gains stand out, and in what follows I will confine my comments only to these two. First, social or collective memory gives us a greater depth and breadth of awareness which can personally enrich us and stimulate creative thought and action. Second, such memory permits us to acquire a standpoint outside the present from which we can better see—and criticize—the shortcomings and aporias of the contemporary age. These two gains come, however, not by enmeshing oneself in the memory of popular culture, but by remembering what is *excluded* from the ruling memory schemata of our time.

Theodor Adorno spoke of the kind of memory I have in mind as "a remembrance of the forgotten." But a better, or at any rate less vague, term than "the forgotten" to refer to the *disjecta membrae* of present-day consciousness might be the "noncontemporaneous." This admittedly cumbersome word denotes that which is "from another time" and thus discordant with the present. The assumption built into most uses of this term is that what is discordant or does not "fit in" with the tenor of the present must be eminently forgettable. Though, to be sure, "noncontemporaneity" as a concept is not always exactly synonymous with "the forgotten" or "the excluded," it is close enough in meaning to serve our purposes here. Hence, what I want to suggest is that the type of memory that carries unacknowledged creative and critical potential today is a memory of the noncontemporaneous. . . .

Before the coming of modernity, people were certainly able to distinguish between the past and the present, but they had a generally weak sense of what really *belonged* to the past as opposed to the present. With the triumph of modernity, the lines between these two temporal domains became much sharper, with the result that people in the West began to understand that some things are "modern" and therefore in tune with the times, while other things are "unmodern" and hence out of step with the age, or noncontemporaneous. What engenders noncontemporaneity is the advance of modernity itself, and the more rapidly the modern replaces the premodern, or the late modern replaces the early modern, the more sizable amounts of noncontemporaneity get produced. Still, not all noncontemporaneity is of uniform weight or importance. To simplify a complicated matter, one could say that today it is possible to delineate three different kinds of noncontemporaneity.

First, there is what might be called *absolute noncontemporaneity*. By this I mean that part of the past that has been completely obliterated except for a few shards or fragments preserved in museums. What we now know of this "lost" past can be ascertained only abstractly, by means of historical or archaeological reconstruction. . . .

Second, there is what might be termed *relative noncontemporaneity*. By this I mean a part of the past that, while also over and done with, has nevertheless left behind more immediately and continuously experienceable physical or cultural traces than those housed in museum displays. . . . Among such lingering residues of relative noncontemporaneity are not only certain physical artifacts still in use despite their obsolescence, but also vestiges of preindustrial habits of mind, residues of old-fashioned codes of honor, antiquated spiritual outlooks, scraps of ancient cosmologies, or shreds of ritual practices from traditions now defunct. Traces of all these superannuated forms of thinking and acting continue on today, but being mere after-effects they are now discontinuous with the past from which they originated. The best way to regard them at the present time is as broken or fractured remains of wholes that have themselves disappeared. None of these fragments should be construed as living, vital traditions because, by being separated from the surroundings of which they were once an integral part, they are not in any true sense natural extensions of the past. Nevertheless, as a result of being alienated from the life- and value-worlds in which they had once made sense, such survivals can become something other than what they were initially; that is, they can become *referents* to a past that is no more. Today this newly acquired referential power might be considered the real value of these surviving remnants of relative noncontemporaneity. For by beginning with traces that are immediately at hand, individuals in the present may work their way back imaginatively to the lost wholes and former registers of meaning that such traces indirectly recall, and in this manner bring back to consciousness the otherwise absent reality of the past.

Third and last, there is *enduring noncontemporaneity*, which denotes those modes of thinking and behaving that have somehow managed to survive not piecemeal but intact into the present age. Where one encounters enduring noncontemporaneity (which will usually be in out-of-the-way places) one comes into contact with the continuous and living presence of the past, however strange or antiquated it may seem by present-day standards. This continuity will by definition be disjunctive with the contemporaneous, since it preserves that which is *unzeitgemässig*, or "out of sync," with the times. To survive at all, elements of enduring noncontemporaneity must often retreat from the mainstream, either to the periphery of social life—to rural enclaves, ethnic subcultures, or religious sects, for example—or, if there is serious risk of suppression or persecution, underground. Yes as difficult as it may be to access many of these hiding places, they do nevertheless serve one important purpose: they sequester and thereby protect still-living modes of noncontemporaneity, enabling them to continue on, in no matter how reduced a condition, within the context of a present that in most respects is antagonistic to them.

What do these three modes of noncontemporaneity have to do with my contention that collective memory is, or can be, a stimulus to creativity? The answer is that by taking note of the referents to the past that have survived into the contemporary era, however few and fragile they may be, one discovers a reality that is temporally much richer and more multilayered than can be known by the forgetter. . . .

A heightened sensitivity toward the noncontemporaneous gives one something else that is unavailable to the forgetter. It gives one a feel not only for what has already passed away, but for what is now in the process of disappearing. The rememberer, one might say, has a better sense of evanescence than does the forgetter, which in my opinion ought to be considered a gain, for it may be that only by grasping the fleetingness of existence, both material and human, does one learn to appreciate the true value of what is perishing.

In a manner not easy to describe, value is often intimately linked to imminent loss. I mean by this that the falling away of something frequently tends to augment its worth, objectively and subjectively. Thus the individual who simply takes things as they come, unobservant of the transience of the people or objects around him and incurious about what that transience might ultimately mean, will probably have a weak or dubious hold on value, while the individual who is highly attuned to what is slipping away will more likely perceive the worth of passing things. If creativity has anything to do with a sensitivity toward fading value, as I believe it does, then the rememberer is surely situated more creatively in the world than is the forgetter. . . .

Earlier I suggested that collective memory, in addition to laying the conditions for creative thought and action in the present, provides us with something else at least equally important: it allows us to develop a much-needed standpoint outside of modernity from which we can better see and critically analyze the deficiencies of modernity itself.

In saying this I do not mean to imply that all kinds of collective memory are critical by their very nature, since it is clearly not true that the recollection of virtually anything from the past carries critical weight. Rather, in referring to the critical power of memory, I have in mind a particular type of memory that does not normally receive much attention because it seems to lack utility, namely the memory of what is estranged from and discontinuous with the present.

As the proverbial locomotive of history has moved forward ever more rapidly, it has left behind modes of thinking, valuing, and experiencing that were once cherished by our ancestors but are now considered obsolete. Obviously, some of the past that has been supplanted dates back to distant times, while other aspects of it, no less "transcended," come from relatively more recent periods. Within the former category one might include the lingering reminders of the classical or medieval periods. Within the latter one could include the world of the preindustrial peasantry in Europe which was still largely intact in 1850 but is now approaching extinction. . . . In Hegelian terms, this cast off "stuff" on history represents merely the refuse of the dialectic, the wreckage left over after the "Worldspirit" (*Weltgeist*) has departed from the scene. Being superseded, such historical debris tends to be seen as irrelevant or irrational, since it no longer corresponds to contemporary realities. Very much like Hegel two hundred years ago, we today also appear to be more interested in the forward-looking side of the dialectic. For the most part, we warm to those aspects of the past that anticipate the present or point in the direction of a future yet to come, and we lose interest in those that have become passé. As for the residues or leftovers of earlier social formations, many now fully agree with the view expressed by Jean Baudrillard when he wrote that it would be best to make the past truly past as quickly as possible so that we can finally do what we should have done long ago—forget it.

In contrast to this perspective, I want to suggest that the transcended past, seemingly comprising unreconciled or unassimilated remains, continues to be important for us at the present time not only because of the qualities of otherness or difference to be found there but because of what I would call the past's generally unacknowledged "truth value." As even a cursory glance at the many earlier struggles over beliefs, convictions, and ways of life will attest neither "truth" nor "value" ever depends simply upon which ideas or systems of thought happen to win out historically. Success alone determines very little for by almost any standard of measurement significant numbers of both true and valuable things have been consigned to the dustbin of history, while much that is worthless has triumphed. But these discarded things perhaps ought not to be neglected and forgotten just because they lost out to purportedly more advanced historical forces. In returning by means of memory to that which is different from the present, one not only pays respect to what has failed or been silenced but also acquires a standpoint from which to criticize the contemporary age— an age that does not seem much inclined to encourage criticism of any kind, above all criticism of itself.

How does one go about critiquing the age in which one lives? Or more precisely, how does one obtain the necessary leverage to make such a critique effective? The brief answer is that one needs a credible vantage point from which to frame what one wants to criticize. Broadly speaking, there are three such vantage points available to any potential critic. The first is one that operates from a position outside of time itself, from the perspective of, for instance, reason in the abstract or even God himself (as with the prophets of the Old Testament who criticized Israel from what they understood to be Jahweh's point of view). The second vantage point is from a projected ideal or utopian future to be arrived at from inside the historical process by the unfolding of certain immanent possibilities thought to be locked within the present. If a critic selects this as his framing perspective, he may censure his era for all the ways in which it blocks its own potential and prevents its most promising tendencies from being actualized. The third vantage point is based not on what might or could be, but on what was. A critic using this approach might juxtapose the strengths of some bygone period to the shortcomings of his own in order to accentuate those deficiencies of the present that would otherwise go unnoticed. Each of these modes of critique has its own degree of effectiveness, but in what follows I will be concerned only with the last of them, which is the one that most relies on memory.

Every substantive critique of the present undertaken from the standpoint of the past must begin with some grasp of what I have called the truth value of the past. Many today have certainly acknowledged the importance of "keeping watch" over superseded values and meanings in order to make sure they do not completely disappear from human consciousness. But simply keeping watch is not enough to engender a critique, since this stance could lead to something merely custodial. In order to move beyond the mere urge to preserve and on to something like a real critique, the eclipsed truths of the past would have to be counterposed to the untruths of the present in such a way as to give what has been discarded real contestatory power. Should this happen, the remembrance of what once had been (extinguished traditions, lost causes, abandoned ways of living or thinking, and the like) might be able to produce, by means of contrasts or comparisons, enough leverage to call many of the givens of the present into question. If one should develop a special attachment or commitment to the absent past because of what one finds there, then a new, still more intense level of critique might result. . . .

Of course, disadvantages may follow from too great an orientation toward the past. For one thing, such a stance obviously hinders a person's ability to fit in, and for another, it has, or seems to have, a dampening effect on one's capacity to be "happy," at least as this term is defined in present-day consumer culture. But the benefits that come with being critically distanced from one's age are arguably more important than the drawbacks. First, thanks to memory a person becomes better positioned to see through reifications, whose workings forgetters especially fail to notice. If it is true, as Adorno succinctly expressed it, that "all reification is a forgetting," then one would expect remembering to be a first and indispensable step toward de-reification. Second, because of the critical effects of memory one becomes less susceptible to manipulation by either the economic or political powers-that-be. Manipulation of any kind occurs more readily, and is generally more successful, when people know only sheer presentness. When one possesses some depth of memory, it becomes easier to break free from the tyranny of the concrete, for a good memory allows one to recall the way things were before the present took shape and consequently to become aware of how one's thoughts and actions can be shrewdly managed unless one takes measures to prevent it. And third, one is better able, should the occasion arise, to go further and actually resist that which is illegitimate in the present, once one has determined that it is in fact illegitimate. When memory is dispensed with, everything tends to be accepted more or less at face value. . . .

To be sure, "hold[ing] on to the debris" in the manner just described does tend to make one untimely, since it places one in contradiction the age instead of permitting one to flow with it. But even though this untimeliness may justly be called beneficial (at least to the extent that it fosters a critical as opposed to a conformist outlook on the present), it is nevertheless true that two potential dangers exist which could nullify the gains that come with memory. One is the danger of so idealizing the past that one becomes excessively mournful about its disappearance. Here the result could be an exaggerated nostalgia for what is no longer present, which, were it to get out of hand, could lead to an unproductive obsession with the past. The other danger is that one might want to raise up the dead and bring back to life what has been left behind, even though the conditions of the present make any such *restitutio in integrum* all but impossible. Both extremes, in my view, need to be avoided. One can remember and abide with what is absent without either pining for the past or believing that it can be reinstated. That particular values or truths now seem to belong to a past that is no more should not prevent one from adopting them as one's own, or even using them with critical intent against the established reality of late modernity. By doing the latter one may be better able to apprehend the present not as some would like it to be, or as others work hard to make it appear, but as it actually is.

Jay Winter (contemp.).

American historian. In his book *Sites of Memory, Sites of Mourning*, Winter provides a detailed historical and iconographic study of World War I memorials in Europe, drawing out the broader relevance for contemporary culture. In a subsequent book *Remembering War*, Winter makes clear the complexities of the connections between war and memory. In this excerpt from the latter, Winter not only makes the case for the war-memory connection but also considers its relevance for memory studies. Additionally, Winter continues the effort to refine the discourse stemming from **Halbwachs**'s concepts, here introducing and refining the concept of "historical remembrance."

From *Remembering War: The Great War between Memory and History in the Twentieth Century*

In the environment of international conflict in which we live today, historians still write about war and all kinds of people still speak of their personal memories of war. Increasingly, though, the space between history and memory has been reconfigured. In between is a varied set of cultural practices that may be described as forms of historical remembrance. It is a field originally formed to commemorate the Great War, but which has been enlarged decade after decade to take account of the upheavals which have followed it, and the millions of men and women who have been injured in wars between nations, civil wars, and insurrections. These are the witnesses—veterans, Holocaust survivors, Guatemalan Indians—whose presence among us we cannot ignore. . . .

But to help sketch out a map of the territory covered by the memory boom, I offer the term "historical remembrance" to help us understand the special features of many of these practices. Historical remembrance overlaps with personal or family remembrance on the one hand and religious remembrance, so central to sacred practices, on the other. But the overlap is only partial. Historical remembrance is a way of interpreting the past which draws on both history and memory, on documented narratives about the past and on the statements of those who lived through them. Many people are active in this field. Historians are by no means in the majority.

Why introduce a new category, historical remembrance? Because the two defining concepts we normally use, history and memory, are insufficient guides to this field. Commemoration requires reference to history, but then the contestation begins. Whose history, written for whose benefit, and on which records? The memory boom is about history, to be sure, but historians are not its sole or even its central proprietors. Witnesses demand the right to be heard, whatever historians say. . . .

Historians do matter, but not as much as they think they do. Those who try to reconstruct their "memory" of past events need historians to establish the boundary conditions of possibility. We can establish with much greater firmness what did not take place than what did, and historians have access to records which—at times—prevent people from either misconstruing or lying about the past. . . .

Historical remembrance is a discursive field, extending from ritual to cultural work of many different kinds. It differs from family remembrance by its capacity to unite people who have no other bonds drawing them together. It is distinctive from liturgical remembrance in being freed from a preordained religious calendar and sanctified ritual forms. And yet historical remembrance has something of the familial and something of the sacred in it. When all three are fused, as in some powerful war memorials . . . historical remembrance is a phenomenon of enduring power.

Adopting the term "historical remembrance" has other advantages as well. Using it helps us avoid the pitfalls of referring to memory as some vague cloud which exists without agency, and to history as an objective story which exists outside of the people whose lives it describes. Historians have memories too, and their choice of subject is rarely accidental. They are part of the memory boom, though not its leading part. When they join other men and women who come together in public to remember the past—their past—they construct a narrative which is not just "history" and not just "memory," but a story which partakes of them both. Historical remembrance is what they do, and how they contribute to a memory boom which extends well beyond the historical profession. . . .

There is clearly a market for historical remembrance. What has triggered it? There are many sources located in the thrust of what we now call "identity politics," in the structure of consumption patterns of educated sectors of the population, and in the spread of what might be termed broadly as psychoanalytic cultures in many parts of the world. . . .

One answer to the question as to why so many people choose to do the work of remembrance lies in the subject of war and its aftermath. Among the most prominent sources of the flowering of public remembrance in the twentieth century has been the desire to recapture the profile and to keep alive the name of those who, because of war, are no longer there. Remembrance is an act of symbolic exchange between those who remain and those who suffered or died. They went through much; they lost or gave much; we give the little we can— starting with recognition and acknowledgment and then moving on, at times, to material expressions of both.

These terms show why the subject of memory has taken on such a powerful collective character. Acknowledgment—understood as active knowledge, expressed in public as the recognition, the rethinking, and the restating aloud of claims—moral, political, material—which other human beings have on us. Among those claimants are victims of war and violence. The least of their claims is that we not let them and their stories vanish without trace, that we face them, that we face what happened to them. That act starts alone. In our individual reflections on an injured or absent person, but acknowledgment, in the sense I am using the term, never ends alone. It is a public act, a kind of remembrance expressed by groups of people prepared to face their shared past together. When they come together, remembrance becomes performative. It is materialized in the gestures and statements of the actors, those whose actions constitute remembrance. . . .

Psychiatric injury is a form of remembrance of a very special kind, one which has taken on many different meanings and associations throughout the twentieth century. To be sure, part of the memory boom is driven by our understanding that perfectly sane people become insane during and after war. Those ex-soldiers "whose minds the dead have ravaged," in Wilfred Owen's phrase, stand in a long line of victims of war and violence whose injuries are not physical but which are none the less crippling. These people are also the subject of the memory boom, and give it some of its tragic features.

And its political ramifications too. For acknowledging an injury in the service of the state is tantamount to accepting the right to material compensation. Pensions—and public expenditure—follow the recognition of the damage done to men and women in war. Since psychological disabilities were hard to diagnose and, even when diagnosed, hard to treat, such injuries were (and remain) the subject of much controversy. Some doctors and pensions officials saw malingering behind every claim of psychological disability. Others were more liberal in their labeling of frequently puzzling sets of symptoms. Over time, what we first termed shell shock and now call post traumatic stress disorder received medical and administrative legitimation, justifying the acknowledgment of injury and the payment of pensions to those suffering psychological injuries related to war service.

In more recent times, there has been much discussion of the claims for compensation for injuries inflicted by violent regimes against their own people or in the course of civil war. Here the problems are multiple. The same mix of psychological and physical injury presents complex problems of medical diagnosis and administrative responses. And now the claimants rarely wear uniforms; they were targets simply because they were there.

But whether we are dealing with the international warfare of the earlier twentieth century or the fragmentation of warfare since 1945, remembrance follows armed conflict, as night follows day. . . .

In the twentieth century, warfare became everybody's business. Before 1900, commemorative statues mostly celebrated individual commanders; after 1900, and even more so after 1914, ordinary people became the focus of commemoration. That is why the preservation of names on war memorials is so important.

Later in the twentieth century, the democratization of suffering changed the face of remembrance. The soldier no longer stands at the center of the narrative of the historical remembrance of war and its victims. Precise figures cannot be established, but it is likely that more women than men died in the course of the Second World War. One million children were murdered in the Holocaust. Genocide since 1945 has targeted women and children, as the future of the population, to be exterminated. Other subject groups—Indians, suppressed minorities, ethnic groups, homosexuals—have asserted their own right to speak, and through their *prise de la parole* they have helped ensure that their stories and their lives were not erased by their persecutors. Their words apper in tribunals, in commissions of inquiry, in autobiographical memoirs, in archives of oral and video testimony. The archives of the memory boom are multiple and growing.

Andreas Huyssen (contemp.)

German American literary theorist. According to Huyssen, the late twentieth century involves a reversal of modern time-consciousness—from a preoccupation with the future to a preoccupation with the past. A central cause of this transformation, Huyssen argues, is the rise of new media. Huyssen, however, is no unalloyed pessimist, as is sometimes the case with postmodernists, but sees the creative potential in new cultural forms. By the same token, he is clear that "the past cannot give us what the future has failed to deliver."

From "Present Pasts: Media, Politics, Amnesia"

One of the most surprising cultural and political phenomena of recent years has been the emergence of memory as a key concern in Western societies, a turning toward the past that stands in stark contrast to the privileging of the future so characteristic of earlier decades of twentieth-century modernity. From the early twentieth century's apocalyptic myths of radical breakthrough and the emergence of the "new man" in Europe via the murderous phantasms of racial or class purification in National Socialism and Stalinism to the post–World War II American paradigm of modernization, modernist culture was energized by what one might call "present futures." Since the 1980s, it seems, the focus has shifted from present futures to present pasts, and this shift in the experience and sensibility of time needs to be explained historically and phenomenologically. . . .

Memory discourses of a new kind first emerged in the West after the 1960s in the wake of decolonization and the new social movements and their search for alternative and revisionist histories. The search for other traditions and the tradition of "others" was accompanied by multiple statements about endings: the end of history, the death of the subject, the end of the work of art, the end of metanarratives. Such claims were frequently understood all too literally, but in their polemical thrust and replication of the ethos of avantgardism, they pointed directly to the ongoing recodification of the past after modernism. . . .

If the time-consciousness of high modernity in the West sought to secure the future, one could argue that the time-consciousness of the late twentieth century implies the no less perilous task of taking responsibility for the past. Both attempts inevitably are haunted by failure. . . . The turn toward memory and the past comes with a great paradox. Ever more frequently, critics accuse this very contemporary memory culture of amnesia—anesthesia, or numbing. They chide its inability and unwillingness to remember, and they lament the loss of historical consciousness. The amnesia reproach is invariably couched in a critique of the media, while it is precisely these media . . . that make ever more memory available to us day by day. But what if both observations were true, if the boom in memory were inevitably accompanied by a boom in forgetting?

What if the relationship between memory and forgetting were actually being transformed under cultural pressures in which new information technologies, media politics, and fast-paced consumption are beginning to take their toll?. . .

Wherever one looks, the contemporary obsession with memory in public debates clashes with an intense public panic of oblivion, and one may well wonder which comes first. Is it the fear of forgetting that triggers the desire to remember, or is it perhaps the other way around? Could it be that the surfeit of memory in this media-saturated culture creates such overload that the memory system itself is in constant danger of imploding, thus triggering the fear of forgetting? Whatever the answer to such questions, it seems clear that older sociological approaches to collective memory—approaches such as Maurice Halbwachs's that posit relatively stable formations of social and group memories—are not adequate to grasp the current dynamics of media and temporality, memory, lived time, and forgetting. The clashing and ever more fragmented memory politics of specific social and ethnic groups raise the question whether forms of collective consensual memory are even still possible today, and, if not, whether and in what form social and cultural cohesion can be guaranteed without them. Media memory alone clearly will not suffice, even though the media occupy ever larger chunks of the social and political perception of the world.

The very structures of public media memory make it quite understandable that our secular culture today, obsessed with memory as it is, is also somehow in the grips of a fear, even a terror, of forgetting. . . . But the fear of oblivion and disappearance operates in a different register as well. For the more we are asked to remember in the wake of the information explosion and the marketing of memory, the more we seem to be in danger of forgetting and the stronger the need to forget. At issue is the distinction between usable pasts and disposable data. My hypothesis here is that we try to counteract this fear and danger of forgetting with survival strategies of public and private memorialization. The turn toward memory is subliminally energized by the desire to anchor ourselves in a world characterized by an increasing instability of time and the fracturing of lived space. At the same time, we know that such strategies of memorialization may in the end themselves be transitory and incomplete. So I must come back to the question: Why? And, especially, why now? Why this obsession with memory and the past, and why this fear of forgetting? Why are we building museums as if there were no tomorrow? . . .

Whatever the social and political causes of the memory boom may have been, one thing is certain: We cannot discuss personal, generational, or public memory separate from the enormous influence of the new media as carriers of all forms of memory. Thus it is no longer possible, for instance, to think of the Holocaust or of any other historical trauma as a serious ethical and political issue apart from the multiple ways it is now linked to commodification and spectacularization in films, museums, docudramas. . . . But even if the Holocaust has been endlessly commodified, that does not mean that each and every commodification inevitably banalizes it as historical event. There is no pure space outside of commodity culture, however much we may desire such a space. Much depends, therefore, on the specific strategies of representation and commodification and on the context in which they are staged. Similarly, the presumably trivial *Erlebnisgesellschaft* of mass-marketed life styles, spectacles, and fleeting events is not devoid of a substantive lived reality that underlies its surface manifestations. My argument here is this: The problem is not solved by simply opposing serious memory to trivial memory, the way historians sometimes oppose history to memory *tout court*, memory as the subjective and trivial stuff out of which the historian makes the real thing. We cannot simply pit the serious Holocaust museum against some Disneyfied theme parks. For this would only reproduce the old high/low dichotomy of modernist culture in a new guise. . . . Once we acknowledge the constitutive gap between reality and its representation in language or image, we must in principle be open to many different possibilities of representing the real and its memories. This is not to say that anything goes. The question of quality remains one to be decided case by case. But the semiotic gap cannot be closed by the one and only correct representation. . . .

The critics of late capitalist amnesia doubt that Western media culture has anything left resembling "real" memory or a strong sense of history. Drawing on the standard Adornean argument that commodification equals forgetting, they argue that the marketing of memory generates nothing but amnesia. Ultimately, I do not find this argument convincing. It leaves too much out. It is too easy to blame the dilemma we find ourselves in on the machinations of the culture industry and the proliferation of the new media. Something else must be at stake, something that produces the desire for the past in the first place and that makes us respond so favorably to the memory markets: that something, I would suggest, is a slow but palpable transformation of temporality in our lives, centrally brought on by the complex intersections of technological change, mass media, and new patterns of consumption, work, and global mobility. There may indeed be good reasons to think that the memorializing drive has a more beneficial and generative dimension as well. However much there is a displacement of a fear of the future in our concerns with memory, and however dubious the proposition may now strike us that we can learn from history, memory culture fulfills an important function in the current transformation of temporal experience in the wake of the new media's impact on human perception and sensibility. . . .

I would like to suggest some ways to think about the relationship between our privileging of memory and the past on the one hand and the potential impact of the new media on perception and temporality on the other. It is a complex story. . . .

Here I would like to turn to an argument first articulated by two conservative German philosophers, Hermann Lübbe and Odo Marquard, in the early 1980s. Already then, as others were in the midst of debating the future promises of postmodernism, Hermann Lübbe described what he called "musealization" as central to the shifting temporal sensibility of our time. Lübbe showed how musealization was no longer bound to the institution of the museum, narrowly understood, but had infiltrated all areas of everyday life. His diagnosis posited an expansive historicism of our contemporary culture, a cultural present gripped with an unprecedented obsession with the past. Modernization, he argued, is inevitably accompanied by the atrophy of valid traditions, the loss of rationality, and the entropy of stable and lasting life experiences. The ever increasing speed of technical, scientific, and cultural innovation produces ever larger quantities of obsolescence, while objectively shrinking the chronological expanse of what can be considered the (cutting-edge) present at any given time. . . .

Historical memory research is international in scope. My hypothesis is that, in this prominence of academic mnemohistory, memory and musealization together are enlisted as bulwarks against obsolescence and disappearance, to counter our deep anxiety about the speed of change and the ever shrinking horizons of time and space.

Lübbe's argument about the shrinking extension of the present signals a great paradox: The more the present of advanced consumer capitalism prevails over past and future, sucking both into an expanding synchronous space, the weaker is its grip on itself, the less stability or identity it provides for contemporary subjects. Filmmaker and writer Alexander Kluge has spoken of the attack of the present on the rest of time. There is both too much and too little present at the same time, a historically novel situation that creates agonizing tensions in our "structure of feeling," as Raymond Williams would call it. In Lübbe's theory, the museum compensates for this loss of stability. It offers traditional forms of cultural identity to a destabilized modern subject, but the theory fails to acknowledge that these cultural traditions have themselves been affected by modernization through digital and commodified recycling. . . .

This conservative argument about shifts in temporal sensibility needs to be lifted from its binary framing . . . and pushed in a different direction, one that does not rely on a discourse of loss and that accepts the fundamental shift in structures of feeling, experience, and perception as they characterize our simultaneously expanding and shrinking present. The conservative belief that cultural musealization can provide compensation for the ravages of accelerating modernization in the social world is just too simple and too ideological. It fails to recognize that any secure sense of the past itself is being destabilized by our musealizing culture industry and by the media that function as central players in the morality play of memory. Musealization itself is sucked into that vortex of an ever faster circulation of images, spectacles, events, and thus is always in danger of losing its ability to guarantee cultural stability over time. . . .

It bears repeating that, as we approach the end of the twentieth century and with it the end of the millennium, the coordinates of space and time structuring our lives are increasingly subjected to new kinds of pressures. Space and time are fundamental categories of human experience and perception, but far from being immutable, they are very much subject to historical change. One of modernity's permanent laments concerns the loss of a better past, the

memory of living in a securely circumscribed place, with a sense of stable
boundaries and a place-bound culture with its regular flow of time and a core
of permanent relations. Perhaps such days have always been a dream rather
than a reality, a phantasmagoria of loss generated by modernity itself rather
than by its prehistory. But the dream does have staying power, and what I have
called the culture of memory may well be, at least in part, its contemporary
incarnation. The issue, however, is not the loss of some golden age of stability
and permanence. The issue is rather the attempt, as we face the very real processes of time-space compression, to secure some continuity within time, to
provide some extension of lived space within which we can breathe and move.

For surely enough, the end of the twentieth century does not give us easy
access to the trope of a golden age. Memories of the twentieth century confront
us not with a better life, but with a unique history of genocide and mass destruction which, a priori, mars any attempt to glorify the past. . . .

In an era of ethnic cleansings and refugee crises, mass migrations and
global mobility for ever more people, the experience of displacement and relo-
cation, migration and diaspora seems no longer the exception but the rule. But
such phenomena do not tell the whole story. As spatial barriers weaken and
space itself is gobbled up by time ever more compressed, a new kind of malaise
is taking root in the heart of the metropolis. The discontents of metropolitan
civilization at the end of the century no longer seem to stem primarily from
pervasive feelings of guilt and superego repression, as Freud had it in his
analysis of classical Western modernity and its dominant mode of subject formation. . . . Our discontents rather flow from informational and perceptual
overload combined with a cultural acceleration neither our psyche nor our
senses are that well equipped to handle. The faster we are pushed into a global
future that does not inspire confidence, the stronger we feel the desire to slow
down, the more we turn to memory for comfort. But what comfort from memories of the twentieth century?! And what are the alternatives? How are we to
negotiate the rapid change and turnover in what Georg Simmel called objective
culture while at the same time satisfying what I take to be the fundamental
need of modern societies to live in extended forms of temporality and to secure
a space, however permeable, from which to speak and to act? Surely, there is no
one simple answer to such a question, but memory—individual, generational,
public, cultural, and, still inevitably, national memory—surely is part of it. Perhaps one day there will even emerge something like a global memory as the
different parts of the world are drawn ever tighter together. But any such global
memory will always be prismatic and heterogeneous rather than holistic or
universal. . . .

The current transformations of the temporal imaginary brought on by virtual space and time may serve to highlight the enabling dimension of
memory culture. Whatever their specific occasion, cause, or context, the
intense memory practices we witness in so many different parts of the world
today articulate a fundamental crisis of an earlier structure of temporality
that distinguished the age of high modernity—with its trust in progress and

development, its celebration of the new as utopian, as radically and irreducibly other and its unshaken belief in some telos of history. Politically, many memory practices today counteract the triumphalism of modernization theory in its latest guise of "globalization." Culturally, they express the growing need for spatial and temporal anchoring in a world of increasing flux in ever denser networks of compressed time and space. As historiography has shed an earlier reliance on teleological master-narratives and has grown more skeptical of nationalist framings of its subject matter, today's critical memory cultures, with their emphases on human rights, on minority and gender issues, and on reassessing various national and international pasts, go a long way to provide a welcome impetus for the writing of history in a new key and thus for guaranteeing a future of memory. In the best-case scenario, the cultures of memory are intimately linked, in many parts of the world, to processes of democratization and struggles for human rights, to the expansion and strengthening of the public spheres of civil society. Slowing down rather than speeding up, expanding the nature of public debate, trying to heal the wounds inflicted in the past, nurturing and expanding livable space rather than destroying it for the sake of some future promise, securing "quality time"—these seem to be unmet cultural needs in a globalizing world, and local memories are intimately linked to their articulation.

But the past cannot give us what the future has failed to deliver. Indeed, there is no avoiding coming back to the downside of what some would call a memory epidemic, and this brings me back to Nietzsche, whose second untimely mediation on the use and abuse of history, often quoted in contemporary memory debates, may be as untimely as ever. Clearly, the memory fever of Western media societies is not a consuming historical fever in Nietzsche's sense, which could be cured by productive forgetting. It is rather a mnemonic fever caused by the cybervirus of amnesia that at times threatens to consume memory itself. Therefore we now need productive remembering more than productive forgetting. In retrospect we can see how the historical fever of Nietzsche's times functioned to invent national traditions in Europe, to legitimize the imperial nation-states, and to give cultural coherence to conflictive societies in the throes of the Industrial Revolution and colonial expansion. By comparison, the mnemonic convulsions of North Atlantic culture today seem mostly chaotic, fragmentary, and free-floating across our screens. Even in places where memory practices have a very clear political focus, such as South Africa, Argentina, Chile, and most recently Guatemala, they are affected and to a degree even created by international media coverage and its memory obsessions. As I suggested earlier, securing the past is no less risky an enterprise than securing the future. Memory, after all, can be no substitute for justice, and justice itself will inevitably be entangled in the unreliability of memory. But even where cultural memory practices lack an explicit political focus, they do express a society's need for temporal anchoring when, in the wake of the information revolution and an ever increasing time-space compression, the relationship between past, present, and future is being transformed beyond recognition.

In that sense, local and national memory practices contest the myths of cyber-capitalism and globalization and their denial of time, space, and place. No doubt some new configuration of time and space will eventually emerge from this negotiation. New technologies of transportation and communication have always transformed the human perception of time and space in modernity. . . . New technologies and new media are also always met by anxieties and fear that later prove to have been unwarranted or even ridiculous. Our age will be no exception.

At the same time, cyberspace alone is not the appropriate model to imagine the global future—its notion of memory is misleading, a false promise. Lived memory is active, alive, embodied in the social—that is, in individuals, families, groups, nations, and regions. These are the memories needed to construct differential local futures in a global world. There is no doubt that in the long run all such memories will be shaped to a significant degree by the new digital technologies and their effects, but they will not be reducible to them. To insist on a radical separation between "real" and virtual memory seems quixotic, if only because anything remembered—whether by lived or imagined memory—is itself virtual. Memory is always transitory, notoriously unreliable, and haunted by forgetting—in short, human and social. As public memory it is subject to change: political, generational, individual. It cannot be stored forever, nor can it be secured by monuments; nor, for that matter, can we rely on digital retrieval systems to guarantee coherence and continuity. If the sense of lived time is being renegotiated in our contemporary cultures of memory, we should not forget that time is not only the past, its preservation and transmission. If we are indeed suffering from a surfeit of memory, we do need to make the effort to distinguish usable pasts from disposable pasts. Discrimination and productive remembering are called for, and mass culture and the virtual media are not inherently irreconcilable with that purpose. Even if amnesia were a byproduct of cyberspace, we must not allow the fear of forgetting to overwhelm us. And then perhaps it is time to remember the future, rather than only worry about the future of memory.

Pierre Nora (contemp.)

French historian. A good deal of the putative memory boom in recent scholarship can be traced to Pierre Nora's signal contributions. Within the crucible of the French Revolution's bicentennial celebration, Nora commissioned and edited an encyclopedic effort to catalogue France's "lieux de memoire," a term Nora theorized, in contrast to "milieux de memoire," to explain the epochal transformations in memory culture over the centuries from the beginning of modernity to contemporary postmodernity. Where once we lived lives suffused with memory, now memory is a special topic. Most famously, in his theoretical and conceptual introduction to the seven-volume encyclopedia he edited, Nora asserted that "we speak so much of memory because there is so little of it left." Nora's project yielded a mixed and heated reception: Was this a conservative effort at recovery? Postmodernist irony? Historically accurate? Whatever one's position, the work's massive influence cannot be underestimated.

Nora's theoretical essay was first published in English in a special edition of the journal *Representations* in 1989 and has been standard reading since then. Given the ease with which the essay can be obtained—and the difficulties of usefully excerpting it—we have opted for a later and much lesser known retrospective essay in which Nora offers his explanation of the rise of interest in memory, for which his project was a founding moment.

From "Reasons for the Current Upsurge in Memory"

We are witnessing a world-wide upsurge in memory. Over the last twenty or twenty-five years, every country, every social, ethnic or family group, has undergone a profound change in the relationship it traditionally enjoyed with the past.

This change has taken a variety of forms: criticism of official versions of history and recovery of areas of history previously repressed; demands for signs of a past that had been confiscated or suppressed; growing interest in "roots" and genealogical research; all kinds of commemorative events and new museums; renewed sensitivity to the holding and opening of archives for public consultation; and growing attachment to what in the English-speaking world is called "heritage" and in France *"patrimoine."* However they are combined, these trends together make up a kind of tidal wave of memorial concerns that has broken over the world, everywhere establishing close ties between respect for the past—whether real or imaginary—and the sense of belonging, collective consciousness and individual self-awareness, memory and identity.

France was quite possibly the first to embark on this age of ardent, embattled, almost fetishistic "memorialism." It was followed, after the fall of the Berlin Wall and the collapse of the Soviet Union, by the "recovery of memory" in

Eastern Europe. And this in turn was followed, after the fall of the military dictatorships in Latin America, and after the end of apartheid in South Africa and the Truth and Reconciliation Commission, by a world-wide "memorialism" and the emergence of all kinds of initiatives that, in one form or another, involved settling scores with the past. . . .

This "memorialist" trend, for which I have suggested the name "the age of commemoration," is so widespread, so deep-seated and all-powerful, that it may be worthwhile—at the risk of confining oneself to generalisations or trivialities—trying to understand the reasons for it. This upsurge in memory intersects, its seems to me, with two major historical phenomena which have marked the age, one temporal and one social. It is these two phenomena that I would like to underline. . . .

The first concerns what is usually referred to as the "acceleration of history." This notion, first put forward by Daniel Halévy, essentially means that the most continuous or permanent feature of the modern world is no longer continuity or permanence but change. And increasingly rapid change, an accelerated precipitation of all things into an ever more swiftly retreating past. We must take the measure of this change for the way in which memory is organised. It is of crucial importance, for it has shattered the unity of historical time, that fine, straightforward linearity which traditionally bound the present and the future to the past.

In effect, it was the way in which a society, nation, group or family envisaged its future that traditionally determined what it needed to remember of the past to prepare that future; and this in turn gave meaning to the present, which was merely a link between the two. Broadly speaking, the future could be interpreted in one of three ways, which themselves determined the image people had of the past. It could be envisaged as a form of restoration of the past, a form of progress or a form of revolution. Today, we have discarded these three ways of interpreting the past, which made it possible to organise a "history." We are utterly uncertain as to what form the future will take. And because of this uncertainly, the present—which, for this very reason no doubt, now has a battery of technical means at its disposal for preserving the past—puts us under an obligation to remember. We do not know what our descendants will need to know about ourselves in order to understand their own lives. And this inability to anticipate the future puts us under an obligation to stockpile, as it were, in a pious and somewhat indiscriminate fashion, any visible trace or material sign that might eventually testify to what we are or what we will have become. In other words, it is the end of any kind of teleology of history—the end of a history whose end is known—that places on the present this urgent "duty to remember" (devoir de mémoire) that is so much talked about. Unlike my friend Paul Ricœur, who keeps his distance from this hackneyed phrase, preferring that of "effort to remember" (travail de mémoire), I am willing to accept the term, provided it is understood in a much broader sense than is usually attributed to it, a sense more mechanical, material and heritage-based than moral, and linked, not to the idea of "debt" but of "loss," which is a very different matter.

For the other effect of this "acceleration of history," symmetrical with that of the future, is to abruptly distance us from the past—we are cut off from it. It has become what an English demographic historian has famously described as "the world we have lost." We no longer inhabit that past, we only commune with it through vestiges—vestiges, moreover, which have become mysterious to us and which would do well to question, since they hold the key to our "identity," to who we are. We are no longer on very good terms with the past. We can only recover it by reconstructing it in monumental detail with the aid of documents and archives; in other words, what we today call "memory"—a form of memory that is itself a reconstruction—is simply what was called "history" in the past. We are dealing here with a radical and dangerous shift in the meaning of words, a shift itself characteristic of the spirit of the age. "Memory" has taken on a meaning so broad and all-inclusive that it tends to be used purely and simply as a substitute for "history" and to put the study of history at the service of memory.

The "acceleration of history," then, has two effects on memory:

- on the one hand, it leads to a kind of *stockpiling*, bound up with this feeling of loss and responsible for the exaggerated importance now attached to memory and the proliferation of institutions and instruments that relate to it; museums, archives, libraries, collections, digitalized inventories, data-banks, chronologies, and so forth;
- and on the other, between an unforeseeable future and a past shrouded in darkness or mist, the *autonomising* of the present, the emergence of the present as a category for understanding our own lives, but a present that is already historical and overlaid with an awareness of its own character and truth. It is this explosion of historical and temporal continuity which, in my opinion, makes memory so topical today: the past is no longer the guarantee of the future, and it is largely for this reason that memory has come to play such an active role in society and been invested with a promise of continuity. In the old days, it was the past and the future that were independent, the present acting as a bridge between them. Today, it is the present and memory that are independent.

The second reason for this outbreak of memory is of a social nature and is linked to what might be called, by analogy with "acceleration," the "democratization" of history. This takes the form of a marked emancipatory trend among peoples, ethnic groups and even certain classes of individual in the world today; in short, the emergence, over a very short period of time, of all those forms of memory bound up with minority groups for whom rehabilitating their past is part and parcel of reaffirming their identity.

Minority memories of this kind are mainly the outcome of three types of decolonization: *international* decolonization, which has allowed societies previously stagnating in the ethnological inertia of colonial oppression access to historical consciousness and the rehabilitation (or fabrication) of memories; *domestic* decolonization, within traditional western societies, of sexual, social, religious and provincial minorities now being integrated with the mainstream and for whom reaffirming their "memory"—in actual fact, their history—is a way of having their "particularism" recognized by a community that had previously refused them that right, while at the same time cultivating their difference and their attachment to an identity threatened with disintegration. . . . Finally, there is a third type of decolonization which followed on the collapse of twentieth-century totalitarian regimes, whether communist, Nazi or just plain dictatorial: an *ideological* decolonisation which has helped reunite these liberated peoples with traditional, long-term memories confiscated, destroyed or manipulated by those regimes: this is the case with Russia and many countries in Eastern Europe, the Balkans, Latin America and Africa.

The explosion of minority memories of this kind has profoundly altered the respective status and the reciprocal nature of history and memory—or, to be more precise, has enhanced the very notion of "collective memory," hitherto little used.

Unlike history, which has always been in the hands of the public authorities, of scholars and specialised peer groups, memory has acquired all the new privileges and prestige of a popular protest movement. It has come to resemble the revenge of the underdog or injured party, the outcast, the history of those denied the right to History. Hitherto, if it did not have truth, it at least had loyalty on its side. What is new, and what it owes to the abysmal sufferings of the last century, to the increase in life expectancy and to the continuing presence of survivors, is the demand for a truth more "truthful" than that of history, the truth of personal experience and individual memory.

History, on the other hand, though it was always *founded* on memory, as a discipline that aspired to scientific status had traditionally been built up in opposition to memory, thought to be idiosyncratic and misleading, nothing more than private testimony. History was the sphere of the collective; memory that of the individual. History was one; memory, by definition, plural (since by nature individual). The idea that memory can be collective, emancipatory and sacred turns the meaning of the term inside out. Individuals had memories, collectivities had histories. The idea that collectivities have a memory implies a far-reaching transformation of the status of individuals within society and of their relationship to the community at large. Therein lies the secret of that other mysterious shift which has occurred, and on which a little light needs to be thrown: the shift in our understanding of *identity*, without which it is impossible to understand this *upsurge in memory.*

The concept of identity has undergone a similar reversal in meaning at the same time as that of memory. It has gone from being an individual and subjective notion to a collective, quasi-formal and objective one. Traditionally, identity characterises all that is unique about an individual—so much so, in fact, that it has acquired an essentially administrative sense relating to law enforcement: our fingerprints are the expression of our "identity," we have "identity" cards and papers. The expression has become a group category, a way of defining us *from without*. "One is not born a woman," Simone de Beauvoir famously remarked, "one becomes one." It might serve as a catch-phrase for all identities created from self-assertion. Identity, like memory, is a form of *duty*. I am asked to become what I am: a Corsican, a Jew, a worker, an Algerian, a Black. It is at this level of obligation that the decisive tie is formed between memory and social identity. Viewed in this light, they are both governed by the same mechanism: the two terms have become all but synonymous, and the fact that they have merged reflects a change in the way that history and society interact. . . .

At this point, of course, it would be important to describe in greater detail how this new memory is organised. . . . Let us make do for the moment, by way of conclusion, with underlining some of the immediate effects of this recent surge in memory. There are two main effects, it seems to me.

The first consists in a dramatic increase in the uses made of the past for political, commercial and tourist purposes. One example of this is a sharp rise in the number of commemorative events. . . . There are all kinds of reasons for this proliferation of commemorative events, but they all go to show that the past has ceased to have a single meaning and that a present that is overlaid with an awareness of its own history necessarily allows for several possible versions of the past.

The second effect of this change in the way memory is organised has been to deprive the historian of the monopoly he traditionally enjoyed in interpreting the past. In a world in which you had *collective history* and *individual memories*, the historian exercised exclusive control, so to speak, over the past. This privilege had even been greatly consolidated over the last hundred years by what is sometimes referred to as "scientific" history. To the historian alone befell the task of establishing the facts, producing the evidence and delivering the truth. It was his profession and his mark of respectability. Today, the historian is far from alone in manufacturing the past; it is a role he shares with the judge, the witness, the media and the legislator. All the more reason, therefore, to speak out loud and clear today on behalf of the "duty towards history," rather than the "duty to remember, the need for which a few of us were proclaiming some twenty or twenty-five years ago.

For the real problem raised by the sacred aura with which memory has now been invested is to know how, why and at what moment the otherwise positive principle of emancipation and liberation on which it is based backfires and becomes a form of closure, a grounds for exclusion and an instrument of war. To claim the right to memory is, at bottom, to call for justice. In the effects it has had, however, it has often become a call to murder. The time has perhaps come to bring against memory the charge that in his *Untimely Meditations* Nietzsche brought a century ago against history, but replacing the word "historical" by "memorial:" "There is a certain degree of sleeplessness, of rumination, of [memorial] significance beyond which any living creature is threatened with collapse, and in the long run destroyed, whether it be an individual, a people or a civilization." It is this message left by memory that we also need to remember.

Charles Maier (contemp.)

American historian. Maier's intellectual history of the German historians' dispute (*The Unmasterable Past: History, Holocaust, and German National Identity*), in which German historians and politicians debated the relevance of memory to German identity and German politics forty years after the end of the war, was a major contribution to memory studies; the German historians' dispute was both a significant occasion in which themes of the memory boom were crystallized and debated, not least by Maier, and a spur to further elaboration of scholarly and political interest in memory. Here Maier extends his reflections, which, following **Nietzsche**, asked what was enough memory and what was too much memory; in turn, Maier asks whether the memory boom in politics and culture has produced "a surfeit of memory," or perhaps even more. A particular issue motivating Maier was the proliferation of revived national identities in European politics following the transformations of 1989, and the interest of their proponents in memory as a source of identity.

From "A Surfeit of Memory? Reflections on History, Melancholy, and Denial"

I believe that we have in a sense become addicted to memory. When I asked in *The Unmasterable Past* whether there might be too much memory. I cited Nietzsche's "untimely meditation" on the use and abuse of history—untimely because it ran against the bourgeois celebratory currents of smug national materialism and "convention." His reflection was out of "sync" with the age, he said because "I even believe that we are all suffering from a distorting historical fever and at least should recognize from what we are suffering." A hypertrophic virtue could be as harmful as a hypertrophic vice. For Nietzsche history might become a cloying excuse not to act and not to accept the fullness of life in the present: a sort of post-Victorian neurasthenia. To live rightly a people needed both to remember and to forget—a sober warning that Freud transformed into the idea that to create one had to repress. These thoughts came to mind when I proposed the question as to whether there might be something inauthentic and unhealthy about the canonization of memory. I think it is time to ask whether an addition to memory can become neurasthenic and disabling. At the least we should ask what characteristics of our time may have helped to bring about this indulgence.

Again, it can be objected that precious few of us cultivate memory. As a society we seem intent on forgetting. Americans are allegedly not interested in history compared with Europeans. But that is false; I think Americans crave history as much as do any Europeans, and I do not think Europeans are really more determined by their memories than we are. In any case, I am not diagnosing American society as a whole, but what might best be called the Republic of Letters or intellectual community.

Moreover, the phenomenon transcends just the explicit preoccupation with memory in its own right. In this regard our interest in memory is part of our general interest in language and discourse. It has analogues throughout the culture. For what is at stake with the focus on memory in its own right is the post-modern dissolution of social transparency. For now we have moved from what is remembered to the rememberer. But our focus on man remembering may well provide only a brief new epistemological equilibrium. The postmodern revolution swallows its own children or at least decomposes its own protagonists. If deconstruction has carried this postmodern problematizing of language to the point where the speaker or writer is himself decomposed, so too the analysis of memory have begun to dissolve, not merely the life that is remembered, but the mind that does the remembering. In any case, memory, as an alternative format for language, has changed from being a medium for reconstructing a world as it was perceived into a semi-opaque and self-referential activity.

Historians, of course, are hardly immune to this epistemological transition. Causal analysis is replaced by representation. The belief that society might play a causal role in historical outcomes gives way to the belief that politics is discourse and symbol and can hardly be explained by any reference outside itself. First social classes and then individuals have been decentered and dissolved in this causal opaqueness. Agency thus dissipates in a sea of discourse; and only the self-enclosed system of symbolic activity can be described, like some serpent swallowing its own tail. . . .

Why . . . does memory now seem to play a larger role in political and civic life? My own belief is that at the end of the twentieth century Western societies have come to the end of a massive collective project. It is not just the project of the communist or even socialist Left or even of the Left *tout court*, although the end of these agendas is apparent. It is also the end, or at least the interruption, of the capacity to found collective institutions that rest on aspirations for the future. Our political representatives do not believe in public goods, that is, commonly held goods that inevitably can be enjoyed by so-called free riders or those who do not pay their own way. And among the public goods that no longer compel our loyalties is the modern nation-state as conceived in the eighteenth and nineteenth centuries. For despite the rhetoric of self-determination, the modern nation was not merely an expression of ethnicity. It was a commitment to values of communal liberty and culture that might have been organized through ethnicity, through linguistic kinship, but that also transcended ethnicity. The ethnic unit as repressed in language or faith or even territory was supposed to provide the basis for nationality, its subsoil so to speak. But ethnicity alone did not incorporate values that the nation-state was supposed to achieve. These values remained future-oriented, not just historically conditioned, they incorporated universal aspirations of law, justice and welfare. The modern nation-state grew out of ethnicity, not toward ethnicity.

I stress this point because I think that as we extend recognition to more and more ethnic fragments—Slovenia, Croatia, Bosnia, Moldova, etc., etc.—we are confused by their claims. Nations in the modern era were more than gene pools; they were layered communities—often hierarchical, to be sure, with subject and ruling ethnic groups. Nonetheless, even when they were hierarchical and stratified by ethnicity and class (as was the American Republic through 1960), they encompassed larger aspirations than ethnicity. The collapse of communism, it becomes clearer as we leave 1991 behind us, involved not just the rejection of totalitarianism and/or the price of economic inefficiency. It was, I believe, part of a broader faltering of all political communities with public collective aspirations—no matter whether these aspirations were distorted and repressive, or generous and emancipatory objectives that sought to extend equality and liberties. In effect, I believe, we are undermining Western nations as well as communist states, throwing out the national baby with the communist bathwater, or letting both go down the drain because of some great exhaustion of civil culture at the end of the second millennium of the Christian era. In that exhaustion, the salvageable political future reduces to ethnicity and perhaps ultimately even kinship. Of course, I may be wrong, or the trend may be reversed. Public trust and future orientations may yet prevail. Jefferson may yet prevail over Calhoun, Mill over Burke. But for the foreseeable future, at least, ethnicity is trump. And ethnic grievances have become the currency of politics. For some these grievances involve past catastrophes. In any case, getting others to pay their respect is a version of national recognition. Respect must be paid, ambassadors must be exchanged, compensatory deals must be arranged, victims must be remembered. In the twilight of Enlightenment aspirations to collective institutions, we build museums to memory, our memory. . . .

[T]he surfeit of memory is a sign not of historical confidence but of a retreat from transformative politics. It testifies to the loss of a future orientation, of progress toward civic enfranchisement and growing equality. It reflects a new focus on narrow ethnicity as a replacement for encompassing communities based on constitutions, legislation and widening attribute of citizenship. The program for this new ethnicity is as symbolic as it is substantive. It aspires preeminently to the recognition by other groups of its own suffering and victimhood. Finally, it cathects to landscape and territory because territoriality has been abandoned as a physical arena for civic action and is nurtured instead as an enclave of historicism.

Are we suffering from too much memory? At the end, let me attempt an answer to the question in another way. I would rather that our society had enough confidence in its future orientation, in its political projects, its capacities to use civic action to meet urgent public needs and diminish the gross inequalities that characterize our life, so that we are all less preoccupied with our memory. The fault is not with memory, but with our current balance of past and future. As a historian I want a decent public awareness of the past and careful reasoning about it. As a historian I want past suffering to be acknowledged and repaired so far as possible by precluding reversions to violence and repression. But I do not crave a wallowing in bathetic memory, I believe that when we turn to memory it should be to retrieve the object of memory, not just to enjoy the sweetness of melancholy. And I am not certain that any memory can retrieve the past.

Fred Davis (1925–1993)

American sociologist. In this 1979 book *Yearning for Yesterday*, Davis provides a detailed sociological account of the meanings and implications of nostalgia. Nostalgia in collectivities, he argues, is a reaction to disruptive and anxiety-producing events, and acts to restore a sense of continuity across such ruptures. For Davis, then, nostalgia is not wholly in service of conservative agendas, though it can be. This argument is in some ways comparable to that of **Samuel** in the context of the British heritage debates.

From *Yearning for Yesterday: A Sociology of Nostalgia*

Nostalgia is from the Greek *nostos*, to return home, and *algia*, a painful condition—thus, a painful yearning to return home. Coined by the Swiss physician Johannes Hofer in the late seventeenth century, the term was meant to designate a familiar, if not especially frequent, condition of extreme homesickness among Swiss mercenaries fighting far from their native land in the legions of one or another European despot. . . .

It is of interest to note in passing that to the medical mind of the early Enlightenment such humble, straightforward terms as the German *Heimweh*, the English *homesickness* and the French *maladie du pays* were somehow found wanting; a *disease* had to be invented to replace what up until that time had, we can assume, been regarded as an unfortunate though familiar vicissitude of life. . . .

Despite the diverse, often bizarre scientistic pretensions of the many military physicians who interested themselves in the subject, it appears that well into the modern era the strong semantic bond between the disease category nostalgia and some commonsensical notion of homesickness remained largely intact. It was only with the word's unmooring from its pathological base, with its demilitarization and demedicalization, as it were, that it began to acquire many of the connotations it has today. . . . [T]his could not have happened much before the turn of the present century, for it is only then, and most notably in America, that one begins to find scholarly reports of a medical or psychological sort that neither treat the condition as a "disease" in the conventional medical sense nor limit its incidence to persons in the military. But once introduced into popular parlance, the process of semantic drift has proved so pronounced that nowadays only a minority of speakers, . . . are likely to associate nostalgia with homesickness *per se*, while almost no one thinks of it as a "disease." . . .

Not only does the word *nostalgia* appear to have been fully "demilitarized" and "demedicalized" by now but, with its rapid assimilation into American popular speech since roughly the nineteen-fifties, it appears to be undergoing a process of "depsychologization" as well. By this I mean that whatever residual connotations of aberrance or mental malfunction—even of a minor or transitory character may have clung to the word following its habitation of two centuries in the realm of psychiatry, these too are rapidly being dissipated through positively tinged popular and commercial usage. So easily and "naturally" does the word come to our tongues nowadays that it is much more likely to be classed with such familiar emotions as love, jealousy, and fear than with such "conditions" as melancholia, obsessive compulsion, or claustrophobia.

Thus, in seeking to understand the nature of the experience from an examination of the etymology of the word, we are confronted with a compound sociolinguistic paradox, to wit: (1) the drift of the word's contemporary connotations from the pathological and occupationally specialized meanings with which it was originally invested and (2) the gradual semantic deterioration of its core referent of *homesickness*. It is almost as if, once lifted from its original context, the word sought of its own accord that murky and inchoate amalgam of sentiments to which so homely a word as homesickness could no longer render symbolic justice.

But, before exploring the new realm of meaning, we may ask how it came to pass that the demedicalized word in the course of the twentieth century acquired such astonishing evocativeness and prominence while gradually shedding that core referent—homesickness—which once distinguished it? . . . [O]ne can only speculate on some of the influences at play. In some small part, perhaps, the sheer phonetic symbolism of the word, its easy association with such like-sounding words as nocturnal and nosegay along with the "-algia" suggestion of malaise and mild affliction, may have helped cloak it in allusive romantic imagery that had been lacking as long as the word was confined to a medical context. More important, probably, is the diminished existential salience of "home" in its concrete locational sense, and hence of "*homesickness*" *per se* in the modern world. As with so many other dimensions of what Karl Polanyi has termed "The Great Transformation," the passing of "home" in the old sense arises from the tremendous mobility of persons in their occupations, residences, localities, and even countries of birth that is characteristic of the industrial order of modern Western society. Increasingly, and at an almost frenetic pace by the mid-twentieth century, this constant movement in sociogeographic space has begun to dislodge man's deep psychological attachment to a specific house, in a specific locality, in a specific region, which over the centuries had been fostered by the more settled and protracted arrangements of a primarily agricultural and small-town society.

In short, *home* is no longer where the hearth is. This, of course, is not to say that for moderns the body of sentiments and images the term conveys no longer exists or is incapable of being experienced. Rather, it points simply to the marked severance of "home-type" sentiments from home *per se*, even if the four-letter word itself has retained many of its geographically specific connotations of place. . . . Because, then, home as such can for so many no longer evoke the "remembrance of things past" it once did, it has fallen to other words, "nostalgia" among them, to comprehend the sometimes pedestrian, sometimes disjunctive, and sometimes eerie sense we carry of our own past and of its meaning for present and future. . . .

[I]t should be made clear that to claim that nostalgic material derives from a personally experienced past is not to claim that the past "causes" or even "explains current nostalgia or, more precisely, that it is the motivational source or triggering circumstance for a nostalgic experience as such. On the contrary, since our awareness of the past, our summoning of it, our very knowledge that it *is* past, can be nothing other than present experience, what occasions us to feel nostalgia must also reside in the present, regardless of how much the ensuing nostalgic experience may draw its sustenance from our memory of the past. . . .

[I]f nostalgia, as it is experienced in today's world by users of the word, locates its objects and events in the past, how does it differ from a variety of other subjective states that are equally, and perhaps even more strongly oriented to the past? History, rememberance, recollection, reminiscence, revivification, and recall are but a few of the words in our language that somehow denote the mental state of a sentient being looking back in time. And yet we sense that, however they may differ among themselves (and of course they do), none conveys quite the same feeling tone as does "nostalgia," the difference being more substantial than the formal hair-splitting of those semanticists who claim that no two words are alike and there is no such thing as a true synonym. Thus, for example, merely to remember the places of our youth is not the same as to feel nostalgic over them; nor does even active reminiscence—however happy, benign, or tortured its content—necessarily capture the subjective state we associate with nostalgic feeling.

Clearly, more than "mere past" is involved. It is a past imbued with special qualities, which, moreover, acquires its significance from the particular way we juxtapose it to certain features of our present lives. . . .

To conceive of nostalgic experience as encompassing some necessary inner dialogue between past *and* present is not to suggest that the two sides in the dialogue are of equal strength, independence, or resonance or that there is even any serious doubt over which way the conversation is destined to go. While both speakers must be present and engaged, as it were, for nostalgia's mise-en-scène to fall into place, in the ensuing dialogue it is *always* the adoration of the past that triumphs over lamentations for the present. Indeed, this is the whole point of the dialogue; for to permit present woes to douse the warm glow from the past is to succumb to melancholy or, worse yet, depression. And, while it may be true that the nostalgic dialogue nearly always entails some risk of this sort to the self, there can be no question that points at issue are intended to arrive at the foregone conclusion of the superiority of times and things past. . . .

I would point to two aspects of nostalgic experience, which I believe are essential for any proper understanding of its relationship to society at large. These are: its sources in the perceived threats of identity discontinuity and its role in engendering *collective* identities among people generally, but most especially among members of "the same generation." . . .

Just as the phasing of the life cycle periodically entails status transitions that in their perceived discontinuity and attendant anxiety evoke nostalgic reactions from individuals, so do untoward major historic events and abrupt social changes pose a similar threat and evoke a similar response from people in the aggregate. The difference, of course, is that historic events and social changes are not institutionally scheduled into the flow of our lives as are the phased events of the life cycle. Nonetheless, even though a noteworthy historic event or profound social change may seem to lie farther outside the mainstream of our lives than, for example, our adolescence, parenthood, or old age, what it lacks in immediacy is often made up for subjectively by the feelings of surprise and strangeness it induces in us. It is as if we were suddenly made aware of a rent in the larger existential fabric of our being-in-the-world, where formerly we perceived a whole. And this, too, is a form of discontinuity with which we must somehow cope. Moreover, unlike the person's passage through the life cycle, the untoward event, although unanticipated, involves a concentration of attention and anxious concern among millions of persons at the same moment of historical time, thereby creating a fertile social psychological medium for the production and diffusion of nostalgic sentiment. Herein lies, too, . . . the powerful generation-delineating properties to which nostalgia lends itself so easily: we summon to mind and communicate among ourselves those comforting images from our pasts . . . which seem to iconically bestow upon that past an age-graded distinctiveness and separableness that mere chronological divisions could never by themselves engender. . . .

Allowing then that we are susceptible to feelings of anxiety and concern for our future selves when we are brought up short by some untoward historic event or intrusive social change, it can be seen how at the most elemental level collective nostalgia acts to restore, at least temporarily, a sense of sociohistoric continuity with respect to that which had verged on being rendered discontinuous. And this period; when the nostalgic reaction waxes strong, may afford just enough time for the change to be assimilated into the institutional machinery of a society (e.g., into the realms of law, politics, religion, and education) as it could not at first and, were it left wholly up to purely *private* feeling, might not for some time thereafter. . . .

[N]ostalgia is, of course, not without its political ramifications, although they, may not be quite what critics of the radical left say they are. Typically, liberals and radicals . . . are disdainful of nostalgia movements, denouncing them as a fatuous form of collective self-indulgence at best and, at worst, a deliberately created, cleverly exploited obstacle on the path to reform or revolution, a somewhat diluted, yet still numbing, "opiate of the people.". . .

[M]any radical and liberal critics . . . carp at collective manifestations of nostalgia . . . for being conservative, if not outright reactionary, for turning peoples' heads away from the "important issues of the day" and incapacitating them for the sustained political action with which to correct the ills and undo the injustices of society. In Marxian terminology it is a subspecies of false consciousness, moreover, a particularly insidious subspecies in that it does not merely serve to obscure further an awareness of class struggle but, in defiance of the logic of historical dialectics, looks longingly backward to obsolete societal arrangements rather than forward to the better ones destined to emerge. Indeed, what more powerful antidote to revolutionary fervor than nostalgia's penchant for believing that the future can only be worse than the past?

All of this may of course be true, notwithstanding the unusual difficulty a historian or sociologist would have in tracing through the long-term political consequences of a particular nostalgia fad or movement or a spate of them as we are now witnessing. At the same time, before liberals and radicals succumb to excessive grimness over the matter it should be pointed out that nostalgia's conservative leaning is qualitatively different from the other ways in which conservatism and reaction manifest themselves. It is, even at the collective level, a good deal more passive, less strident, more inward, and, to be sure, more ephemeral. . . . [I]t defuses what could be a powerful, panic-prone reactivity to jarring change and uncertainty by turning it into tender musing and mutually appreciative self-regard over a shared past. To the extent that constant change, at all levels and in all realms of social life, seems to be endemic to modern civilization, some such "outlet" or "safety valve" may be required. As suggested earlier, this allows time for needed change to be assimilated while giving the appearance, as nostalgia does, of meaningful links to the past. . . .

Nostalgia is more a crepuscular emotion. It takes hold when the dark of impending change is seen to be encroaching, although not *so* fast as to make a monster loom where but a moment ago stood a coat tree. In this sense, collective nostalgia represents a kind of inversion of Harold Lasswell's famous definition of politics as "the displacement of private affect onto public objects." In opposite fashion, nostalgia fads, fashions, and movements drain some of the negative affect and vague discontent generated by identity-jarring change in the public sphere (matters that could well be made the subject of considerable political conflict, as of course they sometimes are) and rechannels them into a more private sphere of shared memories and self-congratulatory sentiment over "the ways things were" and how those who came later made them "go wrong." . . .

Generational nostalgic sentiment . . . creates as it conserves. It creates because the past is never something simply there just waiting to be discovered. Rather, the remembered past like all other products of human consciousness is something that must constantly be filtered, selected, arranged, constructed, and reconstructed from collective experience. And the fulcrum for this great labor can only be the present with its shared anxieties, aspirations, hopes fears, and fantasies. But still, the nostalgic creation is, as I have tried to suggest from a number of different vantage points, a special kind of creation, one powerfully permeated in feeling and thought by a conviction of the essential superiority of what was over what is or appears destined to be. Hence the associated impulse to conserve and recover.

In this manner nostalgic sentiment partakes of one of the great dialectical processes of Western civilization: the ceaseless tension of change vs. stability, innovation vs. reaffirmation, new vs. old, utopia vs. the golden age. Its role in this dialectic is that of a brake on the headlong plunge into the future; a rather tenuous brake, to be sure, since little in contemporary life seems capable of arresting the march of modern technology and rational organization. Nonetheless it is, perhaps, enough of a brake to cause some individuals and peoples to look before they knowingly leap.

At least since the Enlightenment insistent and often strident demands have gnawed at the soul of Western man, demands for change, self-improvement, more efficient organization, modernization, uplift, reform and reconstitution—all those attributes that are in accord with the doctrine of man's almost infinite plasticity and perfectability and that converge finally in the idea of Progress as it was propounded and analyzed by the historian J. B. Bury. Nostalgia fosters a kind of primitive resistance to such urgings, to the probing and poking, to that close examination and magnification which in the view of Max Weber has made for the disenchantment of the world. Nostalgia reenchants, if only for a while until the inexorable processes of historical change exhaust that past which offered momentary shelter from a worrisome but finally inexorable future.

Svetlana Boym (contemp.)

Russian American literary theorist. In this essay based on her book *The Future of Nostalgia*, Boym distinguishes between what she calls restorative and reflective nostalgia, each of which has distinct causes and consequences. In her assessment of postmodern nostalgia, she finds many similarities to earlier moments but seeks to harness nostalgia's dissident potential. See also **Davis** and **Huyssen**.

From "Nostalgia and Its Discontents"

The twentieth century began with utopia and ended with nostalgia. Optimistic belief in the future became outmoded, while nostalgia, for better or worse, never went out of fashion, remaining uncannily contemporary. . . .

The nostalgia that interests me here is not merely an individual sickness but a symptom of our age, an historical emotion. Hence I will make three crucial points. First, nostalgia is not "antimodern;" it is not necessarily opposed to modernity but coeval with it. Nostalgia and progress are like Jekyll and Hyde: doubles and mirror images of one another. Nostalgia is not merely an expression of local longing, but a result of a new understanding of time and space that makes the division into "local" and "universal" possible.

Second, nostalgia appears to be a longing for a place, but it is actually a yearning for a different time—the time of our childhood, the slower rhythms of our dreams. In a broader sense, nostalgia is a rebellion against the modern idea of time, the time of history and progress. The nostalgic desires to turn history into private or collective mythology, to revisit time like space, refusing to surrender to the irreversibility of time that plagues the human condition. Hence the past of nostalgia, to paraphrase William Faulkner, is not even past. It could be merely better time, or slower time—time out of time, not encumbered by appointment books.

Third, nostalgia, in my view, is not always retrospective; it can be prospective as well. The fantasies of the past, determined by the needs of the present, have a direct impact on the realities of the future. The consideration of the future makes us take responsibility for our nostalgic tales. Unlike melancholia, which confines itself to the planes of individual consciousness, nostalgia is about the relationship between individual biography and the biography of groups or nations, between personal and collective memory. While futuristic utopias might be out of fashion, nostalgia itself has a utopian dimension—only it is no longer directed toward the future. Sometimes it is not directed toward the past either, but rather sideways. The nostalgic feels stifled within the conventional confines of time and space. . . .

Historians often consider "nostalgia" to be a negative word, or an affectionate insult at best. "Nostalgia is to longing as kitsch is to art," writes Charles Maier. The word is frequently used dismissively. "Nostalgia . . . is essentially history without guilt. Heritage is something that suffuses us with pride rather than shame," writes Michael Kammen. In this understanding, nostalgia is seen as an abdication of personal responsibility, a guilt-free homecoming, an ethical and aesthetic failure. Nostalgia produces subjective visions of afflicted imagination that tend to colonize the realm of politics, history, and everyday perception.

Modern nostalgia is paradoxical in the sense that the universality of its longing can make us more empathetic towards fellow humans, and yet the moment we try to repair that longing with a particular belonging—or the apprehension of loss with a rediscovery of identity and especially of a national community and unique and pure homeland—we often part ways with others and put an end to mutual understanding. *Algia* (or longing) is what we share, yet *nostos* (or the return home) is what divides us. The promise to rebuild the ideal home lies at the core of many powerful ideologies today, tempting us to relinquish critical thinking for emotional bonding. The danger of nostalgia is that it tends to confuse the actual home and the imaginary one. In extreme cases it can create a phantom homeland, for the sake of which one is ready to die or kill. Unreflective nostalgia can breed monsters. Yet the sentiment itself, the mourning of displacement and temporal irreversibility, is at the very core of the modern condition. While claiming a pure and clean homeland, nostalgic politics often produces a "glocal" hybrid of capitalism and religious fundamentalism, or of corporate state and Eurasian patriotism. The mix of nostalgia and politics can be explosive. . . .

Nostalgia as a historical emotion came of age during the time of Romanticism and is coeval with the birth of mass culture. In the mid-nineteenth century, nostalgia became institutionalized in national and provincial museums, heritage foundations, and urban memorials. The past was no longer unknown or unknowable. The past became "heritage." The rapid pace of industrialization and modernization increased the intensity of people's longing for the slower rhythms of the past, for social cohesion and tradition. Yet this obsession with the past revealed an abyss of forgetting and took place in inverse proportion to its actual preservation. As Pierre Nora has suggested, memorial sites, or *"lieux de mémoire,"* are established institutionally when the environments of memory, the *milieux de mémoire,* fade. It is as if the ritual of commemoration could help to patch up the irreversibility of time.

Instead of a magic cure for nostalgia, I will offer a typology that might illuminate some of nostalgia's mechanisms of seduction and manipulation. I distinguish between two main types of nostalgia: the restorative and the reflective. Restorative nostalgia stresses *nostos* (home) and attempts a transhistorical reconstruction of the lost home. Reflective nostalgia thrives on *algia,* (the longing itself) and delays the homecoming—wistfully, ironically, desperately. . . . Restorative nostalgia does not think of itself as nostalgia, but rather as truth and tradition. Reflective nostalgia dwells on the ambivalences of human longing and belonging and does not shy away from the contradictions of modernity. Restorative nostalgia protects the absolute truth, while reflective nostalgia calls it into doubt.

Restorative nostalgia is at the core of recent national and religious revivals. It knows two main plots—the return to origins and the conspiracy. Reflective nostalgia does not follow a single plot but explores ways of inhabiting many places at once and imagining different time zones. It loves details, not symbols. At best, it can present an ethical and creative challenge, not merely a pretext for midnight melancholias. This typology of nostalgia allows me to distinguish between national memory that is based on a single version of national identity, on the one hand, and social memory, which consists of collective frameworks that mark but do not define individual memory, on the other hand. The rhetoric of restorative nostalgia is not about "the past," but rather about universal values, family, nature, homeland, truth. The rhetoric of reflective nostalgia is about taking time out of time and about grasping the fleeing present.

To understand restorative nostalgia, it is important to distinguish between the habits of the past and the habits of the *restoration* of the past. Eric Hobsbawm differentiates between age-old "custom" and nineteenth-century "invented" traditions. New traditions are characterized by a higher degree of symbolic formalization and ritualization than were the actual peasant customs and conventions after which they are patterned. There are two paradoxes here. First, the more rapid and sweeping the pace and scale of modernization, the more conservative and unchangeable the new traditions tend to be. Second, the stronger the rhetoric of continuity with the historical past and emphasis on traditional values, the more selectively the past is usually presented. "The novelty" of invented tradition is "no less novel for being able to dress up easily as antiquity." Of course, "invented tradition" does not mean a creation *ex nihilo*, or a pure act of social constructivism. It builds on the sense of loss of community and cohesion and offers a comforting collective script for individual longing.

There is a perception that as a result of society's industrialization and secularization beginning in the nineteenth century, a certain void of social and spiritual meaning has opened up. What is needed is a secular transformation of "fatality into continuity, contingency into meaning" [Benedict Anderson]. But this transformation can take different turns. It may increase the emancipatory possibilities and individual choices, offering multiple "imagined communities" and means of belonging, which are not exclusively based on ethnic or national principles. It can also be politically manipulated through newly recreated practices of national commemoration with the aim of re-establishing social cohesion, a sense of security, and an obedient relationship to authority.

Restorative nostalgia knows two main plots: the restoration of origins and the conspiracy theory. The conspiratorial worldview reflects a nostalgia for a transcendental cosmology and a simple premodern conception of good and evil. This worldview is based on a single transhistorical plot, a Manichaean battle of good and evil, and the inevitable scapegoating of the mythical enemy. Ambivalence, the complexity of history, the variety of contradictory evidence, and the specificity of modern circumstances are thus erased, and modern history is seen as a fulfillment of ancient prophecy. Extremist conspiracy theory adherents imagine that "home" is forever under siege, requiring defense against the plotting enemy.

Restoration (from *re-staure*—re-establish) signifies a return to the original stasis, to the prelapsarian moment. While restorative nostalgia returns and rebuilds one homeland with paranoic determination, reflective nostalgia fears return with the same passion. Instead of recreation of the lost home, reflective nostalgia can foster the creation of aesthetic individuality.

Reflective nostalgia is concerned with historical and individual time, with the irrevocability of the past and human finitude. Re-flection means new flexibility, not the reestablishment of stasis. The focus here is not on the recovery of what is perceived to be an absolute truth, but on the meditation on history and the passage of time. Nostalgics of this kind are often, in the words of Vladimir Nabokov, "amateurs of time, epicures of duration," who resist the pressure of external efficiency and take sensual delight in the texture of time not measurable by clocks and calendars.

Restorative and reflective nostalgia might overlap in their frames of reference but do not coincide in their narratives and plots of identity. In other words, they can use the same triggers of memory and symbols, the same Proustian madeleine cookie, but tell different stories about it. Nostalgia of the first type gravitates toward collective pictorial symbols and oral culture. Nostalgia of the second type is more oriented towards an individual narrative that savors details and memorial signs, yet perpetually defers homecoming itself. If restorative nostalgia ends up reconstructing emblems and rituals of home and homeland in an attempt to conquer and spatialize time, reflective nostalgia cherishes shattered fragments of memory and temporalizes space. Restorative nostalgia takes itself dead seriously. Reflective nostalgia, on the other hand, can be ironic and humorous. It reveals that longing and critical thinking are not opposed to one another, as affective memories do not absolve one from compassion, judgment, or critical reflection.

Reflective nostalgia does not pretend to rebuild the mythical place called home; it is "enamored of distance, not of the referent itself" [Susan Stewart]. This type of nostalgic narrative is ironic, inconclusive, and fragmentary. Nostalgics of the second type are aware of the gap between identity and resemblance; the home is in ruins or, on the contrary, has just been renovated and gentrified beyond recognition. It is precisely this defamiliarization and sense of distance that drives them to tell their story, to narrate the relationship between past, present, and future. Through that longing, they discover that the past is not that which no longer exists, but, to quote Bergson, the past is something that "might act, and will act by inserting itself into a present sensation from which it borrows the vitality." The past is not made in the image of the present or seen as foreboding some present disaster; rather, the past opens up a multitude of potentialities, non-teleological possibilities of historic development. We do not need a computer to get access to the virtualities of our imagination: reflective nostalgia opens up multiple planes of consciousness. For Marcel Proust, remembrance is an unpredictable adventure in syncretic perception where words and tactile sensations overlap. Place names open up mental maps and space folds into time. "The memory of a particular image is but regret for a particular moment; and houses, roads, avenues are as fugitive, alas, as the years," writes Proust at the end of *Swann's Way*. It is this memorable literary fugue, then, that matters, not the return home.

In the twenty-first century millions of people find themselves displaced from their place of birth, living in voluntary or involuntary exile. Immigrant's stories are the best narratives of nostalgia—not only because they suffer through nostalgia, but also because they challenge it. These stories are often framed as projections for the nostalgia of others who speak from a much safer place. Immigrants understand the limitations of nostalgia and the tenderness of what I call "diasporic intimacy," which cherishes non-native, elective affinities. Diasporic intimacy is not opposed to uprootedness and defamiliarization but is constituted by it. So much has been made of the happy homecoming that it is time to do justice to the stories of non-return and the reluctant praise of exile. Non-return home in the case of some exiled writers and artists turns into a central artistic drive, a homemaking in the text and artwork, as well as a strategy of survival. Ordinary exiles often become artists in life who remake themselves and their second homes with great ingenuity. Inability to return home is both a personal tragedy and an enabling force. That does not mean that there is no nostalgia there, only that this kind of nostalgia precludes the restoration of the past. Diasporic intimacy does not promise an unmediated emotional fusion, but only a precarious affection—no less deep, yet aware of its transience. . . .

The first decade of the twenty-first century is not characterized by the search for newness, but by the proliferation of nostalgias that are often at odds with one another. Nostalgic cyberpunks and nostalgic hippies, nostalgic nationalists and nostalgic cosmopolitans, nostalgic enviromentalists and nostalgic metrophiliacs (city lovers) exchange pixel fire in the blogosphere. Nostalgia, like globalization, exists in the plural. Studying the sociology, politics, and ethnography of nostalgia, its micropractices and meganarratives, remains as urgent as ever. It is always important to ask the question: Who is speaking in the name of nostalgia? Who is its ventriloquist? Twenty-first century nostalgia, like its seventeenth-century counterpart, produces epidemics of feigned nostalgia. For example, the problem with nostalgia in Eastern Europe is that it seems more ubiquitous than it actually is. This might appear counterintuitive. Western Europeans often project nostalgia onto Eastern Europe as a way of legitimizing "backwardness" and not confronting the differences in their cultural history. . . .

In conclusion, there is not much that is new about contemporary nostalgia. Contrary to the great actress Simone Signoret, who entitled her autobiography *Nostalgia Isn't What It Used to Be*, the structure of nostalgia is in many respects what it used to be, in spite of changing fashions and advances in digital technology. In the end, the only antidote for the dictatorship of nostalgia might be nostalgic dissidence. Nostalgia can be a poetic creation, an individual mechanism of survival, a countercultural practice, a poison, or a cure. It is up to us to take responsibility for our nostalgia and not let others "prefabricate" it for us. The prepackaged "usable past" may be of no use to us if we want to co-create our future. Perhaps dreams of imagined homelands cannot and should not come to life. Sometimes it is preferable (at least in the view of this nostalgic author) to leave dreams alone, let them be no more and no less than dreams, not guidelines for the future. While restorative nostalgia returns and rebuilds one's homeland with paranoic determination, reflective nostalgia fears return with the same passion. Home, after all, is not a gated community. Paradise on earth might turn out to be another Potemkin village with no exit. The imperative of a contemporary nostalgic is to be homesick and sick of home—occasionally at the same time.

Michel-Rolph Trouillot (contemp.)

Haitian American anthropologist. In his book *Silencing the Past: Power and the Production of History*, Trouillot explores the role of power in identifying different events as memorable and relevant, comparing, for instance, the memory of a successful slave revolt, the Alamo, and the Holocaust. In the article from which this excerpt is taken, Trouillot takes up the theme of reparation, particularly the question of apologies and their functions, arguing that public apologies, rather than accommodating the victimized collectivity, serve as screens for those who issue them. They are, by definition, "abortive rituals."

From "Abortive Rituals: Historical Apologies in the Global Era"

Since the late 1980s an increasing number of collectivities throughout the world seem to face one another, demanding, offering, denying or rejecting the explicit recognition of guilt for offences committed from a few years to many centuries ago. Any offer, any request, brings out another one. There is little indication that the wave is likely to stop in the near future. . . .

Collective apologies in our late modern age imply a transfer to collectivities of the attributes that a dominant North Atlantic discourse had hitherto assigned to the liberal subject. Ever since the independent self emerged in liberal discourse in the seventeenth century, it has accumulated a number of properties and attributes, from identity to free will to personality. I contend that the attribution of features of that liberal self to states, ethnic groups and nations is a major condition of possibility of collective apologies as late modern rituals.

Second, this transfer of attributes from individual to collective subjects testifies to the changes in historical perception that make it possible. Third, this transfer and those changes project the protagonists against the background of a global stage where the apology takes on its full significance. We may not have reached the universal history dreamed of by Enlightenment thinkers, but collective apologies are increasing in part because offers, demands, denials or rejections are all projected on to a global stage which is now the ultimate horizon of a new historicity. . . .

As transformative rituals, apologies always involve time—even apologies between individuals. They mark a temporal transition: wrong done in a time marked as past is recognized as such, and this acknowledgement itself creates or verifies a new temporal plane, a present oriented towards the future. Strictly speaking, I cannot apologize for a wrong being—or about to be—inflicted, although I can excuse or explain myself. I can only apologize for things already done. My apology sets a temporal marker between those things—and the past to which they belong—and a present characterized by my new relation to my interlocutor. It creates a new era: I repent, let us now be friends. Or, it registers that a new era has indeed been launched: I can now tell you how remorseful I

am, I was wrong. In short, apologies are premised on the assumption that the
state of affairs to which they refer does not, or should not, obtain in the present
of the actors involved. In claiming a past, they create pastness.

Pastness is, of course, a relation, in the same way that distance is a relation.
In the case of an apology, that relation involves . . . two temporal planes: the
perpetrator and the victim in a first temporal plane—the past; and the repentant and the addressee in a second temporal plane—the present. . . .

The double recognition of numerical identity, . . . which links the two temporal planes, . . . emerges as a necessary condition of the transformation prom-
ised by the ritual. Indeed, it distinguishes the apology proper from related
speech acts that express commiseration without implicating the speaker in the
first temporal plane. At its most felicitous, an apology turns the perpetrator's
expressed regret into remorse acknowledged by the addressee. . . .

[N]ew problems arise when the particular is a collective subject. To start
with, collective subjects never meet each other physically as both collectives
and subjects. They cannot therefore assume identity on pragmatic grounds as
do individual subjects.

Collective subjects are by definition historical products. They cannot precede their own experience. They are not naturally given. This means that we
cannot assume the first temporal plane of a collective apology to be a zero
degree of history in which the particulars existed as such in an eternal present.
We need to establish their existence within that past. We need to establish
when and how our perpetrators—Latin Christendom, the white race, the
Japanese nation or the Hutu ethny—became single historical actors, responsible, as independent subjects, for the wrongs committed in that first temporal order. Second, we need to replicate the operation in the present, aware of
the new difficulties of this second temporal order. What is Christendom today,
regardless of what it may have been in 1492? Third, and only after the first two
operations, we can try to demonstrate a numerical identity between perpetrator and repentant subject. Christendom has changed, yet it is still the same:
it must apologize. Then, of course, we would need to repeat the steps on the
other side of the wrong and establish the numerical identity of victim and
addressee, to make sure that repentant Christendom is indeed apologizing to
the right entity. . . .

On purely formal grounds, collective apologies [thus] imply more than a
simple jump from the one to the many. To be felicitous and transformative,
they require a perplexing relation of identity between subjects who are themselves already very difficult to construct as subjects. They further require that
we maintain these constructions while recognizing their historical nature. . . .

Not surprisingly, then, collective apologies have not been a hallmark of
human history. Indeed, *they have been rather rare.* During most of its history
humankind dealt with clashes between groups and the aftermath of these
clashes mainly on pragmatic terms. To be sure, morality, justice and their
absence—as lived and defined in specific times and places—played their role
in prolonging or ending those clashes. Yet even when such clashes solidified

into long-term feuds and enmities, the expression or resolution of these enmities rarely took the new ritualized forms that typify our times. Indeed, an inherent feature of this ritual wave of collective apologies is its very novelty. Why here? Why now? . . .

Although practices that personalize collectivities by ascribing to them attributes constructed to define or describe individuals may be as old as human society, they took on a different import after the global rise of the North Atlantic in the sixteenth century. As North Atlantic hegemony moved from the Iberian states to Northern Europe, the physical overlap between state and nation, already premised in various versions of the absolutist state, reached a new threshold of both material and symbolic concreteness in the nineteenth century. By the middle of that century, political issues were increasingly couched in nationalist language, and the emerging social sciences, in turn, were becoming increasingly state-centric. . . . Divergent interests aside, social theorists and politicians both assumed the state-nation conflation and sold it to a general public. The habit of treating collectivities as fixed entities, already entrenched in the spheres of knowledge and power, . . . slowly made its way into North Atlantic common sense. The stage was set for collectivities, especially nation-states and ethnic groups—now taken as fixed entities—to be treated as individuals. Yet although some historians and anthropologists ascribed to these individualized collectivities attributes of the subject (such as national character), both the public at large and international law rarely went beyond the need to treat collectivities or institutions such as the state as responsible agents.

Indeed, neither the nineteenth nor the first three-quarters of the twentieth century—which saw an increase in demands for international reparations—witnessed anything close to the wave of apologies that marks our times. Again, this is not surprising when we look back at the formal requirements for a collective apology to obtain as a felicitous performative. Since visions of the person vary considerably across and within populations, . . . any vision of the individual as even remotely constituted in history doubles the requirements for the construction of a collective self that could survive its own history. In short, most visions of the individual make it nearly impossible to move easily from agent to subject and to generate a collective apology as a felicitous transformative ritual.

But let us suppose that the individual self is an unencumbered one, existing prior to its environment and fully formed on its own terms. Collective selves with full attributes of the person become much easier to build on that model since all historical constituents of—and limits to—a fixed identity of the subject have disappeared.

Current collective apologies are premised exactly on that supposedly autoregulating and unencumbered self. Those who propose or request them increasingly ascribe to institutions and collectivities attributes unique to the subject—such as mood, memory, moral responsibility and feelings, down to the possibility of repentance—rather than the practical liability and communal responsibility through time that has long been an attribute of agents. Further, the current wave of apologies does not simply treat collectivities as individuals but as a particular type of individual; more exactly, as a liberal person. Finally, *not any form of liberalism will do.* Rather, behind the discourse about collective apologies today stands the figure of the person in the composite vision of classical liberalism. It is a vision that ties Locke to Kant rather than Montesquieu to Rousseau or to current proponents of a more communitarian liberalism. . . . It is a liberalism of rights rooted in the individual. The collectivities projected in these apologies are not merely subjects. Rather, they are subjects with specific attributes that evoke in turn or together the subject of the market, the subject of civil or criminal law, the ego of psychology, and indeed, the ultimate subject of liberal individualism, an individual united by the memory of past actions yet unburdened by any history that precedes its consciousness. . . .

If we see the global domination of the North Atlantic since the sixteenth century as setting up exactly a unique field of forces—perhaps the first global one in human history . . . —we can also see that practices embedded in this field of forces generate or reinforce conceptual overlaps. From the Caribbean to China, from the spread of plantation work regimes to the diffusion of modern state forms, from the rise of English as lingua franca to the daily renewals of Evangelical commitments, overlapping bundles of practices continue to push forward particular visions of the self.

Central here is the spread of North Atlantic Christianity and its penitent practices. In spite of denominational differences in liturgy and theology, these penitent practices share fundamental assumptions about the redemptive possibilities of singular individuals and the capacity of particular speech acts to actualize this redemption. Yet more obviously material practices, such as wage labour, also presume and reinforce particular framings of the individual. The more such practices spread, the more the visions they embody—and the core they share—compete, on the ground, with pre-existing or parallel visions of the self. Whatever dominant notions of the self may have been in China, Kashmir or sub-Saharan Africa, . . . these localized notions must now accommodate a composite figure of growing international reach.

Key to that composite figure is the unity of consciousness long ago assumed by Locke on the basis of memory of past actions. . . .

The soul of nations—quite a different construct from Montesquieu's spirit—has become, at once, the site of that memory-consciousness and the engine behind both the recognition of past failures and the will to reach a higher moral plane. . . .

The "soul" here is free to choose. Character is self-designed. Inner regulation is in command of change. The collectivities projected in the current wave of apologies are framed outside of history—except of course the history of the encounter on which the apology is premised. Not that this framing denies all historicities. Rather, it requires a particular kind of historicity, notably the possibility of freezing chunks of an allegedly unified past, as in the storage model of memory and history. . . . In other words, history is both denied and heralded.

On the one hand, history is denied as an experience constitutive of the collectivity: no structure precedes the subject. Thus, not accidentally, the current wave favours collectivities assumed to be altogether obvious, eternal and continuous through biological reproduction, such as races and ethnic groups. On the other hand, the history that ties the initial wrong to the possibility of—or need for—an apology is brandished as the sole relevant story. Steeped in a language of blood and soul, collectivities are now defined by the wrongs they committed and for which they should apologize, or by the wrongs they suffered and for which they should receive apology. Further, the historical necessity of joining a collectivity of collectivities best known as "the international community" prompts these newly redefined subjects to play out the liberal social contract on a global scale. Collective apologies today are global apologies inasmuch as they are projected onto a global stage. . . .

The spectacular developments in communications that marked the last two decades of the twentieth century have made possible the creation of a virtual yet global stage on which historical actors—both individual and collective—play out scenarios that are shaped in part by the nature of the stage itself. The "global village" may be an illusion but, if so, it is an illusion through which an increasingly large part of humanity takes consciousness of the new links and hierarchies created by an unprecedented alliance between capital and technologies of communication. The "international community" may be communal only in name, shaped as it is by sheer economic and military force from the North Atlantic, but it remains a powerful trope for the recognition of a new moment in world history.

Particular to this moment is the virtual acceptance that "the whole world is looking at me," a privilege once reserved for the most powerful, who even then retained the right to reject that gaze. That gaze, now virtual yet increasingly hard to escape, global in its pretensions yet parochial in its instrumentalities, frames all discussions of collective responsibility today. It thus helps to set the stage on which collective apologies are performed.

Future historians may debate if, when and how our newest born imagined collective, "the international community," solidified in the minds of a majority of humankind. One can safely suggest that the notion has yet to be inscribed fully in the daily routine of a majority of human beings. At the same time, the endless repetition of this vague and changing concept each and every time collectivities, states or trans-state institutions are involved, the repeated tactical deployment of the phrase, gives this imagined super-community practical and symbolic value. Media references are so frequent that examples may be superfluous here: mentions of the omnipresent "international community" now punctuate all discussions of collective apologies, even those otherwise framed in the most parochial terms. . . .

It is in front of this nebulous entity that collective apologies are being requested, denied, accepted or rejected. Part witness, part audience, this international community functions like a Greek chorus in late modern virtual reality. It is the ultimate listener, presumed yet unseen by the actors, so limited as enforcer yet so powerful as a trope. . . .

[W]ith the development in communications, this assumed international audience helps remove one major obstacle to the performance: the difficulty for collectivities to meet face to face. The virtual chorus is there to fill the gap in communication between the groups involved, wherever they are. Only through it do the actors speak to one another. . . .

Central here is that world, a ghost community, yet the calibrator of a relevance deemed at the same time unique and universal. For on the victim's side one must claim both a unique memory of a unique experience, and the universal relevance of that uniqueness. On the perpetrator's side one must deny or validate that very same combination with the whole world witnessing. . . .

Yet there is an inherent irony. . . . The very discourse of liberal individualism, the tropes of which now allow for the projection of apologetic collective subjects, is fundamentally opposed to the recognition of collective rights, including therefore reparative "affirmative" actions. Further, we need to sever the matter of reparations from the linear relation between time and responsibility which assumes that the effects of past wrongs are necessarily more concrete when the actual victims are still on the ground. That approach rests on a legalistic framework and on a notion of guilt, both of which reproduce the reduction of collectivities to individuals. Yet just as historical authenticity can obtain only in the present of the actors, . . . historical responsibility cannot hark back to an original sin that the collective-individual supposedly committed. Rather, it needs to take into account the structures of privilege unleashed by a history of power and domination and to evaluate the current losses induced by the reproduction of these structures. . . .

From a symbolic viewpoint, . . . collective apologies offer an inherent ambiguity: the request, the offer, the rejection or the acceptance of an apologetic gesture deemed to be felicitous inasmuch as it claims to tie two collective subjects, yet incapable of fulfilling that claim because of the nature of the subjects involved.

The fundamental problem is not one of hypocrisy, although sheer hypocrisy does play a role in the construction of the international community as Greek chorus. My point, however, is subtler. Apologies can be read as rituals in the strictly anthropological sense of a regulated, stylized, routinized and repetitive performance that tends to have both demonstrative and transformative aspects. Their transformative aspect depends fundamentally on a dual identity relation across temporal planes, easily met on pragmatic grounds in individual apologies. Yet in collective apologies, identity is always questionable. It is hard to establish on formal grounds, hard to assume on pragmatic ones. The problem is bypassed through formulas that patch upon collective subjects attributes of a particular kind of liberal individual. Yet the repetition of these formulas has yet to convince the populations involved that the problem has been solved. . . .

464   MEMORY, JUSTICE, AND THE CONTEMPORARY EPOCH

Until and unless the liberal formulas now fundamental in the changing constitution of collective subjects manage to convince the populations on both sides that identity obtains in ways that make the performance meaningful, collective apologies will have little transformative power. For now at least, they are born without the capacity to meet their inherent purpose. The very formulas they use to create their collective subjects—the attribution of the features of the liberal individual—though successful in placing these subjects on stage, make it impossible for them to act. Thus collective apologies are meant not to succeed—not because of the possible hypocrisy of some of the actors but because their very conditions of emergence deny the possibility of a transformation. They are abortive rituals.

Daniel Levy and Natan Sznaider (contemp.)

German-American / German-Israeli sociologists. In their 2001 book, *Memory and the Holocaust in a Global Age*, Levy and Sznaider addressed the effects of globalization on collective memory, arguing that the Holocaust has, over time, become a cosmopolitan rather than merely national memory. This cosmopolitanization, which is driven, they suggest, by a culture of contrition, is not replacing national memory cultures but reconfiguring them. The following excerpt provides a précis of their argument.

From "Memory Unbound: The Holocaust and the Formation of Cosmopolitan Memory"

The study of collective memory usually considers . . . memory structures as being bound by tight social and political groups like the "nation" or "ethnos." What happens when an increasing number of people in Western mass-consumer societies no longer define themselves (exclusively) through the nation or their ethnic belonging? Can we imagine collective memories that transcend national and ethnic boundaries? If so, how do these transnational memory forms come about and what do they consist of?

We suggest that shared memories of the Holocaust, the term used to describe the destruction of European Jewry by Nazi Germany between 1941 and 1945, a formative event of the twentieth century, provide the foundations for a new cosmopolitan memory, a memory transcending ethnic and national boundaries.

Can an event, by many defined as a watershed in European history be remembered outside the ethnic and national boundaries of the Jewish victims and the German perpetrators? Can this event be memorialized by people who do not have a direct connection to it? At the beginning of the third millennium, memories of the Holocaust facilitate the formation of transnational memory cultures, which in turn, have the potential to become the cultural foundation for global human rights politics. . . .

National and ethnic memories are transformed in the age of globalization rather than erased. They continue to exist, of course, but globalization processes also imply that different national memories are subjected to a common patterning. They begin to develop in accord with common rhythms and periodizations. But in each case, the common elements combine with pre-existing elements to form something new. In each case, the new, global narrative has to be reconciled with the old, national narratives; and the result is always distinctive.

Critics of globalization consider it as something that dissolves collective memory and sets up inauthentic and rootless substitutes in its stead. Anthony Smith puts it as follows: "a timeless global culture answers to no living needs and conjures no memories. If memory is central to identity, we can discern no global identity in the making." . . . Why can it conjure no memories? Because timelessness is of its essence: "This artificial and standardized universal culture has no historical background, no developmental rhythm, no sense of time and sequence. . . . alien to all ideas of "roots," the genuine global culture is fluid, ubiquitous, formless and historically shallow." . . . Smith's statement is emblematic of two recurring assertions which: one, restrict memory to the symbolic boundaries of the nation; and two, situate it in a normative dichotomy of real lived experiences and inauthentic mediated representations.

To say that nations are the only possible containers of true history is a breathtakingly unhistorical assertion. Religious traditions and institutions like the Catholic Church and Judaism are good examples. In addition, there is now a vast literature on national tradition, and it is clear that every single national tradition has gone through a moment of "invention." . . . What makes the irony especially rich is that when national cultures were being invented, they were opposed with exactly the same arguments that are being aimed at global culture today: that they were superficial and inauthentic substitutes for rich local culture, and that no one would ever identify with such large and impersonal representations. Notwithstanding the fact that this turned out to be spectacularly wrong, the perception that representations are substitutes for "authentic" experiences persists.

The nation-state, at the turn of the twentieth century, depended for its coming into existence on a process by which existing societies used representations to turn themselves into new wholes that would act immediately upon people's feelings, and upon which they could base their identities—in short, to make them into groups that individuals could identify with. This nation-building process parallels what is happening through globalization at the turn of the twenty-first century. The nation was the global when compared with the local communities that preceded it; however, this did not render it inauthentic. The ability of representations to give a sense to life is not ontologically but rather sociologically determined. So if the nation is the basis for authentic feelings and collective memory—as the critics of global culture seem almost unanimous in maintaining—then it cannot be maintained that representations are a superficial substitute for authentic experience. The nation was literally inconceivable without an imagined community. On the contrary, representations are the basis of that authenticity. And there is nothing inconceivable, theoretically and empirically, about them providing such a basis on a global level. Rather than privileging one form of memory over the other, it seems more fruitful to identify the different historical and sociological conditions of memory cultures.

"Inventions of Nationhood" during the nineteenth century were based on heroic conceptions and formative myths that were transmitted by "traditional" and "exemplary" forms of narrativity. . . . In contrast, the Holocaust has been inscribed in the historical awareness of West European nations (and increasingly also in Eastern Europe) during the last quarter of the twentieth century, a period characterized by a self-critical narrative of their national past. While traditional and exemplary narratives deploy historical events to promote foundational myth, the critical narrative emphasizes events that focus on past injustices of one's own nation. Cosmopolitan memory thus implies some recognition of the history (and the memories) of the "Other." The heroic narrative of First Modernity . . . is the narrative of "acting perpetrators." In contrast, the paradigmatic narrative of Second Modernity becomes the narrative of the "non-acting" victim. In First Modernity this distinction between perpetrator and victim constituted a crucial element for misunderstanding and mutual disdain. In Second Modernity we detect a compromise that is based on the mutual recognition of the history of the "Other." It is this act of reconciliation which becomes the central mnemonic event. Half a century after the Holocaust, it is no longer the atrocities themselves that are at the center of attention (especially in light of the fact that the majority of surviving victims have died), but how the heirs of the victims, the perpetrators and bystanders are coping with these stories and the evolving memories. In other words, the recognition of the "Other" diffuses the distinction between memories of victims and perpetrators. What remains is the memory of a shared past. It is not shared due to some mythical desires and the belonging to some continuing community of fate, but as the product of a reflexive choice to incorporate the suffering of the "Other," constituting what we have referred to here as cosmopolitan memory. Global media representations and emerging interdependencies create new cosmopolitan sensibilities and moral-political obligations. . . . The concept of "cosmopolitan memory" corresponds to the globalized horizon of experiences in Second Modernity. Cosmopolitan memories thus provide a new epistemological vantage point, one that questions the "methodological nationalism" that still prevails in much of the social sciences.

Mark Osiel (contemp.)

American legal scholar. The literature on law and memory, particularly on the role of courts in shaping collective memory, is large and growing, but Mark Osiel's 1997 book, *Mass Atrocity, Collective Memory, and the Law*, remains one of the clearest arguments for law's role in, and obligations to, collective memory. To be sure, others have argued, in contrast to Osiel, that law's role in collective memory is and must be minimal.

From *Mass Atrocity, Collective Memory, and the Law*

Trials of those responsible for large-scale state brutality have captured the public imagination in several societies. Insofar as they succeed in concentrating public attention and stimulating reflection, such proceedings indelibly influence collective memory of the events they judge. More subtly, they influence even our underlying notions of what memory is about, what it is for. It is only a small exaggeration to say, as two political theorists recently have, that the cumulative effect of such trials, from Nuremberg and Buenos Aires to the current proceedings in the Hague, is that "the process of how people are made to vanish has become a distinctive feature of postwar conceptions *of what memory is.*"

By highlighting official brutality and public complicity, these trials often make people willing to reassess their foundational beliefs and constitutive commitments, as few events in political life can do. In the lives of individuals, these trials thus often become, at very least, an occasion for personal stock-taking. They are "moments of truth," in several senses. Specifically, they present moments of transformative opportunity in the lives of individuals and societies, a potential not lost upon the litigants themselves. Prosecutors and judges in these cases thus rightly aim to shape collective memory of horrible events in ways that can be both successful as public spectacle and consistent with liberal legality. . . .

Such trials cannot summon up a "collective conscience" of moral principles shard by all. At such moments, no such consensus on fundamentals is likely to exist. Neither can it be easily created. But criminal trials may nevertheless contribute significantly to a certain, underappreciated kind of social solidarity, arising from reliance on procedures for ensuring that moral disagreement among antagonists remains mutually respectful, within the courtroom and beyond.

To this end, judges and prosecutors can profit from closer attention to the "poetics" of legal storytelling, i.e., to the way in which an experience of administrative massacre can be framed within the conventions of competing theatrical genres. The task of comparative historical sociology is therefore to understand why certain narrative tropes were employed by prosecution and defense in particular trials, and to assess the varying degree to which these were successful in influencing collective memory—both national and international—of the disputed events, often many years thereafter. . . .

In a nutshell, the record of these trials suggests that defense counsel will tell the story as a tragedy, while prosecutors will present it as a morality play. The judicial task at such moments, however, is to employ the law of evidence, procedure, and professional responsibility to recast the courtroom drama in terms of the "theater of ideas," where large questions of collective memory and even national identity are engaged. By helping to put these questions in issue, courts contribute to social solidarity of the sort just described.

Principles of liberal morality can be most effectively inculcated in a society traumatized by recent fratricide if the proceedings are conducted in this fashion. To maximize their pedagogic impact, such trials should be unabashedly designed as monumental spectacles, through rarely acknowledged, considerations of dramaturgy have proven quite valuable to this end. This is because these are "liberal show trials," conducted by what have been called "moral entrepreneurs" and "activists of memory."

The approach advocated here necessarily involves courts in questions of historical interpretation and moral pedagogy generally regarded as beyond their professional competence. It also assumes their capacity to influence political culture and social norms in powerful ways. . . .

All societies have founding myths, explaining where we come from, defining what we stand for. These are often commemorated in the form of "monumental didactics," public recountings of the founders' heroic deeds as a national epic. Some societies also have myths of refounding, marking a period of dsecisive break from their own pasts, celebrating the courage and imagination of those who effected this rupture.

Myths of founding and refounding often center on legal proceedings or the drafting of legal documents: the Magna Carta, . . . the trial and execution of King Louis XVI, . . . and the Declaration of Independence and the Constitutional Convention. "Our country's birthday," reminds Mary Ann Glendon, "commemorates the formal signing of a legal document—a bill of grievances in which rebellious but fussily legalistic colonists recited their complaints, [and] claimed that they had been denied "the rights of Englishmen.'"

To considerable extent, such formations and transformations of collective identity are legally induced. They are not confined to the distant past, moreover. . . .

To do this effectively has increasingly been recognized to require some measure of *son et lumière,* smoke and mirrors, that is, some self-conscious dramaturgy by prosecutors and judges, I contend. For instance, western Allies in postwar war crimes trials deliberately strove "to *dramatize* the implacable contradiction between the methods of totalitarianism and the ways of civilized humanity through a worldwide *demonstration* of fair judicial procedure." . . .

[S]uch efforts can easily sacrifice the rights of defendants on the alter of social solidarity. . . . [T]hey can unwittingly distort historical understanding of the nation's recent past . . . [T]hey may foster delusions of purity and grandeur by encouraging faulty analogies between past and future controversies, readings of the precedent that are often too broad, sometimes too narrow.

. . . [T]hey may fail by requiring more extensive admissions of guilt, and more repentance, than most nation are prepared to undertake. This is because efforts at employing law to instill shared memories sometimes require substantial segments of a society to accept responsibility for colossal wrongs and to break completely with cherished aspects of its past. . . . [L]egal efforts to influence collective memory may fail because such memory—almost by nature—arises only incidentaly; it cannot be constructed internationally. . . . [E]ven if collective memory can be created deliberately, perhaps it can be done only dishonestly, that is, by concealing this very deliberateness from the intended audience.

These obstacles establish the moral and empirical limits within which any liberal account of law's contribution to collective memory must maneuver. . . .

[A]cts asserting legal rights or officially stigmatizing their violation have often become a focal point for the collective memory of whole nations. These acts often become secular rituals of commemoration. As such, they consolidate shard memories with increasing deliberateness and sophistication. These events are both "real" and "staged." In this regard, they seem to problematize the very distinction between true and false representations of reality.

Law-related activities of this sort contribute to the kind of social solidarity that is enhanced by shared historical memory. In the last half century, criminal law has increasingly been used in several societies with a view to teaching a particular interpretation of the country's history, one expected to have a salubrious impact on its solidarity. Many have thought, in particular, that the best way to prevent recurrence of genocide, and other forms of state-sponsored mass brutality, is to cultivate a shared and enduring memory of its horrors—and to employ the law self-consciously toward this end.

Avishai Margalit (contemp.)

Israeli philosopher. In this excerpt from his book *The Ethics of Memory*, Margalit distinguishes between the ethical obligations of individuals and those of collectivities, as well as between the ethics of memory and the morality of memory.

From *The Ethics of Memory*

My question, Is there an ethics of memory? is both about microethics (the ethics of individuals) and about macroethics (the ethics of collectives). What I want to address can be rendered by a series of questions: Are we obligated to remember people and events from the past? If we are, what is the nature of this obligation? Are remembering and forgetting proper subjects of moral praise or blame? Who are the "we" who may be obligated to remember: the collective "we," or some distributive sense of "we" that puts the obligation to remember on each and every member of the collective? . . .

[W]hile there is an ethics of memory, there is very little morality of memory. The drift of this idea—perhaps more appropriately expressed with a question mark than with an exclamation point—obviously hinges on the distinction between ethics and morality. In my account, this in turn is based on a distinction between two types of human relations: thick ones and thin ones. Thick relations are grounded in attributes such as parent, friend, lover, fellow-countryman. Thick relations are anchored in a shared past or moored in shared memory. Thin relations, on the other hand, are backed by the attribute of being human. Thin relations rely also on some aspects of being human, such as being a woman or being sick. Thick relations are in general our relations to the near and dear. Thin relations are in general our relations to the stranger and the remote. . . . Ethics, in the way I use the term, tells us how we should regulate our thick relations; morality tells us how we should regulate our thin relations. . . .

Because it encompasses all humanity, morality is long on geography and short on memory. Ethics is typically short on geography and long on memory. Memory is the cement that holds thick relations together, and communities of memory are the obvious habitat for thick relations and thus for ethics. By playing such a crucial role in cementing thick relations, memory becomes an obvious concern of ethics, which is the enterprise that tells us how we should conduct our thick relations.

Though I confine memory predominantly to ethics, there are cases when morality should be concerned with memory as well. These cases consist of gross crimes against humanity, especially when those crimes are an attack on the very notion of shared humanity. Nazi crimes carried out by an ideology that denied our shared humanity are glaring examples of what morality requires us to remember. Yet, humanity is not a community of memory. Someday it may evolve into one, but today, as a matter of fact—a significant fact—it is not. So who should carry the "moral memory" on behalf of humanity as a whole?

Certainly religions can make a bid on the moral memory of humanity as a whole. Or at least the historical religions can. Judaism, Christianity, and Islam all subscribe to the idea of an autonomous history of humanity that is not merely a part of the cosmic run of events. Man was created for the glory of God, and human history is the goal of creation. It is unfolding under the special guidance of God.

There are secular versions of this picture, to be sure. Hegel's idea of world history with historical laws as a substitute for divine providence is a case in point. But talk about world history does not create a world community of memory. The historical religions claim that they have the potential for creating such a community. The historical religions aspire to shape humanity as an ethical community. . . .

Religion is of relevance here in part because the whole enterprise of an ethics of memory, as well as the politics of memory, is under a cloud of accusation that it is merely a disguised form of religion. The suspicion is that the key notions of an ethics of memory, such as forgiving and forgetting, get their sense and justification only in the religious context of a forgiving God. And the same suspicion holds with regard to the politics of memory, which is viewed as no more than political theology. The most superficial controversy over erecting a public memorial monument adds to this suspicion. . . .

Conflating an ethics of memory with religion is my first worry, though by no means my primary concern. The second worry is of conflating the ethics of memory with traditionalism—that is, conflating the ethics of memory with a doctrine, policy, or mood that is set to defend tradition. The connection between traditionalism and the ethics of memory is straightforward. Traditionalism, by definition, advocates loyalty to the past. It is the business of the ethics of memory to work out what this loyalty consists of in terms of remembering the past. My question is whether doctrines and attitudes that (unlike traditionalism) are oriented toward the future rather than the past can and should be concerned with the ethics of memory.

Marc Augé (contemp.)

French anthropologist. According to Augé, there is a dialectical relationship between remembrance and oblivion that shapes our sense of meaningful time. This excerpt points to the mutually constitutive link of memory and forgetting, outlining a "duty of memory" that belongs to the descendants, consisting of both remembrance and vigilance. Nevertheless, oblivion has its role to play: "Memory and oblivion stand together, both are necessary for the full use of time." See also **Nietzsche**.

From *Oblivion*

A certain ambiguity is attached to the expression a "duty to remember," so often used today. First of all, those who are subjected to this duty are obviously those who have not been direct witnesses or victims of the events of which one intends to preserve the memory. It is very clear that those who survived the Holocaust or the horror of the camps do not need to be reminded of their duty to remember. On the contrary, perhaps their duty has been to survive the memory, to escape, as far as they are concerned, from the everlasting presence of an incommunicable experience. In my childhood I was struck by my grandfather's reluctance to mention life in the trenches, and it seemed to me that I could recognize the trace of that same conviction in the restraint of the survivors of the death camps, in the long delay necessary for those who finally chose to speak of what they had lived. This is the conviction that those who have not been victims of the horror cannot imagine it, no matter how willing and compassionate they are. But also that those who were subjected to it, if they want to live again and not just survive, must be able to do their share of forgetting, become mindless, in the Pascalian sense, in order to find faith in the everyday again and mastery over their time.

The duty of memory is the duty of the descendants, and it has two aspects: remembrance and vigilance. Vigilance is the actualization of remembrance, the effort to imagine in the present what might resemble the past, or better (but only the survivors could do it and their numbers are decreasing every day), to remember the past as a present, to return to it to find the hideous shape of the unspeakable again in the banalities of ordinary mediocrity. Now, official memory needs monuments; it beautifies death and horror. The beautiful cemeteries of Normandy (to say nothing of the various convents, chapels, or museums that will perhaps one day take the place of the concentration camps entirely) align their tombs all along the intertwined pathways. Nobody could say that this arranged beauty is not moving, but the emotion it arouses is born from the harmony of forms, from the impressive spectacle of the army of the dead immobilized in the white crosses standing at attention. Sometimes, among the oldest visitors, it is born from the image they associate with it of a relative or companions who disappeared more than half a century ago. It does not evoke the raging battles, nor the fear of the men, nothing of what would actually restore some of the past realistically lived by the soldiers buried in the Normandy soil. The very ones who fought by their sides cannot hope to find the vanished evidence for one moment, except on condition of forgetting the geometric splendor of the great military cemeteries and the long years across which the images, the events, and the stories have been accumulating in their memory.

Memory and oblivion stand together, both are necessary for the full use of time. Surely, Montaigne tells us, "everything has its season," and it is undoubtedly neither wise nor useful to not want to "be one's age." But it is even more vain to play with it, to identify oneself by it, to alienate oneself from it, to stop by the edge of the road, somewhere between the nostalgia for a truncated or tricked past and the horror of a futureless future. We would plead here against the haughty melancholy of positions stopped in their track, for the active modesty of movement, of exercise, of the mind's gymnastics. We would try to encourage those who intend to struggle against the hardening of the imagination (it threatens all of us) to not forget to forget ill order to lose neither memory nor curiosity.

Oblivion brings us back to the present, even if it is conjugated in every tense: in the future, to live the beginning; in the present, to live the moment; in the past, to live the return; in every case, in order not to be repeated. We must forget in order to remain present, forget in order not to die, forget in order to remain faithful.

Paul Ricoeur (1913–2005)

French philosopher. Ricoeur's integrated approach to hermeneutics and phenomenology led him to focus on issues of narrative and temporality. The publication of *Time
and Narrative* in 1983 was followed by a full-fledged engagement with questions of
memory and the publication of *La mémoire, l'histoire, l'oubli* (*Memory, History, Forgetting*) in 2000. Here Ricoeur tackles the triadic relationship of memory, history, and
forgetting as they pertain not only to the past but also to both the present and the
future, sketching out a critical ethics and politics of remembering. See also **Gadamer**
and **Margalit**.

From "Memory—History—Forgetting"

Before tackling the problem of forgetting directly, I asked myself how it is that
the history as written by historians operates as a critical authority capable of
distinguishing between an excess and a shortage of memory. The first step in our
inquiry involves resituating the entire sequence—memory/forgetting/history—
against the background of a wider dialectic, that of historical consciousness.
Here, the term *historical* does not designate a particular discipline, but rather
the fundamental condition of humanity, commonly known as its "historicity."
Why extend the framework of discussion in this way? Because the three terms
of the triad in question all concern the past, and the past acquires its double
sense of having been and no longer being only in relation to the future. In this
respect, I shall adopt the conceptual framework proposed by Reinhart Koselleck
in *Futures Past*, in particular the fundamental polarity between "space of experience" (*Erfahrungsraum*) and "horizon of expectation" (*Erwartungshorizont*).
Space of experience implies the totality of what is inherited from the past, its
sedimentary traces constituting the soil in which desires, fears, predictions,
and projects take root—in short, every kind of anticipation that projects us
forward into the future. But a space of experience exists only in diametrical
opposition to a horizon of expectation, which is in no way reducible to the
space of experience. Rather, the dialectic between these two poles ensures the
dynamic nature of historical consciousness.

Let us consider now the relation between memory and the history of the historians, which completes, corrects, and sometimes contradicts the memory of
survivors, their ancestors, and their descendants. The privilege that history
cannot take away from memory is that of, on the one hand, preserving—and
even, in the Husserlian sense of the term, of constituting—the relationship
with the past, and also, on the other hand, of bringing out clearly the dialectic
between space of experience and horizon of expectation. This dialectic tends
to be obscured by history, which focuses on the events and human beings of the
past methodically and with, as it were, a gaze that is professionally sharpened to

such a degree that we might well be led to believe it possible to have an interest in history that is cut off from any connection to the present and the future. It is only memory, which turns again, and in a renewed way, to the future, that restores the link between the work of the historian and historical consciousness.

The relation of history and memory can thus be analyzed in three steps. First, memory establishes the meaning of the past. Second, history introduces a critical dimension into our dealings with the past. Third and finally, the insight by which history from this point onward enriches memory is imposed on the anticipated future through the dialectic between memory's space of experience and the horizon of expectation. We shall examine each of these three moments in turn.

1. The original link between consciousness and the past is to be found in memory. This has been known, and repeatedly stated, since St. Augustine: memory is *the present of the past.* . . . People do not remember in isolation, but only with help from the memories of others: they take narratives heard from others for their own memories, and they preserve their own memories with help from the commemorations and other public celebrations of striking events in the history of their group.

These are all well-known phenomena, aptly described by Halbwachs. But to move from these reflections to the assumption that there exists a collective subject of memory, thus going directly against the idea of an individual proprietorship or "mineness" of memories, is a more problematic step to take, for it would imply that the collective memory of a group exercises the functions of conserving, organizing, and evoking that were formerly attributed to individual memory. Halbwachs appears to take this step when, in a sentence that reminds us of Leibniz, he writes that "Every individual memory is a point of view on the collective memory."

My preference, on the contrary, is to use the idea of collective consciousness as a working rather than as a substantive concept. The way that Husserl develops the concept of "personalities of a higher order" at the end of the fifth of his *Cartesian Meditations* is instructive in this regard. By dint of this concept he gives an intersubjective basis to a network of relationships. We objectify this network only if we forget the process by which it was constituted. . . .

It is only by analogy with individual consciousness and its memory that collective memory can be described as assembling together in a unity the traces left by momentous events in the history of the group concerned. This same analogy attributes to collective memory the ability to bring these common memories to life again in public anniversaries, rituals, and celebrations. Once this analogy is acknowledged, nothing prevents us from regarding these "personalities of a higher order" as subjects with inherent memories. Nor is there any barrier to speaking of their temporality or historicity. In short, one extends by analogy the "mineness" of memories to the idea that "we" collectively possess collective memories. This is enough to give historians a starting point for investigating the existence, as phenomena, of groups: the historian of "mentalities" and "cultures" asks for nothing less—and nothing more.

2. We take a step forward in the dialectic between memory and history when we bring in history as a critical authority that is able not only to consolidate and to articulate collective and individual memory but also to correct it or even contradict it. To understand this critical relationship between history and memory one must introduce the linguistic medium of narrative, which memory and history share.

What interests me here is the difference in epistemological status between what might be called *memory narratives* (individual or collective) and *historical narratives*. Memory narratives circulate in conversation and belong to everyday discourse. Admittedly, memory narratives are not devoid of critical second thoughts, since during conversation a play of question-and-answer introduces into a concrete public space an exchange of narratives. But criticism, here, is not raised up to the level of an authority standing above the living exchange of memories.

In contrast, in the case of historical narratives this does happen. Historical narratives break with the discourse of memory on three levels. First and most obviously, they do so in the process of establishing the facts, a level that might be labeled "documentary." Second, historians search for explanations. They do so in two respects: on the one hand they search for causes (more or less as do natural scientists and practitioners of some of the other human sciences), and on the other hand they look for the motives and justifications out of which deeds arose. Even in this second type of explanation the critical spirit of history emerges—from the procedure itself. As Max Weber showed in his discussion of the work of E. Meyer, the historian first assumes, in imagination, the absence of the presumed cause, and next asks himself what the probable course of historical events would have been, as compared to what actually happened. This process of "singular causal imputation" highlights the divergence between historical explanation and the "uncontrolled" explanations of ordinary conversation. . . .

Perhaps, in establishing this distinction between memory and history, one should go further, by denying to history the capacity for the reenactment of the past that Collingwood attributed to it. Far from abolishing temporal distance, history deepens it by making absence the essential sign of the "pastness" of the past, as Michel de Certeau suggests in his *L'Absent de l' histoire*. . . .

The discrepancy between an excess of memory and a shortage of memory . . . can be reinterpreted in terms of the categories of resistance, repetition compulsion, transference, working through, and, finally, "the work of recollection." Following along this line, we can say that excess of memory resembles repetition compulsion, which Freud tells us puts a turn to action in the place of the genuine memory through which the present and the past could be reconciled with each other. How much violence throughout the world is equivalent to an "acting out," instead of a remembering! With regard to such festivals of death we can speak of a repetition-memory (*wiederholendes Gedächtnis*). Following this train of thought, however, one needs to add that repetition-memory is resistant to criticism, while recollection-memory (*Erinnerungsgedächtnis*) is a fundamentally *critical* memory. If this interpretation is right, then a shortage of memory can be interpreted as follows: some people take a sick pleasure in cultivating the repetition-memory from which others flee with a bad conscience. The former like to lose themselves in it; the latter are afraid of being swallowed up by it. But both suffer from the same critical deficiency, failing to achieve what Freud called the work of recollection.

The work of recollection, with its necessary phase of distancing and objectification, can contribute to the interrogating of history. In the end, it is at the "probabilistic" level of large *narration* (as Ankersmit calls them) that historians offer the most powerful alternatives to that "semi-official" history (*offiziöse Geschichte*) into which the grand narratives of collective memory tend to congeal. These controversial *narrations* first of all teach us to see the events of the past simply as "other," and then they teach us how to narrate them from another standpoint, from another perspective. This exercise can lead us even so far as to narrate our own history from the standpoint of the memories of people belonging to other groups, and even to other cultures, than our own. But one must also allow for the two therapeutic suggestions given by Freud. True political wisdom is to be derived from the advice that we ought to exercise patience toward compulsive outbursts in the fictive playground of transference: some peoples need symbolic satisfaction of their fears and hatreds. Great tolerance is required of communities to whom history has given great real satisfaction, or who are far enough advanced along the path of mourning the "lost object" of their past psychic investments. But this advice, offered to those to whom history has given a place comparable to the position occupied by the therapist, does not excuse anyone from Freud's advice to the patient. It is work *on oneself* that induces "repetition compulsion" to give way to "the work of recollection." Critical history can make a contribution to this healing of collective memory.

3. I do not wish to leave the last word to written history as opposed to collective memory. Memory asserts its priority over history not only because it ensures a consciousness of, respectively, continuity between past and present and a feeling of belonging, but, on the contrary, also because it maintains the dialectical connection between what, following Koselleck, we have called space of experience and horizon of expectation. But this dialectic involves an apparent discrepancy, with repercussions for the function of history in relation to memory. The discrepancy is the following: the past, so it is said, cannot be changed, and in this sense it appears determinate; the future, by way of contrast, is uncertain, open, and in this sense indeterminate. If, in reality, events are ineradicable—if one cannot undo what is done or make what has happened not happen—on the other hand the *meaning* of what has happened is not fixed once and for all. Apart from the fact that past events can be interpreted differently, the moral burden attached to the debt that is owed to the past can be increased or lightened, depending on to whether an accusation imprisons a guilty party in a painful sense of irreversibility or a pardon opens the prospect of a deliverance from debt that is equivalent to a transformation of the actual meaning of the past. This phenomenon of reinterpretation, on both the moral

plane and on a simple narrative level, can be considered a case of retrospective action by the expectation of the future on the apprehension of the past.

Memory reinterpreted by this kind of retrospective action serves as a model of historical knowing. Such an instructing of history by memory goes directly contrary to the underlying orientation governing the mode of work of the academic discipline of history. By its nature this work is pure retrospection; it defines itself as the science of human beings in the past. It consequently proceeds by abstracting out "the historical" from the three temporal dimensions of past, present, and future.

Nonetheless, the lessons of memory, as retrospectively transformed by the expectation of the future, are not entirely inaccessible to the historian. After all, it is given to the historian to go back imaginatively to any moment in the past as something that was once present—that is, as it was lived by the people of that time, as the present of their past and the present of their future (evoking Augustine again). Like us, people of the past were subjects with the gifts of retrospection and prospection. The epistemological consequences of this consideration are striking. Knowing that the people of the past expressed expectations (predictions, desires, fears, plans) means breaking up historical determinism and retrospectively reintroducing contingency into history. . . .

More significant for the analysis of forgetting is a distinction between two forms of memory that critical history brings to the fore—repetition-memory and what we call, with Freud, "the work of recollection." One might be tempted to say that there are also two kinds of forgetting, passive and active, although it is less a matter of two distinct phenomena than of a continuum between two extremes, with much overlap between them. At the "passive forgetting" end of the continuum one finds what we designated above by the concept of repetition compulsion, where the patient "acts out" instead of remembering. As we have already suggested, the collective memory of some groups, peoples, and nations seems to have fallen victim to this sort of pathology, which resembles Freud's "substitution discharges" and which is accompanied by forgetting.

More interesting in the present context is how passive forgetting manifests itself as soon as it appears as a shortage of active memory. It is a matter here of *escapist forgetting*—and of bad faith, a strategy of avoidance, that for its part is guided by an obscure desire not to know, not to be informed about, and not to inquire into atrocities committed in one's own neck of the woods. To the extent that this shortage can be considered a shortage of active memory, it might also be classified as passive forgetting. However, as an unacknowledged strategy of avoidance, evasion, and flight, it is in the final analysis an unacknowledged strategy of avoidance, evasion, and flight, it is in the final analysis an ambivalent form of forgetting, as much active as passive. Its active side brings down upon itself the same kind of accountability as do other acts of negligence or omission.

At one end of its range, escapist forgetting turns into active forgetting. Here we first of all encounter the selective forgetting that we have already said belongs to the work of recollecting, and also to the work of history. This form of forgetting becomes subject to criticism when it is practiced by a "semi-official" history (*offiziöse Geschichtsschreibung*), which is essentially the history of the greatness of peoples, the history of what Hegel called "world-historical individuals"—in short, the history of the conquerors. Even when it is method-ologically guided by historical criticism, this forgetting boils down to a forget-ting of the victims. It then becomes the task of memory to correct this systematic forgetting and to encourage the writing of the history of victims.

We move a step further along the spectrum of active forgetting if, like the author of the second *Untimely Meditation*, we dare to offer up a hymn of praise to forgetting . . . "Forgetting," Nietzsche writes, "is essential to action." Here we diagnose a sickness we have not yet named—"historical sickness"—and detect a poison—the excess (*Übermaß*) of the historical, which consists in a perver-sion of the relationship between past and future at the expense of the latter. *History* (*Geschichte*) is endangered precisely to the extent that it is interested in the past alone. The teaching of the second *Untimely Meditation* is that memory, and in its wake history, are first of all and always lifeworks, and only second-arily operations of pure knowledge.

At the other end of the spectrum of active forgetting is forgiveness. Here we must be very cautious. In one sense, forgiveness is the opposite of forgetting, at least of passive forgetting (whether this be a traumatic forgetting or escapist forgetting). In contrast to passive forgetting, forgiveness requires additional engagement in the "work of recollection." Yet despite this, it simultaneously consists in a sort of active forgetting that concerns not events themselves—on the contrary, the traces of these must be carefully protected—but the burden of guilt that paralyzes memory and, by extension, also paralyzes the capacity for a creative orientation toward the future.

Unlike escapist forgetting, forgiveness does not remain enclosed in the nar-cissistic relationship of the self to itself: it always assumes mediation by an-other consciousness, the victim's, which alone is entitled to forgive. Those who bear responsibility for events that have wounded memory can only ask for for-giveness and may have to face the possibility of a refusal. To this degree forgive-ness must always know the unforgivable, the unredeemable debt, the irreparable wrong. Nevertheless, although this is far from obvious, forgiveness is not with-out a certain inner purpose, which has to do with memory. Its intention is not to extinguish memory: on the contrary, the goal it has of canceling the debt is incompatible with that of canceling memory. Forgiveness is a way of healing memory and of completing its period of mourning. Delivered from the weight of guilt, memory is liberated for great projects. Forgiveness gives memory a future. . . .

It is not an absurdity to assert that this kind of forgetting is a strict corollary of the critical memory that we have tirelessly opposed to repetition-memory.

Index